D1256473

HISTORICAL DICTIONARY OF AVIATION

FROM EARLIEST TIMES TO THE PRESENT DAY

DAVID WRAGG

First published in the United Kingdom in 2008
by The History Press
The Mill · Brimscombe Port · Stroud ·
Gloucestershire · GL5 2QG

British Library Cataloguing in Publication Data
A catalogue record for this book is available from
the British Library.

Hardback ISBN 978-0-7509-4527-1

Typeset in Bembo.
Typesetting and origination by
The History Press.
Printed and bound in the United Kingdom.

Contents

Introduction

Aviation is one of today's main industries, a mode of transport that continues to grow, and the foremost component in modern warfare. There are many books dealing with different aspects of its history and development, but no 'quick reference' guide to the way in which aviation has developed, including the work of the pioneers and those aircraft manufacturers that have made a significant contribution to progress.

This is intended to be a quick-and-easy reference book providing answers to the questions that people ask about aviation, and is aimed at the enthusiast as well as others who are searching for answers, such as journalists, politicians, civil servants and those whose business or profession impinges on aviation, but which is not their main activity. It is neither a technical reference book, nor a glossary of technical terminology. It deals with balloons and aircraft, but not spacecraft or space flight, as the length of this volume does not permit such a wide coverage. The book should be seen as complementary to other publications on the market, often dealing with specialised aspects of aviation.

Aircraft are set in context, within the entries for manufacturers or, in the case of military aircraft, the wars and campaigns in which they played a part, as well as for such achievements as transatlantic flights or the Schneider Trophy Races. Space constraints mean that individual aircraft have not been given a separate entry, which in itself would have ignited a debate over which were, and which were not the most significant, but Appendix II gives details of the main aircraft in the two world wars. There are also many other books dealing specifically with aircraft by type, manufacturer or period.

David Wragg

Glossary

AASF	Advanced Air Striking Force	BOAC	British Overseas Airways Corporation
ACV	air cushion vehicle		
AEA	Aerial Experimental Association	BSAA	British South American Airways
AEW	airborne early warning	BWB	blended wing body
AFB	Air Force Base (US)	CAP	Combat Air Patrol
AFC	Air Force Cross	CFT	controlled flight into terrain
airframe	the entire structure of an aeroplane apart from the engines and equipment	CMH	Congressional Medal of Honour
		COD	carrier-on-board delivery
		DFC	Distinguished Flying Cross
airmiss	a near accident when two aircraft would have collided without sharp avoiding action	DSO	Distinguished Service Order
		EAA	Experimental Aircraft Association
		EADS	European Aeronautic Defence and Space Company
airplane	American-English for aeroplane	HDL	Hovercraft Development Limited
AOP	air observation post	ICAO	International Civil Aviation Organization
APU	auxiliary power unit		
ASV	anti-surface vessel radar	IDF-AF	Israeli Defence Force Air Force
ASW	anti-submarine warfare	JASDF	Japanese Air Self-Defence Force
AT&T	Aircraft Transport & Travel	JGSDF	Japanese Ground Self-Defence Force
BAC	British Aircraft Corporation		
base	a term usually used in the United States for a military airfield	JMSDF	Japanese Maritime Self-Defence Force
BEA	British European Airways	JSF	Joint Strike Fighter
BEF	British Expeditionary Force		

LPH	landing platform helicopter	RNAS	Royal Naval Air Service
MAD	magnetic anomaly detector	RNZAF	Royal New Zealand Air Force
MAS	Military Air Service (German)	SAS	Scandinavian Airlines System
MC	Military Cross	SHAEF	Supreme Headquarters Allied
MM	Médaille Militaire (France) /		Expeditionary Force
	Military Medal (UK)	SHAPE	Supreme Headquarters Allied
NACA	National Advisory Committee		Powers in Europe
	on Aeronautics	STOL	short take-off and landing
NAS	Naval Air Squadron	STOVL	short take-off and vertical landing
NASA	National Aeronautics and Space	TWA	Trans World Airlines
	Administration	UN	United Nations
NATO	North Atlantic Treaty	USAAC	United States Army Air Corps
	Organization	USAAF	United States Army Air Force
PR	photographic reconnaissance	USAF	United States Air Force
RAAF	Royal Australian Air Force	USAFE	United States Air Force in Europe
RAeS	Royal Aeronautical Society	USCG	United States Coast Guard
RAFVR	Royal Air Force Volunteer Reserve	USMC	United States Marine Corps
RAuxAF	Royal Auxiliary Air Force	USN	United States Navy
RAE	Royal Aircraft Establishment	VC	Victoria Cross
RAF	Royal Air Force	V/STOL	vertical or short take-off and
RCAF	Royal Canadian Air Force		landing
RFC	Royal Flying Corps	VTOL	vertical take-off and landing
RN	Royal Navy	WDAF	Western Desert Air Force

It took some time for the aeroplane to justify its own specialised press, so in the early 1900s it shared the journal *Flight* with the motor car. Some sixty years later, air cushion vehicles shared aviation magazines until they also justified a magazine of their own.

A

Abruzzo, Ben L. (1937–85) US aeronaut. Having served as a conscript with the United States Air Force, Abruzzo had built a successful real estate empire before joining his friend **Maxi Anderson** in an attempt to cross the Atlantic in a balloon, the *Double Eagle*, in 1977. The ascent ended when the balloon ran into a severe storm which led to a premature splash-down off the northern coast of Iceland. The team succeeded the following year in *Double Eagle II*, a completely new balloon in which they were joined by **Larry Newman**.

Abruzzo failed to make a balloon crossing of the United States, this time as a rival to Anderson, but succeeded in crossing the Pacific in 1981 with **'Rocky' Aoki**, a Japanese restaurateur resident in the United States, and Newman. He was killed in 1985, along with his wife and the other four occupants of the aircraft, flying a Cessna 421 which had developed technical problems after take-off.

aces The concept of the fighter ace evolved during the First World War, and the standard is that to qualify a fighter pilot must have five confirmed kills. Many did far better than this, of course, but much depended on the role. Night-fighter pilots, even with the radar-equipped aircraft that arrived during the Second World War, naturally had a lower 'kill rate' than their daytime counterparts.
See Tables 1 to 11: Fighter Aces – the top-scoring pilots of the major combatants in both wars.

Ader, Clement (1841–1925) French inventor and pioneer. Even when first built, Ader's 20 hp steam-powered flying-machine with a tractor propeller, the *Eole*, was dated. It used a wing resembling that of a bat and had minimal control; the pilot sat behind the boiler and had to peer around the fuselage as if driving a railway locomotive. Despite this, on 9 October 1890 the *Eole* took off under its own power without the aid of a down-ramp run for assistance and made a hop of some 163 ft at Armainvilliers, near Gretz, giving France the distinction of the first heavier-than-air flying-machine to take off entirely under its own power, although it was not the first flight. Two years later, the government awarded Ader a grant to build a further flying-machine, which he named *Avion II*, and his third became *Avion III*, but he failed to complete *Avion II*, and *Avion III* did not match the achievement of the *Eole* when tested on 12 and 14 October 1897. These designs were based on the original *Eole*, although *Avion III* used two 20 hp steam engines driving a single tractor propeller. *Avion III*'s tests were confined to a circular track, and the poor performance may have been the result of not having a straight run into the wind, but even if it had taken off, the lack of control would have still meant that it could not achieve the first flight. Ader inadvertently coined the French word for aeroplane, *avion*, but marred his reputation by making claims in 1906 to have flown *Eole* for 330 ft in 1891 and *Avion III* for 1,000 ft on 14 October 1897.

Aerial Experimental Association (AEA) American pioneering body. Founded in 1907 by a group of pioneers, including **Alexander Graham Bell** and **Glenn Curtiss**, the association was wound up in 1909. It had the unusual feature of each member taking turns to design an aircraft, which was built by the AEA. Its first successful aircraft was the *Red Wing*, designed by **Lt Selfridge**, which flew on 12 March 1908 at Hammondsport, New York, with Canadian **Casey Baldwin** at the controls. The second aircraft was the *White Wing*, designed by Baldwin, which Curtiss flew for five flights on 21 May 1908. Curtiss designed the *June Bug*, which flew the following month.

aerial reconnaissance It is important to note the difference between aerial reconnaissance and **air observation post** activity. The latter is essentially

1

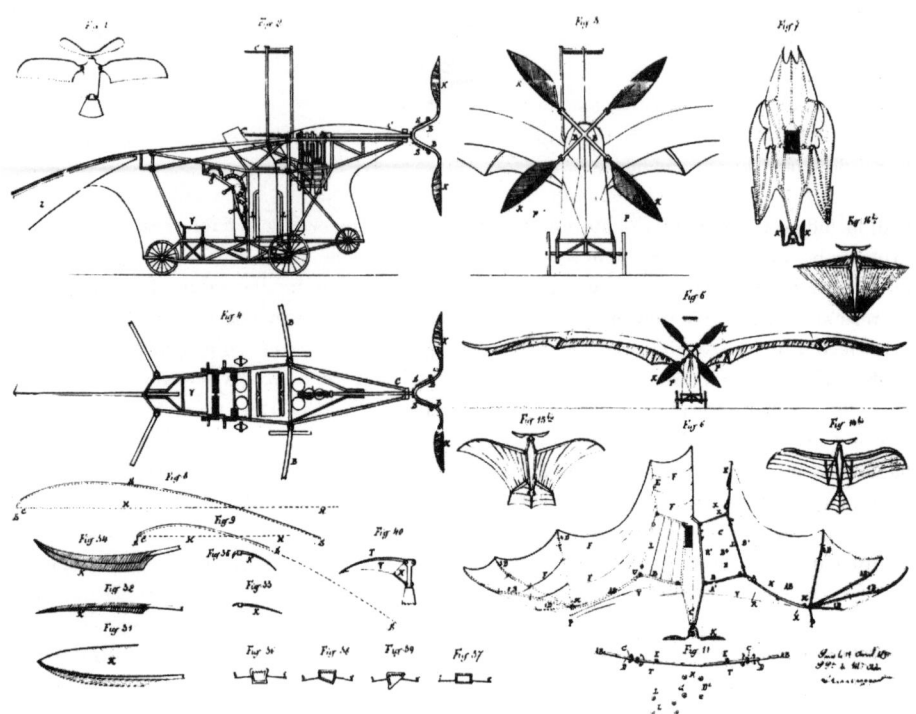

Sectional diagrams of Clement Ader's steam-powered *Eole,* which made a powered hop in October 1890.

passive, keeping watch over a battlefield, while aerial reconnaissance requires penetration of areas either occupied by enemy forces or which may be imminently occupied. It is usually separated out from **maritime reconnaissance**.

Aerial reconnaissance was one of the first duties to fall to the military aeroplane. On the outbreak of the First World War in 1914 it seemed that the main task for the Royal Flying Corps (RFC) would be aerial reconnaissance and the aircraft used were known as **'scouts'.** They were unarmed at first, other than service revolvers for the pilot and observer. Other air arms also prepared for this type of activity. Manufacturers such as **Bristol, Morane** and **Nieuport** produced scout aircraft, and these evolved into the first fighters. Few armies and navies foresaw the aeroplane playing a major role on the battlefield, let alone becoming a weapon of war in its own right.

During the Second World War, aerial reconnaissance continued to be an important function, and special versions of many aircraft were developed for these duties, including the Supermarine Spitfire, Bristol Beaufighter, de Havilland DH 98 Mosquito, North American P-51 Mustang and Northrop P-61 Black Widow, the Focke-Wulf Fw189 and Mitsubishi Ki-46. It was important not only to keep a watch on enemy troop movements, but also on developments such as the construction of factories and launching sites for missiles. Reconnaissance increasingly used photography, with special cameras that essentially provided a double exposure image that enabled highly trained photographic interpreters to be able to assess the height of structures. Photo-reconnaissance was essential before and after a bombing raid. During the war, other types of reconnaissance also became increasingly important, such as meteorological reconnaissance to provide information about the weather conditions over a target, without which a bombing operation could be futile. As an example, the Fleet Air Arm attack on the Italian fleet at **Taranto** was preceded by an RAF Martin Maryland making daily reconnaissance flights before the mission, followed by a post-attack flight.

Postwar, reconnaissance continued to develop, including the use of infra-red technology to identify sources of heat that could provide a clue to the purpose for which a building was being used. Again, variants of fighter and bomber aircraft were used, including the English Electric Canberra, a small number of which continued in RAF service into the twenty-first century. Increasingly, satellite reconnaissance started to impinge on the role of aerial reconnaissance, with some 'spy' satellites capable of reading serial numbers on aircraft, and especially weather reconnaissance. Nevertheless, for many years battlefield commanders found that the results of aerial reconnaissance were more quickly available than those from satellites, and also had the value of being directly under their control and capable of searching for those targets that were of most interest to them.

The Cold War saw aerial reconnaissance applied by both sides, but not without incident, as when a Lockheed U-2, designated as a utility aircraft to avoid giving a clue to its real role, was shot down over the Soviet Union.

The growing use of stand-off weapons to keep aircraft away from heavily defended targets has its counterpart in the use of unmanned air vehicles for reconnaissance. These come in a variety of forms and sizes, with many being very small and difficult to spot, while there are larger and longer range aircraft, such as the American Global Hawk.

Aermacchi/Macchi *See* Finmeccanica

Aéro-Club de France The Aéro-Club de France was founded in 1898 by **Henri Deutsch de la Meurthe** as a meeting place and for the organisation of events, and was based on his experience of l'Automobile Club de France. **Ernest Archdeacon** was one of the early chairmen, and **Octave Chanute** presented a paper announcing the achievements of the **Wright** brothers.

Aero Commander US manufacturer. Part of the North American Rockwell Group, Aero Commander established a reputation as a manufacturer of light aircraft and business aircraft, most of which were based on the high-winged twin-engined Aero Commander 500 series, although the 111A and 112 were single-engined low-wing light aircraft.

Aero Vodochody Czech manufacturer. Originally founded as Aero after Czechoslovakia gained its independence in the wake of the First World War, it produced a number of military aircraft, of which the first were the Aero A-11 and A-12 AOP, then the A-18 fighter, soon joined by the A-24 bomber, for the Czechoslovak Army Air Force. During the 1930s the A-30 and A-100 aircraft were produced as well as the A-32 AOP aircraft. The Aero B-17 bomber was the Tupolev SB-2 built under licence, which entered service shortly before the country was annexed by Germany in 1939.

The company also produced commercial aircraft, including the A-10 of 1921, which could carry three passengers and was operated on the Prague-Kosice route, after which Aero itself operated the ten-passenger A-22 on domestic routes. Later commercial aircraft included the A-23 of 1928, and the A-35 and A-38 during the 1930s.

Postwar, Czechoslovakia became part of the Soviet Bloc. When aircraft manufacture resumed, the company built the L-60 utility and crop-spraying aircraft and the L-200 used for air taxi services. Its most successful postwar product was the L-29 Delfin jet trainer, first flown in 1959 and used by most East European air forces. It was followed by the L-39 in 1968. The break-up of the Warsaw Pact undermined the company considerably with the loss of its main markets, but it is attempting to broaden them with the L-159A light combat aircraft and an advanced trainer derivative of this.

aerobatics A contraction of the term 'aerial acrobatics'. Aerobatics are of considerable importance in the evolvement of fighter manoeuvres, especially in a 'dog fight' between two aircraft, but they are also valuable in training and have an entertainment value.

The first aerobatic manoeuvre was the spin, recovery from which was first performed by the Englishman, Frederick Langham, after stalling while flying in thick fog in an Avro biplane in 1911. Nevertheless, he was not certain as to how he had achieved this 'first'. The first pilot to enter a spin deliberately so as to demonstrate recovery was Lt Wilfred Parke, RN, flying an Avro cabin-biplane. The next aerobatic manoeuvre, the loop, was first performed by Lt (later Capt) **Petr Nesterov** of the Imperial Russian Flying Corps, flying a Nieuport in August 1913. His achievement was acclaimed by aviators elsewhere, but not by his superiors who at first simply viewed him as having endangered government property.

aerodrome *See* airport

***Aerodrome A*, Langley's** In 1898 **Samuel Langley** was awarded a United States Army contract worth US $50,000 to build a heavier-than-air flying-machine. After successful trials with models, the full-sized tandem-wing *Aerodrome A* crashed twice, on 7 October and on 8 December 1903, when it was catapulted off the roof of a houseboat moored on the Potomac river. The problem was that it fouled the catapult mechanism on both occasions, but even if the launches had been successful, the machine lacked any form of control in roll and would have been unable to change direction.

Later, a more successful American aviation pioneer, **Glenn Curtiss**, altered the aircraft substantially, fitting one of his own engines and adding ailerons in 1914. He attempted to fly it, but did little better than make a succession of powered leaps. His intention was to undermine the **Wright** brothers' legal defence of their patents.

aerodynamics The science of flight in heavier-than-air machines is due to the effect of aero-dynamics, which is strictly speaking the science of the motion of air, or any other gas, over a body.

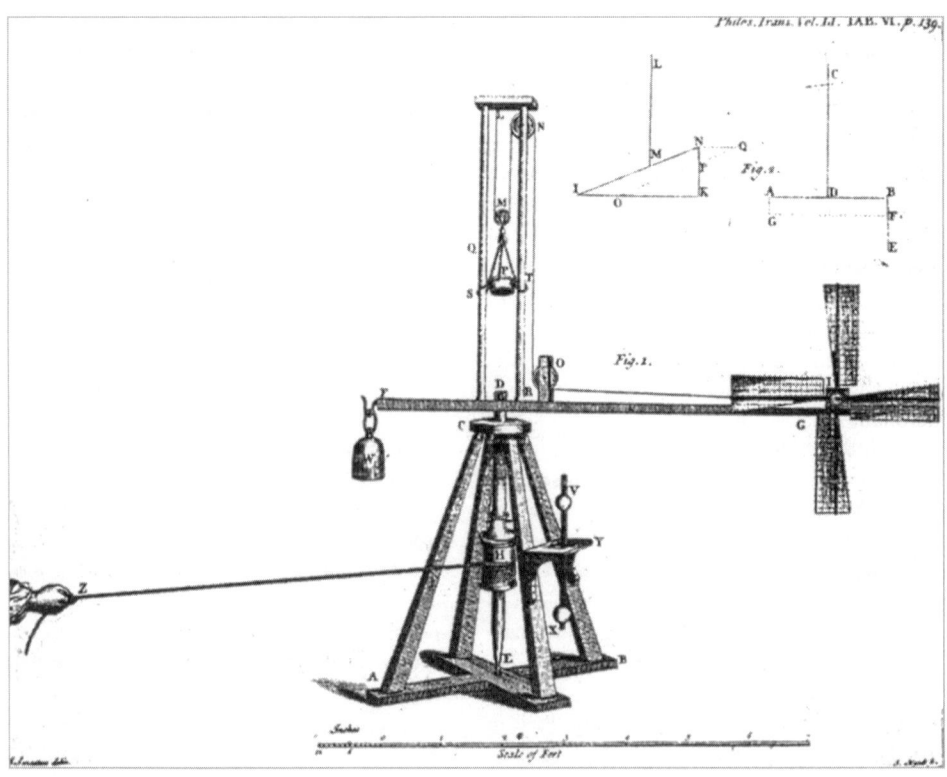

A drawing, possibly for patent purposes, of Smeaton's whirling arm. Originally intended to test windmill sails, it was adapted by Sir George Cayley to test aerofoils. It was the predecessor of the wind tunnel.

Two Englishmen, **Sir George Cayley** and **Horatio Phillips** have been credited with contributing extensively to the development and understanding of the science. Cayley's model glider of 1804 was the first real aeroplane with mainplane, or wings, and adjustable tail surfaces with a fin, giving both control and stability. In a paper, *On Aerial Navigation*, published in 1809, Cayley laid the basis for all subsequent studies of aerodynamics, breaking away from the ornithopter concept and pointing towards the concept of a mainplane, tailplane, fuselage and undercarriage.

Phillips' work on high-aspect cambered **aerofoils** was the basis for all subsequent successful wing design, as well as being an extension of Cayley's work. To Phillips must go the credit for discovering that if an aerofoil is made with a deeply curved upper surface and a shallowly curved lower surface, there will result a high lifting power, the bulk of which is provided by a suction effect on the upper surface, 'lift', rather than by a pressure effect on the lower surface.

aerofoil A surface designed to obtain a reaction from the air through which it is moved. It is usually an alternative expression for a wing, but it can be a **lifting aerofoil fuselage**, a propeller or rotor, or indeed any control surface of an aircraft.

Aeromarine US manufacturer of light aircraft. Products included the PG-1 fighter biplane, but the company was better known for its small flying boats, including the three-seat E.O of 1924.

aeronaut A traveller by air, either as a member of the crew or as a passenger, although more usually referring to a pilot or navigator, regardless of whether their aircraft is lighter or heavier than air.

aeronautics A term coined by the Frenchman Gabriel de la Landelle in the mid-nineteenth century, as an all-embracing word for balloons and airships (aerostation), gliders and aeroplanes (aviation).

Aeronca US manufacturer. A light aircraft manufacturer prominent between the two world wars producing single and twin-seat high-wing monoplanes, including the C-2. During the Second World War, aircraft were built for the military, and postwar the four-seat Sedan and twin-seat Champion entered production for private owners, with the Champion having a military equivalent in the L-16A observation aircraft. The manufacturing rights for the Champion were sold to a company of that name when Aeronca ceased production.

Aérospatiale French manufacturer. Formed on the amalgamation of Nord and Sud Aviation during the late 1960s, Aérospatiale was the nationalised French partner in the Concorde supersonic airliner project and then in **Airbus**, before becoming a major part of the **European Aeronautic, Defence and Space Company** (EADS) in 2000. Aérospatiale was also a significant helicopter manufacturer, with a number of successful designs such as the Dauphin, Gazelle, Ecureil and Puma, Super Puma and Cougar, which were put into the Franco-German Eurocopter company before that too became part of EADS.

Nord itself had been founded as a nationalised concern in 1936. It became reasonably well known after the Second World War for its Noratlas twin-boom transport and for the small 262 twin turboprop feeder airliner, the design of which it inherited when it acquired Max Holste, a manufacturer of military utility aircraft. Nord then became the French partner in the C-160 Transall Franco-German military transport, as well as undertaking subcontracting for other manufacturers.

Sud built the de Havilland Vampire and Venom under licence before producing its own Vatour jet bomber and later moved into helicopter manufacture, including the Frelon, the largest helicopter built in Western Europe for many years. The most significant Sud product was the Caravelle, a short-haul jet airliner and the first of its type to be operated in the West.

aerostat A balloon, regardless of whether it is gas-filled, hot air or a combination of these, or an airship.

aerostation The art and science of designing, building and operating balloons and airships, for which the technical name is **aerostat**.

Agusta/Agusta-Westland Anglo-Italian manufacturer. *See also* Westland. Established in 1907 by Giovanni Agusta to manufacture a range of biplanes. The founder died between the First and Second World Wars, but the company survived, even though at one stage it diversified into motorcycle manufacture. Training aircraft became the main business for a while, and after the end of the Second World War, a basic trainer, the AP-111, was in production. In 1954, licence-production of the Bell 47 helicopter started, and this was followed by the Bell 204 and 205 Iroquois, the 206 JetRanger and the 212, all marketed as 'Agusta-Bell' products. The company also licence-produced the Sikorsky S-61 and the Boeing CH-46 Chinook for the Italian armed forces. At the same time, the company developed its own range of helicopters, including the A106 for the Italian armed forces and the civil derivative, the A109, which remains in production. In more recent years, it developed the EH-101 Merlin medium lift and anti-submarine helicopter in conjunction with the British manufacturer, Westland, which it has since acquired. The Merlin has also been sold to the Canadian armed forces and is in production under licence in Japan by **Kawasaki** for the Japanese Maritime Self-Defence Force. The company is a division of **Finmeccanica**.

aileron A movable surface on the outer trailing edge of an aircraft's wings controlling the rolling or banking movements of the aircraft. Early biplanes sometimes had the ailerons mounted separately between the upper and lower wings, and **gyroplanes** or **autogiros** retained the aileron, even though the conventional wing was replaced by a rotor leaving the ailerons protruding from the fuselage sides. The earliest aircraft frequently used a system of wing-warping or flexing in order to achieve the control now provided by ailerons. Some aircraft, including the Boeing 757, incorporated additional inboard ailerons, or 'flaperons', to enhance control.

air arm While any military aircraft operator is an air arm, in general usage the term is confined to army or, more especially, naval and marine corps air elements used in what is known today as **organic air power**. The first real air arm was that of the British Army, formed in 1878 with a company of the Royal Engineers operating balloons at Woolwich. Later, the RFC was effectively still the army's air arm, while the term gathered its nautical connection when the elements of the RAF's Coastal Area operating from warships became known as the Fleet Air Arm in 1924.

air brake A device used to create extra drag, helping to steady or slow an aircraft. Air brakes are usually fitted to the wings; an extreme form were the dive-brakes fitted to dive-bombers, including the German Junkers Ju87 Stuka dive-bomber. In some cases substantial tailbrakes are fitted to aircraft to reduce speed on landing when runway space is short, such as on the Blackburn (later Hawker Siddeley) Buccaneer carrier-borne bomber, the Fokker F28 Fellowship airliner and the BAe Systems 146 and Avro RJ series of airliners.

air control A form of counter-insurgency operation pioneered by the British in Mesopotamia (present-day Iraq) during the 1920s. It included using aircraft to attack insurrectionists and also to ferry troops around.

air cushion vehicle The correct term for what is commonly referred to as a 'hovercraft', and can be abbreviated as ACV. Hovercraft is inaccurate since a **helicopter** can also hover.

Several engineers attempted to create a craft that eliminated vibration by riding on a cushion of air, and would also be able to travel with equal ease over land or water. The solution lay in finding a system that would contain the air cushion, and this was achieved by **Christopher Cockerell** in 1955. His idea was taken up by the British government after some delay, and **Saunders-Roe** built the prototype SR-N1 which was test flown in 1959 and crossed the English Channel later that year. The ACV developed with larger craft built during the 1960s, by which time the idea of further containing the air cushion using heavy rubber skirts was introduced. Some hovercraft had sidewalls, which improved lift and reduced fuel consumption, but confined them to operations over water. In the United States, Bell Aerosystems became a licensee and built hovercraft for the US armed forces.

Much to Cockerell's dismay, his craft was classified by the British government as an aircraft rather than a ship or a completely new mode of travel. Air cushion vehicles have, nevertheless, a limited field in which they are superior to other modes, ideally areas with shallow waters and swamps or marshes, as otherwise they are slower than helicopters, more expensive to operate than aircraft or ships, and noisy.

air defence Primarily one of the basic roles of any air force or air arm, the concept of air defence came early during the First World War when the First Lord of the Admiralty, Winston Churchill, volunteered the Royal Naval Air Service (RNAS) for the air defence of Great Britain. This soon proved necessary when air raids, first by **Zeppelin** airships and then by German bombers, started. Nevertheless, the power limitations of early aircraft, their poor armament and the much heavier armament of the Zeppelins, meant that success was some time in coming. It was not until the night of 6/7 June 1915 that the RNAS shot down its first airship, near Ghent in Belgium.

An essential part of air defence is in ground-based artillery and, today, missile systems. During the First World War, the Royal Navy also had responsibility for anti-aircraft artillery, but this was transferred to the War Office on 16 February 1916, and the personnel transferred to the British Army.

air force The term air force is generally taken to identify a separate armed service with the specific functions of air defence, aerial attack and reconnaissance, and air transport. It is possible to use the term air force as an alternative to **air arm**, and during the Second World War the air force of the United States was the United States Army Air Force (USAAF), which had been an army corps until 1941, and so was still under army control. At the same time, the Japanese had no separate autonomous air force, but instead army and navy air forces: the terms air corps and air arm were not used.

While the Royal Flying Corps (RFC) as formed in 1912 had army and navy wings, it was effectively under army control and this was a factor in the British Admiralty establishing the Royal Naval Air Service (RNAS) to regain control of its own naval aviation before the First World War. Nevertheless, the war years showed considerable overlap between the RNAS and the RFC, as well as some rivalry, so the British government set up a committee of enquiry, the result of which was the recommendation that a separate autonomous air service be established. The Royal Air Force (RAF) came into being on 1 April 1918, at the height of the war, and was the world's first autonomous air service.

Most nations today maintain an autonomous air force, of which the most recently formed in the developed world is the Royal Danish Air Force, dating from 1950, while the United States Air Force (USAF) dates from 1948. Canada, on the other hand, merged its three armed services in 1967 into a unified Canadian Armed Forces, with separate commands, including air and maritime, but in recent years the merger has been largely reversed and today Canada has a Canadian Air Force, albeit adopting the practice of using army ranks rather than the RAF-pattern ranks used by the Royal Canadian Air Force. Exceptions to the concept of autonomous air forces come in countries with a relatively small population, including Israel, Switzerland and the Irish Republic.

The full range of duties covered by an air force varies. New Zealand has disbanded its fighter squadrons, but most air forces have an air defence and ground-attack capability. Bombers in the old sense are much less common these days, although they remain in the USAF, but the major air forces retain at least an interdictor role. Transport is something that every air force provides to a greater or lesser extent. Most provide at least some search and rescue function, although in the United States this is largely the preserve of the US Coast Guard Service, and in the UK it is shared with the Royal Navy's Fleet Air Arm and the Coastguard, with the latter using chartered commercial helicopter operators. The RAF took over maritime-reconnaissance from the RNAS when it was created, and when the Fleet Air Arm was transferred to the Admiralty in 1939, maritime-reconnaissance remained with the RAF. This is also the case in Australia, New Zealand and South Africa today, but most air forces, including the United States, the Netherlands, Germany and

France, leave maritime-reconnaissance with the navies. Most maritime-reconnaissance aircraft have their origins in transport aircraft, and because their aircrew would have to be extensively retrained for carrier operations, leaving this function with an air force makes some sense, just as long as those involved are trained well in ship recognition.

The advantages of maintaining a separate air force are supposed to stem from an appreciation that air power is a weapon to be used in its own right, and not just in support of naval or ground forces. This is not always the case. During the Second World War, the autonomous Luftwaffe and the Soviet air forces operated in close support of ground forces, while the USAAF, in common with the autonomous RAF, pursued the concept of strategic air power. Both the Allies also provided close support for ground forces, although the British Expeditionary Force deployed to France on the outbreak of war had its own air component in addition to that of the Advanced Air Striking Force also sent to France. Good coordination between air and ground forces took some time to evolve, but can be seen as starting with the Desert Air Force in North Africa and continuing with the Second Allied Tactical Air Force, or 'Second TAF', that was formed in anticipation of the Normandy landings and followed Allied forces across Europe with some units being based in Germany even before that country surrendered.

In some countries, the debate over whether there should be a separate air force has re-emerged, largely as a result of shrinking defence budgets with navies and armies jealously eyeing the share of funds devoted to air power. In others, a form of compromise, with headquarters being merged, has occurred. Many argue that, apart from strategic transport, today most air force activity is in support of ground or naval forces, but this presupposes that a strategic air power threat does not emerge or re-emerge in the future.

air mobility The concept of air mobility has vastly reduced reaction times in warfare and in providing military assistance in a crisis, as well as enabling governments to reduce the number of personnel stationed abroad. Depending on the size and number of aircraft available, air mobility is no longer confined to light forces as even heavy-lift helicopters can be transported in aircraft such as the Lockheed C-5 Galaxy, but the number of tanks and self-propeller artillery required for a major campaign does mean that air mobility for practical reasons is confined to lighter forces. Strong modern armies usually have a proportion of their troops, including paratroops, air-landed troops and support echelons, in air mobile forces ready to be deployed at short notice over long distances. The European Union sees air mobility as being a fundamental feature in the proposed European Rapid Reaction Force, a European federal army in the making.

The concept was first used by the British during the 1920s against insurgents in Mesopotamia, now Iraq, in the operation known as air control, with RAF bomber-transports bombing rebel tribesmen and also ferrying troops and supplies. Nevertheless, the first significant application that marked a change in a campaign, and possibly history, was with the airlifting of troops of the Spanish Foreign Legion from Ceuta in North Africa to mark the start of the nationalist campaign at the outset of the Spanish Civil War (1936–39). During the Second World War, German forces made considerable use of air mobility during the assault phase of campaigns in the Low Countries and over Crete, but air mobility was also used to ferry troops and supplies to support the Chindits in Burma, fighting Japanese forces. Helicopters were used for the first time to transport troops during the Korean War in the early 1950s, and have since become an important element in tactical air mobility in campaigns such as that in Afghanistan in recent years. The distances involved and the lack of sufficient aircraft meant that air mobility was not a factor during the Falklands Campaign in 1982, and the loss of the container ship *Atlantic Conveyor* also meant the loss of heavy-lift helicopters that ended any chance of tactical air mobility after the British task force reached the islands.

air observation post Air observation post (AOP) is the oldest task assigned to **aeronautics** by the military. The first instance occurred on 2 June 1794 at the Battle of Mauberge, when **Jean-Marie Coutelle** made an ascent in a balloon and attempted to observe Austrian troops trying to cross the River Sambre. Far more successful was the second attempt at the Battle of Fleurus on 26 June, when Coutelle was accompanied by Gen Jean-Baptiste Jourdan, who dropped battle orders to his troops on the ground below, making a contribution to French victory.

AOP duties were neglected in some services during the Second World War, including the US Army and US Marines, who had to reinvent these units with their air power more interested in combat operations. Although postwar helicopters were also assigned to this task, in modern times unmanned air vehicles have become more important because of the high risk of deploying aircraft that have to be slow moving over the middle of a battlefield.

air portability A concept that became increasingly important with the growing potential of transport aircraft on military operations. Air portability means the classification given to military equipment that can be flown easily into a forward area. The concept was firmly established during the Second World War with tanks and other vehicles of a size that could be carried by gliders, many of which would break open to release their loads. Items such as the Jeep could fit into a transport aircraft such as the ubiquitous Douglas C-47, but loading and unloading was difficult. Postwar, the potential of the helicopter began to be realised, and at **Suez** in 1956 Citroen 2CV pick-ups were employed because they were big enough to be useful on the battlefield, but light enough to be carried by a helicopter as an underslung load. Land Rover built a specially modified lightweight version of its standard vehicle (today known as the Defender since the product range has widened), but by the time it entered service, new aircraft and helicopters with improved load-carrying capability could easily handle the standard vehicle.

Today, large transports such as the Lockheed C-5 Galaxy can carry heavy-lift helicopters, although often rotors have to be taken off and stowed separately, which delays getting the helicopter into the air after arrival. While tanks and self-propeller artillery can also be carried by air, the numbers required means that often sea transport is just as practical.

air shows The first air show as such was the **Reims Aviation Meeting** held in France during August 1909 and sponsored by the Champagne industry. This was also the setting for the first aviation records. Between the First and Second World Wars, the main aeronautical nations established centres that became the venue for national air shows, with the British initially using Hendon, north of London, and then Farnborough in Hampshire. The early meetings at Reims and Nice were as much social as business, but while aviation garden parties and aerial pageants continued between the wars, after the Second World War air shows became occasions that put business first, and with increasing reluctance provided a high-cost day or few days for the general public to see the aircraft and the flying displays.

At one time the major air shows, including Farnborough, were annual events, but the much longer production life of modern aircraft and the consolidation within the manufacturing industry that has seen far fewer manufacturers, has meant that there are no longer several new aircraft to be shown every year, or indeed even one completely new aircraft. Today, air shows occur on a two or three-year cycle with, in Europe, Farnborough taking its turn with Paris (held at Le Bourget) and Frankfurt. New air shows have appeared in Australia and the Far East.

In the developed world, air show organisers face problems in finding suitable venues with plenty of space on the ground, good access and sufficient space in the air for demonstration flights.

air station *See also* airport. The term for a military or naval air base, of which one of the first will have been Eastchurch on the Isle of Sheppey, off the North Kent coast, used by the RNAS from 1910.

airborne assault Any assault from the air, whether it be by glider-landed troops, **paratroops** or helicopter-borne troops. There were exercises using paratroops between the wars in the Soviet Union, but the first use of such forces was by the Germans in 1940 during the invasion of Belgium and the Netherlands. One of the most daring airborne assaults was the neutralising of the Belgian fort of Eben Emael led by seventy-eight engineers of Kock Assault Detachment on 10 May 1940, who landed on the roof of the fort in gliders and kept the 700 troops inside captive until relieved by ground forces. Less successful was the German glider and paratroop assault on **Crete** in May 1941, where the defenders inflicted heavy casualties and, had the Allies not lost their heavy equipment and communications systems in the evacuation from Greece, might have repulsed the assault.

Later, the Allies used airborne assaults for the invasion of **Sicily**, the Normandy landings, at **Arnhem** and for the crossing of the Rhine.

Today, helicopters have become the method of airborne assault. They were first used in the invasion of the Suez Canal Zone in 1956, but the modern helicopter has considerably greater lifting capacity than the Westland WS-55 Whirlwinds used at that time. This has led many to believe that paratroop assaults are no longer feasible. Certainly, glider-landed troops are no longer necessary as helicopters can be re-used and even at Suez, started the first evacuations of casualties on their return to the aircraft carriers. Whether or not paratroops are also obsolete is a moot point, as the helicopter still has problems of speed, with few capable of more than 150 knots, and, more importantly, range, with a radius of action usually of no more than 300-400 miles, unless it is a genuinely 'one way' trip, in which case this is doubled.

airbus Although today associated with the products of **Airbus Industrie**, the term dates from 1914 and the *Ilya Mourametz* or 'Giant', designed by **Igor Sikorsky**, which was described by one commentator as a 'giant airbus'. In more recent years, early in the wide-bodied era, it was used to describe the Lockheed L-1011 TriStar and the McDonnell Douglas DC-10, but no longer.

Airbus Industrie/Airbus Military Company

European manufacturer. Originally not a company but a common interest group, Airbus is now effectively a subsidiary of **European Aeronautic, Defence & Space Company**. When first founded, it was a partnership between **Hawker Siddeley** of the UK, **Dornier**, VFW and **Messerschmitt-Bolkow-Blohm** of what was then West Germany, and **Aérospatiale** of France. The Hawker Siddeley share of 20 per cent

passed to **British Aerospace**, and later **Fokker** of the Netherlands and **CASA** of Spain joined. Airbus restructured itself as a company, and in 2007 BAe Systems, the successor to British Aerospace, sold its remaining share and the English factories engaged on airbus work. The situation has become complicated with the founding of the Airbus Military Company, initially working on development of the A400 advanced turboprop transport, which has different partners from the civil Airbus, including **Finmeccanica** of Italy.

The original Airbus was the A300B, a twin-engined wide body for busy short-haul routes, which entered service in 1974 and was soon followed by a smaller variant using the same cabin cross-section, the A310, which also ventured on to longer-haul operations. The first single-aisle narrow body was the A320, and variants of this did not follow the Boeing pattern of using a second set of numbers and suffixes to denote different fuselage lengths and ranges, but instead included the A321 stretch and the shortened A319, which was followed by the most recent version, the A318. These are competitors for the Boeing 737 family. Airbus ventured into the long-haul market with the four-engined A340 and twin-engined A330 series, for which Boeing-style sub-category classifications were adopted. The A330 is a direct competitor for the Boeing 777 series. The latest product is the A380, a four-engined double-deck airliner which is currently the largest passenger-carrying aircraft. For the future, the company is also developing the A350XWB as a competitor for the Boeing 787 series.

aircraft The term is normally applied to heavier-than-air flying-machines rather than airships or balloons, although taken literally there is no reason why it should not be applied to anything that flies.

Among those who laid the foundations on which more famous pioneers were ultimately able to build were the Englishmen **Sir George Cayley** and **Horatio Phillips**, while the idea of flight and travel by air was popularised by the efforts of W.S. Henderson and **John Stringfellow**. The first flights were by gliders designed by Cayley, initially with one carrying a young boy and later one carrying his coachman. The first powered aircraft to leave the ground was a steam-powered monoplane built by a Frenchman, **Felix du Temple** in 1874, although it only made a powered leap, meaning that the distance covered was too short for control to be exercised and the engine did not sustain flight, but that the force that counted was the take-off run (or down-ramp run). Ten years later a steam-powered monoplane built by the Russian, **Alexander Mozhaiski**, also made a powered leap. In both cases a down-ramp run provided the acceleration.

The first aeroplane to leave the ground through its own unaided efforts was the Frenchman **Clement Ader**'s *Eole* of 1890. A test-rig designed by the American-born inventor **Sir Hiram Maxim** in 1894 showed considerable potential, but further development was not pursued. The successful first flights by the **Wright** brothers suffered because of their close timing to the unsuccessful efforts by another American, **Samuel Langley**, whose *Aerodrome A* was commissioned by the United States Army.

The first true aeroplane in history was the 'Flyer I', built and flown by the Wright brothers in 1903. Their achievement was not repeated in Europe until 1906 when the Brazilian, **Alberto Santos-Dumont** took his '14-bis' into the air. In the UK, the first flight was that by **Samuel F. Cody** in his British Army Aeroplane No. 1 in 1908. Progress even in the early days was fast, however, so that by 1909 **Louis Blériot** was able to fly across the English Channel from France to the UK and the first international aviation meeting was held at **Reims**, in France.

A fair degree of reliability had been achieved by the outbreak of the First World War in 1914 and the aircraft had become recognisable as such to modern eyes. Already in Russia **Igor Sikorsky** had built and flown the world's first four-engined aircraft, the *Bolshoi* or 'Grand', in 1913, and the following year he developed the even larger *Ilya Mourametz* or 'Giant', which served as a Russian bomber during the war years.

Postwar, the first non-stop crossing of the Atlantic was by a Vickers Vimy bomber in 1919, flown by **John Alcock** and Lt Arthur Whitten-Brown. By the eve of the Second World War, transatlantic scheduled services were planned and much route-proving flying had already been done.

It was even possible to fly from the United States across the Pacific to China.

Aircraft had started to become more specialised during the First World War, and this trend continued between the wars so that airliners and bombers became distinct categories. The Second World War was notable for the reliance placed on air transport, not only for glider-towing and dropping paratroops, but also for carrying supplies. Fighting in China demanded that supplies be lifted over the mountains into that country, while in Burma, air-dropped supplies enabled British and Indian troops to continue to fight the Japanese. In 1948/9, military and chartered commercial aircraft from the Western Allies kept the residents of West Berlin from starvation during the Soviet blockade of rail and road routes.

The advent of the jet age during the Second World War provided greater speed, but was slower in being applied to commercial aircraft, not least because of fatigue problems that grounded the the de Havilland Comet I, the world's first jet airliner. The first turboprop airliner to enter production and service, the Vickers Viscount, was a success, however. By the 1960s, jet transports were becoming the accepted norm for even short-haul flights, while the jet engine developed from the turbojet to the much quieter and more fuel-efficient turbofan. Some types of air transport came and went, with the relatively short-lived carriage of cars and passengers by air being among them, while scheduled helicopter flights have been a rarity, although offshore oil and gas search and production has meant that the world's commercial helicopter fleet is substantial. Supersonic flights, mainly from London and Paris to New York, by the Anglo-French Concorde airliner lasted for some thirty years, but ended in 2004. A serious accident undermined passenger confidence, but environmental concerns were also important.

aircraft carrier A warship designed to carry and operate aircraft, usually predominantly **fixed-wing** aircraft as those designed to carry helicopters are more usually known as helicopter carriers, commando carriers or, these days, landing platform helicopter (LPH). A requirement for the term aircraft carrier is that the flight deck is uninterrupted and runs from stern to stem.

Development of the Aircraft Carrier

The ideal configuration for the aircraft carrier took some time to evolve, but several of the early ships were converted from battleships or battlecruisers, with the first being HMS *Furious*, an unsuccessful design of 'light' battlecruiser. The first conversion was simply to place a flying-off deck forward. This proved unsatisfactory and a landing-on deck was then built aft, with narrow decks either side of the smokestack enabling aircraft to be transferred between the two decks. The ship reappeared in 1925 as a flush-deck carrier and a small island eventually materialised in 1939.

The battlecruiser HMS *Furious* as designed in 1915, with 15 in or 18 in guns forward and aft.

As completed in mid-1917, with a hangar and flying-off deck forward.

The first flights to and from a warship were by the American, **Lt Eugene Ely**, USN, who flew a Curtiss biplane from a platform constructed over the forward gun turret of the cruiser USS *Birmingham* in 1910. The following year Ely landed an aircraft on a platform constructed over the stern turret of the battleship USS *Pennsylvania*. In January 1912 **Lt Charles Rumney Samson**, RN, flew a Short S27 biplane from the battleship HMS *Africa*, which had a platform constructed over one of the forward gun turrets, and then in May of that year he made the first take-off from a ship under way when he flew another S.27 from another battleship HMS *Hibernia*.

Before the First World War, a cruiser, HMS *Hermes*, was converted into a seaplane carrier,

although it was converted back as war approached, and during the war a number of Channel and Irish Sea ferries were taken up from trade and converted to seaplane tenders. A Cunard liner, HMS *Campania*, was extensively converted so that she could launch the Fairey Campania floatplane along a wooden runway, but the ship still had to recover the aircraft from the sea following a sortie. In 1917 a 'light' battlecruiser, HMS *Furious*, was converted while nearing completion with her forward 18-in 'A' turret suppressed and a flight deck built over the forecastle, and this ship took part in the first landings aboard a ship under way, although Lt Cdr E.H. Dunning was drowned on his second landing when his aircraft went over the side. Later, *Furious* had a 'landing-on' deck

As modified in 1918, with a landing-on deck replacing the 18 in gun aft.

As a flush-deck carrier in 1925, on completion of her reconstruction.

As modified in 1932, with the quarterdeck raised and the high angle armament altered.

As modernised in 1939, with a small island and armament of 4 in AA guns.

added aft, with narrow connecting trackways around her funnel linking the two decks. Further modifications in the 1920s meant that she eventually ended up with a through flight deck and a small superstructure on the starboard side.

It took some time before the best configuration for an aircraft carrier could be established. The second carrier, HMS *Argus*, was a converted liner and without an island, although a wheelhouse was mounted on a lift and could ascend and descend as required. The ideal design from the pilot's point of view would be one without an island at all, but this gave rise to problems in conning the ship during flying operations, although several Japanese carriers lacked an island and instead had the bridge under the flight deck, which overhung the bridge and forecastle. A starboard island eventually became the most common as it was discovered that in an emergency pilots tended to veer to port, and when the Japanese built two carriers with islands to port, for operational reasons, it appears that the number of serious accidents doubled. A starboard island also fitted in with maritime tradition, as starboard was derived from 'steerboard', the side on which it would be placed to act as a rudder on early ships. Entry into service of the next two carriers, HMS *Eagle* and *Hermes*, the first to be designed as such from the keel upwards, was delayed while these design issues were settled.

The first American carrier was a converted collier, USS *Langley*, although later two battlecruisers were converted. The first Japanese and a French carrier followed.

Under the Washington Naval Treaty of 1922, carrier tonnage was restricted and so too was the maximum tonnage of individual ships, to 27,000 tons, although two ships of up to 33,000 tons could be built. The maximum carrier tonnage was set at 135,000 tons for the Royal Navy and United States Navy, 81,000 tons for Japan, and 60,000 tons each for France and Italy. The USS *Langley* was regarded as an experimental ship and was not included in the figure for US carriers. The Treaty left the major naval powers with more battlecruiser tonnage than allowed, so the three largest navies immediately set about converting their surplus battlecruisers to aircraft carriers.

One perennial problem with carrier operations was that of aircraft landing while others were taking off. An early attempt to resolve this, seen on the British *Courageous* and *Glorious*, was to have a separate taking-off deck running directly from the hanger and on a lower level than the main flight deck. As aircraft sizes and performance increased, this proved to be unworkable. The problem was not resolved until the advent of the angled **flight deck** in the 1950s. The problems of dealing with ever larger aircraft was eased to some extent by the introduction of hydraulic catapults, more usually known to the British at the time as accelerators. Arrester wires were already fitted, but the British adopted the American idea of a crash barrier across the flight deck so that aircraft that missed the arrester wire did not run into aircraft parked forward on the deck – the barrier could be quickly raised and lowered so that aircraft could taxi across it after landing.

By the late 1930s, navies were building aircraft carriers designed as such rather than converting other ships. In an age of experiment with a new concept, both the RN and the French Marine Nationale built a submarine that could carry a floatplane. The RN lost its *M2* in an accident. The French *Surcouf* was a corsair submarine equipped with twin 8 in guns like the M2, but she was lost during the Second World War. The Japanese had several aircraft-carrying submarines, and some were able to carry two aircraft. Nevertheless, such craft could only carry a small aeroplane and the potential was limited, although a Japanese

submarine-borne aircraft did bomb mainland USA twice, causing no damage.

The Second World War saw the aircraft carrier become the most important type of warship, closely rivalled by the submarine. The Fleet Air Arm attack on the Italian fleet at **Taranto** on the night of 11/12 November 1940, by twenty-two obsolete Fairey Swordfish biplanes from HMS *Illustrious*, showed how the significance of warship types had changed. The point was driven home on the morning of 7 December 1941, when six Japanese aircraft carriers attacked the US Pacific Fleet at its forward base at Pearl Harbor on Hawaii. Nevertheless, within five months the Battle of the **Coral Sea**, 3–5 May 1942, saw the first naval battle in which the opposing fleets did not see each other; it was completely an aerial attack, with losses on both sides. On 3–7 June, just six months after the raid on **Pearl Harbor**, the USN sank four Japanese carriers in one day at the Battle of **Midway**, marking the beginning of the end for Japan's territorial ambitions.

The war years saw some differences in carrier construction emerging. The Royal Navy preferred fast armoured carriers with the hull plated up to the flight deck, which, with the hangar, was part of the hull structure. The United States Navy favoured an open forecastle and openings in the sides of the hangar, with the hangar and flight deck part of the superstructure. The British approach was stronger and more damage resistant, but once damaged repair was more difficult, costly and time-consuming. After experience of tropical storms, however, the USN also started to plate hulls up to flight deck level.

Auxiliary aircraft carriers, more commonly known as escort carriers, emerged during the war years. On most convoy routes, but not that across the Mediterranean to Malta, the slower escort carriers, converted from merchant ships at first but later built from the hull up on merchant ship designs, were adequate. Most of these were built in the United States, with the American ships having welded hulls, which the British Admiralty considered unreliable in Arctic waters (they were not, as experience proved) and so a small number were converted in British yards using riveted hulls. The American-built escort carriers delivered to the Royal Navy were a revelation to British sailors in terms of their accommodation. In theory, the escort carriers should have been easy to convert to merchant tonnage postwar, but in fact hardly any of those operated by the USN were converted, and many became helicopter carriers. The term 'auxiliary' described these carriers better than 'escort carrier' ever could, as they served as carriers for ground-attack aircraft and fighters covering landings in the Mediterranean and the Pacific, as aircraft transports or as the core of an anti-submarine sweep.

An interim stage used by the British was the merchant aircraft carrier, or MAC-ship, which were tankers or grain carriers that remained in Merchant Navy service, but had a wooden flight deck laid and could operate three Fairey Swordfish on anti-submarine duties if the ship was a tanker, or four if it was a grain carrier, with the latter also having a primitive hangar at the stern below the flight deck.

Desperate for more fast carriers, the Americans converted cruisers of the Cleveland-class into light aircraft carriers of the Independence-class, although these were too narrow to be ideal. In fact, building of the large Essex-class carriers proceeded at such a rate that these conversions were probably not necessary, but that was with the benefit of hindsight. By contrast, in looking for a carrier that was cheap and easy to build in yards not accustomed to naval work, the British designed the Colossus-class of light fleet carriers, which arrived too late to see action. These were built to merchant shipping standards, but were real aircraft carriers and looked the part.

While the Japanese had a large aircraft carrier fleet at the start of the Second World War, they were alone among the Axis forces. German and Italian plans included building aircraft carriers and work was well advanced, but a number of factors, including rivalry between naval and air force commanders over who should operate the aircraft, delayed completion, and then it was too late.

Designations of aircraft carriers became CV for a standard aircraft carrier, and CVL for what the Americans would term a light carrier and the British a light fleet. Postwar, helicopter carriers became CVH, and anti-submarine carriers CVS, and for a while the large carriers became CVA, for attack carrier. Now the CVH has been replaced

by the landing platform helicopter, LPH. Nuclear-powered aircraft carriers became CVN.

Postwar, the aircraft carrier benefited from a range of measures designed to make them more effective and capable of operating high-performance jet aircraft. Steam catapults, mirror deck landing systems and angled flight decks, so that aircraft could be recovered and launched at the same time, and those that failed to catch the arrester wire could overshoot and go round again, all helped. All of these were British inventions, but the fully angled flight deck was first introduced on an American carrier.

The postwar world soon found a role for the aircraft carrier. The French used theirs off French Indo-China, British and American carriers operated off Korea during the Korean War, while British and French aircraft carriers were in action at Suez in 1956. The last-mentioned campaign saw the first helicopter assaults, with helicopters flying from the light fleet carriers HMS *Ocean* and *Theseus*. Then the Americans used carriers off Vietnam, and much later in the campaign in 1990 to liberate Kuwait. The British, meanwhile, used two aircraft carriers in the **Falklands Campaign**, and many argue that without them, the Argentine forces occupying these islands could not have been overcome.

Starting in April 1945 the French acquired aircraft carriers to replace the elderly *Bearn*, their sole pre-Second World War carrier, initially using loaned American and British ships, and later building their own. The Royal Canadian and Royal Australian Navies also acquired carriers, as did the Dutch, but eventually these were all withdrawn on the grounds of cost. The Indian Navy acquired an aircraft carrier, and stuck with the concept, as did the Brazilians and the Spanish, with more recent members of the aircraft carrier club being Italy and Thailand. Eventually, after many years, the Soviet Union introduced aircraft carriers, shortly before the collapse of communism. Although they operated two aircraft carriers at different times, the Argentine navy joined the carrier club, but eventually left.

The cost of operating carriers nearly saw an end to the British fleet, but naval fixed-wing aviation was saved by the advent of **vertical or short take-off and landing** (V/STOL) and the BAe Sea Harrier. This enabled ships without arrester wires or steam catapults to be used and were initially known as 'Harrier-carriers'. The performance of the aircraft was enhanced by the ski-jump, a ramp at the end of the flight deck that enabled the aircraft to run along the deck rather than lift off vertically, increasing both range and war load. It is ships like this that have enabled Italy, Spain and Thailand to join the club, while versions of the Harrier, known as the AV-8A and AV-8B are operated by the United States Marine Corps from their helicopter carriers.

aircraft designations There is no standard method of designating aircraft either by manufacturers, operators or nations, and during the Second World War and the Cold War that followed, the Allies even contrived designations for Japanese and then Soviet aircraft for which the true designation was not known. The most widely used system is that introduced by the USAAF and retained by the USAF, and eventually adopted by the other American armed services. This attributes a descriptive prefix to each aircraft type, which is also followed by a number. So 'C-XXX' is a transport aircraft, 'KC-XXX' a tanker conversion of a transport aircraft, and 'F-XXX' is a fighter. The main designations are:

A	attack aircraft (for ground-attack)
AC	gunship variant of a transport aircraft
AH	attack helicopter
B	bomber
C	transport
CH	transport helicopter
E	electronic counter-measures
F	fighter
H	helicopter
KC	tanker
P	pursuit, now obsolete and replaced as below
P	maritime reconnaissance
RA	reconnaissance variant of attack aircraft
RB	reconnaissance variant of bomber
RF	reconnaissance variant of fighter
U	utility
UH	utility helicopter
V	vertical take-off convertiplane, of which the only current example is the Bell-Boeing V-22 Osprey

The list could be endless, and oddities arise, such as the Boeing F/A-18 Hornet, which means that the aircraft can be optimised for the fighter or the attack role, simply by changing a computer module. Suffixes after the aircraft type indicate different versions, so that the original C-130A Hercules was an early version, the C-130H a later standard, and the C-130K one optimised to use as much British equipment as possible. The Hornet was designated originally as the F-18A if single-seat, or F-18B if twin-seat, while the F/A-18C is single-seat and F/A-18D twin-seat, and the same goes for the F/A-18E and F/A-18F. Prototypes and experimental aircraft have an X prefix and pre-production models a Y prefix.

Changes also take place, with the utility helicopter designation UH having originally been HU, which led to the Bell 204/205 Iroquois becoming known as the 'Huey'. Sometimes designations are deliberately misleading, as with the Lockheed U-2, whose utility aircraft designation was intended to conceal its reconnaissance role for as long as possible.

Perhaps the most complicated system of designations was that used by the Japanese between the First and Second World Wars. The first letter denoted the type of aircraft, but it was followed by a figure that denoted the year of the ruling emperor's reign in which the aircraft first appeared. During the Second World War, the Allies used code names to describe Japanese aircraft types, such as 'Betty' and 'Sally'.

Variations of these were created during the Cold War, with Soviet aircraft being given artificial names which remained in NATO use even once the true designation of an aircraft became known in the West. Under this system, names beginning with 'B', such as 'Bear', were reserved for bombers, 'C', such as 'Cub' or 'Crate', were reserved for transport types, 'F', such as 'Fishbed', for fighters, and 'H', such as 'Hook', for helicopters. These were suffixed with an A, B, or C as later variants were identified.

The British tend to follow the aircraft type with a designation that describes the role of the aircraft and the version, so that the Nimrod maritime-reconnaissance aircraft is followed by a suffix MR.3 or MR.4, for example. The Canadians adapt the US system by prefixing it with a C, so that a Hornet would be a CF-18, for example.

Manufacturers use design office numbers or product numbers of names. Sometimes these fit a pattern, as with the Boeing range which has jet airliners in the 7X7 series, but again a second number gives an idea of the size of the aircraft, so that a Boeing 737-300 is smaller than a 737-400, but the 737-500 is smaller than either, or its generation, with the 737-600 and upwards being the 'new generation 737'. There can be suffixes such as 'LR' for long range and 'ER' for extended range. Airbus is even more confusing, with the A318, A319, A320 and A321 all being part of what should be the A320 family.

Using numbers is no guarantee that one will not run out of names. There has been more than one Comet, Corsair, Phantom and Whirlwind, but aircraft numbers are also recycled after a respectable period, with the USAF now back to B-1 and B-2 again.

aircrew The crew of an aircraft as distinct from the ground crew who maintain it. Commercial airlines normally distinguish between flight-deck crew, which today means captain and first officer since navigators have disappeared and flight engineers are a rarity, and cabin crew, the cabin attendants (more popularly known as stewards and stewardesses). Stewards appeared with the first airliners in the 1920s, after these replaced the converted DH4 bombers favoured by many of the first airlines, but in 1930, Boeing, at that time operating an airline as well as building aircraft, introduced stewardesses for the first time on its flights.

airliner A civilian transport aircraft which is not an airship and carries more than eighteen passengers can be regarded as an airliner. Smaller aircraft may claim to be such. The first aircraft to be specifically built to such a specification was **Igor Sikorsky's** *Ilya Mourametz* of 1914, but the outbreak of the First World War precluded its entry into service as such, and with the exception of the prototype, the production models all served as bombers with the Imperial Russian Flying Corps.

After the First World War, the first air services were operated by converted bombers, and even on routes such as London to Paris, the aircraft could only carry a pilot and two passengers. Nevertheless, the heavy bomber had made an appearance towards the end of the war and many of these were converted as airliners, including the Vickers Vimy and Farman Goliath, but these were soon joined by aircraft such as the de Havilland DH66 Hercules. The number of manufacturers of airliners between the wars was considerable, and in the UK alone included **Handley Page, de Havilland, Armstrong-Whitworth, Vickers**, and the flying boat builders **Supermarine** and **Shorts**. In the USA, there was **Boeing, Douglas, Consolidated, Curtiss, Stout**, which was absorbed by **Ford**, and **Martin**. Two of the most successful manufacturers were Ford and **Fokker**, both with trimotor transports, with the latter company's Fokker F.VII/3M pioneering many landplane routes.

At one time, the Americans had a passion for speedplanes for fast transport of passengers and mail, although both were in small quantities and passenger capacity varied between six and eight seats. The aircraft were usually monoplanes, always single-engined and with the sole pilot sitting in what was often an open cockpit. Nevertheless, the aircraft were attractive in appearance. Typical of these was the Lockheed Vega.

A feature of air travel between the wars was that so much of it was by flying boat. This was because of the shortage of airports in many parts of the world and the poor reliability of the aircraft engine of the day, and since more than two-thirds of the world's surface is covered in water, a plane capable of landing on water seemed a good idea. There were also shortcomings with landplane landing gear.

Another feature was that by today's standards, flying was extremely expensive, with a single airline ticket from Cardiff in South Wales to Plymouth in Devon costing the equivalent of an average week's wage for a skilled man. That would have been using a small airliner, a de Havilland Dragon Rapide, with six seats and the comfort equivalent to a small family car of the day. In contrast, on long-haul flights aboard a flying boat the operators and manufacturers tried to give some of the luxury that would be expected on an ocean liner, even down to having libraries. Even so, one passenger flying in the United States was given cotton wool to stuff in his ears to protect them from engine noise, and on landing was sprayed with mud coming through the ventilation vents.

Accommodation for the pilots was also basic, with even the Boeing 80 trimotor of 1928 offering either an enclosed or open cockpit.

Many of the early airliners were of all-metal construction, including the products of **Junkers** and Ford, but others retained fabric skins or were built of wood. The Boeing 247 was an all-metal airliner of sleek appearance, and in 1933 was among the first to employ flaps to reduce landing speeds without stalling and was also Boeing's first airliner with a retractable undercarriage.

Most airliners of the interwar period were in production and service for a very short time by today's standards. The exception was the Douglas DC-3, which first flew in 1936 as the DST, Douglas Sleeper Transport, intended for transcontinental flights in the USA. In its early form it was designed to carry twenty-one seated passengers or fourteen sleeper passengers in bunks. In fact, of more than 10,000 built, mainly as C-47 transports during the Second World War, many were cargo or troop-carrying aircraft, and postwar, many converted to the airline role were usually fitted with thirty-two seats.

By the outbreak of the Second World War in Europe, it was possible to fly from the UK to Australia or South Africa by flying boat, and across the Pacific from the USA to China. Transatlantic air services had been tested, and under wartime conditions became a regular flying boat operation using Poole on the south coast of England as a base. By the end of the war, military landplane transports were crossing the Atlantic and using Prestwick on the west coast of Scotland as their airport. Wartime gave a boost, building airfields, encouraging new routes and also once again increasing the number of air-minded people.

There had been some elegant pre-war airliners, such as the de Havilland Albatross. The Boeing 307 Stratoliner of 1940 was the first to provide a pressurised cabin, but only ten were built and divided equally between Pan American Airways and Trans World Airlines (TWA). Wartime checked the technical development of the airliner, and in the immediate postwar period, air travellers had once

again to endure the cramped and unsatisfactory conditions of converted bombers, such as the Lancastrian, converted from the Avro Lancaster heavy bomber. Even new aircaft borrowed the design of their aerodynamic surfaces, such as tailplane and mainplane, from bombers, with the Avro York based on the Lancaster, the Vickers Viking on the Wellington, and the luxurious double-deck Boeing Stratocruiser based on the B-29 Superfortress. While some new flying boats were built, by 1945 this aircraft was nearing its end.

Some of the early postwar aircraft could hardly be regarded as airliners, 'air ferries' would have been more accurate. With drive-on/drive-off ferries still a rarity, aircraft such as the Bristol 170 Freighter would carry in its stretched version up to twenty passengers and three cars, but this was an expensive operation and as shipping services improved, and hovercraft made their appearance, the business disappeared. Such operations were available across the English Channel and from Spain to the Balearic Islands, but were less successful over the Irish Sea.

The mood of optimism felt on the return of peace was reflected in several large aircraft that were never introduced to service. The Bristol Brabazon was a giant airliner with space for upwards of 200 passengers and was powered by eight Bristol Centaurus engines mounted in pairs in the wings and driving four contra-rotating propellers. A real dinosaur was the last British production civil flying boat, the Saunders-Roe, or SARO, Princess, intended for the South American services of BOAC, although there were also plans for a troop-carrying version. Three were built and flown successfully, but the day of the large long-range flying boat was past. Both these aircraft were too large for the day, and possibly this also inhibited Britain's airlines and aircraft designers in the years that followed when aircraft were introduced that soon proved to be too small.

The jet engine had appeared during the Second World War, but the immediate postwar years were not the start of the jet age for travellers. Douglas produced its DC-4 airliner with four engines for long-haul flights, while the pressurised DC-6 development followed and was then superseded by the DC-7. At first, aircraft had to refuel at

Shannon in Ireland and Gander in Newfoundland at the beginning and end of transatlantic flights.

Piston engines still ruled supreme, and apart from the Boeing and Douglas products, **Lockheed** introduced the Constellation and then the Super Constellation, elegant long-haul aircraft. While used C-47s abounded and the DC-3 was still acceptable, Martin introduced the 440 and Convair, the Metropolitan range of twin-engined airliners for shorter distances.

A false start for the jet airliner followed the failings of the de Havilland Comet I, and despite the rugged structure of the Comet II that followed, airlines and their passengers had been frightened off and it entered service as a military transport. When the Comet IV eventually arrived and commenced the first non-stop transatlantic jet flights on 4 October 1958, it was only just ahead of the Boeing 707 into service, and the larger Boeing had the better economics. In any event, the Comet had been beaten as the first jet airliner to enter service and stay in service by the Soviet Tupolev Tu-104 and its development, the Tu-114, and despite there being a short-haul version, the Comet IVB for BEA, this was beaten into service by the **Sud Aviation** Caravelle.

Far more successful was the Vickers Viscount, the world's first operational turboprop airliner, which introduced new standards of speed, comfort and smoothness on short-haul flights. This was the first British airliner to be exported to the United States, and was bought by many of the leading national airlines in Western Europe, including KLM, Air France and Alitalia. Its success led several manufacturers to follow the four-engined Viscount with a twin-engined airliner for even shorter or less busy routes, using the same engine. These included the Fokker F27 Friendship, the most successful of this breed and also built in the USA under licence, and the Avro, later Hawker Siddeley and then BAe, 748, also produced in India, and the much less successful Handley Page Herald and Japanese NAMC YS-11.

Long-haul turboprop aircraft also appeared, notably the Bristol Britannia, nicknamed the 'Whispering Giant' because of its quietness, and the Lockheed Electra, but they arrived too late and too close to the start of pure jet operations to make an impact on the market.

The advent of supersonic air travel was heralded by the Anglo-French Concorde airliner. At first this appeared to be an aircraft that every airline wanted, and across the world they reserved delivery positions. Boeing planned the 2707, a larger and faster supersonic transport with **variable-geometry**, which would enter service some years after Concorde. The Soviet Union launched the Tu-144, known as the 'Concordski', as it was a crude and unreliable copy of the Anglo-French aircraft. Contrary to popular belief, Concorde used state-of-the-art technology rather than developing new technology, unlike Boeing, and the problems that resulted led to the cancellation of the Boeing 2707. Concorde was not to have the market to itself, however, as problems over noise and the relatively short range, allied to the fact that supersonic flight looked like a cul-de-sac without a second generation aircraft to stimulate the market, resulted in the cancellation of the orders from all except the then state-owned British Airways, as the successor to BOAC and BEA, and Air France.

Concorde entered service with both airlines, mainly between London and Paris and New York, although at different times Bahrain and Rio de Janeiro were also served. At last, a businessman could make a day trip to New York from Europe. There were also excursion flights for enthusiasts and tourists. An accident in Paris on 25 July 2000 led to flights being grounded, even though the BA aircraft had been modified, and when restarted much of the market had gone and transatlantic services were in any case suffering a loss of business traffic following the terrorist acts of 11 September 2001, when the twin towers of the World Trade Center in New York were demolished by two hijacked airliners. After a couple of years' flying at much reduced frequencies, and offering much reduced fares, the aircraft was finally withdrawn.

While waiting for its 2707 to be built, Boeing needed a replacement for the 707. The result was an enlarged version of the aircraft with a flight deck and small passenger cabin on top of the fuselage, the 747, nicknamed the 'jumbo jet' because of its size. This was the first wide-bodied airliner and for many years it was the only large long-haul air transport, dominating the market. Smaller airliners, such as the three-engined Lockheed TriStar and

McDonnell Douglas DC-10, shared the market but were no substitute. Meanwhile, on short-haul services, the main European manufacturers formed a consortium, **Airbus Industrie**, to build a twin-engined short-haul wide-bodied airliner, the A300, which was followed by a slightly smaller aircraft, the A310. Later, an entire range of long, the A340 and A330, and short-haul aircraft, the narrow-bodied A320 series, appeared, with the narrow bodies competing with the Boeing 737 family that had cornered the short-haul market.

European efforts to build airliners were largely doomed to failure. The Vickers VC10 and Super VC10 were popular with passengers, but not with airline accountants. The British Trident series, originally designed by de Havilland and then produced by **Hawker Siddeley**, was the first airliner to be able to land blind in fog, but was too small for the market having been scaled down by BEA, frightened that the aircraft would be too big. Its main competitor, the Boeing 727 trijet was bigger and more economical.

The success for the Europeans was the One-Eleven, the so-called 'bus stop' jet built by **British Aircraft Corporation** (BAC, later BAe), which once again enjoyed a healthy export market. Fokker also enjoyed renewed sales with the smaller F28 Fellowship, the company's first commercial jet. The One-Eleven was produced in several stretches but unlike the Fokker design, which was stretched and re-engined as the Fokker 100, this was never re-engined and eventually after more than 200 had been sold, production ended. Fokker later collapsed.

Even the One-Eleven with several fuselage stretches, failed to match not only the Boeing 737, but the more obvious competitor, the **Douglas** DC-9 in sales. The DC-9's success was so significant that McDonnell bought Douglas as a hedge against future reductions in military aircraft expenditure.

The BAe 146 and its blind-landing successor, the Avro RJ series, enjoyed strong sales at first, despite the economic penalty of using four engines, because of its good short-field performance, and because a range of three fuselage lengths was available from the start. Nevertheless, with an improved RJX already entering production, and orders placed by airlines, the project was scrapped

after more than 300 aircraft had been put into service, again with airlines around the world.

At the other end of the scale from the jumbo jet was the family of small transports built by **de Havilland Canada**, a company originally owned by its British parent, but which eventually passed through a succession of owners, including Boeing, until recent years when it finally secured a settled future with **Bombardier**. The DHC6 Twin Otter proved to be a tough utility aircraft popular with small feeder and outback airlines and the military alike. The larger aircraft that joined it in production were mainly for air forces, until the Dash 7, intended to operate out of restricted airfields but with more comfort and speed than the Twin Otter. The market once again was not ready for the aircraft, but the Dash 8 that followed, with several fuselage stretches, remains in production today and has started a renaissance in the turboprop market because of its lower fuel consumption than jet aircraft.

Even smaller jet aircraft were also introduced by both Bombardier and by a Brazilian company, **Embraer**, that started to make hefty inroads into the world market with its small turboprops, and then with its ERJ series. Rising fuel costs soon showed that the smallest jet aircraft were uneconomical, especially on routes with price competition from the low-fare airlines, but while both manufacturers stretched their original aircraft, Embraer leapt forward with its E-jet family, of which the largest, the E-195, overlaps in capacity with the Boeing 737-600.

In between, other aircraft were developed. The basic Short Skyvan, looking like a box with wings, sold well to civil and military customers, as did the much larger developments, the 330 and 360. The small firm of **Britten-Norman** produced the Islander, which so transformed the economics of operating eight or nine passenger aircraft on thin but socially necessary routes, that the authorities were able to save money by cutting back on ferry services. A stretch, the three-engined Trislander, with the third engine stuck on top of the fin, sold well enough, but nothing like as well as the original, which remains in production with turboprops replacing the original piston engines. **Dornier** also returned to commercial aircraft production with its turboprop 228 utility aircraft, but its larger 328, also available as a jet, was taken over by Fairchild, but the company collapsed and the aircraft is no longer in production.

Throughout the postwar period, Soviet manufacturers failed to make inroads into Western markets. Despite the advances in their military aircraft technology and the space programme, their commercial products lacked appeal and reliability, and were expensive to operate. The Tupolev Tu-134 was no competition for the One-Eleven or DC-9, the Tu-144 Concordski had to be abandoned, and the Tu-154 trijet was no threat to the Boeing 737, and even less to the Boeing 757 twin jet that followed. After the collapse of communism, **Tupolev** developed a direct competitor to the 757, the Tu-204, available at much lower cost and also offered with Rolls-Royce engines and Western avionics as the Tu-214, but has failed to sell in the West, while the 757 production line has now closed. Tupolev and **Ilyushin** continue to offer aircraft to rival specific Western products, but it remains to be seen if they can break into the market.

The next stage in airliner development is the Airbus A380, which entered service with Singapore Airlines in 2008. While this aircraft with its two passenger decks initially offers considerable space, whether or not airlines eventually squeeze in as many seats as possible, replacing the three-class 525-passenger capacity with more than 800, remains to be seen. Will this be the future of air travel, with passengers flying on regional aircraft to a hub airport, or will the Boeing 787 'Dreamliner', with its smaller size able to operate more direct flights between city pairs, be the way ahead? Possibly there is room for both concepts.

airlines An operator of civil transport aircraft, whether passenger or freight or on a charter or scheduled basis, although usually scheduled airlines will carry passengers, freight and airmail. In terms of charter traffic, the term is usually reserved for operators of aircraft that are clearly not intended for executive or business charter, and is rarely applied to operators of helicopters.

Pioneers such as **William Henson** and **John Stringfellow** foresaw air transport. From 1910 there were some services operated by **Zeppelin** airships within Germany, with 40,000 passengers carried and 170,000 miles covered without a single accident of note before the outbreak of the First World War brought services to a halt. In the United States, P.E. Fansler operated a tentative airline in Florida in 1914, largely for tourists with flights 'on demand'. The first airline in the modern sense was Aircraft Transport & Travel (AT&T), a British company founded in 1917, which began operations in 1919. The airline with the longest existence as a single entity is KLM Royal Dutch Airlines, and this probably will hold good for some time despite the merger with Air France as the two companies continue to retain their separate identities. KLM's first flights were, in fact, operated for it by AT&T in 1919 between London and Amsterdam. The Air France/KLM combine is the world's largest airline, but the largest airline in one country is Germany's Lufthansa, in each case on the basis of annual turnover.

The early airlines were generally promoted by individuals, of whom the most famous was the American **Juan Trippe**, founder of Pan American. Nevertheless, by the mid-1920s, governments were becoming involved in Europe, and although the American operators remained in private hands, the award of **airmail** contracts, so necessary to underpin the fledgling air services, effectively ensured that the market was controlled. Indeed, for many years air services both nationally and internationally were tightly controlled by the state, and it was not until 1978 that deregulation occurred in the US, the first major country to allow this. The UK was the next country to deregulate, and the first significant international deregulation was on services between the Netherlands and the UK, which preceded deregulation within the wider European Union by some years. Deregulation, or an 'open skies' agreement between the EU and US, proved elusive, but finally began to take effect in 2007. Other countries that have opened up international services to deregulation have included Dubai and Singapore.

Within Europe, and in many other countries, state ownership was the normal situation for many years, and airlines were treated as an extension of the state and as an expression of national identity. Whether they could afford it or not, and whether it was justified or not, the first thing that many newly independent countries did after designing a national flag was to found a national airline. The one great exception to this has been Scandinavian Airlines System (SAS), with Norway and Denmark each having two-sevenths of the shares, and Sweden the remaining three-sevenths, with each country's stake being held 50:50 by the state and private investors. The Swiss Air Transport Company (Swissair) was for many years the largest completely private enterprise airline within Europe. In the UK, independent airlines grew after the Second World War, but were either confined to charter operations or had to fly scheduled services as 'associates' of the nationalised airlines.

The early development of airlines varied but several were owned by shipping companies, and in many countries, including the UK, domestic air services were largely developed by the railway companies. Between the wars, subsidies were regarded as worthwhile to develop air transport, while today it is more likely to be taxed, usually by means of departure taxes on travellers.

Denationalisation, or privatisation as it has become, took place in many countries, starting with the UK, and followed deregulation. The postwar private enterprise airlines in Europe suffered from instability and the sector was marked by bankruptcies. Comparatively large airlines that emerged, grew and then disappeared in the UK, either through bankruptcy or by being taken over, included British Eagle, Dan-Air, Air Europe, **Laker** Airways, Channel Airways and British Caledonian.

Looking at the development of airlines in Europe and in North America, some distinct differences became apparent during the postwar period. In Europe, before deregulation, half of all air travel was by charter flights as opposed to just 10 per cent in the USA, much of that for the military and their families. The lower air fares of the American scheduled carriers and a common language and currency, all combined to encourage passengers to use the scheduled services. In Europe, the inclusive tour, or package holiday, featuring a charter flight and hotel accommodation, made air travel affordable for the majority. The concept grew up that American air fares were always cheaper than in Europe, but once the charter flights were added, the differential between the

two continents was much reduced. Only in the UK did a European national have a significant 'trooping by air' charter traffic, tendered for by the charter airlines.

Deregulation in the United States saw the arrival of low-cost airlines, of which the first of any significance was South West Airlines. In the UK, pioneering low-cost transatlantic air services were pioneered by Laker Airways with the 'Skytrain' concept, which required passengers to turn up and buy a ticket, without pre-booking, and if they wanted any inflight catering, this had to be paid for separately. The airline collapsed, partly because a railway industrial dispute made it difficult to get passengers to and from the airport. A more enduring low-cost transatlantic service was provided first by Loftleidir and then by its successor, Icelandair, which was particularly useful for passengers from provincial cities in Europe, but required a change of plane in Iceland.

American concepts that carried over to the Old World, included the **shuttle** concept, although only on the UK domestic trunk services, and this has now been abandoned because of the high costs involved and the shortage of capacity at London's Heathrow Airport.

Pioneers of low-cost air transport within Europe have been the Irish airline Ryanair, easyJet in the UK, although founded and owned by a Greek shipping family, and also Flybe, while most European countries are now home to low-cost airlines and the concept has spread to Asia and Australasia. Even so, there have been casualties such as Buzz, Duo and Gill Air in the UK, often because they operated aircraft that were too small to be economically competitive with the Boeing 737 and Airbus 319 aircraft operated by the majors. It may also be that low-cost airlines have as much need of critical mass as the established traditional airlines.

Definition of a low-cost airline varies, as some offer free catering, although usually alcoholic drinks have to be paid for by the passengers, while others charge for everything, even baggage put into the hold of the aircraft. The one factor that they have in common is direct booking, ideally through the internet, cutting out the travel agent. This not only saves the agent's 10 per cent commission, it also cuts out the sales team who visit travel agents and training programmes for agency staff. Tickets are seldom issued, and anyone who would feel more comfortable with one has to pay for the benefit.

While the industry has lost much of its glamour, this can still be found in the small airlines operating small aircraft on 'lifeline' services.

Contrary to popular perceptions, air transport has the greatest impact not in the United States but in countries with poor surface communications, such as Greenland and Iceland.

Several attempts have been made to establish up-market business or even first-class only airlines, mainly in the USA. These tended to fail because of the limited route structure and the elderly aircraft initially used. More recent attempts have been more promising, including PrivatJet in Europe, which provides up-market scheduled services for both Lufthansa and Swiss International.

True low-cost services have been slow returning to the transatlantic routes, although Scottish-based Flyglobespan has done so. Part of the problem is that the traditional scheduled airlines can cover their costs by filling first and business class, and then effectively offer economy class at a marginal price simply to fill the aircraft and ensure that it is trimmed correctly. Flyglobespan has succeeded because of the limited long-haul services from Scotland. Nevertheless, the new 'open skies' agreement between the European Union and the United States suggests that radical change may be on the way.

Over the years, some interesting situations have emerged. West Berlin's isolated position, cut off from West Germany by East Germany, not only gave rise to the **Berlin Airlift** but also meant that only commercial aircraft belonging to the three wartime Western Allies could fly into the city. While Air France eventually operated just from France to West Berlin, BEA and Pan Am, as Pan American had become known, operated from West Berlin to destinations in West Germany. Dan-Air, a British independent airline, operated inclusive tour charter flights to holiday destinations out of West Berlin.

In the United States, Pan Am was not allowed to operate domestic routes until it acquired the ailing National Airways in 1967. The same situation arose in Australia, with Qantas denied domestic routes for many years.

There have also been fashions, one of the most significant being that of a major carrier franchising its name to smaller airlines. British Airways has made much of this with franchisees stretching from Scotland to South Africa, but now there seems to be a change of mood for the future. On rather firmer ground are the feeder airlines that operate, especially in the United States as regional affiliates of the US majors, such as Northwest Airlink and Delta Connection, operating into Northwest and Delta hubs as appropriate. These airlines are limited both by agreements with their unions and with their major airline partner to operating aircraft of no more than a certain size. This is a practical approach as it seems to be the case that an airline with a transcontinental and international route structure finds it uneconomical to operate small aircraft on less busy routes.

Foreign ownership of airlines is still difficult, usually with an upper limit of 49 per cent on foreign investment, and even then voting rights are sometimes limited to just 25 per cent.

Another recent development has been the creation of global alliances, such as the Star Alliance, OneWorld and Sky Team, with the latter claiming to be to global airline. Some believe that these will in time see the airline members merging to become global airlines and that there may be just three or four airlines serving the main routes. That remains to be seen, especially in view of ownership restrictions and legislation designed to maintain competition in many countries. A feature of an alliance is that it involves coordinating schedules, frequent flyer programmes and code-sharing, while in some cases it can extend to maintenance and aircraft procurement.

The airline sector is not typical of business generally. As with other forms of transport, once a service departs any unsold seats are lost forever, unlike 'the butcher, the baker and the candlestick-maker' who have another chance to sell their wares.

airmail Balloons were used for communications purposes during the Siege of Paris in the Franco-Prussian War of 1870–1, with special postage stamps issued, while early attempts at microfiche were also introduced. This was a hit-and-miss affair as the unmanned balloons went wherever the wind took them. Earlier, balloons had been used by HMS *Assistance* in the search for the ill-fated Sir John Franklin expedition in the Canadian Arctic in 1850. Airmail, however, is about sending mail, not simple messages that could be construed as an airborne courier service.

In the early days of powered flight, carrying a small consignment of mail was a gimmick, and a hint of the potential for airmail. In 1911, a Blériot monoplane carried mail for 6 miles in the US between Garden City and Mineola, while in the UK, another aircraft flew mail between Hendon and Windsor. The First World War intervened to delay the introduction of airmail, but it did see a military air dispatch service introduced between Vienna and Kiev in 1918, using Brandenburg biplanes.

In May 1918 the US Post Office introduced an airmail service between Washington and New York. The first international scheduled airmail flight in the world was operated in November 1919 by the British airline, Aircraft Transport & Travel (AT&T), between London and Paris. This was followed by the first international airmail service in the New World in late 1920, when a Hubbard Air Service Boeing Type C aircraft flew from Seattle, Washington State, to Vancouver, British Columbia.

The importance of airmail to airline development between the First and Second World Wars is generally and hugely underestimated. Improved communications were important, and air travel was outside the reach of most of the population, even in the prosperous countries of Europe and North America. Telegraphic communication and, increasingly, long-distance international telephone lines did exist, but had their drawbacks. In the United States, the airline industry received a massive boost when airmail was moved from the United States Army, which had suffered a number of serious accidents while carrying the mail, to the airlines, which tendered for airmail contracts. Before this a transcontinental airmail service had been started in 1921, linking New York with San Francisco.

Britain's first regular domestic airmail service was started in 1934, with Highland Airways flying between Inverness and Kirkwall on the mainland of Orkney. Given the intense railway network in

Europe, overseas airmail was accorded priority, with the British, French and Dutch airlines already benefiting from airmail revenues by this time because so much of their route mileage was aimed at linking their far-flung colonial territories. Perhaps one of the most unusual airmail services was that provided to South America by the new German airline, Deutsche Luft Hansa (DLH – predecessor of today's Lufthansa). Seaplanes were catapulted off the liners *Bremen* and *Europe* on the shipping service between Europe and Brazil while the liner was some 750 miles from its destination, saving a couple of days on the surface mail timings. Initially, DLH used Heinkel He12 and He58 biplanes, but in 1932 Junker Ju46 monoplanes replaced them. The service improved still further in 1934 when the mail was flown from Germany to Bathurst in the then British colony of the Gambia by a Dornier Wal flying boat, and then put aboard one of two cargo ships, either the *Schwabenland* or the *Westfalen*, and again flown off from these ships as they reached a point some 750 miles from the coast of Brazil. The service worked in the opposite direction with mail being flown off as the ships approached the Gambia. Cargo ships were chosen for this improved service rather than divert an ocean liner to call at the Gambia.

A through London to Australia airmail service was agreed in 1934. The British 'Empire Air Mail' scheme was agreed between the participating nations in 1934 and inaugurated in 1937. This allowed cheap-rate airmail letters to be sent to any address in the British Empire, carried by Imperial Airways, and by 1938, Imperial Airways was undoubtedly the world's largest single carrier of airmail. Mail could be flown any distance for the cost of $1\frac{1}{2}d$ (0.625p) per half ounce, or just $2\frac{1}{2}$ US cents at the then exchange rate. The airline had been so encouraged by the prospects offered by airmail that it took the then unprecedented step of ordering no less than twenty-eight of the new Short S23 Empire flying boats straight off the drawing board. In the event, additional aircraft were soon required.

Since the Second World War, the massive growth in air travel and in air freight has reduced the relative importance of airmail to the airlines, and more recently no doubt cheaper long-distance telephone calls and the internet will have played a further part in this. Nevertheless, airmail is still a useful addition to overall earnings. Even during the Second World War, planning for airmail envisaged a premium passenger service, probably with relatively small aircraft. The de Havilland Comet I airliner replaced an earlier project for which the manufacturer had foreseen a transatlantic jet-powered mailplane, but decided that such an aircraft would have been uneconomical. Postwar, BEA operated experimental helicopter airmail services in the West of England and Wales.

airports Usually reserved for locations which handle commercial flights rather than military, in which case the term is air station or air base. For general aviation, the word airfield or the older aerodrome is used.

While there were several centres at which the pioneers congregated and flew their aeroplanes, including Hendon and Brooklands in England and Bagatelle in France, these were at best aerodromes. One of the first airports was Hounslow Heath, to the west of London, from which Aircraft Transport & Travel (AT&T) operated, before the capital's airline operations moved to Croydon, to the south of London, in March 1920. Between the First and Second World Wars, Hythe, on the south coast of England near Southampton, became an important departure point for the Imperial Airways flying boat services to the Empire.

Today, air travel has grown to such an extent that many major cities, not just the capitals, require several airports. Milan, for instance, has three airports. The busiest airport in the world in terms of passenger numbers is Atlanta, Georgia, with more than 88 million passengers in 2005, but add the three main airports for New York together – JFK, La Guardia and Newark, New Jersey – and the combined total comes to almost 100 million. London's main airport at Heathrow handles more international passengers than any other, and London has further airports at Gatwick, Stansted, London City and Luton.

Over the past fifty years, airports have become controversial. Many travellers hate the larger hub airports, while there is always opposition to the construction of a new airport or the expansion of an existing one. Some argue in favour of airports close to the coast or even offshore, but these

bring many drawbacks, including approaches over the sea, which is more dangerous in case an aircraft under or overshoots, and brings bird strike hazards. At some airports, attempts to make the best use of scarce landing and take-off slots has led to charging policies that drive away smaller aircraft, which not only use a slot but require longer separation distances if they are following a much larger aircraft. This has led to some major airports, such as London Heathrow, losing links with destinations that cannot warrant the use of larger aircraft, which is also controversial. The ideal airport has sufficient terminals and runways to cope with the available traffic, a runway or satellite airport within easy reach for smaller **commuter airlines** or regional aircraft, and good road and rail links with the city it is serving. Ideally, it should also have room on the regional runway for business aircraft. Technically, it not only needs air traffic control radar covering its terminal manoeuvring zone, but also a separate system controlling aircraft movements on the ground. If an airline or airlines are based at the airport, good maintenance facilities and room for hangars on the edge of the airport are essential.

airscrew The correct technical term for the propeller of an aeroplane or an **airship**. From the earliest times, these were either of the 'pusher' type, mounted behind the engine as in nautical practice, or 'tractor' propellers, mounted in front of the engine. For many years the latter has been the preferred position, and today the only aircraft in production with a pusher propeller is the Piaggio Avanti II business aircraft. A few aircraft have used both tractor and pusher propellers, of which the most recent was the Cessna Skymaster and Super Skymaster light aircraft, intended to offer pilots all of the advantages of a twin engine without the drawbacks in handling if one engine failed. Airships tend still to use pusher propellers.

In **helicopters**, both propulsion and lift is provided by rotor blades rather than propellers, although some designs have used both to increase speed.

airship The popular term for what is strictly known as a dirigible. The airship was derived from the need to ensure that the early aerostats, simple balloons, could move in the direction of the pilot's choosing. Although there were some attempts to mate balloons with simple **airscrews**, the shape of the craft was wrong and directional control was lacking. Airships have differed widely in type, with the two main types being the rigid and the semi-rigid. The former includes the **Zeppelin** designs that were so effective during the First World War and had a stiff structure. The semi-rigid, with most British wartime airship types being of this kind, had a simple and more flexible structure and was more vulnerable so the RNAS did not use these for offensive operations, but they did prove useful as escorts for shipping convoys. The 'blimp' barrage balloons of the Second World War were simply meant to ascend and descend, and were unpowered.

Early attempts at building airships suffered from both a poor knowledge of aerodynamics and control as well as from the absence of efficient and reliable lightweight power units. It soon became apparent that the early idea of airships being rowed by men with oars was fanciful in the extreme. The cigar shape, so well known from photographs, eventually became standard, although some were more or less pointed at both ends. One of the most famous was the *Dolphin*, so named because of its shape, designed by **Urs Christian Egg** and his partner, **Samuel Pauly** in London. It was never built as Pauly died before it could be completed.

The first recorded attempt to build an airship was in France in 1834, but it was unsuccessful. Success also eluded the first British airship, *The Eagle*, completed the following year and which was to be powered by the crew pulling oar-like levers to power flappers, but it never flew. It was not until 1852 that **Henri Giffard** built a workable airship, making an ascent near Paris and travelling at between 4 and 5 mph using a single steam engine. This was the first true dirigible, or steerable airship, but the low power of its engine meant that only the most limited manoeuvres could be made.

Understanding of the requirements for a successful airship had grown considerably by 1883, when **Albert and Gaston Tissandier** built and operated their electrically powered airship, but this was still not powerful enough and battery charge was inadequate for anything

but the shortest journeys. In 1884, still in France, **Capt Charles Renard** and **Arthur-Constantin Krebs** built another electrically powered airship *La France*, which was powerful enough to be able to travel and return to its point of departure.

In Germany, the great airship pioneer and designer, **Count Ferdinand von Zeppelin** had some difficulty with his early designs at the end of the nineteenth century. At first success seemed elusive. It even appeared as if the airship might be nothing more than an attractive and expensive plaything. Nevertheless, in 1901 **Alberto Santos-Dumont**, a Brazilian living in Paris, circled the Eiffel Tower in one of his small and squashy airships, which he used rather as an urban runabout. The internal combustion engine had arrived and in 1902 the **Lebaudy** brothers produced the first practical airships using Daimler petrol engines. Their first was officially the *Lebaudy 1*, but unofficially was known as *Jaune* because of its yellow colour. This sold to the French Aarmy and one was later acquired by public subscription for the British Army. The first British airship was the British Army No. 1, built at Farnborough in 1906 by the American, **Samuel F. Cody**.

Meanwhile, von Zeppelin had built his Luftschiffbau Zeppelin factory in 1898 and his first airship appeared in 1900, funded by a public subscription. Powered by two 15 hp engines, it enjoyed limited success on its first trial ascent on 2 July 1900. Despite this shaky start, by 1908, a Zeppelin was able to remain in the air for 4½ hours with at least nine passengers, and in 1909 the Imperial German Navy ordered four Zeppelins.

The First World War saw extensive use of airships by both the British and the Germans. Zeppelins were used to bomb London as early as 1915 and presented considerable problems for the relatively slow aircraft of the day which had difficulty in climbing up past the Zeppelin's defensive armament to get into position for an attack. This was a particular difficulty for hydro-aeroplanes because of the weight and drag of their floats, and did much to accelerate the development of the aircraft carrier, which could carry the more agile landplane. The hydrogen used in the gas bag made the Zeppelins highly vulnerable to intense anti-aircraft fire.

The Royal Navy used airships for convoy protection during the war, and postwar the United States Navy not only maintained an active interest in airships, but also experimented with using these to launch fighter aircraft.

Although a British airship, the *R34*, made a successful transatlantic return journey in 1919, the British and the Americans soon favoured the heavier-than-air aeroplane for air services. In 1934 a further double crossing of the Atlantic was made by the British *R100*, but a publicly funded rival, the *R101*, crashed with massive loss of life that same year at Beauvais in northern France, when en route to India. The Germans continued to favour the Zeppelin with one of the most famous and successful being the *Graf Zeppelin*, which entered service in 1928 and operated until 1937. It was withdrawn in the wake of the *Hindenburg* disaster at Lakehurst, New Jersey, that year, again with considerable loss of life when it struck a mooring mast. The scale of the disaster was largely due to a US embargo on the export of the safer, albeit less efficient as a lifting agent, helium to Germany which meant that the Germans were forced to continue using highly combustible hydrogen. The *Hindenburg* tragedy was caught by a newsreel cameraman and was shown in cinemas across the world, accompanied by a distraught commentary by a news reporter as the tragedy unfurled.

The disaster ended the commercial career of the airship just as the military was beginning to realise that the aeroplane was a more efficient tool.

Airships suffered from their huge size and vulnerability. They could not be used in high winds, and even in a stiff breeze handling on the ground was manpower intensive. Despite having engines, real progress still depended on favourable wind conditions. During the Second World War, the main combatants used barrage balloons, or blimps, to protect vital targets by forcing bombers to fly higher to avoid not the airships themselves, but their steel cables which could tear the wings off an aircraft. Even if powered, a blimp would have been extremely difficult to control because it lacked any rigid structure.

In recent years there have been several attempts to revive the airship. They are seen as a means of carrying heavy or outsized loads that could not use the normal highway network, or in providing deliveries to areas with a difficult terrain. Little has come of this so far, and the tourist sightseeing potential has not been fully realised, doubtless due to high cost. Airships have proved to be of some use in carrying advertising at major events, and for this also, the 'blimp' is back.

airspace The air above any country's territory and generally regarded as extending over territorial waters as well. Much airspace in the developed countries these days is controlled, meaning that air traffic control authority is needed to penetrate it. Controlled airspace generally starts at 4,000 ft and rises to 40,000 ft, below which general aviation can usually operate freely except close to airports and military training areas.

airspeed The speed of any form of aircraft through the air, as opposed to its speed over the ground. Airspeed is vital for aircraft to stay in the air and for control, but the speed over the ground is vital for navigation. Early aircraft could often be blown backwards in a strong wind, and even today, light aircraft need to be tied down in high winds otherwise, as the wind reaches their take-off speed, they are likely to lift off the ground. By contrast, balloons drift at the speed of the wind and have no airspeed.

Airspeed British manufacturer, prominent during the interwar period but surviving the Second World War to be acquired by **de Havilland** in the early 1950s. Its products included communications aircraft such as the Envoy and Oxford, often adapted as navigational trainers, while the pre-war Courier was the first British aircraft to have a fully retractable undercarriage. Wartime production included the Horsa troop-carrying glider. Postwar, the company built the elegant twin-engined Ambassador, a high-wing airliner known as the Elizabethan in BEA service. While the Ambassador was piston-engined, the airframe was used to test many of the first generation turboprop engines.

Albatros German aircraft manufacturer. The company first came into prominence when it launched the D.I racer in 1914, which became a First World War fighter. It was followed by the

D.II, D.III, D.IV and D.V, although the last of this line of biplanes was no match for the latest Allied aircraft, and soon the factory was reduced to licence-production of Fokker aircraft. It was one of many that also produced the Rumpler Taube (Dove) early in the war. Not all of the aircraft were fighters, with the C.III being a bomber. Production ceased with the Armistice.

Alcock, Sir John (1892–1919) English aviator. Manchester-born Alcock became an aircraft mechanic at Brooklands, Surrey, in 1910, and after taking flying lessons on Farm Longhorns, he earned his wings in 1912, receiving Royal Aero Club certificate 363. He joined the Royal Naval Air Service in August 1914, and became an instructor at Eastchurch, Isle of Sheppey, before being posted to the Aegean and seeing action over Gallipoli. He was awarded the Distinguished Flying Cross (DFC) for taking on three enemy aircraft single-handed, but fell victim to Turkish anti-aircraft fire in September 1917 and became a prisoner of war. He was repatriated after the Armistice and became a test pilot with Vickers. On 14/15 June 1919, with Lt Arthur Whitten-Brown, he flew a Vickers Vimy bomber to make the first non-stop transatlantic flight from Newfoundland to Ireland, for which achievement both men were knighted. In December 1919 Alcock was killed in a landing accident in heavy fog near Rouen, France.

While in the RNAS, Alcock dabbled in aircraft design, taking salvaged pieces of various Sopwith aircraft, but he became a PoW before he could attempt to fly the resultant hybrid. He received news of the aircraft's flight while in a Turkish PoW camp.

Alenia/Alenia Aermacchi See Finmeccanica

alliances, airline See also airlines. These are formal groupings of airlines, usually from different countries, which have agreed to coordinate schedules and such matters as frequent-flyer programmes. Some may have shareholdings in other members, but this is not necessary. Code-sharing on routes with more than one member operating are also common, and sometimes used to extend an airline's operating area into regions not actually served by it. Some see these alliances

leading to international mergers and eventually the alliances would be the airline, but this does not necessarily have to happen.

The three main alliances are:

OneWorld, which includes American Airlines, British Airways, Cathay Pacific, Finnair, Iberia Airlines, Japan Air Lines International, LANChile, Qantas Airways and Royal Jordanian. Aer Lingus was a member until 2007 but has left to re-establish itself as a low-cost airliner.

Sky Team, which claims to be a global airline, was formed in 2000 by Aeroméxico, Air France, Delta Airlines and Korean Air, but later added Alitalia, CSA Czech Airlines, KLM Royal Dutch Airlines and Northwest Airlines.

Star Alliance, which brings together frequent-flyer programmes and other services for Adria Airways, Air Canada, Air New Zealand, All Nippon Airways, Asiana, Austrian Airlines, Blue1, bmi, Croatia Airlines, Lauda Air, LOT Polish Airlines, Lufthansa, SAS, Singapore Airlines, TAP Portugal, Thai International, United Airlines, US Airways and Varig.

Allied Bomber Offensive In the Second World War, the RAF and the USAAF believed in the concept of strategic bombing, in contrast to the Soviet armed forces and the Axis powers, which lacked true strategic bombers at the outset of the war and instead followed the concept of **blitzkrieg**.

The Americans advocated striking at industrial targets, with emphasis on oil and rubber production and armaments, but the RAF, with its experience of navigational difficulties and finding the targets, had favoured area bombing. So, while sharing the vision of the combined bombing campaign, some flexibility was needed. The combined bombing offensive was soon given the title 'Pointblank'. The US offensive was in four stages. During the first half of 1943 it was primarily concerned with targets within fighter range, including U-boat installations on the French Atlantic coast. The second stage would start in the third quarter of the year, with penetrations into Germany to a depth of around 400 miles, with the main emphasis on aircraft factories, and especially those producing fighters. The third stage, in the fourth quarter of the year, would see other targets being attacked, although pressure would be maintained on the aircraft factories to prevent these from being rebuilt. The fourth stage would occur at the start of 1944, and pave the way for the forthcoming invasion of northern France. The emphasis on curbing fighter production was due to the growing threat from Luftwaffe fighters, which were affecting night and day bomber operations.

The US bombers with their heavy defensive armament were used on day raids and the RAF on night raids, having suffered unsustainable losses early in the war on day raids. This division had two important side-effects. First, had both air forces wanted to operate at the same time there would have been dangerous congestion over the airfields concentrated mainly in the east of England. Second, on certain selected targets, it meant that the USAAF could follow an RAF night raid, preventing the Germans from repairing any damage.

Allison A US aero-engine manufacturer which took over Packard and itself became a subsidiary of General Motors. Just as Packard produced the Rolls-Royce Merlin for the Mustang, Allison produced the Spey for the A-7 Corsair II. The company attained a niche market in producing turboprop engines for the Lockheed Electra and its maritime-reconnaissance development, the P-3 Orion, as well as for the C-130 Hercules, the best-selling postwar military transport. It is now a wholly owned subsidiary of **Rolls-Royce** and its products carry the parent company's name. The acquisition of Allison brought Rolls-Royce back into the market for large turboprops, which it had neglected after its Tyne engine, used on the Vanguard airliner, Belfast and Transall transports, and Atlantique MR aircraft.

Alps, first flights over The first attempt at a flight over the Alps was by the Peruvian, **Georges Chavez**, on 23 September 1910, but this ended in an accident with the pilot dying from his injuries. It was not until 1913 that Oskar Bider, a Swiss, was able to fly his Blériot monoplane over the Bernese Alps, having previously also made the first flight across the Pyrenees. He reported that this flight was no more difficult than that across the Pyrenees.

altimeter The basic instrument that provides the pilot with the height of the aircraft above sea level. Originally altimeters were solely based on barometric pressure, requiring pilots to reset them en route and especially on the approach to their destination, as differences in barometric pressure meant that dangerous variations from a true reading could occur. Radio altimeters provide a more consistently accurate reading of the aircraft's true position relative to the ground, but barometric pressure is still needed in case of failure or interference.

altitude The height of an aircraft above the ground. Safe flying can be achieved most easily by maintaining an altitude that is higher than any obstacle likely to be encountered en route, but this is subject to air traffic control requirements. It is important that the landing approach be such that tall buildings, broadcasting masts and electricity pylons, as well as high ground, can be avoided. Failure to observe this has led to many accidents known as 'controlled flight into terrain' (CFT).

altitude records *See* Table 18: Aeronautical Records.

amphibian Any aircraft that can operate from water or land, regardless of whether it has the hull in the water, as with a flying boat, or has floats. The term was first used by **Charles Rumney Samson** when he fitted a Short biplane with air bags so that it could land on water. The first practical amphibians were designed and built by **Glenn Curtiss** in 1911 or 1912 in the United States, often using a single large float and having fixed wheels. The first amphibian with a retractable undercarriage that could be stored out of the way when operating from water was the Sopwith Bat Boat of 1914.

Until the advent of the helicopter, amphibians provided a high degree of flexibility in operation, but most aircraft continued to be built as landplanes, floatplanes or flying boats because of the higher cost of amphibians. A few aircraft have been offered in amphibian or flying boat configurations, most notably the Convair Catalina, whose PBY-5 or PBY-6 designation had an 'A' suffix added when an amphibian.

To ease maintenance and storage, flying boats could be fitted with beaching wheels to allow them to be pulled up a slipway, but these could not be used for take-off or landing. Helicopters have not generally been built as amphibians, but some types do have hulls that enable them to land on water and the retractable undercarriage sponsons act as stabilizers; typical of these is the Sikorsky S-61 Sea King.

Amundsen, Roald (1872–1928) Norwegian polar explorer. Better known for being the first man to reach the South Pole, Amundsen had also discovered the magnetic North Pole some years earlier. In 1925, sponsored by the American millionaire Lincoln Ellsworth, he tried to use two Dornier Wal flying boats to reach the North Pole, but failed when the aircraft crash-landed short of their destination. One of the aircraft was repaired and flew the crews to safety. In May 1926 he made a further attempt using the airship *Norge*, leased from the Italian government with her Italian crew. Deciding that since **Lt Cdr Byrd** had probably already flown over the North Pole, he would instead make the first transpolar crossing by air. Departing from Spitzbergen, despite disagreements over command with the airship's captain **Umberto Nobile**, they completed the trip and reached Teller, Alaska.

In 1928 Amundsen disappeared searching for Nobile, who had crashed while making a further expedition.

Anderson, Maxi Leroy (1934–83) US aeronaut. Anderson was partnered by his friend **Ben Abruzzo** in an attempt to cross the Atlantic in the balloon *Double Eagle* in 1977, which ended with the balloon drifting into a severe storm and crashing off the northern coast of Iceland. The duo succeeded the following year when they were joined by **Larry Newman** in a new balloon, *Double Eagle II*, ascending from Presque Isle, Maine, on 11 August, and reaching Misery, France, six days later.

Despite this success, Anderson then became a rival to Abruzzo and sought further records with his son. An attempt to cross the United States in a balloon ended in an ascent that took them from San Francisco to Gross Roches, Quebec, which

they tried to present as the first balloon crossing of North America, but this was rejected. Anderson continued ballooning but was later killed in a ballooning accident.

Andes, first flights over On 13 April 1918 Teniente Luis Candelaria of the Argentine army flew a Morane-Saulnier parasol monoplane from Zapala, Argentina, to Cunco, Chile, a distance of about 125 miles, reaching an altitude of around 13,000 ft en route. There is no record of his making the return flight. The first eastbound crossing is believed to have been by a Chilean pilot, Teniente Dn. Dagoberto Godoy of the Chilean Military School of Aviation, who flew a Bristol M1C monoplane from Santiago de Chile to Mendoza in Argentina on 12 December 1918.

Andrée, Salomon Auguste (1854–97) Swedish aeronaut. One-time head of the Swedish patent office, Andrée was inspired by **John Wise** to plan long-distance balloon ascents. From 1894 he started raising funds for a balloon crossing of the North Pole, and although he was ready by 1896, unfavourable weather delayed the ascent until 11 July 1897, when finally he set off from Spitzbergen with two companions. They disappeared without trace. It was not until 1930 that the bodies were discovered by the ship *Bratvaag*, with diaries and photographic film, which produced high-quality prints once developed despite the time that had passed. From the diaries it was discovered that the balloon had grounded while still 500 miles from the Pole, and they had died one by one, possibly from poisoning after killing and eating a polar bear, which may have carried trichinosis.

angled flight deck A postwar British invention that enabled aircraft to land without the danger of continuing on into aircraft either parked forward on the flight deck or waiting to take off, as any aircraft that missed the arrester wires could go round and make a further attempt at landing. This required good reactions on the part of the pilot who would have to move the throttle setting to go round from landing and adjust flap settings. On the other hand, if this was beyond the pilot or there was trouble with the engines, as on a damaged aircraft, ejecting or ditching was also much safer as the crew or the aircraft would land in the water clear of the ship rather than risk being run down. The angled flight deck also enabled aircraft to be launched from this deck as well as forward, increasing the tempo of take-offs when mounting a major mission.

The concept was the brainchild of Capt D.R.F. Campbell, RN, but the first aircraft carrier to have the interim half-angled flight deck was the USS *Antietam* in 1952. The following year the British HMS *Centaur* entered service with a half-angled deck, which could be incorporated into a ship with the minimum of dockyard work.

The fully angled flight deck made better use of space enabling additional catapults to be installed, as when the USS *Forrestal* joined the US fleet in 1955 with two steam catapults on its fully angled flight deck in addition to the two forward. This was only possible on larger ships, and even when refitted with fully angled flight decks, the British carriers HMS *Eagle* and *Ark Royal* could only have a single waist catapult.

anhedral A downward droop of the wings of an aircraft to give an inverted 'V' effect when viewed from ahead or behind. This was discovered by the pioneers to give better control in roll as it countered any natural stability that a design might have. Soviet-era transports and bombers often had this feature, but it could also be seen on the Boeing B-52 Superfortress bomber and Lockheed C-5A/B transport.

Annunzio, Gabriele d' (1863–1938) Early Italian military airman. D'Annunzio had adopted his father's uncle's name in place of his own, Gaetano Rapagnetta. He first became interested in aviation when he was taken into the air by **Glenn Curtiss** at Brescia in 1911, at which time d'Annunzio was a career army officer in the cavalry with a passion for writing poetry. He switched to the Military Aviation Service early in the First World War and was posted to the Lion of St Mark Squadron as a major. He led reconnaissance and bombing raids against the Germans and, more often, Austro-Hungarian forces. His most spectacular operation was when he led seven SVA fighters from Brescia on a 7-hour mission over the Alps to Vienna, considered safe because of its distance from the Allies, to drop propaganda leaflets.

anti-submarine warfare In the twentieth century, two world wars alerted governments to the devastating effects on shipping by even a relatively small number of submarines. During the First World War, maritime-reconnaissance flying boats based on the work of **Glenn Curtiss** in the United States and **John Porte** in the UK, played a part in actively hunting the German U-boats, while coastal convoys were escorted by semi-rigid airships of the RNAS. The Second World War saw ever longer range aircraft used, although at first the only long-range aircraft available to the RAF at the outset of hostilities was the Short Sunderland flying boat. Of the wartime RAF and USN aircraft, the Sunderland and Consolidated Catalina flying boats and the B-24 Liberator, also by Consolidated, were the most effective, so much so that there was considerable friction between the USN and USAAF over allocation of this aircraft, which was also an effective heavy bomber. For convoy escort duties, the carrier-borne Fairey Swordfish biplane was able to operate off the smallest merchant aircraft carriers, the MAC ships, and loiter for a lengthy patrol period, with later versions being fitted with anti-shipping radar. Aircraft and surface vessels learned to collaborate and many 'kills' were the result of this.

At the height of the Cold War, the Soviet Union had ten times the number of submarines available to Germany in 1939, and with many of them nuclear-powered, they were able to dive more deeply, move more quickly and remain on station for far longer than their conventionally powered wartime German counterparts. After the Second World War, anti-submarine technology continued to develop, and while surface vessels with sonar provided a major part of anti-submarine warfare (ASW), augmented by fast nuclear-powered 'hunter-killer' submarines (also known to the RN as fleet submarines), aircraft also continued to play a major part, improved by new technology that vastly increased their effectiveness. No longer were aircrew dependent upon finding a submarine on the surface, or even, with good radar, possibly picking up the periscope or snorkel of a submerged vessel. During the First World War, keen eyesight was the factor, but in the Second World War anti-surface vessel radar (ASV) helped greatly; postwar, other techniques came into play.

The main drawback in detecting submarines was the distortion caused to sonar by the screws, or propellers, of the surface vessel, which also alerted the commander of the submarine to take evasive action. This was overcome by aircraft dropping sonar buoys, including the system known as 'Jezebel' which left a pattern of passive sonar buoys floating on the surface listening for a submarine and using their different positions to give an accurate position for the vessel, which was transmitted back to the circling aircraft. The maritime-reconnaissance aircraft could then drop depth charges or, increasingly, a homing torpedo, to destroy the submarine.

At the end of the Second World War, aircraft such as the Vickers Wellington and the Consolidated Liberator were still in use on maritime-reconnaissance, but these were eventually replaced by the Avro Shackleton, a development of the wartime Lancaster bomber, and the Lockheed P-2 Neptune. A later generation of maritime-reconnaissance aircraft included the Lockheed P-3 Orion, developed from the Electra II airliner, and the Hawker Siddeley (later BAe) Nimrod, developed from the de Havilland Comet IV airliner, while the Franco-German Breguet Atlantique was a purpose-designed submarine hunter. Aboard aircraft carriers, the Royal Navy had the Fairey Gannet, a turboprop anti-submarine aircraft, and the USN the Grumman S-2 Tracker, a twin piston-engined aircraft later replaced by the Lockheed S-2 Viking, and the French Aéronavale had the Breguet Br1150 Alize. The Viking was updated and retained in service, but the Gannet and the Alize were replaced by anti-submarine helicopters. The Soviet Union at the same time used aircraft such as the Tupolev Tu-142, known to NATO as the Bear-F.

Helicopters, usually developments of medium lift machines, used the dunking sonar system, although often in combination with sonar buoys. Dunking sonar enabled a helicopter to hover and lower its sonar to search for a submarine, although the sonar was active rather than passive, and so gave the submariners warning. A homing torpedo or depth charges would then be dropped. The advantage of the helicopter was that it could be deployed on ships without a full-length flight deck, although many of the smaller helicopters,

such as the naval version of the Westland Lynx, deployed from frigates and destroyers, were not always fitted with this equipment. Nevertheless, they could use information from their mother vessel, sonar buoys or surface radar in their hunt. Among the first helicopters to carry dunking sonar was the Sikorsky S-58 and its derivatives, such as the Westland Wessex, but in the 1970s the Sikorsky SH-3D Sea King and the licence-built versions by **Westland** and **Agusta**, were also fitted, as have been the more modern Agusta-Westland Merlin.

For fixed-wing aircraft, autolycus equipment carried aboard can also be use to detect diesel fumes from a conventional submarine using its diesels either on the surface or submerged through the snorkel. Fixed-wing maritime-reconnaissance aircraft also give the observer a clue as to their role by the magnetic anomaly detector (MAD) protruding from the tail, known often as the 'MAD stinger'.

Antoinette French manufacturer. One of the first companies to manufacture both aircraft and engines, the name came from the daughter of **Jules Gastambide**, the owner, but the main driving force behind the firm was the designer **Léon Levavasseur**, an advocate of the monoplane. The early aeroplanes, which appeared in 1907, were not very successful, although the first aeroplane flight in Europe, by **Alberto Santos-Dumont**, had used an Antoinette engine. By 1909 the Antoinette monoplanes were proving themselves to be reliable. Ailerons and wing-warping were used, depending on the model, but by persisting with the tractor propeller and with the mainplane in front of the tailplane, the company set the pattern for aircraft design that has endured to this day. An Antoinette was unsuccessful in an attempt to be first to fly across the English Channel, and while **Louis Blériot** was a customer for the company's engines, he did not use one on his cross-Channel flight. At the 1909 **Reims Aviation Meeting**, an Antoinette set the world's first official speed record of 100 kmph (62.5 mph).

Antonov Ukrainian aircraft manufacturer. As was common in the Soviet Union, originally this was a design bureau rather than a manufacturer, so that its products could, in theory, be built in any Soviet factory. The bureau specialised in transport aircraft, mainly for the military, but its An-2 biplane, known to NATO as the 'Colt', was a utility aircraft also widely used by civil operators and produced under licence in China and Poland. The next design of any significance was the An-10 and its successor the An-12 'Cub', a four-engined high wing transport, while the An-14 'Cold' was an attempt at an An-2 replacement. The An-22 'Cock' four-engined turboprop was at one time the largest transport aircraft in the world, and this tradition has continued with the An-124 four-engined turbofan transport, which holds the world record for the heaviest item of cargo carried so far at more than 150 tons, and the even larger six-engined An-225, although while this has been test flown, it has still to enter production.

Antonov, Oleg K. (1906–84) Soviet aircraft designer. Interested in aeronautics from an early age, Antonov graduated from the Leningrad Polytechnic Institute in 1930 and began working as a designer at a Moscow glider factory, designing the A-7 military glider for carrying troops and supplies, which saw operational service during the Second World War. He moved to the **Yakovlev** design bureau in 1943.

In 1946 Antonov was allocated his own design bureau, producing the design for the robust An-2 utility aircraft in 1947. His An-10 turboprop airliner, which first appeared in 1957, was regarded as being a promising design, far more comfortable than contemporary Soviet transports, but structural failures meant that it was soon withdrawn from service. Antonov's An-22 transport was for many years the world's largest aircraft until the advent of the Lockheed C-5 Galaxy, and today the tradition continues with the An-124, which set a world record by carrying a commercial load of more than 150 tons, and the even larger An-225, although the latter has still to enter production.

Anzani, Alessandro (1877–1956) Italian aero-engine designer. Better known for his motorcycle engines, Anzani had started as a bicycle manufacturer but turned to motorcycles. His lightweight, but simple engines proved reliable and after being chosen by **Louis Blériot** for his cross-Channel flight in

1909, Anzani found a new market among aircraft manufacturers, although eventually his designs were overtaken by those of other manufacturers.

Aoki, Hiroaki 'Rocky' (1938–) Japanese-American aeronaut. A first-generation immigrant, Aoki opened a small restaurant from which he developed a restaurant chain, becoming a millionaire in the process. After taking a keen interest in power boats, in 1981 he joined the *Double Eagle V* team which made the first man-carrying balloon crossing of the Pacific, taking four days from Japan to California, where it crash-landed, briefly knocking Aoki unconscious.

Arab-Israeli air campaigns For most of the second half of the twentieth century there has been tension between Israel and her Arab neighbours, and in some parts of the Arab world this situation continues. Although the Israeli Defence Force Air Force (IDF-AF) dates from 1951, its predecessor, Chel Ha'avir, with its origins in the Zionist Haganah movement, cannibalised aircraft abandoned by the British, including Spitfires and Mosquitoes, when they left what had been Palestine, to counter attacks by Egyptian Spitfires in 1949. In the years following its formation, the IDF-AF bought mainly French aircraft and during the Suez crisis of 1956 gained aerial superiority over neighbouring Egypt with the loss of just eleven aircraft. Again, in June 1967, in a brief conflict, the IDF-AF virtually wiped out the combined Egyptian and Jordanian air forces. After this, the reluctance of France to supply aircraft forced the Israelis to buy most of their equipment from the United States.

A more serious situation arose in October 1973, when the Arabs took the occasion of the Yom Kippur Day of fasting to mount heavy air strikes aimed at neutralising the IDF-AF, which also had to contend with much improved Arab anti-aircraft missiles. Although Israel won the brief war, it was at a cost of 115 aircraft according to its sources, but the USA put the figure at closer to 200.

The easing of tension with both Jordan and Egypt has left Israel with considerable tension with Syria, with Lebanon caught in the middle and often used as a battleground. During the Gulf War of 1991, aimed at liberating Kuwait from

Iraq, Israel was under strong US pressure not to intervene for fear of causing a rift with those Arab regimes friendly towards the anti-Iraq coalition forces. In 2006 Israeli aircraft were involved in strikes against Lebanon, aimed mainly at militants in the south of the country, but which also involved raids on Beirut.

Archdeacon, Ernest (1863–1957) French philanthropist and sponsor of aeronautics. He was always a catalyst for progress than a pioneer, and his sole claim to fame in the air was that of becoming the first European aeroplane passenger on 29 May 1908. A successful lawyer, Archdeacon became interested in aviation and promoted many events that popularised the activity as well as providing capital for many of the pioneers, such as **Gabriel Voisin** and **Ferdinand Ferber**. He was chairman of the influential Aéro-Club de France and organiser of the world's first **air show**, the Reims Week of 1909.

Arlandes, Marquis d' (1742–1809) French aeronaut. A French nobleman, François Laurent, the Marquis d'Arlandes, was at the court of King Louis XVI and also knew the **Montgolfier** brothers. With **Jean-François Pilâtre de Rozier** he made the first man-carrying tethered ascent in a Montgolfière hot air balloon on 19 October 1783, and then pressed for a free ascent, which the two men made on 21 November, rising from the grounds of the Château La Muette in the Bois de Boulogne, near Paris, then passing over the city before descending on the Butte-aux-Cailles, after a trip of some 5½ miles. The Marquis is then reputed to have left de Rozier with the balloon while he hastened back to Paris to take the credit.

armament Despite trials before the outbreak of the First World War, with Wright biplanes fitted with machine guns as early as 1911 when hostilities commenced, most aircraft lacked any armament of their own and were used only for scouting or reconnaissance. In 1914 service revolvers or rifles carried by the pilot or observer constituted an armament. Indeed, many airmen simply saluted or waved as they passed their opponents, until they realised that scout aircraft were a threat because of the information they obtained.

It was not long before machine guns were fitted to aircraft, often fired by the observer, while pilots had to stand up or aim their machine gun skyward to avoid damaging the aircraft propeller. This problem was cured first by fitting deflector plates to aircraft propellers and then by interruptor gear, of which the first was invented by **Anthony Fokker**. The pusher-engined aircraft also enjoyed a brief renaissance with aircraft such as the DH2 giving the pilot a clear field of fire with his machine gun. Meanwhile, the early bombs were often nothing more than artillery shells fitted with fins and dropped over the side by the pilot or observer.

As techniques became more refined, aircraft became specialised, with definite fighter and bomber aircraft emerging. The latter began to grow in size, although bombs were generally no more than 250 lb and often much less. The Germans used their **Zeppelin** airships as bombers before the arrival of the large Gotha bomber biplanes.

The Second World War saw the variety of weapons carried by aircraft grow, but at first fighters used machine guns, ideally four in each wing, and it was not until later that more effective 20 mm cannon were introduced. From the outset, the Messerschmitt Bf109 had an advantage with a cannon firing through the propeller boss, and while the Bell Airacobra also had this feature, the aircraft was not nearly so successful.

The war years saw cannon and rockets increasingly used for anti-armour and anti-shipping operations, while many fighters were able to carry bombs, usually a 250 lb bomb under each wing, so that the fighter-bomber became a reality. Heavy bombers grew in size, and so did their bombs. In 1939, a 1,000 lb bomb was heavy, but this was soon followed by the 2,000 lb bomb, and then in RAF service by the 4,000 lb bomb, known as a 'cookie' and the 8,000 lb bomb, a 'double cookie'. The Lancaster, specially modified, could carry a bouncing bomb, known as 'Upkeep' for the raid on the Ruhr dams (*see* **Dam Busters**), and later a 12,000 lb earthquake bomb, 'Tallboy', and finally a 22,000 lb bomb, 'Grand Slam', which were set to spin on being dropped so that they could burrow into the ground before detonating. These bombs were dropped alongside heavily fortified structures which were undermined and could be destroyed, through the mining effect, even though conventional bombs simply bounced off the top of the fortifications. While bomb sizes grew bigger, the use of quantities of small incendiary bombs proved extremely effective in destroying large tracts of urban areas. In the UK, the firestorm that followed the RAF's bombing of Hamburg is well documented, but the USAAF destroyed many Japanese cities, including Tokyo, by fire-bombing. During 1943 in the Mediterranean theatre, the Germans began to use unmanned glider bombs against Allied warships.

Anti-shipping operations were found to be best conducted by using torpedo-bombers, as at **Taranto** and in the sinking of the German battleship *Bismarck*, and sometimes a mixture of torpedo and dive-bombing proved effective against aircraft carriers.

The ultimate bombs were the nuclear weapons dropped over Hiroshima on 6 August 1945, and on Nagasaki on 9 August.

In the postwar world, missiles began to take over from bombs. Air-to-air missiles became widespread, often with fighter aircraft carrying both short range and longer range types, but the cannon still remained useful. Many of the first generation air-to-air missiles had shortcomings, especially in hot weather when their heat-seeking qualities were downgraded, and for this reason the guns of Indian Gnat fighters proved more effective than the missiles of Pakistani Sabres in combat in 1962 during a war caused by border disputes. Nevertheless, missiles developed and improved. Heavy bombers used stand-off missiles to deliver nuclear weapons, such as Skybolt, and then proceeded to carry cruise missiles capable of operating accurately over very long ranges. Anti-shipping and anti-tank missiles also emerged, and in forms that could be used by helicopters.

For some duties bombs continued to be used. Had the British Isles been invaded by Germany in the Second World War, the Convair B-36 had an enlarged version of the Grand Slam, the 43,000 lb T-12 bomb, on which testing continued after the war and did not end until 1954, by which time the large conventional bomb was replaced by the much smaller nuclear weapons. To rid the Vietnamese jungle of the lush vegetation that offered cover to terrorists at the height of the Vietnam War during the late 1960s and early 1970s, the United States introduced the 15,000 lb BLU-82/B Daisy Cutter.

One of the innovations after the Second World War was the gunship. Helicopters became more specialised. Combat helicopters with a two-man crew carried nose-mounted heavy cannon as well as either unguided rockets or air-to-surface missiles. The USAF also introduced a special gunship version of the venerable Douglas C-47 in Vietnam, from which machine guns could be fired out of the side windows. It was followed by the Lockheed AC-130 Hercules, as used in Afghanistan in recent years, with its high wing making it a more practical aircraft.

Armstrong-Whitworth British manufacturer. First came into prominence during the 1920s with its Argosy airliner for Imperial Airways. Limited interwar defence budgets hindered progress, even though its Siskin fighter and Atlas army co-operation biplane for the RAF were dependable. Links with **Hawker** enabled the company to play a part in production of the Hart light bomber during the early 1930s. The Atalanta four-engined high-wing airliner for Imperial Airways, first flown in 1932, marked a step forward from the earlier biplanes, and towards the end of the decade the four-engined high-wing Ensign of 1938, also for Imperial Airways, was for a time the largest all-metal monocoque aircraft. When the Second World War broke out in 1939, the Whitley was the mainstay of the RAF's bomber strength, but rapidly retired to second-line duties, while some were converted to become transports. A postwar airliner project, the Apollo, made little progress, but the company produced naval Sea Hawk fighters for the Royal Navy, Federal German Navy and Indian Navy on behalf of Hawker and was eventually absorbed into the Hawker Siddeley group in 1960.

Arnhem (September 1944) A bold attempt to shorten the war with Operation Market Garden, part of which was intended to seize a bridge over the lower Rhine in Holland. Intelligence failings missed the presence of a Panzer division close by, and the infant Transport Command could not move all the troops in a single airlift. In an attempt to enable the encircled troops to continue fighting, a massive resupply airlift was mounted at tremendous cost, with No. 48 Squadron losing a third of its aircraft as they flew through intense German AA fire; No. 190 Squadron lost eleven of its thirty aircraft. Flying transport aircraft was not a soft option.

Arnold, Gen Henry Harley 'Hap', USAAF (1886–1950) Pioneering military aviator and USAAF commander. After starting his career as an army officer in the conventional way, graduating from the US Military Academy at West Point in 1907 and then being posted to the Philippines in 1911, 'Hap' Arnold transferred to the US Army's new aviation division. He was taught to fly by **Orville Wright**. He became a pioneer by making the first air-to-ground radio observation reports in 1912, the year in which he also set an altitude record of 6,450 ft. He then organised air operations in the Panama Canal Zone during the First World War.

Between the two world wars, Arnold became one of the leading advocates of military air power and a supporter of **Billy Mitchell**, the controversial advocate of an autonomous US military air service. Despite his army background, Arnold believed in air power as a strategic weapon in its own right rather than simply as tactical support for ground forces. In addition to lobbying the US Congress for additional funding, despite the difficult economic situation, he also kept the US Army's Air Corps in the public eye by organising record-breaking flights.

During the Second World War, Arnold played a vital role in the development of Allied strategy as a member of the US Joint Chiefs of Staff. With a like-minded ally in the RAF's Air Chief Marshal, **Sir Arthur Harris**, he planned the strategic bomber offensive against Germany and, later, Japan. He became the USAAF's first five-star general and postwar he prepared the plans for the autonomous United States Air Force.

arrester hook/wire A retractable hook fitted to the underside of an aircraft fuselage to allow arrester wires to be engaged, mainly when landing on a conventional aircraft carrier, that is one which handles fixed-wing non-V/STOL aircraft.

Trials have involved arrester hooks being used on land-based combat aircraft as a substitute for braking parachutes.

The original deck landings on the first aircraft carriers such as HMS *Furious* used wires running longitudinally along the deck and hooks were attached to the underside of the wings, but these were soon superseded by wires running across the deck. Usually four wires are fitted, and the wires are attached to pulleys under the deck allow some flexibility.

Atlantic, Battle of (1939) A contest between the German U-boats and Allied merchant shipping, which started on the first day of the Second World War, although the Battle of the Atlantic is officially taken as having started after the fall of France. While German surface raiders were meant to be part of the threat, after the sinking of the battleship *Bismarck* on 27 May 1941, in which carrier-borne Fairey Swordfish torpedo-bombers played an important part, the operation became one between U-boats, German maritime-reconnaissance Junkers Ju290 Condor and Focke-Wulf Fw200 aircraft, and Allied ships and aircraft.

The crux of the problem at the outbreak of war was what was variously known as the 'Atlantic Gap', or the 'Black Gap', that part of the North Atlantic in which convoys were outside the protection of shore-based maritime-reconnaissance aircraft. The gap reduced steadily as longer-range aircraft became available, but land-based aircraft always suffered from the disadvantage that for every aircraft flying over and around a convoy, another had to be on its way back to base and yet one more was on its way out. At the base for these aircraft, there would be several more aircraft undergoing maintenance, refuelling and re-arming while their crews rested. The presence of the venerable Swordfish with a convoy forced many U-boat commanders to remain submerged, so that they could not catch up with a convoy, and while the Swordfish often attacked and destroyed U-boats, in many cases the best results came from Swordfish and escort vessels working together.

It was the convoy war and the need to protect trade that saw the birth of Canadian and Dutch naval aviation, brought into being as part of the Fleet Air Arm and at first fully integrated with it.

As an emergency measure, merchant vessels, grain carriers and tankers were converted to become merchant aircraft carriers (MAC-ships), with a wooden flight deck laid so that they could operate Fairey Swordfish on anti-submarine duties. The impact of these was immediate. From May 1943 until VE-Day, MAC-ships made 323 crossings of the Atlantic and escorted 217 convoys, of which just one was successfully attacked. The Swordfish they carried flew 4,177 patrols and searches, an average of thirteen per crossing, or one per day at average convoy speed.

At about the same time, the escort carrier was introduced. These were conversions of merchant vessels, with later ships being built as such. They could carry a larger number of aircraft than a MAC-ship, had RN or USN crews, and usually had fighters as well as anti-submarine aircraft.

Shore-based maritime-reconnaissance aircraft were vital. The Royal Navy was not left entirely on its own to escort the convoys. While the United States was officially neutral from the outbreak of war in Europe until the Japanese attack on the US Pacific Fleet at **Pearl Harbor**, just over twenty-seven months later, in September 1941 American warships and aircraft began to escort convoys to a mid-ocean handover point, officially to ensure that neutral shipping was not engaged by German submarines. The Royal Canadian Navy and Royal Canadian Air Force also moved forces to Newfoundland, as far east as possible, to help maintain anti-submarine cover.

The RAF had bases in Northern Ireland and the south-west of England and South Wales, and moved quickly to establish forward bases in the west of Scotland, including the Hebrides. The situation was helped in May 1940 when British forces occupied neutral Iceland, but even this was not enough to bridge the Atlantic Gap. In 1939 the RAF was ill-prepared for maritime operations, with Coastal Command operating the London and Stranraer biplane flying boats. It was to be some time before the Sunderland became the mainstay of the flying boat force, by which time they were being augmented by Lend-Lease Catalinas. Blenheims and Hudsons, and then Wellingtons became the major landplanes, until the arrival of a small number of ultra-long-range Liberators which closed the gap from August

1942, something that not even Icelandic bases had managed to do.

During the war, RAF Coastal Command alone accounted for 188 out of the 785 U-boats sunk, and shared in the destruction of another 21, while it also sank 343 ships totalling 513,804 tons. This was at a cost of 1,579 aircraft during 235,749 sorties.

Atlantic, first flights Although **Glenn Curtiss** was planning a transatlantic flight before the First World War, the first of this kind was made in May 1919 by a USN Curtiss flying boat, the *NC-4*, which flew via the Azores to Lisbon, taking 58 hours to cover the 4,000 miles. The first non-stop flight followed in June, when **Capt John Alcock** and Lt Arthur Whitten-Brown flew a Vickers Vimy bomber from St John's, Newfoundland, to Clifden, Co. Galway, Ireland, taking 16 hours. Between 2 and 6 July the British airship *R34* crossed the Atlantic from Scotland to New York, and then made the return flight from New York to Norfolk, England, between 9 and 13 July.

The first non-stop solo crossing was made in May 1927 in a Ryan monoplane, *The Spirit of St Louis*, by **Charles Lindbergh**.

The South Atlantic was a more difficult proposition, with longer distances and fewer good bases. The German airline Deutsches Luft Hansa, predecessor of **Lufthansa**, used seaplanes that were catapulted from steamers as they approached the South American or African coasts as a means of speeding the mails during the late 1920s and early 1930s.

It was not until October 1927 that the first non-stop crossing of the South Atlantic was made, with **Dieudonne Costes** and Lt Joseph Le Brix flying a Breguet from St Louis, Senegal, to Port Natal, Brazil, a distance of 2,150 miles, in 19 hours. The Condor Syndicate, a German airline operation, used Dornier X twelve-engined flying boats to make flights to South America from 1932 and onwards, while Zeppelin airships were also used on the route.

Commercial proving flights were started on the North Atlantic in 1937 by Imperial Airways and Pan American, using Short S23 Empire and Sikorsky S-42 flying boats respectively. In July

1938 the Short Mayo composite aircraft, a flying boat that launched a four-engined seaplane at altitude, began to operate on the route. North Atlantic airmail services started in 1939, using Short Empire and Boeing 314 flying boats, but only operated briefly before the outbreak of the Second World War. The Short Empire was also involved with in-flight refuelling to cope with the demands of the route. During the war, a service initially was provided for members of the British government, senior officials and senior officers, from Poole, Dorset, to New York using Boeing 314 flying boats. The new British airline, BOAC, operated these flights, and later augmented them with a service using Consolidated B-24 Liberator bombers, mainly to return aircraft ferry crews to North America. The effect of the war years was to regularise North Atlantic air travel and by the war's end mainly USAAF transport aircraft were operating across the Atlantic, via Prestwick, south-west of Glasgow in Scotland.

Commercial transatlantic flights started in 1946 using US-built aircraft such as the Douglas DC-4 and the Lockheed Constellation, while that same year, the short-lived state-owned British South American Airways (BSAA) started operations to South America. BSAA was later absorbed by BOAC. In 1957, BOAC introduced Bristol Britannia turbo-prop airliners on the transatlantic services, following these with the first jet services using de Havilland Comet IV airliners in 1958, which were very soon followed by Pan American's Boeing 707s.

Auriol, Jacqueline Marie-Therese Suzanne (1917–2000) French test pilot. One of the first women to fly through the sound barrier, Jaqueline Auriol learnt to fly after the Second World War, during which she had been a member of the French Resistance. She was badly injured in a flying accident in 1949, but continued flying and qualified both on fixed-wing and rotary-wing aircraft. She made rapid progress to become a government test pilot and broke the sound barrier in 1955 flying a Dassault Super Mystère. A number of speed records were set by Auriol, and she was awarded the Harmon Trophy.

Auster British manufacturer. A small light aircraft manufacturer that emerged during the Second

World War, initially building **Stinson** high-wing monoplanes under licence for air observation post (AOP) duties. Postwar, it continued in this role with some production for private owners as well. In 1960 it was merged with **Beagle** aircraft.

autogiro The brainchild of **Juan de la Cierva**, who conducted the first flights in his native Spain in 1923. While the term autogiro is commonly used, it emerged as a marketing name for the gyroplanes designed by de la Cierva. The designer was the first person to travel as a passenger in an autogiro when he was flown in one of his own products, a C.6D, in 1926, by which time he had moved his work from Spain to the United Kingdom, later taking British nationality.

The concept was intended to eliminate the risk of an aircraft stalling during take-off and landing. As with the **helicopter**, lift was provided by the rotary wings, but unlike a helicopter, these were not powered but instead rotated freely in the vortex created by the conventionally positioned propeller. Take-off runs were much reduced rather than vertical, with the autogiro running forward and then hopping into the air. Again, in contrast to the helicopter, the control surfaces of a conventional fixed-wing aircraft were retained on the autogiro, with rudders, elevators and ailerons.

While attracting considerable interest at the time, the need for the autogiro was removed by the advent of the helicopter and by improvements to conventional aircraft. The autogiro also suffered from limitations on its speed and on the size of aircraft that could use the technique. In the 1970s, the concept enjoyed a renaissance with single and twin-seat products popularised by their appearance in a James Bond film, but were used mainly as recreational aircraft by private owners.

automatic landing See also 'Fido'. Sometimes referred to as 'autoland', this is a system that enables commercial airliners to land safely in poor visibility, often known as Category IIIB. Originally pioneered in the UK by Smiths Industries on BEA Hawker Siddeley Trident I airliners, the system was triplexed, meaning that three separate systems were used so that if one was inoperative or in error, it was automatically overridden by the other two. A system with a reduced performance was also used on BOAC's Vickers VC-10 airliners: known as autoflare, this was a duplexed system with just operating systems, and could only take the aircraft down to decision height.

The early system was often neglected as it involved costly extra maintenance and pilot training, but in more recent years such systems have become standard on most modern commercial aircraft. Nevertheless, some limitations remain, with the main one being the need for the aircraft to get from the runway after landing to the terminal, so even though the system could cope with zero visibility, the aircraft and their crews would have difficulty once landed. This has become an important issue with aircraft collisions on the ground and the danger of aircraft making runway incursions while other aircraft are landing or taking off. Usually, air traffic control increases the separation between aircraft landings and take-offs in such poor visibility.

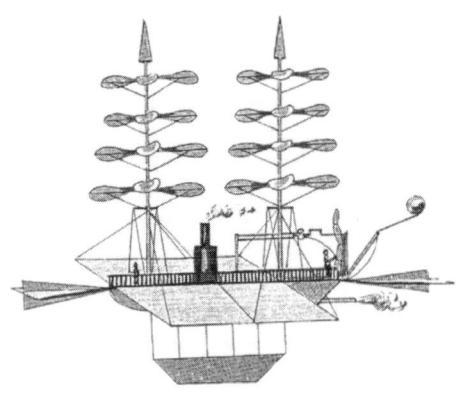

An early design for a helicopter was produced by Gabriel de la Landelle, and may have inspired Jules Verne's *Clipper of the Clouds*. Landelle's true contribution to aviation was the invention of the word *aviateur*.

autopilot The automatic pilot, or autopilot, is responsible for the movement of controls and for maintaining the pre-set course of an aircraft in flight, taking much of the strain out of long-distance flights. The concept was the invention of **Dr Elmer Sperry** in collaboration with **Glenn Curtiss**, and started with an automatic stabiliser for aircraft, with an early automatic pilot demonstrated on a Curtiss flying boat in 1913. After the First World War, autopilots became increasingly popular and early versions included the British Aveline Stabiliser used by **Handley Page**. Today, full flight details are keyed into the aircraft computer before take-off.

auxiliary power unit (APU) The equipment that maintains power on an aircraft when the engines are not in use, providing electrical power and also air for ventilation and engine starting. Originally, this was introduced for operations at airports in remote areas that might not have reliable ground equipment to provide power, but it is now standard. It takes the form of a small low-thrust turbojet engine located in the tailplane. The generator driven by the auxiliary power unit can be used as a back-up in flight if the two generators driven by the engines should fail, but generally the APU can only operate at 20,000 ft or lower.

aviation This term applies to heavier-than-air aircraft. It is usually taken as being confined to powered aircraft, but strictly gliders should also be included. The term comes from *aviateur*, the word for pilots coined by the Frenchman Gabriel de la Landelle.

Avro British manufacturer. Named after its founder, **Alliott Verdon Roe**, Avro produced a number of aircraft before the First World War, including the Type F cabin biplane in which **Lt Wilfred Parkes** was able to make the first controlled recovery from a spin, and the 504, which became one of the most used trainers during the war. Postwar, the company produced the 563, a twelve-seat airliner, the Avenger, which was for a time the fastest fighter, and the Avian, a single-seat sport and racing monoplane which was used for a number of pioneering flights. In the mid-1930s, the Avro 19 was introduced, and achieved success as the Anson light transport and trainer for the RAF. While the Manchester heavy bomber was a failure, it led to the four-engined Lancaster, which carried the heaviest bomb loads of the Second World War, including 22,000 lb 'Grand Slam' earthquake bombs, and was also in use on the **Dam Busters** raid, and became the mainstay of Bomber Command's main force. The Lancaster's aerodynamic surfaces were used for the York transport, while the Lincoln was a development that appeared too late for active service, but the Shackleton, a maritime-reconnaissance development, served for many years and a few had a further life as airborne-early-warning aircraft. The postwar Tudor airliner for British South American Airways suffered from structural failure, but the 748 twin-turboprop feeder airliner was successful and was produced under licence in India as well as remaining in production with first **Hawker Siddeley** and then **British Aerospace**. The most notable aircraft of the postwar period was the Vulcan four-engined delta-wing jet bomber designed to deliver the British nuclear deterrent, and which survived to see action during the **Falklands Campaign** of 1982.

In 1960 the company was merged into the Hawker Siddeley group. The name was revived by **BAe Systems** for the RJ series airliner, a development of the BAe regional jet series, the 146.

B

Bacon, Roger (c.1214–92) British visionary and cleric. Graduating from the University of Oxford, Bacon moved to Paris to continue his studies while also lecturing in Latin. He became interested in physics and introduced the West to gunpowder in 1242. In 1268, he produced the first encyclopaedia, commissioned by Pope Clement IV. His interest in science backfired when the Roman Catholic Church accused him of heresy, mistaking his discoveries for alchemy.

For aviation, Bacon suggested a flying-machine that would be an **ornithopter** powered by a man using a crank. He also appreciated the principles of **aerostation**. His other achievements included envisaging submarines and motor vehicles. All in all, he made many predictions which preceded those of the Italian artist, **Leonardo da Vinci**, but history has accorded him far less credit, possibly because his work was so early and so little of it survived.

Baden-Powell, Major Baden Fletcher Smyth (1860–1937) British Army officer. Brother of Robert Baden-Powell, founder of the Boy Scout and Girl Guide movements, Baden-Powell volunteered to join the British Army's Balloon Section at Aldershot, where he not only participated in ballooning but also began his experiments with man-lifting kites. He became a member of the Aeronautical Society (later the Royal Aeronautical Society) in 1880. Some years later, in 1894, he became the first man to be lifted by a kite, although this particular aeronautical device soon proved to be of limited use. He was the second Briton to fly with **Wilbur Wright** when the Wright brothers visited Europe in 1908.

Bader, Gp Capt Sir Douglas Robert Stewart (1910–82) British fighter ace. Commissioned into the RAF in 1930, he soon became a star performer with the RAF aerobatic team. Bader lost both legs after a flying accident with a Bristol Bulldog fighter biplane in 1931. Refusing to use a walking stick and despite proving that he could still fly with artificial legs, Bader was invalided out of the service and did not return until the outbreak of the Second World War, when he was offered a non-flying role which he rejected and began the fight to return to flying duties. Back in the air, he became first a flight commander, then a squadron commander and eventually commanded a fighter wing of three squadrons of Hawker Hurricanes. When given new squadrons, Bader always led the least experienced unit, while his own personal score reached 22½ confirmed victories. On 9 August 1941, while engaged in aerial combat over France, Bader's aircraft was shot down, and as his right foot was trapped in the cockpit he could only escape by quickly discarding his legs. Becoming a prisoner of war, he received replacement legs which were parachuted to his captors by the RAF. He made two unsuccessful escape attempts while a PoW. Postwar, Bader joined Shell Petroleum in London and became managing director of Shell Aircraft, a subsidiary managing the company's own fleet of business aircraft, while also devoting much of his time to charities helping disabled people.

BAe Systems British manufacturer. The former **British Aerospace**, denationalised in 1982, and which under earlier nationalisation had absorbed the businesses of both the **British Aircraft Corporation** (BAC) and **Hawker Siddeley**, became BAe Systems after acquiring interests in avionics, electronics, shipbuilding and armoured vehicle production. It shed many of its product lines, notably the 125 series executive jet which was sold to **Raytheon Beech**, and closed the last British airliner line, the Avro RJX. It continues to produce the Hawk advanced jet trainer, which has sold to many countries, including production under licence in the US by **Boeing** as the Goshawk, and is a partner in the Eurofighter 2000 Typhoon interceptor. It was the British partner in

Airbus Industrie until it sold its 20 per cent take to **EADS** in 2007.

Baedeker Raids In retaliation for the RAF's area **bombing** of historic cities such as Lübeck and Rostov, chosen because of the number of wooden buildings that would burn easily, the Luftwaffe mounted a series of tip-and-run raids between April and June 1942 against historic British cities, hence the name 'Baedeker' from the series of guide books. Among the targets were Bath, Canterbury, Exeter and Norwich, and because of their relatively small size, many claimed that the experience was more terrifying than the blitz on major centres. It is estimated that these raids accounted for 1,637 civilian deaths and another 1,760 injured.

balance of power Generally regarded as a modern concept, in practice the balance of power dates back to the policy adopted in the United Kingdom during the late nineteenth and early twentieth century under which the country maintained a naval fleet capable of countering that of the two most likely opponents, refined at times to include an alliance with a continental nation. Before the First World War, the *Entente Cordiale* with France was seen as a counter to German ambitions. After the Second World War, the concept became that of a balance of power between the West and the Soviet Bloc. This extended to the size of the armed forces on each side, the equipment used and even the disposition of the forces. A good example came when the Soviet Union modernised its tactical or theatre nuclear weapons, which prompted the United States to deploy cruise missiles and to site these at forward bases in the British Isles. Some maintain that the result was as much a balance of terror.

It became United States policy, with which successive British governments largely concurred, to maintain a balance of power in the Middle East between Israel and the Arab states. This extended to arms supplies, not just to Israel, but also to those Arab states seen as being pro-Western, such as Jordan, Kuwait and Saudi Arabia. In South-East Asia, American policy was to prevent communist takeovers in what had been French Indo-China, which led to the Vietnam War in the 1960s.

These US policies also had their counterpart in an older US policy, the Munro Doctrine, that effectively established spheres of influence. The Soviet Union effectively recognised this when it backed down to US pressure during the Cuban Missile crisis (1961), prompted by Soviet plans to base nuclear-tipped missiles in Cuba within range of the United States. The US also tacitly accepted the same philosophy by earlier not taking advantage of the Hungarian Revolution in 1956 to liberate part of the Soviet Bloc.

Even within NATO, balance of power questions remained strong, with US arms supplies to Greece and Turkey being such that neither country gained a strategic or tactical advantage over the other.

Balbo, Gen Italo (1896–1940) Italian soldier, politician and airman. A member of Italy's elite Alpine troops during the First World War, Balbo was awarded two medals for bravery. An early supporter of Mussolini because he thought that the Fascists could revive Italy's fortunes, Balbo was surprised when in 1926 his loyalty was rewarded with the position of minister for air. Uninvolved with aviation up to this time, Balbo immediately learnt to fly and navigate, before instigating a programme of modernisation and re-equipment for the Italian Air Force, the Regia Aeronautica. He became a popular figure with both the public and his men, with many feats of airmanship, culminating with a mass crossing of the Atlantic in 1933 by twenty-four Savoia-Marchetti seaplanes which made a safe landing on Lake Michigan to coincide with the Chicago Century of Progress Exposition.

His popularity was his downfall, provoking Mussolini's jealousy. The situation was not helped, as war in Europe loomed, by Balbo arguing that Italy should align herself with her First World War allies, the United Kingdom and France. With the country on the brink of war, Balbo was sidelined as governor of Libya, where he preferred to lead combat air patrols rather than undertake his official duties. Returning from a patrol in 1940, his aircraft was shot down by the AA defences of his home base. The official line was that this was an accident, but many maintain that Mussolini had planned Balbo's murder, although in wartime aircraft identification standards among ground gunners were not always all that they could be.

Balchen, Bernt (1899–1973) Norwegian pioneer. Commissioned into the Norwegian naval air service in 1924, in 1925 Balchen was a member of the rescue mission for **Roald Amundsen's** North Pole flight. The following year, he helped Amundsen prepare for his successful transpolar airship voyage, but was prevented from joining because of weight restrictions. That same year, Balchen also helped **Lt Cdr Richard-Evelyn Byrd** prepare for his successful aeroplane flight over the North Pole, and although he did not accompany Byrd on the flight, to show his gratitude the American aviator had Balchen join him on a promotional tour of the United States. While in the USA, Balchen joined **Fokker** and in 1927 flew Byrd's Fokker trimotor, *Atlantic*, to Europe, only just succeeding in reaching France.

A further rescue mission was flown by Balchen in 1928, when he was responsible for rescuing the crew of the *Bremen* who were stranded in Labrador. He flew with Byrd again in 1929, being a pilot and navigator for the successful flight over the South Pole, flying more than 1,600 miles, and later made other Antarctic flights with Byrd and Lincoln Ellsworth. Although he became an American citizen in 1931, in 1935 he returned to Norway to become operations manager for Royal Norwegian Airlines.

On a visit to the United States, when Germany invaded Norway in 1940, Balchen joined the RAF and ferried aircraft from San Diego to Singapore before the Japanese invasion. He moved to the USAAF in 1941 and established Blue West 8 Air Force base in Greenland, conducting search and rescue operations for downed airmen and then taking part in the attack on a secret German meteorological station in the north of the island. In 1944 he started to fly the first of 110 missions between Scotland and Norway, dropping supplies to the resistance and also undertaking rescue flights. He returned to Royal Norwegian Airlines after the German surrender and then joined the newly autonomous USAF in 1948 and commanded a rescue unit based in Alaska.

Baldwin, Frederick Walker 'Casey' (c.1882–1948) Canadian pioneer. As a result of studying engineering with **John McCurdy** at the University of Toronto, Baldwin came into contact with **Graham Bell** and joined the **Aerial Experimental Association** (AEA). On 12 March 1908, at Hammondsport, New York, he flew the AEA's first successful aeroplane, *Red Wing*, becoming the first Canadian to fly a heavier-than-air machine. When the AEA was wound up in 1909, Baldwin joined McCurdy and Bell to found the Canadian Aerodrome Company, although this lasted only a year. Baldwin had come into contact with **Glenn Curtiss** while with AEA and was appointed manager of the Curtiss works in Toronto, producing Curtiss JN-3 Canucks during the First World War. Postwar, Baldwin and Bell resumed their association, experimenting with hydrofoils and setting a world water speed record.

Baldwin, Thomas Scott (1860–1923) American airship pioneer. Orphaned during the American Civil War, Baldwin ran away from his orphanage in 1874 and worked on the railways before joining a circus, where eventually he began making balloon ascents. He came to prominence in 1887 when he made a parachute descent from a balloon using a parachute of his own design. Parachute design was in its infancy and became such an attraction that his fee for a descent is claimed to have been as much as US $2,000 (around £400 at the then rate of exchange).

In 1904 Baldwin completed the first US-built dirigible, *California Arrow*, powered by a Curtiss motorcycle engine, and flew the first circuit outside Europe on 3 August at Oakland, California. One result was that he is generally credited with involving **Glenn Curtiss** in aviation. In 1908, he completed the first airship, *Army Dirigible No. 1*, for the US Army's Signal Corps.

Ball, Capt Albert, VC (1896–1917) British fighter ace. One of the early RFC pilots, while based in France during the First World War Capt Ball scored forty-four victories. His achievements were legendary, as when he encountered two German Albatros fighters and ran out of ammunition, but forced them to flee using his service pistol. He lost his life when his aircraft crashed during combat on 17 May 1917. He was awarded a posthumous VC, Britain's highest award, and the commander-in-chief of the RFC, the later Marshal of the Royal Air Force **Lord Trenchard**, encouraged the press to make him a publicly acclaimed hero, marking a break with earlier British policy not to encourage such treatment for aviators.

balloon A commonly used name for an **aerostat**, of which the main types have been the hot air or **Montgolfière**, or the gas or **Charlière**, named after the inventors. Modern long-distance record-breaking balloons, known as the **Rozier** balloon, are usually a combination of these techniques.

Two Frenchmen, the brothers **Joseph and Etienne de Montgolfier** of Lyon, invented the hot air balloon after observing pieces of paper rising in the heat of a fire. After experimenting with paper bags, they produced paper and linen sphere which, with a wool and straw fire smouldering beneath it, made an ascent on 5 June 1783. The two brothers then sent up an even larger balloon over Paris, carrying three animals, a cock, duck and a sheep, for a 2-mile aerial voyage before landing safely. Further successful ascents were made with tethered balloons, including some in which men were carried up to a height of around 100 ft, before it was decided to proceed with an untethered manned ascent. Initially, it was intended to send two convicts, but two aristocrats, **Jean-François Pilâtre de Rozier** and the **Marquis d'Arlandes** volunteered to make the journey, which turned out to be a successful 5-mile flight over Paris on 21 November 1783.

After centuries of speculation over the possibilities of flight, only a matter of days separated the first and second aerial voyages in history. **Professor Jacques Charles** from the University of Paris, designed a small hydrogen balloon from a rubberised fabric invented by his partners, the Robert brothers, and this made a successful unmanned ascent from the centre of Paris on 27 August 1783. Charles was by this time in competition with the Montgolfier brothers and believed that they were using an unknown gas as a lifting agent, although he realised that it was not as light as hydrogen, still a recently separated gas at the time. Charles had to overcome the very real difficulty of producing hydrogen in sufficient quantity for a man-carrying balloon, and on 1 December such a balloon made a 31½ mile flight, the first 27 miles being with Charles and Aîné Robert, and the remaining 4½ miles being by

Charles alone, after first descending to let Robert alight, at which stage there was just enough gas left for one man to be lifted.

For most of the next 200 years, the Charlière type of balloon was the one most frequently used because hydrogen, being much lighter than air, offered a far superior performance than depending on hot air for lift. It was not until the 1950s, when the American balloon builder **Paul Yost** invented a propane burner, that the hot air balloon experienced a revival that has continued to this day.

Hydrogen is dangerous because it becomes explosive once in contact with the atmosphere, for example through a leak in the fabric of the balloon envelope. During the twentieth century, hydrogen was replaced by the less efficient but safer helium in **airships** and balloons.

Features of the Charlière balloons, copied by subsequent balloons, included a venting valve in the crown, a barometer altimeter, a net slung over the balloon from which could be hung the car or gondola, and ballast that could be jettisoned to lighten the balloon as the journey progressed. However, because of its simplicity and cheapness, the hot air balloon did not disappear completely. The first British aeronaut, **James Tytler**, used a Montgolfière when he made an ascent over Edinburgh in 1784. Indeed, the high cost of hydrogen meant that inefficient, and still not particularly safe, coal gas had to be used as a lifting agent in gas balloons for much of the nineteenth century.

It was left to an Italian, **Vincenzo Lunardi**, to make the first hydrogen balloon ascent in the British Isles in 1784. That same year, the first women made ascents in tethered balloons in Paris on 20 May, and on 4 June a Madame Thible made an ascent with a Monsieur Fleuant at Lyons in a Montgolfière. Pilâtre de Rozier and a companion, Pierre Romain, suffered the unsought distinction of being the first balloon fatalities on 15 June 1785, while attempting a balloon crossing of the English Channel using the extremely dangerous combination of a hydrogen Charlière with a brazier slung under the envelope to heat the gas. Later, using helium and a propane burner, such balloons were used for long-distance record attempts. Using a standard Charlière, a French aeronaut,

Jean-Pierre Blanchard and an American, John Jeffries, had already made a successful crossing of the English Channel from Dover to France on 7 January 1785, although at the cost of having to ditch almost everything, including some of their clothes, to remain aloft until they crossed the coast of France.

The first recorded military use of balloons came in 1794, as **air observation post** for the French Army at the Battle of Fleurus. These balloons were tethered, but nevertheless gave army commanders the equivalent benefit to having an observation post on high ground. An army captain, **Jean-Marie Joseph Coutelle**, was made Chef de Bataillon de Aérostiers de la République. During the American Civil War, between 1860 and 1866, the Unionist Army used balloons for observation duties with the Army of the Potomac.

Attempts to use balloons for communication purposes included that by HMS *Assistance* in 1850, which sent up small unmanned balloons carrying messages giving the ship's position while searching for the ill-fated Sir John Franklin Expedition in the Canadian Arctic. During the Franco-Prussian War of 1870–1, with Paris besieged, sixty-eight balloons were built in a factory set up in the Gare du Nord and were launched, all but one of them manned, to take correspondence and passengers out of the city and over enemy-held territory. Thirty-six reached friendly territory, while the others landed in either Prussian-held territory or in other countries, in one case as far away as Norway.

The British Army started its experiments with balloons in 1878 at Woolwich Arsenal, giving the United Kingdom the longest continuous history of military air power of any country, and by the following year, the Royal Engineers had a fleet of five balloons. The balloons were included in British military expeditions to Bechuanaland in 1884, and in 1885 to the Sudan. The United States established a Balloon Section in the army in 1892, the Netherlands followed in 1896, as did Spain, and then Russia in 1900.

Salomon Andrée's attempt to cross the North Pole in a balloon in 1870 failed because frozen mist on the envelope brought the balloon down.

The balloon has been entirely eclipsed for military and transport purposes by the airship and then by the aeroplane. Until the renewed interest in hot air balloons for recreation, balloons survived mainly as a cheap means of launching meteorological instruments into the atmosphere. They also played a role during the Second World War as a means of raising a radio transmitting aerial to help downed aircrew and shipwrecked seamen send distress calls.

Banfield, Linienschiffsleutnant Godfrey Richard (1890–1986) Austro-Hungarian naval officer and pioneer. Banfield's Irish father was commissioned into the Austro-Hungarian Navy, and Banfield followed him, taking Austrian nationality. Banfield joined the fleet in 1910 and in 1913 was sent to Paris to learn to fly, where he broke his leg in an accident. After Italy declared war on the Austro-Hungarian Empire in May 1915, he undertook reconnaissance patrols over Venice and engaged in air-to-air combat, with his score of Allied aircraft increasing after Italian and French aircraft attacked Trieste. He is credited with single-handedly shooting down three out of a force of eight enemy aircraft on one occasion, earning himself the soubriquet of 'Eagle of Trieste'. His wartime tally has been variously given as between nine and twenty-one enemy aircraft – a wide differential.

After working briefly as an engineer in the UK post-First World War, Banfield moved to Italy and adopted Italian nationality in 1920. He took over the marine salvage company started by his wife's family and in 1956 cleared the Suez Canal after the crisis of that year.

Baracca, Maggiore Francesco (1888–1918) Italian fighter ace. Originally a cavalry officer, Baracca became an aviator in 1912 while serving in Libya. Returning to Italy in 1915, he flew fighters and was soon recognised as an ace, with an official tally of thirty-four kills, but he was shot down and killed in March 1918, strafing Austrian troops.

His personal emblem was a prancing horse and postwar his mother made a gift of this to a racing driver, Enzo Ferrari, who adopted it as his trade mark when he started producing cars.

Barber, Horatio C. (1875–1964) Pioneering British aircraft designer. Designing the Valkyrie, a monoplane canard (i.e. with a small foreplane and large tailplane), Horatio Barber founded the Aeronautical Syndicate in 1909 to build and sell the aircraft. He followed this by founding a flying school at Hendon, north London, in 1910, and the following year the aircraft made the first British air freight flight, carrying a small consignment of electric light bulbs from Shoreham to nearby Hove, winning a prize of £100 which Barber donated to the Royal Aeronautical Club.

Despite these efforts, the Valkyrie did not achieve market success, possibly because monoplanes were regarded as unproven at the time, and in 1912 Barber was forced to sell his company to **Handley Page**, but remained in aviation as a flying instructor and, later, an author.

Barker, Maj William George, VC (1894–1930)

Canadian fighter ace. Having enlisted in the Canadian Mounted Rifles on the outbreak of the First World War, Barker discovered that there was no active role for cavalry and volunteered to join the RFC, becoming a mechanic in December 1914. He progressed to become an observer, at which stage he was given pilot training and made his first solo flight after an hour, becoming operational in January 1916. A natural pilot and leader, over the Western Front in late October 1918 he faced some fifty German aircraft alone and shot down four of them, despite being wounded three times, before crash-landing behind the Allied lines. His tally for the war years was fifty-two aircraft and he was awarded the VC. Postwar he returned to Canada and was a founder member of the RCAF, which was initially part of the Canadian army. Later he formed one of the early Canadian airlines with a friend, **Billy Bishop**. His promising aviation career was brought to an abrupt end when he was killed when the plane he was test-flying crashed.

Barnes, Florence Leontine Lowe 'Pancho' (1901–76)

American aviatrix. Granddaughter of **Thaddeus Lowe**, Florence Barnes had a varied career before becoming interested in aviation. She married a preacher while still in her teens before running away to join a circus. Then she become a tramp and wandered through the Americas, drifting from one job to the next, with such varied occupations as mate on a cargo boat and

associating with Mexican bandits, where she was given the nickname Pancho. It was not until 1928 that she learnt to fly, after which she persuaded Union Oil to give her a job as a pilot. Not content with routine flying, she became interested in racing aircraft and then became a Hollywood stunt pilot during the early 1930s, working on films such as *Hell's Angels*. In the United States between the First and Second World Wars, there were more pilots than jobs and pay was often poor, but Pancho Barnes helped to improve the lot of stunt pilots in the film industry by organising the Motion Pictures Pilots' Association.

Despite all of this, during the Second World War she ran a bar, Pancho's Fly Inn, at what was then Muroc Field near Los Angeles, California, but later officially renamed Edwards Air Force Base, the main centre for US test-flying during the war and afterwards. The 'anything goes' nature of her premises, known unofficially as the 'Happy Bottom Riding Club' by its patrons, caused the USAAF to force its closure.

barnstorming After the First World War the large numbers of ex-service pilots and aircraft contributed to an upsurge in exhibition flying, although this had been popular pre-war and a number of the pioneers made a good living out of it, starting with **Lincoln Beachey** using dirigibles as early as 1906. In the United States, the term 'barnstorming' was used, as one of the early tricks was to fly a small aircraft through a barn with the doors open at both ends.

Barnwell, Capt Frank Sowter (1880–1938)

British aircraft designer. After training as a marine and motor engineer in Scotland, in 1905 Barnwell joined his brother building an aeroplane powered by a 5 hp motorcycle engine, but this failed to fly. His appetite for aviation whetted, in 1911 he became a draughtsman with the British & Colonial Aeroplane Company, predecessor of the **Bristol Aeroplane Company**, designing the Bristol Scout and the Bristol Bullet monoplane, which was rejected by the RFC and RNAS, while the MC1 served with just five squadrons in the Middle East, not only because of its monoplane configuration but also because of its 'high' landing speed (for the day) of 49 mph. Barnwell joined the

RFC in an attempt to understand the requirements for combat aircraft, and as a result he designed the Bristol F-2b Fighter or 'Brisfit'.

Despite his spell with the RFC, Barnwell was a poor pilot, but this did not discourage him from attempting his own test-flying, wrecking a number of prototypes. He designed the Bristol Bulldog biplane fighter, and then the privately funded all-metal monoplane Bristol Blenheim, one of a generation of aircraft that eventually persuaded the RAF to switch from biplanes to monoplanes. Barnwell was killed in 1938 while flying a light aircraft. He had three sons, all killed during the Second World War, two of whom were flying Blenheims.

barrage balloons An anti-aircraft measure used by all the combatant nations during the Second World War, the barrage balloon had a strong resemblance to the airship, although unpowered and unmanned and lacking any means of control. The object was to keep attacking aircraft at a height which not only hampered accurate bomb-aiming, but also presented good targets for anti-aircraft gunners. Any aircraft attempting to dive under the balloons ran the risk of having its wings ripped off by the balloon cables. Mounting an anti-aircraft balloon barrage was no easy task, requiring substantial numbers of personnel to handle the balloons once they were winched down, and facilities had to be provided for maintenance and repair, including keeping gas levels high enough to allow the balloons to ascend lifting their heavy cables.

Batten, Jean (1909–82) New Zealand aviatrix. Her interest in aviation awakened by **Bert Hinckler**'s flights, in 1929 Batten travelled to the UK and trained to become a pilot. In 1932 she attempted to fly from Lympne, Kent, to Australia, but was forced back by engine trouble. A further attempt in 1933 also failed. She made a third attempt in 1934 and set a new record for women pilots by reaching Darwin, in Australia's Northern Territory, in just over two weeks. Other noteworthy flights included the first UK–Australia return flight by a woman, a flight from the UK to Brazil and a flight across the Tasman Sea in 1936.

In later years she faded into obscurity and died after a dog bite became infected.

Beachey, Lincoln (1887–1915) American stunt pilot. The first stunt pilot, Beachey joined **Tom Baldwin**'s aerial circus in 1906 as part of a double act with **Roy Knabenshue** in which they raced each other in dirigibles. In 1910, with aeroplanes available, he joined the **Curtiss** team and soon became its star pilot, being the first American to loop-the-loop and fly upside down. Despite the weakness of the early airframe and poor mechanical reliability, in 1911 he flew below Niagara Falls through clouds of spray and mist. He followed this in 1913 by taking part in a series of staged aircraft versus racing car contests with the then banned motor racing driver Barney Oldfield – they fixed the contests so that aircraft and motorcar victories alternated. In 1914 he set a world record by completing seven successive loops. In March 1915 he was demonstrating his 'dip of death' dive before a large crowd when his aircraft, designed by himself, broke up in mid-air and he drowned in San Francisco Bay.

Beagle British light aircraft manufacturer. Beagle was formed in 1962 from the amalgamation of **Auster**, **Miles**, British Executive and General Aviation, to continue production of the obsolete Auster series of light aircraft and develop the new Beagle 206 twin-engined aircraft. It was also intended to develop a lighter twin, the 246, and a single-engined variant, the 123, but only the 206 entered production and was sold in small numbers, mainly to the RAF whose specification it followed too closely for company buyers. Owned by Pressed Steel, when this company was acquired by its main customer, the British Motor Corporation, Beagle was sold to the British government. Although a light aircraft, the Pup, and its military derivative, the Bulldog, promised much, only the latter sold in significant numbers, and that mainly after the company went bankrupt in 1970 and production was transferred to **Scottish Aviation**.

Beaumont, Wg Cdr Roland Prosper 'Bee', RAF (1920–2001) British fighter ace and test pilot. Born in Enfield, London, in 1920, Beaumont was determined to join the RAF when, as a small child, the pilot of a Hawker Fury waved to him. His passion was confirmed when **Charles Scott** took him for a flight in a de Havilland Fox Moth.

He joined the RAF on a short service commission in January 1939. He went to France where he joined No. 87 Squadron flying Hawker Hurricanes, and as France fell he shot down his first aircraft, a Dornier Do17. Back in England for the Battle of Britain, he shot down two Messerschmitt Me110 fighters over Lyme Regis on 15 August. He was seconded to Hawkers as a test pilot before returning to operational flying with No. 56, the first squadron to fly the Hawker Typhoon, and then after a month to No. 609 Squadron as a flight commander. He pioneered the use of the aircraft on fighter-bomber duties before returning to Hawkers to test-fly its successor, the Tempest. In February 1944 he became leader of No. 150 Wing with Nos 3, 56 and 486 squadrons. He scored the Tempest's first kill when he shot down a Bf109 near Rouen, before his unit was charged with shooting down the V-1 flying bombs, of which he personally shot down thirty-one. When his wing moved to the Netherlands he shot down a Focke-Wulf Fw190 fighter on 2 October 1944. Shortly afterwards, his engine failed over occupied territory and he became a prisoner of war.

On his release he was posted to the Central Fighter Establishment before refusing a permanent commission and joining **Gloster Aircraft** as a test pilot. From there he moved briefly to **de Havilland** before joining **English Electric** as chief test pilot in 1947, where he led the test programme for the prototype of the Canberra jet bomber. In May 1952 he established two transatlantic speed records in the aircraft while making the first ever return flight in one day, taking 10 hours 3 minutes in total. He demonstrated the aircraft with such flair at the 1949 Farnborough Air Show that many give him much of the credit for the aircraft being sold to fifteen air forces. He headed the test programme for the English Electric Lightning interceptor, becoming the first pilot to take a British aircraft to twice the speed of sound. In 1964 he made the maiden flight of the BAC TSR2 bomber, which was later cancelled. Later, from 1970 until his retirement in 1979, he was responsible for the flight testing of the Panavia Tornado. In retirement he became an aviation author and journalist.

Beaverbrook, Lord (1879–1964) British newspaper magnate. Unlike **Alfred Harmsworth**,

Beaverbrook was not known for his interest in aviation, but this Canadian-born entrepreneur was appointed as Minister for Aircraft Production by Winston Churchill when he became prime minister on 10 May 1940. His task was to increase aircraft production, and this he did with production rising from 2,729 aircraft between January and April 1940 to 4,576 between May and August, as a result of which he made a significant contribution to victory in the **Battle of Britain**. Some have accused him of sacrificing long-term advantages for short-term gains, but short-term gains were what were needed at the time. He has also been accused of wanting to scrap Spitfire production in favour of twin-engined aircraft, which would have been a disaster had he succeeded. He retired because of ill health in 1942, but returned to the government in September 1943 as Lord Privy Seal.

Béchereau, Louis (1880–1970) French aircraft manufacturer. After graduating from the Ecole d'Art et Métiers d'Angers, Béchereau founded his own engineering business in 1909. He was approached by **Armand Deperdussin** who wanted a fake aeroplane to be built to publicise his display of textiles in a department store, but the result was so impressive that Deperdussin founded his own aircraft manufacturing company with Béchereau as the chief designer. Initially the aircraft were known as Deperdussins, but later the name SPAD, Société Pour les Appareils Deperdussin, was adopted.

Despite the prejudice against monoplanes during the early years of aviation, Deperdussin designs were successful, adopting the technique of monocoque construction pioneered by the Swiss naval engineer, Eugene Ruchonnet. In 1912 a Deperdussin Monocoque landplane was first to fly faster than 100 mph (160 kmph) and the following year Maurice Prevost won the first **Schneider Trophy Race** flying a floatplane variant.

The Deperdussin name was dropped when another proponent of the monoplane, **Louis Blériot**, bought the company in 1913, but Béchereau continued as chief designer, with his notable wartime aircraft including the Spad VII.

Bedford, Alfred William 'Bill' (1920–96) British test pilot. After serving an electrical

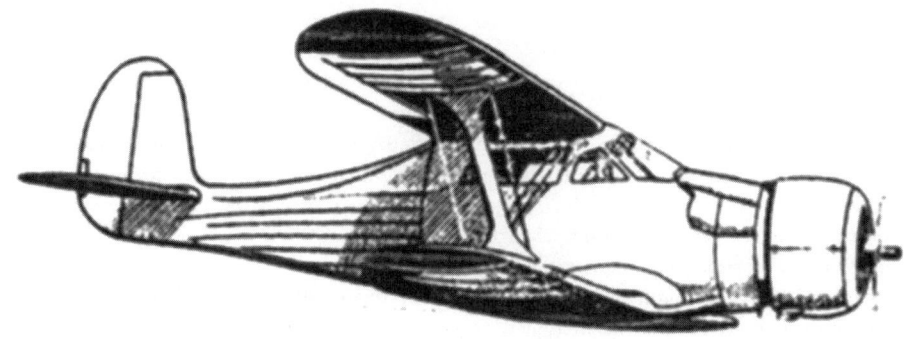

Biplanes came in a number of different forms: the Beech 17 of 1936 was a 'staggerwing', with the lower wing ahead of the upper. It was a successful aircraft used by the military on communications duties, but originally intended for the well-heeled private owner.

engineering apprenticeship, Bedford was commissioned into the RAF in 1940, flying Hawker Hurricane fighters with No. 605 Squadron in 1941, when he was posted to No. 135 Squadron in Burma, and later in India and Ceylon (now Sri Lanka). He returned to England in 1944 to fly North American F-51 Mustangs with No. 65 Squadron. He was awarded the AFC in 1945. Postwar, he remained in the RAF as an instructor before attending the Empire Test Pilots' School, from which he graduated in 1949. He left the RAF with the rank of squadron leader in 1951 to become a test pilot for **Hawker**, and in 1956 took over from **Neville Duke** as chief test pilot, a post which he was to hold for eleven years.

On 22 October 1960 Bedford became the first man to fly the P1127 Kestrel, the prototype for the Harrier V/STOL fighter or 'jump jet', taking the controls with a leg in plaster as a result of a car crash. The first flight was tethered. Later, during flutter tests at 400 mph and 5,000 ft there was a roaring noise and he decided to land, but at 200 mph the aircraft rolled uncontrollably to port and he ejected. On 8 February 1963, he landed the Kestrel aboard the aircraft carrier HMS *Ark Royal* while she was at sea off Portland Bill. At that year's Paris Air Show, during a demonstration flight, the aircraft seemed to fall out of the sky and crashed onto a concrete platform – but Bedford stepped out of the wreckage uninjured.

He retired from test-flying to become an aircraft sales manager for first Hawker Siddeley

and then for **British Aerospace**. He also devoted more time to his hobby: gliding.

Beech, Olive Ann (1903–93), and Walter Herschel (1891–1950) American aircraft designers. Walter Beech's first experience with aircraft design was in rebuilding a **Curtiss** design with a friend in 1913, followed by service as a mechanic in the US Army's Signal Corps at Rich Field, Texas, during the First World War. Postwar, he became an aircraft salesman for Laird, which was later renamed Swallow, and also undertook stunt flying. He left the company with a colleague, **Lloyd Stearman** in 1924, planning to break away from the traditional means of wooden construction and instead to develop aircraft built from steel. With **Clyde Cessna** they established Travel Air. Stearman provided design, Cessna did the test-flying, Beech was in sales, and Olive Mellor handled administration.

After enjoying initial success with the company, Stearman left in 1926 and set up his own business, with Cessna leaving in 1927 to found his company after a design dispute which arose when Cessna wanted to build cantilever-wing monoplanes. Travel Air continued in business for another year until it was sold to Curtiss-Wright in 1929. Both Beech and Mellor remained with Curtiss-Wright, marrying in 1930, but left in 1932 to found the Beech Aircraft Company. The first product was the Beech 17 Staggerwing biplane, with the leading edge of the lower wing far further forward than that of the upper wing. Despite the effects of the Great Depression still being felt, this aircraft succeeded in establishing the company. The Beech 18 twin-engined business aircraft that followed took the company through the Second World War. Initially Beech operated with less than twenty employees.

Demand for aircraft, including trainers when the Second World War started in Europe, meant that production became highly profitable and in 1940 a group of the company's directors attempted to seize control of the business while Walter Beech was in hospital seriously ill and his wife was also in hospital giving birth. Olive discharged herself from hospital, returned to her office and sacked the offending directors, something which she had to repeat in 1953, three years after Walter's death. She continued to run the company until the early 1980s.

Bell US manufacturer. Originally formed in 1935 by **Lawrence Bell**, during the Second World War the company produced the Bell P-59 Airacobra fighter, one of the first aircraft to have a tricycle undercarriage. It later developed the Bell Airacomet, the first US jet aircraft, which was flown for the first time in 1944 but never entered USAAF service. Postwar, a number of research aircraft were flown, including the X-1 and X-2 supersonic aircraft and the vertical take-off and landing X-22. A rocket-powered Bell XS-1, air-launched from a Boeing B-29 Superfortress, was the first supersonic aircraft. Bell also produced the X-5 with **variable-geometry** and variable camber.

The company is renowned as a helicopter manufacturer, with production starting in 1941. The Bell 47 Sioux, first flown in 1945, became the first helicopter to be awarded a federal Aviation Authority Type Approval Certificate in 1946, after which the type remained in production for more than twenty years, with licence-production in Europe by **Westland** and **Agusta**, and in Japan by **Kawasaki**. Many other helicopters also enjoyed outstanding success, including the 204/205 Iroquois, also known as the 'Huey' because of its original designation, and its civil relation, the Two-Twelve, and the 206 JetRanger, which also served with the military as the Kiowa. The first

attack helicopter was a 205 development, the AH-1G Huey Cobra.

While helicopter manufacture remains the mainstay of the business, the company is a partner with **Boeing** in the V-22 Osprey vertical take-off transport, a convertiplane with tilting rotors, and a smaller version for the civil market is under development.

Bell, Alexander Graham (1847–1922) Scottish-American inventor. Bell came late to aviation after an early career teaching deaf children, which led him to take an interest in communicating speech that resulted in his patenting the telephone in 1876. The wealth that came from his successful invention enabled him to take an interest in aviation and he sponsored a scientific association, the **Aerial Experimental Association** (AEA), to build a flying-machine, enlisting the expertise of the engineers **Frederick Baldwin** and **John McCurdy**, and a US Army officer, **Lt Thomas Selfridge**, starting in 1907. The result was an aeroplane with a bamboo structure, the *Red Wing*, which flew. This was followed by the *June Bug*, the first aeroplane to have both ailerons and wheels, which was flown by **Glenn Curtiss** on 21 June 1908, with a second flight on 4 July which was the first public flight in the United States. After such early promise, it seems strange that the AEA was wound up in March 1909 and Bell contented himself with experiments on tetrahedral kites. His advancing age cannot have been the reason for this move as he next took an interest in marine engineering and designed hydrofoil boats, one of which established a world water speed record in 1918.

Bell, Lawrence Dale (1894–1956) US aircraft designer. Bell became involved with aviation as a mechanic for **Lincoln Beachey** and his brother, Grover Bell, both stunt pilots, in 1912. He also converted a Martin biplane into an early bomber for the Mexican rebel, Pancho Villa, before working for **Glenn Martin**, where he eventually became foreman. He suggested that Martin employ a professional engineer and recommended **Donald Douglas**. In 1917, at the age of 23, he was sent to build a new factory for Martin at Cleveland, Ohio, where he stayed until **Rueben Fleet** lured him away in 1928 to become a vice-president of Consolidated Aircraft, where he remained until 1935 when the company moved from Buffalo to San Diego. It was in 1935 that he formed **Bell** Aircraft, which initially developed advanced military aircraft, including the unsuccessful wartime mid-engine Bell Airacobra fighter with propeller hub forward firing cannon. Postwar, the company was involved in research into high-speed flight and set records with its series of rocket planes, before becoming actively involved in the research, development and production of a long series of light helicopters, including such famous designs as the Sioux, JetRanger and Iroquois. The company's largest project to date is the vertical take-off and landing V-22 Osprey, a joint project with **Boeing**.

Bellanca US manufacturer. Bellanca was founded by Guiseppi Bellanca in 1927 and became a leading manufacturer of light aircraft in the 1930s and throughout the Second World War, remaining in business for some forty years afterwards. Its most successful product was the Viking, a low-wing four-seat monoplane.

Bellanca, Guiseppi Mario (1886–1960) Italian-American aircraft designer and manufacturer. Sicilian-born Bellanca studied engineering in Milan before building his first aircraft in 1908, a twin-seat pusher propeller biplane which struggled to fly. His next aircraft was a monoplane, before he emigrated to the United States in 1910. His first successful aircraft was a parasol monoplane completed in 1911, and this prompted him to teach himself to fly. Bellanca founded a flying school at Mineola, Long Island, which proved extremely successful in helping to meet the demand for pilots during the First World War, with students including the future mayor of New York, Fiorella la Guardia, after whom one of the city's airports was later named. Postwar, Bellanca became a consultant to **Orville Wright** and also built a number of aircraft on his own account before founding his eponymous company in 1927. The first official 'Bellanca' product was the *Miss Columbia* of 1926, for which an offer by **Charles Lindbergh** was turned down, although the aircraft did fly across the Atlantic later.

Although Bellanca was formed to build large monoplanes, it became best known for its light aircraft and continued in business throughout the Second World War, shortly after which Bellanca retired, and for some forty years afterwards.

Bellonte, Maurice (c.1896–1984) French aviator and navigator. Although he navigated for **Dieudonne Costes** on record-breaking flights during the 1920s, including a failed transatlantic attempt in 1929, it was for his navigation on the first Paris–New York flight by the *Point d'Interrogation* in 1930 that he became famous. The flight from Le Bourget to Curtiss Field took 30 hours. Happily, Bellonte survived to make a Paris–New York flight aboard a Concorde supersonic airliner.

Bennett, Floyd (1890–1928) USN pilot. Originally trained as a motor mechanic, Floyd Bennett joined the US Navy in 1917, and volunteered for training as a pilot, but was rejected on the grounds that he was too old and lacked adequate education. Nevertheless, he remained in the USN, even after the First World War had ended, and took flying lessons at his own expense. He finally broke through the USN's limitations in 1925 when he was transferred to the then **Lt Cdr Richard Byrd**'s unit, where he quickly made a favourable impression. Byrd took Bennett with him as co-pilot on his transpolar flight over the North Pole in the Fokker Trimotor *Josephine Ford* in 1926, for which they were awarded the Congressional Medal of Honor for this achievement, despite claims that their aircraft had lacked the necessary range. Unfortunately, a serious injury suffered on a test flight prevented Bennett joining Byrd on a New York–Paris flight in 1927. The following year, having made a full recovery, Bennett accompanied **Bernt Balchen** to rescue the crew of the *Bremen*, stranded in Labrador, but en route he became seriously ill and died in Quebec.

Bennett, James Gordon, Jnr (1841–1918) US newspaper proprietor. Bennett inherited the *New York Herald* newspaper empire in 1872, by which time he was already well known as a sportsman and sponsor of sporting events, with what might be described today as a 'nose for a story', as when in 1870 he sent Henry Stanley to find David Livingstone. He was also innovative and made significant developments of his own, including founding a global cable company and a storm warning network for shipping. Despite his achievements, he also had something of a reputation as a playboy and had been rejected by fashionable society in New York after fighting a duel with the brother of an ex-fiancée. In exile in France, where he alternated between Paris and his luxury yacht on the Mediterranean, he turned his attention to the introduction of a European edition of the *Herald*, which laid the foundations for the current *International Herald Tribune*.

He continued his sponsorship of sporting events into the aeronautical age with the Gordon Bennett international balloon races, first introduced in 1906. These continued until 1938, with the exception of 1915–1919 for the First World War and 1931 because of the Great Depression; the 1939 event was cancelled when Germany invaded Poland, that year's host country. An event for aeroplanes was the Coupe International d'Aviation, known informally as the Gordon Bennett Cup, first held at the world's first air show at **Reims** in 1909, when it was won by **Glenn Curtiss**.

Bensen US manufacturer. A small company founded by **Igor Bensen** that produced autogiros or gyrocopters, but failed to enthuse the public for a revival of this aircraft type, despite being used in a James Bond film.

Bensen, Igor Basil (1917–2000) Russian-American engineer. Russian born Bensen was taken from the country by his parents after the Russian Revolution. He completed his education at the University of Louvrain, Belgium, before emigrating to the USA where he worked for **General Electric** between 1940 and 1951 as an engineer and test pilot and was among the first to become involved with helicopters. He worked on a rotor head with automatic stability that made helicopters easier to handle. Bensen moved to **Kaman**, the helicopter manufacturer, in 1951 as head of research, but left in 1953 to found **Bensen Aircraft**, developing and building low-cost gyrocopters for the self-build market. One

of his inventions was the Rotochute, a personal gyrocopter blade that the wearer could use as an alternative to a parachute. He also continued his work on auto-stability systems for helicopters.

Beriev Russian design bureau. The Beriev design bureau became best known in the West during the Cold War for its maritime-reconnaissance flying boats, including the B-6 'Madge' and its B-8 development, as well as the B-10 'Mallow' jet-powered flying boat and the Be-12 'Mail' turboprop, all of which were produced in small numbers. Today it manufactures smaller flying boats and amphibians for the utility market, including fire-fighting.

Berlin, Air Battle of Starting in November 1943, the Second World War Air Battle of Berlin was intended to take the war to the heart of Germany. The idea was that striking at the heart of the German empire would seriously undermine morale during the build-up to the Allied invasion of Normandy. The distance that had to be flown over occupied territory meant that this was a campaign that could only be mounted during the long winter nights, and the sixteen raids to a heavily defended target proved difficult. Worse still, Winston Churchill's pronouncements meant that any element of surprise was lost.

The Air Battle of Berlin consisted of sixteen raids by Bomber Command, with the first on the night of 18/19 November 1943, and the last on the night of 24/25 March 1944. To fool the enemy, Berlin was to be attacked from unexpected angles, even flying past the city and then turning to attack it from the east, so that German night fighters would be ordered to patrol over cities such as Leipzig and Stettin.

To ensure accuracy, Pathfinders were used. On the first raid losses were relatively light, with just 9 aircraft out of the 444 Lancasters and Mosquitoes deployed failing to return, because there was an element of surprise. The ensuing raids became increasingly costly for Bomber Command, with 456 aircraft lost on the 5,000 sorties flown. These losses were far higher than they might have been due to German awareness of the target each night.

All in all, Bomber Command dropped 955,040 tons of bombs during the war in Europe between

1939 and 1945, as well as laying 47,250 mines, which sank more than 1,000 enemy ships. This was at a cost of 9,163 aircraft out of 391,137 sorties, while the human cost was 47,293 lives lost out of the RAF's total of 69,606 men and women.

Berlin Airlift Not only was Germany divided between the four Allied powers at the end of the Second World War, so too was its former capital, Berlin, situated some distance inside what had become East Germany. In spring 1948, the Soviet Union began interfering with surface transport between West Germany and West Berlin, cutting road and rail links for a day or two at a time, before closing all road, rail and inland waterway links with the city on 24 June. The next day a ban was imposed on food supplies from farms in East Germany. This left a city of 2.5 million people with supplies of grain and flour for seventeen days; cereal for thirty-two days; fats for forty-eight days; meat and fish for twenty-five days; potatoes for forty-two days; and skimmed and dried milk for twenty-six days. To maintain these supplies, a daily food requirement existed of 13,500 tons.

The United States Air Force in Europe (USAFE) estimated that its own daily airlift capability was just 700 tons, while with strict rationing a daily requirement of 5,000 tons would be needed to provide a sound, if basic, diet. Using aircraft from other Allied air forces and chartered commercial aircraft would raise the daily total to 3,000 tons, while the difference between this and the daily figure could be substantially reduced by boning meat and dehydrating potatoes.

There were three air corridors into the city, agreed on partition between the Allies and the Soviet Union, but these were only 20 miles wide and had a height restriction of 10,000 ft to prevent them being used for reconnaissance and to allow uninterrupted use of air space by Soviet military flights.

The Berlin Airlift, known to the British as 'Operation Plainfare' and to the Americans as 'Operation Vittles', started two days after the closure of the surface links. USAFE had 102 Douglas C-47s available, each able to carry just 3 tons, and while the RAF believed that it could gather 150 aircraft, the French Armée de l'Air could only provide personnel because the war in

French Indo-China was stretching its transport resources. Other USAF aircraft were gathered from around the world, including 54 Douglas C-54 Skymasters, capable of carrying 9 tons, while the RAF assigned two squadrons of Short Sunderland flying boats (ten aircraft) to operate into the Havel See from Hamburg. The aircraft numbers rose steadily throughout the summer and by August Douglas C-124 Globemasters had joined the airlift, each with a 20-ton capacity. Countries as far afield as Australia and New Zealand sent aircrew to relieve the pressure on the RAF transport pilots. Commercial charter airlines were offered £45 per flying hour for a DC-3/C-47, £8 per hour above the prevailing daily rate.

The airlift continued through the winter, and although some people died because of the cold, for the vast majority that survived there was the consolation of seeing the city formally divided into East and West on 1 December. Flying boat operations were suspended once the Havel See froze.

On 11 April 1949, a daily record of 8,246 tons was airlifted, but on 16 April, the 'Easter Parade' special effort saw 12,940 tons carried.

On 12 May 1949 the Soviet blockade of the city was lifted, almost as abruptly as it had been imposed. The airlift continued into the summer, both to restock supplies and to insure against the sudden re-imposition of the blockade, with the last flights landing on 16 August 1949.

All in all, some 75,000 people were involved, including 45,000 German cargo handlers, while there were eventually 441 USAF aircraft, 147 RAF aircraft, and 104 commercial aircraft. There were 277,804 flights, of which 189,963 were by the USAF, 65,857 by the RAF, including many with Commonwealth aircrew, and 21,984 by chartered aircraft.

USAFE estimated that 2,323,067 tons of supplies were moved by air, while the RAF estimated the total to be 2,325,809 tons. Only 30 per cent of the freight flown in was food; fuel accounted for some 60 per cent. In addition to food and fuel, raw materials were flown in to maintain the economic life of the city, with one estimate being that for every 260 tons flown in, 100 tons of completed manufactured goods were flown out.

Berliner, Henry Adler (1895–1970) German-American engineer. Henry Berliner became involved in aviation when he helped his German émigré father, Emile, build an experimental helicopter using a Bentley motor-car engine. It flew for 90 seconds in 1924. Encouraged by this modest success, in 1926 he founded the Berliner Aircraft Company, which became Berliner-Joyce in 1929. He left in 1930 to found the ERCO engineering company, which initially manufactured tools but later produced light aircraft, of which the Ercoupe was the most successful.

Bermuda Agreement For many years after the Second World War, commercial air transport between the United States and the United Kingdom was governed by the Bermuda Agreement, which regulated the number of carriers and the airports that could be served, as well as overall capacity on the route. These restrictions have been eased in recent years, and in 2007 an 'open skies' agreement was implemented between the United States and the members of the European Union.

Biard, Henri C. (1892–?) British pilot. The son of a French father and English mother, Biard went to the Grahame-White flying school at Hendon, north London, in 1910. Impatient at having to wait for an instructor, on his second day he took off in a Bristol Boxkite and flew for 2 miles before landing safely. He eventually received the necessary instruction and became an instructor himself before joining the Naval Wing of the RFC in 1914 and then becoming a member of the RNAS. He took part in anti-submarine patrols and later shot down a German Albatros fighter over the Western Front. Postwar, he flew for the manufacturer, **Supermarine**, for whom he operated a cross-Channel air service. While with Supermarine, he won the 1922 **Schneider Trophy Race** at Naples in a Sea Lion, but in 1925 was badly injured when his Supermarine S4 monoplane developed wing flutter and crashed.

bilateral agreements For many years, air transport was regulated by a series of inter-governmental air traffic agreements, usually concluded on a bilateral basis. Typically, on any given route the two participating countries would be allocated an equal number of flights, so that if each allowed just one airline on the route, these would also share the flights equally, but if one of them decided to allow a second airline, that would still have to come from the country's total allocation. In some cases the airlines of the two countries would pool receipts. A more liberal version was the **Bermuda Agreement** between the UK and the USA.

The growing trend towards the so-called 'open skies' agreements have stimulated competition and made bilateral agreements largely obsolete, and within certain markets, such as the European Union, completely illegal. The first of these open skies agreements on international services was between the UK and the Netherlands in 1986, which liberalised air transport between the two countries.

biplane Although some early pioneers used this term for aircraft with two tandem sets of wings, that is with the mainplane and tailplane having the same wingspan, it now means an aircraft with two wings, i.e. an upper and a lower wing. Usually the lower wing would be below the fuselage and the upper above it, but in some aircraft, such as the Handley Page HP42 and Supermarine Walrus, both wings were above the fuselage. Biplanes provided high lift, but with higher speeds the drag of the wings and the inter-wing supports became a serious disadvantage. In the early days, before the principle of cantilevered construction was mastered, the biplane was favoured for structural reasons because of problems with early monoplanes.

Even though **Sir George Cayley** proposed biplanes, the first to be built was **Hiram Stevens Maxim**'s test rig. Biplanes are still favoured by many aerobatic teams, but for practical purposes the last biplanes were the Antonov An-2, which entered production in 1947, and its turboprop development, the An-3.

A variation on the biplane was the sesquiplane, in which one of the wings, usually the lower, had a substantially shorter span than the other. In most biplanes, the leading edge of the lower wing is slightly further back than that of the upper wing, but this was reversed on the Airco DH2 of the First World War and later on the highly successful

Beech Model 17 Staggerwing light aircraft of the 1930s and early 1940s.

Birkigt, Marc (1878–1953) Swiss engineer. Swiss-born Birkigt studied engineering and designed mining equipment before moving to Spain in 1898, where he started to design railway rolling stock. At the still early age of 26 years, he became a partner in Sociedad Hispano-Suiza Fábrica de Automóviles and designed a range of dependable motor vehicle engines for the company's cars. In 1913 a second factory was opened in Paris.

After the outbreak of the First World War, with demand for luxury motor cars depressed, the company turned to aero engine design and production and in 1915 Birkigt launched a V-8 engine that combined high performance with low weight, and which was soon adopted for a number of aircraft designs, including the British SE5A. Postwar, Hispano-Suiza adopted the flying stork emblem used by fighter ace **Georges Guynemer**, a friend of Birkigt. While the company reverted to producing motor cars, Birkigt diversified Hispano-Suiza into armaments, designing a 20 mm cannon for aircraft.

Bishop, Maj William 'Billy' Avery (1894–1956) Canadian fighter ace. While training to be a Canadian army officer, in 1914 Bishop was expelled from the Royal Military Academy in Ontario for cheating in an exam, but when war broke out he was recalled and arrived in the UK with a cavalry unit. With the help of a wealthy woman he managed to obtain a transfer to the RFC, although he proved to be a poor pilot and lost several aircraft in landing accidents. He narrowly escaped being grounded and shot down his first aircraft on his next sortie. He then proved to be a natural, fearless, fighter pilot and claimed no less than forty-seven aircraft during the summer of 1917. He also claimed to have attacked a German air station, shooting down three aircraft that took off to defend it, and for this he was awarded the VC.

To this day Bishop remains a controversial character. He is believed to have been attracted to the RFC to get away from the cavalry, because he was allergic to horses rather than by any desire

to fly. He was undisciplined and inclined to exaggerate, and his poor flying skills call his high total of kills into question. Nevertheless, he did shoot down a number of aircraft.

Postwar, he was among the founders of an early Canadian airline. He became one of the first members of the RCAF when it was formed and rose to the rank of air marshal.

Black, Tom Campbell (1899–1936) British long-distance pioneer. Black joined the RFC in 1971 and was trained as a pilot. He rose to prominence postwar, initially in air racing, winning the Mansfield Robinson Trophy on three occasions, and also undertook long-distance flights, mainly to Africa, setting a number of records. Almost as a sideline, he helped to establish Wilson Airways in Kenya, and while there taught **Beryl Markham** to fly.

His reputation as a long-distance pilot resulted in the hotelier A.O. Edwards asking him to fly his de Havilland DH88 Comet in the 1934 McRobertson Miller race from the UK to Australia, with **Charles Scott** as co-pilot. Despite engine problems, the duo won the race. The following year, Black was less fortunate, having to bale out from the DH88 over the Sudan on a flight from the UK to South Africa after a propeller problem. Another propeller proved to be his undoing in 1936 when he was fatally injured after a Hawker Hart taxied into his Percival Mew Gull at Liverpool's Speke airport.

Blackburn British manufacturer. Founded by **Robert Blackburn** in 1914 the company produced some Antoinette-pattern monoplanes and a biplane. During the First World War it manufactured the baby flying boat for the RNAS and later produced a landplane, the Dart biplane torpedo bomber. A long association with the Royal Navy continued between the wars, with the emphasis on carrier aircraft, although a number of civil designs were also built, including the Iris three-engined flying boat. The Lincock biplane fighter was also manufactured for the RAF. The Ripon biplane torpedo bomber entered Fleet Air Arm service during the late 1920s and remained until 1934. During the early years of the Second World War, the Fleet Air Arm had the Skua, first flown in 1937 as a monoplane fighter and dive-bomber. It was badly outperformed in the former role even though it had the distinction of shooting down the first German aircraft and was the first to sink a major warship: the cruiser *Kongsberg* was sunk during the Norwegian campaign. The Skua's successor, the Roc, was little better.

At the end of the war, the Firebrand, a carrier-borne torpedo-bomber, was too late to see active service. An exception to the company's usual designs was the Beverley, a large four-engined high-wing transport for the RAF, which entered service in the mid-1950s, was capable of carrying up to 22 tons and had an impressive short-field performance for its size, but which was also renowned for its slowness.

Perhaps the most outstanding design was the Buccaneer, a carrier-borne jet bomber with later versions capable of carrying up to sixteen 1,000 lb bombs and which was designed to fly low enough to slip under the surveillance of ground-based radar. By the time this joined the fleet in the early 1960s, however, the company was already part of **Hawker Siddeley**.

Blackburn, Robert (1885–1955) British engineer. Inspired by the **Wright** brothers' successful debut in France in 1908, Blackburn completed his first aircraft the following year: a monoplane based on the Santos-Dumont Demoiselle. The aircraft crashed when Blackburn took it for a test flight. His next aircraft in 1911, based on the Antoinette design, was much better. Having proven himself as a reliable aircraft builder, he received a contract to build BE2Cs for the RFC.

Between the wars, Blackburn built a number of undistinguished aircraft for the RAF and the Fleet Air Arm, including the Iris, Skua and the Roc, and when war came again, he built Fairey Swordfish and Short Sunderlands under licence. His company merged in 1949 with General Aircraft, and the merged company's own designs included the large and lumbering Beverley freighter for the RAF and, possibly the sole Blackburn design of real quality, the sturdy Buccaneer carrier-borne jet bomber, capable of delivering up to sixteen 1,000 lb bombs or nuclear weapons, but he died from a heart attack before this aircraft first flew.

Blanchard, Jean-Pierre (1753–1809) French aeronaut. Blanchard's early involvement with aeronautics consisted of experiments with flapping-wing models and testing simple parachutes, with the latter involving tossing sheep off the top of high buildings. He did not become airborne himself until after the invention of the balloon in 1783 by the **Mongolfier** brothers and **Jacques Charles**. He was nevertheless one of the early pioneers, and as early as 1784 he was invited to London to demonstrate his balloons. **Dr John Jeffries** offered him £800 to fly him across the English Channel. As they were about to ascend from Dover in a Charlière, or hydrogen balloon, on 7 January 1785, Blanchard explained that he would have to leave Jeffries behind as the balloon could only lift one man. Jeffries was furious and suspecting that Blanchard wanted the distinction of making the crossing on his own, demanded that he take off his clothes, whereupon he discovered that Blanchard was wearing a belt containing heavy lead weights. Once relieved of this burden, the balloon ascended carrying both men and in front of a crowd reputed to number 250,000. As they were blown across the Channel, Blanchard accidentally released too much hydrogen and the balloon began to descend. The two men were forced to eject not only the ballast sandbags, but also books, luggage, cognac and even their heavier clothes, as well as relieving themselves over the side. This had the desired effect and after 2 hours the balloon had carried them over the Channel. The rising air as they approached the French coast lifted them over the cliffs and they finally descended into some trees.

This was the first aerial crossing of the English Channel and it made both men famous. Blanchard was awarded a pension by Louis XVI, which probably ended with the French Revolution, and later founded a school of aeronautics at Vauxhall in South London, despite still knowing little or no English. He also made a tour of Europe, which ended when the Austrians imprisoned him for spreading propaganda. He then went to the United States, where he made the first balloon descent outside Europe on 9 January 1793. George Washington is credited with providing Blanchard with the world's first passport when he gave him a slip of paper requesting anyone who made contact with him to provide him with assistance. It proved useful when, after ascending from Philadelphia, he descended in Gloucester, New Jersey.

Blanchard died of a heart attack in 1809 during a balloon ascent, but his wife, Madeleine-Sophie, continued to make ascents. Mme Blanchard's ascents included firework displays, with fireworks dropped from the balloon using primitive parachutes, and although such displays were by no means uncommon by this time, they continued to attract large crowds. Mme Blanchard was killed in 1819 during a display over the Tivoli Gardens in Copenhagen, Denmark, when the brazier used to set fire to the fireworks set alight the hydrogen in the balloon envelope. The aerostat made a rapid descent onto the roof of a house, causing the gondola to capsize and topple Mme Blanchard off the roof and on to the ground below.

Bland, Lilian E. (1878–1971) Irish journalist and pioneer. Inspired by **Louis Blériot**'s 1909 flight across the English Channel, Lilian Bland decided to build an aeroplane. She followed the **Wright** brothers in first building and learning to fly on a glider constructed of bamboo, ash and elm, which she named *Mayfly*. After some tentative glides, she ordered an engine from **Alliot Verdon Roe**, but to her dismay, when it finally arrived, it lacked a fuel tank. Clearly a mistress of improvisation, Bland used a whisky bottle that fed into the engine using an ear trumpet. In August 1910, with the engine installed, *Mayfly* made the first flight in Ireland. Bland planned to start her own aircraft company, but was dissuaded by her father who offered her a Ford Model T car if she scrapped the *Mayfly*. She not only accepted her father's offer and abandoned plans to manufacture aircraft, but in 1912 she married and moved to Canada, although she returned to the UK in 1935.

Blériot, Louis Charles-Joseph (1872–1936) French pioneer and aircraft designer/builder. Born in Cambrai in northern France, Blériot trained as an engineer and later established a successful business manufacturing headlamps for motor cars. Attracted by the growing interest in aviation and the developments in gliding, he built

a flapping-wing machine in 1901, but this was a failure. In 1905 he was a spectator when **Charles Voisin** flew **Ernest Archdeacon**'s float-glider off the River Seine in Paris. Blériot and Voisin then entered into a short-lived partnership, which ended in 1906 without producing a single successful design. Further attempts at designing and building a viable aeroplane followed, with Blériot heading a small team that included **Raymond Saulnier** and Louis Peyret, and suffering injuries when he test-flew his own designs, still without success. He crashed almost fifty times.

It was not until Blériot saw **Wilbur Wright**'s successful demonstrations in France in 1908 that he finally grasped the basic principles of flight, and went on to build the Blériot XI monoplane, on which most of the design work was by his associate, Saulnier. Nevertheless, the years of unsuccessful experiments meant that from having ample means and a successful headlamp business, Blériot was short of funds. He was saved by the gratitude of a wealthy friend, whose son had been saved from falling off a balcony by Blériot's wife, Alice, and who advanced him 25,000 fr, enabling him to remain in business.

On 25 July 1909 Blériot took off from France and flew his XI for 37 minutes across the English Channel, winning the £1,000 prize offered by the *Daily Mail*, a London newspaper. Coming so soon on the Wright brothers' triumphant demonstrations, Blériot's flight began to transform attitudes towards aviation, and the interest of the armed forces in aviation rather than aerostation dates from this time.

Blériot established a number of speed records in 1909 before giving up flying to return to his business, his wife and his six children.

'Blitz', the blitzkrieg against British targets (August 1940–May 1941) While the term 'Blitz' is often applied generally to German air raids over British towns and cities during the Second World War, it should only be used for the attacks from summer 1940 to spring 1941, by which time German attentions were turning to the invasion of the Soviet Union.

Night operations were preferred for high-level bombing, since the risk of fighter interception during the early months of the war was minimal. To ensure accuracy, the Luftwaffe used a technique known as *Knickebein*, by which radio beams were transmitted by ground-based stations in occupied Europe, from northern France to the south of Norway, capable of covering the whole of the British Isles. By the end of August 1940 there were twelve of these stations, but by this time, too, No. 80 Wing of the RAF had started jamming the *Knickebein* beams, and later the RAF's countermeasures became more sophisticated and effective, with 'Meacons' bending the beams. The Luftwaffe then introduced more sophisticated radio beams, *X-Geraet* and *Y-Geraet*. The first of these used four beams, with the first pointed at the target for navigation, while the other three crossed the main beam at pre-set points in advance of the bomb release point, assisting accurate bomb-aiming. *Y-Geraet* used a single ground station which produced a complicated beam comprising 180 directional signals per minute, which had to be interpreted by a special device aboard the aircraft whose functions included re-radiating the signal back to the ground station, ensuring that the operators on the ground knew the aircraft's exact position. This meant that they could then signal the aircraft at the bomb-release point. The sophistication of the equipment meant that specially trained crews had to be used, effectively the German equivalent of the RAF's Pathfinders, who worked within a special unit, *Kampfgruppe 100*, flying Heinkel He111s.

Aircraft used on the night attacks on British cities were mainly Dornier Do17 and Heinkel He111s. This was a weakness as neither was a heavy strategic bomber.

The impact of the bombing on those on the ground was considerable. The first heavy daylight attack on London was on 7 September 1940, followed that night by the first heavy German night raid on London, with 318 German bombers sent against the city, with no risk of interception by night fighters. No effort was made to concentrate the attack, which lasted from 20.10 on 7 September until 04.30 the following morning. Finding the target was not a problem, since the fires from the daylight attack were still burning. The Luftwaffe sent another 207 aircraft over the following night, aiming for the fires

which had defeated the fire brigade's efforts, so that by the morning of 9 September, there were no less than twelve major conflagrations. Another 412 people had been killed and 747 seriously injured. The four main railway termini serving the south of England were so badly damaged that railway services could not be operated for a short period. This was the result of two nights' bombing by medium bombers. The Luftwaffe was back for sixty-six of the following sixty-seven nights – the exception being due to bad weather.

Maintaining warfare on this scale required considerable stamina among aircrews. Typical of one bomber crew was that in one three-week period they flew against London on 23 September, twice on 24 September (morning and evening), and then again on the evenings of 27, 28, 29, 30 September and 2 and 4 October, before flying against Manchester on 7 and 9 October, and against Coventry on 12 October. Coventry, in the Midlands, and Manchester, in the north-west, were more distant targets than London, hence the less intensive nature of these operations.

One of the heaviest attacks during the London Blitz was that of the night of 15/16 October, starting at 20.40 on the 15th and continuing until 04.40 the following morning. A force of 400 bombers was sent against the city, approaching it at between 16,000 ft and 20,000 ft. The aircraft came from bases in the Netherlands, Belgium and northern France, crossing the coast at many points between West Sussex and Essex.

London's Blitz lasted from 7 September until the morning of 14 November, a total of sixty-seven nights with just one night without attack from the air. The major raid on Coventry took place on the night of 14 November. No less than 499 bombers approached the target, with one bomber stream coming over The Wash on Britain's East Coast, another over Brighton and a third over the Isle of Wight, both on the south coast. They devastated the city centre; 506 people were killed and 432 seriously injured.

The Blitz continued throughout the winter and into the spring. On the night of 12/13 March, the port of Liverpool was the target.

The Luftwaffe campaign against British cities caused considerable disruption and loss of life, for relatively light German losses at this stage in the war. As war progressed and improved equipment became available, the RAF's night fighters became a more formidable threat. Once again the Germans were paying the price of not having a heavy bomber fleet and lacking the bomb loads, bomb sizes and range to make effective strikes against British cities, despite having the benefit of advance bases in France and Belgium. The constant raids on London showed that even a persistent campaign could not break such a large target without large enough aircraft. It also overlooked the fact that much of Britain's industry had been widely dispersed, with relatively little heavy industry actually based in the capital itself.

blitzkrieg German for 'lightning war', blitzkrieg has come to mean heavy air attack against towns and cities, but in fact refers to the coordination of fast-moving armoured units and tactical air power. This form of warfare was foreseen by Basil Liddell-Hart, the interwar British writer on strategy, and by Charles de Gaulle, and was favoured by both the Germans and the Russians who used it effectively, especially in operations against Denmark and the Low Countries in spring 1940.

Bloch, Marcel (1892–1986) French aircraft designer. Renowned Anglophobe, Marcel Bloch was born in Paris, but instead of following his father into medicine, he studied electrical engineering at the L'Ecole Breguet, founded by **Louis Breguet**, before studying aeronautics at L'Ecole Supérieure d'Aéronautique. He then became an apprentice at the Panhard motor car factory. When the First World War broke out in Europe in 1914 he was conscripted into the Corps of Engineers and posted to the Chalais-Meudon aeronautical research facility where he took the Caudron G-3 design in hand and modified it to make it suitable for mass production. After working for **Maurice Farman** he started his own aircraft factory, although initially he concentrated on propellers, working with **Henry Potez** as a partner under the trade name of 'Eclair'. In 1917 the two partners established a new firm, SEA, to build and market a two-seat scout aircraft, of which the French Army bought more than 100.

After the First World War the drop in demand for new aircraft and the flooding on to the market of former military types meant a sharp fall in business and Bloch diversified into producing low-cost prefabricated housing. He returned to aviation in the early 1930s, building both transport and combat aircraft. Having re-established the company in aviation, the French government started to nationalise the industry, much to Bloch's dismay. His prediction that production would be affected came true, just as the country was attempting to re-arm as the prospect of war with Germany loomed. After the fall of France, Bloch refused to continue aircraft production and was imprisoned at Buchenwald concentration camp, but survived.

At the end of the Second World War, Bloch rejected the family surname because of its German connotations and took the name of Dassault, which translates as 'attack' in English and was the *nom de guerre* of his brother, Paul, who was a leader of the French Resistance movement. While the first generation of French jet fighters were licence-produced British designs, Dassault embarked on a series of increasingly potent aircraft, including the Mystère and culminating in the Mirage family of aircraft, whose outstanding export success kept prices low and enabled the French air force, the Armée de l'Air, to become one of the strongest in Europe. His company also built a series of business jet aircraft, including one of the first to offer true transatlantic range, but as with most European manufacturers, struggled to make headway in the airliner business until the creation of Airbus.

Blohm und Voss German manufacturer. Given that aircraft manufacture in Germany had been banned by the **Treaty of Versailles**, it was not surprising that strenuous efforts were made during the 1930s to re-establish a German aircraft industry. One aspect of this were incentives for companies to diversify into aviation, and one of these was the shipbuilder Blohm und Voss. The company retained its nautical connection by building flying boats, including the Bv138 twin-boom, three-engined, anti-shipping aircraft and the large six-engined Bv222 transport with a range of almost 4,000 miles. The Bv138 was used extensively to attack convoys struggling northwards to the North Cape on their way to Murmansk and Archangel. Postwar, the company was merged into Messerschmitt-Bolkow-Blohm, and today is part of the **European Aeronautic Defence and Space Compnay (EADS)**.

BMW German manufacturer. Although better known as a motor car and motorcycle manufacturer, BMW's connection with aviation dates from the First World War, when its engines were used in the Fokker D.VII. Between the wars, the company favoured air-cooled radial engines and probably the most notable aircraft to use BMW engines during the Second World War was the Focke-Wulf Fw190 fighter. They were also used in the Junkers Ju52/3M transport and Ju88 night fighter, the Arado Ar196 seaplane and were an option on the Ar232 transport and a number of other types, including the Blohm und Voss Bv141. The company can also claim to be the first turbojet engine manufacturer. Postwar, the company's aero-engine interests have been merged with those of MAN.

Bock's Car The USAAF Boeing B-29 Superfortress that dropped the second atomic bomb on the Japanese city of **Nagasaki** on 9 August 1945. It was named after the aircraft's captain.

Boeing/Boeing-Vertol US manufacturer. One of just two manufacturers of large airliners in the western world today, the Boeing Company was originally founded as Boeing and Westervelt, and manufactured just two floatplanes during the First World War. Postwar, the company produced almost every type of aircraft other than those intended for the private flier, and for a while was involved in airline operations before anti-trust legislation forced the separation of manufacturing and transport operations, with its airline business eventually becoming part of United Airlines.

The company achieved early distinction when its Boeing 40, a single-engined passenger and mailplane design, operated the first transcontinental night flights across the USA. During the late 1920s the Boeing 80 was one of many three-engined airliners on the market, in its case carrying up to fifteen passengers at speeds of up to 125 mph. The company also produced the 95, a single-engined mailplane. Boeing established a reputation as a fighter manufacturer as well, starting with the MB-

3A for the US Army and following with its own designs, including the PW-9 biplane, which was developed into the FB series of fighters for both the USN and USMC, and the P-12 for the USAAC. Fighter production continued throughout the late 1920s and early 1930s, after which the company dropped out of this market until following the acquisition of **McDonnell Douglas** in the 1990s.

Boeing did much to establish the form for the modern airliner. In 1933 the 247 first appeared, a twin-engined monoplane with accommodation for ten passengers and a retractable undercarriage, which could fly at up to 180 mph. By the end of the decade the world's first pressurised airliner, the Boeing 307 Stratoliner, entered service with both Pan American and Transcontinental & Western Air, the predecessor of TWA. The 314 flying boat was built for Pan American and the British Overseas Airways Corporation (BOAC). Originally designed for services across the Pacific from the West Coast of America to Hong Kong and Shanghai, the 314 spent its war years mainly on the North Atlantic.

Having abandoned fighter manufacture, Boeing played a role in the development of the bomber. One of the first all-metal monoplane bombers was the B-9, but by the end of the 1930s Boeing was testing the 299, the predecessor of the B-17 Fortress that was to be the backbone of the USAAF's heavy bomber force over Europe during the Second World War. The war also saw the development of the high-flying Boeing B-29 Superfortress, which flew too high for conventional Japanese fighter attack and eventually was used to drop nuclear weapons on **Hiroshima** and **Nagasaki**.

The aerodynamic surfaces of the B-29 provided the basis for the postwar Boeing 377 Stratocruiser, originally intended to be the C-95 transport for the USAAF. A double-bubble double-deck fuselage provided seating for between fifty and a hundred passengers, depending on the accommodation chosen. Bomber and commercial airliner design came close again with the B-47 Stratojet, while the Boeing B-52 Stratofortress in its later versions remained in service into the twenty-first century, gaining a new lease of life as a cruise missile launch aircraft.

Experience gained in developing jet bombers led to the Boeing 717, the prototype for the

C-135 jet transport and its KC-135 tanker derivative, and on to the 707 long-haul jet airliner and its short-haul variant, the 720. This was the first of a series of 707 developments, using as many common components as possible to cut costs and reduce spares holdings, and included the 727 trijet and the 737 twin-jet airliners, with the initial versions of both using the same engine, again to cut spares holdings for airlines. These entered service in 1963 and 1967 respectively. The much updated Boeing 737 remains in production today and orders stretch as far ahead as 2012. The aircraft has outlasted not only the 727, but also its successor, the 757, in production.

While the 707 had competition from Convair, **de Havilland** and **Douglas**, a scaled-up version, the 747, is only now facing direct competition from the Airbus A340. Intended as an interim design while the Boeing 2707 supersonic transport was developed, the 747 has seen four major stretches and enhancements in its design, as well as short-haul and ultra-long-range variants of the original 747-100 series. The first wide-bodied airliner, the 747 was dubbed the 'jumbo jet'. Although Boeing did not enter the market for three-engined long-haul airliners in the 1970s, it did produce the 767, an aircraft of unique cross-section with twin aisles, and followed this with the 777, another true wide-body which is available in many different versions, including one extended range variant capable of flying non-stop between London and Sydney.

The 2707, a **variable-geometry** supersonic transport, was cancelled. It differed from the Anglo-French Concorde in using new technology rather than being simply state of the art.

In 1997 Boeing acquired **McDonnell Douglas**, by that time the third manufacturer of large and long-haul aircraft, as well as a leading military aircraft producer. Boeing was producing just two aircraft, the MD-11 trijet and the MD-95. It soon abandoned the MD-11 and the MD-95, a short-haul jet with two tail-mounted turbofans, was re-designated the 717, for the first time repeating a design classification, but it was withdrawn from production in 2005. This meant that Boeing was once again a manufacturer of combat aircraft with the B-1 bomber inherited from Rockwell and McDonnell Douglas's F-15 Eagle and F/A-18

Hornet, as well as the Goshawk trainer, but the company's XF-32 lost the Joint Strike Fighter (JSF) project.

Meanwhile, Boeing had also developed into a helicopter manufacturer, with the acquisition of Vertol in 1960. Vertol had originated as the Piasecki Helicopter Corporation in 1946, and developed a range of twin-rotor helicopters, of which the most modern have been the medium-lift CH-46 and heavy-lift CH-47 Chinook, both twin-engined machines. It adopted the Vertol title in 1956. Boeing is also a partner with **Bell** on the V-22 Osprey convertiplane, which, if it is successful, may herald the end for the helicopter at some stage in the future.

Looking ahead, Boeing is putting into production an advanced airliner built largely of composite materials, the 787, which will be aimed primarily at services that link cities and by-pass hubs. In terms of size it will be largely a replacement for the 767 series. The company is also working on a maritime-reconnaissance development of the 737 for the USN as a Lockheed-Martin Orion replacement. From 2010 onwards, the company will be looking at a completely new narrow-body design to replace the 737 series, but it is also working on a flying wing or blended-wing design, the BWB, aimed specifically at the air cargo market, and flight trials with a scale model started in 2007.

Boeing, William 'Bill' Edward (1881–1956)

American aircraft manufacturer. Detroit-born 'Bill' Boeing was well educated and a graduate of Yale University who made his fortune by property speculation. In 1914 his involvement with aviation followed his first flight and he took lessons at the **Glenn Martin** flying school. He felt that there was scope for improvement in the design and construction of the early trainers and decided to open his own aircraft factory with a friend, Conrad Westervelt. The first two aircraft, both floatplanes, were completed in 1916. Aircraft production continued after the end of the First World War and in 1927 Boeing founded Boeing Air Transport, a predecessor of United Airlines into which it was merged in 1934 because of US anti-trust legislation banning businesses from both building and operating aircraft.

During the interwar years, Boeing built both fighters for the USN and increasingly large commercial aircraft, but Boeing himself left corporate life in the mid-1930s, although he returned briefly during the Second World War. The company was notable for its Boeing 314 flying boat, used by both Pan American World Airways and the British Overseas Airways Corporation, and the 307 Stratoliner, the world's first pressurised airliner, built on the eve of war for both Pan American and Transcontinental & Western Air, but both these types were built in small numbers. In the popular mind, however, real success came with the B-17 Fortress heavy bomber and the B-29 Superfortress, which dropped the first atomic bombs, used by the USAAF against the Axis powers during the Second World War. Despite the appeal of its Stratocruiser airliner postwar, success came with the jet age, for which Boeing produced both the large B-52 Stratofortress heavy bomber and the Boeing 707 family of jet airliners and, later, the 747, the world's first wide-bodied aircraft, as well as the 737 series, the best-selling commercial airliners of all time with some 5,000 built to date.

Boelcke, Capt Oswald (1891–1916) German fighter ace. Hauptmann Oswald Boelcke first learnt to fly just two weeks after the start of the First World War. Initially he flew Albatros scout aircraft with his brother as observer and was awarded the Iron Cross in 1915. As one of the best pilots in the German Military Air Service (MAS), he was selected to fly the potent Fokker Eindekker, the first aircraft to have synchronised machine guns that could fire through the propeller disc. His success as a fighter pilot led to his rules, *Boelcke's Dicta*, becoming compulsory for all German pilots. His 'dicta' included not firing at an enemy aircraft until the last minute, when effective damage was almost guaranteed. At this time aircraft were not grouped together in units and many different types could be assigned to a base. In 1916 Boelcke persuaded the MAS to group aircraft into units with each operating just a single type and specialising in a particular aspect of warfare. He was given command of Jagdstaffel 2, Fighter Squadron 2, which soon spawned many of the German fighter aces of the war, including

Baron Manfred von Richthofen. Boelcke himself scored forty confirmed kills during the war, including the first American to be lost in aerial combat, Victor Chapman.

Boelcke was awarded the Pour le Merite, but his promising career was brought to a premature end not by combat but by a mid-air collision with a plane flown by a student pilot, Erwin Bohme, who was so stricken by the accident that he had to be physically restrained from committing suicide.

Bolkow *See* Messerschmitt-Bolkow-Blohm

Bombardier Canadian manufacturer. One of the two leading manufacturers of regional jet aircraft, Bombardier was born out of the **Canadair** company when it acquired **de Havilland Canada**, originally formed as a subsidiary of the British manufacturer in 1947, from **Boeing**. The company manufactures railway rolling stock and trams as well as aircraft. The product line includes the CRJ series of regional jet airliners for Canadair Regional Jet and the advanced turboprop Dash 8 family that originated with de Havilland Canada, many of which are fitted with a cabin noise suppression kit and are denoted by a 'Q' prefix between Dash 8 and the variant, being Dash 8 Q100, Q200, Q300 and Q400. The Q400 has a more advanced flight deck than the earlier versions as well as having a much longer fuselage. Rising fuel prices have resulted in a revival of the market for regional turboprops, while the market for smaller regional jets such as the CRJ200 has collapsed.

The company also produces business aircraft such as the Global Express, which has transatlantic capability, and through its acquisition of **Lear Jet** of the USA, which produces smaller business jet aircraft. It acquired **Short** Brothers of Northern Ireland from the UK government and uses its works to produce sub-assemblies.

bombers The first use of bombs, if this means the dropping of munitions from the air, preceded the invention of the aeroplane and even the airship. On 12 July 1849 the residents of Venice were under siege by the Austrians whom they had expelled in March 1848. Balloons carrying 30 lb bombs were launched from Austrian warships offshore with a favourable wind carrying them over the city when timing devices ignited the fuses. As with any attempt with balloons, presumably hydrogen-filled, there was a fair danger that the raid would be 'hit and miss', and so it was. No damage was done from the bombs that fell around the city, with many falling into the lagoon and others on to the Austrians' own positions.

The use of German Zeppelin airships during the First World War as bombers was widely anticipated during the last days of peace, but these large craft presented easy targets and with their hydrogen gas were vulnerable to anti-aircraft fire. At first, the poor performance of the early fighters, especially hydro-aeroplanes with the weight and drag of their floats, made fighter attack difficult against well-armed Zeppelins. Despite the appearance of **Igor Sikorsky**'s *Ilya Mourametz* before the war, which emerged not as the planned airliner but as an early heavy bomber, the true bomber took longer to evolve than the fighter, partly because of the rarity of multi-engined aircraft before the war. A number of effective single-engined bombers did appear, including the Airco DH4 and DH9, and even a bomber variant of the Royal Aircraft Factory's FE2a fighter, the FE2b.

Nevertheless, true heavy bombers began to materialise, with the most successful including the Handley Page 0/400, the Breguet 14 and 19, and the Caproni Ca5, the last being an unusual trimotor with a twin-boom fuselage. The Germans had the Gotha Type 4.

As the war ended, the newly formed RAF in France was planning a heavy bomber raid on Berlin, although given later difficulties and heavy losses in the **Battle of Berlin** during the Second World War, the success of this must have been doubtful. Nevertheless, improved bombers continued to appear, intended for, but too late for, wartime operations, and these included the Vickers Vimy, as well as some of the first significant US combat aircraft, such as the Martin MB and the Douglas T2D-1. The combination of peace and the dire international financial situation between the two wars meant that progress remained slow. Westland Wapitis replaced the RAF's DH9s, while Hawker Hart and Fairey Fox light bombers, Boulton Paul Sidestrand medium bombers and Vickers Virginia and Handley Page Hinaidi heavy bombers entered

service. In the Soviet Union, **Tupolev** designed the giant TB-3 monoplane.

Despite its interest in strategic warfare, including strategic bombing, for many years the RAF was side-tracked by the lure of the light bomber, believing that it was possible to amass a force of such aircraft capable of performing almost as well as a contemporary fighter. When the Second World War broke out, the latest manifestation of this category of aircraft, the Fairey Battle, soon proved itself completely inadequate and highly vulnerable with heavy losses during the Battle of France.

More worthwhile was progress towards establishing effective medium and heavy bombers. The evolution of the Second World War bomber can be traced to the appearance of such significant aircraft of the 1930s as the Boeing B-9 and the Martin B-10, both twin-engined monoplanes. The era of the biplane was drawing to a close and the new aircraft were soon all monoplanes, including the French Bloch MB200 and MB210, the Italian Fiat BR20 Cicogna and Savoia-Marchetti SM79 Sparviero, unusual in having three engines, while the RAF received Armstrong-Whitworth Whitleys, Handley Page Hampdens and Vickers Wellingtons, the latter with strong geodetic construction. While many of the early post-First World War bombers had been bomber transports, for all practical purposes the last of these was the Junkers Ju52/3m, which by the late 1930s was unquestionably a transport aircraft rather than a bomber. Nevertheless, to get around the many restrictions and retain an element of surprise, many German bombers were developed officially as airliners, including the Dornier Do17 or 'flying pencil'. A real glimpse of the future of heavy bombing was the Boeing 299, first flown in 1935 and the direct ancestor of the wartime Boeing B-17 Fortress. Concerned with the close coordination of land and air warfare in the lightning war or blitzkrieg concept, the Germans placed much faith in the Junkers Ju87 Stuka dive-bomber, with little real consideration of strategic bombing, and before the war cancelled their heavy bomber programme.

By this time, aircraft development was such that many bombers were landplanes, and of those land planes, many were intended for operation from aircraft carriers. The Germans and the

Italians produced seaplane bombers, the Heinkel He115 and the Cant Z506B Airone respectively, although these were used mainly for anti-shipping operations. The Royal Navy's Fleet Air Arm had the Fairey Swordfish biplane and Blackburn Skua, while the Imperial Japanese Navy had the Aichi D3A1 dive-bomber, known to the Allies as 'Val', and the Nakajima B5N, known to the Allies as 'Kate'.

The Second World War was the war of the heavy bomber, of which the most powerful in terms of bombload was the Avro Lancaster, one of a trio of British heavy bomber designs. The others were the Handley Page Halifax and the Short Stirling, although the latter's mid-wing configuration meant that the bomb bay was divided in two and heavier bombs could not be dropped. By the end of the war, the Stirlings and many Halifaxes were being used as glider tugs and transports. The USAAF used the Boeing B-17 Fortress, which had a heavy defensive armament for use on daylight raids, and the Consolidated B-24 Liberator, with its remarkably long range that resulted in arguments over whether aircraft should be assigned as bombers or long-range maritime-reconnaissance aircraft. The Americans produced the Boeing B-29 Superfortress, which flew so high that the Japanese were forced to use unarmed (for lightness) fighters on suicide missions to attack it, and which dropped the first atomic bombs. The USSR produced the Petlyakov Pe-8 four-engined bomber.

Neglect of the heavy bomber went against the Axis powers. There were no true Japanese heavy bombers, while the Italians produced the Piaggio P108 four-engined bomber and the Germans the Dornier Do177, which had its four engines mounted in pairs driving two propellers, but was prone to overheating and catching fire.

There were also light and medium bombers, many of which were highly successful. The British had the Bristol Blenheim, which seemed to suffer high losses, but this may have been because they were used during the early years of the Second World War and often deployed in small numbers against targets, and the much-acclaimed de Havilland DH98 Mosquito. The USAAF had the Douglas A-20 Havoc and North American B-25 Mitchell; the Luftwaffe had the Heinkel He111 and Junkers Ju88.

Hitler's obsession with bombing meant that the Messerschmitt Me262 jet fighter entered service as a bomber in 1944, wasting what could have been a significant advantage, while the Arado Ar234 jet reconnaissance aircraft was also used as a bomber.

As the war ended, piston-engined bombers continued to enter service, including the Avro Lincoln and the Convair B-36, a large aircraft originally intended to be able to attack Germany from the United States should the British surrender.

Jet bombers soon began to arrive, with one of the most successful being the English Electric Canberra, widely exported and produced under licence in the USA by **Martin**, and the Boeing B-47 Stratojet. Heavier bombers followed, including the large eight-engined Boeing B-52 Stratofortress, while the RAF received its trio of 'V' bombers to carry the British nuclear deterrent: the Vickers Valiant, Handley Page Victor and Avro Vulcan. The French introduced the Sud Vatour and the USSR saw a succession of designs from the **Tupolev** bureau. Supersonic bombers appeared during the 1960s with the North American B-58 Hustler and the Dassault Mirage IV. The new generation of aircraft saw a change of emphasis, with the aircraft being expected to operate on a hi-lo-lo-hi basis, which meant that they penetrated and left enemy airspace flying low to evade radar, but the first purpose-built low-level strike bomber was the British carrier-borne Blackburn (later Hawker Siddeley) Buccaneer.

Bombers continued to enter service despite the missile age, including the Panavia Tornado developed and operated by the British, Germans and Italians, and the stealth bombers introduced by the USAF, the North American Rockwell B-1 and the B-2. The aircraft also began to change, with many using external stores rather than having a bomb bay, although some compromised with belly recesses or small bomb bays.

See Table 12: First World War Bomber Performance, for war load and range of selected First World War bombers.

See Table 15: Second World War Bomber Performance, for selected Second World War bombers.

bombing Despite some of the pioneers maintaining that they considered that the aeroplane would make future wars impossible, experiments in dropping bombs preceded the First World War, and during the Balkan Wars the Italians were accused of using bombs by the Turks. Many of the early visionaries foresaw bombs being dropped from aircraft or from kites. The advent of the bomber and the bomb meant that no longer would civilian populations living far behind the front line be immune from the hardships and suffering of the war. Indeed, during the Second World War it became imperative to many commanders that the civilians should share the pain, while others saw the bomber as revenge for raids on their own cities.

The bomb first evolved before the First World War, and once hostilities commenced the early air-dropped munitions included hand grenades as well as artillery shells fitted with fins for stability. The concept of strategic bombing evolved with first Zeppelin airships and then bombers operating over towns and cities on the east coast of England as well as raids on London itself. Development was rapid, and by the end of the war 250 lb bombs were available. Between the wars, a combination of peacetime neglect and limited defence budgets meant that little further progress was made, so that by 1939 the main air forces were often operating with much of what was left over from 1918.

In many ways the most potent air-dropped munitions were the torpedoes, first dropped in trials before the First World War and also used in wartime, especially in the Dardanelles. It was not only a case of, as one American admiral put it, being easier to get water into a ship through the bottom than the top, many bombs either broke up on hitting the armour of major warships, or bounced off. The torpedo remained a potent missile during the Second World War, most notably at **Taranto** and **Pearl Harbor**. Earlier, unofficial bombing trials in the United States by **Billy Mitchell** had seen the surrendered German battleship *Ostfriesland* sunk by bombers belonging to the US Army.

During the Second World War, many significant developments took place. From the outset, the concept of dive-bombing to ensure accuracy, most usually associated with the German Luftwaffe

and its Junkers Ju87 Stuka dive-bomber but also used by others, including the Royal Navy's Fairey Swordfish, was important, although it became less so as the war progressed. The concept of area bombing practised by the RAF reflected poor accuracy during the early years of the war, but this improved partly due to better navigational and bomb-aiming aids, partly due to the Pathfinder force marking targets, and partly through the master bomber concept, with the latter proving invaluable in stopping the target area creeping as successive waves of aircraft arrived over it. There were also special highly trained units for the more difficult targets.

Bombs became much larger during the Second World War, and an element in the failure of the Luftwaffe as a strategic bombing force, evidenced during the **Battle of Britain** and the **blitzkrieg** on British towns and cities that followed, was that the Germans lacked a true heavy bomber until much later in the war, by which time it was only possible to produce the aircraft, the Heinkel He177, in limited numbers. While the Germans were limited to 1,000 and 2,000 lb bombs for the most part, the RAF saw its bomb size rise steadily, from the 1,000 lb to the 4,000 lb 'cookie' and then the 8,000 lb 'double cookie'. At the other end of the scale, large quantities of small incendiary bombs were found by both sides to multiply the impact of bombing, often causing huge firestorms that burnt out of control, as at Hamburg and then later at Tokyo, among others. **Sir Barnes Wallis** invented a mine, known as 'Upholder', and popularly referred to as a 'bouncing bomb' for the attack on the Ruhr Dams by the RAF's **Dam Busters**, with a smaller version for anti-shipping duties, although the latter was not introduced to operations.

Later in the war, the British 12,000 lb Tallboy and 22,000 lb Grand Slam, like the bouncing bombs dropped from specially modified Avro Lancaster heavy bombers, were set to spin during their descent so that they burrowed into the ground and produced an earthquake effect on exploding. These bombs, when dropped alongside targets, offered the means of destroying large fortified structures on which smaller weapons simply bounced off or broke up. Typical targets for these large weapons included the U-boat pens and also the German battleship *Tirpitz*, whose deck armour was not proof against them and which caused her to capsise in a Norwegian fjord.

At the outset of the Second World War, the British in particular would often send small forces of bombers against targets which could concentrate their anti-aircraft fire on as few as five or six aircraft, resulting in heavy RAF losses. It became clear later that overwhelming the defences with large formations of closely packed bombers reduced losses by forcing the enemy to divide his fire among too many targets. The concept of 'thousand bomber raids' was born. Daylight bombing also emerged as highly dangerous, forcing the British and the Germans to concentrate on the more difficult night bombing, although it was the Germans who first used aids for accurate bombing, which the British managed on occasions to distort by 'bending' radio signals. When the United States entered the war, daylight bombing returned, not just because of superior defensive armament on their aircraft and, later, the arrival of long-range escort fighters, but because the numbers of aircraft being operated meant that airspace over the airfields in the east of England would have been dangerously overcrowded had both air forces attempted night raids. Night British bombing followed by day American bombing proved devastating, as at Dresden.

The USAAF spent much time trying to evolve bomber formations in which the defensive fire of the aircraft could be arranged to provide effective cover, enabling each aircraft to help protect its neighbours, but this had limited success.

The Germans introduced glider bombs at Anzio, able to strike at targets that were heavily defended, while the United States used the Bat, a stand-off bomb that was radar-guided with a 1,000 lb warhead, effectively one of the first air-to-surface missiles, and used with considerable impact against Japanese warships in 1945. On 6 August 1945, the USAAF dropped the first atomic bomb on the Japanese city of **Hiroshima**, following this on 9 August by a second atomic bomb dropped on **Nagasaki**. Many have criticised the use of a second bomb, but in fact these proved just sufficient as even afterwards there remained a strong anti-surrender faction.

Much improved aircraft performance during the war years meant that bombs were not the preserve of the bomber, but that fighters could, and did, carry a 250 lb or 500 lb bomb under each wing, with these fighter-bombers proving highly effective for tactical strikes. Other fighters carried unguided air-to-ground rockets, effective for anti-submarine warfare, striking at enemy warships and, most of all, were truly effective anti-tank weapons.

Postwar, bomb sizes did not continue to rise in the same way, and the most frequently used conventional bomb proved to be the 1,000 lb bomb. During the Vietnam War, the use of napalm tanks as incendiary weapons was devastating as napalm, liquefied gasoline, was no longer a simple incendiary, but combined blast and an ability to stick to the target. Big 'Daisy Cutter' bombs effectively cleared large areas. Stand-off weapons became an important means of applying the nuclear deterrent, which gradually became a 'thermo-nuclear' deterrent with the advent of the hydrogen bomb, so many times more effective than the atom bomb. Large heavy bombers, such as the Boeing B-52 Stratofortress, found a new lease of life as cruise missile carriers, although this weapon could also be launched from surface vessels and submarines.

Bong, Maj Richard Ira (1920–45) US fighter ace. While training as a school teacher, Bong decided to become a military pilot, joining what was then the US Army Air Corps in May 1941. He qualified and after a spell as an instructor was posted to the Pacific, where he flew a P-38 with the US Fifth Air Force. He scored twenty-eight kills during his first tour of duty and twelve more on his second tour before being posted back to the USA to become a test pilot, flying the first US jet fighter, the Lockheed P-80 Shooting Star. On 6 August 1945 the engine failed on his P-80 and the aircraft crashed, killing Bong. He was America's highest scoring fighter ace.

Boothman, Flt Lt John Nelson, RAF (1901–57) British high-speed pilot. Joining the RAF when it was at its weakest during the early 1920s, Boothman soon showed himself to be a natural pilot and specialised in hydro-aeroplanes as a test pilot. He joined the High Speed Flight for the 1931 **Schneider Trophy Race**, which was unopposed and gave the UK its third victory in a row, allowing it to claim the trophy outright. Boothman's flight around the course set a record of 340.08 mph (547.31 kmph).

During the Second World War, Boothman was a PR pilot, and postwar was seconded to the Ministry of Supply, before returning and eventually becoming head of Coastal Command with the rank of air vice-marshal.

Borel, Gabriel (?–?) French aircraft manufacturer. Relatively little is known about Gabriel Borel, who first appeared on the scene as a partner of **Léon Morane**, before starting his own aircraft factory in 1910. He produced a twin-seat monoplane and in 1913 completed a seaplane with which he intended to win the **Schneider Trophy Race**, although the aircraft did not succeed in qualifying for the French team. His aircraft was bought by the British and Italians for their air services during the First World War. Postwar, his company changed its name to SCIM, and specialised in the design and production of fast, streamlined racing aircraft.

Boulton-Paul British manufacturer. Boulton-Paul came into prominence between the wars with the Sidestrand twin-engined medium bomber, first flown in 1928 for the RAF, although only eighteen were built due to the limited defence budgets of the day, and was replaced by the Overstrand in 1934. In 1937 the Boulton-Paul Defiant fighter appeared with a power-operated rear turret, but the aircraft suffered from the extra weight of having a two-man crew and was eventually relegated to target-towing duties. Postwar it became mainly a component manufacturer, although it produced and flew delta-wing research aircraft, including the PIII fighter prototype. It was acquired by the Dowty Group in 1961.

box kite The invention of the Australian pioneer **Lawrence Hargrave**, the box kite provided additional lift compared to the traditional kite because of the larger number of surfaces. Several pioneering aeroplanes used the box kite concept, including float-gliders designed by the **Voisin** brothers and **Alberto Santos-Dumont**'s Demoiselle. The concept was already obsolete well before the First World War as aircraft speeds increased and the box kite structure provided too much drag.

Boyd, Albert (1906–76) American military test pilot. Sometimes referred to as 'the father of modern flight testing', Tennessee-born Albert Boyd joined the USAAC in 1927, trained as a pilot and eventually was selected as a test pilot. He later specialised in the evaluation of captured enemy aircraft, and postwar was one of a small band of pilots that established Edwards Air Force Base as the world's leading test centre. During his career he flew more than 300 different aircraft types.

Brabazon of Tara, Lord (1884–1964) British pioneer and politician. Henry Moore-Brabazon was the first Briton to fly when he went up in a Voisin in 1908. (The Englishman **Henri Farman** had, in fact, made a circular flight in Europe earlier that year, but he had adopted French nationality and spent most of his life in that country, speaking little English.) The following year Brabazon purchased a Voisin, *The Bird of Passage*, which he took to England, and with **Alliot Verdon Roe** claimed to be the first Englishman to fly in England. On 30 October 1909 he won the £1,000 prize presented by the *Daily Mail* for the first circular mile flown in Britain on an all-British machine. Not surprisingly, he was holder of the then Aero Club of Great Britain's Aviator Certificate No. 1.

Perhaps the exploit that most endeared him to the public was when he took a pig on a balloon ascent to disprove the old retort that 'pigs might fly'.

He joined the RFC during the First World War and played an important part in the development of photographic-reconnaissance, flying with the 1st Wing in France and reaching the rank of lieutenant-colonel.

Postwar, he became a public servant as secretary to the Secretary of State for Air, the department that oversaw the RAF, and then occupied a similar post at another new ministry, that of Transport. He became chairman of the Airmails Committee and an assessor of the inquiry into the loss of the British dirigible, *R101*. He then entered politics, becoming a Member of Parliament, and when the Second World War broke out, he was first Minister of Transport, before the department was renamed War Transport, and then Minister of Aircraft Production. He was elevated to the peerage in 1942. He chaired the so-called Brabazon Committee on the future of British commercial aviation, and while responsible for such white elephants as the giant Bristol Brabazon airliner, he was also responsible for successes such as the de Havilland Dove and the Bristol Freighter.

Brabazon was a keen advocate of safety in the air and when airlines preferred to use aviation gasoline, which he called 'petrol' in their turbine aircraft on grounds of cost rather than the safer kerosene, which he called 'paraffin', he poured out a puddle of kerosene, stood in the middle and dropped a lighted match, which fizzled out, and then defied anyone to do the same with aviation gasoline.

Brabazon was also a chairman of the Royal Aeronautical Society for many years.

Brack-Papa, Francesco (1891–1973) Italian test pilot. After training as a pilot in France, Brack-Papa set a number of altitude records before joining the Italian Military Aviation Service. Postwar, he joined the Italian manufacturer FIAT as a test pilot and in 1922 set an unofficial world air speed record.

Braham, Wg Cdr John Randall Daniel, RAF (1920–74) British night fighter pilot. Initially flying a lumbering Bristol Blenheim night fighter in 1940, which was more usually sent on bomber missions, Braham shot down just two aircraft in seven months, but in 1941, in the faster Bristol Beaufighter, he flew night missions over enemy-occupied Europe and over the next three years his score rose to twenty-nine, which was impressive given the lower rate of kills by night fighter pilots. On 25 June 1944 it was Braham's turn to be shot down and he became a prisoner of war. Much decorated, he not only gained the DSO and DFC, but also two Bars to both of these medals, and the AFC.

Brancker, Sir William Sefton (1877–1930) British pioneer, visionary and public servant.

After being commissioned into the Royal Artillery, Brancker saw service during the Boer War and then in India. Returning to the UK, he learnt to fly in 1913 and in 1914 was appointed Deputy Director of Military Aeronautics with the RFC. Before the First World War ended in 1918, he was planning a heavy bomber raid on Berlin. Postwar, he joined the Aircraft Manufacturing Company, Airco, and helped to inaugurate an air service between London and Paris, before being appointed Director of Civil Aviation. In his new role, he planned an international air service network that would link all of the UK's dominions and colonies, while also promoting long-distance flights and air races. In 1924 he joined **Sir Alan John Cobham** on a flight from London to Rangoon. Inspired by the first flight of the de Havilland Moth training biplane, he advocated government-sponsored flying clubs equipped with the aircraft to provide a pool of pilots ready for an emergency, but this plan was not introduced until after his death, when the Second World War approached. Branker lost his life when the giant *R101* airship crashed in 1930 while flying from London to Egypt and India.

Brantly US manufacturer. Formed during the early 1950s, Brantly produced lightweight helicopters for private owners and for training: the two/three-seat B-2 and then the five-seat 305. It was acquired by **Lear Jet** in 1966, but production of its own designs continued through a new company, Brantly Operators Inc.

Braun, Dr Wernher von (1912–77) German rocket pioneer. Graduating in physics at the University of Berlin, von Braun was obsessed with the potential of the rocket, and so impressed **Walter Dornberger** when they met in 1930 that he was put in charge of a secret rocket research establishment run, contrary to the conditions of the **Treaty of Versailles**, by the German Army. In 1936, after Hitler had taken power and was directing a German re-armament programme, von Braun's research establishment was transferred to Peenemunde on Germany's Baltic coast. At Peenemunde he worked on the first strategic rocket missile, usually known as the V2, but originally designed as the A-4, which from 1944 onwards was fired at London.

As German defeat and surrender became inevitable, von Braun gave himself up to the advancing US forces rather than risk being captured by Soviet forces, and volunteered to work in the United States. It is a measure of his genius that he was welcomed by the US despite his close associations with the Nazi regime. Von Braun became technical director at the White Sands missile range and directed the Jupiter, Juno and Pershing programmes, before moving on to the US space programme with the launch of the satellite Explorer 1 in 1958. He was entrusted with the development of this space programme and especially the plan for a manned landing on the moon, working on the Saturn V booster rocket. Disappointed that the US government would not fund **NASA** for further inter-planetary development after the first moon landing in July 1969, von Braun remained for another three years before joining the aircraft manufacturer Fairchild in 1972.

break-even figure A mythical figure much loved by financial journalists who would write about a new aircraft and provide a 'break-even figure' at which point all research, design, development and production start-up costs would have been repaid. In vain, manufacturers would point out that the aircraft would undergo further development and refinement during its production life, in effect meaning that 'break-even' was a moving target. The term is used much less often today.

The picture becomes even more confused as the manufacturer of an aircraft that has reached maturity has less opportunity to increase prices when competing against newer and more fuel-efficient models. It is also the case that the supply of spares and support during the lifetime of an aircraft for its engines or its systems, can be far more profitable than the original sale.

Breguet French manufacturer. Founded before the First World War by **Louis Breguet**, the Breguet 14 biplane that first appeared in 1916 was one of the more successful French bombers of the war and was among the first production aircraft to incorporate flaps. The successor, the 16,

appeared too late for wartime service, but the 19 entered service with the Armée de l'Air in 1925 and in 1930, a much-modified version made the first non-stop flight between Paris and New York. The company experimented with helicopters, including a co-axial design with contra-rotating rotors that appeared in 1931, but its development was not pursued. The Breguet Saigon flying boat saw service with Air France throughout the 1930s, and the Short Calcutta was built under licence as the Br521 Bizerta for the Aéronavale.

After the Second World War, the company designed a series of double-deck transports for Air France and the Armée de l'Air, including the Br763 Deux Ponts, also known as the Universal. The Vultur turboprop strike-fighter was cancelled, but the Br1050 Alize anti-submarine aircraft was built for Aéronavale's carriers. The company's Atlantique twin-turboprop maritime-reconnaissance aircraft won a competition to replace the Lockheed P-2 Neptune, and was built in collaboration with German industry. The company became involved in other collaborative projects, including partnering the **British Aircraft Corporation** (BAC) in the Jaguar strike-fighter, and with **Dassault** and **Dornier** in the Alphajet advanced trainer, before being acquired by Avions Marcel Dassault in 1972.

Breguet, Louis (1880–1955) Pioneering French aircraft designer and manufacturer. Parisian-born Breguet graduated from the Ecole Supérieure d'Electricité de Paris and worked in the family clock-making business before becoming interested in aviation. In 1907, with his brother Jacques and Prof Charles Richet, he built the first helicopter capable of lifting a man, but the machine was unstable and development was abandoned. Breguet turned his attention to fixed-wing aircraft, and scored another first in the use of steel tubing for the main structure of his successful design of 1909. The plane did not perform well at the **Reims Aviation Meeting** in August, but Breguet built an improved version covered in sheet aluminium, nicknamed the 'Coffee Pot', which flew in 1910. A biplane followed in 1911, which led Breguet to form his own manufacturing company. The Breguet 14 was a successful reconnaissance aircraft during the

First World War. Between the wars Breguet was behind the airline Compagnie de Messageries Aériennes, one of the predecessors of Air France, and made a further contribution to commercial aviation by formulating the Breguet range equation to give operators the costs of operating air routes. One of his aircraft, Nungesser-Coli, made the first non-stop flight across the South Atlantic in 1927, flown by **Dieudonne Costes** and Lt Joseph Le Brix. Breguet struggled to prevent his company being nationalised and in 1972 merged with **Dassault**. The company produced some unusual designs, including the Deux Pont double-deck transport, and the more successful Atlantique maritime-reconnaissance aircraft, a joint venture between France and Germany.

Bristol British manufacturer. Originally founded as the British & Commonwealth Aeroplane Company before the First World War, the firm built aircraft based on the **Henri Farman** biplanes, of which the first was the Boxkite. A number of biplane and monoplane designs followed, culminating in the Bristol Scout biplane of 1914, while during the war the company produced the M1 monoplane and the F2B Fighter or 'Brisfit' biplane that appeared towards the end of the war and remained in RAF service into the 1920s. Between the wars, the company had little success with its civil projects and concentrated mainly on military work, including the Bulldog and Bullpup fighters, used by the RAF and also exported. A twin-engined monoplane, the 142, appeared in the mid-1930s, and a development, the 142M, served as a prototype for the Blenheim light bomber that entered RAF service in 1937 and served during the early years of the war, by which time it was outclassed. The Blenheim was the first of a family of related aircraft, including the Beaufort torpedo-bomber and the Beaufighter nightfighter.

Postwar, the Brabazon eight-engined airliner was too large for the market and was cancelled, but the company had far greater success with the 170 Freighter, renowned for its service as a car ferry across the English Channel, the Mediterranean and in New Zealand, although it was most often to be found on military duties, especially linking East and West Pakistan. A later turboprop airliner, the Britannia, which was popular with passengers

and nicknamed the 'Whispering Giant' by the Americans, was later produced under licence by **Canadair** for commercial and military users. The company also owned **Bristol-Siddeley** engines and produced guided missiles, including the Bloodhound, a first generation mobile surface-to-air missile. The Bristol 188, a stainless steel high-speed research aircraft, passed to the **British Aircraft Corporation** in the industry-wide mergers of 1960.

Bristol-Siddeley British manufacturer. The company was formed out of a merger between Bristol Engines and Armstrong Siddeley in 1959, and later absorbed Blackburn Engines, a subsidiary of **Blackburn & General Aircraft**, in 1962, following this with the aero-engine division of **de Havilland**. In 1966 Bristol-Siddeley was acquired by **Rolls-Royce**, at which time its product range included the Pegasus for the Harrier V/STOL fighter, the Olympus for the Concorde supersonic transport, the Viper for trainers and business jet aircraft, and the Gnome, used in helicopters and some hovercraft. Collaboration on the Olympus was with the French manufacturer, **SNECMA**. The company also led the way in maritime applications for aircraft engines, including the Proteus.

Britain, Battle of (1940) The idea of an air war over the British Isles had been foreseen before the outbreak of the Second World War, and if anything the dangers were exaggerated partly by a belief that the 'bomber would always get through', and partly because German cancellation of their heavy bomber campaign during the late 1930s was unexpected. The closing stages of the Battle of France saw the RAF resisting pressure from the British government to send additional fighter aircraft to France, realising that the land battle was lost and that nothing more could be done, and that scarce resources had to be husbanded for an assault on Great Britain itself. This was a major blow to British planning, as it had been assumed that France would remain in the war with fighting continuing on French and possibly Belgian territory as in the First World War.

After Dunkirk, the RAF had a total of 2,600 aircraft in the UK, of which fighters comprised a minority, facing the Luftwaffe with almost twice that number. The Germans also expected to be able to call upon the Italian Regia Aeronautica, although few of its squadrons engaged in operations over the UK. In contrast to the previous conflict, in 1940 the Luftwaffe found itself with a large number of advanced bases within easy striking distance of southern England. The Germans needed to reorganise and regroup, and settle into their new bases, so there was an interval between the evacuation at Dunkirk in May and June 1940 and the start of the Battle of Britain, which is generally regarded as having started on 10 August 1940. Fighter Command used this interval to redeploy its forces. The conflict was given added importance by the fear that Germany might next attempt an invasion of the British Isles, something confirmed when photographic-reconnaissance produced evidence of a build-up of invasion barges in Channel ports. This meant that the Luftwaffe would be expected to cripple British air power and anti-aircraft defences in advance of the invasion, followed by attacks on communications. While the Luftwaffe was settling into its newly captured bases in France, it was attacked by Bomber Command, but the Germans also managed to commence attacks on British coastal shipping and the south coast ports during June, July and early August, sinking some 30,000 tons of shipping.

Meanwhile, Fighter Command also sent aircraft on anti-shipping strikes and attacked the closer enemy airfields. The Command had suffered from the interwar stress on the supremacy of the bomber, which was seen at first as a deterrent against German ambitions. It was not until 1938 that Fighter Command's needs were given the priority that they deserved, while Hurricane and Spitfire fighters only began to enter service in large numbers in 1939. The mobilisation of industry and the 'shadow' factory system that saw many engineering firms diverted from their normal production to produce war materiel, was sufficiently successful for Fighter Command to have some sixty squadrons ready by September 1940, although many calculated that twice this number would be necessary for security. The RAF started the battle with some 900 aircraft, although only around 600 of these were available

at any one time. The problem was that **Air Marshal Dowding** could not risk exposing his flanks by bringing all the squadrons deployed in Scotland and the north of England, or in the south-west of England, to protect London, the south and the Midlands. He had to make the maximum use of resources and hope that his opponents might make mistakes, even though he was facing three of the most successful, and thanks to their earlier operations and the experience gained in the Spanish Civil War, most experienced air force commanders of the day. His one ace was the Chain Home radar network of fifty stations stretching from the east of Scotland to Cornwall, which meant that early warning was received of incoming enemy formations, together with their location up to a maximum of around 110 miles away. On the other hand, while a shortage of aircraft was never really a problem in 1940, the time taken to train pilots was to be the Achilles heel of the RAF, even with a number of Fleet Air Arm pilots seconded to RAF squadrons.

Field Marshals Kesselring and Sperrle and General Stumpff commanded Luftflotten 2, 3 and 5 respectively, with a total of 800 single-engined and 280 twin-engined fighters, a number of reconnaissance aircraft, 320 dive-bombers and 1,260 medium bombers. Based in Norway and Denmark, Luftflotte 5 was furthest away so its Bf109 fighters could not escort its bombers which would need to concentrate on the east and north-east of England. This reduced the number of fighters that the Luftwaffe could put into the air over the south of England by around a quarter.

The Luftwaffe's basic operational unit was the Gruppe, with thirty aircraft, while Fighter Command at the time generally had twelve aircraft per squadron.

The problems for the Germans were also strategic. The Luftwaffe had not encountered an enemy as well equipped as the RAF before, and had in its previous campaigns depended on close cooperation between ground and air forces to achieve the desired blitzkrieg effect. Never before had it depended on using air power in the strategic sense. During the late 1930s development of long-range heavy bombers had been neglected in favour of larger numbers of dive-bombers and medium bombers. The Messerschmitt Bf109 was the fastest fighter available in 1939 and 1940, and heavily armed with a cannon firing through the propeller boss, but it suffered from short range, was not as manoeuvrable as the Hurricane and Spitfire, and it had a weak tail section. The Me110 twin-engined fighter was not as agile in combat as its opponents.

In fact, the Luftwaffe failed to concentrate its full fire-power on Fighter Command, its bases and its control centres, and paid little attention to the all-important radar stations. Time spent attacking Bomber Command and Coastal Command bases was wasted as neither of these contributed to aerial supremacy in a defensive battle, and could have been picked off at leisure once Fighter Command was finished.

The reality at the time was that the RAF knew the Luftwaffe could be across the Channel in just 6 minutes and be over the first of Fighter Command's No. 11 Group airfields – in southeast England – in a quarter of an hour, and while German aircraft would be picked up by radar as they massed over the French coast, it took 4 minutes for information from the radar station to reach the airfields and 13 minutes for a Spitfire to reach 20,000 ft. Fears that No. 11 Group's aircraft would be lured away by diversionary raids, and that the Luftwaffe would then destroy its airfields, were countered by No. 12 Group, covering an area stretching from Norfolk to North Yorkshire and tasked with protecting No. 11's airfields. It also meant that massive concentrations of fighters were not possible in case the fighters found themselves tackling a diversionary raid, so most Luftwaffe formations were met by a single squadron of fighters initially. It was not until September that No. 11 Group started to mount attacks on the bombers with two or more squadrons, eventually building up to No. 12 Group's 'Big Wing' of five squadrons with sixty aircraft, able to deploy Hurricanes to counter the German bombers and Spitfires to counter the fighter escorts.

The other two groups were No. 13 in the north of England and Scotland, and No. 10 in southwest England.

Starting on 10 August, the Battle of Britain quickly reached a peak on 12 August, with the first concerted attacks on British airfields and the Chain Home radar station at Ventnor on the Isle of Wight being put out of action. Nevertheless, the Luftwaffe failed to press home attacks on the Chain Home network. On 13 August the operation was hit by bad weather, and it was not until 15 August that all three Luftflotten managed to coodinate their attacks, but in 24 hours the Luftwaffe lost seventy-five aircraft compared with thirty-four for Fighter Command. Most of the losses were from Luftflotte 5, with its Me110 twin-engined fighters no match for the Spitfire, which was then withdrawn from the battle.

Both sides overestimated the damage they inflicted on the other. This seems to be inevitable in air-to-air combat with more than one fighter attacking another aircraft, and not necessarily at the same time. Fighter Command rightly believed that it had spent too much effort countering German fighters when instead it should have concentrated on the bombers. The Luftwaffe nevertheless convinced itself that it had cut Fighter Command to just 300 aircraft, when in fact it had twice as many. After poor weather between 19 and 24 August, Goering insisted on air battles between fighters to break what he saw as the remnants of Fighter Command. Small concentrations of bombers were to be heavily escorted, while at night unescorted bomber operations would maintain the pressure. This new tactic proved more successful and British losses started to climb. The RAF was eventually saved by the premature decision to switch from attacks on airfields to attacks on British cities, the start of the **Blitz** which lasted throughout the winter and into early summer 1941, when German attention shifted once again, this time to the invasion of the **Soviet Union**.

British Aerospace (BAe) British manufacturer. Inherited the product range and manufacturing facilities of both the **British Aircraft Corporation** and **Hawker-Siddeley** Aviation on their nationalisation in 1975, then was privatised in 1988. At the outset the company designed and produced the wings for the European Airbus consortium, and its own product range included the Harrier and Sea Harrier V/STOL combat aircraft, with collaboration with **Boeing** on the former, the Hawk advanced jet trainer, and the Anglo-

German-Italian Panavia Tornado interceptor and interdictor, as well as the BAe748 twin turboprop transport and One-Eleven regional jet airliner and BAe125 executive jet. It abandoned One-Eleven production, but put the BAe146, later the Avro RJ, series regional airliner into production. It later became the British partner in the Eurofighter 2000 Typhoon interceptor project.

In recent years it has progressively abandoned many areas of manufacture, selling the BAe125 production line to **Beech** of the United States, scrapping the RJ programme when an advanced RJX range was just about to enter production, and selling its 20 per cent stake in Airbus to **EADS**. With Sea Harrier and Harrier production ended, it remains a partner on the Typhoon and on the **Lockheed-Martin** F-35 JSF, and produces updated Hawks. The company has diversified into wider armaments manufacture and shipbuilding.

British Aircraft Corporation (BAC) British manufacturer. BAC was one of the two main groups into which the bulk of the British aircraft industry was merged in 1960 at the behest of the British government. BAC absorbed such well-known names as **Bristol**, **English Electric**, **Folland**, **Percival** and **Supermarine-Vickers**. It was merged into **British Aerospace** on nationalisation in 1975. During its existence, it collaborated with **Aérospatiale** of France on the Concorde supersonic airliner.

Britten-Norman British manufacturer. Formed by John Britten and Desmond Norman out of their aerial crop-spraying and air transport business to develop the BN-2 Islander utility transport. The twin-engined ten-place aircraft first flew in 1965 and was put into service in 1968, and proved such a success that the British Hovercraft Corporation had to undertake much of the production, although later this was moved to Romania. Less successful was a light aircraft intended for the home-built market, the BN-3 Nymph, but by 1970 a military variant of the Islander, the Defender, was in production as well as a three-engined stretch, the Trislander, of which almost 200 were built. The company went into liquidation in 1971 but was acquired by **Fairey**

Aviation, before later being sold first to **Pilatus** of Switzerland and then to private owners. Plans to re-enter aircraft production by the founders failed when their Firecracker intermediate turboprop trainer was rejected by the RAF in favour of the Brazilian Tucano. The Islander remains in low-volume production, mainly in turboprop form, with components produced in Romania assembled at the company's works on the Isle of Wight.

Brookins, Walter Richard (1889–1953) American pioneer pilot. Brookins became interested in aviation through being a school pupil of Katherine Wright, who introduced him to her brothers. He was taught to fly by Orville in 1909 and proved to be a natural pilot. He was soon left in control of the **Wright** brothers' flying school at Montgomery, Alabama, where he taught other pioneers such as **Arch Hoxsey**. He was among the first stunt pilots and also set records. In 1910 he set an altitude record of 6,175 ft (1,882 m), but his engine cut out and he was forced to make a dead-stick landing. Later that year he made America's first night flight.

Brookins moved into manufacturing when he established the Brookins Aircraft Corporation, but his most significant contribution to aircraft production and design was when he introduced **David Davis** to **Reuben Fleet**, enabling Davis to sell his wing design to Fleet's company, **Consolidated**, which used it on the B-24 bomber.

Brumowski, Capt Godwin (1889–1936) Polish fighter ace. Before Polish independence Brumowski was an army officer in the Austro-Hungarian army. He transferred to the air corps in 1915, initially as an observer, but he taught himself to fly and became a pilot. As commanding officer of Fliegerkampagnie 12, he became a fighter ace and was able to study tactics under **Baron von Richthofen**, where the importance of organisation and operating fighters as groups rather than on solo sorties was learnt. Unlike his mentor, he was unable to change the Austro-Hungarian military air service, but nevertheless continued his career and ended the First World War with a score of forty enemy aircraft. Postwar, he moved into commercial aviation, but was killed in an accident at Amsterdam's Schiphol Airport in 1937.

Bryan, George Hartley (1864–1928)

British researcher and father of aerodynamics. A mathematician, Bryan was among the first to attempt to understand the dynamic forces encountered by aeroplanes, often using models for his research. His first notable work was a paper, *The Longitudinal Stability of Aeroplane Gliders*, presented to the Aeronautical Society (later the RAeS) in 1903. This was before the first aeroplane flights by the **Wright** brothers, so the paper was not fully appreciated at the time, and it was not until he published *Stability in Aviation* in 1911 that his work began to be recognised. The Royal Aeronautical Society awarded him its gold medal in 1915, the year that he presented the Wright Memorial Lecture, *The Rigid Dynamics of Circling Flight*.

Bulman, Paul Ward Spencer (1896–1963)

British test pilot. Originally commissioned into the Royal Artillery, Paul Bulman transferred to the RFC in 1915 and by the end of the First World War had been awarded the MC. Postwar, he flew as a test pilot at Farnborough before joining **Hawker** in 1925, where his first aircraft was the Woodcock biplane. He was the first pilot to fly the Hurricane fighter on 6 November 1935, taking off from Brooklands. He continued as Hawker's test pilot throughout the Second World War, flying the Typhoon and Tempest, before leaving to go into business in 1945.

Burgess/Burgess-Dunne

US manufacturer. An American company that produced the Dunne D8 biplane under licence before the First World War.

Burnelli, Vincent Justus (1895–1964)

American flying-wing pioneer. Burnelli's first recorded contribution to aviation was a biplane designed in association with Carisi in 1915, which was rejected by the US government, although later had the distinction of being the first aeroplane to be bought by a police force when the New York Police Department purchased it. Afterwards, in 1917–18, Burnelli worked for the Continental Aircraft Company, owned by Dr William Whitney Christmas, where he failed to persuade his boss that a flexible-wing aircraft was impractical; the resulting prototype crashed and killed its test pilot on the first flight. Burnelli then moved in 1919 to work on the Lawson Airliner with **Alfred Lawson**, before designing privately a series of flying wings between 1922 and 1950, but he failed to find sponsors to enable these to be built even though he promoted his designs throughout both the USA and the UK.

His flying wings were interesting, but hardly deserved the title. There were both monoplane and biplane designs, but in reality he was advocating thick wing sections and while these contained the cockpit and passenger cabin as well as the engines, a normal tailplane was always featured.

bus stop jet

A term used for the first generation of short-haul jet airliners, including the Boeing 737, Douglas DC-9 and Fokker F28 Fellowship, but with special reference to the BAC One-Eleven. These aircraft were supposed to be able to operate profitably on short sector routes and to operate without fixed airfield equipment, having auxiliary power units and built-in landing stairs. In some countries multi-sector domestic routes were already being flown, but the superior economics of even short-haul jet aircraft when flying point to point, and the high costs of fuel when constantly landing and taking off, meant that the concept rarely took on.

Busemann, Adolf (1901–86)

German aerodynamicist. Lübeck-born Busemann trained as an engineer and qualified in 1924. During the early 1930s, he undertook high-speed wind experiments at the Kaiser Wilhelm Institute, where he discovered that supersonic airflow could be compared with the wake of a ship and that supersonic flight might require swept wings. He presented his theories at the Fifth Volta Congress of High Speed Flight in Rome. While his theories were purely academic at the time, they were applied when Germany started developing jet and rocket-powered aircraft in the 1940s, affecting the design of both the Messerschmitt Me262 jet and Me163 rocket-powered fighters.

After the Second World War, Busemann went first to the UK and then to the USA, where he worked for **NASA**.

business aviation Business aviation began to develop between the two world wars, with wealthy entrepreneurs hiring or buying aircraft, usually aircraft such as the de Havilland Dragon series of biplanes or the Beech 17 Staggerwing, and later the Beech 18. These were in essence often the civilian counterparts of the communications aircraft used by the armed forces. After the Second World War, the market was regarded as being sufficiently large for aircraft to be designed specifically for it, including, notably the de Havilland Dove, a twin piston-engined mini-airliner. While earlier generations of business aircraft had seen the United States produce superior standards of comfort and performance, the Dove was good enough to be exported to American customers. **Beech** continued to be an important manufacturer in this field, while Cessna and Piper started to produce larger aircraft to enter this market. The advent of jet aircraft such as the Hawker-Siddeley HS125, first flown in 1962 and which had started life as a de Havilland project, meant that business aircraft could compete with airline schedules while continuing to offer the flexibility and convenience of flying between airports without a regular air service, or at times when a scheduled flight simply was not available.

A number of major companies acquired fleets of their own, especially in energy and construction, both of which meant doing business in areas where transport links could be poor. Shell ran a substantial aviation section, at one time headed by the wartime fighter ace **Douglas Bader**. A Scottish construction company, Logan, went so far as to develop an airline, Loganair, out of its business operations. For companies who could not justify an aircraft, hire became ever easier with air taxi operators providing often basic piston-engined aircraft or helicopters, while business jet operators also grew in importance. Companies that did not want to be involved with the operation of their own aircraft would have it managed by one of these companies, with the added benefit that the business jet operator could sell unused flying time to other customers.

In the closing decade of the twentieth century, two important trends emerged. One was the availability of business versions of airliners, such as the Boeing Business Jet variant of the Boeing 737, and an Airbus equivalent, and the other was fractional ownership of business jets through schemes such as Net Jets. Even before this, the manufacturers had tried to encourage business to acquire variants of their airliners, with BAC claiming that a One-Eleven could carry twenty passengers in luxury non-stop from Paris to New York for less than the cost of twenty first-class airline tickets.

The success of the market encouraged many other manufacturers to enter it, and **Grumman** at one time did very well with its Gulfstream series, starting with the turboprop Gulfstream I and then the jet Gulfstream II and its successors. Less fortunate was **Handley Page**, which entered the business with its Jetstream business aircraft and small airliner, but went bankrupt, partly because of the difficulty of moving from producing large aircraft in small numbers to producing small aircraft in large numbers. The Jetstream survived with production taken over by BAC.

Butler, Frank Hedges (1856–1928) British aeronaut. Co-founder of the Aero Club, which eventually became the Royal Aero Club, Frank Butler was the heir to a tobacco dynasty. He made more than 100 balloon ascents and set some long-distance records.

Byrd, Rear Adm Richard-Evelyn (1888–1957) American pioneer and USN officer. Disabled by injuries incurred during a game of football, when Richard Byrd graduated from the USN officers' school in 1912 he was sidelined into administrative duties. His career may well have been unspectacular until the USA entered the First World War and Byrd managed to convince the service that he could be trained as a pilot. Postwar, he planned the flight by four NC flying boats across the Atlantic in 1919, but this was led by **Capt John Towers** instead, although it was one of his officers, **Lt Cdr Read**, who completed the crossing, albeit in stages unlike the non-stop flight of **John Alcock** and Arthur Whitten-Brown.

In 1926 Lt Cdr Byrd and **Floyd Bennett** made the first flight over the North Pole in the Fokker Trimotor *Josephine Ford*, and while they both were awarded the Congressional Medal of Honor for this achievement, others claimed that their aircraft had lacked the necessary range. While Byrd tried to become the first man to fly solo across the Atlantic, his aircraft was badly damaged during a test flight and he was beaten by **Charles Lindbergh**. By this time a commander, Byrd then flew across the South Pole on 28/29 November 1929 in a Ford Trimotor, after which he concentrated on developing polar flying and Arctic survival techniques, including exploring the Antarctic by air.

C

cabin The term used for either the enclosed passenger and pilot compartment of a light aircraft, or for the passenger accommodation on an airliner, with the crew in what is increasingly known today as the **cockpit**, but which traditionally was known as the **flight deck**. Early aircraft were completely open, with the **Wright** brothers and others flying their aircraft while lying prone on the wing, although by the First World War, pilots and other crew members sat in open cockpits. The first aircraft to have a cabin was the Avro Cabin biplane of 1912, but in Russia **Igor Sikorsky** built aircraft with cabin accommodation and these were flown in 1913 and 1914. Postwar, many of the early scheduled air services were flown by aircraft with minimal cabin accommodation for passengers and the pilot was left sitting outside for the next decade or more.

cabin crew At first there was no need for cabin crew with aircraft often carrying just two passengers, but during the 1920s, as cabin accommodation became standard and the number of passengers that could be carried rose, stewards began to make an appearance and by 1930, on both sides of the Atlantic, stewardesses had been taken on. From the outset, the role of the cabin crew, strictly cabin attendants, was safety, and on early aircraft included such matters as issuing cotton wool earplugs against the noise of the aircraft engines.

Cabral, Sacadura (1892–1924) Portuguese naval aviator. Although far from a non-stop crossing, Sacadura Cabral and a senior officer, Vice Adm Gago Coutinho, made the first crossing by air of the South Atlantic in 1929. Using a Fairey biplane, their route was from Lisbon via the Canary and Cape Verde islands, but their aircraft crashed when it reached St Paul's Rock, in the South Atlantic off the Brazilian coast. They were offered the use of another aircraft, but this did not have sufficient range to complete the flight, so a replacement aircraft was sent from Portugal, but this was also seriously damaged. A further aircraft was then ordered, and in this they finally managed to reach Pernambuco in Brazil, ten weeks after leaving Portugal. Despite their misfortunes and the change of aircraft, they won the US $50,000 prize on offer for the first flight across the South Atlantic.

Calderara, Mario (1879–1944) Italian naval officer and pilot. Calderara was Italy's first aeroplane pilot. He helped **Ambroise Goupy** design and build the *Goupy II*, which was completed in March 1909, but the aircraft struggled to get into the air when tested at Paris. Disappointed, Calderara returned to Italy and took flying lessons from **Wilbur Wright** in April 1909. He crashed soon afterwards, but recovered and went on to enter a number of flying competitions in Europe. He was appointed air attaché at the Italian embassy in Washington.

Caldwell, Gp Capt Clive Robertson, RAAF (1910–94) Australian fighter ace. Sydney-born Caldwell's first involvement with aviation seems to have occurred when he joined the RAAF on the outbreak of the Second World War: he was trained as a pilot and was sent to the UK. He joined No. 250 Squadron flying Curtiss Tomahawk fighter-bombers in June 1941 in Palestine, where he averaged three enemy aircraft per month up to December. His single best performance was on 5 December when he shot down five Junkers Ju87 Stuka dive-bombers over the Western Desert. In January 1942 he took command of No. 112 Squadron and moved to Kenley, Surrey, where he stayed until September. He was then posted to Australia to command the RAAF's No. 1 Fighter Wing, after which he scored a further eight victories against the Japanese, giving him the grand total of 28.5 victories and making him the top-scoring Australian fighter ace. He was awarded the DSO and the DFC, the latter with Bar.

Camm, Sir Sydney (1893–1966) British aircraft designer. Born in Windsor, Camm took an early interest in aviation and in 1911 began building model aeroplanes, eventually building a full-sized glider before joining the Martinsyde Company as an apprentice in 1914. He came into contact with the chief designer, **George Handasyde**, who recognised his abilities and moved him to the design department to become a draughtsman, from where he left in 1923 to become the head draughtsman at **Hawker**. His first task was to design a powered aircraft, the Cygnet, which was entered for a light aircraft competition at Lympe, and which was widely acclaimed for its efficiency. He became chief designer for Hawker in 1925 and started a long spell as one of the best-known designers in the UK. His aircraft included the elegant family of biplanes based on his Hart design of 1928, which were exported worldwide. Camm went against the ingrained attitudes of the Air Ministry, the government department controlling the RAF, when he designed a low-wing monoplane fighter in 1933, and the project only went ahead because of the financial support of **Thomas 'Tom' Sopwith**, chairman of Hawker, but the result was the successful Hurricane fighter which was to prove to be the mainstay of Britain's fighter defences during the **Battle of Britain**.

Camm's other designs were also successful, although the Typhoon suffered teething problems, but the Tempest was effective against German V-1 flying bombs and the Sea Fury was one of the fastest piston-engined fighters ever, with one Fleet Air Arm aircraft shooting down a MiG-15 jet fighter during the Korean War.

Camm's work continued into the jet age with the Hunter, another export success, and then he experimented with vertical take-off using vectored thrust, which proved to be the key to VTOL in fighter aircraft and which led through the Kestrel prototype to the Harrier and Sea Harrier, the latter being the aircraft that proved to be the mainstay of British operations during the **Falklands** campaign. Camm died in 1966 and

so never saw the success of his VTOL concept. Throughout his life, his designs fully lived up to the old engineering adage, that 'if it looks right, it is right'.

Campbell, Lt Douglas (1896–1990) American air ace. A Harvard graduate, Campbell joined the army's Aeronautical Section in 1917, and after initial training in the USA, he was sent to France where he learnt to fly on a Nieuport. In March 1918 he became one of the original members of the 94th Pursuit Squadron, which despite its combative title sent the first US patrol over the Western Front on 19 March in unarmed Nieuport 28s. Fortunately the patrol did not encounter enemy aircraft since it included not just Campbell, but other future US aces such as **Edward Rickenbacker** and **Raoul Lufbery**. On 14 April, by this time flying an armed aircraft, he shot down a German Albatros scout over France, making him the first member of an American squadron to shoot down an enemy aircraft. He became the first official US ace on 31 May when he shot down his fifth victim, but only a week later was seriously wounded and forced to return to the USA.

Postwar, he entered commercial aviation with W.R. Grace, whose pioneering airline specialised in services to South America and which was eventually merged with Pan American's Latin American operations to form Pan American Grace Airways, PANAGRA.

Canadair Canadian manufacturer. While producing some designs of its own, such as the CL-41 Tutor jet trainer, Canadair mainly produced aircraft under licence for the Canadian armed forces, including Rolls-Royce Avon-powered versions of the F-86 Sabre and CF-5A/B jet fighters and developments of the Bristol Britannia, including the CP-107 Argus, CC-106 Yukon and the CL-44, with the latter also being produced for commercial airlines. Its own designs included the CL-215 twin-engined water-bombing amphibian and its turboprop development, the CL-415. Owned at one time by **General Dynamics** of the United States, it passed into government-ownership before becoming one of the founding companies of **Bombardier**.

canard An aircraft with a tail-first layout. Although this was a feature of the **Wright** brothers' aircraft, the term is normally reserved for modern aircraft of which the first to use this configuration was the SAAB-37 Viggen, but it is also a feature of the SAAB Gripen, the Dassault Rafale and the Eurofighter 2000 Typhoon.

cantilever wing A wing without any external bracing, which was a feature of the early monoplanes produced by manufacturers such as **Blériot** and **Deperdussin**, built not only before and during the First World War, but even during the 1920s. This was despite the fact that one of the first aircraft with a cantilever wing was the Junkers J1 Blechesel of 1915, more usually known as the 'Flying Donkey', and which was also the first all-metal aircraft.

Capper, Col (later Gen) John Edward (1861– 1955) British Army officer, aeronaut and advocate for aviation. The first representative of any government to fully appreciate the work of the **Wright** brothers, Capper was commissioned into the Royal Engineers where he became involved with ballooning and helped to build the British Army's first balloon, *The Sapper* (British Army slang for a member of the Royal Engineers), in 1882. Later he saw service in the Boer War, after which he was given command of the British Army's Balloon Section in 1903. The following year he was sent to the United States, meeting **Octave Chanute**, **Samuel Langley** and the Wright brothers themselves, and was particularly impressed by the two brothers. In January 1905 he wrote to the War Office in London: 'I wish to invite very special attention to the wonderful advance made by the brothers Wright. I have every confidence in their uprightness, and in the correctness of their statements. It is a fact that they have flown and operated personally a flying-machine for a distance of over three miles, at a speed of 35 mph.'

Capper's support helped the cause of heavier-than-air flight at a time when the authorities were sceptical at best. He had already met **Samuel Cody** in 1904 and assisted him in demonstrations of man-carrying kites. He won official backing for the construction of Britain's first airship, the

Nulli Secundus in 1907, and then encouraged Cody to build a powered aeroplane (which had to borrow the engine from the *Nulli Secundus*). Capper's reward was to become the first aeroplane passenger in the UK on 14 August 1909, when Cody took him for a flight.

Despite his achievements, during the First World War Capper had his feet firmly on the ground commanding an infantry unit, and rose to the rank of general.

Caproni Italian manufacturer. Founded by **Dr Gianni Caproni** and active from the middle years of the First World War until the end of the Second World War.

Caproni, Dr Gianni (1886–1957) Italian pioneer and designer. Caproni trained as an electrical engineer, but his interests were switched permanently in 1908 when the **Wright** brothers visited Europe. Initially, he designed components that improved aircraft performance, including one of the first variable pitch propellers, a Wright-pattern glider and a dirigible with a double gas bag. His first aeroplane owed much to an Avro design, but at the time was notable for using tubular metal construction in the wings. During the First World War he developed large triplane twin-boom bombers, which led the way to his postwar flying boat project with nine wings (in three sets) and eight engines, which managed to reach an altitude of 60 ft before crashing. It later caught fire while being rebuilt.

Despite this setback, Caproni later developed into an aircraft manufacturer, producing transport and reconnaissance aircraft, and the Ca73 and Ca101 bombers. The experimental Caproni-Campini 'jet' was first flown in 1941 and then abandoned, despite having made the first cross-country jet flight: the aircraft in fact was not a true jet as a conventional aircraft engine drove compressor fans.

Carmichael, Cdr Peter 'Hoagy' (1923–97) British ace. He joined the Royal Navy in January 1942 and was trained by the USN at Pensacola in Florida. His first operational unit was No. 889 Naval Air Squadron (NAS), a Supermarine Seafire unit aboard the escort carrier HMS *Atheling*,

which he joined in May 1944. In October he joined No. 1834, flying Vought Corsair fighter-bombers from HMS *Victorious*. He flew strikes against Japanese oil refineries in Sumatra during January 1945, and then flew on attacks against islands in the Sakashima Gunto in April and May.

Hoagy remained in the Royal Navy after the war ended, achieving fame by becoming the only Fleet Air Arm pilot to shoot down a jet fighter while flying a piston-engined aircraft. It happened on 8 August 1952 when he was acting CO of No. 802 NAS and leading a formation of four Hawker Sea Fury fighter-bombers from HMS *Ocean* off Korea. They encountered eight MiG-15 jet fighters and Carmichael was set upon by one of them and a dog fight ensued, with the MiG eventually being raked by his cannon fire. The aircraft crashed and another four were damaged. He was awarded the DSC, but sent back to the UK to avoid him becoming a prisoner of war if he were shot down. He remained in the Royal Navy until 1961.

carrier-on-board delivery (COD) Warships in major navies are supported by a fleet train, which can be either part of the navy itself or, as with the Royal Fleet Auxiliary supporting the Royal Navy, manned by civilians. The advent of the aircraft carrier provided an opportunity to have small consignments of urgently required supplies, as well as crew mail and personnel, flown out to the ships while at sea. The USN was first to use the concept with the Grumman Trader, a variant of the Tracker carrier-borne anti-submarine aircraft, and the Royal Navy followed using redundant Fairey Gannet anti-submarine aircraft. Later, the USN used the Grumman Greyhound, a variant of the E-2 Hawkeye airborne early-warning aircraft. For many navies, the concept is a luxury, for even those with carriers often find that aircraft accommodation is too limited, but helicopters can be used and even anti-submarine helicopters have cabin space available for personnel and supplies.

CASA Spanish manufacturer. Established in 1923, Construcciones Aeronauticas SA (CASA) produced a number of its own designs from the 1970s onwards, but was mainly noted for its

licence-production of aircraft such as the Heinkel He111, with Rolls-Royce Merlin engines, during the period after the Second World War, and the Northrop F-5A/B. It designed the C101 Aviojet in conjunction with MBB of Germany and **Northrop** of the USA, and produced components for Airbus. A project of its own is the C212 Aviocar utility aircraft. The company is now part of **EADS**.

CASEVAC Abbreviation for casualty evacuation. The use of aircraft for casualty evacuation dates from the formation of the **Royal Australian Flying Doctor Service,** but did not become widespread until the introduction of larger transport aircraft and the helicopter. In June 1950 four RAF Westland Dragonfly helicopters were deployed to Singapore for rescue and CASEVAC duties in Malaya, and on one occasion, two pilots flew their helicopter for a total of 13 hours to airlift a wounded British soldier to hospital. The **Korean Air War** (1950–3) saw widespread deployment of helicopters for CASEVAC, even using the small Bell 47, with casualties carried in stretchers mounted externally on both sides of the cockpit. The results were impressive. Compared with the Second World War, deaths among casualties fell from 4.5 per cent to 2 per cent. Among soldiers with head or stomach wounds, the death rate fell from between 80 and 90 per cent to 10 per cent. The helicopter brought both speed and smoothness to evacuation, replacing a bumpy ride in a field ambulance.

Most air forces evacuate casualties using their standard military transports, modified to carry stretchers and medical equipment, but the USAF has used specialised McDonnell Douglas C-9A Nightingale transports, developed from the DC-9 regional airliner, which effectively operate as a flying casualty unit.

Castoldi, Dr Ing Mario (1888–1968) Italian designer. An engineering graduate, Castoldi worked in an Italian government aircraft factory at Turin during the First World War, before moving to **Macchi** in 1922. His most famous work was on the series of **Schneider Trophy Race** entrants, which included the sleek M39 in which Mario de Bernardi won the 1926 competition, and the M52. He went on to build successful fighter aircraft. His MC-72 won the record for the fastest piston-engined seaplane in 1934 with 440 mph (708 kmph).

catapult The use of the catapult to enable aircraft to take off from a ship at sea is generally regarded as being part of carrier operations, but its use preceded the aircraft carrier. The first known attempted catapult launch from a vessel on water was when **Samuel Langley** launched his *Aerodrome A* from the roof of a houseboat moored on the Potomac River in Washington, DC, in 1903, although on two occasions the aircraft fouled the catapult and crash-landed in the river. In November 1915 an AB-2 flying boat was launched from the stern of the battleship USS *North Carolina*, and it was not long before most battleships and cruisers were equipped with catapults for launching seaplanes for fleet spotter duties and reconnaissance. Between the wars aircraft carriers were also fitted with catapults, known at the time as 'accelerators', and during the Second World War merchant vessels were equipped with catapults to launch Hawker Hurricane fighters to provide a one-off defence against enemy aircraft.

Postwar, a British invention, the steam-catapult, enabled aircraft carriers to launch ever-heavier aircraft. The concept was also essential for swept-wing jet aircraft with their higher wing loadings. While some smaller aircraft carriers had just one catapult positioned to launch aircraft over the bows, other larger ships had two, and with the introduction of the **angled flight deck**, at least one and sometimes two waist catapults were fitted. The advent of **vertical and short take-off and landing** (V/STOL) aircraft, has meant that many navies can operate fixed-wing aircraft at sea without catapults, but they remain essential for any navy intending to operate conventional aircraft at sea.

Caudron, Gaston (1882–1915) and René (1884–1959) French aircraft designers and manufacturers. The Caudron brothers started building cheap and simple biplanes in 1908, with many of their products being favoured by flying schools for their economy and reliability. After René took aerial photographs of Peking in 1913,

the central government of China bought twelve aircraft for aerial reconnaissance against the many warlords who disputed central power.

An unusual feature of their work was that their aircraft were designed independently rather than jointly, with Gaston's designs being prefixed by the letter 'G' and René's with the letter 'R'. Gaston's work was cut short when he was killed in an accident in 1915, but René continued working until the fall of France in 1940, after which his remaining works were nationalised.

Cavendish, Sir Henry (1731–1810) British scientist. Cavendish discovered that hydrogen was just a seventh of the weight of air, having isolated the gas by pouring sulphuric acid on to hot iron filings. His work was frustrated by the lack of a light but airtight container into which he could isolate the gas and create an aerostat, which had to be left to the Frenchman, **Jacques Charles**.

Cayley, Sir George (1773–1857) British inventor and pioneer. Hailed as the 'father of aerial navigation' by **William Henson** and whose work was generously acclaimed by the **Wright** brothers, Cayley was a wealthy Yorkshire landowner with an unusually inventive mind that extended to such matters as railway signalling and social questions such as the cottage allotment system. Unusually for the period, his work became widely known through publication in engineering and scientific journals.

Estimates of Cayley's main achievements vary, but it is generally agreed that he takes credit for:

1. Clarification of ideas on mechanical flight, and laying down the principles of heavier-than-air flight.

2. Conducting experiments in aerodynamic research for flying purposes, including pressures on surfaces at various angles of incidence, the importance of streamlining, outlining the body of least resistance, showing the movement of the centre of pressure of a surface in an airstream, and discovering that curved surfaces provide better lift than plane surfaces.

3. Drawing attention to the effects of the dihedral angle for wings, and of a movable tailplane and rudder, while also considering the problems of

Mechanics' Magazine,

MUSEUM, REGISTER, JOURNAL, AND GAZETTE.

No. 1520.]　　SATURDAY, SEPTEMBER 25, 1852.　[Price 3*d*., Stamped 4*d*.

Edited by J. C. Robertson, 166, Fleet-street.

SIR GEORGE CAYLEY'S GOVERNABLE PARACHUTES.

Fig. 2.

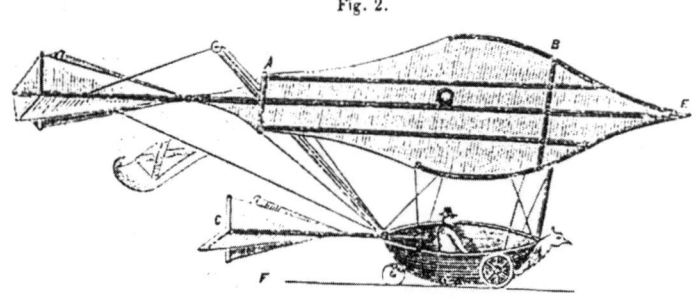

Fig. 1.

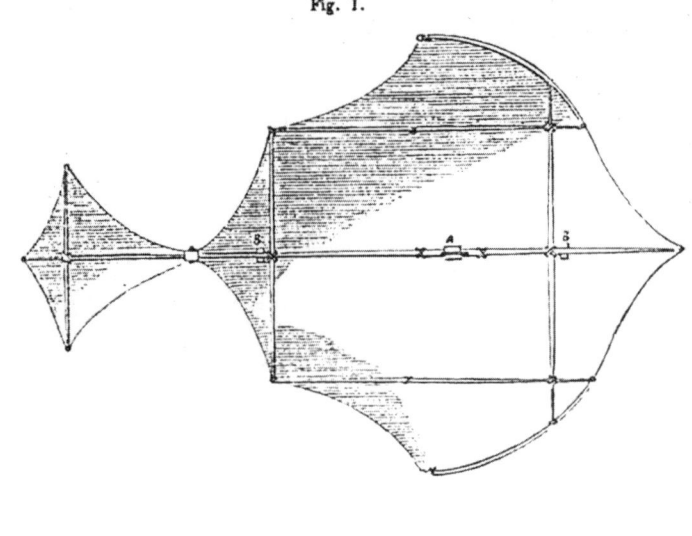

It took some time for aeronautical technical terms to be standardised, so it was not surprising that Sir George Cayley's man-carrying glider was presented to the world in 1852 as a 'governable parachute'. Journals like this ensured that information and news of successful innovations were passed around quickly.

stability, weight control, the significance of the power/weight ratio and the need for a lightweight prime mover.

4. Inventing the bicycle tension wheel and providing the basis for a lightweight undercarriage.
5. Building the first man-carrying glider.
6. Suggesting jet reaction for propulsion and steering.
7. Proposing the internal combustion engine for aircraft.
8. Using a whirling arm for aeronautical research for the first time (although Seaton had used a whirling arm for research into wind resistance for windmills).
9. Studying bird flight and achieving a genuine understanding of this.
10. Suggesting the ideal configuration for an aircraft, with fuselage, undercarriage, mainplane and tailplane.
11. Designing the convertiplane, with a combination of fixed horizontal wing surfaces and vertical lift surfaces.
12. Suggesting water recovery for airships.
13. Inventing the expansion air engine.
14. Inventing the twisted rubber motor for model flying-machines.
15. Inventing the caterpillar tractor.

While some credit Cayley with using the first models for research, it must be remembered that the **Montgolfier** brothers and **Jacques Charles** all dispatched small balloons before scaling up to man-carrying aerostats, but he does appear to have been the first to use heavier-than-air models.

Cayley's first known work was the construction of a helicopter model in 1796, at the age of 23, on similar lines to that of Launoy and Bienvenu, although he would not have known of their work. The results of tests with their model were not published until 1809. In 1799 Cayley had prepared his first glider design, although this was equipped with manually operated flappers of doubtful utility. During the next five years, he made many experiments using a whirling arm, which led to the first known heavier-than-air gliding model in 1809: 5 ft long, with a kite-form mainplane and a tailplane, with a movable weight fitted to alter the centre of gravity, which flew successfully. In 1837 he proposed what amounted to an elementary

turbojet engine with 'a mouthpiece from which the air escapes, the momentum will be in the opposite direction'.

As far as aeronautical interests were concerned, the climax of Cayley's life approached with the construction of a triplane glider in 1849, which made a number of trial flights loaded with ballast before carrying the 10-year-old son of a servant. It was in 1853 that he sent his coachman, John Appleby, on a tentative flight across a valley near Brompton Hall in Yorkshire. Appleby did not enjoy the distinction of making the first heavier-than-air flight, telling his employer that he had been 'hired to drive, not to fly', and threatened to resign.

Cayley suffered some failures. In 1809, he suggested an inverted-cone parachute, not unlike an upside-down umbrella, in an attempt to overcome the oscillations of the Garnerin parachute, first demonstrated in England in 1802.

Cessna US manufacturer. Although **Clyde Cessna** started building aircraft in 1911, he did not found the eponymous company until 1927 after working earlier with **Beech**. The Cessna company was forced to close in 1931 because of the Great Depression, but reopened in 1934 and after the Second World War was for many years the world's largest manufacturer of light aircraft, with its products built under licence in France by Reims Aviation.

The company built the O-1 Bird Dog for the US Army, but became most famous for its light aircraft for flying schools and the private owner. Its best-selling aircraft was the 150, a single-engined high-wing monoplane that first flew in 1957. The company built its first jet in 1954, the T-37 trainer for the USAF and other armed forces around the world. Other significant aircraft included the 336 Skymaster and 337 Super Skymaster, twin-boom aircraft with a tractor and pusher propeller so that the private flier could have the advantage of twin-engined power without the drawbacks of managing to control an aircraft with asymmetric drag should an engine fail. After building light twins for the private owner and the business flyer, in 1968 the company moved up-market into the business jet sector with the Fanjet 500, later re-designated the Citation I, the start of a family of aircraft and at the time of its launch the lowest-cost business jet available. It has also enjoyed considerable success in the utility and regional aircraft market with the 208 Caravan, a single-engined light aircraft which in its current stretched form as the Caravan 675 can accommodate up to fourteen passengers.

Cessna, Clyde (1880–1954) American light aircraft pioneer and manufacturer. Originally trained as a mechanic, Cessna was running his own motor dealership in 1911 when he saw a flying display by Blériot monoplanes flown by the Moisant International Aviators. Cessna ordered a Blériot fuselage and designed and built his own wings, and taught himself to fly during which time he crashed thirteen times. Once he had mastered flying, he became a stunt flyer or 'barnstormer'.

Cessna's first attempt at aircraft manufacture started in 1916, but the company failed to survive the First World War and in 1924 he joined **Walter Beech** and **Lloyd Stearman** in establishing Travel Air, but left in 1927 as he wanted to build monoplanes using fully cantilevered wings, which Beech regarded as too risky at the time. He started his own business, and following **Charles Lindbergh**'s successful solo flight across the Atlantic there was a boom in light aircraft sales so that this time the company was successful. Cessna retired in 1937, handing control to a nephew. The company enjoyed steady growth and during the Second World War provided training and light observation aircraft for the armed forces, while in more recent years its mainstay has become business jet aircraft.

CFM Franco-American manufacturer. A joint venture between **SNECMA** of France and **General Electric** of the USA which dates from 1974. CFM produces a range of turbofans which are available as options on the **Airbus** narrow body range, but are the only engine available on the Airbus A340 series and on the Boeing 737-300 through to the 737-900.

Chadwick, Roy (1893–1947) British designer. Obsessed with flying-machines as a boy, in 1911 Chadwick met **Alliot Verdon Roe** and persuaded

the pioneer to hire him as a trainee draughtsman, working on the successful Avro 504 biplane, originally designed as a scout but which was soon widely adopted as a trainer. His Avro 530 fighter did not enter production, but after the end of the First World War, Avro attempted to diversify into light aircraft with Chadwick designing the Baby biplane, which he, having learnt to fly, crashed into the garden of Roe's brother.

Chadwick remained busy between the two world wars designing a succession of military aircraft, many of which were built in small numbers because of the limited defence budget allowed to Britain's armed forces. His Avro Manchester heavy bomber was a failure due to problems with its engines, but the design was modified and became the Lancaster, the most successful bomber of the Second World War, of which 7,366 were built. Some versions of the aircraft were capable of carrying a 22,000 lb 'Grand Slam' bomb. A commercial derivative was the York transport and airliner, but the Lincoln heavy bomber that followed arrived too late for the war and was soon eclipsed by jet bombers. Chadwick's first postwar commercial aircraft design, the Tudor airliner, suffered from serious problems and he was killed when one of these crashed in 1947.

Chance-Vought *See* Ling-Temco-Vought

Chanute, Octave (1832–1910) French-American glider pioneer. As a guide and associate of the **Wright** brothers, Octave Chanute was one of the most influential men in the history of flight, but one whose role has remained relatively unsung.

Parisian-born Chanute was taken to the United States when he was 6 years old and later trained as a civil engineer specialising in railway bridges. He became interested in flight and started one of the first serious attempts to compile an accurate history of progress, which resulted in the publication of his book, *Progress in Flying Machines*, in 1894. In 1896 he began designing and building gliders himself, using a biplane design and dispensing with the bat-type wings favoured by **Otto Lilienthal** and **Percy Pilcher**. Considering himself too old to fly, he

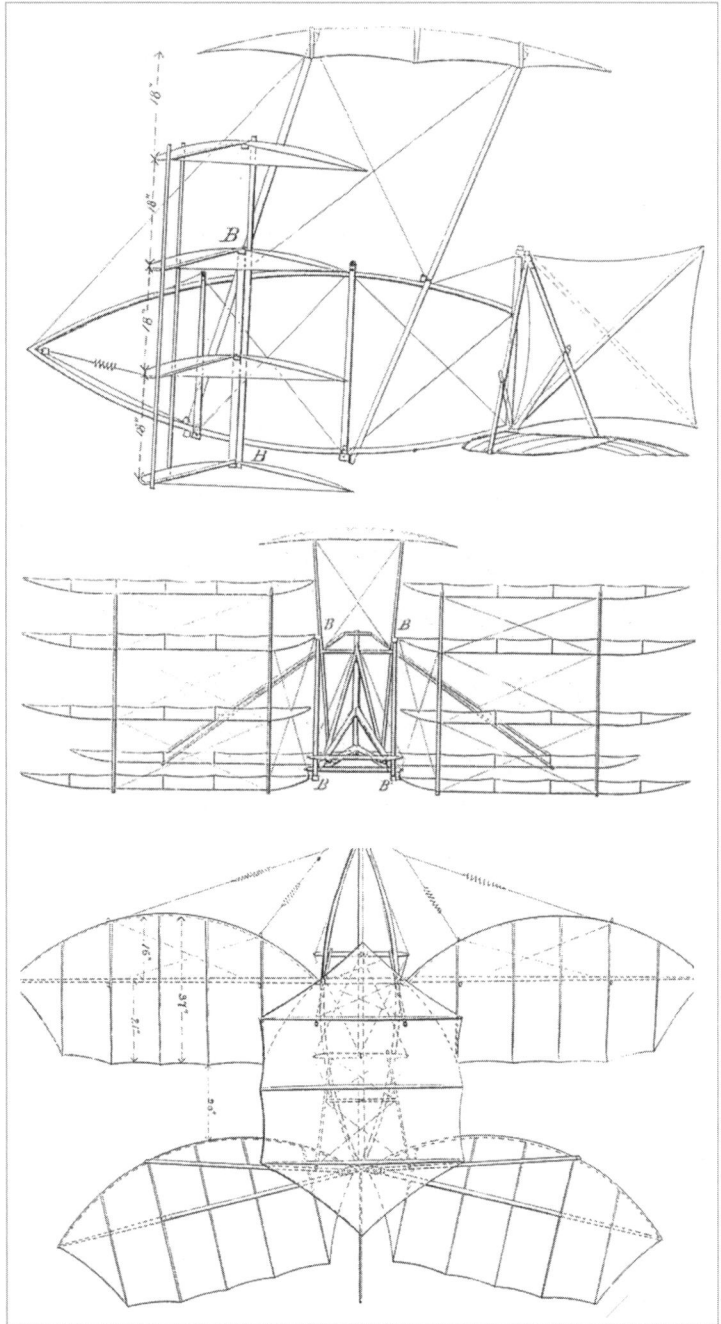

One of the forgotten pioneers, Octave Chanute may have exaggerated his influence on the Wright brothers, but he was a significant glider pioneer in his own right: he designed and built a multiplane hang-glider which flew in 1896. The illustrations show side, head-on and plan views of the apparatus. The use of many wings, as in a multiplane, increased lift but, as speeds rose, also created drag.

hired two pilots, William Avery and **Augustus Moore Herring**. The early flights took place on the shores of Lake Michigan before Chanute moved to Kill Devil Sands, North Carolina.

Among those who had read Chanute's book were the Wright brothers, and from 1900 onwards they corresponded with him and sought his advice. It was Chanute who persuaded them to use the Pratt truss wing structure that he favoured in his biplane gliders. Later, he announced their success to the Aéro-Club de France, but despite his own substantial reputation, he was not believed. Relations with the Wrights were not always harmonious as the brothers felt that he often exaggerated his part in their success, while they were also anxious to protect their patents.

Charles, Prof Jacques Alexander Cesar (1746–1823) French scientist and inventor of the hydrogen balloon. The fact that the first hot air balloon ascents by the **Montgolfier** brothers were followed quickly by those of the first hydrogen balloons was no coincidence. When news of the Montgolfier experiments reached the French Academy of Sciences, the immediate conclusion was that the brothers had discovered a new gas. Determined not to be outdone, the Academy decided to produce a rival balloon design and the geologist Bartholemy Faujas de Saint Fond raised funds for the physicist Prof Jacques Charles to develop the balloon. Charles was aware of the discoveries of Joseph Black, Tiberius Cavallo and **Henry Cavendish** and decided that hydrogen would be the ideal lifting agent. No less important, he knew that the brothers Aîné and Marie-Noël Robert had discovered a means of dissolving rubber using turpentine, which enabled them to apply a rubber coating to other materials, and asked them to build him a 13 ft balloon made of rubberised silk. The balloon was filled with hydrogen and ascended from the Champ de Mars in Paris on 27 August 1783, before a large crowd that included the American scientist Benjamin Franklin. It travelled for 45 minutes and 15 miles to the village of Genoesse, where it descended only to be attacked by frightened peasants who thought that it was a demon.

Charles and the Robert brothers then built a much larger balloon and on 1 December 1783,

Jacques Charles and Aîné Robert ascended from the Tuileries Gardens in Paris, before a crowd claimed to have been as large as 400,000, in the first manned hydrogen balloon voyage. The flight covered 27 miles to the village of Nesle. Here Robert climbed out of the balloon and in the cool evening air, with just one man aboard, the balloon shot up to 9,000 ft and Charles journeyed a further 4½ miles. The abruptness of the ascent and the shock of seeing the sun set for a second time within a few minutes so alarmed the professor that he never set foot in a balloon again.

Charlière The correct term for a hydrogen balloon, or any gas balloon, named after the inventor **Jacques Charles**. Despite the **Montgolfière** balloon being first, it was the Charlière balloon that set the standard for subsequent development of aerostats and in comparatively recent years hot air ballooning has become an international sport. The pressure of the hydrogen meant that the Charlière enjoyed a truly spherical shape, and a valve in the crown ensured that the gas could be vented, while a net was slung over the envelope from which the car or gondolier was slung, equipped with ballast that could be jettisoned to gain altitude, and a simple barometric altimeter gave a rough estimation of height. Later balloons featured an emergency ripping panel.

charter flights The hire of an aircraft and its crew for a flight is the basis of charter operations. There are also leasing arrangements, including dry leasing, which is the lease of the aircraft, and wet leasing, which is the hire of an aircraft with **aircrew**.

Charter operations are as old as commercial aviation itself and the operations are as strictly controlled as scheduled services, with airlines still needing an air operator's certificate; the aircraft requires a valid certificate of airworthiness and the crew must be properly qualified. The growing liberalisation of air transport has meant that the requirements for licences for inclusive tour, or package holiday, charters have gone. The advent of the low-cost airlines has also meant that inclusive tour or package holiday operations are less important than they were. Travellers now often choose to arrange their accommodation and flights themselves, and many of the inclusive tour charter airlines operate their own low-cost services. There is also less need for the public to organise themselves into affinity groups, typically clubs or associations with interests other than travel, to which the members had to belong for at least six months before departure. These restrictions were mainly found on flights between North America and Europe and were intended to protect the established national flag carriers.

It is still possible to organise ad hoc charters, and in the past these have been for such matters as the movement of ships' crews, while there are also corporate charters for business.

The inclusive tour charter was largely a European innovation. The first dated from before the Second World War and was organised by Thomas Cook, the travel agent that later became a major force in the package holiday business. Customers would book a 'package' that included flights, hotel or self-catering accommodation at a holiday destination, and transfers between the airport and the accommodation. This was not the exclusive preserve of the charter airlines, and some of the more expensive packages used scheduled flights. It was a way of enabling independent airlines to by-pass the need to operate under the wing of the national carriers. At the time, the cost of the package holiday generally amounted to no more than the cost of a return scheduled air fare. The package arrangement also had the benefit that, in an era of tight exchange control requirements, as much of the holiday as possible could be paid for in advance to save on the individual's foreign exchange allowance. In the UK these controls were scrapped during the 1980s.

The **International Air Transport Association** (IATA) was for many years strongly anti-charter, even though many of those using charter flights were unable to afford scheduled air travel and so it could not fairly claim that business had been lost. Its stance was largely undermined by many national airlines starting their own charter operation, with the former British European Airways creating British Airtours, for example.

A lower-cost network of scheduled services meant that charter was less important in the USA than in Europe. The result was that, before

the widespread liberalisation and the emergence of low-cost airlines, charter accounted for about 10 per cent of US air travel as opposed to 50 per cent in Europe. Even so, for transatlantic travel, the Americans also had to use charter flights, usually in affinity groups, and were even subjected to inspection and questioning by European officials anxious to enforce the rules.

Chase US manufacturer. Chase came into prominence during the Second World War building troop-carrying gliders, including the all-wood CG-14A of 1943 and the later CG-18A, which in its powered form became the C-122 transport. Postwar, the company built the C-123, known initially as the Chase Avitruc, which first flew in 1949, but production was transferred to Fairchild in 1953.

Chavez, Georges (1887–1910) French-Peruvian pioneer aviator. Georges Chavez was born in Paris of Peruvian parents. He trained as an engineer and at the age of 22 was taught to fly by **Henri Farman**. An enthusiastic flyer, he immediately turned his attention to flying contests despite his inexperience and set a number of altitude records, including one of 8,487 ft on 8 September 1910. His next goal was to be first to fly over the Alps. Chavez took off in his Blériot from Brigue in Switzerland and flew through the Simplon Pass rather than over the mountains. He reached his destination of Dommodossola in Italy after 42 minutes, having endured gale force winds and sub-zero temperatures, but his aircraft either stalled or he had succumbed to the cold, possibly with hands and feet too numbed to control the aircraft, and he plunged some 30 ft to the ground. Chavez died from his injuries two days later.

Some maintain that his last words were 'Arriba, mas arriba' or 'Higher, ever higher', and these became the motto of the Peruvian air force.

Chennault, Maj Gen Claire Lee (1890–1958) American military aviator, tactician and mercenary. Having trained as a teacher, Chennault joined the United States Army during the First World War, but his application to become a pilot was rejected and it was not until after the war that he qualified. He applied considerable thought to tactics, and published *The Role of Defensive Pursuit*, in which he advocated, among other things, fighter pilots operating in pairs. The title of the book seems odd today, but for many years USAAC and, later, USAAF fighter units were known as 'pursuit squadrons', with fighter aircraft designated as 'P' for pursuit until replaced by 'F' for fighter during the Second World War. A practical application of his ideas came with an aerobatic team led by Chennault known as 'Three Men on a Flying Trapeze', which demonstrated close formation flying.

A supporter of **Billy Mitchell**'s ideas for an autonomous air force, which were unpopular with the authorities and which had caused Mitchell to be demoted, hindered Chennault's career between the wars. He retired on health grounds in 1937, claiming to be deaf, but he had been asked by Madame Chiang Kai-Shek to organise a Chinese Nationalist air force. Chennault visited China and returned to the USA in 1940 to gather a force of 300 volunteers, the Flying Tigers, which was given covert support by President Roosevelt and equipped with 100 Curtiss P-40B Kittyhawks, an aircraft with better ground-attack capabilities than aerial combat qualities. Despite the numerical advantage enjoyed by the Japanese Army Air Force in China, and their possession of faster and more manoeuvrable aircraft, Chennault's training and the application of his tactical theories meant that the unit outfought its opponents.

The Flying Tigers, together with Chennault, were integrated into the USAAF in July 1942, and he became commander of the US 14th Air Force in 1943. After the end of the Second World War Chennault resigned from this post to become an adviser to the government of Nationalist China, which had retreated to the offshore island of Formosa (now known as Taiwan). He also established an airline.

Cheshire, Gp Capt Geoffrey Leonard (1917–92)

British bomber leader and philanthropist. Cheshire learnt to fly with the University Air Squadron while an undergraduate reading law at Oxford University, then joined the RAFVR. He had visited Germany before going to Oxford and felt that war was likely. As war became imminent he applied for a permanent commission and was posted to RAF Bomber Command. Although not a noticeably good pilot while with the University Air Squadron, Cheshire flew Armstrong-Whitworth Whitleys with No. 102 Squadron and was awarded a DSO for pressing home an attack on a railway marshalling yard at Cologne after his aircraft had a 12 ft hole torn in its fuselage by an AA shell. He was posted briefly to No. 35 Squadron, flying Handley Page Halifax bombers, a type that suffered from control problems with the early marks, and volunteered to go to Canada to fly back a Lockheed Hudson, before returning to the Halifaxes. Completing his first tour of duty, he was rested as an instructor in 1942, taking the time to write a popular book, *Bomber Pilot*. When he returned to operations he soon added a Bar to his DSO. By this time a group captain, he accepted demotion to wing commander to take command of No. 617 Squadron, which had breached the Ruhr Dams under the command of **Guy Gibson**. He earned the VC in 1944 for his strong leadership rather than any one exploit. By the end of the war with Germany he had regained his rank of group captain and was sent as one of the British observers for the dropping of the second atomic bomb, on the Japanese city of **Nagasaki**.

Postwar, Cheshire founded a network of homes for the terminally ill, initially aimed at war veterans, but in later years the charity's scope broadened.

Chicago Convention on Air Transport (1944)
See Freedoms, air transport

chosen instrument A relic of the days of state ownership and tight control of civil aviation was that an airline would be selected as the 'chosen instrument' for services to a particular part of the world. The airline concerned would be protected from competition and be allocated the national share of traffic rights under the **bilateral agreements** covering services to the countries involved. In some cases, subsidies would be paid, but in any event, the airline concerned received preferential treatment.

Juan de la Cierva's autogiro, developed in the 1920s, was not intended as a true vertical take-off aeroplane, but as an answer to the problems of stalling during take-off.

Cierva, Juan de la (1895–1936) Spanish autogiro inventor. De la Cierva became interested in aviation while still at school, where he designed and built two gliders.

He designed and constructed a trimotor bomber in 1919, but this crashed on take-off, which led him to consider ways of avoiding the risk of aircraft stalling into the ground. His solution was autogiration, but it took some time before he could overcome the tendency of his prototypes to overturn. He cured this by hinging the blades to conquer the problems they presented when advancing and retreating.

The **autogiro** was the first V/STOL aircraft, with a take-off run as short as 15 yd, and landing usually vertically. Rather than building the aircraft himself, de la Cierva licensed the concept to established manufacturers and moved to the UK to continue his work. Ironically he was killed in an air crash at Croydon, south of London, on 9 December 1936, flying as a passenger in an airliner. Postwar, his company was acquired by **Saunders-Roe**.

civil aviation In its strictest sense this is all aviation other than military, but in current usage it normally excludes general aviation and is mainly concerned with commercial air transport.

Clark, Virginius (1886–1948) American aerodynamicist. An American naval officer, Clark learnt to fly in 1910 and became interested in aerodynamics. In 1917 he joined the **National Advisory Committee on Aeronautics** (NACA), where he worked on aerofoil sections, the most notable being the Clark Y, which was used on the Ryan monoplane *Spirit of St Louis* and adopted for many other aircraft because the flat underside gave high lift; it was also easy to build.

Clark later entered the commercial world and pioneered duramould construction using plastic impregnated wood normally chosen for light aircraft but also selected for the Hughes HK-1 'Spruce Goose' flying boat.

close air support The provision of air support for ground forces is one of the most demanding and difficult tasks for combat aircraft. The risks to the aircraft of flying low over concentrations of enemy forces and over a front line that may be highly fluid, or along which an advance or retreat is moving apace, are probably nothing compared to the risks to those on the ground, in danger of falling victim to a 'friendly fire' or 'blue on blue' incident. Nevertheless, close air support is often demanded by ground commanders as it can be brought into play more quickly than artillery.

The idea of close air support and tight coordination with fast-moving ground forces was foreseen between the two world wars by many military strategists and writers, including the Briton Basil Liddell Hart and in France the later General Charles de Gaulle, but their work was largely ignored by the establishment. Due notice was taken in Germany, where the concept of **blitzkrieg**, 'lightning war', actually meant just such a coordinated attack, rather than, as in the UK, when '**Blitz**' became the popular name for the Luftwaffe bombing campaign against British towns and cities from autumn 1940 until early summer 1941.

When the British Expeditionary Force (BEF) was sent to France on the outbreak of the Second World War, it had its own air component comprised of RAF squadrons, as British Army aviation did not exist at the time. The RAF also provided the Advanced Air Striking Force (AASF). The BEF's air component was supposed to provide close air support as well as liaison and aerial observation post (AOP) duties, while the AASF was supposed to attack enemy troop concentrations and, it was thought, targets well behind the front line. In fact, neither the air component nor the AASF was allowed to perform its given task, in part due to French fears of retaliation, and both suffered heavy losses due to the overwhelming superiority in numbers and the quality of the Luftwaffe's equipment, while decision-making and target selection was far too slow to be effective, as were the small numbers of aircraft sent against targets that had to endure the full force of enemy defensive fire.

In the United States, the evolution of first the USAAC and then its successor, the USAAF, into a strategic air force meant that the United States Army had to reinvent tactical air power as the Second World War progressed. The USMC evolved into a force that provided close air support for assault forces as they landed on islands across the Pacific, although at one stage the decision to drop carrier deck training from the syllabus for new pilots (to speed up the flow of new aircrew) threatened this capability. For the USMC, it was the AOP role that had to be reinvented, which they did using borrowed aircraft and by finding members of their non-flying personnel who had

flown light aircraft in civilian life.

Good coordination and cooperation between air and ground forces proved difficult in every country. At Dunkirk in 1940 Goering insisted that the Luftwaffe could finish off the BEF and the French troops amassed in the area, and Hitler allowed this, but despite its experience in Spain and in Poland, as well as in the Low Countries, the Luftwaffe failed to halt the evacuation from the beaches.

It was in North Africa that efficient and well-coordinated cooperation between ground and air forces seemed to emerge during the Second World War. The number of aircraft and personnel available was so low that shore-based Fleet Air Arm units were pressed into operations in support of the British Army in the Western Desert alongside those of the RAF. The experience was to stand all three services in good stead for the years ahead, and the situation was demanding as this was a highly mobile war fought over vast distances, with a front line that moved some 1,500 miles. The exceptions to the mobile element were the siege of Tobruk and the battle of El Alamein, the last victory gained by British arms alone. Essential to victory was close air support and resupply of ground forces.

A new organisation was required for the conflict in North Africa. In October 1941 No. 204 Group of RAF Middle East provided the basis for the Western Desert Air Force (WDAF), initially under Air Marshal Sir Arthur Coningham. Coningham set up his own headquarters in that of the Eighth Army, establishing a close relationship that was repeated right down to the operational squadrons. The WDAF was a truly international organisation, with many of its squadrons coming from the South African Air Force and several other nationalities present. It soon became known for its mobility and it set a fine example of what cooperation between air power and ground forces should be.

Initially the WDAF consisted of sixteen squadrons, of which nine operated fighters, medium bombers, and one reconnaissance squadron. At the start it was ill-equipped and lacked aircraft capable of tackling the Bf109. It was not until summer 1942 that the situation improved with the arrival of Spitfire Vs, followed shortly afterwards by three USAAF Warhawk squadrons. After this the balance of air power began to shift in favour of the WDAF. Within a year the WDAF comprised twenty-nine squadrons, of which nine were from the SAAF, flying Hurricane, Spitfire, Kittyhawk, Tomahawk and Warhawk fighters and fighter-bombers, and Boston, Baltimore and Mitchell bombers. The US fighter-bombers were ideally suited to close air support, but so too were the Hurricanes fitted with four 20 mm cannon or tank-busting rockets.

On 1 February 1943 the WDAF became part of the North West Africa Tactical Air Force, changing again in time for the Sicilian campaign to become part of the Mediterranean Allied Tactical Air Force in July 1943, but only briefly as, on 21 July, it became the Desert Air Force. Despite its designation it participated in the Salerno and Anzio landings, although in the former the distance from airfields in Sicily meant that close air support was initially provided by the Fleet Air Arm from escort carriers offshore. It then remained in Italy for the remainder of the war, developing new close support bombing techniques and joining the Balkan Air Force in supporting Italian and Yugoslav partisans.

The Fleet Air Arm itself cooperated closely with the mainly US troops in the invasion of the south of France, Operation Dragoon, in August 1944, and continued to provide support after the initial landings.

Preparations for the main invasion of France, the Normandy landings on 6 June 1944 (D-Day), had started more than a year before the assault. In the RAF, these came about in the form of the Second Tactical Air Force (Second TAF) in June 1943. RAF Fighter Command was also divided, with some units being attached to Second TAF while the rest remained for home air defence. Both Second TAF and RAF Bomber Command were placed under the overall control of the Supreme Headquarters, Allied Powers in Europe (SHAEF) for the period of the landings. These decisions were based on the experience gained during the North African campaign in which close coordination and good communication between ground and air forces was a major factor in eventual success. Another indication of not simply changing priorities, but of recognising the growing importance of air transport in warfare was the creation of Transport Command in 1943.

Second TAF started life with no less than eighty-seven squadrons of Spitfires, Typhoons, Mustangs, Mosquitoes, Bostons, Mitchells and Wellingtons, and included four squadrons of Fleet Air Arm Seafires. Although it was part of the RAF and commanded by an RAF officer, Air Chief Marshal Sir **Arthur Tedder**, who also served as President Eisenhower's deputy from December 1943 until May 1945, it included airmen and units from every Allied air force.

In preparation for the invasion the squadrons of Second TAF spent much time attacking German air bases in France and the Low Countries, and also attacking other vital installations, with a high priority accorded communications targets. In the months immediately before the invasion, Bomber Command diverted many of its heavy bombers to strike at key targets in northern France, partly to 'soften up' the defences, but also to ensure that rapid reinforcement of forward areas would be more difficult. This continued for some time after the invasion as Bomber Command provided close support for the advancing Allied armies.

The first landing strip in France was ready for operational use on D-Day Plus One, 7 June 1944. Tactics continued to evolve during this period, with the RAF's Typhoons developing the cab rank system of attacking enemy armour and transport with rockets. Patrols also had to be maintained offshore to protect the landing beaches and the ships bringing supplies and reinforcements across the Channel, as well as the vulnerable artificial Mulberry harbours which had been towed from Britain. Second TAF was soon flying strike missions over Germany itself and before the war ended some of its forward squadrons were already based in the country.

After the Second World War, close air support became a feature of every one of the colonial campaigns as well as during the Korean War and in Vietnam. The concept of forward air control evolved, with experienced air force officers operating in light aircraft close to the target to ensure that close air support was accurate and to minimise the risk to friendly forces. Even so, in operations in Iraq and Afghanistan in the twenty-first century such problems continued to emerge, possibly because of poor communications with controllers and also due to poor target recognition.

Clostermann, Pierre H. (1921–2006) French fighter ace. Clostermann was in Brazil when France surrendered in 1940. He joined the RAF in 1942 and after training was posted to No. 341 (Free French) Alsace Squadron at Biggin Hill in 1943. He rose to command No. 3 Squadron flying the Hawker Tempest fighter and was officially credited with thirty-three enemy aircraft. Postwar, he entered industry and became head of Reims Aviation, the manufacturer of Cessna light aircraft in France.

co-axial helicopter A cost-effective attempt to overcome the autogiration effect of a helicopter rotor without wasting power on a tail rotor, the co-axial helicopter first appeared as a **Breguet** project in 1931, but was not taken further. It materialised in a practical form as the Hiller-Copter, which had contra-rotating co-axial rotor blades and was ready for testing in 1944. **Charles Kaman** produced a variation with contra-rotating intermeshing blades, which provided greater stability. He built a demonstrator using an old motor car chassis and engine. His first helicopter, the K-125, made a successful test flight and vindicated his stand, providing a stable hover, and it was ordered by the US armed forces.

Coanda, Henri (1885–1972) Romanian designer. Having been commissioned into the Romanian army, Coanda left to study engineering and at the age of 20 designed a rocket-powered model aeroplane. In 1906, he was persuaded by **Louis Blériot** and **Gabriel Voisin** to move to Paris where he enrolled at the Ecole Supérieure de l'Aérostation, graduating in 1909. His first full-sized design was exhibited at the Paris Salon of 1910, a sesquiplane with a cruciform tail, powered by a ducted fan driven by a 50 hp Clerget engine. Unfortunately the aircraft crashed on its maiden flight, but Coanda was offered a position in the UK at the British & Colonial Aeroplane Company at Bristol, where he worked on military aircraft including the Bristol Fighter.

coast-to-coast, USA Despite the interest shown in flights across the English Channel, the Mediterranean and then the Atlantic, the first transcontinental flight of the United States did not occur until 21–24 February 1921, when an aircraft of the US Army Air Service (USAAS) was flown from San Diego to Jacksonville, at the same time as the first transcontinental mail flight was flown between San Francisco and Long Island. It was not until 4 September 1922 that the journey was made in a single day, when a specially modified USAAS DH4B was used. The following year saw the first non-stop crossing by another USAAS aircraft, a Fokker T-2, flying from Long Island to San Diego on 2/3 May 1924.

Transcontinental services were soon placed on a regular basis, with a daily transcontinental airmail service inaugurated in July 1924. The airline, Transcontinental & Western Air, which later became Trans World Airlines, started the first regular passenger service across the USA on 23 October 1930.

coastguard aviation The United States Coast Guard claims the longest connection with aviation as one of its surfmen photographed **Orville Wright**'s first flight on 17 December 1903. Coastguard aviation, as such, is to be found mainly in the USA, Canada and Iceland, while in the UK, HM Coastguard charters helicopters from commercial operators as well as coordinating the national **search and rescue** efforts.

Cobham, Sir Alan John (1894–1973) British pioneer of in-flight refuelling. Commissioned into the Royal Artillery on the eve of the First World War, in 1917 Cobham transferred to the RFC and learnt to fly. Postwar, he became a stunt flyer and joined a team called Berkshire Aviation Tours. He later joined **de Havilland** as a test and delivery pilot, where he delivered the first Moth trainer to a flying club.

He came to prominence working for Imperial Airways, surveying and route testing the empire air routes and selecting suitable landing sites, preparing the way for regular air services from the United Kingdom to Cape Town, Australia and Rangoon, as well as a route between East and West Africa. He flew with **Sir Sefton Brancker** on the Rangoon flight. In addition to the dangers associated with flying long distances and over the sea or deserts at this time, an added threat emerged when he was flying between Baghdad and Basra and his mechanic was shot and killed by a Bedouin as his aircraft passed overhead. Cobham also endeavoured to promote air-mindedness and encouraged local authorities to build municipal aerodromes, many of which were later to become useful as RAF stations during the Second World War. Cobham next turned his attention to in-flight refuelling, although the pre-war experiments were intended more at extending the range of flying boats for transatlantic operations than, as it turned out, military operations.

Cochran, Jacqueline (1906–80) American aviatrix. From humble beginnings as a foster-child, Cochrane became a beautician and owned her own cosmetics factory before she could afford to learn to fly in 1932. She turned her attention towards aerial racing and after some competitions in the United States during 1933, the following year she entered the MacRobertson air race from the UK to Australia, flying a Gee-Bee racer. Technical problems forced her to abandon the race in Romania and she later sold the aircraft to **Francisco Sarabia**, who was killed flying it.

She became the second woman to win the Bendix Tropy when she took part in 1938, and made the first blind landing by a woman in 1939. During the Second World War she overcame USAAF opposition to found the Women's Air Service Pilots, ferrying aircraft from factories to operational bases. Postwar, in 1953 she became the first woman to fly faster than sound.

Cockerell, Sir Christopher Sydney (1910–99) Inventor of the hovercraft. Born in Cambridge, England, in 1910, his father was curator of the Fitzwilliam Museum, but although his home was visited by many of the leading literary figures of the day, the young Cockerell was more interested in mechanical matters. He graduated from Cambridge with a degree in engineering and afterwards worked for the Marconi Company on the development of aircraft navigational equipment. His father offered him £10 for each

idea he patented, but withdrew the offer when his son reached £100. While at Marconi he produced thirty-six patents for the firm.

He left Marconi in the early 1950s and took over a firm of boat-builders. For some fifty years other inventors had attempted to build craft that would run on a cushion of air, but Cockerell was first to solve the problem of containing the air cushion, initially using a perimeter of higher pressure air. Later he improved on this by using heavy rubber skirts while some air cushion vehicles used sidewalls, although this meant that they lacked true amphibious qualities.

After failing to find a backer for his invention, in 1955 he built a small working model which he 'flew' with it tethered to a piece of string. He took his model to London believing it was his duty to inform the government of anything with a value for defence, only to find that it was immediately classified as secret. When in 1957 he discovered that the Swiss were working on a similar idea, he was allowed to approach the National Research & Development Corporation for funding and was awarded £1,000 (equal to about £12,000 today) on condition that they would have first refusal of any development rights. The government allowed commercial and military development in 1959, and a company, Hovercraft Development Limited (HDL) was formed. **Saunders-Roe** built the prototype SR-N1, which crossed the English Channel for the first time in June 1959. Within a few years, several companies were producing hovercraft and these were merged into the government-backed British Hovercraft Corporation in 1966, much to Cockerell's annoyance as he believed that competition held the best prospects for development, and he resigned from HDL in protest. After a twelve-year fight he received £150,000 for his patents, but when the American government paid the British Technology Group (HDL's successor) £3.7 million in royalties, he received nothing. He was knighted in 1969.

Cocking, Robert (1777–1837) British parachute pioneer. Artist Robert Cocking was one of the few present when **André Garnerin** made his parachute descent in the UK, witnessing the parachute oscillating violently on the way down. Cocking was determined to design a better parachute, but it took him another thirty-five years and when it did appear it followed the inverted design proposed by **George Cayley**. His first, and last, descent came on 24 July 1837, when Cocking lifted off in **Charles Green**'s aerostat, the *Great Balloon of Nassau*, and rose to 5,000 ft, at which point he jumped and released the parachute, which immediately folded, leaving him to fall to earth. He died of his injuries within a few minutes of hitting the ground.

Few of the early pioneers died testing their designs, largely because at this stage they had learnt the importance of tests with models or prototypes. Why Cocking did not do this, possibly sending a weighted parachute for the first descent, or even using an animal, remains a mystery.

cockpit Originally the term used for the seat for the pilot and for the observer or navigator and air-gunner, on an aircraft without a cabin, but today this is increasingly used to refer to the **flight deck** on a transport aircraft. Early aircraft had the pilot lying on the wing, and then sitting on it, but once the aircraft appeared with a fuselage, rather than having the tailplane connected to the mainplane by struts, with the seat enclosed in it, the cockpit also appeared. The first examples were the Blériot and Antoinette monoplanes of 1909. It was some time before a cockpit canopy was provided, with the RAF's first aircraft to do so being the Gloster Gladiator biplane fighter. On early airliners, the pilot, or pilots, would be seated in a cockpit. Many early pilots preferred open cockpits because they felt that it gave them a better sense of sudden changes in flying attitude or speed.

Cody, Col Samuel Franklin (1863–1913)

British-American pioneer and showman. Often confused with 'Buffalo Bill' Cody, but not a relation, Cody was nevertheless a member of a travelling 'wild west' show from an early age. At the age of 30, he took his show to Europe and after touring the Continent, based himself in the south of England. It was not until 1900 that he started his experiments with kites, eventually working on both man-lifting kites and others for meteorological research. His reputation as a showman worked against him when he tried to interest the British Army, which had been disappointed by **Maj Baden-Powell**'s efforts with kites, and it was not until 1904 that senior officers finally saw Cody's work and were able to appreciate that he had a practical invention.

Having gained the confidence of the British Army, Cody became involved with other official projects, including the first British dirigible, the *Nulli Secundus*, and the first British aeroplane to fly. This aircraft was based on a **Wright** design and 'borrowed' the engine from the *Nulli Secundus*, making its first flight on 16 October 1908 on Laffan's Plain, on the site of what is now the well-known Farnborough Air Show.

Cody took British citizenship in 1909 to enable him to enter the competition sponsored by the *Daily Mail* newspaper for the first flight of 1 mile in the UK, but **Moore-Brabazon** beat him to it. In 1913, Cody was killed when the aircraft he was flying broke up in mid-air.

Coffyn, Frank Trenholm (1878–1960) American

pioneer. Coffyn met the **Wright** brothers through his father who was their banker. He was taught to fly by Orville in 1910 and joined their exhibition team, making his first solo flight in front of a crowd of more than 100,000 people. He became a test pilot for Burgess-Curtiss and designed and built the first aluminium pontoons. He flew with the US Army during the First World War, and during the Second World War gained the second US helicopter pilot's licence at the age of 66.

collaborative projects Collaboration has become increasingly common on major aircraft projects, with partners sharing the design, development and production costs as well as sharing the work. This differs from a straightforward licence-agreement under which the manufacturer that designed the aircraft grants another a licence to build and sell it, or from sub-contracting under which one manufacturer takes the lead and commissions another to handle some of the production work, even if the subcontractor takes a share of the risk. The reason for collaborative projects is that the manufacturers concerned want to share the costs without dividing the market. In many cases the concept has been fraught by politics, not least because most collaborative projects are international and partner nations quibble over work-sharing. It is also the case that most of the kudos goes to the country with the final assembly line, although the early projects saw each partner with an assembly line, and one has to have overall **design leadership**.

The first major international collaborative project was the Anglo-French Concorde supersonic airliner, which originated in separate projects mooted by Sud Aviation in France and the **British Aircraft Corporation** (BAC) in the UK, and on which the two manufacturers and their respective governments agreed to proceed jointly in 1962. This was soon followed by a range of military projects between the two countries, including the Jaguar strike aircraft, the Lynx, Gazelle and Puma helicopters, although the last two were based on existing French projects. Of all of these, only the Lynx saw the UK manufacturer, **Westland** Aircraft, hold design leadership. In all of these cases, there were separate final assembly lines in both countries.

Plans for an Anglo-French **variable-geometry** strike aircraft, the AFVG, floundered, and were replaced by an Anglo-German-Italian project, the Tornado, again with three separate final assembly lines. This project highlighted some of the failings of collaboration as the partner nations had differing requirements, with Italy not wanting the interdictor version of this aircraft, just the interceptor, while the Germans at one stage wanted a single-seat version, although this was later dropped. To market the aircraft and oversee development and production, a jointly owned company, Panavia, was established.

The most recent European combat aircraft to be jointly developed has been the Eurofighter 2000 Tornado, which has taken twenty years to reach service and has seen successive delays, including one attempt to cut costs and specifications, and which has involved the UK, Germany, Italy and Spain. Meanwhile, France and Germany collaborated on the Transall, or transport-alliance, C-160 twin-engined turboprop transport and on the Atlantique maritime-reconnaissance aircraft, on which the French manufacturer **Breguet** effectively took the lead. Italy and Brazil collaborated on the AMX strike aircraft.

Despite the importance of these military projects, the biggest international venture of all has been **Airbus Industrie**, which originally featured the UK, France, Germany and Italy, and for the first time saw final assembly centred on one country, initially France, but later some of the single-aisle aircraft were assembled in Germany. The UK retained responsibility for design and production of the wings in all cases. The Airbus operation has now extended to military transports with the A400, which has also added Spain to the list of partners. Some rationalisation of Airbus has followed the complete acquisition of all the production facilities by **EADS**, the European Aeronautic Defence and Space Company. A Franco-Italian regional turboprop manufacturer of regional turboprop aircraft is ATR, which at one stage **British Aerospace** joined, but later opted out.

The UK also collaborated with the United States on the Harrier and Sea Harrier programme, while several European nations and Australia have been involved in the Lockheed Martin F-35 Joint Strike Fighter (JSF) project. The F-35 has thrown up fresh problems, with Italy and the UK wanting their own final assembly lines and disputes arising over the freedom of the partner nations to upgrade the aircraft and in particular its avionics. Once again, there have been disagreements over work-sharing.

Within the United States, **Bell** and **Boeing** have collaborated on the V-22 Osprey convertiplane.

It remains to be seen whether collaboration is the way forward. The problem arises when work-share is allocated on the basis of the number of aircraft ordered by each partner country, and then the decision is taken to cut the size of the order. Costs are increased by at least 20 per cent, although some would say much more, and development times extended. There is the inevitable problem of trying to reconcile not just different requirements, but the replacement cycle for aircraft in service with the respective armed services differing widely. Even Airbus, now in single ownership, has had politicians throughout the countries in which it has production facilities arguing over the future of these factories and their workers. Some of the aircraft produced through these ventures, such as the Airbus series, have sold well, but the Tornado was a political aircraft and the only non-partner to have bought it was Saudi Arabia, and probably as a political gesture to the countries involved.

There are also winners and losers among the nations and the aircraft industries involved in collaborative projects. The Eurofighter Typhoon 2000 has much in common with the experimental Future Combat Aircraft produced and flown by British Aerospace in the late 1980s, but had to share the work and the development of the collaborative project. When collaborative projects started, the United Kingdom had the only aerospace industry in Western Europe capable of producing a full range of civil and military aircraft, with their equipment. Now it is primarily a subcontractor and a collaborative partner.

Collishaw, Sqn Ldr (later AVM) Raymond (1893–1976)

Canadian aviator and pioneer. British Columbia-born Collishaw was a Merchant Navy officer, but on the outbreak of the First World War he volunteered for service with the RNAS. By 1917 he was a squadron commander leading the 'Black Flight' Squadron and flying a Sopwith Triplane named the *Black Maria*. He scored sixty victories over enemy aircraft and was awarded the DSO with Bar, the DSC and DFC.

He remained with what had become the RAF after the war and was sent to support the White Russians during the civil war in 1919, commanding a fighter squadron in the south and shooting down two Bolshevik aircraft. He went on to command the RAF in Egypt at the start of the Second World War.

Commonwealth Aircraft

Australian manufacturer. Originally formed in 1936 by a group of Australian businessmen, its first product was the licence-production of the North American NA-33 trainer, which in Australian form became the Wirraway. In addition to other licence-built aircraft during the Second World War, the company also produced the indigenous CA-2 Wacket trainer and the CA-12 Boomerang ground-attack aircraft. Postwar, the company designed and built the Winjeel basic trainer and also produced North American F-86 Sabre under licence with

Rolls-Royce Avon turbojets. In 1981 it merged with de Havilland Australia and the Government Aircraft Factory to form Australian Aerospace producing a new trainer for the RAAF, but the project was cancelled after serious delays.

commuter airlines/airliners

Originally an American concept for airlines operating over very short distances, in recent years these have become feeders into the major hubs served by the large carriers, and the commuter airlines have often taken the name of the large airline to provide connecting flights, under such operators as Delta Connection and Northwest Airlink. The practice has spread beyond the United States to Europe, Australia and New Zealand, with Scandinavian Airlines System (SAS) and Lufthansa being among the leading proponents.

In many countries, union agreements have limited the size of aircraft that the commuter airlines can operate, and so these are usually smaller jet and turboprop aircraft such as the Embraer and Bombardier regional jet families and the Bombardier and ATR turboprops. Most have less than 100 seats. Slightly larger aircraft include the BAe Systems Avro RJ series and the Embraer E-Jet, which can accommodate up to 116 passengers. As the airliners flying the trunk or mainline routes grow in size, the size of commuter or regional aircraft can also be expected to grow, but the system is flexible enough for the major airlines to be able to transfer routes with limited growth potential to their regional feeders.

composite aircraft

While many modern aircraft are built substantially of composite materials, the term refers to aircraft that are effectively in two parts, with a larger aircraft lifting the smaller one into the air before launching it, thus saving the fuel that would have been burnt during a conventional take-off, and also means launching it at a favourable altitude and speed.

The concept was pioneered during the First World War and continued between the wars with aircraft even being launched from airships to improve fighter performance, especially over the fleet. In 1916 the RNAS used a Felixstowe Baby trimotor flying boat to carry a Bristol Scout fighter which was released from the patrolling flying boat when a Zeppelin airship appeared. One of the most famous of these aircraft was the Short Mayo, which consisted of *Maia*, a large four-engined Short S21 flying boat, and *Mercury*, a four-engined Short S20 seaplane which was launched from the larger aircraft at altitude. In this way a long-standing distance record for non-stop, non-refuelled flight was set between Dundee on the East Coast of Scotland and the Orange River in South Africa in 1938. Imperial Airways used the Mayo experimentally for mail flights on the North Atlantic and African routes. During the Second World War, Japanese Oka flying bombs and their pilots were launched from bombers on kamikaze suicide raids, while Messerschmitt Bf109 fighters were used to launch unmanned Junkers Ju88 bombers close to the target, a project known as the 'Mistletoe' bomb, and one of the rare occasions when the controlling aircraft was smaller than the one released. Postwar, the Convair B-36 bomber, intended to operate with a transatlantic radius of action, took part in experiments in which a republic F-84F Thunderjet fighter was carried ready to provide air defence once beyond fighter range and, unusually for composite aircraft, could return to the mother aircraft afterwards. This was followed by the record-setting Bell X-1 and X-2 series of rocket-powered research aircraft which were launched from under Boeing B-29 Superfortress bombers. Later, the North American X-15 was launched from a Boeing B-47 bomber.

For the future, the concept is likely to be used to provide low-cost sub-orbital flights on the edge of space for tourists.

compound helicopter

A helicopter equipped with a conventional engine and airscrew to provide superior performance in level flight, and often also having fixed wings in addition to its rotors. One of the most promising aircraft of this type was the Fairey Rotodyne, the first true vertical take-off transport other than a helicopter, which was flown extensively during the late 1950s. Two 3,000 shp Napier Eland turboprops were mounted on the wings, with a rotor powered by wing-tip jets. The aircraft was large enough for up to seventy passengers. The project was abandoned during the

consolidation of the British aircraft industry in the early 1960s, while Fairey's new owner, **Westland** Aircraft, had its own plans for a large heavy-lift helicopter, although these came to nothing. The Rotodyne was very noisy and would have been unsuitable for operations from city centre sites, once seen as a possibility for vertical take-off transports.

If the Rotodyne was more airliner than helicopter, other such aircraft have included the Piasecki 16H-1A Pathfinder, a helicopter with a tail-mounted ducted propeller. The concept has been of limited success because of problems with the rotor blades once forward air speed rises, and attention has moved to the convertiplane such as the Bell Boeing V-22 Osprey.

Congreve, William (1771–1828)

British artillery rocket pioneer. Having experimented with rockets for display purposes, the young Congreve turned his attention to military uses, eventually developing a rocket that was both effective and reasonably accurate. An early attempt by the Royal Navy to use his rockets for an attack on Boulogne in 1805 failed due to bad weather, but success followed when a second attempt was made in 1806. On 2–4 September 1807, the Second Battle of Copenhagen saw the city bombarded by rockets and on 5 September the Danes surrendered and handed over their fleet, having lost 200 naval personnel and 1,600 civilians in the attack.

Conneau, Jean (1880–1937)

French aerial racer. Commissioned into the French Navy, Conneau had to race using an assumed name, André Beaumont, for fear of embarrassing the Marine Nationale. He had learnt to fly in 1910 and took a prolonged leave of absence in 1911 to pursue his passion for racing aeroplanes, often winning cross-country races by his navigational skill rather than following roads or railway lines and becoming one of the first to use dead reckoning. He won three out of four races against his rival **Jules Védrines**.

Consolidated/Consolidated Vultee/Convair

US manufacturer. Originally formed in 1923 as Consolidated Aircraft, its first product was a trainer originally designed by Dayton-Wright in 1917. The company spent its early years building trainers until it produced its first airliner, the Fleetster, in 1930. This was followed by a fighter monoplane, the PB-2A and a Vultee-designed ground-attack aircraft. In the years immediately before the outbreak of the Second World War it developed the PBY-5 Catalina, a twin-engined parasol monoplane flying boat which was to prove to be one of the outstanding maritime-reconnaissance and **search and rescue** aircraft of the war years. It was also available as an amphibian, the PBY-5A, and led to an improved development, the PBY-6/6A, with more than 1,200 aircraft of all versions built. The name Catalina was originally coined by the RAF, which along with the Fleet Air Arm gave its American lend-lease aircraft US-sounding names. The other great success was the B-24 Liberator bomber, which was the most widely used American heavy bomber of the Second World War and was in great demand also for maritime-reconnaissance because of its long range, with a radius of action of up to 2,000 miles.

Postwar, the company experimented with the compound or mixed piston and jet-powered XP-81 fighter as well as the giant B-36 bomber, intended to take the war to Germany should Great Britain be invaded. The company enjoyed considerable success with its 240, 340 and 440 range of short-haul twin piston-engined airliners as well as producing the supersonic F-102 Delta Dagger and F-106 Delta Dart fighters, and the first Mach 2 bomber, the B-58 Hustler. It enjoyed less success with the 880 four-engined jet airliner and its successor, the 990, possibly because the fuselage was narrower and less appealing than the **Boeing** and **Douglas** competitors. Plans for a short-haul jet airliner were abandoned and the company was acquired by **General Dynamics** and became a manufacturer of sub-assemblies.

Continental US manufacturer. Now part of Teledyne Technologies, the company was once one of the leading manufacturers of piston engines for light aircraft, being used mainly in Cessna aircraft.

contour flying It soon became apparent that flying at the lowest possible height gave the attacker the advantage of surprise and during the two world wars pilots would fly low, known at the time as 'hedge hopping'. Aircraft flying so low not only presented a target to anti-aircraft gunners for the shortest possible time, they were invisible to the early air defence radars and difficult even for fighters to attack as a fast-moving fighter needed a certain minimum height to be able to pull out of a steep dive safely. The growing use of airborne radars eliminated some of the surprise.

Modern contour flying is often controlled by a radar computer system that safeguards the crew and aircraft by avoiding obstructions more quickly than a human might, and it also involves flying below the tops of hills and mountains, and even around them. One of the first aircraft to utilise these techniques to the full was the Blackburn, later Hawker Siddeley, Buccaneer.

control surfaces *See* aerodynamic surfaces

convertiplane An aircraft that is able to take-off and land vertically, but during flight operates as a conventional fixed-wing aircraft. Early proto-types by **Canadair** and **Breguet** in Canada and France used a tilt-wing system that meant that engines and wings were in the vertical position for take-off and landing, and then moved to the horizontal for forward flight, but the Bell V-22 Osprey uses tilting powerplants and ducted propellers.

Coppens de Houthulst, Willy (1892–1987) Belgian fighter ace. Originally a Belgian foot soldier during the First World War, Coppens volunteered for flying duties and was accepted on condition that he went to England and paid for his own flying lessons. He qualified as a fighter pilot in 1916, but did not shoot down an enemy plane until April 1918. He went on to shoot down eleven enemy aircraft and twenty-six German observation balloons. Despite losing a leg in a landing accident at the end of the war, he remained with the Belgian army until the country was occupied by Germany in May 1940.

Coral Sea, Battle of (5 May 1942) The naval battle between the United States and Japanese forces was the first conflict between aircraft carriers alone, and with the ships of the opposing fleets not coming into sight of one another.

On 3 May the Japanese landed unopposed on Tulagi and Gaudalcanal in the eastern Solomon Islands, but the next day they were surprised by aircraft from the USS *Yorktown*, with Task Force 17, which sank a destroyer and three minesweepers. TF17 then turned its attention to Japanese ships heading for Port Moresby in New Guinea, leaving two Japanese carriers, *Shokaku* and *Zuikaku* to enter the Coral Sea on 5 May. The following day, both sides refuelled at sea, unaware that they were separated by just 70 miles, despite aerial reconnaissance, although later the USAAF reconnaissance spotted the Port Moresby assault force, which included a third Japanese carrier, the *Shoho*.

The *Shoho* was found by American aircraft on 7 May and within minutes, despite the ship desperately circling, she was sunk with the loss of just three USN aircraft. This caused the Japanese to recall the troop convoy. At the same time Japanese aircraft found an American destroyer escorting a tanker, which they mistook for an aircraft carrier and a cruiser, so sent sixty bombers to attack and sank both vessels within minutes.

During the night of 7/8 May the two American carriers *Yorktown* and *Lexington* were so close to the two Japanese carriers that six Japanese aircraft attempted to land on the *Yorktown*. On the morning of 8 May reconnaissance aircraft from both sides discovered each other, with the fleets some 200 miles apart. Both sides launched air strikes at more or less the same time, with the Japanese sending ninety aircraft and the Americans seventy-eight. *Zuikaku* escaped into a rainstorm; *Shokaku* was hit by three bombs, forcing her to withdraw, but she survived due to the poor performance of the American air-launched torpedoes. Meanwhile, Japanese aircraft attacked the two American carriers in three waves, with two attacking *Lexington* from both sides and the third attacking *Yorktown*. Eleven torpedoes were launched at the *Lexington*, but her commanding officer managed to avoid them before two more struck the ship. She began to list to port, before a massive explosion ran through the ship as her aviation fuel tanks ruptured, followed by a further blast 20 minutes later. Further explosions followed, wrecking the

machinery, and at 20.00, the ship having been abandoned, a destroyer torpedoed the burning wreck.

On paper, the battle was a major Japanese victory, with the loss of one small carrier against a major US fleet unit, but *Shokaku* had been damaged and would not be available for the forthcoming **Battle of Midway**, when she would be sorely needed, while the Japanese advance on Port Moresby had been abandoned. The Japanese had also lost many experienced naval airmen and did not have a training programme to replace them quickly or easily.

Cornu, Paul (1881–1944) French helicopter pioneer. After successful experiments with model helicopters, including one powered by a 2 hp Buchet engine in 1905, Cornu built a full-sized machine using a 24 hp Antoinette engine and a lightweight airframe of steel tubes. This managed to reach an altitude of 1 ft on its first test flight on 13 November 1907 at Liseaux, France, which many maintain made him the first helicopter pilot. A shortage of money meant that this was his first and last prototype.

Corrigan, Douglas 'Wrong Way' (1907–1995) Irish-American long-distance pilot. Originally born as Clyde Corrigan, Jnr, his name was changed when his parents divorced. He learnt to fly in return for helping two barnstormers (*see* **barnstorming**) in 1934, and afterwards was employed by the aircraft manufacturer Ryan, as a flying instructor, but also helped prepare the *Spirit of St Louis* for **Lindbergh**'s transatlantic solo flight in 1927. Afterwards he became a barnstormer himself. He then became a transatlantic pilot by accident, taking off from New York on 17 July 1938 to fly to California. Instead he landed near Dublin in the Irish Republic. What was so sensational about the flight was that he used a 9-year-old Curtiss Robin light aircraft, bought for US $325 (£81.25 at the then rate of exchange), in which he had installed a new engine, but he had been unable to fit it out with new instruments or radio and it had been refused permission for flights over the ocean because it was not suitably equipped – it did not even have a fuel gauge. Many believe that he deliberately flew to Dublin and made excuses about reading the compass incorrectly to avoid official action.

During the Second World War Corrigan flew with the US Ferry Command and then became an aircraft salesman.

Costes, Dieudonne (1896–1973) French route pioneer. After flying with the French Army during the First World War, shooting down eight enemy aircraft, Costes became a commercial pilot. During the 1920s, he pioneered air routes across the Mediterranean from France to her African territories, following these with route-proving and survey flights from France to Persia and Argentina, as well as from Senegal in French West Africa to Brazil.

His fame rests mainly on making the first Paris–New York flight in the *Point d'Interrogation* in 1930, with the flight from Le Bourget to Curtiss Field taking 30 hours. Modest to the end, Costes gave credit for his success to his navigator, **Maurice Bellonte**.

counter-insurgency Counter-insurgency operations (COIN) using aircraft dates back to the operations of the RAF in Mesopotamia, present-day Iraq, during the 1920s when the concept known as 'air control' emerged, albeit with only partial success. During the Second World War light aircraft, mainly trainers, were used by the RAF to put down an uprising in that country that had been inspired by the Germans.

Operations by the French in Indo-China after the Second World War soon developed beyond counter-insurgency into all-out war, as indeed did those by US forces in Vietnam during the 1960s and 1970s. Nevertheless, British forces were successful in stemming Indonesian infiltration into what was then Malaysia during the early 1960s. In Southern Rhodesia, now Zimbabwe, government forces operated against terrorists during the 1970s, using light aircraft and helicopters, with the latter often being overloaded with troops and only becoming airborne by making a 'running' take-off.

Many air forces and air arms in different parts of the world include a substantial COIN element, notably Brazil with armed versions of the Tucano trainer deployed to remote areas. Much of modern-day COIN is concerned with infiltration across borders, while anti-drug smuggling operations frequently find that the same type of equipment is necessary, including light aircraft and helicopters, with a number of medium or heavy-lift helicopters essential for the rapid deployment of troops.

Courtney, Frank T. (1894–1982) Irish test pilot and long-distance pioneer. While working as a bank clerk in Paris during the 1900s, Courtney was so keen to learn to fly that he moved to London and worked unpaid for **Claude Grahame-White** at Hendon, where he also learnt to fly. When the First World War broke out, he was rejected at first by the RFC because he wore spectacles, but eventually he was accepted, although this was nearly his undoing as he was badly wounded by shrapnel while on patrol in a Morane Parasol monoplane over the Western Front.

Having recovered from his wounds, postwar he became a test pilot and between the wars flew more than 100 different aircraft on their first flights, making more than 10,000 flights in total, including those for the Cierva Autogiro, for which he suggested hinging the blades. He also became an authority on flying boats. Courtney raced aircraft during the 1920s, winning both the English Aerial Derby in 1920 and the King's Cup air race in 1923. He made two attempts at transatlantic flight, and on the second was forced to ditch because of an engine fire and spent 24 hours in a dingy before being rescued.

Despite his impressive record, he never gained a commercial pilot's licence because of his eyesight and eventually emigrated to the USA where he lectured and wrote on aviation, as well as advising Convair.

Coutelle, Jean-Marie Joseph (1748–1835) French military aeronaut. After the French Revolution Napoleon created a unit, La Première Compagnie d'Aérostiers, with four balloons in 1794 at Chalais-Meudon. The unit was commanded by Coutelle and on 2 June he ascended in the balloon *L'Entreprenant*, during the Battle of Mauberge, where the French were fighting off an Austrian army attempting to force their way across the River Sambre. While this first attempt at aerial observation was of little practical use, far more successful was the second attempt at the Battle of Fleurus on 26 June, when Coutelle was accompanied by Gen Jean-Baptiste Jourdan, who dropped battle orders to his troops on the ground below, making a contribution to French victory.

Despite this early success, when the ship carrying the balloons was sunk during the Battle of the Nile (also known as the Battle of Aboukir Bay) in 1898, Napoleon refused to replace them.

Coxwell, Henry Tracey (1819–1900)

Pioneering British aeronaut. Although trained as a dentist, Coxwell was infected by the glamour of ballooning, building and ascending in his own balloons before founding the first aeronautical journal, *The Balloon or Aerostatic Magazine*, in 1845, which he published and edited under the pen name of Henry Wells. The magazine lasted but a few months.

Coxwell himself almost died just a little later when in 1847 his balloon was engulfed in a thunderstorm and its gas was released by a lightning strike causing it to descend rapidly. Showing great calm, Coxwell climbed the rigging and cut off the bottom of the envelope, allowing it to be inflated like a parachute and descend slowly and safely to the ground. Later he started to develop the concept of the balloon as an offensive weapon, developing and dropping 'aerial torpedoes', which he demonstrated in Germany. In 1870, the Prussians asked him to provide two attack balloons for the siege of Paris.

Attack balloons were doomed to failure, being at the mercy of the wind, but of more practical use were the high altitude ascents made by Coxwell with **James Glaisher** between 1862 and 1865, of which the most spectacular was on 5 September 1862 when they reached an altitude of 34,000 ft. Their craft was loaded with scientific instruments and as they ascended, both men began to feel faint and Glaisher passed out. Coxwell attempted to scrape the ice off the envelope, but his fingers had frozen and his limbs became so stiff that he had to pull the gas venting valve rope with his teeth. Originally, their instruments showed that they had reached an altitude of 37,000 ft, but scientists corrected this later.

Coxwell later published his autobiography, *My Life and Balloon Experiences*.

Crete, airborne invasion of (20 May 1941)

Having occupied Greece, the next step for the victorious German forces was the invasion of the island of Crete, within easy striking distance of the British naval base at Alexandria in Egypt. The island held British, Australian, New Zealand and Greek troops evacuated from mainland Greece. The operation was the first major airborne assault in history, with the main thrust coming from paratroops and air-landed troops, and the German Army was simply ordered to follow up with a seaborne invasion.

'Operation Merkur', or Mercury, had to be postponed from 16 to 20 May as transport difficulties delayed the assembly of the troops at the bases in Greece. It was intended to use 22,750 troops, of which 750 were to land by glider, 10,000 were to be **Gen Kurt Student**'s Luftwaffe paratroops, and another 5,000 were to be landed by aircraft, leaving just 7,000 to be landed by sea. Transport was to be provided by 500 Junkers Ju52/3m transports assigned to Fliegerkorps XI, as well as by eighty DFS230 gliders. Air cover consisted of 280 bombers, 150 dive-bombers and 180 fighter aircraft. Student expected to face 15,000 British and Commonwealth troops, although the real figure was around 30,000, plus 11,000 Greek troops.

The air transport available to Student had a theoretical airlift capability of 6,500 paratroops, but the need to fly in equipment as soon as it was possible to do so meant that the maximum number that could be airlifted at any stage would be 5,000, so it was necessary that the airlift should be in two stages. The first airlift would drop the Western Group, to seize Maleme, and half of the Central Group, which would take Canae. The second airlift would bring the remainder of the Central Group to seize Retimo, and the remainder of the airlift would bring the Eastern Group to take Heraklion. In addition to the paratroops, there would be the men of the army's 5th Mountain Division, with four regiments of three battalions. The weakness in this plan was that the two lifts could not be less than 8 hours apart, so that the defenders would be ready, unless, of course, they did not expect a second lift.

On the morning of 20 May, the first lift took off from its airfields in Greece before dawn with

493 Ju52/3ms and 53 gliders, of which five carried headquarters units, although the one carrying Sussman, commander of the Central Group, broke up in mid-air, possibly through being overloaded. The assault at 08.00 was preceded by heavy bombing, so that only seven of the transports were lost, but the gliders were less lucky, many crashing as they attempted to land and others encountering accurate machine-gun fire. Many of the paratroops were also shot as they dropped, so that before long the olive trees were festooned with the bodies of dead paratroops and their parachute canopies. The German paratroops did not strap rifles or machine guns to themselves as they dropped, and were vulnerable for the first few moments after landing.

The Western Group landed in a light haze at Maleme, and managed to take the bridge over the Tavronitis river while others took the airfield. The Central Group, with more than 2,000 paratroops and 270 glider-borne troops, took the Akrotiri Peninsula and cut the Canae–Akikianou road, but a well-organised British counter-attack wiped out many units, so that by nightfall many of the Germans were badly scattered and fighting as small isolated groups.

Congestion at the airfields in Greece meant that the second airlift was not as well coordinated as the first. While the remainder of the Central Group started their drop onto the airfield at 16.15, slightly late, the full drop was slow and the men widely scattered, while the anti-aircraft fire, such as it was because so much equipment had been left behind in the evacuation from Greece, was more concentrated. The Eastern Group also suffered, with the first aircraft appearing over Heraklion at 14.30, but the last one did not appear until 19.30.

By nightfall German troops were pinned down everywhere and it was only the lack of communications equipment, also left behind in Greece, that prevented the defenders from successfully fighting off the invasion. Student decided to risk everything on seizing Maleme airfield, realising that he needed just one good airfield to establish a bridgehead. At 08.00 on 21 May, six Ju52/3m transports landed on the beach near the mouth of the Tavronitis, and more paratroops were dropped to the rear of the defenders, but many landed on top of the defenders and suffered heavy casualties, leaving just eighty men ready to fight. An air landing in the midst of the fighting at Maleme airfield, regardless of losses, started at 17.00, and the airfield was finally seized. The remainder of the air-landed troops were flown in on 22 May.

The cost of the operation was such that Hitler forbade any further paratroop assaults, with more than 4,000 paratroops and air-landed troops killed and another 327 drowned as they dropped into the sea or their gliders ditched. Forty combat aircraft were lost, but so too were 170 Ju52/3ms. The losses were made worse because the Luftwaffe had crewed its transport aircraft by taking instructors from the bomber training schools, so heavy losses of instructors meant disruption to the training programme.

crop dusting/spraying Aircraft are an effective means of crop dusting or spraying, being able to cover large areas in a single pass and not damaging crops in an attempt to reach those in the middle of an agricultural area.

The application arose shortly after the First World War, with one of the first companies being Huff Daland Crop Dusters, formed in 1925, which became the predecessor of Delta Airlines, today one of the world's largest. Since the Second World War, specialised aircraft have been developed for this work. Great care has to be taken with regard to wind direction to ensure that dusting or spraying does not affect adjoining areas.

cross-Channel flights Not surprisingly, the English Channel was a prime objective for the pioneers. **Jean-Pierre Blanchard** and **Dr John Jefferies** made the first crossing by a balloon in 1784, while soon afterwards **Jean–François Pilâtre de Rozier** became the first balloon fatality while attempting a crossing with a companion.

Louis Blériot made the first aeroplane crossing, winning a prize offered by the London *Daily Mail* newspaper, doubtless to the chagrin of rivals such as the Englishman **Hubert Latham**, although the **Hon. Charles Rolls** had the distinction of making the first return flight. The Channel crossing became so commonplace during the First World War that shortly afterwards the first regular international air services were introduced by a British airline, Aircraft Transport & Travel, in 1919. The Channel also was the location for a completely human-powered flight on 12 June 1979 by the American, **Dr Paul McCready**, which was a record for man-powered flight and for which he later won the US Collier Trophy.

Croydon In the early 1920s British commercial flights were moved from Hounslow Heath, west of London, to Croydon, in the south of London, a new airport which offered better railway connections to the City and West End of the capital. The airport began to decline in importance during the late 1930s with the opening of Gatwick Airport, which was also one of the first airports to have a railway station.

Cunningham, Gp Capt John 'Cat's Eyes' (1917–2002) British night fighter ace. The difficulty of intercepting and shooting down a bomber at night meant that operations during the hours of darkness were favoured during the Second World War by both the Luftwaffe and the RAF, otherwise losses became unsustainable. Early attempts to guide fighters on to bombers in the dark proved ineffective until airborne radar became available. It was an RAF officer, 'Cat's Eyes' Cunningham, who was the first British fighter pilot to shoot down a Luftwaffe bomber in darkness, when on the night of 19/20 November 1940 his Bristol Beaufighter intercepted a Junkers Ju88 medium bomber. At first the British downplayed the role of radar by maintaining that their pilots' eyesight was improved by a diet rich in carrots. Even with radar, night fighter pilots amassed kills more slowly than their day fighter counterparts, but by the end of the war Cunningham had a score of twenty enemy aircraft, of which all but one had been shot down at night.

Postwar, he became a test pilot for **de Havilland**, the company that designed and produced the Beaufighter's successor, the Mosquito, and in 1955 flew the de Havilland Comet III jet airliner around the world, covering 30,000 miles in 56 hours.

Curtiss American manufacturer. One of the first aircraft manufacturers, Curtiss was formed in 1908 by **Glenn Curtiss**. After some success at the **Reims Aviation Meeting** in 1909, the company produced a number of aircraft for training and racing, including the JN-2 and JN-4 biplanes used by the US Army for flying training during the First World War. Postwar, the Curtiss NC series flying boats were the first aircraft to fly across the Atlantic, albeit via the Azores. The company then designed a series of fast seaplanes which produced outstanding results in the **Schneider Trophy Races**, including the CR-3, which set a world speed record of 227 mph in 1924. The Curtiss Sparrowhawk fighter was used in experiments flying to and from US Navy airships. The company produced the last American biplane airline, the Condor, which was also the first aircraft with sleeping accommodation for long transcontinental flights.

During the Second World War, the Curtiss P-40 Warhawk was outclassed as a fighter but proved to be an outstanding ground-attack aircraft, operating in North Africa and the Far East. The SB2C Helldiver was flown from US carriers in the Pacific. The most significant wartime aircraft, however, was the C-46 Commando transport, which offered a wider fuselage than the better known C-47.

Curtiss, Glenn Hammond (1878–1930) American pioneer and manufacturer. If any one individual could be regarded as a viable rival to the **Wright** brothers, it was Glenn Curtiss, not **Samuel Langley**. After earlier experience working for Kodak, Curtiss became a bicycle manufacturer, showing another similarity with the brothers, and then developed into the manufacture of motorcycles, with one of his early designs setting a land speed record of 136.3 mph in 1907 – a staggering record for the time. As the motorcycle had eight cylinders, it was far removed from a practical everyday machine. It was his engines that attracted the attention of **Alexander Graham Bell** who invited Curtiss to join the **Aerial Experimental Association** (AEA) team. Curtiss designed their third aircraft in 1908, the *June Bug*, their first successful design, which made the first public flight in the USA on 4 July 1908, winning a trophy presented by the *Scientific American*. He flew two further 'firsts', winning the Gordon Bennett Cup at the **Reims Aviation Meeting** in 1909 and flying from New York to Albany in 1910.

In the meantime, Curtiss had left AEA and started the first aircraft manufacturer in partnership with **Augustus Moore Herring** in 1909, a former partner of **Octave Chanute**. A further first followed: making the first practical hydro-aeroplane flight on 26 January 1911. Despite this, relations with the Wrights had become fraught, with the brothers desperate to protect their patents, especially for wing-warping, while Curtiss had used the more practical ailerons. In an attempt to discredit the Wrights, Curtiss

modified Langley's *Aerodrome A* with ailerons and flew this successfully.

Curtiss went on to design a multi-engined flying boat, the *America*, hoping to be first to make a transatlantic flight, but while this was prevented by the First World War, his relationship with **John Porte** saw the start of a line of successful maritime-reconnaissance flying boats. Unfortunately, Curtiss did not enjoy the same success in business and a failing working relationship with Herring led Curtiss to put the company into receivership before starting a new company of his own, which was eventually bought out by the motor industry. He then moved to Florida and became a property developer.

D

d'Annunzio, Gabriele *See* Annunzio, d'

d'Arlandes, Marquis *See* Arlandes, d'

da Vinci, Leonardo *See* Vinci, da

Daedalus Daedalus and his son Icarus were prisoners of King Minos on the island of Crete. Legend has it that their only means of escape was by flight. Daedalus made wings from bird feathers and wax, enabling them to fly like birds away from captivity. Icarus ignored the advice of his father and flew too close to the sun, melting the wax in his wings so that he fell to his death.

Daily Mail British daily newspaper founded by Alfred Harmsworth, later **Lord Northcliffe**. It employed the first aeronautical correspondent, **Harry Harper**, who encouraged the proprietor to offer the prizes that did so much to motivate long-distance pioneering flights, including **Louis Blériot**'s flight across the English Channel, a model aeroplane contest won by **Alliot Verdon Roe**, the first circular flight of more than one mile in the UK won by **Henry Moore-Brabazon**, the London to Manchester race won by **Louis Paulhan**, and **John Alcock** and Arthur Whitten-Brown's transatlantic non-stop flight.

Dam Busters One of the most famous bombing raids of the Second World War was the RAF's 'Operation Chastise' against the Ruhr Dams. As early as 1937 the significance of the dams to the German war effort had been recognised. The difficulty lay in finding an appropriate means of attack and suitable weaponry, since the dams were by their very nature extremely heavily built, and the huge reservoirs of water which they contained also helped to protect them from conventional bombing. The driving force for an attack on the dams came not from within the RAF, or even the War Cabinet, but from an inventor named

Barnes Wallis, who had been interested in the destruction of the dams because he saw the disablement of Germany's energy supplies as the key to Allied victory, with the minimum impact on civilian lives.

Wallis developed what is often described as a 'bouncing bomb', but officially was known as 'Upkeep', although within the RAF it was more usually described as a mine. Initially the Air Ministry was doubtful, but eventually the project began to be taken seriously.

The operation was to involve a new squadron within No. 5 Group, at first known as Squadron X but soon re-designated as the renowned 617 Squadron, using twenty Lancasters modified to take the large bouncing bomb. **Wg Cdr Guy Gibson** – a regular RAF officer from pre-war days – was selected as commanding officer.

It was essential that the bouncing bombs should be dropped from an altitude of precisely 60 ft on to flat, calm water. Obtaining such a precise altitude caused some problems at first, until the idea of equipping each aircraft with two spotlights was adopted, one forward and the other towards the tail, which were angled so that the two spots merged into one at exactly the required height. The dams also had to be full of water, and for this reason a date in the middle of May was chosen.

The first of three waves was to consist of nine aircraft attacking the Möhne dam, then those aircraft that were still carrying their bombs were to proceed to the Eder. The second wave would head directly for the Sorpe dam. The third wave would be held in reserve, in case the first and second wave bombs were not sufficient to breach the dams.

No. 617's Lancasters took off on the raid on the night of 16/17 May. On the outward flight, five aircraft were lost, while two others were forced to return early.

The first wave found the Möhne dam. One unusual feature of the raid was that the aircraft did not attack as close together as possible. While Gibson prepared for his bombing run, the other aircraft dispersed to the pre-arranged hiding spots in the hills, so that they would not be seen either from the ground or from the air. After dropping the bomb, Gibson's crew could see a 1,000 ft-high column of white water where the mine had exploded, having been placed accurately by the bomb aimer. Water slopped over the dam, almost as if it had been breached. This impressive start meant that the next aircraft faced a 10-minute delay for the waters to subside. Above them, night fighters had gathered, waiting to attack, but unable to do so while the squadron's aircraft remained at low altitude.

The next aircraft was hit by flak, dropped its mine, which missed the dam and fell on the power house, then as it started to climb there was a sudden bright flash and a wing dropped off. Despite this, Gibson accompanied the next aircraft as it ran in to the attack, and saw another successful strike, even though the aircraft was badly damaged. The fourth and then the fifth aircraft followed, and finally the dam was breached.

The first wave moved on to the Eder dam, which was more difficult to locate as fog was settling in the valleys. After five attempts by the first aircraft, Gibson called in the next aircraft, which dropped its mine on the third attempt, but it was too late, exploding on the parapet of the dam, and sending the aircraft out of control.

The first aircraft returned to make a dummy run, and then hit the target accurately with its mine, but without breaching the walls. The third aircraft, was ordered in, and again after a dummy run, dropped its mine on the next run, collapsing the dam wall.

An American serving with the RAF, Flt Lt Joe McCarthy, led the second wave and his was the only aircraft in that wave to survive to attack the Sorpe dam. Both McCarthy and Flt Sgt Ken Brown damaged the parapet, but the dam remained unbreached. Both the second and third wave leaders were shot down on the return trip, marking a total of eight aircraft lost out of the nineteen which had set out.

The result of the raid on German war production was far less than had been anticipated. The main impact of the destruction of the Möhne and Eder dams lay not in the damage to the hydro-electric stations swept away as the two dams burst, as most German electricity came from coal-fired power stations, or even the flood damage to other industry and communications, but, according to German accounts after the war, the loss of water, itself important for so many industrial applications.

DASA German manufacturer. Effectively the entire German aircraft industry, DASA took over such names as **Messerschmitt-Bolkow-Blohm**, but not **Dornier**. DASA has been absorbed into **EADS**, the European Aeronautic Defence and Space Company.

Dassault French manufacturer. Formed after the end of the Second World War by Marcel Dassault, formerly **Marcel Bloch**, the company produced mainly military and business aircraft, including the Ouragan (Hurricane) fighter-bomber, the Mystère fighter and its Super Mystère successor, and the Etendard and Super Etendard carrier-borne fighters, as well as the Flamant light transport and communications aircraft. These were competent aircraft which enjoyed some success, but it was the Mirage series of fighters and fighter-bombers that made the company a leading exporter of combat aircraft.

The aircraft was extensively developed, with a twin-engined bomber variant, the Mirage IV, to deliver the French nuclear deterrent, and there were prototype **variable-geometry** and VTOL variants. Significant markets included Africa and Latin America. The company has not seen similar success for the Rafale fighter, even though this is available in both land-based and carrier-borne versions.

Dassault also established a firm market niche with its Falcon series of business aircraft, including a three-engined stretched version capable of transatlantic operations. It became the French partner in the Franco-German Atlantique maritime-reconnaissance aircraft after acquiring **Breguet** in 1972, which also brought the company partnership in the Anglo-French Jaguar strike-fighter.

Dassault, Marcel *See* Bloch, Marcel

Davis, David R. (1894–1972) American aerodynamicist and inventor. Davis became interested in aviation after his mother moved the family to California and he helped **Glenn Martin** with his first aeroplane. After service in the US Army during the First World War, Davis learnt to fly and became a stunt flyer (*see* **barnstorming**), and then with **Donald Douglas** formed the Davis-Douglas Airplane Company, although the company failed leaving Davis bankrupt after the 1929 stock market crash.

Despite his difficulties, Davis continued working and after trying to develop a variable pitch propeller, but having to give up because of a shortage of funding, he turned his attention to improving aerofoils, borrowing a car to test wing sections. **Walter Brookins** introduced Davis to **Reuben Fleet**, enabling Davis to sell his wing design to Fleet's company, **Consolidated**, which used it on a number of designs before incorporating it into the B-24 Liberator bomber. The royalties from the wing made Davis and Brookins rich, but the USN was suspicious of the patent because Davis had registered false data and they tried to get him to return the royalties. It was only when the USN was assured that this had only been done to ensure no one copied the design that it relented, but even so it insisted on paying reduced royalties.

de Gusmão, Bartolomeo Lourenço *See* Gusmão, de

de Havilland British manufacturer. Founded after the First World War by **Capt Geoffrey de Havilland**, the company produced a series of airliner, light transport and light aircraft designs between the wars, including the DH66 Hercules trimotor airliner in the 1920s, but became better known for the DH60 Moth series of light aircraft and trainers and the DH84 Dragon series of light biplane transports. In 1934 the DH88 Comet twin-engined racing aircraft appeared. The Second World War prevented further development of two promising airliner designs, the Albatross and Flamingo, but the company's DH98 Mosquito proved to be versatile, being produced in light bomber, reconnaissance and night-fighter variants, with some even used as transports by **BOAC**. It could lift a heavier load than other light bombers,

up to 5,000 lb and was built of wood, a 'non-strategic' material, to make the most of scarce resources. The company's DH82 Tiger Moth was one of the RAF's basic trainers, while the DH89 Dragon Rapide served in the communications role as the Dominie. To assist wartime production, aircraft were also built at a factory in Canada, and postwar this became **de Havilland Canada**.

From 1943 de Havilland built a range of twin-boom jet-engined fighters, including the Vampire, which soon was relegated to become the world's first jet trainer, and its successors, the Venom and Sea Venom. While the success of these aircraft was marred by the structural failure of the world's first jet airliner, the de Havilland Comet I, the company's Dove and Heron light transports proved very successful. The company also produced experimental aircraft, such as the tailless Swallow, and eventually concluded its twin-boomed projects with the DH110 Sea Vixen naval fighter. The Comet I survived its earlier problems, with the Comet II serving as a transport with the RAF and the Comet IV inaugurated transatlantic jet air services with BOAC. The Trident jet airliner that followed made the world's first fully automatic landings, but this, and the 125 business jet, entered production after the company had been merged to form **Hawker Siddeley Aviation** in 1960.

de Havilland Canada Canadian manufacturer. Established in 1947, de Havilland Canada was created from a former **de Havilland** assembly plant at Downsview, Toronto, originally set up to meet wartime demand for the parent company's aircraft. It soon gained a reputation of its own with a series of indigenous aircraft designs. First of these was the DHC-1 Chipmunk basic trainer, used by many air forces and air arms and also built in the UK by the parent company. The company then established a niche for itself, becoming the West's leading manufacturer of STOL utility aircraft and light transports, starting with the DHC-2 Beaver and the DHC-3 Otter. These were followed by the larger twin-engined DHC-4 Caribou and DHC-5 Buffalo, before a stretched tricycle undercarriage development of the Otter, the DHC-6 Twin Otter appeared. Between 1965 and 1988, when production ended, 844 aircraft were built, of which some 600 remain in operation today. An independent manufacturer is attempting to put the aircraft back into production.

The company's penultimate design was the DHC-7, a four-engined STOL airliner that inaugurated services out of London City Airport, but this was followed by the Dash 8 series, which remains in production by **Bombardier**, the company's successor, to this day. Before being merged with **Canadair** into Bombardier, the company was owned by **Boeing** for a short time.

de Havilland, Capt Sir Geoffrey (1882–1965)

British pioneer and aircraft manufacturer. Trained as an engineer, de Havilland initially worked in the motor industry, but in 1908, he borrowed £1,000 from his grandfather to construct an aeroplane, building both the airframe and engine with help from his assistant, Frank Herle. The aircraft was completed the following year, but only managed a few short hops before being wrecked in an accident. A second aeroplane was finished in 1910, and it was in this aircraft, in which de Havilland taught himself to fly, that his reputation began when it was purchased by the British Army for £400 and he was offered a position at the Army's balloon factory.

The balloon factory developed into the Royal Aircraft Factory, where de Havilland designed aircraft such as the FE-2, SE-1, the BE-1 and BS-2 for the RFC. In 1914 he moved to the Aircraft Manufacturing Company (Airco) as its chief designer and test pilot, test-flying all of his own designs until the end of the First World War. Here the aircraft were all designated DH, with his most notable designs being the DH4 and DH9 single-engined bombers, which also provided some of the first postwar air transports.

With the postwar fall in demand for aircraft, Airco collapsed in 1920, but in September de Havilland founded the company that bore his name. Realising that demand for military aircraft was likely to be depressed for some time, de Havilland made a conscious decision to concentrate on commercial designs. His great success was to build the low-cost 60 hp Cirrus engine and a simple biplane, resulting in the DH60 Moth first flown in 1932. This aircraft was an immediate success and aircraft from the Moth family not only enjoyed the boom in private and club

flying, they also took the company back into the military market when it was selected as a trainer. A similar success awaited the Dragon family of biplane small airliners, mostly twin-engined but also including the four-engined Dragon Express favoured by British Airways, one of the predecessors of the British Overseas Airways Corporation (BOAC). He also designed the elegant DH91 Albatross of 1937, a monoplane airliner of wooden construction, for the other BOAC predecessor, Imperial Airways.

The Second World War brought even greater success for de Havilland, with his Mosquito, a twin-engined monoplane initially rejected by the Air Ministry, which many came to regard as the best aircraft of the war. The Mosquito was versatile, as a light bomber capable of lifting a medium bomber warload of up to 5,000 lb, a reconnaissance aircraft, night fighter and escort fighter, and even as a transport for BOAC flying ball bearings from Sweden over enemy-occupied Norway. Before the war ended, the company produced the first Vampire jet fighter, although this was soon superseded by the Venom while most Vampires produced were trainers.

Postwar, the company produced the world's first jet airliner, the Comet I for BOAC, but this promising aircraft had to be withdrawn after a series of accidents, and even though later versions proved rugged and reliable, the setback lost the market to the company and to the UK.

By the time the company was forced to merge into **Hawker Siddeley**, one of two government-inspired major airframe producers, it was producing the Trident airliner for British European Airways (BEA), the first airliner in the world capable of making an automatic landing.

De Havilland lost two of his three sons in crashes caused while test-flying the company's aircraft.

de la Cierva, Juan *See* Cierva, de la

de Montgolfier, Joseph-Michel *See* Montgolfier, de

de Pischoff, Alfred *See* Pischoff, de

de Seversky, Alexander Prokofieff *See* Seversky, de

Deere, Sqn Ldr (later Wg Cdr) Alan Christopher (1917–95) New Zealand fighter ace. Deere left his New Zealand sheep farm in 1937 to join the RAF in the UK. He was flying with No. 54 Squadron during the Battle of Britain when he was the first to shoot down a Messerschmitt Bf109, the first of 21.5 kills. Deere himself was shot down three times during the war, once during the Dunkirk evacuation, but survived and remained in the RAF after the war.

Degen, Jacob (1756–1846) Swiss clock-maker and ornithopter pioneer. Degen was living in Vienna in 1809 when he built an ornithopter using flap valves of a kind pioneered by Melchior Bauer in 1764: these closed on the down stroke and opened up on the upstroke. He was wise enough to test the device slung from deadweight before further experiments with a hydrogen balloon fitted to the ornithopter. The lift of the balloon combined with the ornithoptering motion to provide a number of hops. Unfortunately, illustrations of the ornithopter were circulated with the balloon omitted, which led **George Cayley** to believe that Degen had achieved man-powered heavier-than-air flight, and more seriously, induced Albrecht Berblinger to actually attempt flight.

Delage, Paul-Aristide Gustave (1883–?) French designer. Commissioned into the Marine National (the French Navy), Delage experimented with gliders and qualified as a pilot in 1910. He met **Edouard Nieuport** in 1911, and when the Nieuport brothers died he was offered the position of chief designer in their company, which prompted him to leave the navy in early 1914. He designed a series of Nieuport Scouts, which proved popular with First World War Allied fighter aces, and postwar followed this with a succession of successful racing aeroplanes.

Delagrange, Léon (1873–1910) Early French pilot. A successful sculptor, Delagrange became interested in gliding and in 1905 commissioned **Gabriel Voisin** to build him an aeroplane which he had designed himself. The Delagrange aeroplane would have been difficult to build, so Voisin sold him a conventional Voisin biplane, which he flew in 1908. Taking his aeroplane on a tour of Europe, Delagrange was the first to carry a woman passenger, Mme Therese Peltier, a sculptress, and he also made the first flight in Italy.

On returning home he purchased a Blériot monoplane and was flying this near Bordeaux on 4 January 1910 when he overstressed the aircraft while making a tight turn. The wings broke off and he fell 70 ft to the ground, where he was struck by the aircraft's engine and killed.

delta wing The first recorded delta wing design was that of two Englishmen, J.W. Butler and E. Edwards in 1867, and this also envisaged a form of jet propulsion, first included two years earlier in a practical aircraft design by the Frenchman, Charles de Louvrie. The Butler-Edwards design resembled a paper dart, but the proper definition of a delta wing is that it should represent an isosceles triangle in appearance. Many delta wing designs have omitted a tailplane, using elevons instead of separate elevators and ailerons, but whether or not there is a tailplane has nothing to do with the definition of an aircraft wing as a delta.

Practical delta wing designs appeared in Britain and the United States after the Second World War, with designs from **Avro**, **Boulton Paul** and **Gloster** in the UK, and Convair in the USA. As the Messerschmitt Me163 Komet was not a true delta, but was a tailless aircraft with a swept-wing, the first operational delta-wing aircraft was the Gloster Javelin, which was one of the few to have a tailplane. After its maiden flight in November 1951, it became the RAF's first all-weather jet fighter the following year. Other aircraft that followed included the Avro Vulcan, one of the RAF's trio of 'V' bombers designed to carry the

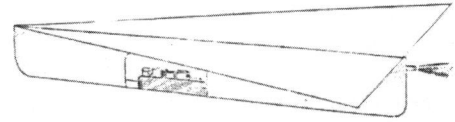

Some pioneers were looking ahead at streamlined shapes. This is not the prototype of the paper dart, but instead a futuristic rocket-powered aeroplane design produced in 1867 by J.W. Butler and E. Edwards.

British nuclear deterrent, the Convair F-102 Delta Dagger and F-106 Delta Dart, both of which were fighters. A world airspeed record was set in 1956 by a British delta-wing research aircraft, the Fairey Delta 2, although this was exceeded in December 1959 by a Convair F-106.

Undoubtedly the most famous and successful delta wing aircraft have been the French Dassault Mirage series (although the Mirage F1 was swept-wing, and the Mirage G had **variable-geometry**), which performed fighter, interceptor, fighter-bomber, reconnaissance and bomber duties. The Anglo-French Concorde supersonic transport was not strictly a delta wing design as the leading edges of the wing were curved. Double delta-wing aircraft are also not true deltas as the angle is changed part way along the leading edge, as on the Swedish SAAB-35 Draken and SAAB-37 Viggen.

Demoyez, Jean (1916–45) French fighter ace. Working as an interpreter for the RAF in 1940 as the Germans advanced across France, Demoyez took the opportunity to escape to the UK, where he joined the RAF and was trained as a fighter pilot, flying Hurricanes and, later, Spitfires, often on fighter sweeps across occupied France. He shot down twenty-one enemy aircraft between 1941 and 1943, as well as damaging ground targets and sinking a minelayer. He was then rested on training duties before transferring to a bomber unit. He was killed in a flying accident after the liberation of France while helping to rebuild the Armée de l'Air.

Denel South African manufacturer. The company was formed in 1992 to maintain and build military aircraft for the South African armed forces during sanctions against the country. It has developed into a significant armaments manufacturer and has built developments of the Mirage as well as developing the Rooivalk combat helicopter.

Deperdussin, Armand (1867–1924) Early French aircraft manufacturer. A textile salesman, Deperdussin had commissioned **Louis Béchereau** to design a mock aeroplane for a department store display of his merchandise, but he was so impressed by the result that he hired Béchereau as a designer and founded his own aircraft company. The

monoplane Deperdussins were a great success and established a reputation for style and speed, with a seaplane variant winning the first **Schneider Trophy Race** in 1913. That same year, at the height of his success, Deperdussin was arrested for fraud and held in custody awaiting trial, causing him to sell his company to **Louis Blériot**. He was finally tried and convicted in 1917, and although he was given a suspended sentence, he was by this time completely broke. Deperdussin committed suicide in 1924.

Deperdussin Monocoque Sometimes known as the Monocoque Deperdussin, this was the first monoplane of monocoque construction, without external bracing for the wings. It took to the air in 1912. A high-wing wooden aircraft, it featured a single seat and a single 160 hp Gnome rotary engine giving the then high maximum speed of 126 mph and allowing it to establish a number of speed records. An unusual feature was that control in roll was through wing-warping.

design competition As the term implies, this is a competition that ensues after a government issues a specification for an aircraft, with the winner being given the opportunity to build the prototype and, usually, put the aircraft into production. At one time it was usual for two or more designs to be built and then for there to be a 'fly-off', but this is seldom the case today, although **Lockheed-Martin** and **Boeing** were able to do this for the Joint Strike Fighter project, the outcome of which was decided in 2001. Improved understanding of aerodynamics has made the fly-off less essential, although the main reason is the very high cost of modern technology and limited defence budgets. It can happen that the manufacturer which produces the winning prototype does not get the contract for production if another company can do it more cheaply, but this is rare.

design leadership When working on collaborative aircraft, it is usual for one of the airframe manufacturers to be given design leadership. This is a prestigious position. On some occasions responsibility for different aspects of the design, particularly complicated areas such as the wings, are left with different partners.

deterrent Although usually associated with nuclear weapons, a deterrent is any weapon or weapon systems, or the size of an armed service or armed services, that can deter an attack by a potential enemy. During the Cold War, the retaliation that could be expected by the Warsaw Pact, and in particular the Soviet Union, from British, American and, possibly, French nuclear weapons was regarded as being the fundamental factor in maintaining peace and preventing conflict that would almost certainly have escalated rapidly to a nuclear exchange. Deterrent does not have to be nuclear, and during the Second World War it is believed that the Germans were inhibited from using poison gases for fear of British retaliation.

The essential feature of any deterrent is the will and the means to use it, but it is equally true that once used, the deterrent effect is ended.

Deutsch de la Meurthe, Henri (1845–1919)

Sponsor and patron of aviation contests. Deutsch de la Meurthe trained as an engineer and inherited considerable wealth from his family who had interests in engineering and oil. One of the men behind the Automobile Club de France, he decided that aviation needed the same type of institution as a meeting place and organiser of events, so he founded the Aéro-Club de France and offered cash prizes to encourage the pioneers. Beneficiaries of his largesse included **Alberto Santos-Dumont**, winning a prize for the first flight around the Eiffel Tower, and **Henry Farman**, for the first circular flight of at least a kilometre in Europe.

These events did much to encourage progress in France and brought French aviators together. For the longer term, his main bequest to French aviation was the founding of the Institute Aérotechnique at St-Cyr to study the science of aviation.

Dewoitine French manufacturer. Active between the two world wars, the company built civil, military and naval aircraft, including the D14 high-wing monoplane that first flew in 1924, the D332 trimotor all-metal fourteen-passenger airliner of 1936. It also built the D500, D510 and D520 fighters for the French air force and navy during the late 1930s, which proved to be outclassed by the Luftwaffe's Messerschmitt Bf109s.

Diamond Austrian manufacturer. Based on a motor-glider manufacturer taken over by Christian Dries in 1990, Diamond has developed a series of single and twin-engined light aircraft and has become the largest manufacturer in its field outside the United States. It specialises in composite materials and in using diesel engines for its propeller aircraft, but also launched a light jet in 2008.

dihedral An upward inclination of the wings from the root (the part that is attached to the fuselage) to the tip, giving a shallow 'V' appearance from front or rear view. The opposite of **anhedral**, the effect is the opposite as well in that it gives increased stability in roll. Some dihedral can be an advantage in passenger aircraft, but it is a drawback in aerobatic aircraft. The **Wright** brothers and other pioneers tended to avoid dihedral.

Dinfia Argentine manufacturer. A small company concentrating on producing aircraft mainly for the Argentina military. Its most famous product has been the Pucara, a turboprop light strike aircraft used in the Falklands Campaign, but it has also produced the IA35 and IA50 light transports for the Fuerza Aérea Argentina (Argentina air force) and the IA53 crop-spraying aircraft.

dirigible *See* airship

dive-bomber This type of aircraft emerged in the late 1920s with a Martin design for the USN being among the first. Essentially, the concept was intended to improve accuracy with the aircraft diving steeply towards the target before releasing the bomb, although the demands on the airframe also meant that the concept was confined to smaller aircraft and could not be applied to heavy bombers. Bomb-rack technology was another factor in delaying the introduction of the dive-bomber, since ideally the main bomb would have to be swung clear of the propeller.

On the outbreak of the Second World War in Europe in 1939, the dive-bomber had reached the peak of its performance. The most famous of these aircraft was the Junkers Ju87 Stuka, but all combatants had dive-bombers, including the Royal Navy's Fairey Swordfish biplane and

Blackburn Skua, and the USN's Curtiss Helldiver and Douglas Dauntless. Even neutral nations such as Sweden had dive-bombers, including the SAAB-17. Nevertheless, the weaknesses in the concept were beginning to show, including the relatively low speeds and the vulnerability of the aircraft against well-trained anti-aircraft defences and fighters, while heavy bombing accuracy was also improving.

Dollfus, Charles (1893–1981) French historian. At the age of 18, Charles Dollfus made his first ascent in a balloon, the start of a life-long passion for aeronautics. He did not become one of the pioneers of aviation, but instead researched and wrote about the subject, becoming a devotee of the **Wright** brothers, and then becoming the first curator of the Paris Musée de l'Air. He was one of the few to also give due credit to the work of **George Cayley**.

Doolittle, Lt Gen James Harold 'Jimmy', USAAF (1896–1993) American pilot, bomber leader and leader. Doolittle joined the US Army in 1917 as an engineering graduate and three years later he was transferred to the then US Army Aviation Section. He had learnt to fly during his early service with the army and in 1922 he attracted attention by making the first transcontinental crossing of the USA in less than 24 hours. He became a member of a number of committees connected with aviation sponsored by the US government. He won the **Schneider Trophy Race** in 1925 flying a Curtiss R3C-2 seaplane at 232.57 mph, the Bendix Trophy in 1931 and the Thompson in 1932. On 24 September 1929 he made the first completely blind flight using aids he had developed himself.

After this string of successes, Doolittle left the United States Army and went to work for Shell, making promotional sales tours of the Americas and also helping to develop new fuels for aviation.

In 1940, after the Second World War had broken out in Europe, Doolittle resumed his military career. He became best known for planning and leading 'Operation Shangri-La', the raid by North American B-25 Mitchell bombers against Tokyo on 18 April 1942, with the aircraft taking off from the aircraft carrier USS *Hornet*. The operation caught the Japanese by surprise as they believed that they were safely out of reach of American bombers. It required great skill on behalf of the pilots as the leading aircraft had little flight deck left in which to make their take-off run. While the attack caused little real damage, in part because the aircraft were dispersed over too many targets, it caused the Japanese to re-assess their strategy, which became more defensive. Doolittle was promoted to major and then lieutenant-general, and in 1944–5 commanded the US Eighth Air Force in England at the height of the advance across Europe towards Germany.

Dornberger, Walter (1895–1980) German ordnance expert. Dornberger had been in the German Army since 1914 when, in 1930, he was given responsibility for rockets as a member of the Army Board of Ordnance. In this position he recruited **Wernher von Braun**, designer of the V-2, as well as being responsible for the V-1 flying bomb. Not the least of his achievements during the Second World War was keeping control of the research establishment at Peenemunde, which the Gestapo wanted to take over, and protecting his scientists from arrest by the secret police.

When the war ended, Dornberger became a British prisoner of war for two years, and after being released he emigrated to the United States where he worked on missile development before becoming a consultant for **Bell** in 1950.

Dornier German manufacturer. Founded by **Prof Claudius Dornier** in 1922, the company initially operated outside Germany as aircraft manufacture was forbidden in the country under the **Treaty of Versailles**. Its best-selling flying boat in the 1920s and 30s was the Wal. The company was also known for the DoX, which first appeared in 1929 and was the largest aircraft in the world at the time, with no less than twelve engines in six nacelles, mounted back-to-back with tractor and pusher propellers. This aircraft made a number of prestigious flights across the Atlantic between 1930 and 1932. The elegant Do24 flying boat was built by Aviolanda in the Netherlands for use by the Royal Netherlands Navy in the Dutch East Indies. Another flying boat, the Do18, used diesel engines.

The company became a vital part of the German rearmament programme during the 1930s, with the Do17 bomber developed initially as an airliner, nicknamed the 'flying pencil' because of its long thin shape, to allay fears of German ambitions. The aircraft proved a useful medium bomber and was further developed as the Do217 later in the Second World War. Towards the end of the war the company produced the Do335, a tandem-engined fighter which appeared in small numbers, suffered from technical problems and was too late to see extensive service.

Postwar, the company was run by Dornier's son, but found itself once again suffering restrictions within Germany. The first aircraft, the Do27 army liaison aircraft, was first built in Spain, but the Do27 and the Do28 that followed were both later built in what was then West Germany for the armed forces once these were reconstituted. Dornier also built under licence the Fiat G91 ground-attack aircraft and Lockheed F-104G Starfighter interceptors for the Luftwaffe, and followed this with licence-production of Bell 204/205 Iroquois helicopters for the German Army. The company built a V/STOL transport, the Do31E, but this project was eventually abandoned. More successful was the Franco-German Alphajet. The company also became a member of the Airbus consortium.

The Do228 turboprop transport enjoyed some success, and was followed by the larger 328, also available as a jet, the 328JET. It was acquired by Fairchild of the United States, but the company collapsed and production has now ceased.

Dornier, Prof Claudius (1884–1969) German

aircraft designer and manufacturer. After graduating as an engineer in Munich, Dornier was employed by **Count Ferdinand von Zeppelin** as a stress engineer working on his airship designs. During the First World War he designed hydro-aeroplanes for the company with what was then the advanced feature of metal **cantilever wings**.

Postwar, the **Treaty of Versailles** banned aircraft manufacture in Germany, so when Dornier established his own company it had to operate from Italy and Switzerland for many years. He continued his work on hydro-aeroplanes, building a series of flying boats including the highly

successful Wal and the DoX, a twelve-engined flying boat which was the first aircraft to be able to lift 100 passengers; on one occasion, in 1929, it carried 169 passengers.

After the rise of the Nazi Party in Germany, Dornier was able to return home and begin to build landplane airliners, with his most famous design being the Do17 bomber. He also designed the twin-engined tractor-pusher propeller Do335 Pfeil, although unlike the Do17 this appeared in small numbers. His wartime work was hampered by shortages of labour and raw materials, which resulted in an excessive degree of standardisation that forced older designs to be kept in production for longer than necessary.

Postwar, the company was taken over by Dornier's son. Work on flying boats and amphibians continued, but its most outstanding success lay in developing small transports, including the 228 twin turboprop, with fifteen seats in the 228-100 and nineteen in the 228-200, and later, after being absorbed by Fairchild of the USA in 1996, the 328, available both as a turboprop and as a jet, but production has now ceased.

Douglas US manufacturer. The company was

founded by **Donald Douglas** in 1924 after the collapse of the Davis-Douglas Company. Fame came to Douglas that same year with the World Cruiser, which was the first aircraft to fly around the world. A steady succession of aircraft followed, including the O-2 observation aircraft for the US Army and the M-2 mailplane. The most significant development came in 1932 with the first flight of the DC-1, a modern all-metal twin-engined monoplane airliner that also marked the start of the 'Douglas Commercial' series. The DC-2 that followed enjoyed considerable commercial success, but it was an order from American Airlines that persuaded a reluctant Donald Douglas to build the DC-3, which was adopted by the USAAC as the C-47, and together these became the most numerous transport aircraft ever built, with more than 10,000 produced during the Second World War. The DC-4 that followed was a large four-engined aircraft, originally with a triple fin and first flown in 1939, but most were built as C-54s for the USAAF. The DC-5 was a high-wing twin-engined aircraft which entered military service, but was produced in limited numbers. Postwar, the DC-6 was a pressurised development of the DC-4. The final piston-engined aircraft was the DC-7, intended for long-haul non-stop services.

Wartime production was not confined to transport aircraft, and the company produced the B-18 bomber, which was a development of the DC-2/DC-3 family, and later the A-1 Skyraider for the USN. After the Second World War, the company's first experience of jet aircraft was the A-4 Skyhawk, a simple, light and inexpensive carrier-borne strike aircraft, while a heavier aircraft was the A-3D Skywarrior and its land-based equivalent for the USAF, the B-66 Destroyer. The company also built the C-133 Cargomaster and the large C-124 Globemaster for the USAF.

In 1959, the company's first jet airliner, the DC-8, entered service, and this aircraft continued in production with extensive fuselage stretches, being especially popular with air freight operators. During the 1960s, the company moved into the short-haul market with the twin-engined DC-9 series, with engines mounted at the tail, again stretching the aircraft. It found favour with a number of European operators, including Alitalia, Iberia, KLM and Swissair.

Cash-flow problems led to a merger in 1967 with McDonnell, which was anxious to end its dependence on military work, to form **McDonnell Douglas**. The new company continued to develop the product range and in 1971 the DC-10 three-engined wide-bodied airliner first flew. This was further developed as the MD-11, while the twin-engined DC-9 series was developed into the MD-80 and MD-90 family. In 1997, McDonnell Douglas was acquired by **Boeing**, and MD-11 production quickly came to an end. The last of the MD-90 series entered production as the Boeing 717, but this also ended in 2005. Some former Douglas facilities remain operational building sub-assemblies for their new owner.

Douglas, AM Sir William Sholto, later Lord Douglas of Kirtleside (1893–1970) British ace and fighter leader. Douglas learnt to fly in France during the last days of peace before the outbreak of the First World War when he joined the Royal Flying Corps (RFC). He was posted to No. 2 Squadron, a reconnaissance unit, where

he flew unarmed BE 2As. The reconnaissance aircraft or 'scouts' eventually transformed into 'fighting scouts' and then fighters, and before the war ended Douglas had commanded two fighter squadrons. In one aerial battle he engaged with **Hermann Goering**, the German ace and future Nazi air minister.

Postwar, Douglas was chief test pilot for **Handley Page** in 1919 and 1920, before returning to the RAF and commanding units in the Sudan. He rose rapidly to senior rank during the Second World War, taking over from **Hugh Dowding** as head of Fighter Command in 1940, and then commanded the RAF in the Middle East before returning home to head Coastal Command in 1944–5. After German surrender, he was military governor of the British Zone of Occupation. On retirement from the RAF, he became managing director of the nationalised long-haul airline, BOAC, before becoming chairman of the nationalised British European Airways (BEA), holding this position for fifteen years.

Douglas, Donald Wills (1892–1981) Scottish-American engineer and manufacturer. While training at the US Naval Academy, Douglas was present when **Orville Wright** demonstrated the US Army's Wright I biplane at Fort Myers. Inspired, he left the academy and moved to the Massachusetts Institute of Technology, working under **Jerome Hunsaker**. After graduating, Douglas worked first for the Connecticut Aircraft Company before going to California where he was employed by **Glenn Martin** as chief engineer. After Martin moved the business to Cleveland in 1918, Douglas left because he did not like the climate and returned to establish a new company in California in 1920 with **David Davis**, known as the Davis-Douglas Company. The company was wound up after the first aircraft, the *Cloudster*, crashed in Texas while attempting to fly non-stop across the USA.

It was time for Douglas to set up his own company, and he was fortunate to win the order for torpedo aircraft for the US Navy. In 1924 two Douglas aircraft made the first aerial circumnavigation of the globe, taking 175 days. The company survived the years of the Great Depression, although production was on a small scale. This changed in 1932, when the first of the DC (Douglas Commercial) range of airliners was built for Transcontinental & Western Air (the predecessor of Trans World Airlines) and this led to developments, including the DC-2, and then to the most popular airliner ever built, the DC-3 and its military version the C-47, known in the British armed forces as the Dakota but to the Americans as the Skytrain. More than 10,000 C-47s were built during the Second World War, in addition to those manufactured under licence in the Soviet Union as the Lisunov Li-2. Ironically, Douglas was reluctant to build the DC-3 as he regarded the DC-2 as adequate for the market, but he was persuaded by the then president of American Airlines with an order for twenty aircraft.

The company's series of piston-engined air transports produced just one flop, the DC-5, a twin-engined aircraft and the only one to have a high wing, but its four-engined DC-4, DC-6 and DC-7 aircraft brought ever longer range operations into existence. Its first jet airliner was the DC-8, a rival to the Boeing 707. The DC-9 series of short-haul airliners followed and eventually developed into the MD-80 and MD-90 series. The company had by this time merged with McDonnell in 1967 as the latter company sought to protect its business with a stake in the commercial market. The DC-10 long-haul airliner was relatively successful, but the successor, the MD-11, although selling steadily, had its production terminated by **Boeing** after it acquired **McDonnell Douglas**, possibly because it overlapped with the new owner's 767 and projected 777 series.

Douhet, Guilio (1869–1930) Italian aviation strategist. Commissioned into the Italian Army, Douhet took an early interest in air power and in 1909 published a paper on its future. He was soon transferred to the aviation unit and when Italy went to war with Turkey in 1911 he was in command of an air squadron that made the world's first air raid, bombing Turkish positions in Libya. The Italian aviation activities became known as the Battagliore Aviatori (Aviation Battalion) in 1912. Douhet took this as an opportunity to lobby for a strategic bombing capability and commissioned **Gianni Caproni** to begin design and construction of a trimotor bomber, far exceeding his authority

and for which he was court martialled and sent to prison for a year.

In 1921, in his book *Il Dominio dell'Aria* (*The Command of the Air*), he advocated the creation of large air forces with strategic bombing capability, insisting that such forces would be able to fly everywhere unopposed and in attacking defenceless cities would force them to surrender. Not only did this mean that he sided with the prevailing interwar notion that the 'bomber would always get through', but it ignored the potential for fighters and anti-aircraft defences. His theory impressed the Italian dictator Mussolini so much that Douhet was appointed commissioner for aviation, but this was an unhappy position as it brought him into conflict with the public hero, **Italo Balbo**.

Dowding, AM Lord 'Stuffy' (1882–1970) British fighter strategist. No one could be more different from the public image of the British fighter pilot, as a laid back and informal individual, than their leader Hugh Dowding during the crucial first few years of the Second World War. Dowding was known as 'Stuffy' for his over-precise manners and standoffish character.

Like many RAF officers of his generation, Dowding had been commissioned into the British Army. He served with the artillery during the Boer War as Hugh Caswall Tremenheere and was posted to a number of units scattered around the British Empire in the years that followed. He did not return to the UK for any appreciable length of time until shortly before the outbreak of the First World War in 1914, but he did find time to learn to fly in the remaining months of peace. After the outbreak of war, he volunteered to be transferred to the Royal Flying Corps (RFC) and flew on active duty, rising to the rank of brigadier-general by the end of the war, then becoming an air commodore in the newly formed RAF.

Many attribute his slow further progress between the wars to his inability to make friends, but the 1920s were a period of dramatic reductions in the size of the RAF, which at one time consisted of no more than twelve squadrons, so opportunities for rapid promotion, especially among more senior officers, were limited. He did at least have the consolation of his hobby, skiing, and became head of the Ski Club of Great Britain.

In 1930 Dowding joined the Air Board, becoming the Member for Supply and Research, and this supposedly tame-sounding role was to prove to be ideal for him. He was responsible for driving research into radar. He also insisted that the aircraft industry should switch from building wooden aircraft to using metal, this at a time when aircraft orders were for small quantities and infrequent, and supported the Hurricane and the Spitfire. Under Dowding, the ultra-conservative biplane mentality was replaced by a forward-looking service based on the monoplane. It was a just reward that his next appointment in 1936 was as head of the RAF's newly formed Fighter Command. This gave him the chance to put into effect all of the developments he had fostered as Air Member for Research and Supply, reorganising the country's fighter defences around the Chain Home radar network.

After the outbreak of the Second World War, once the fighting had started in spring 1940, he successfully resisted Winston Churchill's demands for still more fighters to be deployed forward to France when it was clear that the German advance could not be stopped, and ensured that he had adequate numbers of aircraft and pilots ready for the **Battle of Britain**. In November 1940, with the battle won, he moved on from what had been an exhausting position and retired in 1942, a much under-rated leader who had made the right decisions over a period when there was little past experience to learn from.

Dowty, Sir George Herbert (1901–75) British industrialist. At the age of 17 Dowty entered the aircraft industry with Heenan and Froude, before moving to **Avro** and then **Gloster**. He founded his own company in 1931, specialising in undercarriages at a time when these were changing, with the widespread adoption of retractable undercarriages. Since Dowty's death the company has merged with Messier of France.

drag Anything that interferes with the smoothness of an airframe constitutes drag, even the operation of the ailerons to turn an aircraft causing it to slow down and climb, as was shown during the **Schneider Trophy Races** when aircraft lost speed while making turns along the circuit. Early

biplanes had heavy drag from the struts and bracing between the wings, sometimes referred to as a 'built-in headwind', but this was also a problem with the early monoplanes, which before cantilever construction had such extensive external bracing that many believed that the biplane was a safer option.

External stores, usually meaning the warload such as bombs or missiles, also constitute drag and affect the performance of the aircraft, so considerable effort is put into streamlining these to minimise the effect on performance.

du Temple, Felix *See* Temple, du

Duke, Sqn Ldr Neville Frederick (1922–2007) British ace and test pilot. Born in Tonbridge, Kent, Duke's fascination with flying started early and as a small boy he saved his pocket money for joy-riding flights. Shortly before the outbreak of the Second World War he applied to join the Fleet Air Arm, but was turned down as too young and instead joined the RAF in 1940. Commissioned in April 1941, he joined No. 92 Squadron at Biggin Hill, flying Supermarine Spitfires on fighter sweeps over northern France. His first kill was over Dunkirk in June, shooting down a Messerschmitt Bf109, with a second kill a few weeks later. In November 1941 he was posted to No. 112 Squadron in the Middle East flying the Curtiss Tomahawk. The Tomahawk was a better ground-attack aircraft than a fighter, and within six days he was shot down twice. By the end of the year he had shot four aircraft and damaged others and after his eighth victory he was awarded the DFC.

He spent nine months as an instructor at a fighter school in Egypt before rejoining No. 92 Squadron, which had been moved to Egypt in January 1943, as a flight commander. He shot down two enemy aircraft over Tunisia before his ammunition ran out, and a few days later he shot down a Junkers Ju87 Stuka. He was awarded a Bar to his DFC. Over the first three months of the year he shot down twelve enemy fighters and two bombers and was awarded a DSO, was promoted to squadron leader and returned to the fighter school as chief instructor. In February 1944 he was posted to command No. 145 Squadron in Italy, flying the Spitfire VIII. Over a few weeks he shot down another five aircraft and was awarded a second Bar to his DFC. On 7 June, during a low-level strafing sortie, his engine caught fire, and he had difficulty baling out as his parachute snagged, but he eventually got free and landed in the middle of a lake behind enemy lines. He was rescued and hidden by Italian partisans until the arrival of American troops. Returned to his squadron, his final success was shooting down two Bf109s over Rimini on 7 September. On three tours of duty he had flown 486 sorties, shot down twenty-seven enemy aircraft confirmed, and in all probability another three. He was the RAF's highest scoring pilot in the Mediterranean theatre.

In January 1945 he became a production test pilot at **Hawker**, flight testing aircraft as they came off the assembly line, and early in 1946 he was selected to attend the fourth course at the Empire Test Pilots' School, where he flew the Gloster Meteor jet fighter, his first jet. In June 1946 he was posted to the RAF's High Speed Flight. While flying a Meteor at its maximum speed at just 120 ft, an engine failed, but he managed to retain control and land the aircraft safely. Later, while on a mission to demonstrate a Meteor to the Czechoslovak armed forces, he was awarded the Czech Military Cross for his war record. Posted to the Fighter Test Squadron at Boscombe Down, he began research at high altitude, reaching 50,000 ft and high Mach numbers, for which he was awarded the AFC.

He left the RAF in August 1948 to join Hawker as a test pilot, but remained a member of the RAuxAF, flying Spitfires and Meteors. Delivering Hawker Furies to Pakistan, he set new speed records for London to Rome, to Cairo and to Karachi. He tested the new family of prototype aircraft that led to the naval Seahawk fighter and the Hunter. He test flew the Hunter, and was at the Farnborough Air Show on 6 September 1952 when John Derry flew the de Havilland DH110 over the airfield at high speed. The aircraft broke up, killing Derry and his observer and twenty-eight spectators. As soon as the runway was cleared, Duke took off in his Hunter, performed his display and finished with a sonic boom. A year later, on 7 September 1953, flying an all-red Hunter, he set a world air speed record of 727.63 mph. While carrying out firing trials in a

Hunter in August 1955 the aircraft's engine failed, but he managed to land safely, for which he was awarded the Queen's Commendation for Valuable Services in the Air. He was less lucky when, two days later, using the same aircraft after an engine change, there was a serious loss of thrust shortly after take-off and he crash-landed at 200 mph on the grass at RAF Thorney Island, suffering serious back injuries. He never fully recovered from his injuries and left Hawker in October 1956. For his exploration of supersonic flight, he was awarded an OBE.

He continued freelance flying and consultancy and formed Duke Aviation, which he sold in 1982. He also became personal pilot to the industrialist **Sir George Dowty**. Duke wrote books on flying and published his war diaries. He sold his medals, many believed to pay for a hip operation for his wife, but in reality because his home had been burgled three times and he wanted to keep the collection together. He continued flying in retirement and with his wife flew to airshows and reunions. On 7 April 2007, while flying a light aircraft with his wife as passenger, he became unwell, but managed to land safely. He collapsed as he left the aircraft and died that evening.

Dunne, John William (1875–1949)

British swept-wing and tailless aircraft pioneer. Wounded serving with the British Army during the Boer War, Dunne was brought back to the UK where he took an interest in aerodynamics. He was encouraged by the author and visionary H.G. Wells to experiment, and then met **Col Capper**, who employed him at Farnborough as the chief designer for military kites. His role and his ambitions differed, and he left to establish his own company.

He wanted to build a completely stable aircraft and in 1908 succeeded in flying his first powered design, a swept-wing and tailless biplane. A development of this aircraft was built by the **Short** brothers in 1910, which could lift 600 lb, a considerable payload for the day. In 1912 a further development, the D8, flew, with the pilot leaving the cockpit while in the air and climbing on to the wing to demonstrate its stable handling. Dunne did not build many further aircraft himself, but licensed his design to **Burgess** in the USA, who used it as the basis for a hydro-aeroplane, and to the French fighter designer and manufacturer, **Nieuport**.

Dupuy de Lôme, Henri (1816–85) French airship pioneer. Although a naval architect, Dupuy de Lôme was commissioned by the French government during the Prussian siege of Paris in 1870–2 to build an airship capable of reaching the city. The resulting airship did not make its first ascent until February 1872, after the siege was lifted, which was just as well, as the 100 ft-long craft was powered by eight sailors turning a crankshaft driving a single 30 ft pusher propeller, and despite their extra ration of rum, progress was slow even in calm weather. This was clearly far from being a practical airship.

Durant, Charles Ferson (1805–73) Pioneering American aeronaut. Durant visited Paris to study the work of the French aeronauts.

On his return to the USA, Durant became the first to make an officially recognised cross-country balloon voyage in his home country, ascending from Castle Garden, New York, on 9 September 1830.

Dutrieu, Hélène (1877–1961) Pioneering Belgian aviatrix. In 1909 Dutrieu learnt to fly on the diminutive Demoiselle and despite a crash succeeded in becoming the second woman to learn to fly and later made the first flight by a woman lasting an hour. She was also the first woman to fly with a passenger.

E

EADS *See* European Aeronautic Defence and Space Company

Eaker, Gen Ira Clarence (1896–1987) US bomber leader. On the outbreak of the First World War, Eaker gave up teaching to join the infantry before transferring to the Signal Corps where he learnt to fly. The formation of the US Army Air Service in 1920 was followed by a number of publicity flights, and Eaker was involved with these, including the first dawn-to-dusk flight from the US to Panama City, a Pan American goodwill tour in 1926–7, and in 1929 a flight over California with a Fokker trimotor, *The Question Mark*, which Eaker and Carl Spaatz kept airborne for 150 hours.

Shortly before the US entered the Second World War, Eaker was given command of the Twentieth Pursuit (i.e. fighter) Group, and in January 1942 he was promoted to full general and transferred to command the US Eighth Air Force's bomber squadrons. Despite his rank, he led the first US bomber raid over German-occupied Europe with Boeing B-17 Fortresses striking at the Rouen railway yards – a risky venture with serious implications had he been shot down and captured. In 1944 he was put in command of all Allied air forces in the Mediterranean, introducing shuttle raids with a northern base in the Soviet Union. Finally, as a five-star general, he became Chief of the US Air Staff until his retirement in 1947.

Earhart, Amelia (1898–1937) American aviatrix and pioneer. Earhart became interested in aviation following her first flight in 1920. She paid for flying lessons by working as a telephone switchboard operator, and afterwards, with help from her mother, she bought a light aircraft and flew aerobatics at shows. Throughout this period she toyed with studying medicine, having worked as a nurse during the First World War,

and also attempted to become a professional photographer. It was not until 1928 that her career as a pilot became a possibility, when a wealthy Englishwoman, Mrs Frederick Guest, was forced by her family to withdraw from a plan to become the first woman to fly across the Atlantic, albeit with a professional crew at the controls of her Fokker F.VII/3M. Earhart became her stand-in, simply because she lived in Boston from whence the flight was due to depart. She had to accept being flown, but even so, when the aircraft landed in Wales on 18 June 1928 Earhart became a celebrity.

With the money earned from making endorsements, Earhart began to make a number of aerial 'firsts' of her own, and while many of them were simply that the flight was the first to be made by a woman, as when she flew from the east coast of the USA to the west and back again, others, such as an autogiro altitude record of 18,415 ft in 1931, were records in their own right. There were some worthwhile firsts, such as being first to fly from Hawaii to California. She gained further publicity and credibility when she became the first woman to fly herself across the Atlantic, which she did in 1932 flying a Lockheed Vega.

In 1937 she set off from Miami with a companion, Fred Noonan, as navigator, in a Lockheed 10E, intending to become the first woman to fly around the world. Despite problems with the chronometer, they took off from New Guinea on 1 July 1937 to fly the 2,556 miles to Howland Island, a difficult piece of navigation over such a long distance given the aids available at the time. They were never seen again and the wreckage of the aircraft was never recovered.

The fate of the two aviators has been the source of much speculation over the years. One of the wilder theories is that they were forced down by the Japanese, but their course was far from Japanese territory. If they did survive and fell into Japanese hands during the Second World War, there could be some basis for another theory, which is that they were executed by the Japanese.

Eckener, Hugo (1868–1954) German airship pioneer. Originally a journalist, Eckener was strongly critical when he reported on the first ascent by a Zeppelin in 1900, but in just six years he had become a firm advocate of airships to the extent that **Count Ferdinand von Zeppelin** hired him. Eckener not only learnt how to fly the large airships, he also used his journalistic experience to publicise the Zeppelins. He became the company's managing director and also directed Delag, the subsidiary that was the world's first airline, operating scheduled services within Germany. During the First World War Eckener's talent extended to airship design, as well as overseeing the training of military airship pilots.

Postwar, his work had to take place outside of Germany because of the ban on aircraft production and operation imposed by the **Treaty of Versailles**, but he designed the US Navy's airship *Los Angeles* before returning to Germany when the Nazis began their rise to power. Hitler's deputy and minister for aviation, **Hermann Goering**, bought the Zeppelin company. One of the new German airships, the *Graf Zeppelin*, was captained by Eckener on a commercial flight across the Atlantic in 1928 with twenty passengers, and the following year he flew it around the world, covering 21,500 miles in twenty-one days, including flying 7,000 miles non-stop from the factory at Friedrichshafen to Tokyo. When the *Graf Zeppelin* was shown at the Chicago World's Fair, Goering insisted that the swastika be painted on the tailplane, but Eckener, who was anti-Nazi, painted the emblem on the left-hand side only, then flew around Chicago clockwise so that those on the ground could not see it. He was sacked by Goering, and many believe that he escaped prison or possibly execution simply because he had become a popular hero.

Eckener made some 2,000 airship ascents.

Edwards, Sir George Robert (1908–2003) British aircraft designer and industrialist. Born in Chingford, Essex, Edwards graduated in engineering from the University of London. He worked initially in engineering workshops before joining **Vickers** at Weybridge in 1935. When the Second World War broke out he was promoted to experimental works manager and one of his first tasks was to design an aerial minesweeping system for RAF Coastal Command. He became chief designer in 1945 and the following year learnt to fly. His designs included the Vickers Viking, based on the aerodynamic surfaces of the Wellington bomber; the Viscount, the world's first turboprop airliner; and the Valiant, the first of the RAF's trio of 'V' bombers.

He became managing director of Vickers-Armstrong (Aircraft) in 1953 and when the company was merged into the **British Aircraft Corporation** (BAC) he became its first managing director. He worked on a large transatlantic transport for both the RAF and commercial airlines, the V1000 and VC7 respectively and afterwards maintained that these could have beaten the Boeing 707 and Douglas DC-8 into service. He was involved with the Vanguard, a commercial failure, the TSR2 bomber, cancelled by the British government, and the Anglo-French Concorde supersonic airliner. More successfully, he was behind the BAC One-Eleven regional airliner. He retired in 1975 as chairman, anxious to leave before BAC was merged into the nationalised **British Aerospace**. He was knighted in 1957.

Egg, Urs Christian 'Durs' (1748–1831) Swiss aeronaut and visionary. Relatively little is known about Egg or his partner, **Samuel Pauly**. A gunsmith, Egg was working in London when he learnt about a dirigible design produced by Pauly, and hired him to build one for him with the intention of using it on an air service between London and Paris, which Egg believed would take 10 hours. The result, named the *Dolphin*, because of its fish-like shape, was built in Brompton, London, in a large shed and was intended to be propelled by men pulling on oars. Pauly died before the project could be completed and it became known as 'Egg's Folly'. It would not have worked.

elevator/elevon Controls that enable an aeroplane or glider to climb or descend. In many of the early machines, the elevators were mounted ahead of the pilot, and to some extent this now happens with **canard** profile aircraft such as the SAAB Viggen and the Eurofighter 2000 Typhoon. On a delta wing, elevons replace ailerons and elevators.

Ellehammer, Jacob Christian Hansen (1871–1946) Danish inventor. Ellehammer's interests and inventions were widespread and included clocks, telephones, motorcycles and X-ray machines, many of which were simply improvements on existing designs. In 1905 he took an interest in heavier-than-air flying-machines and completed a delta wing biplane using an engine of his own design and construction, which succeeded in making a short hop while running around a circular course tethered to a central pole. He built further aircraft, including experiments with helicopters between 1912 and 1916.

Ely, Eugene (1886–1911) Pioneering US naval pilot. Ely became involved in aviation flying with the Curtiss Exhibition Company, but a more serious contribution to aviation came on 14 November 1910 when he took off from a wooden platform built over the forward deck of the cruiser USS *Birmingham*, anchored at Hampton Roads, Virginia, in a Curtiss pusher biplane. He was originally intended to make his take-off once the ship was under way, but being impatient he did not wait. On 18 January 1911 he made the first landing on a ship, again at anchor, touching down on the battleship USS *Pennsylvania*, on which ropes weighed down by sandbags had been stretched across her quarterdeck so that hooks under the aircraft could snag on the ropes.

Ely was killed in an accident in October 1911, flying in an exhibition at Macon, Georgia.

Embraer Brazilian manufacturer. Embraer is one of today's two main manufacturers of jet-powered regional aircraft in the western world. It was founded in 1969 as a joint private and state enterprise to take over the work of CTA, a government-sponsored design organisation. The name is an abbreviation of Empresa Brasileira de Aeronáutica SA. The first product was the CTA-designed Bandeirante light transport, but the company also produced the EMB-200 agricultural

aircraft and built the Aermacchi MB326 armed jet trainer under licence for the Brazilian air force. The Bandeirante enjoyed considerable export success, the first Latin American aircraft to do so, and was followed by a larger transport, the 30-seat EMB-120 Brasilia. In conjunction with Fiat of Italy, the company also embarked on a collaborative programme to produce the AMX strike aircraft. The Tucano turboprop trainer became a considerable success, being exported to a number of countries, including the UK, where it was built under licence by **Bombardier** in Belfast.

Despite these successes, the big boost to the fortunes and reputation of Embraer came in the 1990s with the launch of first the EMB-135 and then, in 1997, the EMB-145, regional jets, sales of which were boosted by the fashion for feeder and commuter airlines for the major operators in both the United States and Western Europe. These aircraft, with one and two-abreast seating and two tail-mounted jets, proved so successful that the company then embarked on a new programme of regional jets, the 'E' series with two and two-abreast seating, wing-mounted engines, and a double-bubble fuselage design that provides improved headroom and cabin luggage space as well as underfloor baggage and cargo capacity. This has taken Embraer into a new league with the largest aircraft, the E-195, accommodating up to 116 passengers in a high-density configuration, overlapping with the bottom of the Boeing 737 range. The economics of the aircraft are such that it is the first regional jet to be ordered in quantity by low-cost carriers.

A move into military air transport is imminent with the design of the C-390, a twin turbofan transport incorporating the wing of the E-190, intended to be a replacement for the Lockheed C-130 Hercules.

ENAER Chilean manufacturer. ENAER is a producer mainly of basic trainers, including the T-35A/B Pillan. It also upgrades imported combat aircraft such as the Dassault Mirage 5, now known as the Pantera or Mirage 50.

English Electric British manufacturer. This broad-based British heavy engineering company's interests included railway and heavy electrical engineering as well as computers. It entered the aircraft industry at the end of the Second World War and found early success with its Canberra jet bomber and reconnaissance aircraft, which was also built under licence in Australia and in the United States by **Martin** as the B-57. Its next major project was the P-1A, which developed into the Lightning, a Mach 2.0 twin-engined interceptor, but by the time this aircraft entered full production for the RAF, the company had been merged into the **British Aircraft Corporation** in 1960. The Lightning had limited export sales to Kuwait and Saudi Arabia.

Enola Gay The USAAF Boeing B-29 Superfortress, that dropped the first atomic bomb on 6 August 1945 over the Japanese city of **Hiroshima**, was named *Enola Gay* after the mother of the aircraft commander Colonel Paul Tibbets.

Esmonde, Lt Cdr Eugene, VC (1909–1942) British naval pilot. A major threat to British shipping in the Atlantic and the Bay of Biscay during the Second World War were the fast German battlecruisers *Scharnhorst* and *Gneisenau*, which in 1940 had accounted for twenty-two ships lost, totalling 116,000 tons. The Royal Navy forced the battlecruisers to take refuge at Brest, in occupied France, with the heavy cruiser *Prinz Eugen*, where the RAF repeatedly bombed them, causing some damage but failing to ensure their destruction. Germany decided to return the three ships to northern waters where they would be safer and could be used against the Arctic convoys. Instead of taking the long route around the west of Ireland, on Hitler's orders the ships were sent through the Straits of Dover. British delays in detecting the ships and communications difficulties over mounting an attack meant that a force of just six Swordfish from No. 825 Naval Air Squadron was all that was available to attack the three ships, which were escorted by a combat air patrol of thirty Luftwaffe fighters.

On 12 February 1942 Lt Cdr Eugene Esmonde took his six aircraft into the air, but instead of the escort of sixty Spitfire fighters that he had been promised, just ten Spitfires turned up. In poor light, they located the three warships and their escort

of ten destroyers. The lumbering Swordfish were caught in a hail of fire from the fighters above and the warships below, but they pressed home a torpedo attack. Esmonde's aircraft was badly damaged in the heavy fire, but he kept the aircraft airborne long enough to launch its torpedo before it crashed into the sea; his target, the *Prinz Eugen*, avoided the torpedo. All six Swordfish were shot down, with the loss of Esmonde and twelve out of the eighteen naval airmen involved in the attack. His body was recovered on 26 April 1942. He was awarded a posthumous VC.

Esnault-Pelterie, Robert Albert Charles (1881–1957) French pioneer and designer. After studying both sculpture and engineering, Pelterie began experiments with **Wright**-pattern gliders in 1905, before designing and building his first aeroplane, the REP1, which made a few short hops in 1907. He continued working on and developing his designs, putting ailerons on his Wright glider to replace the wing-warping of the original, and adding seat belts, steel tube airframes, radial engines and brakes, among a host of items, to his aircraft. Despite selling some aircraft to the French Army, his designs never had a major impact or great commercial success. After the First World War he became better known as a lecturer and writer on space flight.

Etrich, Igo (1879–1967) Austrian designer. Trained as an engineer, but also a keen naturalist, Etrich was inspired by how the seed leaf of a variety of cucumber plant floated to earth, believing that it could offer the ideal shape for an aeroplane wing. After testing models, he built a full-sized machine, basically a flying wing, which he flew first as a glider and then as a powered aeroplane in 1907 and 1908. He was disappointed by the lack of stability and in 1909 added a tailplane, creating a stable and easy-to-fly monoplane which he named the *Taube*, or Dove. He sold the rights to the aircraft to the Rumpler concern, and the aircraft was later built by many German manufacturers, including an all-metal version, the *Stahltaube*. It was in widespread service with both the German Military Air Service and Naval Air Service during the early years of the First World War. One of these aircraft reconnoitred Russian troop strengths before the Battle of Tannenberg, one of the first hostile uses of an aeroplane during the war.

Eurocopter *See* below

European Aeronautic Defence and Space Company (EADS) European manufacturer. Established in July 2000, the biggest amalgamation of European aeronautical and defence interests, bringing together **CASA** of Spain, **PZL** of Poland, Eurocopter, **Aérospatiale**, Daimler-Chrysler of Germany, and initially 80 per cent of **Airbus Industrie**, although this was increased to 100 per cent in 2007 when the **British Aerospace** interest was acquired.

Eurocopter brought together the helicopter manufacturing interests of MBB, with its BO-105 light helicopter, and Aérospatiale, which manufactured the Puma transport and Gazelle light helicopter jointly with **Westland** of the UK, as well as the Dauphin and Ecureuil (Squirrel), and had earlier produced the Super Frelon and Alouette II and III. The company soon began to rationalise its range by offering new models, including the EC120 and EC135 light helicopters and the NH90 military transport and Tiger combat helicopter. Many of the older models remain in production, including the BK117, now re-designated as the EC145.

Experimental Aircraft Association (EAA) Founded in 1953 by Paul H. Poberezny, EAA has 170,000 members throughout the world representing recreational aviation, including homebuilt aircraft. The association's headquarters and EAA AirVenture Museum are based at Oshkosh, Wisconsin.

F

Fabre, Henri (1882–1984) French hydro-aeroplane pioneer. When Fabre learnt about the experiments with float-gliders by **Blériot** and **Voisin** in 1905 he decided to design and build a hydro-aeroplane of his own, which he completed in 1909. His first design failed to become airborne, but he worked on a radically different **canard** (tail-first) design, the *Hydravion*, which he attempted to fly for the first time on 28 March 1910 at Le Mede, near Marseille, and found that it flew well. This was the world's first successful take-off from water. No further development of aircraft was made by Fabre, but instead he turned his attention to designing and building floats for the products of other manufacturers.

failsafe A concept that appeared during the early 1960s with the first generation of short-haul jet aircraft, which introduced failsafe structures so that fatigue in any one area would not lead to a catastrophic failure. Previously, aircraft had operated within strict flying lives, either for the airframe as a whole, or for certain vital components, such as wing spars, and to some extent such limitations continue.

Fairey *See* below

Fairey, Sir Charles Richard (1887–1957) British manufacturer. Trained as an engineer, in 1910 Fairey won a contest with a model aeroplane of his own design, but inadvertently infringed **John Dunne**'s patents. Impressed by Fairey's knowledge, Dunne recruited him as manager for his workshop which was building his stable biplanes. Fairey then moved to **Short** brothers and worked on seaplanes. In 1915 Fairey set up his own company, initially building Sopwith designs under licence, but then began to incorporate modifications, inventing trailing edge flaps and using these for the first time on a modified floatplane version of the Sopwith Baby biplane, which he named the *Hamble Baby*.

After the First World War Fairey became a prominent manufacturer and was at one time chairman of the Society of British Aircraft Constructors. Dissatisfied with the products on offer from British manufacturers, he imported the American Curtiss D-engine and the Reed metal propeller, upsetting his main customer, the Air Ministry, which resented the import of American equipment during the Depression. He also opened a factory in Belgium, Avions Fairey, in 1931. During this period, his biggest success was the Swordfish torpedo-bomber and dive-bomber intended for carrier operations, and which were needed in such quantities that many were built by other manufacturers. Although they were regarded as obsolete when the Second World War broke out, the aircraft nevertheless mounted a successful attack on the Italian fleet at **Taranto** in November 1940, putting three battleships out of action for the loss of just two out of twenty-one aircraft, and later became an invaluable anti-submarine aircraft operating from merchant aircraft carriers and escort carriers. The aircraft's successors, the Albacore and Barracuda, were not nearly so successful or well-loved, while the company's naval fighters, the Fulmar and Firefly, were too heavy to be successful in air-to-air combat. Rather better was the Gannet, originally an anti-submarine aircraft but later an airborne-early-warning aircraft, operated from carriers. The most successful design was probably the Delta 2, the last British aircraft to set and hold a world air speed record and which many believe inspired the Dassault Mirage III, and the Rotodyne, a vertical take-off compound aircraft that was too far ahead of its time.

Falklands Campaign (2 April–14 June 1982) Argentina had long laid claim to sovereignty over the Falkland Islands, or Las Malvinas, in the South Atlantic, attracted possibly by the fishing rights and valuable oil and natural gas resources. Argentine forces invaded the Falklands on Friday

2 April 1982. Initial landings by Argentine troops were from landing craft and smaller warships, including corvettes, and were followed by reinforcements flown in aboard the Fuerza Aérea Argentina's Lockheed C-130 transports, augmented by chartered civilian Fokker F27 Friendship airliners.

Landings on South Georgia, 1,500 miles from Argentina and governed as part of the Falkland Islands, also took place, using the ice patrol vessel *Bahia Paraiso*, 9,600 tons, with an Aérospatiale Puma and two Alouette III helicopters operating from the vessel. The Royal Marines machine-gunned the Puma until it retreated across a bay and crash-landed. They shot down one of the Alouettes.

When the news of the invasion reached London, it took just 72 hours for a Task Force to be hastily assembled and its first units put to sea. The Royal Navy centred the force around its two remaining aircraft carriers. The flagship was the larger of the two, the elderly HMS *Hermes*, which had been refitted with a 'ski-jump' so that she could operate the new British Aerospace Sea Harrier. The other carrier was the new, purpose-designed 'Harrier-carrier', HMS *Invincible*. Between them, these two ships carried twenty Sea Harriers. Later, this force was augmented by two landing dock assault ships, *Fearless* and *Intrepid*, fitted with stern docks that could flood to enable landing craft to be floated off, and helicopter landing platforms. A container ship, *Atlantic Conveyor*, was modified to carry helicopters.

Surprise was impossible. The departure of the Task Force was shown across the world on television. Many were pessimistic about the chances of regaining the Falkland Islands.

In the ensuing conflict, the British lost two destroyers, including the class lead ship of the Type 42 destroyers, HMS *Sheffield*, which sank after being hit by an air-launched Exocet missile, and two frigates. In terms of the success of the operation, the worst loss was that of the converted container ship, *Atlantic Conveyor*, which took most of the Task Force's troop-carrying helicopters with her. It meant that once ashore, British troops had to cross East Falkland, the more populous of the two main islands, on foot.

On 21 April a small British force was landed on South Georgia. An Argentine submarine, *Sante*

Fe, was so badly damaged by missiles, fired from a helicopter as South Georgia was retaken, that she had to be beached.

At no time could the Task Force bomb Argentine bases on the mainland. The attempts by the RAF to mount long-distance strategic bombing raids from Ascension Island using Hawker Siddeley Vulcan bombers were costly, needing twelve refuelling aircraft for each aircraft sortie, and did relatively little damage to the runway at Port Stanley, the islands' capital, although a radar station was destroyed on one attack. Nevertheless, Argentine use of the base was limited to Pucara light attack aircraft, leaving its air force and naval pilots operating from the mainland, 400 miles away, at a disadvantage. While the Argentine ground forces struggled to cope, their pilots showed great skill and courage, earning the respect of their opponents. Despite this, no Sea Harriers were shot down by enemy aircraft. On 15 June British troops entered Port Stanley and the Argentine forces surrendered.

One outcome was that planned cuts to the Fleet Air Arm were not fully implemented, eventually leaving the Royal Navy with three aircraft carriers, two of which are intended to be available for operations at any one time. The two assault ships were reprieved, and two replacements, HMS *Albion* and *Bulwark*, built. The Royal Navy also gained a helicopter carrier, specifically for commando operations, HMS *Ocean*.

Farman *See below*

Farman, Henry/Henri (1874–1958) and Maurice Alain (1877–1964) Anglo-French aircraft designers and manufacturers. Born in France to British parents, the brothers were both cycling enthusiasts. Maurice Farman, the younger and quieter of the two, was the first to take to the air, initially as a balloonist, and introduced his brother to aeronautics. Maurice met **Captain Ferdinand Ferber** and helped design the Kellner-Neubauer aeroplane in 1909. He opened his own factory in 1912 and began to compete with his brother's business, with his most successful product being the Longhorn, so named after its landing gear, which became one of the first great trainers. He designed First World War bombers.

Henry preferred to be known as Henri; he spoke little English and later took French nationality. His interest in cycling was soon extended to cars and with a third brother, Richard, he became a dealer, but his enthusiasm was blunted by a serous accident. Inspired by **Voisin**'s float-glider experiments, he bought his first plane in 1907 and by the following year was the leading pilot in France, earning his spurs by making the first circular flight in Europe at Issy on 13 January. Later the same year he made a 17-mile cross-country flight.

When Henri's second Voisin aircraft was sold by Voisin himself to **J.T.C. Moore-Brabazon**, without Henri's permission, he retaliated by establishing his own company at Billancourt and building the first of a series of successful biplanes. At the 1909 **Reims Aviation Meeting** he was the major prize-winner, taking 63,000 fr.

After Henri and Maurice merged their two companies in 1916 they produced the Farman Goliath, originally designed as a bomber, but postwar became one of the first large airliners. During the Great Depression years, they diversified into motor car production, but without success, and later the company fell prey to the wave of nationalisation that swept France in the immediate pre-Second World War years.

Farre, Henri (1871–1934) Pioneering French aviation artist. Living in Argentina at the outbreak of the First World War, Farre returned immediately to France and volunteered for the Aviation Militaire. He flew as an observer and bombardier and soon began to jot down sketches which he turned into oil paintings when off duty, using an impressionist style. He provided some of the best illustrations of the war in the air.

Fedden, Sir Alfred Hubert Roy (1885–1973) British engine designer. Fedden trained as an engineer. He worked for the Brazil-Straker Company from 1906, where he successfully persuaded his employers to build their own engines and was appointed chief engineer. **Rolls-Royce** and Renault engines were built under licence during the First World War for the aircraft industry, but postwar Fedden was instructed to design radial engines, with his first, the Jupiter,

being a success. In 1920, the company was acquired by **Bristol**, the airframe builder, and over the next twenty-two years Fedden headed Bristol engines and produced a series of well-regarded designs, including the Hercules and Centaurus.

Fédération Aéronautique Internationale (FAI) The international body responsible for verification and confirmation of all aerospace records. It was founded in 1905 by the **Comte Henri de la Vaulx** and for many years was based in Paris, but has since moved to Geneva. The FAI works through the national aero clubs and is responsible for notification of a new record, which originally had to be by telegram within two days. **Records** are divided into categories and today comprise spacecraft, as well as balloons, **gliders**, **airships** and aeroplanes of widely differing types, including model aeroplanes and **air cushion vehicles**.

Felixstowe British manufacturer. Felixstowe was the name given to the products of the Seaplane Experimental Establishment. Based on the work of **Glenn Curtiss** and **Charles Porte**, RN, the state enterprise produced a series of up-to-date maritime-reconnaissance flying boats for the RNAS during the First World War, after which most of the work was handled by the emerging private manufacturers.

Felixstowe-Porte F2A The first fruit of the collaboration between **Glenn Curtiss** and **Charles Porte**, RN, was this twin Rolls-Royce Eagle-powered biplane flying boat, with the lower wing on top of the fuselage, which entered service in 1917. The aircraft had a Porte hull and the wings of a Curtiss H12, and was manned by a crew of five. It was heavily armed for the time and could also carry a useful warload of bombs. *See* Tables 12–17 for aircraft performance.

Ferber, Capt Ferdinand (1862–1909) French pioneer. Commissioned into the French Army, Ferber began to take an interest in flight from 1899, building hang-gliders based on the work of **Otto Lilienthal**. He enjoyed little success, partly through not fully appreciating the techniques, but also due to the poor construction of the aircraft. Matters changed little after he contacted

Octave Chanute and as a result he switched to the **Wright** brothers' techniques, including wing-warping, but again poor construction held him back. Ferber's contribution to progress largely lay in opening the way for Chanute to communicate the Wrights' successes to European pioneers, and in helping **Ernest Archdeacon** and **Gabriel Voisin**. In 1909 he took part in the **Reims Aviation Meeting** under the name 'de Rue', but without success. On 19 September 1909 he was killed in a flying accident at Boulogne.

Ferguson, Harry George (1884–1960) British pioneer. A motor mechanic and motorcycle racer, Ferguson attended the **Reims Aviation Meeting** in 1909 and was immediately convinced that aviation was the industry of the future. He built his first aircraft based on the design of an Antoinette but encountered a seemingly endless series of problems, including difficulties with airscrews, of which he tried at least a dozen. He finally made his first tentative flight in the aircraft on 31 December 1909, flying just 400 ft. He spent the next three years attempting, without success, to improve his aeroplane, before turning his attention to the farming implements, on which his fame now rests.

Fiat/Fiat Aero *See* Finmeccanica

'Fido' Originating as the Fog Investigation Dispersal Operation (Fido), the RAF later proclaimed that it stood for 'Fog, Intensive, Dispersal Of'. The subject had been under discussion for years before the early experiments into Fido began in 1937 using alcohol, but they enjoyed little success. Fido was not ready for full operational use until January 1943, having adopted Haigas (Hartley Anglo-Iranian Gas) burners using petrol, which ran through pipes on either side of the runway. Fifteen RAF stations were so equipped and Fido was credited with saving 2,500 aircraft and 10,000 aircrew, at a cost of 30 million gallons of petrol.

Many frustrated airline travellers in the years that followed, before automatic landings in fog became possible, argued that Fido should have been introduced at the main airports, but neither aircrew nor airlines favoured this. Apart from the immense cost, the dangers to any aircraft that came off the runway, and to its passengers, were too great for peacetime or for civilian travellers.

Fieseler, Gerhard (1886–1987) German ace and manufacturer. Fieseler was one of the Military Air Services' aces during the First World War with twenty-two victories. Postwar Fieseler became a stunt pilot and in 1928 was one of the first to demonstrate the outside loop in the UK and France. He bought a glider manufacturer in 1930 and in 1932 renamed it the Fieseler-Flugzeugbau. One of his early products was designed by **Alexander Lippisch**: a delta monoplane with pusher and tractor propellers, known as the Vespe. The company was best known for the light utility Storch (Stork) of the Second World War, an army cooperation plane with a remarkable short-take-off performance. The factory also worked on both the V-1 and V-2 'revenge' weapons.

fighter/fighter-bombers The fighter evolved early during the First World War. It is the second oldest military aircraft type and the aeroplane that is most often the first to be replaced by missiles. Despite trials firing machine guns from aircraft before the First World War, the fighter reputedly emerged when the pilots and observers of scout aircraft started firing at each other with their service revolvers and rifles. The fighter itself later produced a number of offspring in the fighter-bomber, photo-reconnaissance fighter, interceptor and ground-attack aircraft.

It did not take long for suitable aircraft to be fitted with machine guns and these emerged as the first true fighters. The machine guns were often fired by the observer, usually sitting behind the pilot. In some aircraft the pilot could fire a forward-pointing machine gun, initially mounted in the upper wing which involved him standing up to fire it over the blades of the propeller disc. Deflector blades were fitted to the propellers of aircraft to allow the machine gun to fire through the disc, giving better control of the aircraft and more accurate fire. A major step forward was the propeller-synchronised machine gun, reputedly rejected by the Allies but offered by the Dutchman **Anthony Fokker** to the Germans. When the Central Powers acquired this and fitted it to the Fokker E.III fighter, it was the beginning of the

'Fokker Scourge', with the RFC pilots describing themselves as 'Fokker fodder'. An alternative to the synchronised machine gun with its interruptor gear was the pusher-propeller fighter such as the Airco DH2 and Vickers Gunbus, as well as the Farman, in which case the observer sat in front of the pilot and worked the machine gun. It did not take long for suitable Allied aircraft with propeller-synchronised machine guns to emerge.

While the rate of progress was much slower between the First and Second World Wars, a number of developments did take place. Slowly, monoplanes became the usual configuration for a fighter, although in 1939 and 1940 the RAF and the Fleet Air Arm still had Gloster Gladiator biplanes. Most fighters became single seat, although the British had a number of twin-seat fighters with a rear-gunner, until it became apparent that such aircraft were too heavy to be effective fighters. Enclosed cockpits became standard. As the fastest aircraft, fighters were among the first to have flaps and retractable undercarriages. Significant fighters at the start of the Second World War included the Hawker Hurricane and Supermarine Spitfire, the German Messerschmitt Bf109 with its propeller-boss fitted with a cannon, and later the Focke-Wulf Fw190, and the American Curtiss Hawk, Republic P-47 Thunderbolt and North American P-51 Mustang. Speeds rose towards the 400 mph mark, and armament improved from eight machine guns to either two cannon and four machine guns or four cannon.

One of the most significant developments of the war years was the advent of the night fighter, initially with the Bristol Beaufighter and then the de Havilland Mosquito, as well as the German Junkers Ju88, all of which were twin-engined aircraft with a radar operator. The Hawker Typhoon with anti-tank rockets became a potent element in providing close air support, while the Mustang and the Lockheed P-61 Lightning provided long-range fighter escorts. Many fighters were able to adapt to the fighter-bomber role with a 250 lb bomb under each wing, although the Consolidated Corsair operated off aircraft carriers with a 500 lb bomb under each wing. The Messerschmitt Me262 jet fighter appeared in 1944, but on Hitler's orders it was often confined to the bomber role, and was joined by the first

rocket-powered interceptor, the Me163 Komet. The British Gloster Meteor jet fighter entered service in 1945.

Not all of the wartime fighters had equal qualities. The Bf109 had speed and a high rate of climb, and with its propeller-boss cannon was a potent interceptor by the standards of 1939 and 1940. However, it was kept in production for too long and was dated by the later years, and it had a weak tailplane. The Hawker Hurricane was highly manoeuvrable with a tight turning circle, while the Supermarine Spitfire was fast and reasonably manoeuvrable, but also very strong, with its weakness being the landing gear that, in the naval Seafire, was not up to repeated carrier deck landings.

Following the war, many jet fighter designs appeared, including the SAAB-21, which had originated as a twin-boom fighter with a pusher propeller, and became the only fighter aircraft to be built in both piston and turbojet forms. The United States Navy received the compound Ryan Fireball with a piston engine and a ram jet to improve performance, while the Supermarine Attacker was the first jet specifically designed for carrier operation, although the first jet carrier deck landing was Cdr Eric 'Winkle' Brown's de Havilland Vampire landing aboard HMS *Ocean*. In the USA, the Lockheed F-80 Shooting Star entered service and was then followed by the Republic F-84 Thunderjet and the North American F-86 Sabre. In the Soviet Union, **Yakovlev** produced a number of jet fighters but his design bureau was eclipsed by Mikoyan-Gurevich with the successful series of MiG fighters.

The **Korean War** saw MiG-15 fighters, flown by Russian pilots, confront American F-86 Sabres, while the Gloster Meteor was already outclassed. The early jets did not always have it all their own way as was driven home when a British naval pilot, **Lt Peter Carmichael**, shot down a MiG-15 while flying a piston-engined Hawker Sea Fury.

The post-Second World War years saw increasing emphasis on interceptors able to climb quickly to reach high-flying jet bombers, on all-weather fighters and on ground-attack and fighter-bomber developments. Notable designs included the Dassault Mirage series of fighters, the flexible McDonnell F-4 Phantom II and Northrop F-5

Freedom Fighter, intended as a low-cost jet fighter for poorer countries, and the British Aerospace Harrier and Sea Harrier, with **V/STOL** and the Soviet MiG-21. The Americans then developed the air superiority fighter – something of a misnomer as this is the role of any fighter – and produced **variable-geometry** McDonnell Douglas F-15 Eagles for the USAF, and Grumman F-14 Tomcats for the USN and a number of air forces as well. When these proved too expensive they had to be augmented with the Lockheed Martin F-16 Fighting Falcon for the USAF and other allied air forces, and the Boeing F/A-18 Hornet for the USN and a number of air forces. The latter aircraft was originally a fighter but gained an attack role in its F/A-18C/D development.

British fighter development in the 1950s was badly disrupted by a belief that future fighters would be made redundant by the use of guided missiles. After producing the successful Hawker Hunter, the country had no successor for the English Electric Lightning, an aircraft with a remarkable rate of climb, but range and radar limitations, leaving Britain to buy the Phantom II.

A number of joint fighter projects have been introduced: the Panavia Tornado was a poor interceptor, with the design emphasis favouring the interdictor variant, while the Eurofighter 2000 Typhoon has taken some twenty years to get into service. It remains to be seen whether the US-led Joint Strike Fighter (JSF) project, being led by the Lockheed Martin F-35, will be the success that it is expected to be.

See Tables 12–17 for the speed of selected First and Second World War fighters.

fin Also known as the vertical stabiliser, the fin became an accepted part of aeroplanes and gliders from the **Wright** brothers onwards, but a number of flying wing designs have dispensed with this feature.

Finmeccanica Italian manufacturer. Major Italian aerospace and engineering group with diverse interests. It now includes the aviation ranges of both Alenia, formerly Aeritalia, which was in turn created from Fiat, and Aermacchi, as well as **Agusta/Agusta-Westland**, the helicopter manufacturer.

Fiat entered aviation in 1918 with the R-2 reconnaissance-bomber biplane. Between the First and Second World Wars the company benefited from the Regia Aeronautica being maintained at a greater strength than most European air forces, with Fiat producing a range of fighters designed by Celestino Rosatelli, including the CR20, CR30 and CR32 biplanes, as well as a number of light aircraft. In 1939 the company was producing the CR50 Freccia monoplane fighter. The Regia Aeroanutica also had the CR40 and CR42 fighters, the BR20M Cicogna bomber and G12 trimotor transport. Other notable wartime Fiats were the G52 and G55 fighters.

Founded as Macchi, later Aermacchi, the company came into prominence during the First World War with the Macchi M14 fighter and the Nieuport-Macchi M7 and M8 fighter-bombers; the M8 and the M9 were available for commercial and private use postwar. After Mussolini assumed power in 1923, the company produced seaplanes for the **Schneider Trophy Race**, including the M33 and M39, the latter being a mid-wing monoplane and winner of the 1926 contest. The Macchi C200 Saetta of the late 1930s was one of the better Italian fighters of the Second World War, despite engine shortcomings which were solved by re-engining with Mercedes Benz engines to produce the C202 and C205.

After the Second World War, trainer versions of the G46 and G59 were produced. De Havilland Vampire jet fighters were manufactured under licence by Aermacchi and Fiat, followed by the North American F-86 Sabre and partnership in the European production of the Lockheed F-104 Starfighter. Aermacchi produced its own design, the MB326, as an advanced trainer and light strike aircraft. Fiat produced its own G91, winning a NATO competition for a strike-fighter and entering production for the Italian and German air forces during the late 1950s. The MB326 was developed into the MB339. Finmeccanica is now offering the M-311, a turbofan jet trainer. Fiat's G222 light transport has led to the development with **Lockheed-Martin** of the C-27 Spartan tactical transport.

fixed-wing Any aeroplane that is not a helicopter is described as fixed wing, as opposed to **rotary-**

wing, even if it has **variable-geometry, variable-incidence** or folding wings, as many carrier-borne aircraft have so that they can be struck down into the hangar deck.

Flack, Gp Capt Martin (1882–1931) British

aviation medicine pioneer. Qualified as a doctor in 1908, Flack was commissioned into the Royal Army Medical Corps on the outbreak of the First World War. He took an interest in aviation and began to study the medical effects of flying. When the RAF was formed, Flack transferred to the Medical Service and became its first director of research.

flag carrier A close relation to the **chosen**

instrument although less restrictive in practice, as any one nation may have several flag carriers operating on different routes or, more usually, to different parts of the world. When the United Kingdom operated three flag carriers – BEA, BOAC and the private enterprise British Caledonian – the first was confined to the UK and Europe, the second operated long-haul, and the third flew to Africa as well as having a small UK domestic and European network. At the same time, France had Air Inter for domestic routes and Air France for international routes, except to parts of Africa and the Pacific served by the privately owned Union Transports Aeriens (UTA).

flaps Flaps are usually found on the trailing edge

of an aircraft wing, but there are also leading edge flaps, and the object is to increase both lift and drag during landing and take-off – the flap settings are different for landing with more flap required than during take-off. The early aircraft did not need flaps, but these became important as both speed and aircraft weight increased.

In 1915 **Charles Fairey** was building Sopwith designs under licence, but then began to incorporate modifications, inventing trailing edge flaps and using these for the first time on a modified floatplane version of the Sopwith Baby biplane, which he named the *Hamble Baby*. Later, the sleek all-metal Boeing 247 airliner of 1933 was among the first to employ flaps to reduce landing speeds without stalling.

Fleet *See* below

Fleet, Reuben Hollis (1887–1975) American

aircraft manufacturer and entrepreneur. After university Fleet qualified as a teacher and also joined the National Guard, the US Army's main source of reservists. He was mobilised during the First World War and put in charge of pilot training for the US Signal Corps, which included the aviation units. He also introduced an airmail service between Washington and New York.

His military experience taught him that the Curtiss Jenny, the main training aircraft, was difficult and even dangerous for novice pilots, so he set out to provide a safe training aircraft, founding his own aircraft company in 1923, the **Consolidated** Aircraft Corporation. His company grew and soon had a wide product range that included flying boats and bombers. Fleet, tired of problems with trade unions and high US taxes, sold the company just ten days before the Japanese attack on **Pearl Harbor**.

Fletcher, Vice Adm Frank Jack 'Black Jack'

(1885–1973) American naval commander. Fletcher gained a reputation for being over-cautious during the early naval battles in the Pacific in the Second World War, although this may have been largely due to the dominance of the aircraft carrier at a time when most naval officers on all sides had been trained to handle a battle between surface vessels. In December 1941 he delayed his force's arrival at Wake Island in order to refuel, and this allowed the Japanese to seize the island unopposed. However, in May 1942 he succeeded in turning back Japanese forces at the **Battle of the Coral Sea**, although the US suffered heavier losses than the Japanese. The following month he had his flagship sunk at **Midway**, allowing **Rear Adm Spruance** to take most of the credit for the USN's first great victory of the war. His real failings were at Guadalcanal in August 1942, where he left the US Marines ashore isolated by withdrawing his carrier force too early. He showed the same caution in the Eastern Solomons. He lost his command in October 1942, but returned for the invasion of Okinawa.

flight deck (1) The name traditionally given to the compartment on a cabin airline occupied by the pilots and, when such people existed, the navigator, flight engineer and wireless operator. The early airlines, even multi-engined aircraft such as the Vickers Vimy, did not have flight decks, but these became more commonplace during the 1920s and all new airliners during the 1930s were designed in this way. Today the term used is **cockpit**.

flight deck (2) The deck used for take-off and landing on an aircraft carrier (on smaller ships the term is usually helicopter deck or platform). The first ship to be completed with a through flight deck to minimise turbulence from the funnels and superstructure was the second carrier to be built, HMS *Argus*, converted in 1918 from a liner being constructed for an Italian shipping line.

floatplane Hydro-aeroplanes have either used floats, hence floatplane, or had their hull resting in the water, hence **flying boat**. The more common term for the former is 'seaplane', believed to have been coined by Winston Churchill when First Lord of the Admiralty.

The floatplane evolved from the float-glider, first built and flown in 1905 by **Gabriel Voisin** or **Ernest Archdeacon** and **Louis Blériot**, using a combination of the **Wright** brothers and **Lawrence Hargrave** designs, and which was successfully towed off the River Seine in Paris by a motorboat. The first flight of a powered floatplane was by **Henri Fabre** in 1910, and this was followed by the first truly practical floatplane, built in 1911 by **Glenn Curtiss** in the United States.

The term lingered on for some years for float conversions of landplanes, such as the de Havilland DHC-6 Twin Otter. While most such aircraft were civil, military aircraft also available with floats included the Fairey Swordfish.

flying boat A development from the early **floatplane**, but the big difference was that the hull settled in the water and acted as an undercarriage. The most important of the early pioneers was **Glenn Curtiss**, who built the world's first flying boat in 1912. He collaborated with the retired British naval officer, **Cdr John Porte**. Porte and

Curtiss designed and built the *America* flying boat with Porte intending to fly it across the Atlantic. The outbreak of the First World War brought an end to the plan, but Porte returned to England with authority to build Curtiss flying boats. A flying boat factory was established at Felixstowe, on the Suffolk coast, which also became a base for patrols over the North Sea. The base at Felixstowe turned into the Seaplane Experimental Station and it was one of its designs, the F5, built under licence by the **Short** brothers, that had the first metal hull.

Curtiss continued working in the United States, building the HS-1 and then the NC class. The NC-4 was the first heavier-than-air aircraft to fly across the Atlantic, albeit in stages via the Azores to Lisbon, in 1919.

Between the two wars was the period when the flying boat ruled supreme, with a large number of manufacturers producing civil and military designs, with the former doing much to open up the air routes of the world and make longer distance air travel a reality. Noteworthy aircraft included the Dornier Wal and then the giant DoX, as well as the trimotor Do24. In the United States, not only Curtiss but also **Sikorsky** and **Martin** produced a series of successful designs, including the Martin *China Clipper*, before **Boeing** produced the 314 for transatlantic services just before the Second World War broke out in Europe. During the war years, this aircraft flew regular transatlantic air services for the new British Overseas Airways Corporation (BOAC). Meanwhile, in the UK **Supermarine**, **Saunders–Roe** and Shorts produced the Supermarine Walrus amphibian, the Short Calcutta and Rangoon, and then the long-range Empire flying boat for the Empire Airmail Service operated by Imperial Airways. With so much of the world's surface covered by water, the lack of airfields and the poor reliability of the aircraft engines of the day, the flying boat was the ideal tool for the development of air services.

The Second World War saw the maritime-reconnaissance flying boat operated on anti-submarine warfare and search and rescue duties, including the Short Sunderland and, the most successful flying boat series ever, the Consolidated PBY-5 and PBY-6 Catalina. In Germany, **Blohm und Voss**, a shipbuilder, had taken up aircraft production and produced the Bv138 and Bv222 flying boats.

Postwar, the flying boat went into decline. The number of airfields had grown rapidly under the demands of wartime, the new turboprop and turbojet engines were offering much improved reliability, aircraft ranges were extended and the landplane was far more economical to operate than the flying boat. Shorts built the Sandringham and Solent as commercial developments of the Sunderland. Saunders-Roe produced the giant Princess flying boat with ten engines, but after four were built the project was abandoned as being too large for the market. Saunders-Roe also built the SR.A1 jet flying boat fighter, but this was abandoned after successful trials as it could never compete with carrier-borne aircraft. In the United States the Hughes Hercules, the largest wooden aeroplane ever built, nicknamed the 'Spruce Goose', made just one flight before being abandoned and put into storage.

For a period Martin continued to build maritime-reconnaissance flying boats, as did **Grumman**, with search and rescue amphibians for many years, while in the Soviet Union, **Beriev** continued to build flying boats and amphibians. In Japan, **Shin Meiwa** built the PS-1 maritime-reconnaissance flying boat in small numbers. **Canadair** built the 214 amphibian for fire-fighting duties, although other versions were also offered, and eventually many of these were converted to turboprop propulsion and then succeeded by the 414. Beriev also built aircraft for this role in later years.

flying bomb The predecessor of the stand-off guided missile, the flying bomb was effectively a device used during the Second World War. The Germans employed glider-bombs for the first time during the landings at Salerno, while they also used unmanned Junkers Ju88s which were controlled by Messerschmitt Bf109 fighters before being released towards the target. The Japanese used **kamikaze** aircraft flown on suicide missions by their pilots both to attack Allied warships and to counter the high-flying Boeing B-29 Superfortresses attacking Japanese cities. Later, Japanese Oka flying bombs were launched with their pilots from bombers, although the parent

aircraft could rarely get close enough to the target to be successful.

The V-1 revenge weapon launched by the Germans towards London and the south-east of England was a flying bomb, but also a predecessor of the cruise missile. Untargeted, it inflicted much damage, although not to any against targets of real strategic significance.

flying wing A concept meant to improve aerodynamic efficiency and also increase interior space. Much work was done on the flying wing by **Northrop** after the Second World War, but no commercial or military application resulted, although experiments with **lifting body** designs helped to pave the way for the US space shuttle. Currently, **Boeing** is working on a blended wing design (the BWB) intended for the air cargo market, with the possibility of a commercial aircraft ready for service late in the first quarter of the twenty-first century.

Flynn, John (1880–1951) Australian missionary and medical air service pioneer. An Australian cleric and physician, Flynn had travelled the Australian outback since 1911, providing medical care for dwellers in remote settlements and preaching. He usually travelled by camel, although in later years he used a car. In 1925, with the help of Queensland & Northern Territories Aerial Service, the predecessor of today's Qantas, he founded the Australian Inland Mission with the purpose of improving communication with remote farms and settlements, and to purchase an aeroplane to carry a doctor quickly over the vast distances. The service provided the basis for the Royal Flying Doctor Service of Australia.

Focke/Focke-Achgelis/Focke-Wulf German manufacturer. Focke-Wulf came into prominence during the interwar period after Germany restarted aircraft production. The founder, **Heinrich Focke**, soon fell out with the Nazi regime and worked on his own to produce the Focke-Achgelis Fa61 helicopter, which was not made full use of by the Germans, almost certainly due to financial, raw material and production constraints. The company he founded continued, under the leadership of its talented designer, **Kurt**

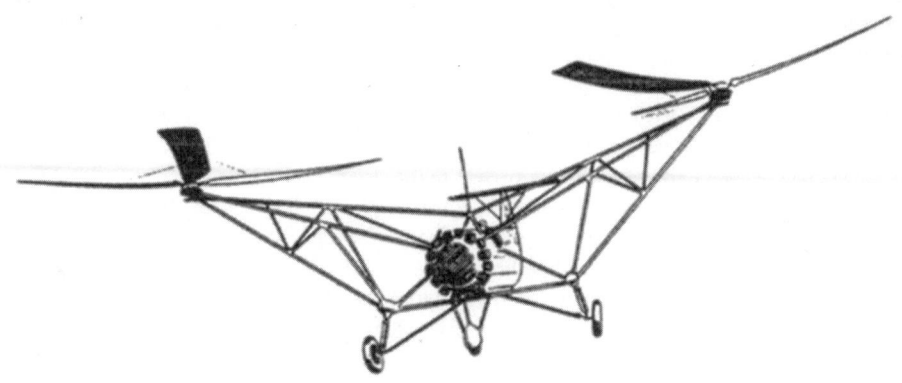

The Focke-Achgelis helicopter was capable of flight with the offset rotors providing stability, but it was not developed by the Nazis, probably due to pressure on budgets and industrial capacity that would have accorded an experimental machine a low priority.

Tank, initially producing the Fw44 Stieglitz training biplane, and the Fw58 Weihe (Kite), a twin-engined light transport, communications and navigational training monoplane. Before the outbreak of the Second World War, the Fw200 Condor airliner entered service with Deutsche Luft Hansa (*sic*), and during the war years this became the main Luftwaffe maritime-reconnaissance aircraft. The Fw190 single-engined fighter was the most successful Luftwaffe fighter of the war, with more than 20,000 built. Before the end of the war, the Ta152 appeared, designated as a Tank design and successor to the Fw190. The company also built a twin-boom, twin-engined reconnaissance aircraft, the Fw189. Postwar, the company became a subcontractor to a number of European programmes based on the licence-production of American designs before a merger with Wesser in 1963 to form Vereinigte Flugtechnische Werke, which **Heinkel** also joined in 1964.

Focke, Heinrich Karl Johann (1890–1979)

German aircraft designer. At the age of 18 Focke built his first glider. When the First World War broke out, he joined the German Military Air Service but was injured in a flying accident and discharged, and he returned to aircraft design. He took an engineering degree postwar, and helped to design a number of light aircraft. In 1924, with

Georg Wulf, he founded the aircraft manufacturer Focke-Wulf, initially building light aircraft and small airliners. Wulf was killed in 1927 flying an Ente trainer designed by Focke.

One of Focke's wisest moves was to recruit **Kurt Tank** in 1931, allowing Tank to design the company's range of fixed-wing aircraft and leaving Focke free to pursue his interests in **autogiros** and **helicopters**, including a licence-built Cierva design in 1933. At this time Hitler had come to power. Focke fell out with the new regime and his company was nationalised, although he was permitted to continue working on helicopters in a new company, Focke-Achgelis. His Fa61 helicopter of 1936 proved to be successful and the following year made the first helicopter flight of more than one hour. Focke designed several other helicopters, including one that was essentially a glider for observation flights from U-boats, but none saw widespread use during the Second World War, possibly due to Germany's constant shortage of raw materials and manpower.

Fokker Dutch manufacturer. After the death of the founder, **Anthony Fokker**, in 1939, the company was known officially as the Royal Netherlands Aircraft Factory. Fokker founded his enterprise in 1919 having designed a series of successful wartime fighter aircraft for the German Military Air Service. The first notable commercial design from the company was the F.VII, a single-engined airliner that appeared in the mid-1920s. Considerable success came with the development of a trimotor version, the F.VIIB/3M. This was followed by the twin-engined F.VIII, the F.IX and F.XX trimotors, and the F.XXII four-engined airliners before the outbreak of the Second World War. The company also built small numbers of military aircraft, although the Dutch belief in neutrality and the presence of a strong pacifist movement in the Netherlands, meant that production was limited, with the Royal Netherlands Air Force only having a small number of modern D.XXI fighters in service in 1940.

Production was interrupted by the war, but postwar, the company produced the S.11 Instructor basic trainer, as well as manufacturing British and American designs under licence. From the late 1950s onwards, great success followed the introduction of the twin-engined F27 Friendship, the first turboprop regional airliner, which was also built under licence in the United States by Fairchild-Hiller, although less successful was the jet follow-up, the F28 Fellowship. A brief amalgamation with **VFW** of Germany failed, and afterwards the company produced the F50, an updated and re-engined version of the F27, as well as the 100, a stretched and re-engined development of the F28, and a smaller version, the F70. The company went bankrupt in 2000 and attempts to revive it failed, although Rekkof was created to provide product support for the many Fokker aircraft still in service worldwide.

Fokker, Anthony Herman Gerard (1890–1939)

Dutch pioneer and manufacturer. Born in Java, Fokker returned home to the Netherlands with his parents at the end of the nineteenth century. After he had completed his schooling he trained as an engineer in Germany, choosing his school because it planned to build an aeroplane. The aeroplane crashed on its first flight, but Fokker was already convinced that he could do better and persuaded his parents to support him in establishing his own company in Germany. His first aircraft was the perhaps inappropriately named Spin, which fortunately did not live up to its name but actually flew well. Small volume military sales of the Spin

encouraged Fokker to remain in Germany once the First World War started. He was, in later years, to maintain that he offered his services to the Allies, and especially his propeller-synchronised machine gun that was able to fire straight ahead through the propeller disc, but this seems to have been a convenient lie. As it was, he produced a series of outstanding aircraft for the German Military Air Service, including his Eindekker monoplane and a triplane. It is difficult to be sure how much of this work was due to Fokker himself and how much to **Reinhold Platz**, who took over as chief designer, while Fokker's own great strength was as a salesman.

After Germany's defeat, Fokker was unable to build aircraft in the country. He was also forbidden to move his machinery out of the country, but he hired several long freight trains, bribed the border guards and, overnight, transferred his factory to the Netherlands.

Back in his home country with Platz, a series of commercial aircraft with tubular steel fuselages and cantilever wooden wings were produced, with the most notable being the F.VII/3M, a high-wing trimotor monoplane used for many pioneering and route-proving flights as well as by the early airlines. Despite the glut of surplus military aircraft and, later, the Great Depression, Fokker aircraft sold so well that he established a second factory in the United States, which he eventually sold to General Motors, whereupon it was renamed the General Aviation Corporation, and later became North American Aviation. All went well until one of his aircraft crashed in 1931, killing the famous football coach Knute Rockne. Orders were cancelled and the public refused to use his aircraft – a strange over-reaction considering the poor safety standards of the day.

Back in the Netherlands, both commercial and military aircraft continued to be built by Fokker, and in the late 1930s, the Douglas DC-2 was also assembled there. Fokker died from a throat infection in 1939.

Folland *See below*

Folland, Henry Phillip (1889–1954) British

aircraft designer and manufacturer. Folland was **Geoffrey de Havilland**'s successor as chief designer at the Royal Aircraft Factory, where his first design was the SE-4 biplane, apparently successful but eclipsed by his next aircraft, the SE-5 and the even better SE-5a, which confirmed his reputation. After the Royal Aircraft Factory team broke up, he worked first for British **Nieuport** and then for **Gloster**, designing the Gauntlet and the famous Gladiator, before designing the F.5/34 monoplane, advanced as a rival to the Hurricane and Spitfire. Despite his abilities, Folland remained a firm advocate of the biplane, suggesting that his potential was becoming limited.

It was not until 1937 that he established the company that bore his name at Hamble, near Southampton, which acted as a subcontractor throughout the Second World War. After his retirement in 1951 it produced the famous Gnat jet trainer, which achieved fame when used by the RAF's Red Arrows aerobatic team, and also when it became a potent light fighter with the Indian Air Force, which nicknamed it the 'Sabre Slayer' after its performance in conflict with neighbouring Pakistan.

Fonck, Capt René Paul (1894–1953) French fighter ace. Trained as an engineer, Fonke was an admirer of the early aeronauts. His background notwithstanding, when he joined the French Army in 1914, he was sent to dig trenches, and it was not until 1915 that he began flying training. He soon proved to be a natural pilot, and on one occasion forced an enemy aircraft to land and be captured. He downed six enemy aircraft in one day and he was renowned for his marksmanship, usually using no more than six rounds per victim. He ended the war as France's top-scoring fighter ace with 75 confirmed kills, but many believe that he was probably the greatest ace ever with more than 125, if unconfirmed kills are added.

Postwar, Fonck became a stunt flyer and like many others attempted to set record and trail-blazing flights, although an attempt to be first to fly from New York to France in a Sikorsky failed when the aircraft crashed, killing the other two crew members. In 1937 he rejoined what had become the Armée de l'Air as inspector of fighter aviation, reorganising France's fighter defences, but retired in 1939 due to ill health.

Ford American manufacturer. The Ford Motor Company entered aircraft production during the early 1920s with the Flivver, a single-engined, single-seat low-wing monoplane intended for the budget-conscious private flier, but then acquired Stout, and produced the Ford-Stout Pullman single-engined airliner in 1924, following this with the 5-AT Trimotor in 1930, capable of carrying up to twelve passengers. Despite the success of the Trimotor, aircraft production ended in the mid-1930s in the face of recession and strong competition from **Boeing**, **Douglas** and **Lockheed**, but the company remained a manufacturer of aero-engines for some time later, including licence-production of the Rolls-Royce Merlin at one of its UK factories near Manchester.

Forlanini, Enrico (1848–1930) Italian helicopter pioneer. Trained as a civil engineer, Forlanini completed a steam-powered model helicopter in 1877, which rose to a height of 42 ft on a flight that lasted for 20 seconds. He switched to the internal combustion engine in 1909 when he completed a dirigible. He does not appear to have pursued either of these flying-machines further, and spent the rest of his time working on hydrofoils.

Foss, Maj Joseph Jacob (1915–2003) US fighter ace. After joining the USMC following **Pearl Harbor**, Foss trained as a fighter pilot and took part in the Battle of Guadalcanal, so that by the end of 1942 he had amassed a score of twenty-three kills out of his eventual Second World War total of twenty-six. His score would have been higher but he was repeatedly sent on tours of the US to boost public morale.

Postwar, he was involved in general aviation and helped to organise the South Dakota Air National Guard, part of the USAF's reserves. He became involved in state politics, becoming governor, and later worked for KLM Royal Dutch Airlines in the USA.

Foulois, Maj Gen Benjamin D. (1879–1967) American advocate of air power. After joining the US Army in 1898, Foulois was commissioned in 1901 and became involved in aeronautics in 1908 when he joined the Aeronautical Section of the Signal Corps. He was trained on the army's first dirigible before being taught to fly aeroplanes in 1909 by **Orville Wright**, qualifying the following year. He then worked on developing aerial observation and radio communications techniques, which were seen as the main role of the aeroplane in wartime. After the First World War broke out in Europe, he was in command of US air units along the border with Mexico. When the USA entered the war, Foulois was sent to Europe to command what had become the US Army Aviation Section, but a clash of personalities with **Billy Mitchell** resulted in him being sidelined commanding support and training functions. Foulois never forgave Mitchell and played a leading part for the prosecution in the famous courts martial of the American officer for criticising the US Army.

Despite his disagreements with Mitchell, which owed more to two head-strong personalities than to differences in belief, Foulois was a strong advocate of air power, and on one occasion organised an air display at Mineola, Long Island, with 600 aircraft airborne at the same time. In 1934 he boasted to President Roosevelt that the US Army could provide a country-wide airmail service, but its cause was undermined by a spate of accidents that resulted in the important mail contracts being given to the airlines. Rather more positively, that was the year he took the bold step of advocating a long-range bomber with four engines, meaning that when the Second World War came, the USAAC, later the USAAF, was well placed for the exercise of strategic air power, with the Boeing B-17 Fortress. Foulois retired in 1935 and spent the rest of his life lecturing.

Fowler, Harlan Davey (1895–?) US aero-dynamicist. Relatively little is known about Fowler, despite his working for the Naval Aircraft Factory in the United States on the **Shenandoah** dirigible programme between 1922 and 1925. He moved into the private sector designing for Pitcairn, and followed this by working for **Fokker**'s US factory, for **Glenn Martin** and **Consolidated**. His one big contribution to aviation was the Fowler flap, which provides high lift on a small wing.

Frantisek, Sgt Josef (1914–40) Czech fighter ace. The Munich Agreement of 1938 was intended

to prevent the outbreak of war in Europe by forcing Czechoslovakia to cede the Sudetenland to the Germans, but Frantisek disobeyed orders, took off in his fighter, and strafed the occupying German troops. This was a serious offence that could have resulted in war between the two countries, a war that the Czechs were ill-prepared to fight, and Frantisek had to take his aircraft to Poland to avoid arrest. He joined the Polish Air Force, and shot down two or three Luftwaffe aircraft when Poland was invaded in September 1939. When Poland was defeated he fled to Romania, but was interned. He escaped to France via Syria and joined the Armée de l'Air, once again becoming a fighter pilot. After the fall of France in 1940, he escaped to the UK and joined the RAF, eventually becoming a member of No. 303 Polish Squadron, equipped with Hurricanes. He shot down seventeen German aircraft in just five weeks, giving him a total score of twenty-eight kills and making him the highest-scoring Czech pilot. He was killed in a landing accident on 8 October 1940.

Frantz, Sgt Joseph (1890–1979) French fighter ace. After learning to fly in 1911, Franz set an endurance record of 4 hours 27 minutes. He joined the Aviation Militaire in 1912 and at the outbreak of the First World War was posted to a Voisin squadron as a spare pilot. On 5 October 1914 while flying with his mechanic, Quenault, as a bombardier, he spotted an Aviatik over French territory; he manoeuvred so that Quenault could take aim and while the gun jammed after firing a few rounds, the Aviatik, attempting to escape, went into a spin and crashed. The two men became instant heroes. Postwar, Franz worked in the aircraft industry.

freedoms, air transport Although seldom referred to today, the Chicago Convention on Air Transport in 1944 established the basis for international air transport regulation in the postwar world. These were subsequently implemented by the **International Civil Aviation Organization** (ICAO). One of the main agreements from the Convention was the concept of 'five freedoms of air transport' – a further three freedoms were recognised but denied official support – they were:

The First Freedom allows an airline to operate over foreign territory without landing.

The Second Freedom allows an airliner to land at a foreign airport to refuel, or for any purpose other than the setting down or picking up of passengers, mail or cargo.

The Third Freedom allows an airliner to set down passengers, mail or cargo, having been taken on board in the airline's own country, at a foreign airport.

The Fourth Freedom allows an airliner to pick up passengers, mail or cargo at a foreign airport and fly them to its own country.

The Fifth Freedom allows an airliner to set down passengers, mail and cargo from a second country at an airport in the airline's own country, and then fly them on to a third country – in short, an international connecting flight.

The Sixth Freedom combined the third and fourth freedoms.

The Seventh Freedom is the right to fly passengers, cargo and mail between two countries using the airline of a third country.

The Eighth Freedom is the right to cabotage traffic, which is the right to carry traffic between two domestic points within a foreign country.

An example of the eighth freedom was the right exercised by Pan American and British European Airways to fly passengers from West Berlin to destinations within West Germany during the Cold War, although the Soviet Union always denied that West Berlin was a part of West Germany. The deregulation of air services within the European Union has made this once rare privilege commonplace, with the Irish airline, Ryanair, operating domestic services within Great Britain, as well as international services from that country.

Frise, Leslie George (1897–1979) British designer. Instead of joining the RNAS in 1918, Frise was persuaded to join the **Bristol** Aeroplane Company, initially working on such projects as a balance control for ailerons, the Frise aileron, which maintains control despite extremely high angles of attack and helps to prevent spin. He also designed aircraft such as the Bristol Fighter, Bulldog, Blenheim, Beaufort and Beaufighter.

After the Second World War, he worked for the comparatively small Hunting Percival concern, working on the Pembroke transport and the Provost trainer.

fuel early attempts at flight used a variety of fuels, including coal, coal gas, gunpowder and battery power, but it was the internal combustion engine and petrol that proved the best combination and the only one to combine light weight with adequate power. The Germans during the 1930s and in the Second World War used diesel aircraft engines on some aircraft, and the tendency for untreated diesel fuel to 'wax' in very low temperatures may have adversely affected the performance of some Luftwaffe aircraft during Operation Barbarossa. Initially, the turbojet showed that it could work efficiently with gasoline or kerosene, but the latter proved to be much safer as it does not explode on ignition, although at first it was more expensive. **Lord Brabazon** campaigned after the Second World War against the use of gasoline in turbine engines. He demonstrated by pouring out some kerosene, which he called paraffin, standing in the puddle and dropping a flaming match into it. After the match fizzled out he stepped away from the puddle, challenging someone to try the same with gasoline, which he called petrol.

Fuji Japanese manufacturer. The company moved into aircraft production in the early 1950s with the re-establishment of the Japanese armed forces as 'self-defence agencies', producing the Beech T-34 Mentor trainer under licence and then using its design as the bases for the LM-1/2 Nikko four/five-seat cabin monoplane. An intermediate trainer, the T-1, was built between 1958 and 1963 as a replacement for North American T-6 Harvard trainers. Later, Fuji built the Bell 204 Iroquois helicopter under licence and also produced other **Bell** designs for the Japanese market, as well as constructing a number of its own light aircraft designs.

Fullard, Capt Philip Fletcher (1897–1984) British fighter ace. Between May and November 1917, Fullard scored at least forty-two kills and some estimates maintain that his score could have been as high as fifty-three, flying both an SE-5 and a Nieuport. He was injured in a soccer match at his airfield and invalided back to the UK. Postwar, he made a publicity tour of the United States and later served with the RAF in Germany. During the Second World War he served in an administrative role with the RAF.

fuselage The main part of an aeroplane to which the wings and tailplane are attached and which is usually referred to by the insurance market as the 'hull'. The very early aeroplanes did not have a fuselage as such, but this became apparent on the Blériot and Antoinette aircraft, and by 1912 the concept was standard for all aircraft types.

G

Gabreski, Francis (1919–2002) Polish-American fighter ace. In 1940 Gabreski abandoned his preparations to study medicine in France and returned to the United States, where he joined the USAAF and was posted to a Curtiss P-40 Kittyhawk squadron based in Hawaii. He was one of the few fighter pilots to get into the air when the Japanese attacked **Pearl Harbor**. In 1942 he was posted to the UK to study RAF fighter tactics and spent some time with No. 315 (Polish) Squadron, before returning to the USAAF to command the 61st Pursuit Squadron with Republic P-47 Thunderbolts. His experience with the RAF proved its worth, with Gabreski shooting down thirty-one Luftwaffe aircraft. Posted to Europe, he was shot down on 20 July 1944 over enemy-occupied territory, and became a prisoner of war.

Postwar, he remained with what became the USAF and saw action over Korea flying North American F-86 Sabre jet fighters, shooting down 6.5 MiG-15s. On retirement, he became a transport consultant.

Gabrielli, Prof Guiseppe (1903–87) Italian designer. A student of **Theodore von Kármán** at Aachen, on graduation Gabrielli went to work for **Piaggio** in 1929, before moving to **Fiat** in 1931. He produced almost 130 designs while at Fiat, of which around sixty entered production, including the first Italian jet fighter, the G-80.

Galland, Gen Adolf (1912–96) German fighter ace. Galland began his flying career as a commercial pilot for the German national airline Deutsche Luft Hansa (now Lufthansa), but joined the Luftwaffe at the time of the **Spanish Civil War** and took part as a member of the Condor Legion, flying more than 300 ground-attack sorties. With this invaluable experience, when he returned to Germany early in 1939 he was able to instruct pilots.

In spring 1940, just before Germany invaded Denmark and Norway, Galland was posted to a fighter unit as adjutant of Jagdgeschwader (JG) 27. His first kill in air combat came on 12 May when he shot down a Belgian Aviation Militaire Hurricane over Belgium. After the fall of France, he was given command of Gruppe III of JG 26, which he led throughout the Battle of Britain, and when **Werner Moelders** died in 1941 he was given command of the Luftwaffe's fighters while still only 29 years old. This brought him into the political arena and he spent much of his time trying to persuade first his superior **Goering** and then the Führer himself that the role of the fighter should be aerial superiority rather than ground attack, but the latter role fitted well with the **blitzkrieg** strategy of 'lightning war', coordinating air and ground forces, while Hitler's obsession with the theory meant that the first German jet fighter, the Me262, was often used for light bombing duties. The Führer's irritation resulted in demotion, but he was spared an even worse fate because of his hero status with the German public, and was given command of a jet fighter squadron. He ended the war with 104 confirmed kills.

In 1955, he was recalled to rebuild the Luftwaffe when Germany was once again allowed armed forces and then later became an airline director.

Garnerin, André Jacques (1769–1823) French parachute pioneer. After the French Revolution Garnerin joined the Committee for Public Safety and was sent to Austria on a secret mission, but was captured and imprisoned in Budapest in 1795. He had developed an interest in ballooning, inspired by the **Montgolfier** brothers' ascents, and while in custody he worked on a plan to escape using a parachute, but was repatriated to France before his scheme could be implemented.

Back in France, he resumed his experiments with balloons and then with parachutes, before making the world's first parachute descent from a balloon on 22 October 1797. His parachute was attached beneath a balloon and was of ribbed parasol design, 24 ft across, with Garnerin standing in a bucket under the parachute canopy. He made his descent from 3,000 ft before a large crowd, injuring his leg slightly when the bucket hit the ground. Despite his experiments, making the first descent was an act of outstanding courage. Apart from the injured leg, the only other side-effect was that the oscillations of the parachute during the descent had made him ill. Garnerin then started to tour, making demonstration parachute descents including the first in England in 1802 where he met **Robert Cocking**. Napoleon appointed Garnerin the French Republic's official aeronaut.

By this time his wife had already become both the first woman to pilot a balloon and, in 1798, the first to make a parachute descent, while a niece, Eliza Garnerin, became the first woman professional parachutist, performing at fairs and shows.

Garros, Roland (1888–1918) French fighter ace. While in Paris studying to become a concert pianist, Garros had his head turned by the excitement of the **Reims Aviation Meeting** in 1909, and began flying training. His first aeroplane was a Clement-Bayard Demoiselle which he flew at Issy. On qualifying, he became a display pilot and joined the Mosiant International Aviators in 1910, visiting the United States. He made the first non-stop flight from France to Tunisia, 453 miles across the Mediterranean, on 23 September 1913.

The outbreak of the First World War caught Garros in an uncomfortable position – inside Germany advising on the use of aircraft in warfare. On the first night of war he took his aircraft out of the hangar, started the engine and took off for Switzerland, flying in the dark over the Alps. He then returned to France and joined the Aviation Militaire as a scout pilot with Escadrille MS23. He was one of the first to fit deflector plates to his airscrew so that he could fire through the propeller disc, and on 1 April 1915 shot down a German Albatros. He followed this with four more victories over sixteen days to become a hero. The story is that he was credited with being the first ace – until this time a sporting term – and the definition of an ace as having five or more kills dates from this time.

This mounting tally of German aircraft was brought to an abrupt end on 18 April 1915 when German ground fire damaged his engine's fuel lines and he had to make an emergency landing behind enemy lines. The Germans captured his aircraft before he could destroy it and discovered the secret of the deflector plates. Garros became a prisoner of war until escaping in 1918. He was retrained and took to the air again, but air combat had moved on and once again he was a vulnerable novice, being shot down while flying a Spad in October 1918.

gas balloons *See* Charlière

gas turbine In its essence, this is a mechanical power plant that rotates in reaction to a current of gas passing through or over it, and as the gas can include the earth's atmosphere, this also defines a turbojet, turbofan, turboprop or turboshaft. *See also* jet.

Gastambide, Jules (?–1944) French engineer. Trained as a civil engineer, in 1902 Gastambide was the owner of an electricity generating station in Algeria. While taking a holiday in France he agreed to support financially a new engine design being built by **Léon Levavasseur**, who showed his gratitude by naming the engine after his patron's daughter, Antoinette. The engine lived up to expectations, powering racing motorboats and a new company was created in 1906. **Louis Blériot** joined the two men as a partner, but dropped out the following year when the decision to build aircraft was made. The first aircraft, a **canard** with a single engine driving twin pusher propellers, was not completed, but the second was a tractor monoplane named after Gastambide and another director, Mengin, and known as the Gastambide-Mengin I. After testing at Bagatelle in the Bois de Bologne in 1908, it was modified and given the far more elegant name of Antoinette II. It made the first passenger-carrying flight by a monoplane in August that year.

After the First World War, Gastambide and Levavasseur designed a monoplane with a variable camber wing using leading and trailing edge flaps of advanced design. It was built by Jean Latham, **Hubert Latham**'s cousin. The aircraft was largely overlooked but could have revolutionised aviation at the time.

general aviation Any aspect of aviation that is not military or airline, and includes police, agricultural, training, air ambulance, air taxi or business and executive aviation, as well as private flying. The initial flights by the pioneers would have been regarded as general aviation.

General Dynamics American manufacturer. The company itself appeared in 1952 when Electro Dynamics was renamed, but a connection with aviation dates from as early as 1908 and the establishment of the Gallaudet Aircraft Company. The company acquired many of the leading names in aircraft manufacturing, including Thomas, founded in 1909; **Consolidated**, founded in 1923 and which became the corporation's Convair division; **Stinson**, founded in 1925; Thomas-Morse, founded in 1929, and Vultee, founded in 1932, while for a period **Canadair** was owned. The most famous products were the F-111 **variable-geometry** strike aircraft used by the USAF and RAAF, and the F-16 Fighting Falcon, now produced by **Lockheed Martin**.

General Electric American manufacturer. One of the world's three leading aero-engine manufacturers, the company has undertaken turboprop, turbojet, turboshaft and turbofan production since the end of the Second World War, and its products have been produced under licence in the UK, where they were manufactured by **Bristol Siddeley**, and in France, where the licence was held by **SNECMA**. It is a partner with SNECMA in the CFM series of engines. The CF-6 advanced technology engine was used in the Airbus A300 and the McDonnell Douglas DC-10, and for many years the company was a leading supplier to Airbus.

Genet, Dr Edmond-Charles (1763–1834) French-American visionary. Genet was the chief interpreter for the French government at the time of the Revolution, after which he emigrated to the USA where he became the holder of the first aeronautical patent to be issued in the United States. His patented idea was the highly improbable one of using aerostats to raise and lower canal barges rather than waste time and water using locks.

Gibbs-Smith, Dr Charles Harvard (1909–82) British aeronautical historian. Gibbs-Smith worked initially at London's Victoria and Albert Museum in 1932, before being employed by the Ministry of Information during the Second World War. He gained a reputation for accurate and meticulous research and had several books published on aviation history, confirming the achievements of **George Cayley** and the **Wright** brothers. He become curator of London's Science Museum.

Gibson, Wg Cdr Guy Penrose (1918–44) British bomber leader. Commissioned into the RAF in 1937, Gibson was posted to No. 83 Squadron flying Hampden bombers when the Second World War broke out. He was transferred to a Beaufighter night-fighter unit before being moved back to bombers with No. 106 Squadron, flying the Avro Lancaster four-engined heavy bomber.

In 1943 he was asked to lead a new squadron specifically formed for special duties, which became No. 617 Squadron. The role envisaged for the squadron was a raid on the dams in the River Ruhr using a new form of air-dropped mine, more usually known as the 'bouncing bomb'. On the night of 16/17 May 1943, he led his squadron against the Möhne, Eder and Sorpe dams, with Gibson dropping his first bomb against the Möhne; it took four more bombs to breach the dam. He then took the surviving aircraft to the Eder, which was destroyed after three bombs, but the Sorpe remained intact. Not only did Gibson show superb leadership during the attack, he also remained present throughout the raid circling low both to distract the enemy AA fire and to direct the attacks by following aircraft, a role later to be known as that of the master bomber. For his part in this attack he was awarded the VC to add to his existing DSO and DFC.

An immediate public hero, Gibson toured the USA to raise support for the British war effort. He declined offers of a staff job, but the reward for his desire to remain on active service was to be killed in action when his plane was shot down during a raid on München-Gladbach and Rheydt on 19 September 1944.

The raid on the dams was successful, but while the British believed that it would deprive German industry of hydro-electric power, most of Germany's electricity needs were met by coal-fired power stations and it was the lack of water for heavy industry that was the main impact of the operation. *See also* **Dam Busters**.

Giffard, Henri (1825–82) French aeronaut and designer. An engineer, Giffard attempted to build a viable dirigible using a 3 hp steam engine of his own design which was attached to a cat-walk suspended from the 144 ft-long elongated gas bag of his airship. On 24 September 1852 this craft ascended and travelled from Paris to Trappes at 6 mph. The low speed meant that the craft was far from practical and only minor changes to direction could be made, not full turns, but this airship was by far the best-performing at the time.

While Giffard continued to experiment, his work was hindered by an eye infection that left him blind and depressed. He committed suicide by taking chloroform.

Glaisher, James (1809–1903) British scientist. Glaisher headed the meteorological department at the Royal Observatory at Greenwich, east of London, and was interested in weather forecasting, at the time an almost unknown science. He realised that the use of hydrogen balloons had potential and formed an association with **Henry Coxwell**, one of Britain's leading balloonists. Between 1862 and 1865 the two men made a number of ascents, of which the most spectacular was on 5 September 1862 when they reached an altitude of 34,000 ft. Their craft was loaded with scientific instruments and as they ascended, both men began to feel faint. Glaisher passed out and the envelope became covered in ice. They only survived because Coxwell was able to pull the gas venting valve rope with his teeth. Originally their instruments showed that they had reached an altitude of 37,000 ft, but scientists later corrected this to 34,000 ft.

Glaisher was a founding member of the Meteorological Society and in 1866 helped to found the Aeronautical Society, now the Royal Aeronautical Society.

glider An unpowered fixed wing aeroplane that can be used for gliding or soaring, in the past sometimes referred to as a sailplane. The inventor of the glider was the Englishman, **Sir George Cayley**, who designed and built a series of model gliders before constructing a full-sized glider that in 1849 took off carrying a 10-year-old boy after being towed downhill into a stiff breeze. In 1853 he sent his coachman, John Appleby, on a similar glide across a valley. No control was applied in either case, and it was not until 1891 that a German, **Otto Lilienthal**, produced a series of hang-gliders in which the pilot hung by his shoulders from the glider and controlled it by moving his body. Lilienthal built two biplane and five monoplane gliders before being killed in a gliding accident. One of his followers, **Percy Pilcher**, also enjoyed some success with hang-gliders before being killed, and had been working on a powered glider.

An Englishman, **F.H. Wenham**, also conducted several experiments with gliders during the nineteenth century, and from these evolved a theory about weight distribution in aircraft. The American, **Octave Chanute**, developed and flew gliders, influencing the **Wright** brothers who, after experiments with models, built and flew three gliders between 1900 and 1902 before embarking on their first powered aeroplane.

After the First World War, gliders were used in tests for the feasibility of rocket propulsion in Germany, including a number by the Rhon-Rossitten Gesellschaft in 1928 and by the German Sailplane Research Institute in 1938. During the 1920s and 1930s, gliding was used as a means of training pilots in Germany without infringing the restrictions on German military aviation imposed by the **Treaty of Versailles**.

The Second World War saw the introduction of large troop and even vehicle-carrying gliders. These were used initially by the Germans for the assault on the Low Countries, including the daring attack on the Belgian fort of Eben-Emael, and later were used in the invasion of **Crete**. In turn, the Allies used gliders for the landings in Sicily, although bad weather meant that a number landed in the sea, and then for the invasion of Normandy, as well as at **Arnhem** and for the crossing of the Rhine. The largest glider operated was by **Messerschmitt** and led to the Me323 Gigant powered transport. Large British and American glider designs also influenced the Bristol 170 Freighter and Fairchild C-123 Provider transports of the postwar period.

The introduction of the **helicopter** made the glider redundant, as the helicopter could be reused time and time again during an operation, and indeed in the **Suez Campaign** in 1956, troop-carrying helicopters returned to the aircraft carriers offshore with the first casualties.

Gliding has become a low-cost means of flying and many maintain that the meteorology that is so important to the glider pilot results in a higher standard of airmanship. High performance gliders have been developed for competition flying, while at the other extreme, the **hang-glider** has made a reappearance as a cheaper means of gliding.

glider-bomb A low-cost and low-technology predecessor of the stand-off bomb or the air-to-surface missile, the glider-bomb made its operational appearance during the Second World War. At Salerno, Henschel Hs293 glider-bombs were launched unsuccessfully, on 25 April 1943, against British escort carriers operating offshore to provide fighter defence over the beachhead. Two days later, another attack against a British corvette resulted in the ship being damaged. In these cases, the bombs were launched from Dornier Do217 bombers.

Gloster British manufacturer. The company first came into prominence in 1923 with the Grebe fighter biplane, and a development in 1925, the Gamecock. The Gloster IV seaplane was a runner-up in the 1927 **Schneider Trophy Race**, although the gauntlet fighter-biplane of the 1930s was slower than the IV. The Gladiator, designed by **Henry Folland**, was the RAF's last fighter biplane and still in service in 1940, seeing action over Norway and France, while the Sea Gladiator was operated off HMS *Eagle* in the Eastern Mediterranean and three of these aircraft provided the sole fighter defence of Malta during summer 1940. During the Second World War, Gloster produced other company's designs, including the Hawker Tempest. Gloster also built Britain's first jet-powered aircraft, the E28/29, known as the Gloster Whittle, and followed this with the world's second operational jet fighter, the

Meteor, and while this aircraft established several postwar speed records, by the time of the **Korean War**, it was outclassed. Gloster next produced the RAF's first all-weather jet fighter and the first operational delta wing fighter, the Javelin. The company became part of **Hawker Siddeley** Aviation in 1960.

Goering, Reichsmarschall Hermann Wilhelm (1893–1946) German air strategist and politician. Having enlisted in the infantry in 1912, Goering applied to join the Military Air Service (MAS) when war broke out in 1914, but failed the entrance exam. Nevertheless, he served with distinction even though he found life in the trenches extremely difficult due to arthritis. Eventually he realised his ambition of joining the MAS through the intervention of a friend. Despite the earlier rejection, once in the MAS Goering turned out to be a natural pilot with a penchant for painting his aircraft all white, and by the end of the war he was commanding the fighter ace **Manfred von Richthofen**'s former squadron and had a score of twenty-two Allied planes to his credit.

Postwar, with a defeated Germany in turmoil and communist insurrection breaking out in a number of cities, Goering joined the Nazi Party and became a close friend of its leader, Adolph Hitler, becoming involved in the Beer Hall Putsch of 1923. After Hitler took power in 1933, Goering became his deputy and while he had specific responsibility for the new air force, the Luftwaffe, he was also the founder of the Gestapo and of the concentration camp system. He enjoyed the trappings of power, adopting an ostentatious lifestyle, including an all-white uniform.

Goering's belief in air power remained unabated even though it led to costly German strategic mistakes: at the time of Dunkirk he insisted that the Luftwaffe rather than the army should finish off the British and the French, but it failed to do so and well over 300,000 men escaped to continue fighting. During the **Battle of Britain** he switched targets and effectively started the **Blitz** of London and other British cities, giving the RAF a much-needed respite. That the Blitz was cut short was not his fault, but down to Hitler's invasion of the **Soviet Union**. Like Hitler,

Goering ignored strategic realities, and tempted fate with the preposterous declaration that no enemy plane would fly over the Reich, but British aircraft had flown over Germany from the start of the war and by autumn 1940 Berlin had been bombed in retaliation for a raid on London. By the time the war ended, he had lost Hitler's confidence and Karl Doenitz, commander-in-chief of the German Navy, became the Führer's successor, leaving Goering to be captured and imprisoned awaiting trial as a war criminal. He received a death sentence, but cheated the hangman by swallowing a cyanide capsule.

Goupy, Ambroise (1876–1951) French pioneer. After having his first aeroplane built for him by Voisin in 1908, which managed a few tentative hops, Goupy worked with **Mario Calderara** and **Louis Blériot** on his own design, the *Goupy II*, which incorporated a Blériot fuselage with biplane mainplane and tailplane, and was built at Blériot's works. The aircraft's sole distinguishing feature was that it was the first tractor biplane. After modifications and renaming as the *Goupy III*, it flew reasonably well and entered limited production for a flying school.

Government Aircraft Factory (GAF) Australian Manufacturer. Based at Fisherman's Bend, New South Wales, GAF was formed in 1946 from the Department of Aircraft production and later produced the Nomad utility aircraft as well as carrying out assembly and overhaul work. It was acquired by Rockwell International of the United States in 1995.

Grade, Hans (1879–1946) German pioneer. An engineer, Grade founded his own motorcycle factory in the early years of the twentieth century. Inspired by reports of the early pioneers, he built a triplane in 1908, but this seems to have been unsuccessful. Rather better was his tractor monoplane of 1909, which gave him the distinction of making the first flight in Germany of a German aircraft. Despite designing and building further aircraft, Grade and his company faded into obscurity.

Grahame-White, Claude (1879–1959) British pioneer. Grahame-White's first passion was for motor vehicles. The scion of a wealthy family, he qualified as an engineer and by 1909 was running his own Renault dealership in London and, coincidentally, selling **Blériot** headlamps. At the **Reims Aviation Meeting** in 1909 he was impressed by Blériot's machine and bought one, and when Blériot refused to take the time to teach him to fly, he taught himself, becoming the holder of British certificate No. 6. A year later he had become one of the UK's best known pilots and attempted the London to Manchester night flight for which the *Daily Mail* was offering a prize, but was beaten by **Louis Paulhan**. A natural businessman, he opened flying schools at Brooklands and Hendon, and at Pau in France.

Grahame-White was anxious that his country should realise the potential and the threat of aviation, and in 1912 he started a campaign design to arouse public awareness, flying across England in a Farman biplane on which was painted the rallying cry 'Wake up England', outlined in light bulbs.

On the outbreak of the First World War, he joined the RNAS and among his operations was one against German bases in Belgium, but he then left the service to start his own aircraft factory. Postwar, he returned to his first love, motor vehicles, and started his own company which failed. He lost his base at Hendon to the government, but managed to obtain compensation, and then moved into the London property market.

Granville, Zantford D 'Granny' (1901–34) American designer. Self-taught and unqualified, Granville was sacked from his first, and last, job in aviation. He had been inspired by a flight in a Curtiss flying boat in 1921, and although he then opened a garage, he sold out in 1925 and went to work for the company running Boston airport. He was sacked after a dispute with the proprietor and set up a mobile aircraft repair business, using an old car converted to carry his tools. It was from his experience of working on a variety of aircraft that he learnt about aircraft design.

In 1929 Granville designed his first aircraft, a two-seat side-by-side biplane with flaps on all wings and an overhead control column, and to complete the novelty he conducted his first test flight in darkness at 03.00 hours on 3 May

1929, possibly to avoid interference from his four brothers who had helped him to build the aircraft. The aircraft was a success, and 'Granny' Granville and his brothers were able to form the Gee-Bee Company, producing a series of designs that swept the board in air races throughout the USA. The run of successes, although spectacular, was short, and in 1933 the company's products were involved in an unfortunate series of accidents, not all of which were due to the aircraft, but orders stopped and the factory closed. Before this happened, Granville had started to experiment with **canard** aircraft. After the company folded, he opened a design office in New York and appeared to be about to restart production when he was killed flying a Gee-Bee, which stalled at low level when he attempted to avoid a group of workmen standing in the middle of the runway. His brothers remained in the aircraft industry.

Greece Air Campaign (1941) For the Greek campaign in the Second World War, an initial four RAF squadrons were transferred to the Balkans from North Africa, where they had achieved aerial superiority over Italian forces. One interesting aspect of the campaign was the use by the RAF of a 'secret' air base at Paramythia, used by No. 30 Blenheim and No. 37 Wellington Squadrons to attack Italian forces in Albania, and these were later joined by No. 815 Naval Air Squadron with its Swordfish for attacks on Italian shipping in the port of Valona. The base was so remote that fuel had to be flown in by Douglas Boston bombers, but losses due to accidents and enemy action were high. As Axis forces advanced, the base had to be abandoned on 17 April 1941.

The cost of transferring so much of the RAF's strength to Greece from North Africa meant that the RAF was left with just six squadrons with which to stem the initial advance by the Afrika Korps, which quickly reversed the gains made by the Eighth Army against Italian forces. In Greece, nine squadrons with less than 200 Blenheims, Gladiators, Hurricanes and Lysanders faced more than 1,200 Luftwaffe aircraft of the latest types. The outcome was a foregone conclusion, with heavy losses. The few surviving aircraft were evacuated to Crete.

Green, Charles (1785–1870) British balloon pioneer. On 19 July 1821 Green made the first ascent in a hot air balloon using coal gas, in a stunt designed to celebrate the first anniversary of the coronation of King George IV. Coal gas was much cheaper than hydrogen and readily available as it was being piped to light street lamps. He later sat astride a pony lifted on a platform hung beneath a balloon on 29 July 1828.

Despite these stunts, he also made a number of significant ascents, with the most famous being the 480-mile night aerial voyage from London to Weilburg in the German Duchy of Nassau. This made his reputation and the ballon was subsequently named the *Great Balloon of Nassau*. Less happily, the balloon was used for **Robert Cocking**'s first parachute descent on 24 July 1837. Cocking jumped when the balloon reached 5,000 ft and released the parachute, but the parachute immediately folded and he fell to earth. He died of his injuries within a few minutes of hitting the ground.

Grey, Charles Grey (1875–1953) British aviation journalist. Dublin-born Grey studied engineering and then joined the staff of the motoring magazine *Autocar*, which at the time also reported on developments in aviation. He was sent to Paris in 1908 to cover the Aeronautical Salon, where he was so impressed by the potential of the aeroplane that on his return he pressed his publishers to launch a new magazine, *Aero*, which he edited until 1911, leaving to found *Aeroplane*. He edited this magazine until 1939. He also edited *Jane's World's Aircraft* between 1916 and 1941.

As a journalist, Grey was incisive and perceptive, never short of criticism over the state of aviation in the UK, which made him many friends and many enemies, some of whom regarded his criticism as unpatriotic when it was intended to be quite the opposite. In later years, *Aeroplane* specialised in commercial aviation only, before being acquired by its long time rival *Flight*, and became a monthly magazine aimed at enthusiasts.

Griffith, Dr Alan Arnold (1893–1963) British turbojet designer and vertical take-off pioneer. Griffith worked for the Royal Aircraft Factory before moving to do research into structural fractures at the University of Liverpool, where he eventually became involved in turbine research. He laid the foundations for the axial flow turbojet in a paper published in 1926, *An Aerodynamic Theory of Turbine Design*. He joined **Rolls-Royce** in 1939 as chief scientist on its jet engine development programme, with his work showing fruit in the postwar period when it led to the Avon and Conway turbojets. He was also a pioneer of vertical take-off and in 1954 he directed the so-called *Flying Bedstead*, which used two Nene engines to lift a test platform. The work led eventually to the Short SC1 vertical take-off aircraft, although it was a test programme and the aircraft did not enter production, allowing the first practical V/STOL aircraft to be the Harrier, which used the different system of vectored thrust for vertical take-off and landing.

Grob German high-performance glider manufacturer that has made a successful move into building light aircraft, mainly for training, with extensive sales for the G115 and G120 two-seat aircraft, mainly built of composite materials.

ground attack The concept of ground attack dates from the First World War, mainly with attacks against enemy airfields and the aircraft parked there. **Junkers** produced an early all-metal monoplane for this role.

During the Second World War, aircraft were evolved especially for this type of duty. They were more rugged than straightforward fighters or even many fighter-bombers, and included the Commonwealth Aircraft Boomerang and the Hawker Typhoon and Tempest, and in the Soviet Union the Ilyushin Il-2 Stormovik. Refinements to ground-attack and anti-tank operations involved sending fighters to strafe enemy airfields and aircraft in a role known as 'fighter ramrods'. It soon became clear that on this type of action only one pass could be made over heavily defended airfields as by the time an aircraft was ready to make a second attempt, the AA gunners would have got its altitude and speed and their defensive fire would be so much more deadly.

Grumman *See* Northrop/Northrop Grumman

Grumman, Leroy Randle (1895–1982) American engineer and manufacturer. An engineering graduate from Cornell University, Grumman initially worked for the New York Telephone Company until America entered the First World War, when he joined the USN with the ambition of becoming a pilot. He was wrongly diagnosed as having flat feet, and so at first he was rejected. He eventually qualified as a flying instructor, but was then posted to the Naval Aircraft Factory at Philadelphia as a test pilot, where he met **Grover Loening**, the chief designer. Postwar, Grumman was taken on by Loening as an engineer at his own factory, where he stayed until it was sold in 1929.

It was at this stage that Grumman decided to start his own factory with a group of business associates and financial backers, with the latter including Loening. Desperate to keep the new factory busy during the Great Depression, Grumman took on any work available, building floats, canoes and vehicle trailers from aluminium, and in this way they eventually were awarded a USN contract. As the years progressed, the company became increasingly associated with a long series of carrier-capable aircraft for the USN, many of which were also adopted by the Royal Navy's Fleet Air Arm, which during the early years of the Second World War was desperately short of high performance aircraft. It also manufactured superior light aircraft for business users or wealthy private flyers, and a long series of amphibians.

Guggenheim, Daniel (1856–1930) American patron of aeronautical science. Although moderately wealthy from their business activities, the Guggenheim family finally achieved considerable wealth from their investments in silver mines in California. Guggenheim believed firmly that philanthropy was the duty of the rich, and when through his son, a First World War naval aviator, he learnt that there was a need to fund aerodynamics research and training at the University of New York, he was easily persuaded to provide a donation of US $500,000 (£125,000 at the then rate of exchange, more than £2.5 million at today's values). This resulted in the birth in 1926 of the Daniel Guggenheim Fund for the Promotion of Aeronautics, for which the funding eventually reached US $3 million, training engineers and scientists and helping research into the development of many advanced devices for aircraft and rockets.

Gulf War, Iraq and Iran (1981–89) The war between Iraq and Iran started in 1979 and continued throughout the 1980s. It was an inconclusive struggle between two more or less evenly matched opponents, both with considerable oil wealth, but with neither having the benefit of an indigenous aircraft industry. The Iraqi Air Force had been purchasing Soviet equipment, with MiG-23 and MiG-25 aircraft in service alongside a number of Chengdu F-7s, developments of the MiG-21. Relations with the West improved during the war years as Iran was viewed as the greater threat, and Iraq was able to buy helicopters from France, the USA and Germany, as well as Dassault Mirage F1EQ attack aircraft. Iran moved closer to the Soviet Union during these years, buying Sukhoi Su-24 strike aircraft and MiG-29A interceptors, as well as Ilyushin Il-76 and Antonov An-74 transports. The pace of operations fluctuated and was sometimes heavy, but the conflict ended in 1989 with no clear outcome.

Gulf War (1991) Sometimes referred to as the 'First Gulf War', although many historians reserve that title for the conflict between Iraq and Iran, this war was caused when, on 2 August 1990, Iraq invaded Kuwait, over whose territory it had long staked a claim.

Faced with the overwhelming might of Iraq's armed forces, and having little room in which to fight and delay the invasion, Kuwait's own armed forces were soon overwhelmed. The forces gathered initially for the defence of Saudi Arabia and then for the liberation of Kuwait were referred to as the 'Coalition' forces. In addition, the essential command and control mechanisms vital to creating an effective operational force out of so many different national forces were based on the tried and tested systems of the **North Atlantic Treaty Organisation** (NATO). The backbone of the combined air, land and sea operation was provided primarily by the United States, but with strong support from the United Kingdom and France. Many other nations also provided forces, including a number of the Arab states.

The two stages of the operation were known as 'Desert Shield', protecting Saudi Arabia, and 'Desert Storm', the campaign to liberate Kuwait. The British armed forces referred to their role as 'Operation Grandby'. The earlier conflict between Iraq and Iran was widely believed to have weakened the armed forces of both countries, but, as events proved, any weakness was exaggerated.

Although forces started arriving in Saudi Arabia and offshore in the Gulf within days of the invasion, the need to assemble substantial ground forces with heavy armour and to stockpile substantial quantities of munitions, fuel and spares, meant that it took some time before the conflict could start. The war began with Coalition air attacks on 17 January 1991, preparing for the start of the ground war on 23 February. A feature of the early days of the conflict was that cruise missiles were used extensively for the first time, with astonishing accuracy.

For the first time, the air war started with an attack by eight AH-64 Apache attack helicopters of the US Army's 1st battalion, 101st Aviation Brigade. These destroyed Iraqi air defence radar, creating a black hole corridor between two Iraqi radar stations. The priorities for the Coalition air forces were to neutralise Iraqi airfields, thus gaining air supremacy, and then to attack other strategically important targets. The first wave of attacks was at night, and despite the large number of targets available, the air attacks had to be staggered. This was partly to avoid the problems of congestion with so many aircraft available to the Coalition, partly to maintain steady pressure on the Iraqi Air Force around the clock, and last, but by no means least, to avoid IFF (identification, friend or foe) hazards with so many different types of aircraft from a wide number of air forces and air arms. The greater use of 'smart' or stand-off weapons by the USAF also helped to ensure both accuracy and lower aircraft and aircrew losses. On the other hand, the use of the JP233 runway denial weapon by the RAF's Tornados was a weakness, as the aircraft had to fly straight and level while the JP233's varied munitions load was dropped over the target.

Strike aircraft operated under the protection of three E-3 Sentries, with combat air patrol provided by USAF and RSAF F-15 Eagles, and RAF and RSAF Tornado F3s. Defence suppression was by F-4G 'Wild Weasel' Phantoms, with radar jamming by USAF EF-111A Ravens and USN EA-6B Prowlers.

While some Iraqi aircraft put up a fight and were shot down, most of the air force's aircraft were sent to Iran – transformed into something approaching an ally, for safety. Not all of them were returned at the end of the conflict.

The USN deployed aircraft carriers, including the USS *Kennedy*. It was the only navy to deploy aircraft carriers during the Gulf War – the Royal Navy did not send any of its Invincible-class carriers, ostensibly because they were designed for a different kind of war, but the limited range of the Sea Harrier would have meant that these ships would have had to have been within range of Iraqi missile attack. In any event, they were not needed as sufficient ground bases were available.

This was a short but violent conflict, taking just 100 hours of fighting to eject Iraqi forces from Kuwait. It ended on 26 February.

Gulf War (17 March–7 April 2003) Unusually, Iraq was not invaded by the Coalition formed to liberate Kuwait, and so, while the country was defeated, the regime remained intact. There was no peace agreement, not even a peace conference. UN sanctions were applied as the regime continued to oppress its opponents within the country, and there was evidence of genocide against minorities. British and US aircraft had to remain in the area, mounting strike missions against Iraqi munitions plants and defence installations. As the situation deteriorated, the United States and its allies prepared to invade the country and depose the dictator, Saddam Hussein.

Heavy air attack preceded the invasion, which was led on 20 March by forces moving over the border with Kuwait while helicopter-borne troops seized oil rigs offshore and landed troops on the enemy-held coastline. Cruise missiles were used, with 300 fired from US surface ships and British submarines, while others were fired from Boeing B-52 bombers flying from RAF Fairford in England. The war lasted three weeks, during which the Iraqi army and the Republican Guard suffered large-scale desertion, even though many of those who attempted to desert were executed. With most of its heavy equipment destroyed, even

before the ground war started, Iraqi resistance crumbled. Bridges over the rivers Euphrates and Tigris were seized before they could be destroyed.

The demand on the US and its allies was considerable, especially as many of the countries involved were heavily committed to operations in Afghanistan, invaded two years earlier.

gunship A development by the US armed forces during the **Vietnam War**, initially with heavily armed helicopters with air gunners firing from the open cabin door. The next stage was to adapt fixed-wing aircraft with machine guns and cannon set to fire through the window openings, and initially a number of Douglas C-47 transports were so modified, becoming AC-47, but it soon became plain that high-winged aircraft were vastly superior. A number of different types were used, including the Fairchild AC-119 and AC-123, but the most enduring has been the Lockheed AC-130 Hercules, which has more recently seen service in Afghanistan. A single aircraft can bring down a devastating hail of fire on counter-insurgency operations.

Gurevich, Mikhail I (1882–1976) Soviet aircraft designer. Born in Kursk, Gurevich graduated as an engineer from the Paris Ecole Supérieure de l'Aéronautique where he was in the same year as **Marcel Bloch**. He completed his studies at Kharkov in 1925 and in 1929 was assigned to help Paul Richard, a French designer who had opted to work for the Soviet Union, although the design team only stayed together for a year. In 1937 Gurevich was appointed head of design at Moscow's Aircraft Factory No. 1 and in 1940 he began a long association with **Artem Mikoyan** from which sprung a long series of fighter aircraft, beginning with the MiG-1 of the Second World War.

Gusmão, Bartolomeo Lourenço de (1686–1724) Brazilian balloon pioneer and visionary. Having trained for the Roman Catholic priesthood in Lisbon, de Gusmão experimented with a series of small hot air balloons and was eventually, in 1709, invited to demonstrate one of his balloons before King John V of Portugal. The small balloon, the *Passarola*, ascended briefly before catching fire and dropping in flames. Nevertheless, King John was so impressed that de Gusmão was awarded all patents in flight and granted exclusive rights to further development, which he appears to have never used. For many years, drawings purporting to show the *Passarola* as an open boat beneath a billowing sail were dismissed as fantasy. It could be that his work was no more significant than setting alight the tissue wrappings from biscuits and causing them to ascend.

Guynemer, Capt Georges Marie Ludovic Jules (1894–1917) French fighter ace. During the First World War Guynemer was rejected by the French Aviation Militaire twice on health grounds, but eventually succeeded in entering as a mechanic and managed to train as a pilot. On 19 July 1915 he scored his first victory. When squadrons were organised, his, the N3, was nicknamed the Cigones, or storks, and became known for producing many good pilots. While Guynemer scored fifty-four kills, his record was somewhat tarnished by being shot down seven times, once by an artillery shell passing through his aircraft, and a number of landing accidents. Noted for his aggression in the air, he flew into cloud while chasing a German aircraft, and was never seen again. The Germans claimed to have shot him down, but of this there was no proof.

gyroplane *See* autogiro and de la Cierva

H

Haenlein, Paul (1835–1905) German engineer. In 1865 Mainz-born Haenlein patented a semi-rigid airship, which he later built and which made an ascent in 1872 at Brunn in Austro-Hungary. He used coal gas as a lifting agent and to power a 3.6 hp internal combustion engine, which must have reduced the duration of any ascent considerably. The airship remained tethered and little is known about further development.

Hafner, Raoul (1905–?) Austrian helicopter pioneer. Hafner started his experiments with helicopters during the 1930s, working with Bruno Nagler. In 1933 he visited the UK to demonstrate a single-seat machine and decided to stay, setting up his own company in 1935. That same year he developed an improved **autogiro**, incorporating for the first time collective and cyclic pitch control in the rotor hub. In contrast to many of the helicopter pioneers, his work entered production during the Second World War, with unpowered autogiro units that could be towed carrying troops. In 1944 he was offered the role of head of the helicopter department at Bristol Aeroplane, where his work eventually bore fruit as the Bristol 171 Sycamore light helicopter.

Hall, Robert Leicester (1905–91) American engineer and test pilot. After working for **'Granny' Granville** as a stress engineer, Hall set up his own company in early 1932 with the financial support of Marion Guggenheim. His first aircraft, the *Bulldog*, was unreliable, although it finished sixth in the Thompson Trophy in 1932. Hall then worked briefly for the light aircraft manufacturer **Stinson**, and then for **Grumman**.

Hall, Sir Arnold Alexander (1915–2000) British engineer and industrialist. Born in Liverpool, Hall originally intended to become an electrical engineer, but was so convinced by the lectures of Sir Melvill Jones, Professor of Aeronautical

Engineering, that he eventually graduated in aeronautics, despite fainting during the examinations with appendicitis. He moved into research, initially at Cambridge, where he helped **Frank Whittle** in building the jet engine, being responsible for stressing the compressor. In 1938 he was appointed Principal Scientific Officer of the Royal Aircraft Establishment (RAE) at Farnborough. Remaining at Farnborough during the Second World War, he was involved with aerodynamic research and then with developing and building wind tunnels for speeds of up to 600 mph. He also helped to develop a gyro-electric gun sight that automatically worked out ranges and deflections, enabling the RAF to double its rate of kills.

Postwar, Hall became Zaharoff Professor of Aviation at the University of London, and in 1947 was appointed a member of the Air Safety Board. In 1951 he returned to Farnborough as Director of the RAE, where he led the investigations into the failures of the de Havilland Comet airliners, correctly proving that metal fatigue was to blame. He was knighted in 1954. In 1955 he joined the board of **Hawker Siddeley** and became chairman in 1963. During his time with the company it developed the Harrier V/STOL jet fighter and the Hawk advanced trainer, and also chaired the committee overseeing the development of the engines for the Concorde supersonic airliner. He remained with the company when its aerospace activities were removed and merged with those of BAC to create the nationalised **British Aerospace**.

Halsey, Adm William F. 'Bull' (1882–1959) American naval airman and commander. Graduating from the US Naval Academy in 1900 with an indifferent record as a student, Halsey did not qualify as a pilot until after the First World War. In 1941 he was a vice-admiral and the most senior carrier admiral in the Pacific. His aircraft carriers were at sea when **Pearl Harbor** was attacked and this enabled him to take the initiative immediately, attacking Japanese-held islands early in 1942. With the official title of Commander of Carriers, Pacific Fleet, from April 1942, he was partly responsible with **Doolittle** for the daring raid on Japan launched from the USS *Hornet*, which distracted the Japanese from their original objectives. He missed the **Battle of Midway** because of illness, but from then on proved to be an aggressive commander and leader of the carrier forces in the Pacific. His nickname 'Bull' reflected his toughness and enthusiasm for battle as much as his rugged appearance. He was promoted to admiral in November 1942. To allow intervals for planning, the USN attack carrier force in the Pacific was known as the Third Fleet when commanded by Halsey and the Fifth Fleet when commanded by Spruance. He was in command of the carriers at **Leyte Gulf**, but his desire for active combat lured him into attacking the Japanese decoy carrier fleet, and later his judgement was questioned after he took his fleet into two severe typhoons, losing three destroyers in one of them and with several of his carriers suffering considerable damage. Nevertheless, his career was unaffected and on 2 September 1945 the Japanese surrender was signed aboard his flagship, the battleship *Missouri*. He was promoted to the five-star rank of fleet admiral in December.

He was a highly regarded and well-liked fighting admiral, but doubts remain about his abilities as a strategic planner and his precipitous behaviour.

Hamel, Gustav (1889–1914) British pioneer pilot. The son of German parents, Hamel learned to fly in 1910 and became the first Englishman to loop and the following year carried the first British air mail, flying from Hendon to Windsor to celebrate the coronation of King George V. In 1913 he announced plans to fly across the Atlantic using a specially-built Martin-Handasyde monoplane, but the following year he disappeared in an accident while flying across the English Channel.

Hamilton, Charles Keeney (1881–1914) American stunt pilot. After leaving home in Connecticut to seek adventure in 1899, Hamilton met Israel Ludlow, a New York solicitor who experimented with kites and gliders towed behind boats and motor cars, and offered to be his test pilot. This was hardly an auspicious start to a flying career as the kites and gliders frequently ended their flights by crashing. His next move was to join **Frederick Baldwin** who allowed him to pilot his *California Arrow* airship, which started Hamilton on a four-year stint as a showman flying dirigibles and making parachute descents. He visited Japan in 1909, but returned to the United States after learning about the **Reims Aviation Meeting**. **Glenn Curtiss** gave him lessons on one of his aircraft at Hammondsport. Despite not having qualified as a pilot, in the absence of Curtiss on business, Hamilton took one of his aircraft for a lengthy flight and after Curtiss had got over his anger at the 'joy ride' he hired Hamilton as a display pilot. He was also allowed to fly stunts in return for sharing his fee with Curtiss.

Hamilton was a reckless pilot who flew in any weather and led an equally uncontrolled lifestyle. He was sacked by Curtiss in a dispute over money owed to the designer, and subsequently Curtiss won a court judgment against his former pilot. In 1912 Hamilton ceased flying because of poor health. He died in 1914.

Handasyde, George Harris (1877–1958) British manufacturer. In 1908 Handasyde formed a company called Martinsyde with H.P. Martin, intending to manufacture aeroplanes. Their first designs were based on the Antoinette monoplane and were faster with less drag. The third aircraft was sold to **Thomas Sopwith**. They sold two aircraft to the British Army in 1912, followed by fighter biplanes for the RFC during the First World War. They also built the Elephant bomber.

In 1920 Handasyde set up his own company, but it collapsed in 1924. Nevertheless, he returned to aviation in 1928 to work for Desoutter, where he modified the Koolhaven Coupé for the British market.

Handley Page British manufacturer. Founded by **Sir Frederick Handley Page** in 1909, the company produced a number of aircraft before the outbreak of the First World War, including the

HP5 'Yellow Peril' monoplane in 1911, and the HP6 of 1912, before building a biplane, the HP7, in 1913. During the war, the company produced the HP O/400 twin-engined heavy bomber biplane, which appeared in 1916 and was one of the first successful heavy bombers. Postwar, the company produced a number of military designs, but the first notable aircraft of the interwar period was the HP42 biplane commercial airliner of 1930. During that decade, the company produced the HP50 Heyford bomber and the HP52 Hampden, known as the 'Flying Pan Handle' because of its shape, for the RAF. A tailless aircraft, the HP75 Manx was also flown experimentally.

The Hampden was one of the RAF's more effective bombers at the outset of the Second World War, but later the Halifax became one of the three heavy bomber types operated by the service, although by the end of the war many had been switched to target towing and transport duties.

Postwar, the company produced the Hermes four-engined airliner for BOAC and the Hastings, a four-engined transport, for the RAF. A light transport was the four-engined Marathon, a high-wing monoplane, and its successor became the prototype for the twin-turboprop Herald airliner. **Miles** Aircraft was acquired in 1948 and operated briefly as Handley Page (Reading) before being absorbed by the parent company. The military connection was maintained during the late 1950s and early 1960s by the Victor, one of the trio of four-engined jet bombers designed to deliver Britain's independent nuclear deterrent.

No new defence contracts were awarded to the company during the 1960s in retaliation for its refusal to take part in the industry mergers inspired by the British government in 1960. Unable to launch a major airliner project without state assistance, the company instead launched the HP137 Jetstream, a small twin-turboprop aircraft for executive and feeder airliner use, taking up to eighteen passengers. Unfortunately, cash-flow problems during development and early production led to the company's collapse, but Scottish Aviation, which became part of **British Aerospace**, built the aircraft as the Jetstream 31 and later in its development, the stretched Jetstream 41, both of which sold well worldwide.

hang-glider Pioneered by **Otto Lilienthal** in Germany and **Percy Pilcher** in England and Scotland, the hang-glider has seen renewed interest in recent years as a low-cost means of gliding. Powered hang-gliders have also paved the way for the microlight, ultra-light aircraft.

hangar Essentially a shed for storing and maintaining aircraft, some attribute the first hangar to the **Samuel Pauly** and **Urs Egg** who started to build an airship at Brompton in London, but this was really no different from any other structure used for what would have been a substantial project by the standards of the day. With the advent of the airship, which was extremely difficult to handle in high winds, the hangar became a necessity, although at first the term 'airship shed' was widely used. One of the largest hangars was in the UK at Cardington, Bedfordshire.

Light aircraft see relatively little use, so hangar accommodation is useful to protect them from high winds that may overturn them. For large commercial aircraft, hangars are needed only for major maintenance, and in some cases the tailplane is left outside through a gap in the doors because of the high cost of accommodating ever larger aircraft. At sea, the difficulty of conducting maintenance work on deck, and the need to protect aircraft from spray, means that carrier-borne aircraft need to be 'struck down' into the hangar deck of a ship. Larger aircraft carriers often have two hangar decks, one above the other, and during the 1920s and early 1930s, many had flight decks leading from the hangar decks to enable aircraft to take off without having to be put on deck lifts to take them to the flight deck. As aircraft sizes and weights grew, the hangar deck take-off became impractical as it was impossible to provide a long enough take-off run.

Unusual hangars were the small structures appended to the conning tower of submarines capable of operating aircraft, such as the British M2 and French *Surcouf*, and a number of Japanese boats, some of which could accommodate two aircraft. Aboard the M2, much was made of the fact that the inner and outer hangar doors could not be open at the same time so that sea water could not flood into the submarine, but the system did not work and in 1932 she sank with all hands. Today, frigates and destroyers usually have a hangar so that they can operate one or two helicopters.

Hanriot, René (1872–1925) French designer and manufacturer. The son of a wealthy family, Hanriot had established a reputation as a racing driver when he became interested in aviation, and started to build a monoplane in 1907. He exhibited his aircraft at the 1909 Salon de l'Aéronautique in Paris, where it won acclaim for its clean lines. He opened a flying school at Bethaney in 1910 although still unable to fly himself.

At the outbreak of the First World War, Hanriot switched to biplanes, but was refused orders by the French Aviation Militaire as they regarded his aircraft to be inferior to those of **Nieuport**; his business survived by exporting to Belgium and Italy. Postwar, he switched to all-metal aircraft, but died suddenly and his firm was taken over by his son.

Hargrave, Lawrence (1850–1915) Australian pioneer and inventor of the **box kite**. A first-generation English emigrant to Australia, he qualified as an engineering draughtsman; he also explored New Guinea. He became an assistant astronomer at the Sydney Observatory, then in 1883 an inheritance left him free to experiment with flying-machines.

In 1884 that he published his studies into wing design, proposing that an efficient wing should have a centre of pressure located at around 25 per cent of its chord. He appreciated the significance of aluminium for lightness and the importance of dihedral and ailerons, and the superiority of curved wings compared to flat wings. Some credit him with inventing the rotary engine (not to be confused with the Wankel of more recent times), and he certainly built a working model. He was best known, however, for his discovery of the box kite as an efficient and strong lightweight design for high lift, flying his first model in 1893. Later, using a train of four box kites, he lifted himself 16 ft into the air. His work was published and well known in both the United States and in Europe, which he visited on a lecture tour in 1899. Eventually his work proved too expensive and he abandoned it.

Harmon, Clifford Burke (1868–1944) US millionaire and pioneer. A property millionaire and developer from New York, Burke took up ballooning as a sport suitable for a wealthy gentleman, and won a number of balloon races before setting an endurance record of 48 hours, 26 minutes, 30 seconds in 1909. He then bought an aeroplane from **Curtiss** and set out to fly at exhibitions and in races, including participation in aviation meetings in 1910 at Los Angeles and at Harvard-Boston, where he flew a Farman. Also that year he made the first flight across Long Island Sound. He helped others enjoy his enthusiasm for flight in 1926 when he founded the Harmon International Trophy for achievement in aeronautics.

Harmsworth, Alfred *See* Northcliffe, Lord

Harper, Harry (1880–1960) British aviation journalist. The son of a magazine editor, Harper followed his father into journalism, working on a local newspaper and eventually moving on to a national newspaper as an entertainment critic. He had, meanwhile, developed a keen interest in aviation, and in 1906 wrote to a number of wealthy businessmen looking for sponsorship for construction of a glider he had designed. One of those to whom he wrote was Lord Harmsworth, proprietor of the London *Daily Mail*, who turned his request down after having the glider design evaluated by experts. Some time later, however, he contacted Harper and offered him a position as the world's first aviation correspondent.

Harper was well qualified for his new role, already having many contacts among the pioneers, and it was Harper who proposed that the newspaper should sponsor aeronautical achievements which not only provided good copy for the newspaper, but did much to advance flying in the early years. Harper was also a prolific author on aviation.

Harris, ACM Sir Arthur Travers 'Bomber' (1892–1984) British bomber strategist and leader. Having emigrated to Rhodesia when he was young, Harris joined the infantry on the outbreak of the First World War and saw action against German forces in West Africa before returning to the UK and joining the RFC, where he became a fighter pilot. He remained in the newly formed RAF after the war, and served in Palestine and the US as well as playing a part in the development of the policy of 'air control' in Mesopotamia (present-day Iraq) using bomber transports. It was here that the nickname 'Bomber' was gained.

On the outbreak of the Second World War, Harris was commanding No. 5 Group in Bomber Command, before being appointed deputy chief of the air staff in 1941. He became commander-in-chief of RAF Bomber Command in February 1942. Harris was a strong proponent of bomber warfare and blind to the requirements of the other services or other theatres of war, which led him to demand the use of Coastal Command aircraft. He has been criticised for his policy of area bombing, but that in itself is unfair as the technology of the time meant that accurate bombing was difficult, and when it was possible, was restricted to a number of highly trained crews. On the other hand, he was resistant to change and to new ideas, such as the Pathfinder Force, and suspicious of what he described as 'panacea targets' such as oil and transport. All in all, he commanded and defended his men at a time when the bomber force was the only means the UK had of tackling Germany directly. The bombers could not guarantee victory, but they made an effective contribution.

He retired in 1946. Knighted in 1943, he was ignored in the victory honours list but was awarded a baronetcy in 1953.

Hartmann, Col Erich Alfred (1922–93) German fighter ace. Hartmann joined the Luftwaffe in 1940 and trained as a fighter pilot. He first flew in combat with JG52 over the Soviet Union, and, unusually, remained with the unit throughout the war, scoring the incredible total of 352 confirmed kills, making him the highest scoring fighter pilot ever.

The Soviet forces were so desperate to have this potent foe disposed of that they put a price on his head, contrary to any of the rules of war. He was captured at the end of the war and sent to a prisoner-of-war camp where he was subjected to hard labour, contrary to the Geneva Convention, and not released until the USSR bowed to international pressure in 1955.

On his release, Hartmann immediately joined the newly reformed Luftwaffe and played a part in its reconstruction.

Hawker, Harry George (1889–1921) British designer. Born in Australia, Hawker left school at 12 years old and worked to save his fare to the UK, planning to go into aviation, but on his arrival could only find employment in the motor industry. His luck changed in 1912 when he joined **Sopwith**, working long hours to save the money to pay for flying lessons. In October 1912 he won the British Michelin Cup by flying for 8 hours, 23 minutes. In 1913 he set an altitude record, and then won the Mortimer Singer Amphibious Prize flying a Sopwith Bat Boat.

Back on the ground, he designed every one of the First World War Sopwith scout and fighter models and then gave each its first test flight. When the Sopwith Triplane was ready, he looped it three times in succession to show his faith in it.

Postwar, with MacKenzie-Grieve as navigator, Hawker flew the Sopwith entrant in the transatlantic contest sponsored by the *Daily Mail*, but crashed mid-ocean after the radiator leaked. The men were missing for a week, but had been rescued by a Danish steamer without a radio, which also managed to salvage the remains of their aircraft. On their arrival in the UK, they were fêted and the wreckage of their aircraft went on display at Selfridge's department store in London.

During the postwar slump in aircraft orders, the Sopwith company went into liquidation, but was rescued and reformed as Hawker to avoid confusion and doubts over its solvency. Hawker himself resumed competitive flying and also took up motor racing at the famous Brooklands course near Weybridge in Surrey. While practising for the Aerial Derby at Hendon on 21 July 1921 his plane suddenly dived into the ground while being flown at low level and he was killed. The reason for the accident has never been established, although some have suggested that he may have suffered a sudden haemorrhage.

Hawker, Maj Lanoe George, VC 1890–1916 British fighter ace. No relation to **Harry Hawker**, Hawker was born into a naval family and had attended the Britannia Royal Naval College at

Dartmouth, but poor health meant that he was later commissioned into the Royal Engineers instead. He learnt to fly and in 1913 was able to transfer to the RFC.

After the outbreak of the First World War, Hawker flew scout sorties over Belgium. His first air-to-air engagement was on 31 October, when he was armed with nothing more potent than his service revolver; he also had to modify hand grenades to make small bombs. On 18 April 1915 he made a solitary attack on the Zeppelin shed at Gontrode, which earned him the DSO. Ever inventive, he rigged a Lewis gun to the cockpit of his Bristol Scout at an angle of 45 deg so that it could shoot past the propeller blades, enabling him to shoot down three enemy aircraft on 25 July 1916 for which he was awarded the VC and given command of his own squadron, No. 24, equipped with DH-2s. He made his squadron the most successful in the RFC, shooting down the deadly Fokker Eindekkers. Despite his undoubtedly gung-ho attitude, he was one of the few to recognise that the role of the scout was not air-to-air combat per se, but the protection of the reconnaissance aircraft engaged on the all-important task of aerial photography over and behind enemy lines.

He was regarded as being so valuable that during summer 1916, he was ordered not to fly over enemy lines, but continued to do so by omitting references to over-flying from his reports. Knowing that he was to be posted back to the UK on 23 November, he led a patrol to bomb Bapaume, and after attacking two German aircraft, his flight was itself attacked by Albatros scouts, one of which was the mount of **von Richthofen**. The two aces then engaged in a fierce 35-minute battle, the toughest he had ever flown according to the German, which ended with Hawker being killed by a bullet in the head. His relatively short career meant that Hawker did not become one of the top ten British aces of the war.

Hawker Siddeley British manufacturer. Formed in 1960 in a government-inspired merger of British aircraft manufacturers, Hawker Siddeley Aviation (HSA) incorporated **Avro, Armstrong-Whitworth, Blackburn, de Havilland, Folland** and **Gloster** as well as Hawker. A sister company,

Hawker Siddeley Dynamics (HSD), worked on missile development and was based on the guided missile interests of de Havilland. Engine manufacturing subsidiaries of these companies were merged into Bristol Siddeley. HSA and HSD were subsidiaries of what had become a large industrial manufacturing group with interests extending from power generation to railway equipment.

The oldest of these companies was Avro, dating from before the First World War, while Hawker itself dated from the immediate postwar period when it was formed to take over the former Sopwith works following that company's collapse. **Tom Sopwith** continued to play a major part in the company's development following the death of its founder, **Harry Hawker**. A variety of designs appeared during the early 1920s, including the Cygnet light aircraft, but the company soon started to concentrate on military aircraft, with the emphasis on fighters and light day bombers.

The first of a series of distinctive biplane fighters appeared in 1925 with the Hornbill, followed by the Hornet and Woodcock, with the latter also built under licence in Denmark as the Danecock. The Hart day bomber was so successful that a variety of versions were produced for fighter, observation, ground-attack and training duties, and one of these, the Fury, became the first RAF aircraft capable of exceeding 200 mph. The Hart was one of the first major designs by **Sir Sydney Camm**, who remained as chief designer for many years and was responsible for most of its more successful products.

The famous Hurricane monoplane fighter first flew in 1936, and up to 1944 some 14,000 Hurricanes of all types were built, despite being outpaced by later and faster German fighters. Most of the British fighters in the Battle of Britain were Hurricanes, and the aircraft showed outstanding manoeuvrability in combat. From 1941, Hurricane production was supplemented by that of the Typhoon fighter, itself replaced before the end of the war by the Tempest, one of the fastest piston-engined fighters ever produced, although many were built by Gloster to ease the pressure on Hawker's own production facilities.

Postwar, the Hawker Sea Fury was built for the Royal Navy's aircraft carriers and one of these aircraft shot down a MiG-15 jet fighter during the **Korean War**. The jet age also saw Hawker developing the Sea Hawk jet fighter for the Royal Navy, although most of these aircraft were actually built by Armstrong-Whitworth. Its outstanding success, developed from the P1052 experimental aircraft, was the Hunter jet fighter for the RAF. This aircraft established an air speed record and was produced under licence in Europe and demand, even for second-hand examples, remained strong for more than two decades afterwards. The company was also responsible for the Harrier and Sea Harrier V/STOL aircraft, developed from the experimental Kestrel. The Sea Harrier has been credited with British success in the **Falklands Campaign**.

Post-merger, HSA relied heavily on the development work of its predecessor companies, with the HS125 executive jet and Trident airliner inherited from de Havilland, the HS748 feeder airliner from Avro, the Buccaneer from Blackburn and the Harrier and eventually the Sea Harrier from Hawker, while the Gnat advanced jet trainer came from Folland. The company became a major subcontractor for the European **Airbus** consortium's first design, the A300, after the British government abandoned the project, while also postponing development of a jet successor to the HS748: the HS146 itself; although this was later resurrected and put into production by **British Aerospace**. The company also suffered cancellations when a supersonic development of the Harrier was cancelled by the British government, along with a promising jet military transport with STOL capabilities, the HS681, which would have rivalled, and outpaced, the Lockheed C-130 Hercules. The Nimrod maritime-reconnaissance aircraft was a development of the de Havilland Comet 4 jet airliner.

The company was merged into the nationalised British Aerospace in 1975.

Hawley, Alan Ramsay (1869–1938) American

aeronaut and fighter leader. A wealthy stockbroker and enthusiastic motorist, who helped found the Automobile Club of America, Hawley visited France in 1906 and gained an aeronaut's licence. He celebrated his success by making an ascent in a balloon to voyage from Paris to England. On his return to the USA, he took **Wilbur Wright** for an ascent in 1907.

An accomplished balloonist, in 1910 he won the **Gordon Bennett** Balloon Trophy by journeying 1,171 miles from St Louis to Chilogoma in northern Quebec, Canada. The balloon crash-landed and Hawley suffered a knee injury, which slowed his progress as he and his assistant, A. Post, had to walk back to civilization.

As war in Europe drew closer, Hawley took the lead in organising an air national guard, the air equivalent of the National Guard forces spread across all US states. He was also behind a unit of volunteers who would leave for Europe, which later became the Escadrille Lafayette, an American unit in the French Aviation Militaire.

Heath, Edward Bayard (1888–1931) American

manufacturer. Believed to have worked at the **Curtiss** Hammondsport factory at one time, in 1910 he returned to his native New York and experimented with a Blériot-type monoplane, which he had to rebuild when it fell apart the first time it taxied. Some time after this he became an aircraft parts dealer in Chicago and resumed his experiments with aircraft so that by 1918 he had a light biplane known as the 'Feather' on the market. He next wanted to market a low-cost aircraft, but it was not until 1925 that he created the Heath Parasol which used a lightweight fuselage mated to the wing designed for the Thomas-Morse Scout, with a 25 hp engine. Initially the aircraft was sold complete from the factory, but to make flying affordable, in 1927 it also became available in kit form.

The next product was smaller and had a mid-wing. Known as the 'Bullet', it won the 300-cubic-inch class at the National Air Races in Los Angeles during 1928.

Heath's knowledge of structural engineering had failed him with his first design in 1910 and it failed him again with his last design in 1931. This was to have been a low-wing single-seat monoplane, but for the lack of a secure structure for a wing-strut, the aircraft wing folded while in flight, crashing and killing Heath as he flew it.

Heinemann, Edward Henry (1908–91)

American designer. The Douglas World Cruiser's

round-the-world flight in 1926 encouraged Heinemann to become a draughtsman in the aircraft industry and he started work with **Douglas**. He moved to Northrop in 1930, a company in which Douglas took a substantial stake in 1936 so Heinemann ended up back with Douglas. He was given the task of improving a bomber design that had originated with Northrop and the result was the Douglas Dauntless. Other aircraft designed by him included the A-20 Havoc and A-26 Invader, and his work continued into the jet age with the Skyrocket, the first aircraft to fly at twice the speed of sound.

Heinkel *See* Heinkel, Ernst

Heinkel, Ernst (1888–1958) German designer and manufacturer. While an engineering student, Heinkel was so impressed with the sight of a Zeppelin in 1908 that he decided to design aircraft. His first aircraft was a home-built biplane based on **Hargrave**'s box kite principles, which took to the air in July 1911, but after several flights it crashed, seriously injuring Heinkel. Once he had recovered, he worked first for LVG, then Albatros and finally Hansa-Brandenburg, where he was approached by a wealthy Austrian, Camillo Castiglioni, who wanted Heinkel to work for him. When Heinkel refused, Castiglioni bought the company to secure the young designer's services. Heinkel produced a long series of hydro-aeroplane designs for Hansa for the German Naval Air Service during the First World War.

He established his own aircraft factory in 1922. One of his early designs was the He25, which used a launcher-rail for take-off, a concept that dated back to the **Wrights**. Heinkel himself gained a reputation for unconventional and pioneering designs. The company was noted mainly for its elegant He111 bomber which was the mainstay of the Luftwaffe's bomber force for most of the war, and later for the unsuccessful He177 four-engined bomber, with the engines in two nacelles, which was prone to catch fire, as well as for a small single-engined jet prototype.

helicopter Often referred to as a rotary-wing aeroplane, since the rotor blades provide lift and control as well as propulsion, the practical

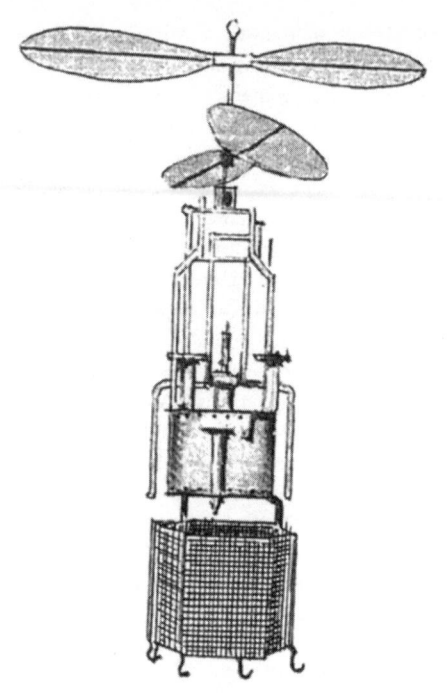

Co-axial rotors were clearly in mind with the Vicomte Ponton d'Aemcourt's 1861 helicopter design, patented in 1861 and flown in model form from 1863, sometimes using clockwork motors, sometimes steam.

helicopter was a relatively late arrival, although the concept had engaged the attention of many pioneers and would-be pioneers. The first known helicopter designs were those of **Leonardo da Vinci**, while others interested in the helicopter included **Sir George Cayley** and **Horatio Phillips**. A significant milestone along the way to developing the practical helicopter was the gyroplane, but this differed significantly from the helicopter by having unpowered rotor blades that rotated in the slipstream from the conventional propeller, giving a reduced take-off but not true vertical take-off, while separate ailerons also had to be provided.

While Cayley and Phillips both produced models of their helicopters, the first capable of lifting a man off the ground was one built by **Louis Breguet** in France in 1907, which used a

50 hp Antionette engine. This was not a practical machine as it lacked any means of control and only made a tethered flight. In Argentina, during the early 1920s, the Marquis de Pescara produced another helicopter, but it lacked any means of stability. The first practical helicopter was the Focke-Wulf Fw61 in 1936, which used two laterally displaced rotors, but this machine did not enter production, although a development, the Focke Achgelis, first flown in 1940, was produced in small numbers.

The conventional helicopter as it appears today, with a main rotor and tail rotor, was developed by the Russian émigré **Igor Sikorsky** working in the United States during the 1930s and 1940s, culminating in the first flight of his VS-300 in 1939. Wartime development of the helicopter in the United States, and further intensive work by **Bell Aerosystems**, gave the USA a considerable lead by the end of the 1940s, although since then the French and the Russians have made considerable strides, with the latter also developing and building the world's largest machines.

Variations on the configuration of the helicopter have included twin rotors, as favoured by **Piasecki**, which was acquired by Vertol and then again by **Boeing**. In this, the tail rotor is driven by the engines and the forward rotor has a drive shaft off it, as opposed to the conventional helicopter which devotes around 10–15 per cent of its power to driving the stabilising tail rotor. Intermeshing rotors were chosen by **Kaman** to provide stability, and some designs, including some from the Russian **Kamov** design bureau, use contra-rotating rotors. Eurocopter preferred an enclosed 'fenestrom' tail rotor, while in the United States, first **Hughes** and then, after it was acquired by **McDonnell Douglas**, MD Helicopters, favoured replacing the tail rotor with a ducted efflux from the engine, reducing power loss to the tail rotor and also noise levels, and increasing safety for those close to the helicopter when landing and taking off. The helicopter quickly proved itself an outstanding and versatile machine, and many duties became its own, including search and rescue and anti-tank operations, while it also relieved fixed-wing aircraft of many anti-submarine duties.

The use of heli-borne troops has replaced the glider and poses a challenge to the use of paratroops, but helicopters still suffer limitations on range and speed. The development of offshore oil and gas supplies would have been much more difficult and costly without helicopters to carry workers to and from the exploration and production rigs. Helicopters have also secured a significant niche in executive transport.

The one area in which the helicopter has made only a marginal impact has been in scheduled air services. Early attempts by BEA with experimental mail services in the West of England, and a service between London's Heathrow Airport and central London, were soon dropped, and operations in Belgium by Sabena and in Pakistan by Pakistan International Airways also had a short life. A service linked London's Heathrow and Gatwick airports for some years, but was dropped when a new motorway was built. One of the few remaining services links Penzance in Cornwall with the Isles of Scilly off the extreme south-west point of England, and is operated by Brintel using Sikorsky S-61s.

Henschel German manufacturer. One of the smaller German aircraft manufacturers active before and during the Second World War, the company produced the Hs126 army cooperation aircraft and the Hs292 rocket-assisted glider-bomb, which was first used operationally on 23 August 1943.

Henson, William Samuel (1812–88) British designer and visionary. An engineer and successful inventor who worked in the linen trade, Henson took a keen interest in the work of **Sir George Cayley**, and experimented with model gliders. He believed that a full-size aircraft would be possible and designed a model monoplane with a lightweight steam engine, by his friend **John Stringfellow**, which was patented in 1842. In 1843 the two men formed the Aerial Transit Company with two other investors, intending that this should be the world's first airline.

The design featured a fuselage-mounted steam engine driving two propellers, a high monoplane wing and a tricycle undercarriage. When the model was built in 1845–7 it succeeded only in trundling down its launch ramp, possibly making a hop at the end, but failing to get airborne.

The aircraft, known as the *Ariel*, captured the public imagination so much so that it appeared in magazines and newspapers for many years and became firmly embedded as the likely shape of travel by air. It also succeeded in becoming a matter for caricature, even in one case on a silk handkerchief. Disappointed, Henson married in 1847 and emigrated to the USA.

Hero of Alexandria (c.AD 62) Hero discovered that a jet of steam could provide reactive propulsive power, but was unable to find a practical application.

Heron, Samuel D. (1891–1963) British engine designer. During the First World War, Heron was already an established engine designer and was working at the Royal Aircraft factory on research into making air-cooled engines lighter. When the Royal Aircraft Factory was diverted to research, he moved to Armstrong-Siddeley, where he continued his work with a practical application in the Jaguar radial engine. His next move was to work for the United States Army at McCook Field, but he found the same frustrating lack of purpose as he had found in the UK and in 1926 joined the Wright engine company. It was the Heron-designed Wright Whirlwind engine that powered the *Spirit of St Louis* to Paris in 1927.

Herring, Augustus Moore (1867–1927) American glider pioneer. Born into a wealthy family, Herring studied to be an engineer at the Stevens Institute of Technology in New Jersey. At the same time, he built two unsuccessful gliders, but failed to graduate when the institute rejected his graduation treatise on heavier-than-air flying-machines. He then used part of an inheritance to purchase one of **Lilienthal's** gliders, making a number of flights and also using the design as the basis for some further work of his own. He was employed for a while by **Octave Chanute** and then by **Samuel Langley**, although he resigned from the latter's employment in 1895 in a dispute over wing design and returned to Chanute. Herring proved to have abilities both as a designer and as a glider pilot, but once again he was too opinionated for his employer and left Chanute. With the support of a wealthy enthusiast, he built

a glider of his own and then applied power to it, but even so all that resulted were some extended glides.

He resumed the connection with Chanute in 1902, and they went to Kitty Hawk where he met the **Wrights**, but failed to impress them. After their successful first flights in December 1903, he offered them a partnership, which they rejected. He was far more successful with **Glenn Curtiss** in 1909, who was persuaded that Herring's patents would put his competitors out of business, and they formed the Herring-Curtiss Company, with almost all of the money being found by Curtiss. When Curtiss discovered Herring's deception, he forced him out and dissolved the partnership, but Herring sued and won a judgement against Curtiss, although he died before the damages could be paid.

high wing Monoplanes can be high, medium or low wing. The high wing has three advantages: greater stability, improved vision for the pilot and the other occupants, and it offers a better and unbroken interior to the fuselage. High wing configurations enabled bombers to have a longer and uninterrupted bomb-bay, allowing larger bombs to be carried. Purpose-designed military transports favour a high wing so that large loads can be carried and because the fuselage can be closer to the ground, loading and unloading becomes easier. Some aircraft have a high wing to provide extra clearance for the propellers or to enable turbines to be sufficiently far off the ground not to ingest material off the runway. **Variable-incidence** and **variable-geometry** both require high wings to work.

A drawback inherent in the high wing is that it can make structural integrity in a large and heavy aircraft difficult to achieve.

Low wings provide a firmer structure and less drag, and a higher floor, which on large commercial aircraft provides space under the cabin floor for baggage, cargo and, of course, fuel. Most large aircraft wings, whether high, low or mid-wing, are 'wet', that is to say that they include fuel tanks.

Hill, Geoffrey Terence Rowland (1895–1956) British designer. After serving in France during the First World War, Hill returned to the UK as a test pilot for the Royal Aircraft Factory. Postwar, he joined **Handley Page** as a test pilot and also worked on the design of leading edge slots. His experience of design seems to have kindled an enthusiasm for the work, and he started to design aircraft on his own account, becoming especially interested in tailless aircraft with a swept wing. He built and flew such an aircraft in 1926 which proved to have the safe handling that its designer was hoping for. **Westland** commissioned him to build three aircraft of this design, but none of them were ever developed beyond the prototype stage.

After the Second World War Hill worked for **Short** Brothers, where he developed the aero-isoclinic wing which used tip controls to regulate wing distortion which proved to be a problem on early thin-wing high-speed aircraft. Nevertheless, the history of Shorts postwar was mainly devoted to relatively low speed transport aircraft.

Hiller *See below*

Hiller, Stanley, Jr (1924–2006) American helicopter manufacturer. With a father who was both wealthy and interested in aviation, Hiller received the encouragement he needed, while having considerable talent of his own. At just 15 years old he started to produce gas-powered model cars, and at 18 was starting to design helicopters. An employee in the model car business built a helicopter based on Hiller's design, the Hiller-Copter, with contra-rotating co-axial rotor blades, which was ready for testing in 1944. To obtain the support necessary to get his designs into production Hiller made an arrangement with the Kaiser Company, but in 1945 struck out on his own as United Helicopters, which eventually adopted the name of Hiller in the 1950s, before being purchased by Fairchild in 1964.

Hillman, Edward Henry (1889–1934) British airline pioneer. Coming from humble origins, Hillman worked his way up from being a band boy in a British cavalry regiment to the rank of sergeant during the First World War, after which he started a cycle repair business. He invested his earnings in buying a bus and introduced a service between Romford and Chelmsford in Essex, and by 1930 had a fleet of 200 vehicles operating services from Essex into London. He introduced an air service in the early 1930s using Romford as a base, and by 1933 was operating a twice-daily Romford–Paris schedule, with his main base convenient for north London. His need for an economical but comfortable six-seater passenger aircraft lay behind **de Havilland**'s development of the Dragon series. In 1934, he won the contract to provide airmail services from London to Belfast and Glasgow.

Hillman died suddenly in 1934, but his company survived to be almagamated into a new airline, British Airways, which was set up as a rival on UK and European services to the state-sponsored Imperial Airways. Eventually both airlines were merged by the government to form the British Overseas Airways Corporation (BOAC) in 1940.

Hindenberg A successor to the famous *Graf Zeppelin* airship, the *Hindenberg* was destroyed in the world's worst airship disaster while mooring at Lakehurst, New Jersey, on 6 May 1937, at the end of a transatlantic crossing from Frankfurt in Germany. Thirty-three of the ninety-six passengers on board were killed when the airship collided with the mooring mast and caught fire. The disaster was due in part to an American embargo on helium gas sales to Germany, preventing the airship from using this much safer lifting agent over the highly flammable hydrogen. The disaster was caught on newsreel camera and shown in cinemas throughout the world, which undoubtedly led to a loss of interest in airship development as a mode of transport.

Hindustan Indian manufacturer. Originally founded at Bangalore before the Second World War to undertake maintenance and assembly work, Hindustan Aeronautics produced the first Indian-designed aircraft, the HT-2 basic trainer, after the war. It was followed by the HAOP-27 Krishnak AOP aircraft, the HJT-16 Kiran jet trainer and HF-24 Marut jet fighter, as well as by licence-built examples of the Folland Gnat light jet fighter, the HS-748 transport and the MiG-21 interceptor, and the Jaguar strike aircraft.

Hinkler, Herbert John Louis 'Bert' (1892–1933) Australian long-distance pioneer. Queensland-born 'Bert' Hinkler began building gliders while still a teenager. He moved to the UK and joined the Royal Navy, serving as a petty officer (the equivalent of an army sergeant) artificer (skilled tradesman) at the beginning of the First World War before moving to the RNAS and training as a pilot. Postwar, he became a test pilot for **Avro**, and in 1920 flew the 650 miles from London to Turin in northern Italy, non-stop in an Avro Baby biplane, which used the 35 hp Green engine that **Roe** had used in his 1910 triplane, winning the Britannia Trophy. He followed this by winning the 1920 Aerial Derby at Hendon.

Hinkler's reputation was largely based on flying solo over 11,000 miles from the UK to Australia in just 15½ days, between 7 and 22 February 1928, in an Avro Avian, earning him an honoury commission as a squadron leader in the RAAF. He followed this with a horseshoe-course flight from Toronto to South America, across the Atlantic to West Africa and then north to England in 1931. In 1933 he attempted to lower his UK–Australia record, but was killed when his aircraft crashed in the Alps.

Hiroshima (6 August 1945) As US forces fought their way across the Pacific, they not only had to endure kamikaze suicide attacks from the air, they also faced fanatical resistance whenever they attempted to reclaim territory occupied by the Japanese. There were suicide attacks by troops, and anyone who did not join the resistance efforts could expect to be shot in the back. With this experience, invasion of the Japanese home islands appeared to be exceptionally costly and prolonged. Nevertheless, the Allies had a weapon that they hoped would force the Japanese to surrender.

A special unit had been formed ready for the possibility of using nuclear weapons: this was the USAAF's 509th Composite Group. The unit had been established as early as 1944 in view of the possibility that nuclear weapons might have to be used against Germany. Once German defeat was seen as inevitable without recourse to the nuclear option, the force was moved to Tinian Airfield in the Marianas in May 1945, and was ready to use nuclear weapons by 1 August.

On 6 August, at 0245, the Group's Commanding Officer, Colonel Paul Tibbets, took off in his Boeing B-29 Superfortress, **Enola Gay**, followed by two observation aircraft. Weather conditions were important to ensure that the bomb would fall on the right target, and as he became airborne Tibbets did not know which of three Japanese cities would be his target. Shortly after 0700, he was directed to Hiroshima. A little more than an hour later, at 0815, while flying at 31,600 ft, the U-235 atomic bomb, known as *Little Boy*, was released, exploding at an altitude of 1,000 ft. Within seconds 78,000 people were dead, another 51,000 were injured and 176,000 were made homeless. More than 70,000 buildings were destroyed.

Hispano/Hispano-Suiza French manufacturer. Originally Franco-Spanish, the company was a noted manufacturer of automobile and aircraft engines between the wars, and postwar became a subsidiary of **SNECMA**, the main French aero-engine manufacturer, building rocket projectiles. In Spain, the remnants of the company pursued a separate existence as Hispano Aviación, building the Messerschmitt Bf109 fighter under licence with Rolls-Royce Merlin engines, as well as producing its own trainer designs before eventually being absorbed into **CASA**, now **EADS**.

Horten, Reimar (1915–94) and Walter (1913–98) German glider pioneers. Like **Hill**, the Horten brothers were interested in building tailless aircraft, but were inspired by **Alexander Lippisch**'s glider in 1931. They built a glider of their own, which they named the Horten I. They joined the Luftwaffe from 1936–8 and when they left became glider designers, building a series of five plywood aircraft. They continued design work during the Second World War, although their flying wing jet fighter was never built. Postwar, Reimar emigrated to Argentina and Walter helped to rebuild the Luftwaffe.

hot air balloons *See* Montgolfière

hovercraft *See* air cushion vehicle

Hoxsey, Arch (1884–1910) American pioneer. A mechanic, Hoxsey was compelled to learn to fly in 1910 when he saw his first aeroplane. He was taught alongside **Walter Brookins** by **Orville Wright**, at Orville's flying school in the United States. He then became an exhibition pilot with the Wright team, and the newspapers created a rivalry between Hoxsey and fellow team member **Ralph Johnstone**. In September 1910 the two men flew at shows throughout the United States, billed as the Heavenly Twins, with such daring that on one occasion **Wilbur Wright** grounded Hoxsey. Even so, in October 1910 Hoxsey took former US president Theodore Roosevelt for a flight. In December, flying at Dominquez in California, while attempting to set an altitude record, he lost control of his aircraft and was killed when it fell out of the sky.

Hughes American manufacturer. Although better known for the 'Spruce Goose' flying boat, the Hughes Tool Company also designed and built a range of helicopters. These included the 300, first flown in 1955 and adopted by the USN as a trainer, and the five-seat 500, first flown in 1963 and which provided the basis for the US Army's OH-6A Cayuse observation helicopter. Experiments with helicopters using ducted efflux from the turboshaft instead of a tail rotor were conducted on the 500, before the company developed the eight-place 900 Explorer. The concept provided greater safety and reduced noise. The company was sold to **McDonnell Douglas** before the takeover by **Boeing**, which decided not to remain in the light helicopter market. Hughes products are now produced and sold by **MD Helicopters**.

Hughes, Howard Robert (1905–76) American air racer and aircraft designer. Having inherited a fortune while only 19 years old, Hughes continued his education and qualified as an engineer. Later he made a film, *Hell's Angels*, about flying, which proved to be a spectacular success. He then set out on a career as a film producer. He took up air racing in the 1930s as a hobby and began designing

his own aircraft, with his H-1 monoplane setting a landplane speed record of 352.3 mph on 13 September 1935, and in 1937 the same aircraft set a transcontinental speed record flying from Los Angeles to Newark, New Jersey, in less than 7½ hours. In 1938 he flew a Lockheed 14 around the world setting a new record of 91 hours.

He was responsible for the design of the Lockheed Constellation airliner, a great postwar commercial success, before working on his HK-1 Hercules, an all-wood flying boat known as the *Spruce Goose*. This 150-ton aircraft made its one and only flight in 1947, with many critics claiming that it had failed to meet the requirements of flight. It had, although it was doubtful if it was a practical aircraft. He also designed the fast XF-11 reconnaissance aircraft, in which he crashed and although he survived, he became a recluse. He died in 1976 while being flown in an air ambulance from Mexico to the USA.

Hunsaker, Jerome Clarke (1886–1984) American scientist. Commissioned into the USN when he was 22 years old, in 1909 Hunsaker was sponsored by the service for a course at the Massachusetts Institute of Technology (MIT) and afterwards visited France where he worked with Eiffel using a wind tunnel. In 1913 he returned to the USA and built America's most advanced wind tunnel, which was followed by the first course in the USA on aeronautics at MIT. In 1916 he became head of the Navy Bureau of Construction and Repair where he took part in the design of the Curtiss NC-4, which became the first aircraft to cross the Atlantic in 1919. In 1923 he produced the dirigible *Shenandoah*, as well as work on carrier-borne aircraft and their engines. He also worked on catapults, at the time known as accelerators, to allow ever heavier and faster aircraft to be operated from carriers. In 1926 he left the USN and joined Bell Laboratories, working on radio for aircraft, before joining the **National Advisory Committee on Aeronautics** (NACA) and being appointed chairman in 1941.

Hunting *See* Percival Aircraft

hydro-aeroplane *See* floatplane *and* flying boat

I

Icarus *See* Daedalus

Ilyushin *See* below

Ilyushin, Sergei Vladimirovich (1894–1977)
Russian designer and bureau head. Of humble origins, Ilyushin became a mechanic in the Imperial Russian Flying Corps where he met **Igor Sikorsky**, and then chief mechanic for the fleet of Ilya Mouramtez ('The Giant') bombers converted from the pre-war airliner design. While the flying corps was among the last of the Russian services to join the revolution, Ilyushin himself was quick to join the Bolsheviks. In post-revolutionary Russia, he was sent to the Zhukovsky Air Academy, graduating in 1924.

In 1929 he produced the first high-performance glider to be designed in Russia and was put in charge of his own design bureau. His first project was a large long-range transport aircraft that flew non-stop from Moscow to New Brunswick in Canada; just the sort of prestigious project to endear him to his political masters. During the Second World War, he was responsible for the Il-2 Sturmovik, a rugged ground-attack aircraft that proved devastating against German tanks in the long fight westwards, that led to eventual German defeat.

Postwar, Ilyushin's bureau concentrated on transport aircraft and bombers, and Ilyushin alone is believed to have worked on more than fifty aircraft.

Immelmann, Lt Max Franz (1890–1916)
On the outbreak of the First World War, Immelmann joined the German Military Air Service and the following year found himself in the same squadron as **Oswald Boelcke**. Both men were fortunate enough to receive machine-gun fitted Fokker Scouts, and on 1 August Immelmann shot down a French bomber, giving the German his first confirmed kill of the war. Fighter tactics had still to be developed, and the two men played a part in this, sending aircraft in two-man teams and developing the concept of the wingman to protect the tail of the leader, as well as sending aircraft into the air as a unit. Immelmann himself invented the Immelmann turn. Based at Douai, after Boelcke was transferred, he became known as the 'Eagle of Lille', while the RFC pilots soon claimed that they were 'Fokker Fodder'. In 1916 Immelmann won the 'Blue Max', but on 18 June 1916, after downing his sixteenth victim, his aircraft broke up in mid-air. For propaganda purposes, a member of the RFC was credited with Immelmann's downfall, but it is generally believed that a synchroniser malfunction enabled him to shoot off his own propeller.

Immelmann did not match the popular image of a fighter pilot; he was moody, a teetotaller and vegetarian, the latter being most unusual at the time.

inclusive tour operations
First operated by Thomas Cook before the Second World War. Postwar, inclusive tour holidays became popular due to the desire of the public in the more prosperous countries of Western Europe to take advantage of low-cost holidays in and around the Mediterranean. Sometimes known as package holidays, the customer pays one single sum for travel and accommodation, usually including at least one, sometimes two or even three, meals per day, except when self-catering accommodation is booked. Optional extras include items such as car hire. Both scheduled and charter flights can be used and the concept is not unique to air travel.

The concept became popular partly because of foreign currency exchange controls, which meant that travellers were limited in the amount of currency they could take abroad; paying in their own currency for as much as possible before leaving home was attractive, and partly because of the tight **bilateral air transport agreements** in Europe that kept fares high compared to those in the USA. For the airlines, charter traffic was a way of staying in business rather than becoming involved as 'associates' of the nationalised flag carriers.

The growing popularity of the low-cost airlines in Europe has meant that inclusive tours are less significant now than in the past.

India–Pakistan, air campaigns Until relatively recently, there has been considerable tension between India and Pakistan, often over the status of the Indian state of Kashmir, but also over other border issues. Both countries developed substantial defence forces because of these border tensions, while those of India were also prompted by border disputes with Communist China. Procurement differed, with India initially favouring British, then French and later Russian equipment, while Pakistan initially preferred American equipment and then, in more recent years, Chinese combat aircraft.

Indian-produced Folland Gnat lightweight fighters gained the name 'Sabre-slayer' when they outfought North American F-86 Sabres, largely because the Sabres relied on air-to-air missiles which in the early heat-seeking versions were unreliable in tropical conditions. The most significant war between the two nations was in 1971, which started on 3 December with a Pakistan Air Force strike against ten Indian Air Force bases, including two in Kashmir, and concluded with East Pakistan declaring independence to become the new state of Bangladesh early in 1972. In this conflict, the air war extended to using aircraft from the Indian Navy's aircraft carrier, INS *Vikrant*, with Sea Hawk fighter-bombers attacking Chittagong and Cox's Bazaar.

interceptor Essentially a development of the fighter, an interceptor is a fast combat aircraft with the emphasis on both speed and a fast rate of climb, both of which are more important than manoeuvrability. The first purpose-designed interceptor was the Messerschmitt Me163 Komet, but the jet age and the need to counter high-flying bombers ensured that these qualities remained important for many years. The Lockheed F-104 Starfighter was even advertised as the 'missile with a man in it'.

The concept became far less important with the tendency for bombers to fly low and release stand-off weapons while still clear of the target, and then even more recently to release cruise missiles capable of flying some considerable distance. It is also the case that traditional heavy bomber operations are unlikely in the future. Today, the emphasis is on all-round performance and a high maximum speed is becoming less important for combat aircraft.

interdictor An aircraft capable of interdiction bombing, which means precision attacks on vital military and communications targets. The concept became possible during the Second World War, for while bombing accuracy was generally very poor during the early years, highly trained crews were able to mount raids against specific targets. Two of the most significant examples of interdiction bombing were the RAF's attacks on the prison at Amiens, which had to be so precise because the object of the exercise was to knock the walls down and shake the cell doors off their hinges in order to release members of the French Resistance held prisoner there, and the Gestapo Headquarters in the Hague, which was next to a school. The **Dam Busters** raid could be cited as another example.

The concept is attractive, but difficult in practice, and the USAF and USN suffered heavy losses during the Vietnam War attempting interdiction bombing. Eventually, a combination of blanket bombing and precision attacks with 'smart' bombs (guided weapons) proved the way forward.

International Aero Engines (IAE) Manufacturer. A multinational company founded in 1983 to manage development, production and support for the V2500 aero-engine available with between 22,000 and 33,000 lb thrust. The partners are **Pratt & Whitney**, **Rolls-Royce**, the Japanese Aero Engines Corporation and MTU Aero Engines. Each partner contributes an individual module to the V2500 engine, which powers the Airbus A319, A320 and A321, and the McDonnell Douglas MD-90 aircraft.

International Air Transport Association (IATA) Formed in 1945, the International Air Transport Association remains the main organisation representing the interests of airline operators, but it is specifically aimed at the large national flag carriers. While IATA was criticised for many years for keeping fares high and effectively imposing an industry standard that inhibited true competition or even differentiation between member airlines, it also created a truly international standard ticketing system, acted as a clearing house to settle airlines' accounts with one another, and has done much work to ensure good operational practice. Its control of member airlines' fares and provision for passengers is far less than once was the case.

international civil aircraft markings All civilian aircraft have a registration index with a national prefix. Practice varies between nations, with most European nations having all letter registrations, while the United States has the national prefix followed by numbers, and also uses a letter suffix, which for major airlines can be the abbreviated name of the operator. Other countries that have numbers following the national letter include China and Taiwan.
See Table 19: International Civil Aircraft Markings

International Civil Aviation Organisation (ICAO) Originally formed as a result of the 1944 Chicago Convention on Air Transport to implement the convention's decisions, ICAO is part of the United Nations. The Chicago Convention produced ninety-six articles to which all nations are expected to subscribe and include the **freedoms** of air transport as well as standards for en route equipment and standards for navigation and ground formalities. Overall, ICAO involvement has been beneficial, raising standards and ensuring compatibility.

international consortia/projects *See* collaborative projects

Israeli Aircraft Industries (IAI) Israeli manufacturer. Formed as Bedek (Hebrew for maintenance and repair) Aircraft in 1953, the company expanded into licence-production and major upgrades of aircraft. It produced the indigenous Arava, a twin-boom, twin-engined, light transport, and acquired the rights to build an executive aircraft from North American Rockwell in 1967. A modified Mirage V led to the production of the multi-role combat aircraft, the Kfir; the company also produces guided weapons. In the complex tangle of relationships in the Middle East, IAI has also upgraded McDonnell Douglas F-4 Phantoms for the Turkish Air Force.

J

Jabara, Capt James (1923–66) American jet fighter ace. Although Jabara joined the USAAF to make his full mark during the Second World War, with 3.5 victories, he remained in the service postwar and, flying North American F-86 Sabre fighters with what had become the USAF during the Korean War, shot down fifteen enemy aircraft. He became the first US jet fighter ace when he shot down his fifth MiG-15 on 20 May 1951.

Jacobs, Eastman N. (1902–87) US aerodynamicist. A graduate from the University of California, he joined the Pacific Telephone and Telegraph Company before moving in 1925 to the **National Advisory Committee on Aeronautics**. Using wind tunnel research, he developed high-performance aerofoils, discovering how to lower the pressure across the chord and enable the development of laminar-flow wings.

Japan, US bomber campaign (March–August 1945) The US bomber campaign had to await the seizure of suitable bases within flying distance of the Japanese home islands with the occupation of the Marianas. The USAAF had initially been reluctant to attack civilian targets, but the long and costly struggle to re-take occupied territory across the Pacific persuaded the chiefs of staff that such attacks were inevitable. The campaign started with a series of incendiary raids; the first was on Tokyo on 15 March, on Nagoya the following night, a similar raid on Osaka the night after that, then Kobe and then a return visit to Nagoya, after which the USAAF ran out of incendiaries.

These raids were just a preliminary for a sustained bomber campaign. The USAAF stepped up its attacks on Japanese cities so that there were sixty major raids between June and August, 1945, destroying some 60 sq miles of Japanese cities, and concentrating on the sixty-five Japanese towns and cities with more than 100,000 inhabitants.

In this short bombing campaign, the USAAF dropped 154,000 tons of bombs on Japan.

These raids used the new Boeing B-29 Superfortress. On some raids, the aircraft left their gunners behind, with the exception of the tail-gunner, who would act as an observer only because all the guns were removed. This saved 3,000 lb per aircraft, enabling a heavier bomb load to be carried. Some attacks were made at night, with take-off at 1800, reaching the target around midnight. On approaching the target, they would find that it had been marked by a force of twelve 'pathfinder' B-29s, which would have dropped flares around it, leaving the main force to bomb within this 'ring of fire'.

This intense rate of bombing had little impact on the country's military leadership, even though it forced more than 8 million Japanese to flee the urban areas and seek what refuge they could in the countryside. Rations were at starvation levels, at 1,400 calories per day per person. Fuel was scarce, and the little that remained was reserved exclusively for the military, and especially for the final kamikaze onslaught of 5,000 aircraft, many of which were unsuitable second-line training or communications types.

Jeffries, Dr John (1744–1819) American pioneering balloonist. A Boston physician who graduated from Harvard in 1763 and then continued his studies in Aberdeen and London, he returned home in 1769. During the American War of Independence, he took the side of the loyalists and eventually became Surgeon-General to the British forces. In 1779, with defeat looming, he moved back to London and took an interest in science. He sponsored the first balloon voyage across the English Channel in 1785 with **Jean-Pierre Blanchard** as pilot, for which he paid £100 (at least £5,000 by modern values) plus £800 (£40,000) for equipment. As mentioned in the entry for Blanchard, most of this equipment was thrown overboard as the two men struggled to keep their balloon aloft. By carrying a letter to Benjamin Franklin, then in Paris, from his son who was in London, Jeffries effectively carried the first airmail.

Jeffries returned home to Boston in 1789. His earlier support of the British cause seems to have been overlooked or forgiven and he spent the rest of his life living comfortably in his home town.

Jeschonnek, Gen Hans (1899–1943) German air commander. Chief of the Luftwaffe General Staff from February 1939. Unlike many career officers who were apolitical, he was a strong admirer of both Hitler and Goering, but had a poor relationship with **Erhard Milch**. A strong supporter of the blitzkrieg concept, he neglected other aspects of air power, leaving the Luftwaffe unprepared for a strategic air war, and refused to countenance heavy bombers or an air transport organisation. His failings meant that Germany lacked adequate fighter defences and that an air re-supply operation at Stalingrad failed. Hitler blamed Goering, who in turn blamed Jeschonnek, who blamed Goering. The day after the RAF bombed Peenemünde and the USAAF bombed Schweinfurt, he wrote a paper attacking Goering and then shot himself.

jet The jet engine was the result of independent research in the United Kingdom by **Air Commodore Sir Frank Whittle** and in Germany by **Dr Hans von Ohain** during the 1930s. Their work was largely ignored at first, but eventually came to fruition in the Gloster E28/39 and the Heinkel He178 respectively – and not surprisingly these two aircraft were remarkably similar in appearance. The world's first operational jet combat aircraft was the Messerschmitt Me262, followed by the Gloster Meteor, while the first jet transport was the de Havilland Comet I airliner.

Jet engines can be divided into five major types, of which the original was the turbojet – a series of turbine blades suck air into the engine, compress it, and after ignition the hot efflux gases drive a final set of turbine blades and power is provided by the thrust of these gases. Today, most commercial aircraft are powered by turbofans, which include a set of large first-stage fans with a substantial proportion of the air actually bypassing the compression and ignition stages, a system that provides additional thrust and improved fuel economy as well as reducing noise levels by blanketing the hot efflux gases. A variation on the turbofan is to have twin- or triple-spool engines that ensure the different sets of turbine blades rotate at their optimum speeds. The one drawback of the turbofan is that the additional drag makes it unsuitable for operation at very high speeds or very high altitudes. One reason for the failure of the Tupolev Tu-144 supersonic airliner was that it used turbofans and thus had to maintain reheat rather than simply use this to accelerate to supersonic speeds, as on the Concorde airliner.

The big advantage of the jet engine has been that the lack of reciprocating movements has created both greater smoothness compared to piston engines and far greater reliability. Inflight engine failures are now rare indeed, with one estimate being that only one airline pilot in three will experience an engine failure during his career (airline pilots fly far longer hours than military pilots, who are constrained by budgetary factors). By contrast, piston engine failures were such that even after the Second World War, pilots could expect two or three a year.

A simple jet engine with no moving parts is the ramjet, and it has been used to boost the performance of piston-engined aircraft, such as the Ryan Fireball, but cannot be used to move an aircraft until a reasonable air speed has already been attained as air cannot be drawn into the engine. The most usual application of the ramjet is in the tailpipe of supersonic aircraft to provide reheat of the efflux, thus boosting power, in a process sometimes referred to as 'after-burning'. The use of a ramjet in this way can be clearly seen as a hot orange glow in the tailpipe. Ramjets can also be used to power missiles either launched at speed from aircraft or boosted to operational speed by rockets.

A variation on the jet engine is the turboprop, with a large gearbox reducing the engine speed to drive propellers, offering better acceleration on the runway and improved performance at lower altitudes. There have been relatively few turboprop combat aircraft, although one of the first was the Royal Navy's Westland Wyvern strike aircraft, but it has proved ideal for maritime-reconnaissance aircraft which spend much time at lower altitudes. The first successful turboprop aircraft was the Vickers Viscount airliner, which first flew in 1951, and the most common is the Lockheed C-130 Hercules military transport. Rising fuel prices have led to a revival in turboprop aircraft for regional and feeder services with the main manufacturers being Bombardier of Canada and the Franco-Italian ATR. The drawback of the turboprop is that maximum speeds are usually below 400 mph, and cabin noise can be a problem, although this can be reduced by using different types of propeller and by introducing white noise to the cabin.

The turboprop has its own variant, the turboshaft, which is used to drive the rotor blades of helicopters. The improvement in helicopter performance has been such that turboshafts can be found powering helicopters as small as three seats.

Johns, Capt William Earl (1893–1968) British

author. Served with the RFC and the RAF, from which he retired in 1930. Famous for the series of books featuring a pilot hero, Biggles, which spanned the period from the First World War well into the Cold War. The books are unpopular today among the politically correct elite for their racism and chauvinism, but these features were an accurate representation of the times.

Johnson, Amy (1903–41) British aviatrix. A

secretary in London, Johnson was supposed to have been attracted to flying when she saw the film *Wings*, the first to win an academy award, at a cinema in 1927. She saved from her wages until she could afford to join the London Aero Club, where she not only learnt how to fly and to navigate, but also how to repair aeroplanes. Unable to afford advanced tuition, she became an aeroplane mechanic so that she could exchange her skills for lessons. She was not content with simply flying, but wanted the fame and fortune of being seen to set records.

Despite her desire for fame, on 5 May 1930 her departure on the first solo flight by a woman from Croydon, south London, to Australia went almost unnoticed, possibly because few ever believed that

she would get far. It was not until her de Havilland Moth arrived in India that media attention was alerted, and again it was the London *Daily Mail* that was first with the aviation news. It took another nine days for her to reach Port Darwin on 24 May, where she was accorded the welcome that she craved. This was the start of a number of record attempts, with her reaching Cape Town, Tokyo and Moscow.

She married **Captain Jim Mollison** in 1932, who already had a reputation for record-breaking flights, and they began to operate as a team, but not always successfully or harmoniously. In 1933, they set out to fly from Wales to the United States, hoping to reach New York, but had to crash-land at Bridgeport, Connecticut, low on fuel. Mollison had insisted on being the pilot for the entire trip, and when exhaustion had begun to take over, had refused his wife's repeated offers to relieve him at the controls. The whole affair erupted into an argument, leading to the accident. Not surprisingly, they divorced in 1937.

During the Second World War, Johnson became a member of the Air Transport Auxiliary Service, whose main role was to deliver aircraft from the factories to the air stations where they were needed – a highly demanding role as the members had to cope with a wide variety of aircraft types. In January 1941, while flying an Airspeed Oxford, a twin-engined communications or navigational training aircraft, she ran low on fuel and had to bale out over the Thames estuary. Landing in the water, her flying gear became waterlogged and she drowned.

Johnson, Clarence Leonard 'Kelly' (1910–90)

US aircraft designer. Graduating as an aeronautical engineer from the University of Michigan in 1932, he went to work for Studebaker, a name more usually associated with motor cars. The following year, studying for his MSc, he was working in a wind tunnel while the Lockheed 10 transport was being tested, and his recommendation that the aircraft's stability problems could be cured by a twin-fin saved the design, earning him a position with the company in California. He became its chief research engineer in 1938.

Some forty aircraft designs were handled by Johnson, including the P-38 Lightning long-range fighter and the P-80 jet fighter, designed in just five months, which he handled concurrently with the Constellation airliner.

Postwar, he worked on both the F-104 Starfighter, known as the 'missile with a man in it', and the high-flying U-2 reconnaissance aircraft, which used the 'U' for utility designation to keep the aircraft's true role secret as it was one of the products of the 'Skunk Works', as Lockheed termed its top-secret facility. Both of these were launched in 1956. In 1960, he worked on a successor to the U-2, the aircraft initially designated as the YF-12A. Later designated the SR-71, this could not have been more different from the U-2, having a delta wing and being capable of Mach 30.

Johnson, Gp Capt (later AVM) James Edgar 'Johnnie' (1915–2001) British ace. On qualifying as a pilot, Johnson was posted to No. 616 'South Yorkshire' Squadron, originally a RAuxAF unit, scoring his first kill during summer 1941. He became the UK's highest scoring ace by the end of the Second World War with thirty-eight confirmed kills and the rank of group captain. He remained in the service postwar and retired as an air vice-marshal.

Johnson, Lt Col Robert Samuel 'Bob' (1920–99) US ace. Johnson joined the USAAF in 1941 and by 1943 was in the UK flying Republic P-47 Thunderbolts, an aircraft known as 'the Jug', and being given intensive air combat training as the aircraft was regarded as inferior to the German Bf109s.

Johnson scored his first kill in June 1943, after which he scored a total of twenty-eight kills over the next twelve months. He also took an interest in fighter tactics, maintaining that close escort of bomber formations was impractical and instead argued successfully that fighters should drive off approaching enemy aircraft.

Johnstone, Ralph (1886–1910) American pioneer. Touring Europe and the United States as an exhibition trick cyclist, he was introduced to **Orville Wright** by a friend, who taught him to fly and then gave him a job as an exhibition pilot. He joined **Arch Hoxsley** and together they

were known as the Heavenly Twins. In September 1910, after competing in the Boston meet, he set an altitude record of 9,741 ft.

In November he was killed when his Wright biplane broke up at 800 ft over Denver. He tried to regain control but was thrown out of his seat, and although he grabbed a strut, he died when the aircraft hit the ground.

Joubert de la Ferté, ACM Sir Philip B. (1887–1965) British air commander. Before the Second World War, Joubert de la Ferté was air adviser to combined operations and then assistant chief of air staff responsible for the introduction of radar. In this role he is credited with the successful application of radar equipment which enabled the RAF's fighters to be where they were needed during the **Battle of Britain**. He was knighted in 1938.

In June 1941 de la Ferté was promoted to air chief marshal and became commander-in-chief of RAF Coastal Command, a post that he had held in peacetime. He arrived in post at the height of the **Battle of the Atlantic**, his aircraft having shared in the destruction of just two U-boats, but by February 1943, it had accounted for twenty-seven. He did much to reduce the 'Atlantic Gap' and centralised his command to ensure the efficient use of scant resources, as well as overseeing the introduction of the more effective Torpex-filled depth charge, an improved and much more accurate low-level bomb sight, and, after some hesitation, was responsible for the introduction of the Leigh light.

De la Ferté was a controversial figure who was frequently involved in disputes with the Admiralty. He commanded Coastal Command, and with Bomber Command he not only sought to borrow his units for the Thousand Bomber Raids, but also competed for longer-range aircraft such as the Consolidated Liberator.

In February 1943, he was appointed inspector-general of the RAF, almost a non-post. He retired in October, but was recalled to serve in South-East Asia Command as a deputy chief of staff to Lord Louis Mountbatten.

Joukovsky/Zhukovskii, Nikolai Yegerovitch (1847–1921) Pioneering Russian aerodynamicist.

Graduating in mathematics and physics, his first job was teaching physics, and it was not until the early 1900s that he appears to have become interested in aeronautics. He built Russia's first wind tunnel in 1902, making significant discoveries on aerofoil sections and lift, similar to the findings of Martin Kutta, but arrived at independently. Following the Russian Revolution, he founded the Central Institute for Aerodynamics, but did not live to see it develop.

Jullien, Pierre (1814–77) French pioneering designer. A clock repairer, Jullien built a model dirigible in 1850 using watch springs for power, which succeeded in flying when launched at the Paris Hippodrome. Eight years later, he demonstrated a model aeroplane with a metre wing-span powered by rubber bands to the French Society for the Encouragement of Aviation; the model flew 12 metres – the first French-built flying model. This encouraged him to raise funds to build a full-sized aeroplane that would have been powered by an electric motor, but he could not find the backing he needed and, having poured all of his own money into the project, he died in poverty.

Julliot, Henri (1856–1923) French airship designer. An engineering graduate, in 1901 he was working for the **Lebaudy** brothers, who were sugar refiners, when they told him to design a dirigible. An envelope, 187 ft long, was built at the Surcouf balloon works, while Julliot designed a nacelle with a 40 hp Daimler-Benz engine at the Lebaudy works. This was the famous *Lebaudy I*, nicknamed 'Jaune', because of its yellow paint, and the world's first successful semi-rigid dirigible (in contrast to the rigid **Zeppelin**s). It could travel at 25 mph and its many cross-country flights led to it being bought by the French Army in 1905, while in the UK a fund was established by the London *Morning Post* newspaper to buy a Lebaudy for the British Army, which naturally enough was named *The Morning Post* airship.

jumbo jet A term coined for the Boeing 747 when it first flew in February 1969. The term is still used, but dated, as the aircraft has been overtaken by the larger Lockheed C-5 Galaxy and the slightly larger still Antonov An-124, while the largest aircraft to fly so far has been the An-225, although this has still to enter production. The largest passenger aircraft today is the Airbus A380.

Junkers German manufacturer. Founded by **Professor Hugo Junkers**, the first aircraft was the J.1 which appeared in 1915, the world's first all-metal aeroplane. Working outside Germany immediately after the First World War, the company produced a series of all-metal airliners and Junkers also started production of diesel engines for aircraft, the only company to do so commercially until recently. His F.13, which appeared in 1919, was the first all-metal commercial aircraft. His early designs used corrugated steel rather than sheet aluminium, which was difficult to work with at the time. He founded an airline in 1921, and this was later merged into the new Deutsches Luft Hansa (*sic*). Returning to Germany, Junkers retired from business to concentrate on research in 1930, and when Hitler came to power he refused to collaborate with the Nazi regime and the company was confiscated and nationalised in 1934. It continued to build transport aircraft, including the famous Ju52/3M trimotor, which was also adopted as a bomber transport and was last used operationally in the combat role during the Spanish Civil War. It proved the mainstay of the Luftwaffe's transport effort throughout the Second World War, with more than 3,000 being built. The company also moved into warplane production, with the Ju87 Stuka dive-bomber, which was followed by the Ju88, a medium-bomber and night fighter, and its development, the Ju188. The last commercial transport was the elegant Ju90 for DLH, and this was developed into the Ju290 maritime-reconnaissance aircraft during the Second World War.

Junkers, Prof Hugo (1859–1935) German designer. After studying thermodynamics at Berlin, Karlsruhe and Aachen, Junkers opened his first factory in 1889 to produce engines and followed this with thermal heating devices. He started teaching thermodynamics at Aachen in 1897, and moved from this to a study of aeronautics. In 1910, he patented a design for a fully cantilevered flying wing, a concept that was barely understood at the time and which was not to see a practical application for more than thirty years. He followed this in 1915 with the J.1, the first all-metal aeroplane, using corrugated steel rather than sheet aluminium, which was difficult to work with at the time. The J.1 flew, despite its ugly appearance.

In 1919 he produced the F.13, which was the first all-metal commercial aircraft, and this aircraft entered production outside of Germany, since Germany itself was banned from aircraft production by the **Treaty of Versailles**. Like a number of manufacturers, Junkers also ventured into the air transport business, founding an airline in 1921 which was later absorbed when the new national airline, Deutsches Luft Hansa (not Lufthansa, as today), was founded. His next move was to introduce diesel engines for aircraft, and, until recently, he was the only manufacturer to do so on a commercial scale. He followed this by building the G.38, regarded as a large aircraft at the time with its capacity of thirty passengers.

Junkers retired from business in 1932 to pursue scientific research. After Hitler came to power, he refused to collaborate and as a result had his company taken from him in 1934.

K

Kaman American manufacturer. One of the smaller US manufacturers, the company was founded in 1945 and produced the HUK-1 and HOK light helicopters, followed by the H-43 Husky rescue and fire-fighting helicopter, all of which used contra-rotating intermeshing blades for greater stability. More conventional was the single rotor UH-2 Seasprite for the USN, a small ship helicopter for operations from frigates and destroyers. The most recent project has been the single-seat K-MAX helicopter, described by the company as an aerial truck and designed for repetitive lifting, as in forestry operations. The company also builds aircraft structures as a subcontractor and now also distributes musical instruments in the USA.

Kaman, Charles H. (1919–) American helicopter designer. A graduate in aeronautical engineering, he went to work for United Technologies on helicopter blades, where he came to the conclusion that his employers were wrong to back **Igor Sikorsky**'s single rotor design as he felt that contra-rotating intermeshing blades provided greater stability. He built a demonstrator using an old motor car chassis and engine. Realising that United would not back him, he left and started his own company in 1945.

His first helicopter, the K-125, made a successful test flight and vindicated his stand, providing a stable hover, and it was ordered by the US armed forces. His K-225 of 1951 was the world's first turbine-powered helicopter.

kamikaze (1) record-breaking aircraft The name given to a distance record-setting aircraft of the 1930s.

kamikaze (2) suicide aircraft The term kamikaze or 'divine wind' referred to an event in Japanese history when a storm destroyed a Mongol invasion force. During the Second World War, it was used for suicide attacks, of which the best known were the use of aircraft as manned missiles against Allied warships, but there were also kamikaze assaults by infantry and even submarine attacks. In the air, because the Japanese fighters lacked the power to reach the high-flying USAAF Boeing B-29 Superfortress bombers, aircraft were stripped of all unnecessary weight, including armament, and flown into the bombers.

At first, the Japanese were reluctant to resort to kamikaze attacks when suggested by Admiral Arima, however, Ensign Shoichi Ota of the Naval Air Technical Depot began the design of a human flying bomb, the Oka, following the American invasion of the Marianas. This first appeared in September 1944, and was intended as a mass-produced disposable aircraft that had the advantage of the pilot being committed to carrying out his attack knowing he would not return. Powered by five rockets and of flimsy construction, the single-seat Oka had to be carried to within range of its target by a land-based bomber, and after being released it could fly under power for up to 11 miles before diving or gliding on to its target with its 2,600 lb of explosive. The big weakness was that the mother aircraft had to get close to the target, well within range of Allied radar and fighters.

The name kamikaze was chosen by Vice-Admiral Takijiro Onishi, who introduced the concept on his own initiative after he became commander of the Fifth Base Air Force in the Philippines on 19 November 1944. He started the attacks using Zero fighters, which were manoeuvrable indeed, but could only carry a bomb of 550 lb (250 kg) and were completely wasted on vessels with armoured decks.

Most pilots were senior ratings or very junior officers, and strategic sense was lacking. They would aim for a destroyer or escort carrier. The preferred spot when attacking a carrier was the join between the island and the flight deck, which often caused considerable loss of life, but the lifts, even on the armoured British carriers, would have been more vulnerable, not only putting ships out of action but with the very real possibility of setting aircraft in the hangar below on fire, and starting a chain of events that could end in the loss of a carrier.

Later, when the concept received official backing, it became known as Operation Sho.

Rear Admiral Arima himself flew the first officially recorded kamikaze mission on 13 October 1944, crashing his aircraft into the carrier USS *Franklin*. It was also at this time that volunteers were called for from 201st Air Group based in the Philippines at the base known to the Americans as Clarke Airfield. In calling for volunteers, the Japanese commanders made it clear that they were looking for men without family commitments, but the entire unit volunteered, becoming the 1st Special Attack Force or *Tokhai Tai*. Lt Yukio Seki was given command of the first group of twenty-three petty officer pilots. Seki himself had to fly four missions before finding a suitable target. This was an option open only to those flying modified aircraft as the pilots of the Oka flying bombs had no chance of turning back. Tactics varied. A pilot could either opt for an attack from high altitude, around 20,000 ft, or make a lower approach at around 3,000 ft. The high altitude attack meant that the aircraft could not dive at a very steep angle for fear of losing control, making accuracy difficult, but from 3,000 ft a steep dive was possible.

Anti-ship kamikaze missions were usually escorted by fighters, who as well as fighting off the Allied fighters were also expected to report back on the success of the mission. The more cynical believe that one duty of the escorts was to discourage any kamikaze pilot who had second thoughts and wished to return. There could be some truth in this as not all of the 'volunteers' seem to have been genuine and others seem to have signed up under peer pressure, as when entire units 'volunteered', and those who were reluctant to volunteer were sometimes found dead after an air raid. Even Christian Japanese airmen volunteered for kamikaze missions, maintaining that it was their duty to die for the emperor.

Japanese propaganda claimed that every kamikaze sank a ship, but this was a gross distortion of the truth. Even so, at Leyte Gulf, four escort carriers were damaged by Kamikaze attacks and a fifth, USS *St Lo*, sunk. It seems that one in four kamikaze inflicted damage while one in thirty-three sank a ship.

Kammhuber Line A name given by the Allies to the German night fighter defence system organised by Gen J. Kammhuber during the summer of 1940. Initially, the line consisted of three zones, each of which had anti-aircraft and searchlight units, and two radar sets. One of these radar sets tracked the bombers and the other the German night fighters, who initially circled a radio beacon while waiting for the fighter controller to direct them towards their targets. This worked well, and was expanded into the system known officially as *Raumnachtjagd*, sector night fighting, which consisted of overlapping defensive areas. These areas stretched from Denmark to south of Paris, and in some areas were double depth to protect the most important cities.

In July 1943, the RAF used 'Window' (aluminium foil strips) for the first time to jam the radar and by August the Kammhuber system had to be abandoned in favour of directing the German night fighters towards the bomber streams in a tactic known as *Wilde Sau*.

Kamov Russian design bureau. The design bureau founded by Nikolai Kamov specialised in light utility and shipboard helicopters using the Kamov co-axial contra-rotating rotor. Among its early designs was the Ka-15 of 1952, designated 'Hen' by NATO, which was followed by the Ka-20 'Harp' during the early 1960s, and then the Ka-25 'Hormone' and Ka-26 'Hoodlum'.

Kármán, Theodore von (1881–1963) American-Hungarian aerodynamicist. Having studied engineering in Budapest and Göttingen, he worked for the Austro-Hungarian Army's aviation units during the First World War designing helicopters, although none of his designs entered service. After the First World War he started to teach aerodynamics at Göttingen, where he also became involved in research, discovering the von Kármán Vortex Street. He also travelled, advising **Junkers** and **Zeppelin**, and lectured in the United States at the invitation of the **Guggenheim** Foundation, as well as being an aeronautical consultant in Japan.

He moved to the USA during the early 1930s and continued his consultancy work, handling airship design, curing turbulence problems on the Douglas DC-3 airliner and even helping in balancing the giant Palomar telescope. He made extensive use of wind tunnels in his research. He became a professor at Cal Tech, and with colleagues founded Aerojet Engineering, which produced rocket motors. At the end of the Second World War he was assigned to assessing captured German and Japanese aircraft.

Kartveli, Alexander (1896–1974) American-Russian designer. Russian-born Kartveli studied engineering at the Paris Ecole Supérieure d'Aéronautique, and although he returned home, he was one of many who escaped to the West following the Bolshevik Revolution. He worked with **Blériot** and **Fokker** before going to the United States in 1934 where he was employed by another Russian émigré, **Alexander de Seversky**. He worked on two fighters, the P-35 and P-43, and although these were never popular, he was responsible for the more successful P-47 Thunderbolt which was built after Seversky's company was relaunched as **Republic Aviation**.

Postwar, Kartveli designed the Republic F-84 Thunderjet.

Kawanishi Japanese manufacturer. Active during the interwar period and the Second World War, the company usually specialised in flying boats and seaplanes, including the ESK1 reconnaissance seaplane of the early 1930s, followed by the H6K1 Type 97 four-engined flying boat of the mid-1930s. Wartime aircraft included the Ki4 and Ki61 Type 3 fighter landplanes, and the H8K2 four-engined flying boat, codenamed 'Emily' by the Allies, which was reputed to be the best Japanese flying boat of the war.

Kawasaki/Kawasaki-Bell Japanese manufacturer. It was part of a major industrial group that became involved with aviation after the First World War. Between the wars it produced a number of aircraft for the Japanese Army Air Force, including licence-building the Dornier F, which became

the Type 87 in Japanese service, the Type 88 and 93 bombers, and Type 95 fighters. Later aircraft included the twin-engined Ki45 night fighter known as the 'Dragon Slayer' to the Japanese, but codenamed 'Nick' by the Allies.

The company returned to aircraft manufacture during the mid-1950s to supply aircraft for the self-defence forces, including licence-built Bell, Boeing-Vertol and Hughes helicopters, and the Lockheed Neptune maritime-reconnaissance aircraft, which it later developed into the P-2J, with turboprop engines and stretched fuselage. In more recent years, it has built the Boeing CH-46 helicopter under licence for the JASDF and the JGSDF, and also builds the OH-1 armed scout helicopter, while the JASDF operates the C-1 jet transport. More recently, it has started deliveries of the Agusta-Westland EH101 Merlin for the JMSDF.

Kazakov, Alexander Alexandrovich (1891–1919) Russian fighter ace. Commissioned into the cavalry, he transferred to the Imperial Russian Flying Corps in 1914. Even given the lack of understanding of fighter tactics at the outset of the First World War, his attempts to down enemy aircraft using a grappling iron at the end of a long steel cable were unrealistic. On the one occasion when he came close enough to snag a German Albatros, he failed and had to destroy the aircraft by crash-landing on top of it. Despite this unpromising start, by the end of the war he had seventeen confirmed kills, before continuing in the service of the White Russian counter-revolutionaries, destroying three Bolshevik aircraft. He was killed on 3 August 1919 in an accident during take-off, although some maintain that he committed suicide because he was depressed by the advance of Bolshevik forces. A deeply religious man, he always wore a St Nicholas icon while flying, and attended the funeral of every enemy pilot brought down over Russian-held territory.

Kerwood, Charles W. (1897–1976) US fighter ace and mercenary. Kerwood was a member of the Escadrille Lafayette, the American force raised to fly with the French Aviation Militaire before the United States entered the First World War. He was wounded twice in combat and became a PoW after being shot down. He was wounded yet again when he attempted an escape.

Postwar, he commanded the Royal Hellenic Army Air Force units fighting the Turks, before returning to France where he organised American volunteers for a Franco-Spanish campaign in Morocco against Berber tribesmen, with the air element commanded by **Sadi-Joseph Lecointe**. Finally, during the Second World War, he joined the USAAF.

Kesselring, FM Albert (1885–1960) German military leader. Commissioned into the German artillery, where he saw combat during the First World War, Kesselring remained with the much-reduced German Army post-Versailles, but transferred to the newly formed Luftwaffe after Hitler came to power in 1933. When the Second World War broke out, he commanded the Luftwaffe forces deployed first for the invasion of Poland and then for the invasion of the Low Countries and France. He was posted to North Africa in 1941 where he supported Rommel's ground forces for two years. He was made commander-in-chief of all German forces in Italy from 1943, and succeeded in delaying the Allied advance northwards even after Italian surrender.

He was arrested in 1945 and tried for war crimes at Nuremburg, charged with atrocities against Italian hostages, and given a death sentence. The sentence was commuted to life imprisonment but he was released in 1952.

Kimmel, Adm Husband E. (1882–1968) American naval commander. One of the unluckiest naval commanders in history, Kimmel was commander-in-chief of the US Pacific Fleet when the Japanese attacked **Pearl Harbor** on 7 December 1941. He was relieved of his post, found guilty of dereliction of duty and forced into retirement. A naval board of inquiry cleared him in 1944, but a further investigation by Congress did not, although it decided that rather than dereliction of duty, he was guilty of errors of judgement. The truth was that the United States and its armed forces had failed to recognise the gathering tension in the Pacific, that radar in Hawaii was not used to its full potential, and that adequate reconnaissance was not mounted.

Kindelberger, James Howard 'Dutch' (1895–1962) US designer. Although he left school with a basic education, Kindelberger took a correspondence course to become a draughtsman with the Army Corps of Engineers. He transferred to the Signals during the First World War and was trained as a pilot. Postwar, he worked first for **Glenn Martin** as a designer, and then for **Douglas**, to which he moved in 1924 and later designed both the DC-1 and DC-2 airliners.

He was appointed President of the General Aviation Manufacturing Corporation in 1934, before the company changed its name to **North American**. He worked on, or oversaw, the design of the BT-9 and T-6 Texan trainers, the P-51 Mustang long-range fighter and the B-25 Mitchell light bomber. Following the Second World War he diversified the company into the new technologies of missile design and rocket motors, while also designing new aircraft, such as the famous F-86 Sabre fighter and the naval FJ-1, the B-45 Tornado bomber, and the X-15 rocket plane and XB-70 supersonic bomber.

King, AF Ernest (1878–1956) Wartime USN commander-in-chief. Born in Ohio to Scottish immigrant parents, he served in destroyers during the First World War and then on the staff of the admiral commanding the Atlantic Fleet battleships. He spent the years between the two world wars as a submariner and learning to fly, determined to understand every facet of seapower. He was an acting vice-admiral by 1938.

In December 1940, with the USN taking an increasingly active role in the Atlantic, he was put in command of the Atlantic Squadron, despite this effectively being a demotion, but he was promoted back to full vice-admiral early in 1941, and then to admiral in February when his command was given the status of the US Atlantic Fleet. The USN was by this time escorting convoys to a mid-Atlantic handover point to ease the pressure on the Royal Navy and Royal Canadian Navy, and King's skill and determination led President Roosevelt to appoint him commander-in-chief of the entire US Navy which then entered the war in December 1941. Despite this, the relationship between the two men was never easy and King was denied the chance of reorganising the Navy Department.

It was King who decided US strategy in the Pacific, holding Hawaii and ensuring that Australia was not isolated, and then advancing island group by island group towards Japan. He did not neglect the Atlantic, and reinforced the Atlantic Fleet by creating the Tenth Fleet in May 1943 specifically to counter the German U-boats. He was promoted to the five star rank of fleet admiral in December 1944, and retired on 15 December 1945.

Kingsford-Smith, Sir Charles Edward (1897– 1935) Australian pioneer and airline founder. During the First World War, Brisbane-born Kingsford-Smith served as a motorcycle dispatch rider at Gallipoli and then in Egypt before joining the RFC in 1917, initially as a mechanic. He was later trained as a pilot and commissioned, being awarded the MC. Postwar, he worked as a stunt pilot in Hollywood and planned a transpacific flight, although this never happened due to a lack of financial support.

He returned to Australia and began setting national records in the air. At the same time he met another aviator, Charles Ulm, and revived the idea of a transpacific flight. This time they found a wealthy American backer who enabled them to buy a Fokker F.VII/3M, in which they flew from the United States across the Pacific to Australia between 31 May and 10 June 1928. On the back of the publicity and interest in aviation created by their flight, the two men established Australian National Airways, while continuing to make their record-breaking flights to demonstrate the safety of air travel. It was ironic, therefore, that Ulm was killed in an accident in 1934, and Kingsford-Smith died the following year when his aircraft disappeared in the Gulf of Martaban, off Burma.

kite Although at one time used as the slang term for an aeroplane, the true kite is the most basic form of heavier-than-air flight, with propulsion being provided by the tow-line, and lift by the incidence of the kite to the wind. The origins of the traditional kite are lost in antiquity, but the concept is believed to have come from China. **Lawrence Hargrave** invented the box kite in 1893, combining the biplane and tandem-wing concepts and boxing these at the wing ends in a design that produced both lift and stability. Several

of the early pioneers were influenced by this work, and aircraft using the box kite configuration included those by the **Voisin** brothers.

Knabenshue, A. Roy (1876–1960) American pioneer. After little success with his own glider designs, he changed to airships and finally got into the air, demonstrating his dirigibles at the 1904 St Louis World's Fair. He met the **Wright** brothers and **Frederick Baldwin**, and the latter recruited him to pilot his dirigible, the *California Arrow*. After a few months, Knabenshue returned to working on his own at shows and exhibitions.

When he learnt of the Wrights' successes, he proposed that he should become their exhibition manager, which they accepted and found to be an extremely profitable arrangement. In 1913 Knabenshue built the *White City*, the first US passenger-carrying airship.

Knight, James H. (1893–1945) American airmail pioneer. After flying with the US Army Aeronautical Section during the First World War, he went to work for the US Post Office as a pilot working on airmail flights. On 22 February 1921 he was involved in an attempt to maintain airmail services, by night as well as by day, to raise public awareness of the service, but bad weather nearly ruined the effort. His DH-4 flew the leg of the transcontinental service between North Platte and Omaha where Knight's relief pilot was not ready, so he continued and flew the Omaha to Chicago leg, through snow and fog. His intermediate landing place at Des Moines was closed due to thick fog so he used his emergency reserves of fuel to fly on to Iowa City. Fortunately, a night-watchman at Iowa City heard the plane and lit a flare, enabling him to land and refuel before flying on to a hero's welcome at Chicago.

Later, the airmail services were operated first by the US Army and then by the airlines, which he joined in 1928 when he went to work for United Airlines in their press office.

Kollsman, Paul (1900–82) German-American instrument specialist. Kollsman was the founder of the New York-based Kollsman Instrument Company in 1928, having earlier emigrated from Germany with his brother Otto. Driven by the conviction that the existing instruments were crude and badly made, he started by designing an altimeter using switch watch gears to drive the hands. The following year **Jimmy Doolittle** tested the device to see if it was suitable for night flying, and found that it was twenty times more accurate than anything else available.

Kondo, Vice Adm Nobutake (1886–1953)

Japanese naval commander. Despite being a gunnery specialist, he commanded the Imperial Japanese Navy's Southern Force responsible for the invasion of Malaya, Singapore, the Philippines and the Netherlands East Indies, as well as the attack on Ceylon, while his ships were brought to battle at the **Coral Sea** and **Midway**, at a number of other actions and finally at **Leyte Gulf**. He showed excessive caution and an inability to grasp the importance of naval air power.

Koolhoven, Frederick (1887–1946) Dutch

designer. Having learnt to fly on Farmans in 1910, Koolhoven went to work for **Deperdussin** as an assistant to **Louis Béchereau** and was then sent to England to work with the English subsidiary. After the company was wound up, he moved to **Armstrong-Whitworth**, initially as works manager but eventually becoming chief designer. His first design, the FK.1 was unsuccessful, but he soon gained a reputation for innovation before moving to the British Aerial Transport Company, where he designed a fighter, the BAT Bantam, although peace meant that there were no orders for this aircraft.

Returning to the Netherlands, he became designer for the Nationale Vliegtuigindustrie, which he reorganised and ran until the fall of the Netherlands in 1940.

Korean Air War (1950–3) At the end of the

Second World War, Korea was liberated from the Japanese, who had occupied the country since early in the twentieth century. After the Soviet Union had belatedly entered the war against Japan, it was agreed that the United States would take the surrender of Japanese forces in the southern part of the country, leaving the Soviet Union to take the Japanese surrender in the north. An arbitrary line was drawn between the two zones at the 38th

parallel. After UN-supervised elections in the south, in May 1948, the new Republic of Korea came into existence in July, but while it laid claim to be the government of the entire country, the north remained firmly in the Communist camp as the Democratic People's Republic of Korea, which also claimed to have jurisdiction over the whole country.

The scene was set for confrontation. Korea was to be one more postwar area of tension. Yet, on the morning of Sunday 25 June 1950, a sudden invasion by North Korea of its southern neighbour found few senior commanders at their posts, leaving the North Koreans free to sweep south, supported by strong air cover. This was to be the first conflict in which the UN formally deployed troops, due largely to a Russian boycott of the Security Council, which meant that the Soviet Union's veto could not be enacted.

Proposals for the creation of a South Korean Air Force had been rejected by the United States. As a result, the country was left with an embryonic air arm operating training aircraft, and little else. The Republic of Korea (RoK) Army, trained and equipped by the United States before withdrawal of its own armed forces, was little more than a gendarmerie. It had 95,000 men in 1950, nominally comprising eight divisions although only half of these were up to strength. It had war-surplus American equipment, including rifles and light mortars. While there were some anti-tank mortars and guns, these were obsolete and ineffective against modern armour. Ammunition stocks were limited.

The excuse was that the United States believed Korea had no strategic value in the confrontation that had emerged between East and West. It was thought that any North Korean aggression against the south would extend to no more than terrorist attacks. North Korea, by contrast, was heavily armed. Its armed forces included the North Korean People's Army (NKPA) with eight full-strength divisions and another two at half strength, with at least 135,000 men under arms and its own artillery and armour, and the Korean People's Armed Forces Air Corps. This included a number of fighter types, the most modern of which were piston-engined Yakovlev Yak-9 fighters as well as

Ilyushin Il-10 ground-attack aircraft. The Yak-9 would not have been a match for the North American F-51 fighter-bombers which had been proposed for the putative RoK Air Force.

The United States had pulled out without making anything other than the most rudimentary preparations for the South Koreans to defend themselves. It was argued that creating stronger RoK armed forces, including an air force, would add to the tension in the area. In fact, tension was a part of life for the area. What existed was a serious military imbalance. This would not have mattered had the United States still maintained forces on the ground in Korea, but most of the USAF's equipment in the region was by this time deployed on to Okinawa, one of the smaller Japanese islands, and to the Philippines.

The United States Far East Air Force was not at the state of readiness that could have been expected given the tension in the area. This followed similar slackness in Korea, so that FEAF's headquarters in Japan did not receive notification of the invasion until some 6 hours after it had started. Most of its personnel were away for the weekend. The news was relayed to the component air forces, which included the Twentieth in Okinawa and the Thirteenth in the Philippines. No decisions were taken for some time and at first hesitation and confusion reigned.

When operations did start, the priority lay not in attacking the invaders, but in evacuating US nationals. Even this did not start until 0330 on Monday morning, with the air evacuation not starting until 27 June. The orders were that the FEAF could only attack North Korean forces if the evacuation itself was attacked. Meanwhile, South Korean ground forces were being pushed back by the invaders although they had managed to slow the pace of the advance. After a preliminary skirmish on 26 June, fighter combat flared up on 27 June between Yak-7s and Lockheed F-82 jet fighters. The first FEAF bomber sorties were the following day.

The result was a three-year war, which on at least one occasion came close to seeing the use of nuclear weapons. Substantial forces from both sides of the East–West divide had to be deployed to rectify a situation which would not have occurred if South Korea had been equipped with

one of the basic requirements of a nation state, the ability to defend itself, or if outside assistance had been timely. This was not so much a failure of deterrence, as so many wars could be described, as a complete absence of it. The signals sent to the Soviet Union and Communist China suggested that they could get away with the annexation of South Korea.

After the initial series of defeats, the US commander in the area, Gen Douglas MacArthur, achieved a successful landing on occupied South Korean territory with the landings at Inchon, although many commentators believe that he took unjustifiable risks in the process.

Ignoring Chinese warnings, MacArthur pushed the UN forces northwards through North Korea to the Yalu River, beyond which lay China itself. The Chinese crossed the Yalu and inflicted a devastating defeat on the UN forces. Many commentators believe that this period saw MacArthur undergo a series of violent mood swings in which he first refused to believe that China could threaten American forces, and then believed that they were about to be overwhelmed by Chinese forces. By this time, his inaction meant that Chinese forces had been able to cross the Yalu and surround his positions. His reaction to this was to demand to be able to use nuclear weapons against the Chinese, or saturate large areas of Korea with radioactive material so that the Chinese could not occupy it.

MacArthur, was eventually relieved of his command and retired, leaving his successor, General Ridgway, to stabilise the position.

During the conflict, air power by the UN forces was often exercised from Okinawa or the Philippines while aircraft from British and American carriers operated over Korea, a result of so few bases ashore being available, especially when the northern forces almost overran the south. The aircraft deployed aboard the British carriers were piston-engined Hawker Sea Furies and Fairey Fireflies, although in one case the former managed to shoot down a North Korean MiG-15. Most, if not all, of the MiG fighters deployed by the North Korean forces were in fact flown by Russian pilots. When eventually shore bases became available, it was soon realised that the British-built Gloster Meteor jet fighters deployed under US command by the RAAF were no match for the more agile

MiG-15s. There was little involvement by the RAF in the war due to its heavy commitments elsewhere, with operations against Communist bandits in Malaya (now Malaysia) and colonial policing duties.

Kosovo Air Campaign (27 March–3 June 1999) The end of the Communist Tito regime in Yugoslavia meant the break-up of the country into a series of small Balkan states, with their newly found independence marred by strong ethnic divisions between Orthodox Serbs, Muslims and Roman Catholics. The Serbian leader, Slobodan Milosevic, resisted attempts by Kosovo to break free from central control, and the resultant ethnic cleansing meant that the United Nations became involved and many of the member nations positioned troops in the area as peace-keepers, although not always very effective. It was decided to remove Milosevic from office and allow the Kosovar population to return to their homeland. Faced with the difficulty of landing and maintaining troops in the difficult terrain, with a UN resolution behind it, the NATO members prepared a bombing campaign.

The air campaign started slowly, with just fifty sorties in the first 24 hours. It took twelve days for the number of sorties to match those of the first 12 hours of the air campaign that started the Gulf War for the liberation of Kuwait. The impression was that the NATO forces were using air power selectively, aiming at key targets to force Milosevic to negotiate and curb ethnic cleansing of the Kosovo Muslims. The pace of bombing using both smart and dumb weapons accelerated until at the peak some 1,200 aircraft were available, many operating from US carriers cruising in the Adriatic, but Northrop Grumman B-2A stealth bombers were also deployed from their base in Missouri. Inevitably, not all of the bombs fell on Serbian targets and at least two refugee convoys were hit, as was the Chinese embassy, destroyed on 7 May. Lacking significant air power of their own, on 3 June Milosevic agreed to a complete withdrawal of Serb troops from Kosovo.

NATO losses were light, but included a Lockheed Martin F-117A Nighthawk stealth fighter, used in the ground attack role, shot down by a ground-to-air missile due to poor tactics.

Kozhedub, Maj Ivan Nikitovich (1920–91) Soviet air ace. During training, Kozhedub proved to be such a good pilot that the Soviet air force wanted to keep him on instructional duties, and it took much pressure from him before he was finally posted to a fighter squadron. He was with the 16th Air Army at the Battle of Kursk in 1943, and by the end of the war had sixty-two confirmed victories, having flown 520 sorties. He was awarded the Gold Star.

Postwar, he remained with the service, and was active during the Korean War commanding MiG-15 units deployed secretly, with Russian pilots and the aircraft in North Korean markings.

Krebs, Arthur-Constantin (1850–1918) French engineer. **Charles Renard** asked Krebs, who was at the time a captain in the French Army's corps of engineers, to build an electric motor to power his dirigible, *La France*. The 8 hp motor designed by Krebs weighed just 211 lb, and allowed the airship carrying the two men to make the trip of 2.5 miles from Chalais-Meudon to Villacoublay, and then back again, on 9 August 1884, reaching a speed of 13 mph.

While the craft was a success, the weight of its electric batteries meant that this was not the way forward.

L

Lahm, Lt Frank Purdy (1877–1963) American pioneer. Commissioned into the United States Army, Lahm was sponsored by his father, a ballooning enthusiast, in the 1906 **Gordon Bennett** balloon race, which he won by travelling 402 miles from Paris to Yorkshire. He returned to France to take a course at the Cavalry School at Saumur, and at the same time was ordered to provide an overview of aeronautical development in Europe.

Back in the United States, he became the first US Army officer to be taken up in an aeroplane when he was flown by **Orville Wright** at Fort Myers, Virginia, on 9 September 1908. In October 1910 he was one of the first two officers to be trained to fly by **Wilbur Wright**. Much of his time between learning to fly and American entry into the First World War was spent surveying sites for future air stations, but he was later sent to Europe in command of the American Expeditionary Force's aerostats.

Laird, Emil Matthew (1896–1982) American pioneer. A lowly paid hotel worker, Laird became fascinated by aviation when he saw **Walter Brookins** fly past his hotel. At first, he could only afford to build models, but he attended the 1912 **Gordon Bennett** race in Chicago and studied aircraft design so that the following year he started to build a full-sized monoplane, for which he bought an engine on credit. Unfortunately, it crashed on its first flight. He built two further aircraft which were successful and he became a display pilot, often flying at night with headlamps fixed to the wings of his aircraft.

He spent most of the First World War in hospital recovering from injuries received when he had crashed another pilot's plane, but when he was discharged, he started his own aeroplane factory in Chicago. This was promptly abandoned when he received backing to build a factory in Kansas, where he founded the Laird Airplane Company. His first product was the three-seat Laird OX-5

biplane, which failed to sell in the depressed postwar market. After a disagreement with his backer, he returned to Chicago and once again started his own company in 1923, but it was not until the 1930s that his Laird Solution and Super Solution racing planes met with success, winning the Thompson and Bendix Trophy races.

Laker, Sir Frederick 'Freddie' (1922–2006) British low-cost air travel pioneer. Born in Canterbury, Kent, Laker became an apprentice at the **Shorts** aircraft factory in Rochester in 1938, and then an engineer in the Air Transport Auxiliary during the Second World War, where he also learnt to fly and how to manage an airline.

Laker qualified as a commercial pilot postwar and started flying with the state-owned British European Airways (BEA), but he soon left to become a freelance pilot while also trading in government surplus. In 1948 he bought twelve Handley Page Halifax bombers that had been converted to carry cargo, and used them during the **Berlin Airlift**, where they transported 11.6 per cent of the cargo carried by commercial aircraft. Afterwards his company, Aviation Traders, reverted to buying and selling government surplus. He designed and built a small airliner, the Aviation Traders Accountant, but failed to find a manufacturer that would build it under licence. He started a small charter airline, then in 1960 his businesses were merged into British United Airways in an attempt, with others, to establish a strong and viable British private enterprise airline.

As BUA's first managing director, Laker ordered Vickers VC-10 airliners for its African routes and placed the first British orders for the successful BAC One-Eleven short-haul jet airliner. He extended the company's vehicle ferry services, inherited from Silver City, by adding Carvairs, converted DC-4s, to the fleet of Bristol Freighters. In 1965 he resigned and a year later formed his own charter airline, Laker Airways. Shortly afterwards he pressed to be allowed to run low-cost transatlantic services, which did not materialise until September 1977 when he launched Skytrain.

Skytrain was a no-frills airline, with customers having to pay for refreshments, but in addition there were no bookings and passengers bought a ticket at the airport, waiting for the next flight if the aircraft was full. Over the next five years, operating McDonnell Douglas DC-10s, Skytrain grew to become the fifth largest carrier on the North Atlantic. Laker also ran International Caribbean Airways on behalf of the government of Barbados.

In the winter of 1981–2, with oil prices rising, the established airlines on the North Atlantic cut their economy fares by two-thirds, forcing Skytrain into liquidation. In an unprecedented move, his passengers started a fund that eventually reached £3.5 million, and he succeeded in fighting an anti-trust battle in the courts to obtain £80 million for his creditors and £8 million for himself, but it was too late to save his airline.

In 1992 he set up Laker Airways (Bahamas), initially with two Boeing 727s, flying American tourists to the islands, again as a low-cost operator.

Lambert, Comte Charles de (1865–1944)

Russo-French pioneer. During the closing years of the nineteenth century, de Lambert, a Russian aristocrat, whose ancestors had flown in the French Revolution, became interested in both speed boats and flying-machines. He experimented with hydrofoils in both England and France. Later, in 1909 he was the first European to be taught to fly by **Wilbur Wright**. De Lambert was an exceptionally worthwhile pupil. He bought two Wright aircraft, crashing one of them in an attempt to fly the English Channel, but flying the other at the **Reims Aviation Meeting**, coming fourth in the Grand Prix distance event. His claim to fame lies in his flight, in a borrowed Wright machine, around the Eiffel Tower on 9 October 1909.

Lambert, William Carpenter (1896–1982)

American ace. Flying with the British RFC during the First World War, Lambert scored twenty-two victories but failed to make the list of British aces because of his American nationality. He also failed to make the American list because he flew with the RFC.

Lana de Terzi, Francesco de (1631–87)

Italian priest and visionary. A Jesuit priest from Brescia, de Lana de Terzi was interested in science and in 1670 published *Prodromo Overo Saggio di Alcune* in which he envisaged lighter-than-air aircraft. His plan was for four 25 ft diameter copper spheres beneath which hung an open boat, which would be raised by the spheres once the air was evacuated from them. While this plan was impractical, as the copper spheres would have collapsed under the air pressure as they 'emptied' of air, it did recognise that an object could rise if it weighed less than the volume of air it displaced. This was before the discovery of hydrogen, which would have made his idea feasible.

He took his vision further, suggesting that the ability to fly would change warfare.

Lanchester, Frederick William (1868–1946)

British engineer. Having worked as an industrial engineer, Lanchester built the first all-British motor car in 1895, and in 1899 founded the Lanchester Engine Company with his brother George. The company became famous for its luxury cars.

Meanwhile, he had become interested in aviation, having begun by building model aeroplanes in 1890. He also discovered some of the basic laws of aerodynamics, and in 1897 presented his findings to the Physical Society of London, which included a description of the way in which a wing derived lift. His work was taken less seriously than it should have been because he was not a trained scientist and his terminology was confusing. Later, in 1909, he met **Ludwig Prandtl** at Göttingen and discussed aeronautical theory.

Langley, Samuel Pierpoint (1834–1906)

American scientist. Although originally an engineer and architect, Langley became interested in astronomy and made a number of discoveries in his new field, eventually enjoying the distinction of heading the Smithsonian Institution in Washington. He became interested in aviation in

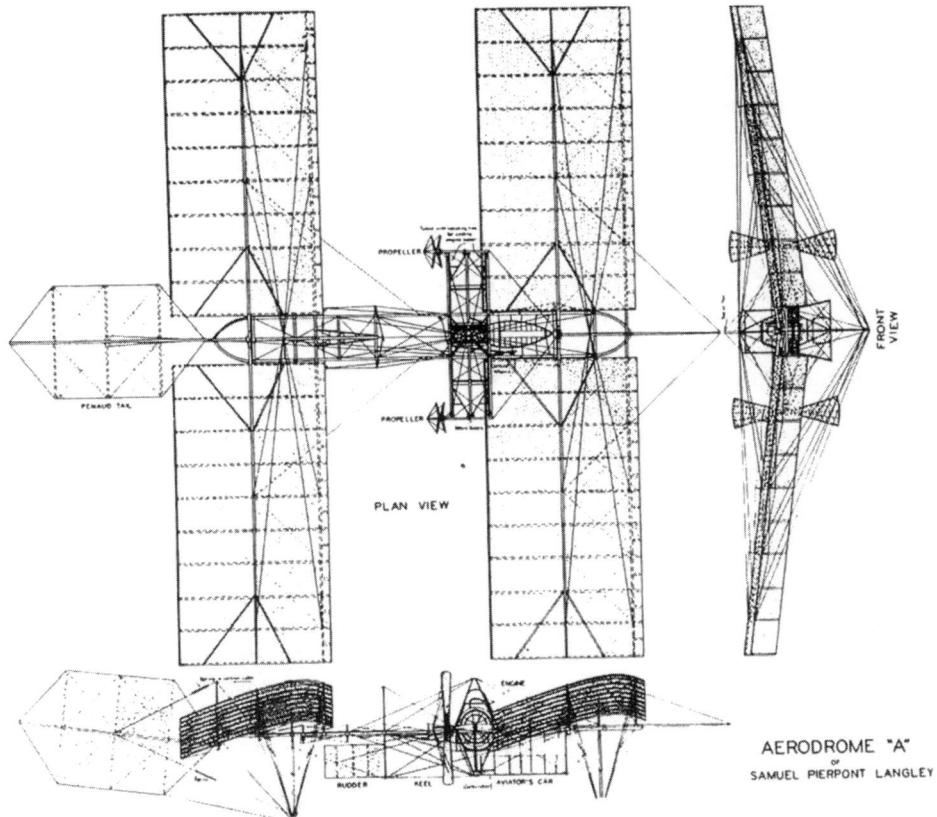

FRONT VIEW

PLAN VIEW

AERODROME "A"
OF
SAMUEL PIERPONT LANGLEY

Samuel Langley's 'Aerodrome A' looks as if it could have flown, and models certainly did, but until Glenn Curtiss modified the basic design, it was flawed.

the late 1880s and followed this with experiments of model aircraft, many of which were quite large. His first steam-powered model, in 1891, was unsuccessful but he eventually tested a further seven models between 1896 and 1903. These proved to be increasingly successful, with one flying for 3,000 ft. His work so inspired the War Department, that it sought US $50,000 (worth £10,000 at the then rate of exchange, or £67,000 in today's money) from Congress for him to build a full-sized powered aeroplane. His aircraft was a tandem-wing monoplane, which he called the *Aerodrome A*, with an engine built by Stephen Balzer and later developed by **Charles Manly**. In October and then again in December 1903, two attempts were made to launch the *Aerodrome A* from the roof of a houseboat moored

on the Potomac river, but on both occasions the aircraft collapsed into the river giving Manly, who had elected to fly the machine, a ducking. The problem was that the aircraft lacked 'control in roll' that might have made flight possible, as Langley belonged to the 'chauffeur' category of designers who did not truly understand the three-dimensional aspect of flight.

The failure of a project on which so much public money had been spent aroused strong press criticism and doubts over the possibility of heavier-than-air flight. The *Aerodrome A* was nicknamed 'Langley's Folly', and the War Department refused to believe the claims by the **Wright** brothers that they had achieved it. The value of Langley's work can be judged by the fact that once fitted with ailerons, **Glenn Curtiss** was able to fly the machine.

Latécoère, Pierre (1883–1943) French manufacturer and airline pioneer. After manufacturing munitions and aircraft during the First World War, Latécoère planned his own airline, which started operations as the Compagnie Latécoère on 25 December 1918. The first flights were from Toulouse in south-west France to Barcelona in Spain, and this was gradually extended to Morocco and then to Dakar in West Africa, which received its first air services in 1924. In 1927 the company was sold and renamed Aéropostale, later becoming one of the predecessors of Air France.

The airmail service finally reached South America on 12 May 1930, when **Jean Mermoz** reached Brazil from Dakar, although a regular service did not follow until 1934.

Throughout this period Latécoère manufactured a series of large transport and bomber aircraft, which continued up to the fall of France in 1940, and included the Latécoère 521 flying boat of 1935. In recent years the company has specialised in aerostructures, mainly building fuselages, such as those for the Airbus A380.

Latham, Hubert (1883–1912) British pioneering pilot. A motor boat racing driver and big game hunter, Latham was reckless with his life as he had been warned that he would die early from tuberculosis. He was impressed by **Wilbur Wright**'s flights at Le Mans and was taught to fly on an Antoinette by **Léon Levavasseur**, whom he knew from his interest in motor boats. After buying a stake in the company, Latham became **Antoinette**'s chief test pilot. His ambition was to be first to fly across the English Channel, winning the *Daily Mail* prize in an Antoinette, but he crashed into the sea twice due to engine problems. His disappointment was assuaged to some extent by winning 42,000 fr. at the **Reims Aviation Meeting** later that year, coming second only to **Henri Farman**. His spell of glory was short-lived, despite a demonstration tour. He went on safari in French Equatorial Africa where, on 16 July 1912, he was killed by a wild buffalo.

La Vaulx, Comte Henri de (1870–1930) French aeronaut. A wealthy Paris banker, de La Vaulx took up ballooning as a hobby in 1900 and in October of that year set a new distance record of 1,193 miles, travelling from France to Russia whereupon he was arrested as a spy and jailed. He was soon released and the following year took three friends on the first balloon crossing of the Mediterranean, travelling from Marseille to Algeria on 13 October. These were the most significant of more than 250 balloon and dirigible ascents which were made in the years that followed, many of them in the Zodiac dirigible that he purchased in 1909. He also took a passing interest in aeroplanes, sponsoring **Victor Tatin**'s 1907 monoplane, which was unsuccessful.

While La Vaulx was vice-president of the important Aéro-Club de France for a number of years, his enduring legacy was as founder of the **Fédération Aéronautique Internationale (FAI)** in 1905, which was established as the official body that confirms all aeronautical records.

He was killed in an airliner accident in 1930, flying from New York to Montreal.

Lavochkin, Syemyon Alexander (1900–65) Soviet designer. He trained at the Joukowsky Air Academy. There are few details of Lavochkin's early career, and it was not until he started to design fighter aircraft with Gorbunov and Gudov, with the designation LaGG-1 etc., that he came into prominence. He was given his own design bureau in 1943, which produced the La-5 and La-7 fighters, reputed to be the best Soviet aircraft of the Second World War.

Lawson, Alfred W. (1869–1954) Anglo-American pioneer and mystic. Lawson was the son of English parents who emigrated to the US when he was a child. In November 1908 he founded *Fly*, the first aviation magazine in the United States. Two years later he founded a second aviation magazine, *Aircraft*, and is credited by some for having invented the term 'aircraft'. He learnt to fly and in 1917 he founded an aircraft factory in Green Bay, Wisconsin, which built a small number of MT.2 trainers. One of his engineers was **Vincent Burnelli**, and postwar Lawson asked him to design an airliner, the C-2, which was similar in appearance to the Handley Page 0/400. This aircraft flew from Milwaukee to New York and on to Washington in August–September 1919. In 1920 Lawson won the first US Post Office airmail contracts.

Lawson raised the capital for his company to build a bigger aircraft, the L-4, which he dubbed the 'Midnight Liner', a trimotor which could carry twenty-four passengers. His shareholders were impatient for a return on their capital, and the aircraft was hurried towards its first flight before it was ready. It crashed on its first test flight in March 1921. This marked the end of Lawson and aviation as the business nearly brankrupted him. In later years, he proposed a new theory of economics and founded his own religion, Lawsonomy, with a popularist approach. Having rebuilt his fortunes, he purchased Des Moines University in 1943, renaming it Des Moines University of Lawsonomy.

Le Bris, Jean-Marie (1808–72) French glider pioneer. A former master mariner, Le Bris had been fascinated by the soaring and gliding of the albatross on his voyages around the two capes, and even caught one and dissected it to study its wing construction. In 1857 he built a full-sized glider based on the albatross wing, constructed from wood with a fabric-covered airframe. Despite its 50 ft wing-span, it weighed just 92 lb. The tail could pivot up and down, and there was also a form of **variable incidence** on the wing. Launched from a horse-drawn cart, the glider is believed to have lifted off with Le Bris at the controls at just 15 mph. The second flight saw the glider dropped from a mast erected over a quarry, but it oscillated, probably a series of stalls, as it fell and Le Bris suffered a broken leg.

The glider left Le Bris virtually destitute, but in 1867 a public subscription enabled him to return to his experiments, designing a glider similar to his original design, and which could lift off in a gentle wind. Persuaded not to fly it himself, in 1868 Le Bris had it towed into the air, where it crashed as there was no one at the controls.

That seems to have been the end of his attempts at flight. He became a war hero during the Franco-Prussian War, but was murdered during an argument in 1872.

Lear Jet Corporation American manufacturer. Originally founded in 1961 as the Swiss-American Aviation Corporation by **William Lear**, the company intended to build the Learjet

23 in Switzerland, but moved to Wichita, Kansas in 1962, and the title of Lear Jet Corporation was adopted. Lear's plan was to prove that the jet airliner could be scaled down for business use, and in 1963 the Learjet 23 was formally launched. The company started to produce a series of business jets and in 1965 acquired the light helicopter manufacturer, **Brantly**, before itself becoming part of the Gates Corporation. The company has continued to develop and expand, and is now the main US subsidiary of the Canadian-based **Bombardier** group.

Lear, William Powell (1902–78) American inventor and manufacturer. Lear's first passion was radio and he started building small sets as early as 1912. By 1916, when he left school to join the US Navy, he was already adept at Morse code. During the First World War he was a radio operator at the Great Lakes Naval Air Station, the USN's main training centre. Postwar, he left the USN and established an electronic laboratory, developing a practical car radio which entered production under the Motorola brand. He also developed avionic equipment such as air radios, autopilots and direction finders. Even in the 1960s he continued to invent, producing the eight-track cassette player.

Lear's most famous contribution to aviation came in 1963 with the launch of the **Lear Jet**, the first viable business jet which confounded sceptics who refused to believe that the commercial airliner could be scaled down.

Lebaudy, Paul (1858–1937) and Pierre (1861–1924) French airship pioneers. Wealthy sugar refiners, the Lebaudy brothers had their chief engineer, **Henri Julliot**, design and build the semi-rigid dirigible the *Lebaudy I*, known popularly as 'Jaune' because of its colour. The craft made its first ascent in 1902 and made a number of cross-country passages before being purchased for the French Army in 1905. The brothers continued to manufacture dirigibles but could not match the success of the rigid Zeppelins of their German rival, which proved stronger and easier to control.

Leblanc, Alfred (1869–1921) French pioneer. Having taken up ballooning as a hobby, by 1907

Leblanc was sufficiently proficient to set up an endurance record of 44 hours 2 minutes during the **Gordon Bennett** race. He was a friend of **Louis Blériot**, and had the distinction of being the person to awaken the aviator on the morning of his cross-Channel flight with a weather report. He bought the first production Blériot XI and became an exhibition pilot, winning the 490-mile Circuit de l'Est long-distance race in 1910 and being one of just two pilots to finish. He tried to repeat this success in the United States that same year with the Statue of Liberty Race, but while he was in the lead, he ran out of fuel and crashed, receiving serious injuries. He later accused others of having sabotaged his machine.

Lecointe, Sadi-Joseph (1891–1944) French racing pilot. Having learnt to fly on Blériot aircraft before the outbreak of the First World War, Sadi Lecointe flew combat sorties for eighteen months before being posted to a training unit, instructing more than 1,500 students before the end of the war as well as becoming a test pilot. Postwar, he raced for Spad and then for Nieuport-Astra, winning the 1920 **Gordon Bennett** Trophy and the Beaumont Trophy in 1924 and 1925.

After attempting to enter politics in 1924 as a radical socialist, in 1925 he led a group of volunteers in a Franco-Spanish expedition to Morocco to crush a Berber uprising. Afterwards he became a test pilot and then inspector general for French civil aviation. Following the fall of France, he commanded an Armée de l'Air base in North Africa until he was removed by the Vichy regime for his pro-Allied sympathies.

Leduc, René-Henri (1898–1968) French engine designer. Trained as a motor mechanic, when the First World War broke out Leduc was initially sent to serve in the infantry before being sent to a military engineering school. Postwar, he continued his studies at the Ecole Supérieure d'Electricité. After graduation, he was recruited by the Breguet concern in 1924 where he worked on ramjet engines. He started the design and construction of a full-sized ramjet-powered aircraft in 1937, at a time of upheaval in the French aircraft industry. His work was then halted by the outbreak of the Second World War, with his

prototype hidden after the fall of France in 1940. Following the Second World War his project, the Leduc 010, was resurrected and made its first flight on top of a transport aircraft, as with the space shuttle transporter, in 1947. It was not until 1949 that it flew under its own power, reaching a speed of 450 mph – the first flight of a manned ramjet aircraft. His Leduc 021 first flew in 1953, but the French government lost interest and the project was abandoned in 1957.

Many believe that Leduc spread himself too thinly on too many projects, including ejection-seat design, and blame him for the slow pace of development, but the essential weakness of the ramjet was simply that of gaining sufficient speed for the ramjets to work.

Lefébure, Eugène (1878–1909) French engineer. After assembling a Wright machine at the Hague, Lefébure taught himself to fly and in July 1909 made the first flight in the Netherlands. He then took part in the **Reims Aviation Meeting** and became a test pilot for the Wright's French subsidiary. It was in this latter role that he was killed on 7 September 1909, when the aircraft he was flying broke up in mid-air.

Leigh-Mallory, ACM Sir Trafford L. (1892– 1944) British air leader. Originally joining the British Army and transferring to the RFC, Leigh-Mallory remained with the newly created RAF when the war ended. By 1938 he was already an air vice-marshal commanding No. 12 Fighter Group, which at the height of the Battle of Britain was responsible for the air defence of the Midlands. His group also supported **Park**'s No. 11 Group when that came under pressure. He became an advocate of the 'big wing' tactic, using large numbers of fighters to overwhelm attacking forces, which proved controversial and brought him into dispute with both Park and their commander, **Dowding**. After Dowding was replaced, Leigh-Mallory relieved Park, and then pressed for 'big wing' tactics over occupied France, which many believe were of doubtful value.

Promoted to air marshal in July 1942, the following month he was responsible for air cover over the failed Dieppe amphibious operation, but in November became commander-in-chief of

Fighter Command. He was knighted in 1943 and that December he became Commander-in-Chief, Allied Expeditionary Air Force in preparation for the Normandy landings, with the rank of air chief marshal. His role in coordinating the tactical air forces was over by October 1944, and in November he was sent to be air officer commander-in-chief for South-East Asia Command, but en route his aircraft crashed and he was killed.

LeMay, Gen Curtis Emerson (1906–90) US
bomber leader. Rejected by West Point in 1924, LeMay joined a reserve officer training unit and finally was commissioned into the then USAAC in 1930 as a pilot and navigator. He took the 305th Bombardment Group to the UK in 1942. In July 1945, back in the USA, he was put in charge of the planning for the first nuclear bombs to be used against Japan. Postwar, by this time a lieutenant-general, he had the task of organising the Berlin Airlift, the success of which resulted in him being appointed chief of the Strategic Air Command, SAC, with full responsibility for America's nuclear deterrent.

After retiring from the USAF in 1965, he attempted to enter politics as vice-president to George Wallace, the independent candidate who failed to break the Republican-Democrat duopoly.

Lenormand, Louis-Sébastien (1757–1839)
French parachutist. Lenormand made the first verified parachute jumps in December 1783 when he descended from the tower of the Montpellier Observatory. It is believed that he may have made earlier jumps from tall trees. His aim was not for escape from a flying-machine but as a means of escaping from high buildings which were on fire.

The challenge to his claim to be first came from Fausto Veranzio, a Hungarian living in Italy in the sixteenth century, and whose claims were supported by detailed drawings.

LET Czech manufacturer. Established in the 1970s
as Let Kunovice, the company's first product was the L-410, a nineteen-seat regional turboprop airliner, which initially entered service with Slov-Air. The company went bankrupt in 2000 and was rescued by a local company, Morovan Aeroplanes and re-established as Letecke Zavody Aeronautical

Industries. Production has been relatively small scale, but the company has managed to penetrate western markets with its aircraft, doubtless due to the lack of competition in this size category.

Levavasseur, Léon (1863–1922) French
engineer. Graduating as an engineer having originally gone to Paris from his home in Cherbourg to study art, Levavasseur initially worked as an arc lamp designer, but by 1903 he had been sponsored by the French government to build an aeroplane. The aeroplane was a failure, and a second design was built but never flown.

Meanwhile, he had also been commissioned by **Jules Gastambide** to design an engine, which was built and named the 'Antoinette' after his patron's daughter. The engine's light weight was due to the extensive use of aluminium. It had fuel injection and air cooling, all advanced features for the day, although the early fuel injectors were prone to clogging. Completed in 1903, it was available as a 24 hp or a 50 hp unit. The first application for this engine was in powerboats, proving successful in the races held at Monaco in 1904 and 1905. The latter year also saw the engine being used in the boat that towed the Voisin float-gliders off the River Seine.

In 1904 a company was formed to build the engines with Gastambide and Levavasseur joined by **Louis Blériot**. One of their early customers was **Alberto Santos-Dumont**. When Levavasseur declared his intention to build another aircraft, Blériot left the partnership to work on his own. The first aircraft, the Gastambide-Mengin monoplane was another failure, but the design was refined and developed leading to the elegant Antoinette IV of 1909 with its slender fuselage reminiscent of a boat, and which became a successful exhibition and racing aircraft.

Levavasseur's later designs, including the Monobloc introduced in 1911, did not repeat the Antoinette IV's success, and the company was soon overtaken by its rivals, leaving Levavasseur to fade into obscurity and poverty.

Leyte Gulf, Battle of (23–25 October 1944)
Often described as the 'biggest naval battle in history', Leyte was an attempt by the Japanese to make some use of their major surface units, but

it was yet another battle in which carrier-borne aircraft played the dominant role. It was also the first use of massed **kamikaze** attacks.

The battle arose because US forces were ready to re-take the Philippines. The operation called for one of the biggest efforts so far. On 20 October, General MacArthur's forces landed, with the Seventh Fleet of 300 landing ships and transports putting the US Sixth Army ashore on Leyte, one of the smaller islands in the Philippines. Heavy fire support was given by six battleships and cruisers, supported by destroyers and no less than eighteen escort carriers with aircraft to provide close air support and fighter protection. The Seventh Fleet was commanded by Rear Admiral Sprague, and was divided into three groups: 'Taffy One', led by Sprague himself, 'Taffy Two' and 'Taffy Three' led by subordinate commanders. Japanese airfields were kept under constant attack by aircraft from **Admiral William Halsey**'s US Third Fleet, with Mitscher commanding TF38 with its four carrier groups and eight fleet carriers, *Lexington*, *Wasp*, *Hornet*, *Hancock*, *Intrepid*, *Essex*, *Enterprise* and *Franklin*, and another eight light carriers, *Monterey*, *Cabot*, *Cowpens*, *Independence*, *Langley*, *Princeton*, *Belleau Wood* and *San Jacinto*, supported by major surface units. The Third Fleet's carriers had 1,000 aircraft between them.

Japanese concern now reached its peak with a desperate plan calling for four aircraft carriers, the recently repaired *Zuikaku* and the light carriers *Zuiho*, *Chitose* and *Chiyoda*, with just 116 aircraft, and nine battleships, nineteen cruisers and thirty-five destroyers. The primary objective was to finally bring the Japanese battleships into action.

Overall, the battle of Leyte took place in four parts: an air-sea battle in the Sibuyan Sea on 24 October; a night battle in the Surigao Straits on 24–5 October; a battle off Samar, and an air-sea battle off Cape Engano that same day. The grand design was called Operation Sho-Go, meaning 'to conquer'. The action was known to the Japanese as the Second Battle of the Philippine Sea, and to the Americans as the Battle of Leyte Gulf.

On 23 October 1944, two American submarines, *Dace* and *Darter*, discovered the First Striking Force and torpedoed three heavy cruisers including the flagship *Atago*, which sank almost immediately, as did the *Maya*. Fighting had started on 24 October, when aircraft based on Leyte attacked the most northerly of the American carrier groups in the Battle of the Sibuyan Sea. This attack was intended to draw the US Third Fleet away and allow the Japanese battleships a clear run at the transports, but the aircraft failed to find the American ships and, running short of fuel, attempted to fly to bases on Luzon where many of them were intercepted by American fighters on the way. The shore-based aircraft managed to hit just one of the American carriers, the USS *Princeton*. A single 550 lb armour-piercing bomb shot straight through the flight deck just forward of the aft elevator, punching a neat hole in the flight deck as it continued down into the ship, eventually reaching the ship's bakery, where it exploded and killed everyone present. The explosion reached up into the hangar deck where six aircraft were being refuelled and rearmed, setting them alight, the heat causing their torpedo heads to explode. The bomb had struck the ship at 0935, and at 1010, fire threatened the aviation fuel. Two-thirds of the ship's company were ordered to abandon the ship, leaving behind fire-fighters and AA gunners, but the latter were also ordered to leave once the ship's AA ammunition started to explode in the heat. By 1330, the only part of the ship still ablaze was that near to the aft magazine. The light cruiser USS *Birmingham* was ordered alongside to provide further fire-fighting assistance and then to provide a tow, but this was delayed until 1530 by alerts. The cruiser drew alongside with many of her crew on her decks, either helping the fire-fighters or simply watching, but, without any indication of what was about to happen, the aft magazine exploded, tearing off the carrier's stern. On the cruiser, 233 men were killed and 211 were seriously wounded, with just 25 having minor injuries. Aboard the carrier 108 were killed, mainly fire-fighters and 190 wounded.

Meanwhile, two US carrier groups had found Japanese warships steaming through the Sibuyan Sea. The carriers sent four waves of aircraft throughout the day. Among the targets was the giant battleship, *Musashi*, a sister ship of *Yamato* and thus one of the two largest warships in the world at that time, with the heaviest main armament, 18.1-in guns. *Musashi* was hit by eleven torpedoes and nineteen bombs and so badly damaged that she eventually sank, slipping beneath the waves as she steamed slowly in circles, her steering gear jammed. Damage to a battleship from a direct hit by a bomb tended to be rare as bombs usually bounced off the armour plating but even so, *Musashi* was unfortunate. Other Japanese ships were badly damaged, with the heavy cruiser *Myoko* forced to turn back. The other giant battleship, *Yamato*, was also hit as was another battleship, *Nagato*, but both managed to remain operational.

During the night of 24/5 October, the Japanese Southern Force was attacked by American motor torpedo-boats, although only one ship, the light cruiser *Abukuma*, was damaged. At 0200, the US Seventh Fleet mounted a torpedo attack by destroyers, sinking the battleship *Fuso* and three Japanese destroyers. It was not until 0420 that a classic naval gunnery engagement got under way, with Vice-Admiral Nishimura's flagship, *Yamashiro*, suddenly blowing up, and the cruiser *Mogami* damaged. USAAF aircraft attacked shortly after daybreak, sinking the crippled *Abukuma*. This was followed by an attack by aircraft from the Seventh Fleet's escort carriers, which sank the *Mogami* and the remaining destroyers.

At 0645 on 25 October, American reconnaissance aircraft discovered the battle fleet east of Samar, a large island to the north-east of Leyte. Just 13 minutes later, the Battle of Samar began, with the Centre Force battleships discovering and starting to shell Sprague's 'Taffy One' group of escort carriers, the most northerly. Sprague ordered all of the aircraft to be flown off and withdrew his ships to the south. A number of the escort carriers were able to put up smoke, while the remainder attempted to improvise a smokescreen by changing the fuel-air mixture for their boiler fires, but this was a dated tactic as the Japanese flagship *Yamato* now had radar, as did some of the other ships; this was the best opportunity the Japanese ever had of destroying part of the American carrier fleet. The escort carrier USS *Gambier Bay* was sunk and another three, *Fenshaw Bay*, *Kalinin Bay* and *White Plains*, were damaged. Then the Japanese broke off the one-sided engagement and turned away.

The second group of six escort carriers were next to be attacked by the Japanese, as kamikaze attacks started. Four aircraft from shore bases dived on to the Second Escort Carrier Group, hitting both *Suwanee* and *Santee*, with the second ship also being hit by a torpedo from a Japanese submarine. Further kamikaze attacks blew up the escort carrier *St Lo* and damaged both *Kalinin Bay* and *Kitkun Bay*. It was not until later that the Americans realised that they were the targets for suicide attacks. The first few aircraft were seen either as having crashed out of control or having been deliberately flown into the ships by pilots who were frustrated after their aircraft had been badly damaged.

At 0800 Mitscher sent the first of six waves, with a total of 527 aircraft, to attack Vice-Admiral Ozawa's Japanese Northern Force with its four aircraft carriers to the east of Luzon. This was to become the Battle of Cape Engano. Against the overwhelming American attack, Ozawa had just twenty fighters left, and these were shot down almost as soon as the attackers arrived. The light carrier *Chitose* was sunk quickly, slipping beneath the waves at 0937. With *Zuikaku*, *Zuiho*, *Chiyoda* and a light cruiser all damaged, Ozawa moved his flag from *Zuikaku*. The three remaining carriers, now with no fighter defence at all, inevitably fell victim to the succeeding waves, with *Zuikaku* on fire and burning out of control after the third wave of 200 aircraft had attacked. Halsey then turned his attentions to the Centre Force, and later that day on 25 October and the following day, carrier aircraft from the Third and Seventh Fleets found the Centre Force and attacked, sinking two cruisers.

Overall, the Japanese lost three battleships, four aircraft carriers, six heavy and four light cruisers, eleven destroyers, a destroyer transport and four submarines, while the Americans had lost a light carrier and two escort carriers as well as three destroyers. The Japanese had lost 150 aircraft, both shore-based and carrier-borne, compared to 100 US aircraft. Some 10,000 Japanese had lost their lives compared with 1,500 Americans. After Leyte, the Imperial Japanese Navy was a spent force.

The big failing at Leyte went far beyond the question of who won the naval battles. The objective had been to catch the American transports at sea and inflict such heavy losses among them that the United States would be forced to think again. Yet, the battle did not develop until several days after the first landings.

licence-production The manufacture of equipment, including engines or airframes, designed by another company. The first significant example of licence-production was when the **Short** brothers obtained a licence to build the **Wright** 'A' biplane. During the First World War, the Rumpler Taube was built under licence for the German Military Air Service by several manufacturers. Licence-production has a number of benefits, including easing pressure on the original manufacturer's production facilities, or saving foreign exchange, and is generally far less troublesome and costly than **collaborative projects**. During the Second World War, the Rolls-Royce Merlin engine was produced in the United States by Packard under licence. For many years **Sikorsky** licensed European manufacturers to produce its helicopters, including **Westland**, as did **Bell** with **Agusta** in Italy and Kawasaki in Japan.

lifting aerofoil fuselage An aircraft in which the fuselage is designed to act as a part of the aerodynamic surface, or which uses a deep section wing as part of the accommodation. Few in number, typical aircraft in the past have included the Junkers G38, with accommodation for a dozen of its passengers in cabins in the wing inboard leading edges, and the French DB71 trimotors, in which a twin-boom fuselage was adopted, with accommodation in the wings between the booms and the centre fuselage – both aircraft appeared around 1930. In recent years several proposals have been made for such aircraft, but these have not progressed for a number of reasons, including questions over fitting the aircraft into existing airports and the likelihood of claustrophobic interiors due to the lack of windows.

lifting body During the late 1960s, the American **Northrop** concern produced a lifting body design for NASA, the HL-10, which was used to simulate the control methods necessary for the US space shuttle orbiters when returning to the earth's surface. Rocket propulsion was used but descent was by gliding.

Currently, **Boeing** is working on a similar concept, the blended wing, for cargo operations.

Lilienthal, Otto (1848–96) German gliding pioneer. As a youth, he experimented with strap-on wings, accompanied by his brother. Later, Lilienthal studied engineering as well as spending several years in a workshop as an apprentice gaining a practical insight into mechanics before founding his own factory. His products included marine signal lamps and small steam engines. Once his factory had established itself, he returned to his ideas for flight. While being a firm believer in the ornithopter, he was realistic and believed that gliders were an essential preliminary. His first real glider, a hang-glider, was completed in 1891 and over the next two years he made a number of other gliders with the best travelling 750 ft. His work became well known as reports, accompanied by photographs, were widely published and while his work was noted by both **Octave Chanute** and the **Wright** brothers, he also had a disciple in the British glider pioneer, **Percy Pilcher**.

In 1895 Lilienthal became interested in the possibilities of the biplane, which he envisaged as having the same wing area as his monoplane gliders but without the control problems associated with a mass of unwieldy wing. Three biplanes were built, two, Nos 12 and 14, in 1895, and one, No. 15, in 1896. They achieved considerable success and had a particular influence on Chanute. He also investigated more advanced means of control than simply swinging the pilot's body around, including simple wing-warping or flexing, an all-moving fin and wing-tip airbrakes, and he was working on an elevator design at the time of his death.

He had earlier built a powered glider, his No. 16, using ornithoptering flight with six movable slats on each wing-tip to provide propulsion and power provided by a 2 hp carbonic acid gas engine. This made a number of glides, but powered flight does not seem to have been attempted. He returned to the idea of powered flight during the winter of 1895–6, again with ornithoptering wing-tips and again with a carbonic acid gas engine although this time of 5 hp. This and a new monoplane glider, No. 18, were untested at the time of his death.

During his life he made more than 2,000 glides, but on 9 August 1896, while flying his No. 11 glider, he was gusted to a standstill in generally favourable weather conditions, attempted to dive to gain speed, but instead stalled and side-slipped into the ground, breaking his back. He lingered on during the night and the following day but died that evening.

Lindbergh, Charles Augustus (1902–74) First to fly solo across the Atlantic. Lindbergh left the college where he was studying engineering to learn to fly in 1922, and afterwards joined a flying circus, although he was more likely to wing-walk or parachute than be the pilot. This soon palled and in 1924 he joined the USAAC, becoming an airmail pilot in 1926. His parachute experience came in useful as he had to jump from aircraft on a couple of occasions before they crashed.

In 1927, he prepared to compete for the Orteig prize for the first New York–Paris non-stop flight. After persuading some St Louis businessmen to sponsor his attempt, he helped **Tubal Ryan** build the aeroplane he wanted, which was designed and built in under two months. He chose a single-engined single-pilot aircraft to save weight. Naming the aircraft *Spirit of St Louis* in deference to his sponsors, he flew it from San Diego in California to New York, setting a transcontinental speed record of 21 hours 20 minutes. He took off from Roosevelt Field on Long Island on 20 May 1927 and then flew steadily eastwards for 33 hours 30 minutes, increasingly in danger of falling asleep and crashing into the sea. He made landfall over Ireland and was then able to navigate a course to Paris. His welcome at Le Bourget was beyond his expectations, as was the adulation and enthusiasm aroused by his flight, and he was pressed with offers to endorse products. All he was interested in was convincing people that flying was safe.

Lindbergh received the CMH, and embarked on a tour of the Americas, meeting and then marrying the daughter of the US ambassador to Mexico. He then pioneered and surveyed commercial air routes, and became an adviser to Pan American Airways, but in 1932 their son was kidnapped and murdered. To escape from excessive public and media attention, the Lindberghs went to Europe, where **Hermann Goering** asked him to inspect the Luftwaffe, which so impressed Lindbergh that he warned the United States to stay out of any future European conflict. In the row that followed, he incurred the wrath of President Roosevelt

and felt compelled to resign his USAAC reserve commission.

Once the United States entered the Second World War, Lindbergh did indeed return to the then USAAF, and played a part in teaching bomber pilots how to get the maximum range from their aircraft. Postwar, he returned to his work with Pan Am and also won the 1953 Pulitzer Prize for his autobiography, *The Spirit of St Louis*. He was also responsible for as advising against the building of an American supersonic transport rival to the Anglo-French Concorde.

Ling-Temco-Vought American manufacturer. The company emerged when Chance-Vought was purchased by Ling-Temco in 1961 while the aerospace company was engaged in production of the variable-incidence wing F-8 Crusader carrier-borne fighter for the USN and the Aéronavale.

Chance-Vought dated from 1917 when Vought Aircraft was founded, concentrating on aircraft for the USN. Among its early designs was the UO-1 biplane seaplane that was catapulted from battleships and cruisers for fleet-spotting duties. Later, the first aircraft to carry the Corsair name, the UO-2, also a biplane seaplane, entered USN service. The company's most famous product was the F4K Corsair of the Second World War, a crank-wing high-performance fighter-bomber used extensively by the Royal Navy and the USMC, although it also provided a significant part of the RNZAF's strength towards the end of the war. A number were brought out of storage for use in the **Korean Air War**. During the late 1940s the company experimented with aircraft with circular wings, but none entered production. The first jet produced by the company was the F7U-3 Cutlass for the USN during the early 1950s. After being acquired by Ling-Temco, production of naval aircraft continued with the A-7 Corsair strike aircraft, which was also bought by the USAF. The group also built and test flew the XC-142 V/STOL transport, but this four-engined tilt-wing aircraft did not enter production.

Today, the company works on aero-structures for other manufacturers.

Link, Edwin Albert (1904–81) Inventor of the flight simulator. Angered by the attitude of his flying instructor and the cost of lessons when he learnt to fly in the late 1920s, Link set out to design a simulator that would enable people to teach themselves to fly. It took just a year to design and build and teach his brother to fly. Unable to find a manufacturer interested in the simulator, he toured the USA with it and sold rides for 25 cents. His fortunes changed within a few years as the US Army recognised the potential for cost savings using the 'Link Trainer' during the 1930s, and the equipment went into widespread production to meet orders from the US and further afield. Link left the company after the Second World War and took an interest in oceanography, designing and building several vehicles for underwater exploration.

Lioré-et-Olivier French manufacturer. Active between the two world wars, the company became prominent during the late 1920s with the LeO 20 fighters and LeO 206 four-engined bomber for the French Aviation Militaire. During the 1930s, the company produced the LeO 45 bomber for what had become the Armée de l'Air and the LeO 257 seaplane for the Service Aéronautique, while Air Orient, a predecessor of Air France, received LeO 242 flying boats. Production ceased with French surrender in 1940, and was not restarted after the war.

Lippisch, Prof Alexander Martin (1894–1976) German pioneer aerodynamicist. Lippisch graduated as an engineer from both Berlin and Heidelberg universities. When the First World War broke out, he served in the army, later being posted to the Military Aviation Service. Postwar, he experimented with different wing designs and investigated the issues connected with high-speed flight, designing the Delta 1 flying wing, which was rejected by the re-born German aircraft industry in 1931. It took until 1939 before he could convince his critics after demonstrating a rocket-powered swept-wing model. He was assigned to **Willy Messerschmitt** under whom he was able to develop his concept, eventually producing the Me163 Komet rocket-powered interceptor, capable of 600 mph. The aircraft was available too late and in too small numbers to influence the outcome of

the Second World War, and was prone to sudden explosions.

Postwar, Lippisch returned to research and worked on supersonic delta wings, mainly in the United States, where his work influenced many designs. Later, he investigated the possibilities of using vectored thrust in aircraft.

Litvak, Jnr Lt Lydia (1921–43) Soviet woman ace. The highest-scoring Soviet woman fighter pilot during the Second World War, she had twelve confirmed German kills during the Battle of Stalingrad flying a Yakovlev Yak-1. She was shot down and killed in combat over Orel.

Lockheed/Lockheed-Martin American manufacturer. The merger of two of the oldest names in US military aircraft production, to which was also added **General Dynamics**, created a company strong in both military air transport and combat aircraft, as well as having experience in maritime-reconnaissance.

The older of the two companies was Martin, originally known as the Glenn Martin concern but in later years as the Martin Marietta Corporation. The company was formed in 1909 and produced a number of biplane designs before the outbreak of the First World War. In common with many US manufacturers, the company did not get aircraft into service with the US Army before the war ended, but the twin-engined MB-1 bomber served with the USAAC for many years afterwards. A development, the NBS-1, had up-rated engines and was also available as a transport. During the 1920s, Martin also built the MO-1 single-engined observation monoplane for the USN, and the MS-1, a small floatplane with folding wings for stowage aboard submarines. Also, in the early 1920s the P2M trimotor flying boat entered service with the USN and airlines. Later, the company developed a biplane dive-bomber for the US Navy. During the 1930s, considerable variety was apparent in the product range which included the M-130 'China Clipper' flying boat that helped Pan American extend its services across the Pacific and also the B-10, a twin-engined, all-metal, mid-wing twin-engined bomber monoplane that could lay claim to be the first modern bomber. One development of the B-10 concept was the B-26 Marauder of the Second World War. The company also produced the PBM-3 Mariner flying boat for the USN.

Following the Second World War, Martin made a rare attempt at the civil landplane market with the twin-engined 404 intended for domestic air services in the USA. The company also produced the P5M Marlin flying boat for the USN. Despite experimenting with jet aircraft, the company's main project was the licence-production of the English Electric Canberra jet bomber as the B-57, but the company also made improvements to the aircraft's structure. Following the end of B-57 production, the company left aircraft design and production to concentrate on armaments and space research.

Lockheed was formed in 1926 by **Allan Loughead** after the failure of an earlier enterprise and the following year saw the first flights of the Vega, a single-engined high-wing monoplane with accommodation for six passengers or mail. A development of the Vega, the Air Express, established a number of transcontinental speed records in the USA, while **Charles Lindbergh** used a later aircraft, the Sirius, on a number of record-breaking flights. The company's first twin-engined airliner was the Electra, which appeared in 1930 and was followed by a number of developments of the basic design, producing the Lockheed 10, 12 and 14, and the Lodestar for civil use, and the Hudson, a maritime-reconnaissance variant of the 14, used by the USN and RAF during the late 1930s and early years of the Second World War.

The war years saw a number of significant aircraft produced by Lockheed, including a twin-boom, twin-engined long-range escort fighter, the P-38 Lightning, as well as the Ventura and Harpoon maritime-reconnaissance aircraft and the first Constellation transports. The company produced the first operational US jet fighter, the F-80 Shooting Star and a jet trainer development, the T-33, which also entered service after the war with many Allied air forces. The wartime Constellation developed into a commercial airliner which was further developed into the Super Constellation and the Starliner during the early 1950s.

Postwar, the company retained its connection with maritime-reconnaissance aircraft with the P-2 Neptune and later the four-engined Orion, both of which served with many Allied air forces and navies. The Orion was a development of the turboprop Electra II airliner, which was not as successful as the company expected as interest was switching to jet aircraft for longer-haul services. The outstanding success of the 1950s was the appearance of the first Lockheed C-130 Hercules, a four-engined military transport, which remains in production in a much upgraded form throughout the first decade of the twenty-first century. A variant of the Hercules was the largest aircraft to ever take off from an aircraft carrier, but the aircraft was too large for regular carrier operation. A small number of Hercules have been sold to airlines, such as the L-100. Larger transport aircraft included the four jet-engined C-141 Starlifter. The company also produced the U-2, which despite its utility designation was a high-altitude reconnaissance aircraft, and its successor, the SR-71 Blackbird.

The company ventured into the executive market with the unusual JetStar, also known to the USAF as the C-140, with four tail-mounted engines. A new airliner, the long-range L-1011 TriStar, a wide-bodied aircraft with three turbo-fans, encountered problems when the engine manufacturer **Rolls-Royce** went bankrupt. It was generally highly regarded but missed much of the market while the problems at R-R were resolved. There were also problems with the AH-56 Cheyenne combat helicopter and the C-5A Galaxy four-engined transport, which for a time was the largest aircraft in the world. The company also produced the S-3A Viking anti-submarine aircraft for the USN's carriers.

A fighter programme, the F-16 Fighting Falcon, for the USAF developed into an international project with the aircraft built under licence in Europe and entering service with many Allied air forces. The latest variant of the Hercules, sometimes known as the Hercules II but more usually as the C-130J, remains in production, and a joint project with **Alenia** of Italy has produced the twin-engined C-27 Spartan, an updated Fiat 222, which uses the same engines and flight-deck layout to provide compatibility between the two aircraft.

The company's contender for the Joint Strike Fighter (JSF) project was the successful XF-35.

Lockheed/Loughead, Allan Haines (1889–1969)

US manufacturer. Born Loughead, Allan and his brother were car mechanics in California when Allan went to work for a dealer in Chicago who was diversifying into selling aircraft, and took the opportunity to learn to fly on a Curtiss pusher. Loughead started to build aircraft in Chicago before returning to California where, in partnership with his brother Malcolm, he opened an aircraft factory, the Alco Hydro-Aeroplane Company, with their first design known as the Model G to give purchasers the idea that this was their sixth design. Despite this, while the aircraft flew successfully on 15 June 1913, there were no orders and the prototype was put into storage.

When the First World War broke out in Europe, the brothers offered to build hydro-aeroplanes for the USN forming a new company, Loughead Aircraft, at Santa Barbara. **John Northrop** joined them as their chief engineer. Despite building a number of different designs, the USN bought just two aircraft and the company collapsed in 1921, even though they had built a monocoque biplane of plywood construction for the postwar racing market. Malcolm set up his own company producing hydraulic brakes for motor cars.

It was not until 1926 that Allan Loughead returned to aviation, again with Northrop as his engineer and chief designer. The new company was given the name Lockheed and used the advanced plywood monocoque construction pioneered with their 1921 design to produce the Vega monoplane, which flew in 1927 and which was aimed at the market for mail planes. The Depression was upon them by this time, and in 1929 they merged with the Detroit Aircraft Company before being sold to an investment group in 1932, which developed the company that survives to this day, albeit now merged with Martin. The company produced many transport aircraft, including the Constellation and Electra airliners and the C-130 Hercules transport, as well as maritime-reconnaissance aircraft such as the Hudson of the Second World War and the postwar Neptune and Orion.

When the company merged with Detroit in 1929, Loughead left and once again started his own company, Loughead Brothers Aircraft Corporation, in 1930, which lasted until 1934 during which time it produced just one aircraft. He changed his name to Lockheed in 1934, and in 1937 formed yet another company, Alcor, but it was also unsuccessful.

Locklear, Ormer Leslie (1891–1920)

American stunt pilot. After working as a stuntman with horses and motorcycles, Locklear's interest in flying was aroused by **Calbraith Rodgers'** call at Fort Worth, Texas, on his transcontinental flight. Locklear had some success with a home-built glider before joining the US Army Aviation Section which trained him as a pilot. He remained in the USA because of the shortage of suitable aircraft wih the US forces in Europe and began stunt flying. He is believed to have been the first to wing-walk, eventually climbing on to the upper wing of a Curtiss Jenny biplane while another pilot kept the aircraft flying steady, and on 18 November 1918 he became the first to transfer from one aircraft to another in mid-air. He was encouraged by his commanding officer in these stunts because it was thought that it would give trainee pilots confidence.

Newspaper reports of his stunt led to offers from Hollywood and he resigned his commission in May 1919. Despite his initial success in the film industry, his original contract was not renewed. Ironically, it was when he was still staging the final shots of a film, after dark on 2 August 1920, that while standing on the wing of his aircraft, his pilot became blinded by the spotlights, misjudged his height and lost control. The aircraft plunged to the ground so fast that the engine was forced 5 ft into the ground. Both men were killed.

Loening, Grover Cleveland (1888–1976)

Manufacturer and designer. One of the first to graduate in aeronautical science, he went to work for **Blériot's** US licence-holder in 1910 before moving on briefly to the **Wright** Company as factory manager in 1913, and then joined the Aviation Section of the US Army's Signal Corps in 1914. The following year he became a vice-president of Sturtevant. In 1917 he founded the

Loening Aeronautical Engineering Corporation specifically to tender for a USN scout contract. He later built a number of amphibians, including one designed for the private aircraft owner. The company was sold in 1928 for US $3 million (£750,000 at the then rate of exchange, worth as much as £30 million today) to a group of investors who merged it with Curtiss-Wright, leaving Loening to invest in **Grumman**, but work as a consultant.

Longmore, ACM Sir Arthur (1885–1970) RAF commander. Australian-born, Longmore went to the UK where he joined the Royal Navy as one of its first pilots, and had the distinction of making the first aerial torpedo drop during trials before the outbreak of the First World War. When the RNAS was merged into the RAF, he remained with the service. He commanded RAF Training Command from 1939 and was largely responsible for the Empire Air Training Scheme that ensured pilots and navigators could be trained in the friendlier skies of the Dominions. He became Commander-in-Chief, Middle East Air Forces, based in Egypt, but friction between himself and Winston Churchill saw him recalled. He served as inspector general of the RAF from May 1941 until he retired in 1942, the same year that he was knighted.

Lorin, René (1877–1933) French artillery officer. Commissioned into the artillery, he was probably the first to appreciate that the exhaust gases from in-line engines could be utilised to provide additional thrust. He then experimented and developed the concept of the ramjet, although aircraft speeds were too low at the time for such a device to function effectively.

low-cost carrier Over the years, many attempts have been made to reduce the cost of air travel, including **inclusive tour** charters. At one time, coach-air and rail-air services enjoyed some popularity with lower cost railway travel and even lower cost coach travel covering part of the journey, keeping the flight as short as possible. Examples of this were the Silver Arrow service provided by British United Airways, and later British Caledonian Airways, between London Victoria railway station and London Gatwick airport, with a flight to Le Touquet and then a train to Paris. Another British airline, Skyways, operated a coach-air service from UK points to French airports by way of Lympne Airport in Kent. These were a few routes serving a small number of passengers.

The true low-cost airline provides a direct service, and in some cases uses the same airports as the traditional airlines, although a few favour remote airports some distance from their passengers' destination. The basics of a low-cost airline are dispensing with travel agents, saving commission and sales and training costs; charging for bookings not made through the internet; charging for food and drink aboard the aircraft; charging for baggage put into the hold; and charging for changes of flight times as well as having a no refunds policy.

Early attempts at low-cost airlines were not trouble-free. There was the collapse of Laker Airways in the UK, which operated a no-frills, no booking, 'Skytrain' service from Gatwick to the USA; and refinancing was needed by Ryanair in Ireland.

The first modern low-cost airline was South West Airlines in the United States, followed by a revived Ryanair and also by easyJet in the UK.

The concept is now almost universal, although given the rapid growth of the sector, some of the airlines can be expected to encounter financial difficulties. Many traditional airlines are trying to restructure themselves as low-cost carriers, but this will be easier said than done.

Lowe, Thaddeus Sobieski Constantine (1832–1913) US aeronaut. Born into a farming community, Lowe left New Hampshire for Boston intending to study chemistry but, after illness interrupted his studies, became a travelling showman and began to become involved in ballooning. In 1859 he started to raise funds to attempt a transatlantic crossing in a balloon, building the *City of New York*, with a 104 ft diameter envelope. The envelope was badly damaged in a storm and Lowe repaired it, but so badly that when reinflated it exploded.

At the height of the American Civil War Lowe started cross-country flights, straying into

Confederate territory where he was imprisoned as a Union spy. He was later released and repatriated.

He offered his services to Abraham Lincoln, but despite being referred by the president to the army, he found that the generals could not appreciate the value of aerostats as surveillance platforms, regardless of the earlier French experience. On his own initiative Lowe pressed ahead and used his balloons as aerial observation posts, employing a total of five altogether, and telegraphing his findings to a ground post. He was present at the first battle of Bull Run, at Chancellorsville and during the Peninsula campaign. Despite this he never gained the recognition he deserved from the generals and in 1863 turned to other activities, including such contrasting areas as smelting ovens and refrigeration.

Lucas, Wg Cdr Percy Belgrave 'Laddie' (1915–98) British fighter ace. Born at Sandwich, Kent, he acquired his nickname as a child. He graduated as an economist from Cambridge but went into journalism as a sports writer. He volunteered for the RAF on the outbreak of the Second World War and was sent to Canada where he was among the first to learn to fly under the Empire Air Training Scheme. In 1941 his first operational posting was to No. 66 Squadron in Cornwall, mounting fighter-bomber strikes against German shipping. In February 1942 he was posted to No. 249 Squadron in Malta which he eventually commanded and led to hold the highest number of kills of any unit involved in the defence of the Maltese islands. He was awarded the DFC for the destruction of three Italian bombers which had a fighter escort of eighty aircraft.

On his return from Malta, he served on the staff of Fighter Command. He took command of No. 616 Squadron and then moved to command the Spitfire Wing at Coltishall, Norfolk, where he was awarded the DSO. In 1944 he commanded No. 613 (City of Manchester) Squadron flying de Havilland Mosquitoes on low-level interdictor missions, winning a Bar to his DSO. He remained in the RAF until entering business in 1946 running a greyhound racing company and becoming a professional golfer. He entered politics in 1950 as Conservative MP for Brentford and Chiswick, but

abandoned it in 1959 and returned to business. He also started to write books.

Lufbery, Maj Raoul Gervais Victor (1885–1918) French-American ace. At the age of 6 years old, Lufbery emigrated to France with his father, and in 1902 began to travel the world. He acquired US citizenship and in 1908 joined the US Army and was posted to the Philippines. He left the army in 1910 and continued his travels, eventually reaching Saigon in what was then French Indo-China, and became a mechanic for a stunt pilot. When the First World War broke out, the two men were back in France, but initially Lufbery could only join the French Foreign Legion, although later he was able to transfer to the French Aviation Militaire and assume his role as mechanic to the stunt flyer. In May 1915 he was trained as a pilot, initially flying bombers, but he was soon posted to a fighter unit and in May 1916 became a member of the Escadrille Lafayette, the American unit raised to fight alongside the French. When the unit was finally incorporated into the Aeronautical Section of the US Signal Corps in February 1918, he was already an ace and had a reputation as an outstanding pilot, so he was given the rank of major and command of the 94th Aero Squadron. On 19 May his plane burst into flames when it was hit by an incendiary, and rather than be burnt to death he jumped out; not having a parachute he fell to his death. His score was seventeen confirmed kills but it is generally believed that the true figure was higher.

He gave his name to a defensive formation known as a 'Lufbery', in which aircraft form up and fly in a circle making it impossible for another aircraft to penetrate without being shot down, as each member of the 'Lufbery' effectively guard the tail of the plane in front and in turn are protected by the plane behind.

Luft-Verkehrs Gesellschaft (LVG) German manufacturer. Founded before the outbreak of the First World War, LVG built biplanes with conspicuously clean lines for the day, some of which were developed into bomber and reconnaissance aircraft during the war. The most famous of these aircraft were the CIII and CV reconnaissance-bombers. The company was also one of many undertaking production of the Rumpler-Etrich Taube for the German Military Air Service early in the war.

Luke, Lt Frank, Jnr (1897–1918) US ace. Joining the Aeronautical Section of the US Army Signal Corps in 1917, he qualified as a pilot and was posted to France in March 1918. He earned himself a popular reputation as a 'sausage buster', shooting down fourteen German balloons, but was unpopular with his comrades because of his boasting and with his commanders because he frequently abandoned patrols as he went looking for air-to-air combat. With a court martial for insubordination looming over him, he went on a solo sortie on 29 September 1918. Over Toul he shot down three German observation balloons and then came under heavy AA fire which forced him down; he was injured in the crash-landing. He then used his pistol to evade capture but was shot by German infantry.

Lunardi, Vincenzo (1759–1806) Italian aeronaut. In 1783 he was secretary to the ambassador of the Kingdom of Naples in London when he heard news of the Montgolfier brothers' first ascents. He designed and built his own hydrogen balloon in which he made the first balloon ascent in England on 15 September 1784. He travelled from the Honourable Artillery Company's parade ground at Moorfields in the City of London, to North Mimms in Hertfordshire, jettisoning his ballast and his sole passenger, his pet cat, before ascending again and eventually touching down at Standon Green, near Ware. In June 1785 he arranged the first ascent by a woman in the British Isles; he originally intended to take Mrs Letitia Ann Sage, George Biggin and a Colonel Hastings from St George's Fields, London, but because of the lady's weight, Lunardi and Hastings gallantly gave up their places and the balloon travelled as far as Harrow, Middlesex.

M

Macchi *See* Finmeccanica

MacCready, Paul B., Jnr (1925–2007) Designer of man-powered flying-machines. A successful aeronautical engineer, in 1976 he decided on an attempt to win the Kremer Prize for the first man-powered flying-machine to fly over an officially verified course. With the help of volunteers from the California Institute of Technology he designed and built the Gossamer Condor, which on 23 August 1977 was successfully flown by Bryan Allen over a figure-of-eight course. In 1979 his Gossamer Albatross man-powered aircraft was successfully flown 21 miles across the English Channel.

Mach, Ernst (1838–1916) Austrian physicist. Although born in Moravia, while still a child Mach moved with his family to Vienna. While studying ballistics, he noticed the change in airflow as objects approached the speed of sound and wrote many papers on this phenomenon, which were largely ignored at the time.

During the 1930s, after Mach's death, with supersonic flight becoming a tempting possibility his work began to receive the recognition it deserved and in commemoration the speed of sound, regardless of altitude, was classified Mach 1, with twice the speed of sound as 2.0.

Malan, Gp Capt Adolph Gysbert 'Sailor' (1910–63) South African ace. Born in South Africa, Malan initially qualified as an officer in the Merchant Navy before joining the RAF in 1935. He proved to be a natural pilot and was given command of No. 74 Squadron, flying Spitfires during the **Battle of Britain**, shooting down eighteen German aircraft. In 1942, he became commanding officer at Biggin Hill and over the war years he became the RAF's third highest-scoring fighter pilot with a confirmed total of thirty-two kills. Postwar, he returned to South Africa and took up farming.

Malta, air war of (1940–3) In 1940 the territory of Malta was a British colony comprising four islands – three inhabited and one uninhabited – of 127 sq miles in total, with a civilian population of 270,000. The RAF had three airfields on Malta: at Luqa, Hal Far, which was also used by the Fleet Air Arm, and Takali. Another airfield was added at Safi, between Luqa and Hal Far. There was also a flying boat base at Kalafrana, on the shore close to Hal Far. Given adequate naval and air power, its geographical position meant that whoever occupied Malta could control the Mediterranean, but it was just 80 miles from the air bases of Fliegerkorps X in Sicily. Fliegerkorps X had been moved from Norway, where it had extensive experience in anti-shipping operations. Some relief for Malta came with the start of Operation Barbarossa, in which Germany focused on the invasion of the Soviet Union, but when the winter made operations over Russia difficult, the Luftwaffe turned its attention back to the island.

During the Second World War Malta was under almost constant attack by the Luftwaffe and the Italian Regia Aeronautica. While the first six months after Italy entered the war were relatively calm, once Fliegerkorps X arrived in Sicily at the beginning of 1941, the situation changed dramatically. Convoys to Malta came under increasing aerial attack, with some losing all ships and others being forced to turn back. The relief of the island, besieged by enemy forces, with 34 per cent of babies in 1942 not living to see their first birthday, did not come until the massive convoy of Operation Pedestal in August 1942. Even this convoy, regarded as a success, lost nine out of fourteen merchant ships as well as an aircraft carrier, with two others badly damaged, and two cruisers. Malta convoys did not have escort carriers but fleet carriers.

Despite this, the RAF and Royal Navy between them at one stage almost cut the supply lines between Italy and Axis forces in North Africa.

Two Fleet Air Arm Swordfish squadrons were based on the island, but, after losses, were merged to form the Naval Air Squadron, Malta.

The fighter defence of Malta in 1940 was non-existent, despite the threat from Italy. Anti-aircraft defences were also minimal and primarily concerned with the defence of the main fleet base at Grand Harbour. Flying boat pilots from RAF Kalafrana flew three Gloster Sea Gladiators, the famous *Faith*, *Hope* and *Charity*, found in crates at Grand Harbour, as the island's sole fighter defences in June 1940.

Fighter squadrons were soon flown in to defend the island but their Hurricanes were no match for the German Bf109s. Fighters had to be flown off aircraft carriers within range of the island, usually with a Fleet Air Arm Fairey Fulmar to provide navigation, but on arrival it was not unknown for most of the aircraft to be destroyed or badly damaged while refuelling ready for their first sorties. Spitfires were later added and the American carrier, USS *Wasp*, made two trips across the Mediterranean to fly off aircraft to Malta. Offensive operations from the island were flown by Blenheims on anti-shipping missions, along with a Fleet Air Arm Swordfish squadron, and by Wellingtons, which bombed the Italian fleet in harbour at Naples after the surviving ships had moved there from **Taranto**. Later, Beaufighter and then Mosquito night fighters provided air cover over Malta.

Malta's plight eased with the Allied landings in North Africa and the victory at El Alamein, followed by the landings in Sicily. While Malta-based aircraft played a part in the latter, the limitations of the airfields meant that most of the airborne element was based in North Africa.

man-powered flight For centuries, man-powered flight was seen as the way into the air, largely because, until the advent of the steam-engine, only clockwork-power or man-power was available. The early tower jumpers often attempted to fly using wings strapped to their arms, and it was the connection between man-power and ornithoptering flight, i.e. emulating bird flight, that was one of the fundamental drawbacks which prevented man-powered flight realising its potential.

The way forward came by using ultra-lightweight structures, airscrews or propellers, and cycling. **Dr Paul MacCready**, an American aeronautics engineer and gliding champion, built the Gossamer Condor, and on 23 August 1977 this won the Kremer Prize for man-powered flight by completing a figure-of-eight course. His next machine was the Gossamer Albatross, which became famous for making the first man-powered flight across the English Channel on 12 June 1979. MacCready was later awarded the Collier Trophy for his work in the record-breaking project. The following year he built and flew the first solar-powered aircraft, the Gossamer Penguin.

Manly, Charles Matthew (1876–1927) US engineer and pioneering pilot. Manly was put forward as an engineer to help **Samuel Langley** by the Dean of Engineering at Cornwell University. He joined Langley and Stephen Balzer, who was building an engine for Langley's proposed flying-machine, the *Aerodrome A*. He redesigned the engine, which was initially a rotary (not to be confused with the Wankel engine) but became a radial, and increased the power from 8 hp to 42 hp, while retaining the low weight of 208 lb.

In 1903 Manly made two attempts to fly the *Aerodrome A*, launching it off the roof of a houseboat on the Potomac river, but in each case the lack of 'control in roll' meant that the effort failed and he received an unwanted ducking.

Mannock, Maj Edward 'Micky', VC (1887–1918) British ace. Irish-born Mannock came from an army family but was working in Turkey at the start of the First World War. Interned, he was released and repatriated because of poor health. Despite a serious defect in one eye he managed to join the RFC and train as a pilot, joining No. 40 Squadron on 1 April 1917 flying Nieuports. He was a natural pilot and soon began scoring kills, and within a year, on 31 March 1918, he became CO of No. 74 Squadron. Within four months he was killed, when on 26 July a bullet fired by a German soldier hit his fuel tank and his aircraft crashed in flames. While his tally of confirmed kills stood at fifty, his comrades, who had seen him allow victories to other less experienced pilots when more than one pilot had been involved, put pressure on the RAF who relented and granted him the total of seventy-three kills, making him the leading British ace of the war – and yet he had only been flying operationally for sixteen months. He was also awarded a posthumous VC.

Mantz, Albert Paul (1903–65) US stunt pilot. Like many stunt pilots, Mantz wanted to fly for the cinema, and although he tried to break into Hollywood, it was not until **Pancho Barnes** helped him that he eventually succeeded. He set up a company, United Air Services, to serve the industry and also acted as a consultant to **Amelia Earhart**. Less successful were his attempts to win the Bendix Trophy before the Second World War in a Lockheed Orion.

When the US entered the Second World War he headed the army's First Motion Picture Unit and worked with US actor and future president Ronald Regan. Much of his work for the army consisted of training films but he also produced the documentary *Memphis Belle*.

Postwar, he was the only pilot to win the Bendix Trophy on three consecutive occasions using a modified North American F-51 Mustang. In what seemed odd at the time, he paid US $55,000 (£20,000) to buy 475 war surplus aircraft, recouping the outlay by selling the fuel left in the tanks. He was killed flying the modified Vultee trainer used for filming *Flight of the Phoenix*, after insisting on making one last pass before the cameras.

Marey, Etienne Jules (1830–1904) French physician and photographer. Many of the pioneers believed that imitating bird flight held the answer to heavier-than-air flight, but had no real idea of how the wings functioned. Marey took a series of photographs using multi-exposure, a new technology at the time, which revealed just how a bird's wings work. He later employed a wind tunnel which used steam injection to demonstrate how the air flowed around structures.

maritime-reconnaissance *See* anti-submarine warfare

Markham, *née* Clutterbuck, Beryl (1902–86) British aviatrix. At the age of 4 she was taken

by her father to Kenya where she was brought up on a farm. Taught to fly by **Tom Campbell Black**, during the early 1930s she provided an air courier service throughout East Africa using a de Havilland Moth before being inspired to set a record, in this case making the first east–west solo crossing of the Atlantic by a woman. Leaving RAF Abingdon on 4 September 1936, she flew her Percival Gull across the ocean despite bad weather, but was forced to land in Nova Scotia short of fuel and short of her declared destination of New York. She was given a ticker-tape parade when she finally reached New York.

Already twice married and divorced, she married Raoul Schumacher, a writer, in California and in 1942 published her acclaimed autobiography, *West with the Night*.

She eventually returned to Kenya.

Marseille, Capt Hans-Joachim (1919–42) German ace. Although born into a military family, Marseille had not planned a military career but joined the Luftwaffe just before the Second World War. He was a fighter pilot during the Battle of Britain and claimed seven Allied aircraft before being posted to North Africa. On 1 September 1942 he shot down an unrivalled seventeen aircraft in one day, averaging just fifteen rounds per victim. Eventually, his total reached 158 Allied aircraft and he was awarded the Knight's Cross with Swords. He was killed by the tailplane of his Bf109 as he baled out of the burning aircraft.

Marseille's secret had been to dive at his opponents at high speed, but it was the combination of this with an unerring degree of accuracy that enabled him to make every round count.

Martin *See* Lockheed-Martin

Martin-Baker *See* Martin, Sir James

Martin, Glenn Luther (1886–1955) US designer and manufacturer. At the age of 19 Martin moved with his parents from Kansas to California where he started a car dealership, although his first passion was flight. His first glider was finished in 1907 but was a disappointment. Undaunted, he decided to build a powered aeroplane with the help of his mother, using a disused church as his workshop. The plane, a pusher-propeller biplane, completed in 1909, enabled him to become a stunt pilot although he claimed to be the first to shoot a movie film from an aeroplane and would use his aircraft to deliver newspapers. He also used oranges for mock-bombing raids and shot coyote from his aircraft.

He felt confident enough to found his own company in 1911 although this merged with Wright in 1917 leaving him free to set up a second company using his own name in Cleveland that same year. The company relocated to Maryland in 1929. Martin built aircraft mainly for the military market, but an outstanding commercial aircraft was his Martin 130 China Clipper flying boat for Pan American. He retired in 1952.

Martin, Sir James (1893–1981) British engineer and ejector seat inventor. Ulsterman Martin qualified as an engineer and founded his own aircraft company in 1929, specialising in fighter aircraft. He received financial support from Captain Valentine Baker in 1934, and the company adopted the Martin-Baker title. None of the fighter aircraft produced by the company entered production, but it was claimed that its MB-5 was the fastest piston-engined aircraft of the Second World War being capable of 460 mph.

He was commissioned to design an ejector seat in 1944 by the Air Ministry (the parent department of the RAF) as rising aircraft speeds made escape from an aircraft in mid-air increasingly hazardous. On 24 July 1946 the first manned ejection was made from the rear seat of a Gloster Meteor jet fighter. In return, Martin was knighted.

Some 200 lives a year have been saved by ejector seats and later developments included seats that could eject safely at zero altitude and those that would work under water. The company is one of just two ejector seat manufacturers qualified to tender for USN contracts.

Maxim, Sir Hiram Stevens (1840–1916) British-American inventor. Largely self-educated, Maxim worked as a carriage-builder, engineer, instrument-maker and draughtsman before inventing a number of electrical devices which ensured that from the mid-1870s onwards he enjoyed a steady income.

He settled in the UK in 1881 where he invented his machine gun and rapidly became a millionaire. He then turned his attention to powered flight. Using a revolving arm he experimented with wing shapes before building two lightweight 180 hp steam engines. He used the steam engines to power a large biplane that was run on a circular test track, and on 31 July 1894 this managed to lift itself and three men off the track, before fouling an overhead guide rail. Maxim seems to have been content with this, considering it a step forward which in some respects it was, and the biplane was then scrapped. He took British nationality in 1900 and was knighted in 1901.

It was not until 1910 that he returned to aviation, building a powered aeroplane which was less successful than his test rig of sixteen years earlier.

Maybach, Wilhelm (1846–1929) German engineer. Despite being orphaned at 10 years old, Maybach managed to obtain a technical education and qualified as a draughtsman, working for Nikolaus Otto who invented the Otto-cycle for four-stroke engines at Deutz, where he also met Gottlieb Daimler. Otto did not envisage the internal combustion engine being used in road vehicles and eventually Maybach and Daimler left and moved to Bad Canstatt, where they worked to produce a motor vehicle. The first four-stroke motorcycle materialised in 1885, with their first motorcar following in 1886.

Maybach's own contribution to progress was a practical and reliable carburettor, which was copied so widely that he was forced to act to protect his patents. After Daimler died in 1900 it was Maybach who deisgned the first Mercedes car the following year, naming it after Daimler's daughter. With the financial backing of Zeppelin he started his own company in 1907 at Friedrichshafen, building engines for the giant airships before and during the First World War, and then building motor vehicles from 1922 until the outbreak of the Second World War.

The Maybach name has since been resurrected for an up-market range of motor cars built by Mercedes Benz.

McConnell, Capt Joseph, Jnr (1922–54) US ace. Highest-scoring fighter ace during the

Korean War, McConnell flew North American F-86 Sabres with the USAF's 51st Fighter Wing, shooting down sixteen MiG-15s while flying 106 sorties. He was shot down once himself.

Postwar, he became a test pilot at Edwards Air Force Base, but his F-86H crashed on 26 August 1954 killing him.

McCudden, Maj James Thomas Byford, VC (1895–1918) British ace. Born in Kent, he joined the Royal Engineers at the age of 15 as a bugler before transferring to the RFC in 1913 to train as a mechanic. He later became an air-gunner and observer before qualifying as a pilot in 1916. He soon showed himself to be a natural pilot and leader, studying fighter tactics and passing these on to his men, and he became CO of No. 56 Squadron. He had fifty-seven confirmed victories; he was awarded the Military Medal before commissioning and then later the DSO and Bar and the MC. He was was also awarded the VC. Transferred to command No. 60 Squadron, he was taking off in an SE-5A when the engine failed and in an attempt to turn and return to base, his aircraft stalled and he was killed.

McCurdy, John A. Douglas (1886–1961) Canadian pioneer. McCurdy's father was secretary to **Alexander Graham Bell** and the engineering student was invited by Bell to join the **Aerial Experimental Association** (AEA) in September 1907. McCurdy specialised in structures, and the AEA invited each of its members design an aeroplane. McCurdy's *Silver Duck* was the last to be built, making the first aeroplane flight in Canada from the frozen surface of a lake at Baddeck, Nova Scotia, on 23 February 1909, with the designer at the controls. The AEA disbanded that year and McCurdy formed his own business, the Canadian Aerodrome Company, not to operate airfields but to build aircraft; it built just two.

McCurdy had the distinction of making the first radio transmissions from an aircraft as he flew a Curtiss biplane over Sheepshead Bay, New York, on 27 August 1910. Less successful was his attempt to fly 96 miles from Key West, Florida, to Havana in Cuba the following January, as he ran out of fuel and had to ditch in the sea some 10 miles short of his destination; he was rescued by an American

destroyer. Despite this, Cuba's President Gomez decided to award him the US $8,000 prize for making the attempt.

When the United States entered the First World War, McCurdy managed Curtiss's Canadian factory producing JN-3 trainers. Postwar, he became a politician and was eventually made lieutenant-governor of Nova Scotia. At the age of 73 he was guest of honour when the RCAF flew a replica of his aircraft off the same lake to commemorate the first aeroplane flight in Canada on 23 February 1959.

McDonnell Douglas *See* below *and* Douglas, Donald Wills

McDonnell, James Smith, Jnr (1899–1980) US engineer and manufacturer. Graduating from MIT, McDonnell joined the United States Army Air Service and trained as a pilot. In 1924 he left to join Huff Daland, the crop-dusting pioneers, before moving into manufacturing with Consolidated in 1925. After working there briefly he joined Stout and worked on the design of an aircraft that would become the famous Ford Trimotor. He then worked for a number of different companies over the years before the Second World War, designing the Metalplane for Hamilton. Here, he also built the Doodlebug, a competitor in the Guggenheim Safe Aircraft Contest with such features as extensive flaps and leading edge slats, but unfortunately it had an unreliable engine which meant it was not placed. After three years with other companies he joined **Martin** in 1933, becoming chief engineer for landplanes before leaving in 1938 to start his own company.

While his company concentrated on sub-assembly work for other manufacturers throughout the Second World War, in 1943 it won the contract to build the first jet fighter for the USN, the FH-1 Phantom. It was a much later and supersonic aircraft of the same name, the F-4 Phantom II, that proved to be an outstanding success during the Vietnam War, and although originally designed as a naval carrier-borne fighter it entered service with many air forces, including the USAF and RAF. The company later designed the McDonnell Douglas F-15 Eagle and F/A-17 Hornet. Realising that the concentration on military aircraft left the company vulnerable, it acquired the predominantly commercial **Douglas** in 1967, becoming McDonnell Douglas.

McGuire, Maj Thomas Buchanan, Jnr (1920–45)

American ace. Joining the USAAC in 1941, shortly before it became the USAAF, he was trained as a pilot and initially posted to Alaska, before moving on to the Pacific Theatre. He became known for his aggressive attitude towards both the enemy and his fellow squadron members making him deeply unpopular, although, it was while attempting to help a comrade in trouble on 7 January 1945 that his Lockheed P-38 Lightning stalled and crashed into the sea. Despite his short period on the front line he accumulated thirty-eight Japanese aircraft and became the second highest-scoring US ace of the war.

McPhetridge von Thaden, Louise (1905–79)

American aviatrix. After learning to fly in San Francisco in 1927, Louise McPhetridge persuaded **Walter Beech** to lend her one of his Travel Air Speedwings for the first Women's Air Derby from Santa Monica to Cleveland. She also set a record of 198 hours in the air, stopping only for refuelling, with Frances Marsalis. In 1936 she came first in the Bendix cross-country race, beating a male-dominated field by stressing consistency so that the Beech Staggerwing was flown on only 65 per cent throttle.

She married Herb von Thaden in the late 1920s, and during the late 1930s she became an aircraft saleswoman and managed a flying school.

MD Helicopters

American manufacturer. MD currently builds and sells the former **Hughes** 500 and the 900 Explorer helicopters.

Mermoz, Jean (1901–36)

French pioneer. Joining one of the early French airlines, Lignes Aériennes Latécoère, a subsidiary of the aircraft manufacturer, during the 1920s he soon proved himself to be one of their most capable pilots. Engine problems led to a forced landing in the Sahara Desert in 1926, where he was taken hostage by nomads who demanded, and got, a 50,000 fr. ransom. He returned to the airline and helped to plan and survey many routes in South America, of which the most important and demanding lay across the Andes to Chile. He also made a number of pioneering transatlantic flights starting with the first mail flight between Senegal and Brazil on 12 May 1930, and then the first transatlantic passenger flight with six passengers flown between Senegal and Brazil in 1933 using a Couzinet Arc-en-Ciel. It was on a later transatlantic flight in 1936 that he disappeared.

Merriam, Frederick Warren (1880–1956)

British pioneer. His wife's death prompted him to switch from being an antiquarian book dealer to a pilot, completing training in 1912. He worked for **Bristol** as an instructor at its school in Brooklands, south of London, and when war broke out instructed recruits to the RNAS before being posted to maritime-reconnaissance.

Postwar, he became a test pilot, initially for Saunders, the flying boat builder for whom he tested the Kittiwake, and then designed, built and flew a glider. He attempted to establish a flying boat sightseeing company, but it was not a success so he set up the first employment bureau in aviation.

He rejoined what had become the Royal Navy's Fleet Air Arm in 1939, once again becoming an instructor, but retired on the grounds of bad health in 1956.

Messerschmitt/Messerschmitt-Bolkow-Blohm

See Messerschmitt, Prof Willy Emil

Messerschmitt, Prof Willy Emil (1898–1978)

German designer and manufacturer. At just 12 years old he began building model gliders, and at 15, along with an architect, began building full-sized gliders. He was not fit enough to join the German armed forces during the First World War and instead received an engineering training at Munich. He set up his company in 1923, initially using his father's premises, a restaurant and wine merchant's business, to build a monoplane glider, but was pushed out to a disused brewery where he built several more gliders. He built his first powered aircraft in 1924. By 1927 he had an established reputation and entered into an agreement with the Bavarian Aircraft Company, BFW, that allowed him to design aircraft which BFW would then build – this is why his 109 is often designated the Bf109 rather than the Me109.

In 1934 he designed the Bf108 light cabin monoplane for the private-owner and sport market before beginning work on the Bf109. This aircraft was to set the last official speed record before the outbreak of the Second World War and then become the mainstay of the Luftwaffe's fighter force. He enjoyed the support of **Hermann Goering** but not of **Erhard Milch**. His Bf109 was kept in production and service too long because of the need to standardise to maintain production in the face of a labour and materials shortage, although there were a number of improvements that enhanced its performance. His next major project, the Me110 twin-engined long-range fighter and night fighter, was troublesome and lacked the manoeuvrability of a single-engined aircraft.

He produced Germany's first rocket-powered interceptor, the Me163 Komet, which was almost as much of a threat to its pilot as to the enemy bomber formations, and the first jet fighter, the Me262, although the potential of this aircraft was compromised by Hitler's insistence that it be used as a bomber. The Second World War saw him return to work on gliders, producing the giant Me321 troop-carrying glider that could carry 130 fully equipped troops and required three Me110 tugs to become airborne. This then led to a powered version: the six-engined Me323 Gigant.

After the war he moved to Argentina and helped establish an aircraft industry, before returning to what had become West Germany in the mid-1950s, re-establishing his company and moving into the motor industry with his small bubble cars.

Meusnier de la Place, Gen Jean-Baptiste Marie (1754–93) French pioneering military aeronaut. Commissioned into the engineers, in 1784 he proposed the first streamlined airship using manpower to drive the propeller and which incorporated such features as an internal ballonet and a suspended nacelle. He also proposed balloon sheds to store airships and balloons away from the weather, especially high winds.

He must have favoured the French Revolution because afterwards he rose quickly in rank from lieutenant to general before being killed at the Battle of Mainz.

Midway, Battle of (3–7 June 1942) Just six months after the attack on **Pearl Harbor**, the Battle of Midway came as no surprise to the Americans whose intelligence had given them enough warning to know both the objective and the likely date. This meant that **Admiral Chester Nimitz**, commander-in-chief of the US Pacific Fleet, did not have to spread his forces but instead could risk concentrating them to defend Midway atoll. The Japanese did at least anticipate a strong defence and, apart from a diversionary raiding force sent north to the Aleutians, concentrated their available naval forces for a long-sought decisive battle with the Americans.

The first move by American forces took place on 3 June when, during the afternoon, USAAF Boeing B-17 Fortress bombers were sent to attack the Midway invasion force, but the heavy bombers enjoyed little success against ships under way at sea. At the outset, the Japanese failed to fly effective reconnaissance missions leaving large areas of sea uncovered.

The first wave of Japanese aircraft left the four carriers, *Akagi*, *Kaga*, *Hiryu* and *Soryu*, at dawn, with more than a hundred aircraft heading for Midway to destroy the defences. At the same time, shore-based aircraft of both the USAAF and USN flew from Midway and, finding the Japanese carriers, attacked, disrupting the formation of the fleet and killing a number of crewmen working on the open decks. The Japanese mounted an intense AA barrage and scrambled Zero fighters, with these defences accounting for seventeen American aircraft.

The Japanese attack on Midway's shore installations caused considerable damage but failed to put the airfield or the AA defences out of action. The Japanese commander, **Vice-Admiral Chuichi Nagumo**, decided to send a second wave to complete the operation and keep the US forces under pressure. The second wave could not be sent off immediately, however, as the aircraft had been armed with torpedoes expecting to launch an attack against US warships; these had to be removed and replaced with bombs for the second attack on Midway itself. As this was being done, a reconnaissance aircraft finally discovered American warships and radioed with a report that there were ten, a sufficient number to cause Nagumo to change his mind and reverse his order so that the bombs now had to be replaced with torpedoes. Nagumo also decided that the second wave should wait until the first wave, by now returning with aircraft short of fuel, had been safely recovered. Meanwhile, in the hangar decks of the carriers, the armourers had left the bombs on the decks rather than sending them back to the magazines.

At 0900, a reconnaissance aircraft radioed that it had seen an American aircraft carrier, which it believed to be the *Yorktown*.

The first wave finally returned and the aircraft were struck down into the hangars while the second wave aircraft were brought up and ranged on the flight decks ready for take-off. None of the Japanese ships had radar and there was no time to react when the first of the American aircraft were spotted. **Rear Admiral Raymond Spruance**, commander of USN Task Force 16, had put up the entire force from the *Enterprise* and *Hornet* while **Rear Admiral Fletcher**, of Task Force 17, had sent half of the *Yorktown*'s aircraft, making a force of 156 aircraft in all.

Flying low over the sea towards the Japanese ships, no less than thirty-five of forty-one Douglas Devastator torpedo-bombers were shot down, with their crews having little time to escape before their aircraft crashed into the sea. Radar would have caught the second wave of American aircraft as they flew high towards their targets but the Douglas Dauntless dive-bombers remained unnoticed as they approached at 19,000 ft and the Japanese remained distracted by the low-level attack. At 1022 the first dive-bomber peeled off and began its dive towards the *Kaga*. Twelve 1,000 lb bombs were dropped at the ship, four of which hit her.

Akagi was next to be hit and the order was given to abandon Nagumo's flagship, but the vice-admiral wanted to go down with her and was only persuaded with difficulty that his real duty would be to continue to direct the battle. He transferred his flag to a light cruiser, *Nagara*.

Rear Admiral Yamaguchi immediately ordered a strike against the *Yorktown* and the aircraft took off from *Hiryu* at 1100. Just eight Aichi D3A 'Val' bombers managed to penetrate *Yorktown*'s fighter screen and intense AA fire, but they succeeded in dropping three 500 lb bombs on to the carrier. The first bomb exploded among parked aircraft ranged on the flight deck and set them alight, while the second hit the funnel and blew out the fires for five of the carrier's six boilers. The third penetrated the flight deck and travelled down three decks to ignite an aviation fuel tank. Prompt damage control saw the aviation fuel fire smothered with carbon dioxide while the magazines were flooded as a precautionary measure. It looked as if the *Yorktown* would survive.

That afternoon Yamaguchi ordered his remaining aircraft to make a second attack on *Yorktown*. It was now the turn of the *Yorktown*'s captain to give the order to abandon ship. Yamaguchi immediately jumped to the conclusion that a second American carrier had been hit and that there were now no American carriers in the Pacific. *Hiryu* prepared yet another strike against the Americans but before this could be flown off, Dauntless dive-bombers from *Enterprise* and *Hornet* found her and attacked, with at least four bombs hitting the ship as she manoeuvred in a desperate bid to escape; another four were near misses. Once again, aircraft burst into flames and fires swept across the flight deck and the hangar.

Later that afternoon, *Soryu*, abandoned and burning, blew up. Fifteen minutes later, *Kaga* blew up as the fires reached her magazines. *Akagi* survived the night and was sunk in a torpedo attack by Japanese destroyers at dawn; a similar treatment was dealt out to *Hiryu*, but the ship remained afloat and managed to survive an attack by Boeing B-17 Fortress bombers before finally slipping beneath the waves at 0900 with her captain and Rear Adm Yamaguchi still aboard.

On learning of the loss of all four carriers, commander-in-chief of the Imperial Japanese Navy's First Fleet, Admiral Yamamoto, abandoned the invasion of Midway and withdrew westwards. Efforts to save the crippled *Yorktown* continued with a destroyer providing an escort, but on 7 June both ships were found by the Japanese submarine *I-168* and torpedoed, delivering the *coup de grâce* to the carrier and also sinking the destroyer.

The Americans might not have won the war in the Pacific at Midway as they still had a long way to go to reach the Japanese home islands, but the Japanese had lost any chance of winning because of their heavy losses of equipment and, no less important aircrew, for which they lacked a training system capable of replacing them. The early advantages of surprise attack and superior forces had been lost, as had the impression of Japanese invincibility created in the first few frantic weeks of war as the emperor's forces spread rapidly across the Pacific and westwards through South-East Asia and Indonesia.

Mignet, Henri (1893–1965) French designer.

From an early age Mignet studied bird flight and was inspired by the **Wright** brothers to build gliders, contacting **Lilienthal**'s brother, Gustavus, for advice. He was trained at the Bordeaux School of Electricity and when the First World War broke out was immediately assigned to the Signal Corps. His unit was based close to an airfield where he mixed with the mechanics and also managed to be taken up for his first flights, although this probably stopped after he taxiied a Spad Scout, went too fast and overturned the aircraft.

Postwar, he returned to work on electronics and earned enough to fund building a series of gliders, but was less fortunate with powered aircraft until he built his HM-8 in 1928. This was a simple monoplane and was successfully publicised by Mignet as the ideal low-cost and safe aeroplane for home builders.

His fame today rests on a later design, the **Pou-de-Ciel** or 'Sky Louse' of 1934, a tandem-wing machine with a pivoting forward wing that enabled the plane to be controlled without pedals. Hundreds of these were built across Europe and beyond, with many doubtless also suffering the designer's professed lack of coordination because he dispensed with the pedals. Unfortunately, either because of the aircraft defying convention or attracting too many would-be pilots lacking sufficient ability, the 'Pou' suffered a large number of crashes throughout 1935, with the aircraft suddenly diving straight into the ground. Wind tunnel tests showed that if the front wing lost lift and the rear wing continued to generate lift, the aircraft would suddenly dive. Mignet soon found a solution, but not before many had scrapped their aircraft.

Despite continuing to design aircraft he had lost credibility. He moved briefly to the United States in 1937 intending to set up an aircraft factory in Chicago, but returned to France in 1939. His wife was murdered by the French Resistance during the Second World War after which he left his homeland and attempted to set up aircraft factories in Argentina, Brazil and Japan, but again returned home.

Mikoyan, Artem I. (1905–70) Soviet designer.

Armenian Mikoyan graduated from the Zhukovsky Air Academy in Moscow in 1936 and was recruited by the ZAG1 Bureau to work on transport aircraft. His abilities were soon recognised, doubtless due to his arrogant and aggressive stance, and he was assigned to a bureau with **Gurevich** working on fighter aircraft. Their first project was the MiG-1. In 1944 the advancing Red Army found German designs for rocket and jet-powered fighters which were handed over to Mikoyan and Gurevich who produced the MiG-KB rocket-powered fighter and, in 1947, the MiG-15.

Mil Soviet design bureau. Named after the

founder when it was formed in 1947, the Mil design bureau has produced a series of single-rotor helicopter designs, and at times has had the distinction of building the largest helicopter of the day including the Mi-6 of 1957, known to NATO as 'Hook', and the Mi-12 'Homer' of 1969, which strayed from the usual Mil design principles by having two tandem rotors. The bureau also produced the giant Mi-10 'Harke' flying crane, which unusually for such a machine also had a cabin with accommodation for up to twenty-eight passengers. The most famous of the bureau's products has been the Mi-24 'Hind', the first combat helicopter to enter service in substantial numbers, differing from most such machines by also having accommodation for up to eight armed troops. Undoubtedly the most numerous has been the Mi-8 'Hip' transport helicopter which has now been superseded by a development, the Mi-17.

Mil, Mikhail Leontyevich (1909–70) Soviet helicopter pioneer. While still little more than a school-leaver, Mil started to experiment with gyroplane design and continued to do so for some twenty years before he was finally assigned his own bureau in 1947. It took just a year for the first fruit of the new venture to appear, the GM-1, a simple machine that acted as the prototype for the production Mil-1, which entered production in 1951. He then started a long series of helicopters, of which the Mi-8 transport was probably the most successful, but which included many giant and heavy-lifting machines, and the Mi-24 'Hind', an attack helicopter also capable of carrying a small number of troops.

He was awarded the Lenin Medal in 1969.

Milch, FM Erhard (1892–1971) German air force leader. Milch was one of the first airmen to command a squadron, even though he was an observer rather than a pilot with the German Military Air Service during the First World War. Postwar, Milch helped found an airline for Junkers. He took charge of the new national airline, Deutches Luft Hansa (now Lufthansa) in 1929, and gained favour with the emerging Nazi Party by giving Hitler and his senior party leaders free air travel, quite illegally. When the Nazi Party finally took power they gave Milch the task of secretly establishing the new Luftwaffe. He did this and at the same time bullied the aircraft industry into bending itself to his will, in some cases forcing the owners, including **Hugo Junkers**, to hand over their assets to the state. He also built an air transport infrastructure within Germany.

In 1935 the Luftwaffe was unveiled, not only making it clear that Germany intended to impose her will on her neighbours, but making it difficult for the poorly armed Allies to intervene. He assumed control of all aircraft production during the Second World War and ensured that the Me262 jet fighter entered production. However, he was sacked by Hitler for insisting that the aircraft should be used as intended: as a fighter rather than a bomber.

Miles *See* Miles, Frederick George, George Herbert and Maxine Francis Mary

Miles, Frederick George (1903–76), George Herbert (1911–99) and Maxine Francis Mary (1901–84) British manufacturers. Frederick started a motorcycle rental business towards the end of the First World War, and after the war ended built a small biplane and started a flying school with some friends. His brother George joined him on leaving school and the company grew steadily. In 1932 Frederick married Lady Maxine 'Blossom' Forbes-Robertson who was already interested in aviation. She wanted her husband to build her an aeroplane for which she handled the stress analysis, and so the first real Miles aircraft was born: the Hawk. Lacking production facilities they had it built by Phillips and Powis. The aircraft was an immediate success being faster and more comfortable than the Moth, as well as cheaper, although training took longer because of the higher wing loading. A number of racing and cabin monoplanes followed but as the Second World War approached they were awarded contracts for trainers.

During wartime, the company employed 6,000 people and postwar hoped for a promising future, but the dire state of the British economy meant that despite a promising light commercial design, the Aerovan, a radical twin-tail transport nicknamed the 'Flying Tadpole', the company went bankrupt for lack of sufficient orders and its business was acquired by **Handley Page** in 1948. Frederick started a design consultancy while George went to work for **Airspeed**. When the two started to work together again in 1951 they managed to produce a few aircraft, but Britain had been effectively pushed aside in the light aircraft market by this time.

Miller, Jessie Maude (1902–65) Australian aviatrix. She was the first woman to fly from England to Australia as a passenger with her lover Bill Lancaster. The resulting fame took the couple to Hollywood and Miller began to build herself a reputation as a pilot, winning the speed event at the National Air Races in 1929. She was given a contract by Fairchild. In 1930 she flew an Alexander Bullet to set a transcontinental speed record. An affair with a writer, who was later found dead, placed Lancaster under suspicion and although cleared, the couple left the USA for the UK.

After Lancaster disappeared during a flight over the Sahara Desert in 1933, Miller stopped flying. His decayed body was found next to his Avro biplane in 1962.

Mitchell, Brig Gen William 'Billy' (1879–1936)

American strategist and visionary. Commissioned into the US Army in the Philippines, he spent much of the early years of the twentieth century travelling. He learnt to fly in 1915 and then demanded that US Congress should start devoting funds to military aviation. He convinced Congress of the case, and the US Army Aviation Section became an entity in its own right in 1916, having been part of the Signal Corps. Mitchell was one of the commanding officers when the Aviation Section went to France in 1917, and he led the first US air patrol over the Western Front in May 1917. He organised and then led offensive operations, and was planning paratroop operations when the war ended.

Postwar, Mitchell lobbied hard for the continued support of military aviation and in fact his constant pressure and aggressive demands became counter-productive. He also made enemies when, in 1921, he led a small formation of aircraft to bomb and sink a captured German battleship, the *Ostfriesland*, arguing that this disproved the theory that a capital ship was immune from aerial attack. However, the USN argued that the ship was at anchor and did not have its AA defences manned. Mitchell also pressed for an autonomous US air service along the lines introduced in the UK. In 1925, the loss of the *Shenandoah* airship saw him accuse the War Department, which was responsible for the US Army, of criminal negligence, and for this he was court-martialled. He was completely unrepentant. Only one member of the panel did not vote for conviction, and many believe that this was his old friend from childhood, the future General Douglas McArthur.

Despite the lack of autonomy, between the wars the USAAC concentrated increasingly on the development of strategic air power so that when the US entered the Second World War, it did so with a strategy that had much in common with that of the RAF. The disgrace of Mitchell also meant that much of his writing and speech-making was overlooked, including his belief, expressed during the early 1920s, that war with Japan was likely and that it would start with a carrier-borne attack on **Pearl Harbor**.

Mitchell, Reginald Joseph (1895–1937)

British designer. One of Britain's greatest aircraft designers was largely self-taught, being an apprentice at a steam locomotive works before being taken on by the then small firm of Supermarine in 1916. It took him three years to become chief engineer and to start work on the company's family of flying boats. His fame springs from the successes in the late 1920s and 1930s with the family of seaplanes, the S5, S6 and S6B, that won the **Schneider Trophy Race** on three consecutive occasions, winning it outright for the UK, and set a world air speed record.

His ill-health began in 1933 with cancer of the rectum, and the colostomy that followed left him in discomfort for the rest of his life, although he continued working. During the winter of 1934/5, he encountered pilots of what would soon be unveiled as the Luftwaffe and was convinced that war with Germany was inevitable.

He returned to work on the fighter, eventually named the Spitfire, that he was designing and which owed its origins to the S6 series. He threw all his energy into the new aircraft and many believe that overwork shortened his life but, in 1940, the Spitfire was the latest and best fighter that the RAF possessed and the only British fighter capable of encountering the Messerschmitt Bf109. He lived to see it fly as a prototype but died before it could enter service.

Mitsubishi Japanese manufacturer. Part of an industrial group that became involved in aviation during the 1920s, the company initially produced European designs under licence. One of the first of its own designs was the Type 10 carrier-borne fighter for the Japanese Navy Air Force in 1925, but this was followed by **Blackburn** and **Junkers** designs built under licence. A number of other fighters were built for both the JNAF and the JAAF before the company turned to its most famous design, the A6M2 Type O carrier-borne fighter, the famous 'Zero', which was ready before Japan entered the Second World War. Mitsubishi also produced the Ki67 Type 3 bomber for the

JAAF and the D5Y1 kamikaze suicide aircraft for the JNAF.

Postwar, aircraft production was banned until 1952, when the company returned to licence-production, initially building **Sikorsky** helicopters. During the 1960s the Mu-2 communications aircraft was put into production and followed in the 1970s by the T-2 jet trainer. The most recent product has been the F-2A/B jet fighter, based on the Lockheed Martin F-16, but with a new composite wing.

Moelders, Oberst Werner (1913–41) German ace. Commissioned into the German Army, Moelders was, it seems, air sick during his early flights yet he transferred to the Luftwaffe and in 1938 was sent to Spain with the Condor Legion supporting the Nationalists in the **Spanish Civil War**. Within four months he had shot down fourteen enemy aircraft. While honoured on his return and favoured by **Goering**, he concentrated on developing fighter tactics and replaced the 'circus' formations of the First World War with the leader/wingman pair, or the 'finger four'. He commanded Gruppe III/JG53 during the invasion of France and the **Battle of Britain**, and by the end of the second winter of the war he had become the first fighter pilot to score more than 100 kills. He also played a prominent role in Operation Barbarossa, the invasion of the Soviet Union, taking his score to 115 kills. Recalled in November 1941 to attend **Gen Ernst Udet**'s funeral, he was killed when his aircraft ran out of fuel as he was searching for a landing site in a storm.

Moisant, John B. (1868–1910) US pioneer. Born in the USA to French-Canadian parents, Moisant and his brothers became sugar growers in El Salvador and also adventurers. His brothers were arrested for political intrigue by the country's dictator and it took two attempts by Moisant to get them released. Moisant was sent by the dictator to France to buy arms and aircraft and, while in Paris, he learnt to fly and made two fruitless attempts at designing and building his own aircraft. He did, however, become the first to fly from London to Paris carrying a passenger.

He returned to the United States and took part in the **Gordon Bennett** Belmont Park Meeting,

and when his own machine was damaged, paid US $10,000 (£2,000 at the then rate of exchange, worth £105,000 today) to buy **Leblanc**'s Blériot, which the Frenchman could not fly because he had been injured for the race around the Statue of Liberty. His entry broke the rules, but he won, beating **Claud Grahame-White**. At first he was allowed to retain the prize but was later disqualified after protests from the other competitors.

He next gathered together a group of French and American aviators and established the Moisant International Aviators, a stunt and display team that toured the United States. They were seen in Texas by the president of Mexico who asked them to fly reconnaissance flights against rebel positions close to the border between Mexico and the USA, which they did. All went well until December; when visiting New Orleans, Moisant's aircraft overturned during landing, throwing him out and breaking his neck.

Mollison, James Allan (1905–59) British long-distance pioneer. Scottish-born Mollison was commissioned into the RAF in 1923, but left later to go to Australia where he flew airmail services for Australian National Airways. In 1931 he moved into competitive flying and set a new Australia–UK record of 8 days 21 hours. He then embarked on other long-distance flights setting a record of 4 days 17½ hours for London to Cape Town and 3½ days for Lympne, in Kent, to Rio de Janeiro, which was also the first flight between the UK and South America.

He was married briefly to **Amy Johnson** but their rivalry prevented this from being a happy marriage or a successful partnership. He also set a speed record between New York and London in 1936, of 19 hours 59 minutes. Like his ex-wife he delivered aircraft during the Second World War, although in his case he was part of the RAF's Ferry Command.

monoplane An aeroplane with one set of wings. To be precise it has one wing, as the wing structure is taken as running from wing-tip to wing-tip. With the exception of some aerobatic aircraft, all aircraft in production today are monoplanes. The monoplane is almost as old as powered flight itself, with **Langley**'s *Aerodrome A* being a tandem-wing

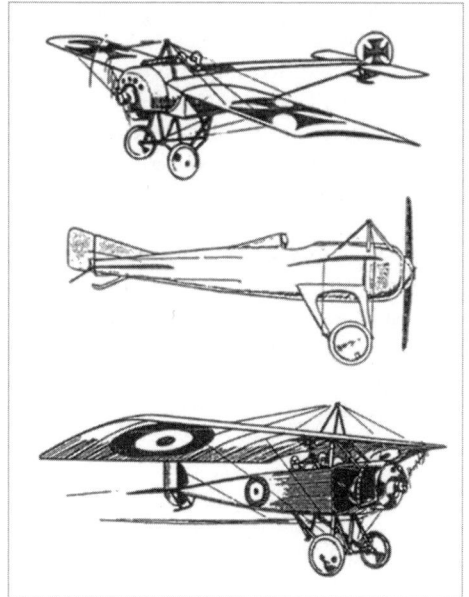

The early monoplane required so much rigging it was barely better than a biplane, as the Fokker EIV (top) shows, and so too does the streamlined Deperdussin *Monocoque* (centre). The Morane Parasol monoplane (above) also needed stressing.

monoplane, although rather more successful was the aircraft in which **Louis Blériot** flew across the English Channel. During the First World War, the French Deperdussin and the German Taube and Fokker Eindekker were all monoplanes. Nevertheless, the First World War was a biplane, and occasionally triplane, war, and the biplane remained dominant for many years afterwards. The reason was that the early monoplane needed external bracing for its wing, which persuaded many that they should opt for the superior lift of the biplane. The bracing also made mounting a machine gun more difficult. It was not until the advent of the **cantilever wing** that the monoplane became truly viable, and despite early work by **Junkers** in Germany before the First World War, many air forces continued to be sceptical about the monoplane, even ordering biplanes during the 1930s.

The wing can be low, high or medium, although the latter is least effective as in many aircraft types its intrusion into the fuselage is a nuisance. An aircraft with the wing mounted above the fuselage with a gap between is known as a parasol monoplane.

Montgolfier, Joseph-Michel de (1740–1810) and Jacques-Etienne de (1745–99) French inventors of the hot air balloon. The brothers were paper-makers from Annonay, near Lyons, and had noticed ash and unburnt particles rising in the smoke and heat of a fire. They experimented, placing paper bags in the smoke, and noticed that they inflated and rose. Next they made a large paper and linen sphere, which was placed over a fire of chopped wool and straw in the market place at Annonay, from which it made an ascent on 4 June 1783 before a large crowd. In Paris later that summer they constructed a larger balloon, which made an ascent on 19 September from the Palace of Versailles, carrying a cock, a sheep and a duck on an 8-minute, 2-mile voyage, ending with a safe landing in the Bois de Vaucressan. The ascent was watched by Louis XVI of France and his wife Marie Antoinette, and a crowd reputed to have been 130,000 strong.

On 15 October 1783, **Jean-François Pilâtre de Rozier** made the first manned ascent using a tethered Montgolfière, as the hot air balloons had become known. For the first aerial voyage it was intended to use two convicts, but de Rozier and the **Marquis d'Arlandes** volunteered, ascending from the gardens of the Château la Muette in the Bois de Boulogne, near Paris, on 21 November 1783, journeying over Paris and then descending on the Butte-aux-Cailles, some 5 1/2 miles from their starting point. Control over the fire was through sponges and buckets of water, and again the fuel was a mixture of straw and wool, a combination that the Montgolfier brothers credited with considerable properties.

As far as it is known, of the two brothers only Joseph ever made an ascent and that was just once, rising in the giant aerostat *Le Flesseles*, at Lyon in 1784.

Montgolfière A hot air balloon as invented by the brothers **Joseph-Michel** and **Jacques-Etienne de Montgolfier**. Modern hot air balloons use propane gas burners rather than the braziers of paper and wool originally favoured by the brothers. While for most of ballooning history the gas balloon was favoured, especially after safer helium was substituted for hydrogen, the application of the propane gas burner has revived interest in the hot air balloon, which has become a popular sporting and recreational air vehicle.

Mooney American manufacturer. Famous for building single-engined light aircraft, the company started after the Second World War and became known for innovations such as producing the first single-engined pressurised light aircraft, the Mk22 Mustang. It became part of Butler Aviation International in the early 1970s, and began trading under the name of Aerostar International.

Morane/Morane-Saulnier French manufacturer. Founded before the outbreak of the First World War, the company was initially a proponent of the monoplane and its products had distinctive all-moving tail surfaces. The company's Parasol reconnaissance aircraft became one of the first fighters. A Morane-Saulnier *monoplane de chasse* was the first Allied aircraft to have a machine gun firing through the propeller disk, with the propeller being protected by deflector plates.

Between the wars, the company produced military aircraft for the French armed forces including the MS225C fighter of the late 1920s and the MS406 fighter of the late 1930s, judged to be one of the better aircraft in service with the Armée de l'Air in 1939. Production ceased with the fall of France but re-started after the war ended with the MS733 Alcyon basic trainer and later the MS760 Paris jet trainer. These were joined by a number of light aircraft but production passed to *Aérospatiale* when the company went out of business.

Morane, Léon (1885–1918) and Robert Charles (1886–1968) French manufacturers. Léon Morane's original involvement with aviation was as competition manager for **Louis Blériot**, but in 1911, with his brother and **Gabriel Borel**, he set up his own factory. The trio built one monoplane but then split up following disagreements over design. The Moranes were then joined by **Raymond Saulnier** who had worked

for Blériot designing the Blériot XI. The company became Morane-Saulnier and concentrated on monoplanes, with **Roland Garros** as their star competition and test pilot. The company survived the nationalisation programme of the late 1930s and the Second World War, but was forced out of business in 1966.

Moss, Dr Sanford A. (1872–1949) US engineer. Graduating from Cornell University with a PhD in engineering, Moss started work at **General Electric** developing more efficient turbines, including gas-driven turbines. Rather than following this to its logical conclusion and developing the jet engine, during the First World War the priority was to turbo-charge piston engines to derive the maximum power from them and improve the performance at altitude. Turbo-charging enabled a Liberty engine to operate at altitudes in excess of 14,000 ft, while postwar a turbo-supercharged Liberty allowed a Le Pere biplane to set an altitude record of 38,180 ft. The full benefit of this research came during the Second World War when it played a major part in providing the high altitude performance of US heavy bombers.

Mozhaiski, Alexander Feodorovitch (1825–90) Russian pioneer. Given the need for the old Soviet Union to demonstrate that Russia led in everything, it was not surprising that Mozhaiski was claimed to be the inventor of the aeroplane and had made the first flight. A naval officer, Mozhaiski's design was similar to that of **Henson** and used two British-built steam engines to drive three propellers, with one tractor propeller forward and two pusher propellers at the rear. The machine was launched down a ramp and, when tested in 1884 in St Petersburg, it did manage a hop due to the down-ramp momentum, but it was unable to sustain flight and lacked controls.

multiplane The name given to any heavier-than-air flying-machine with four or more wings, although the description is usually applied to aircraft with a 'Venetian blind' arrangement of aerofoil surfaces, such as the test rig built by **Horatio Phillips**. The problem with the multiplane was the considerable drag generated and the difficulty in establishing a suitable location for the control surfaces.

Munk, Max Michael (1890–1986) German scientist. A graduate of the Technische Hochschule Hannover and of Göttingen University, Munk worked on research for German aircraft manufacturers until after the First World War when he decided to emigrate and joined the **National Advisory Committee on Aeronautics** (NACA) in 1920. One of his most significant discoveries was that wind tunnel airflow was often different from that experienced on full-scale tests because the wind tunnel airflow was at a different density. His solution was to factor in the Reynold's Number to scale results and also to use variable density wind tunnels, one of which was later built at Langley and proved its worth.

He left NACA in 1927 to teach, usually at relatively minor posts.

museums, aviation A complete list of aviation museums would require a directory of their own, but most countries have at least one museum devoted to aeronautical history. Few can be as comprehensive as the National Air & Space Museum at the Smithsonian Institution in Washington DC. In the UK civil aviation is neglected, although the Museum of Scottish Aviation at East Fortune, near Edinburgh, and the Farnborough Air Sciences Trust remedy this to some extent. The Imperial War Museum shows some military aircraft in London, but the majority of its collection is on display at Duxford, Cambridgeshire. There is the RAF Museum at Hendon, north London, the Fleet Air Arm Museum at Yeovilton in Somerset, and a Museum of Army Aviation at Middle Wallop in Hampshire. In the United States it is also possible to board a preserved aircraft carrier in New York.

N

Nagasaki (9 August 1945) Three days after the first atomic bomb was dropped on the Japanese city of **Hiroshima** on 9 August, a second Boeing B-29, named **Bock's Car** after its captain, dropped another atomic bomb, this time on the city of Nagasaki. Meanwhile Japan's leaders still debated Truman's call of 6 August to surrender, or face complete ruin from repeated attacks by the new weapon. Nagasaki was a major industrial centre with more than 250,000 inhabitants, many of whom worked in the Mitsubishi factories. The bomb dropped on Nagasaki was more powerful than that used at Hiroshima and was known as 'Fat Man' due to its shape, which resulted from a different fission technique. It killed 50,000 people and injured 10,000 more, a lower figure than that at Hiroshima since Nagasaki's terrain offered many buildings in the valleys protection from the burst.

The RAF had an observer in *Bock's Car*, **Gp Capt Leonard Cheshire**, a former commander of the famous 617 squadron. In contrast to his earlier experiences flying in the RAF's bombers, the B-29 was a revelation to Cheshire with relatively little internal noise; he was dressed in shirt sleeve order, without an oxygen mask and flying at 39,000 ft at almost 400 mph. Weather conditions were perfect, with a clear blue sky.

Nagumo, Vice-Adm Chuichi (1887–1944) Japanese naval commander. Nagumo led the audacious raid by six Japanese aircraft carriers against the US Pacific Fleet in its forward base at **Pearl Harbor** on 7 December 1941. A torpedo specialist rather than a naval airman, he expected to lose a substantial number of the aircraft sent against Pearl Harbor, with them having to fight their way there and back again, but despite low losses, he refused to send a third and possibly even a fourth wave later in the day, leaving Pearl Harbor functioning as a naval base. His fear was that of an engagement with the Pacific Fleet's two

carriers. He had gained a reputation in peacetime for daring but in war he proved over-cautious. Early in 1942 he was largely responsible for the occupation of the Netherlands East Indies, and also ventured into the Indian Ocean and attacked the Australian port and city of Darwin. His forces were decisively defeated at the **Battle of Midway**, losing four carriers in a single day.

He was relieved of his command in 1943 and posted to the Mariana Islands. He committed suicide just before US forces invaded Saipan in July 1944.

Nakajima Japanese manufacturer. Another industrial group to enter aircraft production in post-First World War Japan, the company initially built British and French designs under licence before building its own designs, which included the Type 5 advanced trainer, the A2N1 carrier-borne fighter and later the Type 91 fighter monoplane. During the late 1930s, the B4Y1 Type 96 fighter and B5N1 Type 97 strike aircraft were built for the JNAF's carriers, while the JAAF received the Ki-27 Type 97 fighter and the Ki-34 Type 97 transport. Wartime aircraft included the J1N1 Type 2 fighter and reconnaissance aircraft for the JNAF and the Ki-44 Type 2 and Ki-84 Type 4 fighters and Ki-49 Type 0 bomber for the JAAF. The Kitsuka turbojet-powered and Ki-115 and Ki-201 suicide aircraft were also produced by this concern. Production ceased with Japanese surrender.

National Advisory Committee on Aeronautics (NACA) Formed between the wars to coordinate US research into aviation, NACA was a direct predecessor of NASA. Among its innovations were cowlings to streamline the profile of radial engines, inevitably known as 'NACA cowls', which had hitherto simply left their cylinder heads open to view, and the appearance of aircraft was considerably improved.

National Aeronautics & Space Administration (NASA)

National Aeronautics & Space Administration (NASA) Replacing the earlier **National Advisory Committee on Aeronautics (NACA)**, NASA was founded in 1958 and over the intervening years has become firmly associated in the public mind with the US space programme. It continues to be involved in aviation research, including such matters as supercritical wings, and has an extensive research facility at its Dryden Research Centre.

naval aviation Before the First World War, naval aviation was established in the United States, the United Kingdom and France, with all three navies having converted ships for the operation of hydro-aeroplanes. During the war, the RNAS successfully attacked and sank a Turkish ship with a torpedo, while the service was also responsible for the initial air defence of the United Kingdom and provided escorts for convoys using airships. Meanwhile, in many other countries, naval aviation was proceeding alongside army aviation.

The Royal Navy was first to operate **aircraft carriers**, but the overlap between the RNAS and RFC during the war years, and the duplication of effort, led to pressure for a single autonomous air service which emerged on 1 April 1918 as the RAF. Many believed that there remained a need for navies to have control of their own aviation, and a look at the aircraft operated by the USN during the late 1930s compared with those operated by the Royal Navy shows the benefits of having a dedicated naval air arm. Nevertheless, the Royal Navy regained full control of its Fleet Air Arm in 1939. During the Second World War, the most important naval battles were conducted by carrier-borne aircraft with the opposing fleets not coming into sight of one another, as at the **Coral Sea** and **Midway**. Aircraft were also important at other battles, such as Matapan. The Fleet Air Arm attack on the Italian fleet at **Taranto** showed that naval air power was indispensable, even when using obsolete aircraft, and this was confirmed at **Pearl Harbor**. Without naval aviation, the Japanese would not have been able to attack Pearl Harbor, but also the United States would have had considerable difficulty fighting back over the long reaches of the Pacific Ocean.

Postwar, naval aviation proved important during the war in French Indo-China, Korea and Vietnam when air bases ashore became too vulnerable. It was a significant feature in the Anglo-French campaign at Suez, and without it the Falkland Islands could not have been recovered from the Argentine.

Navarre, Sous Lt Jean Marie Dominique (1895–1919)

Navarre, Sous Lt Jean Marie Dominique (1895–1919) French ace. The outbreak of the First World War found Navarre learning to fly and in September 1914 he joined MF8, a Maurice Farman squadron with the French Aviation Militaire. He soon showed himself to be an over-enthusiastic and undisciplined pilot, so when bored with reconnaissance he applied to transfer to a fighter unit; his request was denied. He persisted and in 1915 was transferred to a Morane fighter unit, shooting down an Aviatik on 1 April – only the third aircraft to be shot down by a French unit and so was awarded the Medaille Militaire.

He was transferred to a Nieuport squadron in 1916, painting his aircraft bright red to bait the Germans so that by June he had twelve confirmed kills. He also used his aircraft to shoot wild ducks and geese using a shotgun. His days of aerial combat, and hunting, were cut short in June when he was shot down and so badly wounded that he took two years to recover. Officially back on duty in summer 1918, he was kept from operational flying by his superiors who realised that his recovery was not complete.

After the war, during practice for a victory display in which he planned to fly illegally through the Arc de Triomphe in Paris, his aircraft hit a telephone pole and he was killed.

Nesterov, Capt Petr Nikolaevich (1887–1914)

Nesterov, Capt Petr Nikolaevich (1887–1914) Russian ace. Flying a Nieuport at Kiev on 20 August 1913, Nesterov flew the first loop, for which he was placed under arrest for ten days by his commanding officer on a charge of risking government property. Fortunately, he was soon released once aviators in France and Great Britain heard of his achievement, and was promoted from lieutenant to captain.

During the First World War, Nesterov commanded the XI Corps Air Squadron. On 26 August 1914 he confronted a flight of Austrian aircraft that had just bombed his airfield, even though his aircraft was unarmed, ramming the leading Austrian aircraft so that both planes plummeted earthwards and both pilots were killed.

Netherlands and Belgium, German invasion of (8 May 1940)

From the outset the odds were stacked against the defenders. The Luftwaffe had 3,834 aircraft, including 1,482 bombers and dive bombers, 42 ground-attack aircraft, 248 fighter destroyers or Zerstorer (fighter-bombers) and 1,016 fighters. By contrast, the RAF had 456 aircraft, of which 261 were fighters, 135 bombers and 60 reconnaissance aircraft. Somewhat larger, the French Armée de l'Air had 1,604 aircraft, many of them also obsolete or obsolescent, of which 260 were bombers, 764 fighters, 180 reconnaissance aircraft and another 400 or so aircraft in army support duties. Belgium had just 180 aircraft, of which 81 were fighters while the Netherlands had 132 aircraft, of which 35 were fighters and 23 fighter-destroyers.

The Germans scored in both quality and quantity and through having combat-hardened aircrew. The situation was not helped by the French insisting that neither of the two Allied air forces should press heavy bombing raids against German industry for fear of German reprisals against French targets.

Typical of the actions that took place was on 12 May when six AASF Battles, with an escort of two Hurricane fighters, were sent against the Vroenhoven and Veldwezelt bridges, across which the German forces were streaming. Four of the aircraft were shot down as they approached the targets, which were left undamaged. By 21 May the air component of the BEF was down to its last few Lysanders, while the few surviving Battles were limited to night operations to keep losses to an acceptable level. As the Germans swept through Belgium and the Netherlands, causing British forces which had ventured into Belgium to retreat back into France, the British soon started to husband scarce resources and trained aircrew for the defence of the British Isles.

Newman, Larry (1947–)

US aeronaut. Qualified as a commercial pilot, Newman took up hang-gliding as a hobby in 1974. With **Ben Abruzzo**, whom he met in Albuquerque, he started a hang-glider manufacturing company and in three years this became the largest of its kind anywhere. In 1978 he joined Abruzzo and **Maxi Anderson** in the transatlantic balloon, *Double Eagle II*, which ascended from Presque Isle in Maine on 11 August and reached Misery in France six days later. They intended to hang-glide to earth once over France but were forced to jettison the hang-glider to save weight as the balloon neared the French coast.

Newman returned to commercial aviation although he also started a company building ultralight aircraft to put an advanced machine built of composites into production – but the high price meant that it was out of reach of its market.

In 1981 he joined **'Rocky' Aoki** and Abruzzo on the first man-carrying balloon crossing of the Pacific, but failed in his ambition to make the first circumnavigation by balloon.

Nieuport/Nieuport-Delage See below

Nieuport (de Nie Port), Edouard (1875–1911)

French manufacturer. Trained as an engineer, he founded his company in 1909 at Issy and although born de Nie Port, he changed his name for business reasons. His first monoplane in 1910 attracted considerable attention because of its small size and streamlining. The following year, flying one of his own aircraft, he set a speed record of 82.73 mph, but on 15 September he was killed during a demonstration flight for the French military. His brother Charles took over the business, but in 1913 he was also killed in a crash.

Nimitz, Adm Chester W. (1885–1966)

American naval commander. Born in Texas to German immigrant parents, his early career was spent in the submarine service. He was promoted to rear admiral in June 1938, and in 1939 became head of the Bureau of Navigation which brought him to the notice of President Roosevelt. He succeeded **Rear Admiral Kimmel** as commander-in-chief of the US Pacific Fleet (Cincpac) after **Pearl Harbor**.

His first task was to create a strong staff and team of fighting commanders, and these included **Halsey**, Mitscher, **Spruance** and Turner, and the USMC commanders Holland Smith and Vandegrift. He supported initiative, and after ordering Halsey to attack Japanese-held islands early in 1942, he also backed the **Doolittle** raid, 'Operation Shangri-La', on Japan in April. Also in April he was given command of all Allied forces in the Pacific, including air and land forces. He was responsible for the victories at **Midway** and at Guadalcanal and encouraged the use of ULTRA intelligence, eventually leaving the Imperial Japanese Navy all but destroyed after the fiasco at **Leyte Gulf**. An outstanding naval strategist, one of his least recognised achievements was the successful deployment of the submarine fleet which cut Japan's supply lines feeding the home islands with food and raw materials as well as fuel. By the end of the war, shipping in the Inland Sea was vulnerable and he had succeeded in sinking the largest aircraft carrier built outside the United States, the *Amagi*, before she could even become operational. He signed the Japanese surrender document on behalf of the US government, was promoted to fleet admiral in December 1944 and took over from **FA Ernest King** as chief of naval operations in November 1945.

Nobile, Gen Umberto (1885–1978) Italian aeronautical explorer. Trained as an engineer he became an airship designer for the Italian government, but when an airship was sold to **Roald Amundsen**, the Norwegian polar explorer, Nobile accompanied it as the captain. Named the *Norge*, Amundsen planned the airship to make the first journey over the North Pole but was beaten by **Richard Byrd**. Instead, the two men decided to make the first transpolar voyage leaving Spitzbergen on 11 May 1926 and taking three days to reach Teller in Alaska. Nobile as captain and pilot became the hero, much to Amundsen's dismay.

Nobile organised a second polar crossing with a new dirigible, the *Italia*, to explore the ice cap. Ascending on 23 May, severe icing conditions made the operation dangerous and eventually it crash-landed, but not before a Russian farmer picked up their distress signal on a crude radio set. A massive international search effort was launched which resulted in Amundsen, searching in a flying boat, becoming lost. On 23 June, a Swedish aircraft located the crash site and landed. The pilot had been ordered to rescue Nobile and leave the rest

of the crew for other rescue aircraft, which were supposed to have been close behind. Nobile wanted other crew members to go first but eventually gave in and took the flight. Unfortunately, other aircraft were not close behind and it was not until August before the rest of the crew could be rescued, after one of them had died.

Nobile was charged with dereliction of duty on his return to Italy, with those members of the Regia Aeronautica who favoured aeroplanes rather than airships working against him; he was at risk of being executed. Although convicted, he was imprisoned rather than executed and allowed to go to the Soviet Union where he designed airships before moving to the United States in 1939. There he taught aeronautics. He returned to Italy after the Second World War and cleared his name.

Noorduyn (Noorduijn), Robert Cornelius (1893–1959) Anglo-Dutch pioneer and manufacturer. With a Dutch father and English mother, Noorduyn studied in the Netherlands and Germany before joining **Sopwith** in England in 1913 and then moving to **Armstrong-Whitworth** the following year. He worked with **Frederick Koolhoven** and followed him to BAT in 1917. He went to work with **Fokker** in 1920 and then in 1924 went to the USA to found a Fokker factory in New Jersey using the name of the Netherlands Aircraft Manufacturing Company. In addition to upgrading the F.VII from one engine to three he also designed the Universal utility aircraft while still with Fokker in the USA.

In 1929 he went to work for **Bellanca**, and then in 1931 he joined Pitcairn. He adopted the spelling 'Noorduyn' between 1931 and 1934 when he founded his own factory across the border in Montreal. His Universal had sold well in Canada and he built upon its success with a series of single-engined utility aircraft, of which the most famous was the Noorduyn Norseman which first flew in 1935 and was the first of 919 built.

Nord *See* Aérospatiale

North American/North American Rockwell American manufacturer. The result of a merger between North American Aviation, which dated from 1934, and Rockwell Standard, whose aerospace interests included guided weapons production and the Aero Commander range of executive and light aircraft. Many of the most notable North American aircraft designs entered service during the Second World War and included the B-25 Mitchell medium bomber, the F-51 Mustang fighter and the T-6 Texan trainer. These were followed by the T-28 Trojan advanced trainer and the F-86 Sabre jet fighter, which was highly successful during the Korean War and was built under licence in Australia, Canada, Italy and Japan. A number of experimental aircraft were also built postwar including the X-15 and the XB-70A Valkyrie high-speed research aircraft. Later in the 1950s, the company produced the supersonic F-100 Super Sabre, the T-2 Buckeye jet trainer and the T-39 Sabreliner navigational trainer, and in the 1960s the A-5 Vigilante carrier-borne bomber entered service with the USN. The company also produced the OV-10A Bronco counter-insurgency aircraft. The final major project by the company was the B-1B Lancer supersonic bomber for the USAF, before production passed to **Boeing**.

North Atlantic Treaty Organisation (NATO)

Dating from 1949, NATO is the most successful and enduring alliance of all time. The membership initially included Belgium, Canada, Denmark, France, Iceland, Italy, Luxembourg, the Netherlands, Norway, Portugal, the United Kingdom and the United States. Greece and Turkey joined in 1952, followed by West Germany in 1955. During the de Gaulle era, France opted out of active membership, forcing the alliance to move its European headquarters from Paris to Brussels. Spain joined in 1975.

Control of the organisation is through the North Atlantic Council. Subordinate to the Council are two major commands, ACLANT for the North Atlantic and SHAPE for Europe, and below these are subordinate commands. NATO members not only exercise together, they hold a number of joint operations to improve inter-operability such as the naval standing forces in the Atlantic, the English Channel and the Mediterranean. After the break-up of the Warsaw Pact, many of its members applied to join NATO, including Poland, while others took advantage of the 'Partnership for Peace', a form of associate membership.

Despite being a Cold War alliance intended to deter a Soviet invasion of Western Europe, NATO operational deployments have followed the end of the Cold War, with NATO organising the invasions of Iraq to liberate Kuwait and then Kosovo. The justification for this was that only NATO had the organisational structure and experience of the international commands that these operations required.

The European Union is now planning a European Rapid Reaction Force, and many fear that this might undermine NATO by withdrawing increasingly scarce military resources from it.

Northcliffe, Lord (1865–1922)

British newspaper proprietor. Born Alfred Harmsworth, his career in journalism developed as he started to found small news magazines aimed at the growing mass of people with the education and the time to be able to read, and the money to buy them. He acquired the ailing London *Evening News* in 1894. Two years later he founded a sister morning paper, the *Daily Mail*, and also made further acquisitions in the years that followed. In 1905 he was ennobled as Baron Harmsworth. The following year he hired **Harry Harper** as the first aeronautical correspondent, and with encouragement from his protégé started to offer the prizes that did so much to motivate long-distance pioneering flights, such as Blériot's flight across the English Channel, and through them inspire the public and politicians with the potential of aviation. In addition to the cross-Channel flight, other milestones in early aviation that can be attributed to Harmsworth's generosity included the model aeroplane contest won by **A.V. Roe**, the first circular flight of more than one mile in the UK won by Henry Moore-Brabazon (*see* **Lord Brabazon of Tara**), the London to Manchester race won by **Paulhan**, and **Alcock** and Brown's transatlantic non-stop flight.

He died in 1922 having lost his powers of reasoning the previous year.

Northrop/Northrop Grumman

American manufacturer and merger of Northrop and Grumman in 2002. Originally formed in 1930,

Grumman's first aircraft was the FF-1, a tandem twin-seat carrier-borne fighter biplane with a retractable undercarriage. In 1933, the first of many Grumman amphibians, the J2F-1 Duck, appeared. During the period before the United States entered the Second World War, the company produced the F2F and F3F carrier-borne fighter biplanes, the F4F Wildcat carrier fighter monoplane and the Goose amphibian. Wartime aircraft included the Widgeon amphibian, the F6F Hellcat fighter and the TBF Avenger, regarded by many as the best torpedo-bomber of the war, followed by the company's first twin-engined fighter, the F7F Tigercat, and the F8F Bearcat, again carrier-borne aircraft.

Postwar, the company continued with Tigercat and Bearcat production before producing its first jet fighter, again for the USN, the F9F panther, followed by a swept-wing development of the aircraft, the F10F Cougar. Amphibian production continued with the Mallard and the HU-16 Albatross. Work also started on carrier-borne anti-submarine aircraft with the S-2 Tracker and its AEW and COD developments, the E-1B Tracer and C-1A Trader. During the late 1950s, Grumman produced yet another carrier-borne attack aircraft, the A-6 Intruder, and an electronic counter-measures variant, the EA-6B, as well as the company's first civil landplane, the turboprop Gulfstream I, one of the largest business aircraft available at the time.

Turboprop successors to the Tracer and Trader followed with the E-2A Hawkeye and C-2 Greyhound, as well as a jet successor to the Gulfstream I: the Gulfstream II. A STOL observation and attack aircraft for the US Army was the OV-1 Mohawk. Naval fighters also continued with the F-14A Tomcat while the company designed the lunar landing modules for the NASA Apollo programme.

Northrop was slightly earlier, with its first aircraft being the Alpha, a six-passenger single-engined monoplane that entered service in the late 1920s, followed in 1933 by the Gamma mailplane and in 1935 by the T-17. During the Second World War the company's most important aircraft was the P-61 Black Widow night fighter, also known as the F-15 Reporter in its reconnaissance role. Postwar, Northrop experimented with tailless aircraft and

also produced the F-89 Scorpion fighter. The early 1960s saw the successful lightweight and low-cost F-5A/B jet fighter and its related T-38 Talon advanced jet trainer, with the former seeing service in many air forces worldwide.

Northrop, John Knudson (1895–1981) US manufacturer. Joining the **Loughead** brothers in 1916, he worked on the F-1 flying boat before serving in the US Army's Signal Corps in 1917 and 1918. He returned to Loughead Aircraft postwar, and when it collapsed, moved to **Douglas** and helped with the design of the World Cruiser. Meanwhile, Loughead had been re-established as Lockheed and Northrop rejoined the brothers, designing the Vega.

He set up his own company in 1928 under the name of Avion but this was purchased by United Aircraft and Transport and renamed Northrop. He designed the Alpha and Beta monoplanes for the new company, but when the owners merged the business with Stearman and relocated to Kansas, he refused to leave California. Instead, he had Douglas establish a new Northrop company as a subsidiary and resumed designing and building aircraft such as the Delta and Gamma, while the XBT-1 prototype became the Douglas Dauntless dive-bomber.

The company had to be fully merged into Douglas after labour disputes in 1937, hence the Dauntless becoming a Douglas product, but in 1939 Northrop launched yet a third company bearing his name and gained a reputation for flying-wing research.

Norway, Allied campaign (April–May 1940) Norway and Denmark were of immense strategic importance to both sides during the Second World War. Seizing both countries allowed the Germans safer movement between the Baltic and the Atlantic and meant that a repeat of the First World War British naval blockade would be more difficult. They could also move iron ore from Sweden all year round, as the Gulf of Bothnia froze in winter. Operations against British shipping in the North Atlantic were easier from Norway and, although this was not apparent at the time, the German occupation of Norwegian ports would make support of the Soviet Union by British and

American forces more difficult. The Allies had been planning an invasion of Narvik in Norway during the Russo-Finnish War of 1939-40 under the guise of aiding Finland, but the plans had to be dropped after an armistice. The Germans had obtained intelligence about the plans which made them determined to seize Norway. Meanwhile, the Anglo-French Supreme War Council, under pressure to do something as the 'phoney war' dragged on, decided that if a pretext to establish a presence in Norway could not be found, then mines should be laid in Norwegian waters to force German merchant shipping out of territorial waters and onto the high seas, where they could be legally attacked by British and French forces. While the first mines were being laid on 8 April it became clear to the Allies that Germans were themselves planning a major move against the two Scandinavian countries.

The German invasion was a textbook example of how to mount an assault on territory with difficult land communications. Despite the loss of the cruiser *Blücher* to Norwegian shore batteries at Oslo, by noon the Germans were in control of Bergen, Kristiansand, Narvik, Stavanger and Trondheim.

After the Norwegian government accepted British and French promises of support, an Anglo-French expeditionary force was immediately dispatched. Before the advance formations of British and Free Polish troops arrived at Narvik on 12 April, the Royal Navy had already enjoyed success in the First Battle of Narvik and had used shore-based aircraft to sink the light cruiser *Konigsberg*. Improvised airstrips and frozen lakes were all that the country could offer by way of airfields.

The campaign would have been well suited to the use of carrier-borne air power, had sufficient ships and high-performance aircraft been available. As it was, aircraft had to be moved by sea aboard the aircraft carrier *Glorious*, which took the Hurricanes of No. 46 Squadron to Norway. When the aircraft were flown off, two crashed on the soft landing ground so the rest were moved north to Bardufoss where they provided fighter cover for Narvik. Meanwhile, No. 263 Squadron arrived with its Gloster Gladiator biplanes but all of these obsolete aircraft were either destroyed or

badly damaged within three days. The squadron returned home to re-equip, but again still with Gladiators so that when it returned, the outcome was much the same.

Bombing sorties were mounted from Lossiemouth by the Wellingtons of No. 9 Squadron, while No. 224 from Leuchars mounted anti-shipping strikes with its Lockheed Hudsons. These were small forces with which to contest the well-equipped Germans, and clearly British equipment was insufficient and dated. Many fighter units were being held back in the UK in expectation of a German aerial attack.

Despite British and French troops pushing the German forces back towards the Swedish border, it soon became clear that the air and ground forces deployed in Norway were more urgently needed in France as the German assault on the Low Countries and then France forged ahead. On 7 June the members of Nos 46 and 263 Squadrons were ordered to destroy their remaining aircraft and join the aircraft carriers HMS *Glorious* and *Ark Royal* for the passage home. The pilots of No. 46, without arrestor hooks or carrier-deck landing training, succeeded in flying their aircraft aboard *Glorious* by the expedient of fitting sandbags to the tail wheels. On 8 June, while the ship was steaming at a leisurely pace towards Scapa Flow in Orkney, she was caught by the German battlecruisers *Scharnhorst* and *Gneisenau*, shelled and sunk. Many members of the RAF were among more than 1,500 men who died, either during the action or in the cold seas afterwards.

Norway, Neville Shute (1890–1960) British manufacturer and novelist. Norway was born in London. He joined the infantry during the First World War after being rejected by the RFC because of a stammer. At the end of the war he took a degree at Oxford and in 1923 went to work for **de Havilland** as a stress calculator, while also learning to fly. He joined **Vickers** in 1924 and worked with **Barnes Wallis** on the R-100 airship. In 1926 Norway published his first novel using his Christian names as his pen name.

In 1931 he founded his own aircraft manufacturer, **Airspeed**, with a group of friends, but left in 1938 to concentrate on writing. The company produced the Oxford communications aircraft and navigational trainer and the Horsa troop-carrying glider, both of which saw demanding service during the Second World War. In 1948, the company was acquired by de Havilland.

Norway himself moved to Australia after the Second World War and his later novels were all set there, including *On the Beach*, about the aftermath of a nuclear war.

Nowotny, Maj Walter (1920–44) Austrian ace. Trained as a pilot by the Luftwaffe he became operational in February 1941, but his first confirmed victory was not until July flying over the Soviet Union. In 1942 he was flying with JG54, a fighter unit, and by the end of the year he had more than fifty victories; a year later this had more than doubled. **Adolf Galland** selected him to lead the first jet fighter squadron, Kommando Nowotny, which meant adjusting to the new technology and developing new tactics, but he was killed in air-to-air combat in November 1944, by which time his score was 258 confirmed kills.

Nungessor, Sous Lt Charles Eugene Jules Marie (1892–1927) French ace. Travelling the world before the First World War, Nungessor was working as a rancher when war broke out, but immediately returned home. He joined the cavalry but in 1915 was transferred to the Aviation Militaire and flew Voisin bombers before being posted to Escadrille N65 as a fighter pilot. He had a mixed career with fighters, scoring forty-five confirmed kills to become the third highest scoring French ace, but he was also wounded several times in action and suffered many landing accidents; he was even involved in a car crash. At one stage, insisting on returning to operations, he had to be carried to and from his aircraft in a chair.

Postwar, he capitalised on his reputation, becoming an exhibition and stunt flyer in the United States and marrying an heiress. As his reputation waned with the passing of time he decided to stage a comeback by making a transatlantic flight in 1927. Flying with **François Coli**, they took off from Paris in a Levavasseur biplane, *L'Oiseau Blanc*, planning to fly to New York, but they disappeared in mid-ocean.

O

Ohain, Dr Hans Pabst von (1911–98) German engineer. Having completed a seven-year course for a doctorate in just four years in 1933, Ohain was taken with the idea of continuous combustion, effectively meaning the jet engine. He built a prototype with the help of a mechanic to enable him to patent the idea, and although the engine was too poorly assembled to work well, he received the support of **Ernst Heinkel**. From April 1936, von Ohain enjoyed the use of Heinkel's extensive facilities, and a year later he had a hydrogen-fuelled small engine; Heinkel was sufficiently impressed to order a full-scale prototype. On 27 August 1939 the new engine powered the new He178 making the world's first jet-powered flight. This promising lead that could have prolonged the war was, however, frittered away by the German leadership and even when **Messerschmitt** developed the Me262 and put it into production, too little too late, the aircraft was wrongly assigned as a bomber rather than as a fighter.

Olds, Brig Gen Robin (1922–2007) US ace. Born into an air corps family in Hawaii, Olds joined the USAAF during the Second World War and flew Lockheed P-38 Lightnings and North American P-52 Mustangs over Europe, qualifying as an ace with thirteen confirmed kills and another eleven or twelve aircraft destroyed on the ground. Postwar he remained with the service and flew the first American jet fighter, the Lockheed P-80, coming second in the Thomson Trophy Race in Cleveland in 1946. He then went on exchange with the RAF in the UK, commanding No. 1 Squadron, a fighter unit, and also served in Germany, North Africa and Thailand with what had become the USAF.

During the Vietnam War, in 1966 he was given command of the 8th Tactical Fighter Wing based in Thailand flying McDonnell F-4 Phantom IIs. He flew 105 sorties over enemy-held territory, shooting down two MiG-17s and two of the much more capable MiG-21s before being posted back to the USA to become commandant of the Air Force Academy.

Opel, Fritz von (1899–1971) German pioneer of rocket-powered flight. Born into the Opel motorcar business, von Opel's interests extended to aviation. His first attempts with rocket-propulsion, however, were by using a cluster of rockets designed by F.W. Sander installed in a racing car, which was successfully tested as the first rocket-propelled car on 15 March 1928. Von Opel made the second rocket-powered flight (the first had been made in an aircraft deisgned by **Alexander Lippisch**) using a Hatry glider, RAK-1, on 30 September 1930.

organic air power The modern term for the aviation forces, attached to and a part of, surface forces such as armies and navies and including air corps and air arms. While initially military aviation was completely organic, with scout aircraft flying reconnaissance for armies and others doing the same and observing the fall of shot for the fleet, the strategic element became apparent even during the First World War. While the Luftwaffe's operations were closely integrated with those of the German Army in the blitzkrieg concept, this was not an example of organic air power and indeed the Luftwaffe fiercely resisted granting the other two services control of their own air power. In the United States, with the USAAF having become a strategic force, the United States Army had to reinvent organic air power as the Second World War progressed, as did the USMC.

ornithopter An aircraft propelled by flapping wings, often based on an incomplete understanding of the working of a bird's wing, and which consistently failed to provide true flight. It was discredited long before the first flights by the **Wright** brothers.

Osborn, Earl Dodge (1893–1988) US manufacturer. When the USA entered the First World War, Osborn, a Princeton graduate, served as an ambulance driver in Europe. Postwar, he was one of those behind the short-lived Aero Marine Airways, after which he became editor of *Aviation* from 1924 until 1929. While editor he formed a company, EDO, to build a modern flying boat and although it flew successfully in 1925 he decided to concentrate on the manufacture of floats, with the first set fitted successfully to a Waco 9 in 1926.

Osterkamp, Oberleutnant zur See Theodore (1892–1975) German ace. Rejected on medical grounds by the German Military Air Service at the start of the First World War, Osterkamp managed to join a volunteer unit of the Naval Air Service and train as a pilot. He flew observation aircraft throughout 1916 before transferring to fighters the following year. His first sortie as a fighter pilot started badly, with him wrecking his aircraft on take-off and being grounded by his commanding officer, but after the rest of his squadron had taken off he seized a spare aircraft and followed, vindicating himself by shooting an SE-5. In little more than a year he shot down thirty-two Allied aircraft, although he was shot down once himself. When the war ended he volunteered to help the White Russians during the Russian Civil War.

He joined the Luftwaffe at the start of the Second World War and added six more aircraft to his tally before being taken off the front line on grounds of his age.

Ovington, Earle L. (1879–1936) US pioneer. While still studying he became an assistant to Thomas Edison and in 1911 learnt to fly at the Blériot School at Pau. He bought a Blériot XI and took it back to the USA. He became the first to carry official airmail in the USA, flying a Queen – a licence-built Blériot XI – on 14 September 1911 during the International Aviation Tournament at Garden City, New York. He carried the mail from Garden City to Mineola, 3 miles away. Later that year he won the *Boston Globe* newspaper's prize for an air race. Afterwards, he withdrew from aviation, and after serving as a lieutenant-commander in the USN during the First World War, became a consultant. He later operated an aerodrome at Santa Barbara, California.

Ozawa, Vice Adm Jisaburo, (1886–1966) Japanese naval commander. The last commander-in-chief of the Imperial Japanese Navy's Combined Fleet, he had earlier in the war commanded the Malayan Force or Southern Expeditionary Fleet that covered the landings that eventually saw the fall of Thailand, Malaya and Singapore. He was a rarity in that he was a supporter of naval air power and many believe that he was Japan's foremost tactician. Aircraft under his control sank HMS *Prince of Wales* and *Repulse* on 10 December 1941. He also provided support for the invasion of the Netherlands East Indies and his ships entered the Indian Ocean to attack Ceylon, now Sri Lanka. During the Battle of the Philippine Sea, in June 1944, he commanded the First Mobile Fleet, and at **Leyte Gulf** his carriers lured **Adm Halsey's** Third Fleet away from the invasion beaches.

He refused promotion to admiral on the grounds that rank was unimportant.

P

Pacific, first flights Between 31 May and 10 June 1928, flying a Fokker F.VII/3M, Charles Kingsford-Smith captained the first flight across the Pacific, flying from the USA to Australia. Ten years later, Juan Trippe pushed Pan American's route network out across the Pacific to China and Hong Kong with the first through flight from San Francisco to Hong Kong leaving on 2 November 1936 in the fifty-two-seat Martin M-130 flying boat *Philippine Clipper*. After this, routine scheduled flights had passengers change at Manila in the Philippines on to the smaller Sikorsky S-42 *Hong Kong Clipper*, as this was more economical for the numbers wishing to fly the entire transpacific route.

Page, Sir Frederick Handley (1885–1962) British manufacturer. After studying electrical engineering, in 1906 Page became chief designer at electrical manufacturers Johnson & Phillips, but was really more interested in aviation. He experimented with **Jose Weiss** on model gliders then started out on his own in 1909. His first powered aeroplane was the *Blue Bird* completed in 1909, and in 1910 he built and flew the *Yellow Peril* with its unusual crescent-shaped wing.

During the First World War, Murray Sueter, the first Inspecting Captain of Naval Aviation at the Admiralty, asked him to build 'a bloody paralyser of an aeroplane to stop the Hun in his tracks'. The result was the 0/100 heavy bomber. From this time onwards, the company name became synonymous with heavy bombers.

Following the war, Page invented the leading edge slot that lowered landing speeds and increased safety. Always concerned about safety, his HP42 commercial airliner of 1930, a large biplane with a built-in 'headwind' of struts and wires, operated for Imperial Airways for ten years without a single fatal accident. As the Second World War approached, his Hampden twin-engined bomber was one of only two decent bombers serving with RAF Bomber Command and during the war his Halifax four-engined heavy bomber was an important part of the main bomber force, although it suffered from early handling problems. After the Second World War his Hastings military transport for the RAF and Hermes airliner for BOAC kept the company going until the crescent-wing Victor four-engined jet 'V' bomber entered service as part of the British nuclear deterrent.

Page had to fight another battle during the postwar period: to keep his company independent. Refusing to merge with a larger group, the Victor was his last government order. The Herald twin-turboprop regional airliner sold in small quantities, despite being regarded as economical (but in later years suffered from pressurisation problems), but some years after his death in 1962, the company's undoing was the Jetstream, a small turboprop feeder airliner of high performance, of which the costs of developing and producing forced the company into bankruptcy. The Jetstream was taken over first by Scottish Aviation and then **British Aerospace**, and produced in quantity at Prestwick in Scotland with a stretched version, the Jetstream 41, later introduced.

parachute While **Leonardo da Vinci** drew parachutes, his work on aeronautic topics was not known for some centuries afterwards, and so the parachute eventually emerged at around the same time as the first balloon ascents. This was not because balloonists necessarily needed parachutes, more probably because the structure of the hot air balloon provided a clue; once the fire began to die down and the amount of heat diminished, the **Montgolfière-**type of balloon would behave almost like a parachute.

The first successful parachute descent was by a Frenchman, **Sebastian Lenormand** in December 1783, when he jumped from a tower in Montpellier. The concept moved a step forward in 1797 when a compatriot, **André Jacques Garnerin**, made a descent of 3,000 ft from a balloon.

The first descent from an aeroplane was made in the USA in March 1912 by Capt Albert Berry. Parachutes were available during the First World War, but the leaders of the Allied air arms objected to their provision, allegedly on the grounds that it would encourage airmen to leave their aeroplanes or airships rather than fight. The modern parachute was developed by another American, Leslie Leroy Irvin, who made a descent in April 1919 from an aircraft in Dayton, Ohio. In later years, the Irving Parachute Company (a clerical error resulted in the wrong name being used) became one of the leaders in the development and production of parachutes. During the interwar period exercises were conducted in the use of paratroops, mainly in the Soviet Union in the mid-1930s, but it was the German Luftwaffe that used paratroops effectively in the early stages of the Second World War. In both the UK and the USA, during exercises and demonstrations in the late 1930s, supplies were parachuted to the ground.

Today, the parachute remains an essential item of safety equipment in military aircraft since it still has to be used after ejection from an aircraft. The parachute has moved on from being simply a functional piece of equipment, however, and has become an addition to the sporting element of flight, including delayed opening and group drops, usually with the participants joining up in mid-air before eventually opening their parachutes for their final descent. Not only military supplies and equipment can be parachuted, but so too can relief aid, although items such as water and grain are often dropped without parachutes. Parachutes are also used to drag heavy items out of transport aircraft in the initial stage of air dropping. A number of military aircraft have also used parachutes for braking once on the runway, with the first known use being by the German Arado Ar234 jet bomber of the Second World War. One of the most interesting modern safety innovations has seen experiments with the parachute recovery of light aircraft. On the other hand, paratroops have become less important with the advent of the helicopter for airborne assaults.

paratroops Airborne troops dropped by parachute are known as paratroops and remain in most modern armies. The use of paratroops on exercises was pioneered in the Soviet Union in the mid-1930s, although the early experiments that had the 'paras' climbing out of the fuselage onto the top of a Tupolev G-2 bomber before jumping were hardly practical or likely to lead to a mass airborne assault. Nevertheless, the right aircraft was available at the outset of the Second World War in the shape of the Junkers Ju52/3M, a trimotor that had started operational life as a 'bomber-transport', but by the outbreak of war was simply a transport and very effective. Uniquely in Germany the paratroops were part of the Luftwaffe rather than the army. Paratroops were used alongside glider-landed troops in the German assaults on the Low Countries in May 1940, with varying degrees of success for the former. The biggest operation mounted by the Germans during the war years was Operation Mercury, the airborne assault on the Greek island of Crete on 21 May 1941, when some 10,000 paratroops were deployed by the Luftwaffe. The operation nearly failed and casualties were high. Only the fact that the defending British and Greek troops had left most of their heavy equipment, and in particular their communications equipment, behind in the evacuation from Greece enabled the Germans to win the battle. Hitler was so shocked that he banned further paratroop assaults.

The Allies, on the other hand, had learnt much about paratroop assaults and deployed paratroops for the invasion of Sicily – albeit with poor results because of bad weather – and then for the invasion of Normandy, where they secured vital bridges before the Germans could sabotage them. They again used paratroops at Arnhem in Operation Market Garden, where they encountered heavier German forces than anticipated, before finally deploying them for the Rhine Crossing. Postwar, paratroops were used in the colonial war in French Indo-China by the French and in the Anglo-French landings at Suez in 1956, as well as in the Belgian Congo by the Belgians.

Techniques varied, with British and German paratroopers jumping from around 500 ft, in which case only one parachute was worn as there was no time to open a second if the first failed. This had the advantage of being exposed to ground fire for as short a time as possible. Russian and American paratroops jumped from 1,000 ft and carried two parachutes, as there was time to use a second.

The use of paratroops has the advantage of speed and surprise, but the weakness is that they arrive with only light weapons and despite the increased performance of military transport aircraft in recent years, this remains true today. The plan has to be to secure vital airfields so that follow-up transport aircraft with heavy equipment and air-landed troops can be flown in, and also to secure bridges for ground formations to surge forward. The latter scenario suggests that ground forces should not be too far away, in which case the helicopter becomes the preferred means of assault.

Even so, for the deployment of special forces the paratroop attack has a place. Instead of mass attacks at low altitude, small numbers of men are dropped from high altitude and are able to drift for long distances before landing on enemy-held territory.

Park, ACM Sir Keith Rodney (1892–1975)

New Zealand ace and leader. Moving to the UK, Park joined the army in 1911 and transferred to the RFC in 1917. Despite his late transfer he accounted for twenty enemy aircraft before the First World War ended. He remained with what had become the RAF between the wars, and was commanding No. 11 Fighter Group during the Battle of Britain defending London, and he often led his men into battle in a Hawker Hurricane. Later, he was the AOC in a number of important areas, including Malta and Egypt, before becoming Allied Air Commander-in-Chief, South-East Asia. Postwar, after leaving the RAF, he returned to his native New Zealand and represented **Hawker Siddeley**, the aircraft manufacturer.

Parseval, Maj August von (1861–1942)

German pioneer. Commissioned into the German Army, von Parseval is credited with inventing the kite balloon or *Drachenballon*, which provided a steadier platform than a spherical balloon on its own, and was used by both sides during the First World War. In 1906 he invented the flexible airship which could be transported deflated behind an advancing army and then inflated when needed.

In retirement after the First World War, he became a professor at the Berlin Technical Academy.

Patterson, William Allan (1899–1980)

Airline president. Although intended by his father to have a military career, Patterson ran away from a military academy and found work with Wells Fargo in San Francisco in 1914. By 1924 he was able to authorise loans and one customer was Pacific Air Transport which operated an air service along the West Coast of America. Increasingly absorbed by air transport, he joined Boeing Air Transport in 1929, and when the airline was split off from the manufacturer by anti-trust legislation he found himself working for the new United Airlines, becoming its president in 1934; a position he held until 1963. His innovations included the first stewardesses and, much later, the first order for jet airliners from an American airline.

Pattle, Sqn Ldr Marmaduke Thomas St John (1914–41)

South African ace. Pattle went to the UK where he joined the RAF, making his first kill while flying with No. 80 Squadron in North Africa in 1940. He was with the British forces deployed to Greece in November, and between then and April 1941 steadily built up a large number of victories with a confirmed total of twenty-eight, but as much of his combat was over water, the true total could well be very much higher. He was killed when he was shot down over Athens in April 1941 attempting to help a fellow squadron member who was being attacked by a Luftwaffe Bf109.

Paulhan, Louis (1883–1963)

French pioneer. He served with the French Army's balloon section early in the twentieth century, and once back in civilian life he worked as a mechanic at the Astra balloon works outside Paris. The first flight by **Alberto Santos-Dumont** inspired him to switch to aeroplanes, and in 1908 he won a model glider contest prize, a Voisin biplane, albeit without an engine. With the help of friends he bought a Gnome engine and taught himself to fly on the aircraft during July 1909 at Douai. The next month he took part in the **Reims Aviation Meeting** and, despite his inexperience, came third in the Grand Prix. Early in 1910 he went to the USA, winning US $10,000 (£2,000 at the then rate of exchange, or £114,000 in today's values) for a flight in California. Later that year he beat **Claude Grahame-White** to the *Daily Mail* prize for the London to Manchester race. He built an aircraft of his own in 1911, *L'Aéro-Torpille*, working with Victor Tatin.

When the First World War started he attempted to become an aircraft manufacturer but without success, so he joined the Aviation Militaire and became a fighter pilot in 1916.

Pauly, Samuel Johannes (1766–1819) Swiss aeronaut. Pauly moved to London during the Napoleonic Wars, attracted by the brisk business in armaments, and among his achievements while in London was the first centre-fire brass cartridge, in effect the first modern bullet. He was employed by **Urs Egg**, who had set up business as a gunsmith with workshops in Pall Mall, counting King George III among his clients, to build a dirigible.

Egg had earlier built a dirigible while in France. Pauly's design had the gas bag made of goldbeater's skin, said to consist in this case of 70,000 cow stomachs, stretched over a wooden frame in the shape of a large fish, leading it to be called the *Dolphin*. Trim control was featured, probably for the first time, in the form of a sandbox that could be moved along a rope stretching from the nacelle to the tail. Built in a large balloon shed in Brompton, London, not far from today's Science Museum, it was not completed because Pauly died during the final stages of construction in 1819. Egg lost his massive investment.

Had it been completed, Egg planned to use the *Dolphin* on a London to Paris air service which he estimated would take 10 hours. Instead, uncompleted, the project became known as 'Egg's Folly'. Not all was lost, however, as the showman, P.T. Barnum, purchased the inner ballonet which was inflated and used to lift the circus performer, Tom Thumb, during his circus act.

payload The maximum revenue-earning weight that can be carried by an aircraft, which has grown considerably since Horatio Barber flew a Valkyrie on the first British air freight flight, carrying a small consignment of electric light bulbs from Shoreham to nearby Hove. The record

today stands at more than 150 tons for a diesel railway locomotive, including a section of track and heavy chains to keep the load steady in flight and carried from Japan to Australia aboard an Antonov An-124. Routinely all-cargo loads of 45 tons or so are carried on Airbus A300 freighters, while an all-cargo Boeing 747 can carry in excess of 100 tons. Passengers are included in the payload for passenger aircraft, which will also carry cargo and often mail as well. Traditionally, the average passenger has been taken as weighing 140 lb but in many countries this is under review as passenger weights have increased, especially in the more prosperous countries.

On most aircraft there can be a trade-off between payload and range, but a limiting factor on just how far this can be done is the landing weight of the aircraft, which for most fixed-wing aircraft is always considerably lower than the take-off weight. Helicopters have the same take-off and landing weights.

Pearl Harbor, Japanese attack on (7 December 1941) The Japanese caught the Americans off guard by attacking the United States Pacific Fleet as it lay in Pearl Harbor, on the Hawaiian island of Oahu, on a Sunday morning. They also had the advantage of surprise, approaching undetected through a tropical storm and launching their aircraft in conditions that would have seen most exercises cancelled. The Americans were aware that the Japanese fleet was at sea, but had convinced themselves that it was heading for South-East Asia. When a radar operator at the station on the northern tip of Oahu reported blips, no action was taken as the duty officer was expecting a flight of B-17 bombers and the radar station was about to close for the day.

Even if the alarm had been sounded, the attack could not have been stopped, but American defences would have been prepared, the men could have gone to action stations and fighter aircraft could have got off the ground. The Japanese commander, Vice Admiral Nagumo, had expected his aircraft to have to fight their way to the target and was surprised to learn that they reached it unscathed. Despite the rising tension between the two countries, the US ships in the harbour did not even have torpedo nets in place.

Japanese aggression in China during the 1930s had not been conducive to stability in the Far East. While at first the Americans were reluctant to act, to many Japanese it had seemed for some time that war with the US was inevitable. American opinion changed as the extent of Japanese ambitions became clear. Japanese atrocities in China could not be ignored, especially after the rape of the former Nationalist Chinese capital of Nanking, which fell to Japanese forces in December 1937.

In December 1940 the US had imposed an embargo on the sale of scrap metal and war materials to Japan. This was followed by the freezing of Japanese assets in the US in July 1941, after Japan invaded Indo-China. The United Kingdom followed, denying Japan the currency with which to purchase oil and raw materials. Japan was left with a strategic reserve of 55 billion barrels of oil, enough for eighteen months of war. The only way to extend this was for Japan to find another source of oil by invading the Netherlands East Indies.

Although many Japanese were resigned to war with the US, there were others who realised the enormity of the task and were opposed to hostilities, including none other than the commander-in-chief of the Imperial Japanese Navy's First Fleet, Admiral Isoroku Yamamoto. He believed that Japan would not be able to match the US either militarily or, no less important in modern warfare, in industrial output. His view was that Japan could win a major victory during the first year of war, but that by the second year the US would have recovered and could move to the offensive. Although the Imperial Japanese Navy was superior in strength to the US Navy in the Pacific, it was weaker than the combined strength of the US Pacific and Atlantic fleets.

The government of Japan was in the hands of the army-dominated pro-war faction. The need for crude oil meant that Japan had to either abandon its plans for what amounted to an Asian empire, the so-called 'Greater Asia Co-Prosperity Sphere', or go to war and achieve its needs by conquest. Japan had few friends, and Germany and Italy were too far away to be able to provide any worthwhile assistance.

Yamamoto chose to strike a crippling blow at the US Pacific Fleet by attacking its main base on Hawaii. If Pearl Harbor could be knocked out and major units of the Pacific Fleet destroyed, it would take time for the US to re-establish a significant naval presence in the area. Given the vast distances involved in the Pacific, control of the seas had to take precedence over everything else. The successful British raid on the Italian fleet at **Taranto** had proved that an attack on Pearl Harbor was feasible.

The Japanese were able to devote considerable resources to the operation, employing six aircraft carriers with 423 aircraft, all modern monoplanes. The forces included the famous Mitsubishi A6M, the 'Zero', but this was a fighter and the real work was to be done by dive-bombers and torpedo-bombers, and the so-called 'level bombers', which dropped bombs in the conventional manner.

Japan intended to attack without first declaring war on the US. It sent 353 of its aircraft to Pearl Harbor. Flying at 10,000 ft, the first wave passed over the northernmost point of Oahu at 07.30, and at 07.49 the attack began. There was no anti-aircraft fire at first. The sky was completely clear of fighters. Freed from any need to defend the bombers, the Zeros dived and raced across the dockyard and airfields in a strafing attack. Dive-bombers swept down on Ford Island, their bombs causing fires and sending debris into the air. Torpedo-bombers flew low to attack 'Battleship Row'.

Not until the second wave second wave mounted its attack were American fighters in the air. The strike aircraft in the second wave consisted entirely of bombers and dive-bombers, as torpedo-bombers were seen as being too vulnerable once the defences had been alerted. Almost all of the twenty-nine Japanese aircraft shot down over Hawaii that morning belonged to the second wave.

The attack set the battleship *Arizona* on fire, capsized *Oklahoma*, along with the target ship *Utah*, counted by Japanese intelligence as an active battleship, and both *California* and *West Virginia* were left sinking. The light cruiser *Helena* was crippled. *Pennsylvania* and two destroyers, all in dry dock, were damaged.

The commanding officer of the battleship *Nevada* decided that his ship would be safer at sea than sitting as a target in the harbour. The Japanese attempted to sink her in the harbour mouth and block the port, and dive-bombers attacked *Nevada* in the face of heavy AA fire. The commanding officer did well to beach his ship, keeping the base functional and saving his vessel.

The original plan was for the aircraft to return to the Japanese carriers to refuel and re-arm, before making a further attack in the afternoon. Instead, Nagumo ordered a withdrawal to the north-west, anxious to avoid the US Pacific Fleet's aircraft carriers which were, by their absence at Pearl Harbor, obviously at sea. As a result, the Imperial Japanese Navy lost any chance of victory. The only possible justification would have been an attack on the Panama Canal to delay reinforcement of the Pacific Fleet. As it was, at no time was Pearl Harbor unavailable to the US Navy, while the airfields ashore were quickly repaired. A further raid on Pearl Harbor might have given the Japanese the breathing space they so desperately needed.

Pearse, Richard William (1877–1953) New Zealand pioneer. He completed a monoplane and engine in 1904 that managed to make a few powered hops, leading some of his fellow countrymen to claim that he had flown before the **Wright** brothers, even though he later confirmed that the trials had been unsuccessful. His design was notable for its use of a tricycle undercarriage with steerable noise wheel and a rudimentary aileron. He did not attempt to build a second aircraft until 1925, intending it to have short take-off features due to a tilting engine, while it also had the then advanced feature of a variable-pitch propeller and a tail-rotor to counter torque. Had it flown it would have been the first convertiplane, but it did not.

Pégoud, Célestin-Adolphe (1889–1915) French pioneer. A mechanic with the French Aviation Militaire, he left in 1913 to work for **Blériot** and then learnt to fly. Like many of the pioneering pilots he enjoyed stunt flying. On 20 August 1913 he took a Blériot monoplane that was due to be scrapped and flew it to 2,000 ft before abandoning the aircraft, baling out with a parachute and landing safely, the first time this had happened. On 1 September he flew another Blériot upside down for several seconds, something that the experts had claimed to be impossible. On 21 September he looped the loop at 10,000 ft, following Nesterov's achievement in Russia.

He returned to the Aviation Militaire when the First World War broke out but this time as a pilot, but he was shot down and died from a bullet wound in his neck.

Pemberton-Billing, Noel (1881–1948) British designer and manufacturer. A yacht salesman who had been involved in gun-running, Pemberton-Billing built no less than three monoplanes in 1908, with the third having a tricycle undercarriage and the only one to even manage a hop. He famously demanded that a reporter from *Flight* confirm the fact, which he did using a magnifying glass to look at the wheel tracks. In 1912 he founded his own company, building both aircraft and racing yachts near Southampton. Not modest, he once boasted that any man with the sense to come in out of the rain could learn to fly in one day, and wagered **Frederick Handley Page** £500 that he could do so. He was given half an hour of instruction on a Farman, took off and flew the aircraft completing the manoeuvres, although he nearly stalled, and landed safely to pocket his £500.

At the outset of the First World War he contacted Captain Murray Sueter, the Inspecting Captain of Naval Aviation, regarding the needs of the RNAS. In great secrecy he designed and built the PB IX biplane, claiming that the design was chalked upon the walls of his workshop and that it took just 6 days, 10 hours to complete. He served briefly with the RNAS and was involved with the attack on the Zeppelin sheds at Lake Constance on 21 November 1914, before entering politics to argue the case for better air defences. He was largely responsible for ending aircraft production at the Royal Aircraft Factory and for improved anti-Zeppelin air defences around London, and is credited with inventing the term 'Fokker Fodder' to describe the inferior quality of British fighters.

Meanwhile, in 1916 his company adopted the title **Supermarine** from its telegraphic address.

Pénaud, Alphonse (1850–80) French pioneer. Denied a career in the French Navy due to ill-health, Pénaud spent the last ten years of his life on aeronautics. He took the twisted rubber motor for models, the brainchild of **Sir George Cayley**, and brought it to wider public attention, applying it for the first time to a successful model contra-rotating helicopter in 1870. The following year he unveiled his model 'planophore', the first inherently stable monoplane design, with a mainplane forward, a tailplane at the rear and a rubber-powered pusher propeller. The mainplane had some dihedral for stability. The model was demonstrated to prominent members of the Société d'Aviation on 18 August 1871, flying for 131 ft.

In 1876, with the help of his mechanic Paul Gauchet, he designed a twin-engined monoplane amphibian which in appearance was well ahead of its time. It had contra-rotating propellers mounted one in each wing to counter any directional stresses, elliptical wings with cambered surfaces, slight dihedral and incidence, a tailplane with fixed fin and movable rudder, and elevators, with all of these surfaces moved by a single control in the glass-domed and instrumented cockpit. It also had a retractable undercarriage with shock absorbers and tailskid, and a planned air speed of 60 mph.

Whether or not the aeroplane would have flown had it been built is doubtful. Apart from the difficulty of finding a suitable powerplant, the stability that was a feature of Pénaud's designs would have countered the need for 'control in roll'. Depressed by his poor health, he committed suicide in 1880.

Percival, Edgar Wikner (1897–1984) Australian

designer and manufacturer. An engineer by profession, during the First World War he enlisted with the Australian Light Horse and was posted to the Middle East before transferring to the RFC, going solo after just half an hour's flying training. He flew with **Billy Bishop** in No. 60 Squadron and later, in 1918, flying with No. 111 Squadron in Egypt, he modified a Bristol F2B Fighter.

Returning to Australia postwar, he won a government-backed aircraft design contest in 1926 but could not find the support to build it, and in 1929 he moved to the UK. In 1932 he launched his first aircraft, the Gull, a low-wing monoplane that was an instant success and noted for its efficiency, and after being put into production by Percival's own company, was used by many of the record-setters for their flights. Developments included the Mew Gull and Vega Gull.

More than 3,000 Proctor trainers were built during the Second World War but Percival left the company in 1944. He did introduce the high-wing EP-9 in 1954 but found industrial life difficult and beset by union problems, and while he continued to design aircraft, including a STOL design in the 1960s, these were paper proposals and did not lead to production aircraft.

The notable achievements of his company include the Provost piston-engined trainer, used by many air forces, and the turbine version, the Jet Provost, while the One-Eleven jet airliner built by the British Aircraft Corporation (BAC) and its successor, **British Aerospace** (BAe), originated as a Percival design. The company was merged into BAC during the government-inspired mergers of the 1960s.

Phillips, Horatio Frederick (1845–1926)

English inventor and engineer. Phillips proved **Cayley**'s theory that a cambered wing would make the ideal aerofoil. He tested a variety of double-surface aerofoil sections, described as 'blades for deflecting air', with different thicknesses and camber and at different angles of attack in what was only the second practical wind tunnel. In 1884 Phillips registered his first and most influential patent for aerofoil design, proving that a higher degree of curvature on the upper surface created lift, with lift mostly coming from the suction effect provided by the reduced pressure on the upper surface. To demonstrate his findings he built two models and two full-sized machines.

In 1890 Phillips patented a design for a cigar-shaped fuselage surmounted by a tandem multi-wing structure, in which the two sets of wings comprised a 'Venetian blind' of thirteen slats, which he built in 1893. Although the chord for both wings was just 1.5 in (3.8 cm), the wing-span of 19 ft (5.8 m) gave a total wing area of 140 sq ft (130 sq m). Power was provided by a steam engine driving a 6.5 ft (2 m) tractor propeller. Installed on a test track of 323 ft (98 m) circumference, in May the tethered machine rose 2–3 ft off the ground, but the front wheels remained on the track. A larger model, using a track of 628 ft (191 m) circumference, managed to lift a weight of 385 lb (175 kg). In 1907 Phillips' only flying-machine made the first tentative hop in the British Isles, using four 'Venetian blind' frames in tandem with a 20–22 hp engine driving a single tractor propeller.

Despite his contribution to greater understanding of the shape of the wing on lift, Phillips lacked a full appreciation of the broad principles of flight.

Piaggio Italian manufacturer. Formed in 1964 to build the P136 amphibian designed by Rinaldo Piaggio, the company also built the P19 single-engined trainer and P166 light transport, before collaborating with **Douglas** on the PD-808 executive jet. In 1979, following the rapid rise in fuel prices, the company developed a high-performance turboprop business aircraft, the Avanti, with three lifting surfaces, including both a canard layout and a tailplane with twin pusher-turboprops. This sold slowly for some years, before eventually bankrupting the company in the 1990s, but the company was rescued in 1998 by a consortium that included the Ferrari sports car family. An updated aircraft, the Avanti II was then launched, which is selling well today. Another aspect of the business is the manufacture of aeroengines for companies such as Rolls-Royce Turbomeca and Pratt & Whitney.

Piasecki, Frank Nicholas (1919–2008) US helicopter designer. After working for Kellett Autogiro while still a student, and then for Platt-LePage Aircraft, he graduated from New York University and joined Budd, pioneers of stainless steel railway carriages. He gathered around him a group of enthusiasts, styling themselves the 'PV Engineering Forum' with the objective of designing and building a helicopter, which eventually appeared as the successful PV-2. The forum became Piasecki Helicopters and in 1944 was awarded a contract to build a larger helicopter, a tandem-rotor machine known officially as the PV-3, and unofficially, because of its shape, as the 'Flying Banana'. American financiers backed a massive expansion of the company after the Second World War, but by 1955 its founder was ousted and the company renamed Vertol, later being taken over by **Boeing**.

Piasecki continued working in a new design company he had established, including the development of a helicopter-dirigible composite aircraft, which was lost during a test flight.

Piccard, Prof Auguste (1884–1962) Record-setting Swiss aeronaut. Qualified in both mechanical engineering and natural sciences, Piccard saw aeronautics as a means to an end because of his interest in the upper atmosphere. In 1913 he ascended in a balloon to 10,000 ft. In 1930 he had a pressurised gondola that would allow ascents to even higher altitudes, but the first attempt failed because of its weight. In 1931 it took him and an assistant to 52,500 ft and allowed Piccard to conduct experiments on cosmic rays and ionisation. Later, he completely reversed course and conducted experiments in deep sea oceanography.

Pietenpol, Bernard 'Bernie' H. (1901–84) US homebuilt pioneer. After learning to fly in a Curtiss Jenny, Pietenpol started to build his own aircraft which flew in 1923, powered by a Ford car engine. He also built an aircraft with a Gnome rotary engine before building a series of aircraft starting in 1929, all powered by a Ford A engine, despite many sceptics maintaining there was no future in using motorcar engines for aircraft due to their weight.

He convinced the editor of *Modern Mechanix* magazine of the potential, so much so that he was invited to prepare plans for a homebuilt aircraft that the editor designated as the Air Camper, a two-seat aircraft of simple design intended to help the less well-off fly; this appeared in 1932 using a Ford A series engine. The next year a single-seat aircraft followed, the Sky Scout, with a Model T engine, although this was built in lower numbers.

After serving as a flying instructor during the Second World War, he left aviation and ran a television repair business.

Pilâtre de Rozier, Jean-François (1757–85) French aeronaut. Apprenticed to an apothecary, once qualified de Rozier left his home town of Metz and moved to Paris, where he began to experiment. In 1780 he founded the first science museum in Paris and conducted lectures and demonstrations. He volunteered to be the first aeronaut once he heard of the **Montgolfier** brothers' achievements, but the Academy of Science rejected his offer so he by-passed it and approached the brothers directly. He made his first tethered ascent on 15 October and on 21 November 1783 he made the first balloon voyage with the **Marquis d'Arlandes**.

The following year, de Rozier had the ambition to be first to cross the English Channel in a balloon, which soon became a contest with **Jean-Pierre Blanchard**. Due to the distance and limited understanding of aeronautical science at the time, the choice of a **Charlière** or a **Montgolfière** was resolved by combining the key elements of both: a hydrogen balloon with a brazier burning under the envelope. It ascended near Boulogne, France, on 15 June 1785 with de Rozier and Pierre Romain aboard. As it reached 5,000 ft it exploded and both men fell to their deaths in front of a large crowd that included de Rozier's English fiancée, Susan Dyer, who died shortly afterwards.

While the technology of the day let him down, the concept of gas and heat has been used in many modern record-breaking balloons, which are known as **Rozier** balloons.

Pilatus Swiss manufacturer. Founded in 1939, in recent years the company has been a subsidiary of Oerlikon. In addition to licence-production of aircraft for the Swiss Air Force, it has also built a series of successful utility aircraft and trainers, including the single-engined turboprop PC-6 Porter STOL utility aircraft and PC-9 trainer, which is now being superseded by the PC-21. At one time the company owned the small British manufacturer, **Britten-Norman**.

Pilcher, Percy Sinclair (1867–99) English hang-gliding pioneer. Pilcher joined the Royal Navy at 13 years old and left at 18 to study engineering, after which he took an interest in gliding and was influenced by **Otto Lilienthal**. In 1896 he became a consultant to **Hiram Maxim**'s project. After building his first glider, the Bat, he visited Lilienthal in Germany and on his return modified the design. He changed the tailplane and reduced the dihedral of the mainplane, after which he made a series of reasonable glides at Cardross, on the River Clyde in Scotland. It was disappointing that his second glider, the Beetle, completed in 1895, was a failure and his third, the large Gull completed the following year, only showed limited potential. It was not until he completed his fourth

glider, the Hawk, in 1896 at Eynsford, Kent, while he was working for **Maxim**, that the real potential of his hang-gliders could be seen. A monoplane, the Hawk had a substantial undercarriage and was usually launched by towing: Pilcher would sit wearing the glider on one hilltop while the towing mechanisim was placed on the top of a neighbouring hill. Many good glides followed and Pilcher patented a modified version with an engine, although for want of a suitable powerplant this was never built.

In 1899, doubtless having been preoccupied by his work for Maxim, he built a triplane glider and had by this time designed, built and bench-tested a 4 hp internal combustion engine. The triplane was never to be tested. On 30 September Pilcher arrived at Lord Brayne's estate at Stanford Hall, Market Harborough, Leicestershire, to make demonstration glides with his new triplane, the Hawk and a Lilienthal glider. Bad weather meant that he could not fly the triplane or the Lilienthal, but he later made two glides with the Hawk. On the second of these, the weight of the water-logged structure proved too much and the tail assembly snapped, leaving Pilcher to fall 30 ft to the ground; he died two days later from his injuries.

pioneers The pioneers are included in this book by name in alphabetical order. They include the inventors of the balloon, the **de Montgolfier** brothers and **J.A.C. Charles**, as well as the pioneers of the airship, including the **Tissandier** brothers, the **Lebaudy** brothers and **von Zeppelin**. For heavier-than-air flight, the fathers of the science of aeronautics such as **Sir George Cayley**, **Horatio Phillips**, **Lawrence Hargrave** and **Alphonse Pénaud**, are accompanied by the visionaries such as **da Vinci** and **de Lana de Terzi**, and the gliding pioneers, including La Bris, **Chanute**, **Lilienthal** and **Pilcher**, as well as the **Wright** brothers themselves. The pioneers of heavier-than-air flight included **Ader**, **du Temple**, Moy, **Mozhaiski**, **Langley** and the Wrights. Many of these gained fame in more than one aspect of the subject. The work of **Garnerin** and Irvin on parachutes is also mentioned, as is that of **Congreve** on rockets and **Martin** on ejection seats, and **von Ohain** and **Whittle** on the jet engine. Nor should we forget the helicopter and the work of **Sikorsky** and

Piasecki. The leading pilots are also mentioned, along with the first flights across the oceans and the continents.

Piper American manufacturer. Formed in 1937 by William Piper from the former Taylor Aircraft Company, which dated from 1931, Piper initially concentrated on building the Cub high-wing monoplane, and did not add to its range until the Tri-Pacer was launched after the Second World War ended. Piper's first low-wing aircraft was the PA-6 Sedan, but this did not enter production. The first production low-wing aircraft was the twin-engined PA-235 Apache during the mid-1950s. This was followed in 1956 by the single-engined PA-24 Comanche, and in 1959 by the PA-25 agricultural aircraft and the PA-28 Cherokee, intended as a low-cost replacement for the Tri-Pacer. The Apache was developed into the Aztec while the Cherokee was stretched to become the Cherokee Six and then offered with a retractable undercarriage as the Cherokee Arrow, before a twin-engined version was put into production, the PA-34 Senaca. Earlier, the Comanche also had a twin-engined version developed, the PA-30 Twin Comanche.

While concentrating on the lighter end of the market, the company also produced the PA-31 Navajo with up to nine seats.

Piper, William Thomas (1881–1970) US engineer and manufacturer. Returning from fighting in the Spanish-American War, he studied engineering at Harvard and on graduating worked for US Steel. When the USA entered the First World War he served with the engineers and postwar amassed a fortune in the oil industry.

He did not become involved with aviation until 1931 when he was living in Pennsylvania and a local light aircraft manufacturer, Taylor, went bankrupt. Piper bought it for US $761 (£185 at the then rate of exchange). Initially the company manufactured and sold a light aircraft, the E-2 Cub, in small quantities. The designer, **C. G. Taylor**, left in 1936 and was replaced by Walter Jamouneau. The factory was destroyed the following year and the business moved to Lock Haven, where the Cub was updated as the J-2 Cub and the company took Piper's name, making him a further fortune.

Pischoff, Alfred de (1882–1922) Austro-Hungarian pioneer. While working in France, de Pischoff built his first full-sized aeroplane in 1905 with an associate, Koechlin, using a box-kite format albeit with dihedral on the lower wing and anhedral on the upper wing, with the pilot expected to fly lying flat. The aircraft was a failure, but in 1907 he built the first tractor biplane in a factory belonging to Lucien Chauvière, whose propeller design was used with an Anzani engine, and it managed to make a few powered hops. Chauvière and de Pischoff founded a workshop together at Billancourt, building aircraft to customers' own designs or offering them their designs, which included a successful monoplane produced in 1909.

piston engine Essentially all non-turbine engines are piston engines, including radial engines, rotary engines and 'V' engines, but the term is generally used to describe modern in-line or horizontally opposed engines.

plane guard One of the earliest duties for the helicopter was to relieve escort vessels of the task of providing a plane guard for aircraft carriers during flying operations. The helicopter would patrol astern of the carrier, ideally off the port quarter, ready to rescue the crew of any aircraft that has to ditch in the sea or eject. The practice started in the late 1940s. Advantages include speed and ease of transfer to the carrier with its superior medical facilities, but it also frees the escort vessel for its proper role rather than leaving it almost as a sitting target.

Platz, Rheinhold (1886–1966) Dutch designer. Originally a welder, in 1912 he went to work for **Anthony Fokker** and is credited with getting Fokker to adopt steel tube construction, combining lightness with strength. Working together, they created the successful series of First World War fighters. Postwar he designed the all-wood cantilever wings of the Fokker VII and VIII airliners.

Many believe that Platz was the guiding genius behind Fokker's success, and while he was well rewarded by his boss, his efforts were largely unrecognised. He left the company in 1931.

Pocock, George (1796–1846) English kite pioneer. A schoolmaster whose hobby was flying kites, he was a headmaster at the early age of 22. He started to investigate the possibility of man-lifting kites, initially using his children as passengers, strapping them into armchairs which were then lifted by large kites and also rigged to act as parachutes. His kites worked well, on one occasion lifting his daughter Martha (later mother of the famous cricketer, W.G. Grace) to 300 ft, and on another taking his son out over the Bristol Channel. In 1822 he designed a kite-drawn carriage which he called the **Char-Volant**, which proved light to steer and worked successfully provided the wind was blowing in the right direction, running between Bristol and Marlborough in 1827 at speeds up to 20 mph. It was also demonstrated before King George IV at the Ascot race meeting the following year.

Pocock wrote about his invention and even wrote hymns praising his **Char-Volant**.

Pointblank Directive The name given to the Anglo-American 'Combined Bomber Offensive' (*see* **Allied Bomber Offensive**) during the Second World War, presented by **General Ira Eaker**, commander of the USAAF's Eighth Air Force, who was convinced that it was better to saturate certain targets. He argued that it 'was better to cause a high degree of destruction in a few really essential industries than to cause a small degree of destruction in many industries'. The American Air Staff had selected six vital targets – submarine construction yards and bases, the aircraft industry, ball-bearings, oil production, synthetic rubber and military transport.

From February 1943, the Combined Bomber Offensive priorities for the RAF and the USAAF initially gave first priority to the destruction of the German aircraft industry, followed by the ball-bearing industry. Later, oil production was to be the top priority, followed by rubber production. However, objectives changed to match the strategic situation. A good example of this was the need to restrict the operations of the *Kriegsmarine* (German Navy), and the commander of the RAF's Bomber Command, ACM Sir Arthur 'Bomber' Harris, had earlier ensured that regular mining sorties had been conducted throughout much of 1942,

especially during the run up to Operation Torch, the Allied invasion of North Africa. Now the rule was that mining was to be conducted by all groups whenever the weather was too bad for an attack over the Continent. Mines had proved effective, and before the North African landings had often delayed U-boat sailings. Harris was convinced that mines were more effective than attacking the U-boat bases, and was undoubtedly right until the large Tallboy and Grand Slam bombs appeared.

The Americans agreed with Harris's target of a joint force of 3,000 bombers and the plan called for some 950 heavy bombers to be in the United Kingdom by 1 July 1943; 1,200 by 1 October; 1,750 by 1 January 1944 and 2,700 by 1 April 1944. In addition, US medium bomber strength would rise from 200 to 800 over the same period. Although, unlike Harris, he did not openly claim that the offensive could win the war, Eaker believed that without it a cross-Channel invasion was impossible.

The RAF shared Eaker's vision of the combined bombing campaign, given the title Pointblank, provided that there was some flexibility in the plan. Harris had also been allowed to attack German cities with a population of 100,000 or more. The first of these attacks had been with 442 bombers which attacked Essen during the night of 6/7 March 1943. Further attacks followed, although not at the frequency which would occur later in the war, taking place on 12/13 March, 3/4 April and 30 April/1 May, so that during the two months there were 1,552 bombing sorties against Essen, dropping a total of 3,967 tons of bombs. Production at Krupps was very seriously damaged.

By this time the Pathfinder units were using H2S, which could show on a cathode tube pictures of urban/rural or land/sea contrast, and were particularly effective over targets where a city had a water frontage. This was an advantage on operations over the Ruhr where so often the target was obscured by industrial haze, even on an otherwise clear night. The new Mk.XIV bombsight was also giving Bomber Command shorter runs into the target, cutting the period when the bombers were at their most vulnerable. Harris replaced the original turrets in many of his aircraft with a new design capable of taking heavier .50-calibre guns, which were far more effective against German fighters than the original .303 guns.

Damage to another major German industrial organisation came on 20/21 July, when the former Zeppelin plant at Friedrichshafen, on the shores of Lake Constance, was attacked using some of the still-limited supply of H2S sets fitted to Pathfinder aircraft. The attack was reasonably successful, destroying half the plant, and might have been more successful still had the maps provided for the crews to recognise the target area from the H2S image been more up-to-date. Losses amounted to just 4.6 per cent, despite the short summer night which meant that the aircraft had to continue to North Africa after the raid in an operation which later became known as 'shuttle' bombing.

Meanwhile, the RAF had been back over the Ruhr, treating Wuppertal so roughly with 700 bombers that five out of the six main factories were destroyed. The Ruhr received much attention during the summer months, since the short nights of the northern summer made flying to and from targets further afield much more dangerous. At the end of the Battle of the Ruhr, Lord Cherwell, the British Government's Chief Scientific Adviser, was able to reassure Churchill that bombing accuracy had improved. In 1941 RAF Bomber Command had managed to get just a fifth of its bombs within 5 miles of the target, but by 1943 almost 70 per cent were within 3 miles.

There can be little doubt that the raids on the Ruhr were extremely successful and, along with the Thousand Bomber Raids, showed that the RAF had overcome its early difficulties to provide an effective bombing strategy. By 1944, German production of tanks would be down to 17,625 against planned production of 38,400 while for fighters it would be 25,822 from 57,600, and when production of all aircraft types is taken into consideration there would be 39,925 built against plans for 93,600.

Much has been made of the way in which German industry managed to overcome its difficulties, and it is true that under its Armaments Minister, Albert Speer, a genius in maintaining production, Herculean efforts were made to maintain and even increase production. Careful selection of statistics will sometimes show production even increasing. Nevertheless, such massive raids, which are well targeted and repeated so that repair work is affected, create major problems which accumulate and cannot be easily or quickly overcome.

Pokryshkin, Alexander Ivanovich (1913–85) Soviet ace. The Soviet Union's second highest-scoring fighter ace, and indeed, from 1941 to 1944 the highest scoring. His first kill was a Messerschmitt Bf109 on 23 June 1941. He was frequently taken away from front-line duties to train new pilots, and more than thirty of those he taught became aces in their own right. Overall, he scored fifty-nine kills with forty-eight gained while flying a Bell Airacobra which was hardly the best Allied fighter of the war. Postwar, he remained with the Soviet military, becoming deputy commander of the air defence forces between 1968 and 1971 and then heading the civil defence organisation.

polar flights In 1925 the famous Norwegian explorer, **Roald Amundsen**, was sponsored by the American millionaire Lincoln Ellsworth for an attempt to reach the North Pole. He used two Dornier Wal flying boats but failed when the aircraft crash-landed short of their destination. In May 1926 he made a further attempt using the airship *Norge* with her Italian crew leased from the Italian government, deciding that since **Richard Byrd** had probably already flown over the North Pole, he would make the first transpolar crossing by air. Departing from Spitzbergen, despite strong disagreements with the airship's captain **Umberto Nobile** over command, they completed the trip and reached Teller, Alaska.

Byrd and **Floyd Bennett** had indeed made the first flight over the North Pole in the Fokker Trimotor *Josephine Ford*. Byrd completed his achievements in 1929, when he flew across the South Pole on 28/29 November in a Ford Trimotor, after which he concentrated on developing polar flying and Arctic survival techniques, including exploring the Antarctic by air.

Polikarpov, Nikolai (1892–1944) Soviet designer. Graduating from an aeronautics course run by the Imperial Russian Navy, in 1916 he was recruited by the Russo–Baltic Wagon Factory to start a production line for the Sikorsky S-16. After the Bolshevik Revolution he was ordered to build copies of the Spad VII and was put in charge of State Aircraft Factory No.1. During the 1920s he began designing aircraft and anxious to match Western products, suffered several failures. The Soviet dictator, Stalin, accused him of treason and gave him eighteen months to produce a fighter, otherwise he would be executed. With his design team, he spent the time working under house arrest. Fortunately, the I-5 biplane fighter was good enough for the threat of execution and the house arrest to be lifted.

A later design, the I-16 of 1933, was a monoplane with a retractable undercarriage and a Bristol Jupiter engine built under licence.

Porte, Cdr John Cyril (1884–1919) British flying boat pioneer. Invalided out of the Royal Navy in 1911, Porte started flying for the British subsidiary of **Deperdussin**, and later became acquainted with **Pemberton-Billing** and the White & Thompson Company before joining **Glenn Curtiss** in the United States to work on flying boat development.

Porte and Curtiss designed and built the America flying boat with Porte intending to fly it across the Atlantic. The outbreak of the First World War meant an end to this plan but Porte returned to England with authority to build Curtiss flying boats. A flying boat factory was established at Felixstowe, on the Suffolk coast, which also became a base for patrols over the North Sea.

Towards the end of the First World War, Porte was accused of receiving money from Curtiss from the licence fees paid to the American and he was prosecuted, but after a long trial he was acquitted and a guilty government granted him the Order of St Michael and St George, which he received from King George V. He died in 1919 from tuberculosis.

Post, Wiley (1898–1935) US pioneer. Brought up as a farmer, he used the proceeds from a cotton crop to study mechanical engineering, after which he went to work in the oilfields. After losing an eye in an industrial accident, he used the US $1,600 (£400 at the then rate of exchange) compensation to learn to fly and buy an old aeroplane. In 1928

he became the personal pilot of F.C. Hall, an oil magnate, and in 1931 Hall offered to sponsor him on a round-the-world flight. On 23 June 1931, he took off with Harold Gatty as navigator in a Lockheed Vega, *Winnie Mae*, named after the sponsor's daughter. They circled the world in 8 days, 15 hours, 51 minutes. This was no mean achievement, but Post was disappointed as he had wanted to make the flight on his own. His chance came in 1933, making the first solo circumnavigation of the globe and also cutting 21 hours off the time.

The following year he began experiments with supercharged aircraft engines and high-altitude pressure suits. During this work he has been credited by many with the discovery of the jet stream, a river of wind flying several miles high, when on 7 December 1934 he flew into the stratosphere over Bartlesville, Oklahoma, wearing a rubber pressurised suit and flying an aircraft made of plywood. The following year he used the 'discovery' to add an extra 100 mph to his aircraft's cruising speed. In fact, a Japanese meteorologist, Wasaburo Ooishi, had discovered the jet stream ten years earlier using weather balloons, but his report was published in Esperanto and was, therefore, widely overlooked.

Post's work ended in 1935 when his plane crashed in Alaska, not on a research flight but on a holiday excursion to Russia with Will Rogers, the comedian, as a passenger who was also killed.

Potez *See* below

Potez, Henry Charles Alexandre (1891–1981) French manufacturer. A graduate of L'Ecole Supérieure de l'Aéronautique, where he met **Marcel Bloch**. Both men were recruited at the outbreak of the First World War to conduct research work at Chalais-Meudon. Potez was then seconded to work for the **Caudron** brothers. At the same time, Bloch had designed a more efficient airscrew and invited Potez to join him in founding a factory, Helices-Eclair, in 1916. In 1917 the partners found backing to start manufacturing observation aircraft. The business was wound up at the end of the war.

Potez founded his own company in 1919 to continue producing observation aircraft, and the firm prospered until nationalisation in 1937. The company collapsed with the fall of France and in 1953 it was restarted, but while it purchased another manufacturer, Air Fouga, in 1958, a few years later it was absorbed into Sud Aviation, one of the predecessors of **Aérospatiale**.

powered flight Strict definitions apply to powered flight, most significantly that flight must be sustained by the aircraft's engine after the momentum of the take-off run has disappeared and that flight must be controlled. These requirements distinguished the first flights by the **Wright** brothers in December 1903 from the powered hops, with the most noteworthy being those by **du Temple** in 1874 and **Mozhaiski** in 1884, in which the power that counted was the take-off run. A flight through the air of at least a quarter of a mile is necessary if sustained powered flight is to be proved – the distance over the ground is irrelevant because of the impact of head and tailwinds.

Prandtl, Prof Ludwig (1875–1953) German aerodynamicist. Graduating in engineering from the University of Munich, he became a professor of mechanics at Hanover, before moving on in 1904 to found a course in aerodynamics at Göttingen, which he established as the leader in research in the world at the time. He discovered boundary layer flow and the phenomenon of induced drag and wing-tip vortices. He was commissioned to design the shape of the **Parseval** dirigible in 1906 and had a wind tunnel built at Göttingen so that air flow could be studied. Among his students, many of whom rose to prominence, was **von Kármán**.

Pratt & Whitney/Pratt & Whitney Canada US manufacturer. One of the 'big three' aero-engine manufacturers, the company has a long history of piston and jet engine development, favouring the former in its radial form. It built the JT8 turbojet for the Boeing 707 and McDonnell Douglas DC-8, following this with the JT9 turbofan for the Boeing 747. Military engines have included the F100 for the Boeing F-15 Eagle air superiority fighter. Over the past twenty-five years, a major project has been the civil aero-engine manufacturer, **International Aero Engines**

(IAE), with international partners, each with a share of the product. A Canadian subsidiary has a dominant position with its PT6 series engine available as a turboprop and for helicopters as a turboshaft.

pressurisation Pressurisation of aircraft permits higher altitudes to be reached and extends the range of aircraft as lower air pressure reduces fuel consumption and also allows higher speeds to be flown. The first pressurised airliner was the Boeing 307 Stratoliner which entered service with both Pan American Airways and Transcontinental & Western Air in 1940, with each having just five aircraft. After the Second World War the higher altitudes required by jet and turboprop aircraft meant that pressurisation became the standard, although the piston-engined Douglas DC-6 was a development of the DC-4 and like the DC-7 that followed it, was pressurised. A number of utility and feeder airliners have been turboprop-powered but unpressurised, such as the Short Skyvan and 330/360 series, and the Dornier Do228, but none of these remain in production and passengers now expect the comfort afforded by pressurisation.

PZL/PZL-Swidnik Polish manufacturer. Founded after Polish independence from Russia following the Bolshevik Revolution, the company initially built foreign designs under licence before developing its own range, mainly for the armed forces, with the PZL P-1, P-6, P-7 and P-11 fighters entering service during the 1930s, as well as the P-23B reconnaissance bombers. The most up-to-date aircraft in service with the Polish air force before the outbreak of the Second World War was the P-37 bomber, although defence budgets had been pared to the bone between the wars and only limited production of any of these aircraft had been possible. Postwar the company restarted by building **Mil** light helicopters under licence, including updated versions of the Mi-1, and later graduated to building trainers such as the PZL-130 Turbo-Orlik. Plans to build the PZL-3 armed helicopter were abandoned in 1998.

The company has now become part of the **European Aeronautic Defence and Space Company** (EADS).

Q

Quimby, Harriet (1875–1912) American aviatrix. Despite her humble origins, she became a drama critic for the San Francisco *Dramatic Review*, and then in 1903 moved to New York to work on *Leslie's Weekly*. It was in New York that she met **John Moisant**, who taught her to fly in 1911 at Garden City. She then became a member of the touring display group, the Moisant International Aviators, before visiting Europe intending to be the first woman to fly an aircraft across the English Channel. She bought a Blériot and had it delivered to England. She also hired **Gustav Hamel** as a consultant, but his advice was for him to fly the aircraft across the Channel in her clothes while she hid on the French coast, and after landing they could swap. This advice was immediately rejected and on 16 April 1912 she took off from Dover planning to land near Calais, but instead drifted off course by 25 miles and landed in Normandy. Her flight was no mean achievement, but lost its impact as the press was overwhelmed by news of the *Titanic*'s sinking. She did receive some attention on her return to the USA.

Anxious for publicity, she took part in the Harvard–Boston aviation meeting in late June, and then planned an attempt on the speed record. On 1 July she took off with a passenger to test her Blériot for the record attempt, but while over the harbour at Boston the aircraft suddenly dived and the passenger was thrown out. Quimby managed to regain control before the aircraft dived again and she was also thrown out. When rescuers reached the scene, they found both passenger and pilot had died. **Earle Ovington** conducted an investigation on the wreckage of the aircraft and found that it did not have the standard controls, that the rudder and wing-warping wires had become entangled and that the dive had been caused by stalling as the aircraft pulled to one side.

R

radial engine An air-cooled engine with the cylinders, usually an odd number, radiating from the crankshaft which also acts as the propeller shaft. Radial engines were light and the components accessible but suffered from drag, although on later versions this was overcome to some extent by the streamlined 'NACA cowls' placed over the cylinders.

ranks Most air forces use army ranks, but the RAF and a number of other air forces in the British Commonwealth use their own special ranks. The South African Air Force has never followed RAF practice, and Canada no longer does so.
See Table 20: Comparative Ranks – Royal Air Force, Royal Navy and Army

Raynham, Frederick Phillip (1892–1954) British pioneer. Taught to fly by **Alliot Verdon Roe** in 1911, he became Roe's test pilot before fulfilling the same role for Martinsyde during the First World War. After the war, Martinsyde built a transatlantic aeroplane to compete for the *Daily Mail* prize, which Raynham took to Newfoundland hoping to beat his rivals, **Harry Hawker** and **John Alcock**. His first attempt ended with the aircraft crashing and his navigator being seriously injured when glass shards from the compass were driven into his head when it hit the instrument panel. The navigator had to be sent back across the Atlantic leaving Raynham to rebuild the aircraft without adequate facilities. On 17 June, with a replacement navigator, he made a second attempt, which also ended in a crash.

On his return to the UK he was sent to demonstrate a Martinsyde Semiquaver fighter to the Spanish and Portuguese armies, and returned with half-a-dozen orders. He used a Semiquaver in the 1920 **Gordon Bennett** race, but was forced out when an oil pump failed. He joined **Sydney Camm** and **George Handasyde** in building a glider for the Britannia Trophy, but while the glider

flew, nothing came of it. Camm and Raynham joined **Hawker**, the aircraft manufacturer, in 1924 and he test flew the Cygnet before joining the Air Survey Company helping to map New Guinea and Sarawak.

Read, Lt Cdr Albert Cushing 'Putty' (1887–1967) American long-distance pioneer. Commissioned into the USN in 1906, he learnt to fly in 1916 at Pensacola and the following year was put in command of a naval air station and led anti-submarine patrols. In 1919 he was selected to captain a Curtiss NC flying boat on a transatlantic attempt; on 8 May three aircraft took off from Rockaway, Long Island, but only Read's aircraft, NC-4, managed to reach Lisbon on 27 May after stopping at Newfoundland for an engine change and later at the Azores.

Nevertheless, Read was promoted to full commander and later held the rank of captain in which he commanded aircraft carriers. Early in the Second World War he was captain at Pensacola, the USN's flying training school, where he presided over the training of many British Fleet Air Arm pilots sent to the USA under the Towers Scheme. Later he taught at the Naval War College and served in the Bureau of Aeronautics.

records Since 1905, aeronautical records have been verified by the **Fédération Aéronautique Internationale (FAI)**, but it is left to the national aero club to apply for certification of a national record as a world record, and this must be done within two days of the completion of the attempt. Records are classified regarding scope and aspect of performance, such as altitude, endurance or speed, but the aircraft and apparatus are classified as well, with Class A for free balloons; Class B for dirigibles or airships; C for aeroplanes, seaplanes and amphibians; D for gliders; E for rotorcraft; F for model aircraft; G for parachutes; H for jetlift aircraft; I for man-powered aircraft; K for spacecraft; L for air cushion vehicles. There are sub-classes for each class with, for example, aeroplanes being divided into those that are piston-engined, turboprop-powered, turbojet-powered or using rocket propulsion.

In the case of absolute speeds, the records are set over a distance of 3 km with a restricted altitude of 100 m (328 ft), but there are other categories without altitude restriction from 15 to 25 km; or over circuits of 100, 200, 500, 1,000, 2,000, 5,000 or 10,000 km. The 3-km rule dates from 1923. Originally records were set over varying distances, but after the First World War a 1-km rule was introduced and this became 3 km in 1923. After the First World War the speed was the average of two runs over the course, but in 1922 this became four runs and in recent years it has become two in each direction, without landing and within a time lapse of 30 minutes. Regardless of the record sought, needless to say, the pilot is not allowed to leave the aeroplane or aerostat during an attempt, and everyone aboard must remain alive for the next 48 hours. Any new record must be at least one per cent better than the preceding record. *See* Table 18: Aeronautical Records.

Reims Aviation Meeting (22–29 August 1909)

As the first aviation meeting, Reims attracted many

The first air show at Reims, 22–29 August 1909, was as much a social occasion as a business one, and it also saw the first endurance and speed records set. There is a strong sense of Edwardian style and glamour in this poster.

of the major public and political figures of the day, from the President of France downwards. Held on the Plain of Bethany just outside the city, it was sponsored by the champagne industry and was known officially as La Grande Semaine d'Aviation de la Champagne. It was the venue for the first official records for altitude, endurance and speed. The champagne industry's prize money totalled 200,000 fr., which proved sufficient inducement to bring thirty-eight aircraft to the meeting, of which twenty-three actually took part. The only disappointment was the weather, with the programme interrupted by high winds, but the few accidents did not result in any fatalities.

There were 120 take-offs, with 84 flights of more than 3 miles. **Henri Farman** won the Grand Prix for a flight of 180 km which took him 3 hours 5 minutes in his Farman III. **Hubert Latham** challenged the award because Farman had changed the aircraft's Vivinus water-cooled engine for an air-cooled Gnome rotary, but many believe that **Levavasseur** prompted him to this action. **Glenn Curtiss** set a record of 43.35 mph flying on 23 August, despite high winds, but the following day **Blériot** raised this to 46.18 mph, and then on 28 August he won the **Gordon Bennett** Cup Race with 47.83 mph. On 27 August Farman made the first flight carrying two passengers, flying 6 miles in 10 minutes.

Reitsch, Hanna (1912–79) German aviatrix. Reitsch switched from training as a physician during the 1920s to flying. Initially she flew gliders but later moved on to powered aircraft and demonstrated outstanding ability, becoming a test pilot at the German Institute for Glider Research. She was sent on propaganda tours to Latin America and Africa, but her most notable pre-war achievement was flying the Fa-61 helicopter inside the Deutschland-Halle in Berlin in 1938.

She became Hitler's personal pilot for a time, and also test flew the Messerschmitt Me321 Gigant glider, which was capable of lifting 130 fully equipped troops. She next tested the same company's Me163 Komet rocket-powered interceptor but in 1943, while flying one of these aircraft, she noticed that the take-off gear had failed to jettison, and despite trying to make a safe landing she crashed and broke her skull

in six places. In just five months she was back at work, flying a piloted V1 rocket to identify control problems that had already killed several test pilots. She identified the problem, but then proposed leading a squadron of manned V1s to conduct suicide missions; the idea was rejected by the Luftwaffe.

Her most dangerous mission was probably fetching General von Greim to a meeting with Hitler, who was by this time besieged in his Berlin bunker. A Luftwaffe pilot flew a two-seat Focke-Wulf Fw190 to Gatow airport with Reitsch stuffed into the radio compartment behind the rear seat. The aircraft was attacked by Soviet fighters which were fought off by Luftwaffe escorts. At Gatow, the general was transferred to a Fieseler Storch which he flew with Reitsch towards central Berlin. Soviet AA fire shattered one of the general's feet, so Reitsch took over the controls. On arrival, Hitler put the general in command of what was left of the Luftwaffe.

At the end of the war, Reitsch was captured by the Allies but released. Her father allegedly shot her mother, sister, her nieces and the family maid before committing suicide to avoid capture by Soviet forces.

Renard, Capt Charles (1847–1905) French aeronaut. Commissioned into the French Army's engineering corps, in 1884 he had an idea for an electric-powered airship. With the help of a friend, **A.C. Krebs**, he obtained funding from the Ministry of the Interior, largely because the then minister, Léon Gambetta, had escaped from Paris by balloon during the siege in 1870. The airship was built in just two months and made its first ascent on 9 August 1884, travelling 5 miles from Chalais-Meudon to Villacoublay and then returning, the first controlled aerial journey. While the motor was light, the weight of the batteries and their poor range meant that this combination did not represent the way forward, but it was a significant step at the time.

Rentschler, Frederick Brant (1887–1956) German-American engineer. A graduate of Princeton, during the First World War he worked for Wright-Martin (later simply Wright) inspecting engine castings. Postwar, he was a keen advocate of advanced air-cooled engines, but his ideas were turned down by the board and when in 1924 he had to take time off for an operation, he used his convalescence to seek financial support for his ideas. He was successful and left Wright, taking two of their designers, George Mead and Andy Wilgoos, who designed a new engine called the Wasp. In 1925 Rentschler bought a bankrupt tool and die company in Connecticut, Pratt & Whitney, for US $253 (£63 at the then rate of exchange) and started production of the Wasp engine in its workshops. Four years later, the company was worth US $35 million.

Republic Aviation US manufacturer. Dating from the early 1930s, the company was formed out of the **Seversky** business. One of its own designs to reach production was the F-47 Thunderbolt fighter, which showed strong signs of its Seversky ancestry. Postwar designs included an experimental PR aircraft, of which just two were built, but the company returned to prominence with the F-84 Thunderjet and its developments, the RF-84 Thunderflash and F-84F Thunderstreak, all of which were supplied to many European NATO countries. These were followed by the first supersonic fighter to enter squadron service, the F-105 Thunderchief.

The company was acquired by Fairchild in 1965.

Reynolds, Osborne (1842–1912) British engineer. Belfast-born Reynolds graduated from Cambridge with a degree in mechanical engineering in 1867, and a year later was professor of engineering at Owens College, Manchester. While he made many important discoveries, his most important as far as aviation was concerned lay in fluid dynamics, discovering the relationship between fluid density and streamlined flow, later expressed as the Reynolds Number, enabling later researchers to scale the results of wind tunnel tests from models to full-sized aircraft.

Riabouchinsky, Dimitri Pavlovitch (1882–1962) Russian aerodynamicist. Abandoning a business education to study science in Heidelberg when he returned to Moscow in 1904, Riabouchinsky opened a research institute using his family's

considerable wealth. The Aerodynamic Institute of Koutchino gathered many of the best scientists in Russia and was responsible for discovering some of the fundamental laws of aerodynamics, although at first they dropped model aircraft from towers and only later used wind tunnels.

He fled to Paris following the Bolshevik Revolution.

Richthofen, Rittmeister Manfred von (1892–1918) German ace. Commissioned into the German Army, he initially served in the 1st Uhlan Regiment, a cavalry unit, before transferring to the infantry and then to the Military Air Service as an observer. He hated flying at first, but later sought training as a pilot although he was not an adept student and wrote off several of his training aircraft. He then found navigation difficult and the story is told that during his first sortie over the Western Front he had to land and ask for directions. A spell flying bomber missions over the Eastern Front bored him and he asked for a transfer back to the Western Front. At this early stage he did not impress his superiors, and **Oswald Boelcke** at first refused to allow him to join his unit Jagdstaffel 2.

The transfer to Boelcke's unit was the making of von Richthofen, improving his flying and combat abilities. His first confirmed victory was an FE 2b on 17 September 1916. He made spectacular progress and, when his mentor and commanding officer was killed, he took over the unit. His aircraft were painted red gaining him the nickname of the Red Baron. More than half of the eighty Allied aircraft he shot down were two-seaters, which were easier prey and yet often more valuable to the war effort than single-seat scouts. Not all two-seaters were easy targets however, for he was shot down and wounded on 16 July 1917 by the rear gunner in a British aircraft. He had a bullet glance off his skull and had to fight to remain conscious in order to land his aircraft safely. He returned to combat after a month and by 20 April 1981 his score reached eighty aircraft, all of which were British but for one Belgian aircraft.

Von Richthofen had always ensured that he had an exit available during aerial combat, but on 21 April he chased his victim down to low altitude, just above the trenches, where he was caught by a Sopwith Camel flown by Roy Brown, a Canadian. The Red Baron was caught between the camel's gunfire and that of an Australian unit on the ground below, and his aircraft crashed into the ground at high speed. The wreckage was soon stripped by souvenir hunters so today no one knows exactly who accounted for him. Respected by his enemies, he was buried with full military honours.

Rickenbacker, Capt Edward Vernon (1890–1973)

American ace and airline chief. Born to poor Swiss immigrants as Richenbacher, he changed his name during the First World War. His first job in 1903 was working in a car factory, and he became the company racing team's mechanic before becoming a racing driver himself, and then a car salesman. During the First World War he was an army driver, and one day he spotted a broken down Mercedes by the roadside. He stopped and repaired the car, which belonged to **Billy Mitchell**, and as a result was permitted to train as a pilot. Once qualified he was posted to the 94th Squadron, known as the 'Hat in the Ring', and flying with it he shot down twenty-six German aircraft, becoming an ace.

He left the army after the war and started building cars, with the unusual feature for the day of brakes on all four wheels, but a whispering campaign by his competitors saying that this design led to accidents, meant that sales slumped and his company collapsed. He next worked for Cadillac's La Salle division before joining **Fokker**'s US subsidiary in 1928, which was later acquired by General Motors. Later he worked for American Airlines and then for North American's airline operation which he joined in 1933, and in 1935 when the airline, Eastern Airlines, was sold off, he remained with it and became chairman.

During the Second World War he was sent by the US government on a special mission to the Soviet Union. Later, he was sent on a tour of US bases in the Pacific flying in a Boeing B-17 Fortress, which was forced to ditch, leaving those aboard adrift for twenty-two days in the ocean before being rescued. Postwar, he returned to Eastern Airlines.

Rockwell, Kiffin Yates (1892–1916)

American ace. A college dropout, he had learnt to fly but, looking for adventure, joined the French Foreign Legion in 1914 and became involved in the First World War. At the first opportunity he joined the Escadrille Lafayette in April 1916 and shot down his first German aircraft, the first to be shot down by an American, on 18 May.

He was shot down and killed over Luxeuil in September 1916.

Rodgers, Calbraith Perry (1879–1912)

American pioneer. Denied a naval career because of ill health, he went to Columbia Unversity and achieved fame as a footballer. On graduating he raced yachts and motor cars. He was taught to fly at the **Wrights'** school in June 1911, going solo after just 90 minutes of instruction. He won the endurance prize at the Chicago International Aviation Meeting in August 1911, which encouraged him to ask Ogden Armour to sponsor him for the first transcontinental flight, intending to win the prize of US $50,000 (£10,000 at the then rate of exchange, around £58,000 today) offered by the Hearst newspaper group for a successful flight before 10 October. Ogden Armour promised sponsorship of $5 per mile provided that the aircraft was painted with the logo of a new grape soda, so the Wright EX biplane was named *Vin Fiz*. Taking off from Sheepshead Bay, Long Island, on 17 September 1911, his cross-country flight involved six inflight engine failures and fifteen accidents, broken bones and even concussion. He therefore did not reach Long Beach on the coast of California until 10 December. He had spent the money Armour had given him and failed by two months to meet the Hearst deadline.

The following year in April he flew into a flock of seagulls in California; one of the birds jammed his rudder, causing his Wright biplane to crash, breaking his back and neck which killed him.

Roe, Sir Edwin Alliot Verdon (1877–1958)

British engineer and manufacturer. After leaving school at 14 years old, Roe spent some time in Canada on a variety of jobs before returning to England in 1892 and taking up an apprenticeship for the Lancashire & Yorkshire Railway at the

Horwich locomotive works near Manchester, during which time he also became a successful bicycle racer. He left the railway to work in a boat yard before taking a degree in marine engineering at the University of London. He went to sea between 1899 and 1902 as a ship's engineer, where he started to study bird flight. Between 1902 and 1906 he experimented with flying models, before going to the USA to help a Mr Davidson construct a helicopter. He returned to England in 1907.

He won £75 in the *Daily Mail* contest for a model aeroplane in 1907, and this money, equal to around £4,500 today, funded his work on a full-sized biplane, although it left him with just 5s a week for food. The biplane was ready in September, and Roe took it to Brooklands for testing. Self-taught as a pilot, he suffered a number of accidents before finally making a powered hop in the biplane on 8 June 1908. His next aircraft was a triplane on which he was helped by an associate, but the arrangement ended and in frustration Roe simply auctioned off the unfinished aircraft before starting another triplane on his own, which was completed in 1909 under the railway arches at Lea Marshes, East London. The fact that his money had all been spent meant that this aircraft had wings covered in packing paper rather than cloth, but even so, when it was tested it flew well.

After this success, he founded his own company, A.V. Roe & Co. in 1910, which traded as **Avro**. Among the notable aircraft built before the outbreak of the First World War was the Avro Cabin Biplane in 1912, the first cabin aircraft. It became famous because it was on this aircraft that Lt Wilfred Parke, RN, became the first pilot to demonstrate a deliberate spin and recovery, flying at 600 ft on 25 August 1912. There was more to this aircraft than spin recovery, however, for it also had considerable endurance, remaining airborne for a record 7½ hours in October. The following year, the Avro 504 first appeared and was to be one of the great aircraft of the First World War as a mainstay of the training schools with 8,340 built.

In 1928 Roe sold all of his shares and bought a stake in the S.E. Saunders Company, creating **Saunders-Roe**, which built flying boats before concentrating on floats. His original firm built a variety of mainly military aircraft, including

the Anson light transport and trainer and the Lancaster bomber, the latter regarded by many as the best heavy bomber of the Second World War. Bomber production ended with the Vulcan, a delta-wing bomber built to deliver the British nuclear deterrent, but airliners were also built, including the ill-fated Tudor and, towards the end of the company's independent existence before it was merged into Hawker Siddeley, the 748, a twin-turboprop feeder airliner that was also built under licence in India.

Rogallo, Francis M. (1912–) American aerodynamicist. He entered aviation working for **NACA** in 1936, and was based at the Langley Centre at Hampton, Virginia, after the Second World War when he became involved with concepts for simplifying flight. He visited California in 1948 and interviewed other engineers and aerodynamicists to find ideas for simplified flight, which he developed himself at home in his kitchen using paper models and an electric fan. With his wife's help, he developed a wing made from cloth in which NACA failed to find any possibilities and after it was patented was sold as a sophisticated toy kite. It was not until **Dr Wernher von Braun** saw the possibilities held by the wing for the recovery of spacecraft that the wing was accepted.

Rogallo built an aircraft, the Flexwing, in 1961 incorporating what had by this time become known as the Rogallo wing, but it did not attract any potential buyers. It was not until 1971, when two hang-gliders were built using the Rogallo wing and appeared at the world's first hang-glider meeting at Los Angeles, that his invention eventually found an application.

Rohrbach, Adolph (1889–1939) German engineer. Trained as an engineer with a diploma in shipbuilding, Rohrbach went to work for **Blohm und Voss**, at that time purely shipbuilders. He then moved to Zeppelin, attracted by the huge dirigibles they were producing. There, during the First World War, he designed heavy bombers, the Zeppelin-Staaken series. Postwar, he set up his own company to build all-metal aircraft, but favoured smooth-skin construction rather than the corrugated airframes built by **Ford** and **Junkers**.

Unable to build aircraft in his native Germany, he started work in neighbouring Denmark and by 1929 demand was such that he opened a factory in the USA, although too late to catch the market which was taken by competitors who had adopted his techniques.

He died in 1939 from a heart attack.

Rolls-Royce British manufacturer. Strictly, Rolls-Royce (1971) because the original company went bankrupt working on the RB211 turbofan.

The origins of the company lay in motor car manufacture and the company became involved in aviation with its car-derived Eagle engine during the First World War. Postwar, it worked on a series of in-line engines that led ultimately to the Merlin which powered, among many other aircraft, the Hurricane and Spitfire fighters and the Mosquito and Lancaster bombers, and which was produced under licence in the USA by Packard for the North American F-51 Mustang. Following the Second World War it powered Spanish-built Messerschmitt Bf109s and Heinkel He111s.

While the Merlin was superseded by the Griffon, the company grew rapidly, establishing a strong position in first turboprop and then jet manufacture. The Dart turboprop, developed for the Vickers Viscount airliner, was also used in the Argosy transport, Handley Page Herald, BAe748, Fokker F27 Friendship and NAMC YS-11, as well as the Breguet Alize ASW aircraft, the Grumman Gulfstream I, and re-engined Convair Metropolitans. Jet engines such as the Avon, Conway and Spey were also used by several different types of aircraft each. In 1961 one of its old competitors, Napier, was acquired, followed in 1968 by the other remaining British aero-engine manufacturer, **Bristol-Siddeley**, which brought R-R the Pegasus vectored-thrust engine for the Harrier and the Olympus for the Concorde supersonic airliner, as well as helicopter engines and marine versions of the BS engines. During this period, the motor car division produced Continental piston engines for light aircraft under licence.

Aviation and motor interests were separated after the bankruptcy, with the aero-engine interests becoming state-owned until the company was privatised in the 1980s. First Vickers, and now BMW, produce Rolls-Royce cars under licence in order to use the name from the aero-engine manufacturer.

Concorde was the first of a large number of collaborative projects, but the company was late on the Airbus range and did not produce engines for the airframe manufacturer until the advent of the A330. It also lost its leading role in turboprop production during the 1960s until it acquired **Allison** of the United States some years later. The US company, whose engines are used on the Lockheed P-2 Orion, C-130 Hercules and the Alenia C-27 Spartan, now trades under the Rolls-Royce name. Despite the problems developing it, the RB211 became a successful engine, and in addition to the Lockheed l-1011 TriStar for which it was developed, became the most popular engine choice on the Boeing 757, and has also been used on the Boeing 747 and 767 and the Tupolev Tu-214. It has been superseded by the even larger Trent, available on the Airbus A330, Boeing 777 and the Airbus A380.

Rolls, The Hon Charles Stewart (1877–1910) British pioneer and salesman. Graduating from Cambridge University with a degree in engineering, he raced first bicycles and then racing cars and was a friend of Henry Moore-Brabazon (*see* **Lord Brabazon of Tara**). He pressed for an increase in the 4 mph speed limit on motor vehicles in 1896, and with other enthusiasts was successful in having the limit raised to 12 mph. He learnt to fly both balloons and aircraft and in 1901 formed the Aero Club. Despite coming from a wealthy family, he earned his own living and in 1903 started to sell imported and expensive French cars. He was introduced to **Henry Royce** who was starting to build high-quality motor cars and, despite having little in common, they became firm friends. In 1904 they established Rolls-Royce, with Rolls selling the cars that Royce built.

Rolls continued to fly and gained the Aero Club's certificate no. 2 in 1910, the year that it became the Royal Aero Club. He celebrated on 2 June by becoming the first man to make a return flight across the English Channel, but on 12 July he was killed flying at Bournemouth when his French-built Wright biplane broke up in mid-air.

Romaero Romanian manufacturer. A state-owned aircraft manufacturer that came into prominence building the **Britten-Norman** Islander and also the British Aerospace One-Eleven 500srs as the Rombac One-Eleven. Work on Islander kits continues.

rotary engine In modern times, confused by being the alternative term for the Wankel engine, the original rotary engine was an internal combustion engine in which the cylinders, and therefore also the pistons, rotated around a static crankshaft with the propeller attached to the cylinders. Invented by Australian **Lawrence Hargrave** in 1887, it was adapted for the aeroplane by Laurent Seguin in 1907. The first production example was the 50 hp Gnome, but the concept was also adopted by several other manufacturers. Many First World War aircraft were powered by the rotary engine, but postwar, as power continued to increase, the problems of control and stability inherent in the design made it unsuitable and most subsequent engines were either liquid-cooled (water or glycol) in-line engines, as favoured by **Rolls-Royce**, Daimler-Benz and **Junkers**, or air-cooled radial engines, as produced by **Bristol** and many American manufacturers.

The Wankel engine has also found limited use in light aircraft. It replaces the reciprocating piston with a roughly triangular revolving piston.

rotary wing The current term for a **helicopter**, used because the rotor combined the functions of both wing and propulsion.

Royal Flying Doctor Service of Australia Founded in 1925 by the **Revd John Flynn** and Qantas Airlines, the service brings medical care to isolated communities and sheep or cattle stations in the Australian outback.

Royce, Sir Frederick Henry (1863–1933) British engineer. Born into deep poverty at Alwalton, near Peterborough, and an orphan at 9, he had a number of jobs before finally being apprenticed at a railway locomotive works where he was already notable for his precision as a machinist. After a further job, in 1880 he went to London having taken months to save up the

cost of a railway ticket. On arrival in the capital, he worked at an electricity generating station by day and went to technical school at night. After three years he went north to Manchester and set up a workshop producing electric motors and dynamos. His passion for quality ensured that the business prospered. When he was 39 he bought a used Decauville motor car hoping to use it for leisurely trips, but the frequent breakdowns caused him to decide that he could build something much better, which he did within a year. His new car was so good that he then resolved to become a motor vehicle manufacturer and, in search of someone who could sell his cars, he met the **Hon Charles Rolls**. Despite their different backgrounds, the two men became friends as well as business partners.

In 1906 the firm, by this time **Rolls-Royce**, produced the iconic Silver Ghost, which by itself firmly established the company's reputation. Once the First World War broke out, the Admiralty asked Royce if he could manufacture a Renault aircraft engine under licence for their aircraft and airships. When he examined the engine, Royce knew he could do better and promised the Admiralty that he would. He produced the Eagle, a 20 litre engine producing 225 hp, and followed it with the Falcon and the Hawk. These were so reliable that by the end of the war Rolls-Royce was producing 60 per cent of all British-built engines, although imports of Gnome and Clerget engines continued, especially for fighters and scouts.

Postwar, Royce remained in control of the company until his death in 1933, by which time R-R had powered the world's fastest aircraft.

Rozier balloons A gas balloon to which heating is applied, effectively combining the **Montgolifière** and **Charlière** concepts, and so called because the first was used in a disastrous attempt by **Pilâtre de Rozier** to cross the English Channel in 1784. The concept has been revived in recent years for record-breaking attempts, notably the first solo round-the-world balloon ascent, completed on 2 July 2002 by the American Steve Fossett, taking two weeks for the 19,428.6 mile aerial voyage.

Rudel, Col Hans-Ulrich (1916–82) German ace. Filled with the ambition to fly from childhood, he joined the Luftwaffe to train as a pilot, but it was with difficulty that he eventually qualified and to his disappointment he was sent to an observation squadron rather than a fighter unit. Once Operation Barbarossa, the invasion of the **Soviet Union**, got under way, he was transferred to a Junkers Ju87 Stuka dive-bombing squadron, where he became noted for his determination and his daring. Although designed as a dive-bomber, a tank-busting version of the Stuka entered service in 1943, just in time for the Battle of the Kursk Salient, and Rudel's unit was the first to fly it into combat. His eventual score on the Eastern Front was 519 tanks, more than 2,000 other vehicles and many gun positions. He even achieved what many would have considered impossible, sinking the Soviet battleship, the First World War veteran *Marat*, 23,000 tons, in Kronstatt harbour on 23 September 1941. Stalin, the Soviet dictator, put a price on his head contrary to the rules of the Geneva Convention.

Not surprisingly, he received numerous honours and medals from the Nazi regime and, in 1945, Hitler himself ordered that a new medal be struck, the Knight's Cross with Golden Oak Leaves, of which Rudel was the only recipient. Rudel's luck eventually ran out shortly before the end of the war when anti-aircraft fire wounded him so badly that he lost a leg below the knee. His reputation was such that, despite the lack of facilities and medicines at this stage of the war, he received the best medical care. He repaid the attention by returning to operations and is claimed to have been flying on the last day of the war. Some even maintain that Hitler, with Goering in disgrace, saw Rudel as his successor as Führer, although this does not really fit with the transfer of power to Doenitz.

When the war ended, Rudel was taken prisoner briefly but later moved to Argentina.

Ruhr, Bomber Campaign *See* Pointblank Directive

Rumpler German manufacturer. The Rumpler Flugzeugwerke produced a number of designs for the German Military Air Service before and during the First World War, including the Rumpler-Etrich Taube (Dove) fighter monoplane. This was designed by **Igo Etrich** and demand for it was such that its production had to be shared between several other firms. The company also produced the *Stahltaube*, a steel version of the Dove and a 'C' series of fighter biplanes, of which the CIII and CIV were the most successful. Production ceased with the end of the war.

Rutan, Elbert Leander 'Burt' (1943–) American designer and engineer. Graduating as an engineer from the California Polytechnic Institute, he worked for **NASA** as a technician at Edwards AFB. During the late 1960s he began experiments with delta aeroplane models and canard configurations, eventually building a full-sized aircraft, the VariViggen, constructed mainly of wood, and then in 1975, the VariEze, made of foam and glass fibre which he intended for the homebuilt market. The VariEze used a pusher propeller and was designed to provide 200 mph using an engine of just 100 hp. Better still was the Quickie of 1977, a single-seat aeroplane that could fly at 125 mph on an 18 hp engine. The VariEze and Quickie designs sold in substantial quantities while Rutan continued working for NASA, building military test aircraft using similar materials to his homebuilt designs, including the AD-1, a jet with a pivoting wing based on an earlier German concept.

Perhaps an even greater contribution to aviation development was the Voyager, a twin-engined canard which, with assistance from John Ronz on the wings and propellers, he designed for his brother, Dick, and Jeanna Yeager, to make an unrefuelled circumnavigation of the globe. The project started in 1982 and the completed aircraft finished its circumnavigation at Edwards AFB on 23 December 1986. The entire project was privately funded.

Ryan, Tubal Claude (1898–1982) American designer and manufacturer. Inspired by seeing **Calbraith Rodgers** on his transcontinental flight, he flew with the United States Army Air Service for two years before starting a flying school at San Diego, California, in 1922 and in 1925 diversified into airline operations with a service between San Diego and Los Angeles. His 'airliners' were open-cockpit aircraft that he modified by building a passenger cabin, and the conversions were so successful that in 1926 he started to design and build his own aircraft. His first aircraft, designed in conjunction with his business partner, B.F. Mahoney, was the M1, a high-wing cabin monoplane, but disagreements over the company's future course saw Ryan sell his stake and leave. The following year, the company built the famous *Spirit of St Louis* for **Charles Lindbergh**.

After leaving the company, Ryan worked as an aero-engine salesman until he founded his new company, Ryan Aeronautical, in 1931. The company built trainers including the ST and the Fireball. The Fireball, built in 1945, was a compound piston-engined fighter with a ramjet, one of which made the first 'jet' landing on an aircraft carrier after the piston engine failed. It also built the X-13 vertical take-off jet in 1957.

S

SAAB Swedish manufacturer. Possibly more famous to the layman as a car manufacturer, the company is in fact Svenska Aeroplane AB, and was formed in 1937 to ensure a steady supply of aircraft to neutral Sweden in the event of a major European war. During the Second World War the company produced the SAAB-17 light bomber, the SAAB-18 bomber and the SAAB-21 fighter, with the latter having the distinction of being the only piston-engined fighter to also be produced as a jet fighter after the war.

Postwar, the company diversified into motor manufacture, but continued to develop and build aircraft for the *Flygvapnet*, Royal Swedish Air Force, including the SAAB-29 Tunnan fighter, followed by the SAAB-32 Lansen during the mid-1950s and the SAAB-91 Safir trainer. These were followed by the SAAB-35 Draken during the 1960s, the SAAB-105 jet trainer and then the SAAB-37 Viggen (Viking). The Viggen was followed by the JAS37 Gripen light fighter, currently in production and with which the company has become associated with **British Aerospace**, which now has a stake in the aircraft production side of SAAB.

An attempt to diversify into airliner production, with the SAAB-340 regional turboprop, followed by the larger SAAB-2000, saw the aircraft ordered by a substantial number of airlines, but the venture was not financially successful and the company has returned to military work. Nevertheless, military variants of these aircraft have also been developed for airborne-early-warning duties.

Sadler, James (1751–1828) British aeronaut. Encouraged by reports of the first balloon ascents in 1783, he built his own balloon, starting with a scaled down model. He next built a full-sized balloon with an envelope 63 ft in diameter, which ascended from Oxford on 4 October 1784 and journeyed for 6 miles, making it the first balloon ascent by an Englishman in an English-designed balloon. He toured the country displaying his balloon and making numerous ascents, but in 1812 his attempt to cross the Irish Sea failed, largely because the balloon was mishandled. His son, Windham succeeded in crossing the Irish Sea on 22 July 1817. He was killed in 1824 when ballooning, after his basket hit the side of a house and he was thrown out. His father lived for another four years but appears to have abandoned any further attempts at ballooning.

SAFRAN French manufacturer. A French group that includes companies in a wide range of activities, including aero-engine manufacturers **SNECMA**, **Turbomeca** and **CFM**, as well as Messier-Dowty, the undercarriage manufacturers, acquired in 1994.

Saint-Exupery, Antoine-Marie-Rodger de (1900–44) Pioneering French commercial pilot. After failing to be selected as a cadet officer for the French Navy, he joined the French Aviation Militaire in 1921 and proved to be a natural pilot. On leaving the military he joined Compagnie Latécoère and became an airmail pilot. Initially, he flew on the services linking France and North Africa, but he later went to South America and helped survey and pioneer air services there, mainly flying in Argentina and Brazil under difficult conditions and survived a number of accidents. On his return to France in the 1930s, he worked initially as a test pilot before joining Air France's publicity department. He also became a successful novelist, often featuring aviators, although he also wrote a book for children.

When the Second World War broke out, he joined what had become the Armée de l'Air, mainly flying reconnaissance sorties. After the French surrender he went to the USA and joined the USAAC shortly before it became the USAAF. He disappeared on a photo-reconnaissance mission over the Mediterranean while flying a Lockheed P-38 Lightning, most probably shot down by a Focke-Wulf Fw190.

Sakai, Saburo (1916–2000) Japanese ace. After joining the Imperial Japanese Navy in 1933, he was trained as a pilot in 1937 and eventually flew more than 200 combat sorties during the Second World War becoming Japan's highest scoring ace with sixty-seven confirmed kills. He lost an eye in the fighting over Guadalcanal during August 1942, but despite terrible agony managed to fly some 600 miles back to his base.

Samson, Cdr Charles Rumney (1883–1931) Pioneering British naval aviator. Commissioned into the Royal Navy, he initially served at sea before becoming one of 200 applicants competing for four places for pilot training offered by the Royal Aero Club in 1911. He proved to be a natural pilot and impressed the Admiralty to the extent that he was given command of the world's first naval flying school at Eastchurch on the Isle of Sheppey. He went far beyond his official duties by campaigning for up-to-date aircraft and researching into the full potential for naval aviation. He was protected from the wrath of his superiors by the interest and support of people such as the First Lord of the Admiralty, Winston Churchill.

He earned fame by making the first take-off from a British warship on 10 January 1912, flying from a launching platform of planks over the forecastle of the battleship HMS *Africa* using a Short S27, a Wright-type biplane, which had been fitted with air bags in case an emergency landing in the River Medway proved necessary. He flew back to the airfield at Eastchurch. Later that year, at the Annual Naval Review held at Portland in May, he flew a Short biplane which he had fitted with three torpedo-shaped floats and named HMS *Amphibian*. He flew over the fleet while still at anchor and later, during the review, carried a messenger with a letter for King George V, landing alongside the Royal Yacht *Victoria and Albert*. More important still, he flew an S27 from a ramp built over HMS *Hibernia's* forecastle while she steamed at 10.5 knots into the wind in Weymouth Bay.

On the outbreak of the First World War, he was given command of the first unit of what had become the Royal Naval Air Service (RNAS) to be sent to Europe, being based near Ostend in Belgium. What was perceived as the ill-disciplined activities of his unit resulted in them being ordered home again within a few days, but on the way back Samson claimed to have lost his bearings and landed at Dunkirk, claiming that bad weather prevented them from flying across the Channel. Unable to attack the Germans without bombs, he had boiler plates welded onto civilian vehicles and created an armoured car squadron.

In 1915 he was sent to Gallipoli as a commander flying photo-reconnaissance missions, spotting for the guns of warships and even making a few raids against enemy positions. On one occasion he narrowly missed killing Kemel Ataturk, the Turkish commander and future dictator, when his bombs fell wide of the staff car transporting him. He also commanded a flotilla of ships fitted with planks from which to fly aircraft, and operated against enemy shipping in the Eastern Mediterranean. He later proposed the use of lighters towed at speed by destroyers to launch fighter aircraft.

When the RAF was formed, Samson transferred and was given the rank of colonel before the service introduced its own ranks. His career was cut short by a heart condition and he died aged 48.

Sanger, Dr Eugene Albert (1905–64) Czech rocket scientist. Graduating from the technical university at Vienna with a doctorate in engineering and physics, Sanger began working in Germany on rocket propulsion, making important advances in liquid hydrogen fuels and metal powder additives. Working with Irene Bredt, whom he later married, he developed the concept of an antipodal bomber which would be launched into earth's orbit and on descending be able to bomb any target, and which eventually found a peaceful application in the space shuttle.

He left Germany at the end of the Second World War to work in France, before returning to Germany and finally working in Egypt on a ballistic missile programme that was eventually abandoned.

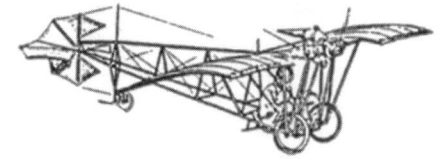

The Brazilian pioneer Alberto Santos-Dumont built this diminutive, but successful Demoiselle in *1909*. The pilot sat inside the bamboo fuselage.

Santos-Dumont, Alberto (1873–1932)

Brazilian pioneer. Having learnt mechanical engineering through helping to maintain the locomotives of the internal railway on his father's enormous coffee plantation, his interest in aviation was whetted by the novels of **Jules Verne**.

At the age of 18, on a visit to Paris, he saw a number of aerostats and this confirmed his desire to pursue a life in aeronautics. It was another six years before he made his first balloon ascent, which encouraged him to have a small balloon, *Brazil*, made – at the time, the smallest hydrogen balloon ever to lift a passenger. The following year, 1898, he designed his first dirigible, but he was at first hampered by low-powered engines; he also failed to produce gas bags that were sufficiently robust. Nevertheless, in 1901 he won the prize offered by **Henri Deutsch de la Meurthe** for the first balloon trip around the Eiffel Tower, with his No. 6 ascending from St Cloud and rounding the tower before making its safe return. This made him a hero throughout France. From this time on, Santos-Dumont used his dirigibles as others might use a car, even landing in Paris boulevards for coffee, but his craft were still too small to have commercial applications.

On learning from **Octave Chanute**'s report of the achievements made by the **Wright** brothers, he designed an aeroplane which he asked **Gabriel Voisin** to build for him. When completed, he had a large and ungainly canard configuration biplane with **Hargrave**-type box-kite wings, powered by a 24 hp engine. At first it failed to fly, even though it was launched from balloon No. 14 in July (and so the aircraft was designated the 14-bis), but when fitted with a 50 hp Antoinette engine, it managed a short flight on 13 September 1906 at Bagatelle. It was little more than a powered hop and covered just 80 ft. Better was to come on 12 November when it made the first flight in Europe, covering some 700 ft. The Europeans, still largely ignorant about the Wright brothers and their achievements, claimed this as the first ever flight and were not disillusioned until the brothers arrived in France in 1908 and flew with what, compared to European standards, was complete ease.

The superiority of the Wrights simply inspired Santos-Dumont to greater efforts. In 1909 his new aeroplane, the diminutive Demoiselle, appeared so small that the pilot sat within the bamboo framework of the fuselage. The aircraft was shown at the **Reims Aviation Meeting** that August and so inspired people that it entered limited production the following year. That was the year that Santos-Dumont learnt that he was suffering from multiple sclerosis and that as his muscles began to waste, he would have to give up flying. He returned to Brazil and became a recluse. In addition to his illness, he became depressed at the way in which the aeroplane became a machine of war, and eventually committed suicide using his tie to hang himself in his bedroom.

Sarabia, D.A. Francisco (1900–39)

Mexican pioneer. Combining his duties as personal pilot to Mexico's President Cardenas with running a small airline, he was anxious that his country should share some of the glory that aviation had bestowed, mainly on the Europeans and the United States. He purchased Jacheline Cochran's Gee Bee racing aeroplane, *QED*, and on 24 May 1939, flew from Mexico City to New York, covering 2,350 miles and setting a new record of 10 hours 37 minutes. This achievement won him the title of 'Mexico's Lindbergh', and he was honoured in both New York and Washington, where he met President Franklin Roosevelt.

He started his homeward flight on 7 June, planning to fly directly to his mother's home at Lerdo in Mexico, and was seen off by his wife and a group of American dignitaries, but as the aircraft climbed through 100 ft, the engine failed. He attempted to glide down and ditch in the Potomac river but, without a shoulder harness, his face knocked into the instrument panel on impact and he lost consciousness; he drowned before he could be rescued. There were accusations of sabotage, but in reality an oily rag had been sucked into the carburettor air inlet. Students in Mexico rioted, in response to Sarabia's death believing that he had been killed deliberately.

Saulnier, Raymond (1881–?) French designer. Trained as an engineer at the Ecole Centrale in Paris, he went to work for **Louis Blériot** in 1908 and designed the Type XI, which was the aircraft in which Blériot flew across the English Channel and was subsequently licensed to other manufacturers. The **Morane** brothers invited him to join their new aircraft manufacturing venture in 1911, which became Morane-Saulnier and produced many outstanding scout aircraft during the First World War. He also worked on an interruptor device to allow machine guns to fire through the propeller arc but, although patented, this was not refined enough for practical use.

Saunders-Roe (SARO) British manufacturer. Formed when **Sir Alliot Verdon Roe** left Avro during the late 1920s and teamed up with the Saunders boat-building concern, jointly producing a series of flying boats and amphibians, starting with the twin-engined Cutty Sark of 1929. Much of its pre-war work was building floats for other manufacturers, but postwar it returned to aircraft production with the ten-engined Princess flying boat (which was cancelled because it was too big, although several examples were built and took to the air) and the world's only jet-powered flying boat fighter, the SR.A1 (also cancelled).

The company acquired **Cierva** and moved into helicopter production, developing the Skeeter in the 1950s which was intended for AOP work with the British Army. It developed a later helicopter that was eventually to enter production as the Westland Scout and Wasp. The company was chosen by the government-sponsored National Research and Development Corporation to build the first full-sized hovercraft, the SR.N1 of 1958, but in 1960 the company became part of **Westland** following the government-inspired mergers of the British aircraft industry.

Savoia-Marchetti Italian manufacturer. Originally an interwar manufacturer of seaplanes, postwar the company concentrated mainly on light aircraft, including basic trainers. One of its earliest designs won the 1919 **Schneider Trophy Race**. More notably it produced the S65, a twin-boom design with engines mounted fore and aft of the cockpit driving tractor and pusher propellers. It was entered for the 1929 Schneider Trophy. The SM55X flying boat, a twin-boom twin-hull design, made a number of record-breaking mass flights during the early 1930s, including a formation of twenty-three aircraft that flew from Rome to New York and Chicago in 1933.

During the Second World War the company produced the SM79 Sparviero (Hawk) trimotor bomber, regarded as the best Italian bomber of the war, and the SM95 transport, which remained in production after the war for the national airline Alitalia. Postwar, the mainstay of production was the SF260, a single-engined low-wing monoplane for training and for the private owner.

Schnauferr, Heinz-Wolfgang (1922–50) German ace. Leaving college to join the Luftwaffe in 1939, he became a night-fighter pilot and first saw operations in spring 1942, becoming known as the Night Ghost of St Trond (a base in Belgium). He normally flew a Messerschmitt Me110 equipped with upward firing machine guns, and achieved the very high success rate, on average, of scoring a kill on every three out of four sorties, so that by the end of the war he was the world's highest-scoring night-fighter ace with 121 confirmed victories.

He was killed in a motoring accident after the war when a lorry pulled out in front of his car. Although he was thrown clear, the lorry's load of oxygen bottles fell and crushed him.

Schneider, Jacques (1879–1928) French sponsor. Heir to an armaments empire, and trained as a mining engineer, he was more interested in motorboat racing and flying. He was taught to fly by **Louis Blériot** in 1909 and was convinced that the hydro-aeroplane showed the most potential for the advancement of the aeroplane. His own contribution to the pioneering days was limited to setting a French altitude record of more than 30,000 ft in 1913, ascending in his balloon *Icare*.

With an arm crippled in a high speed motor boating accident, and unable to fly gliders or aeroplanes, he decided that his contribution to aviation would be through sponsorship of an annual contest for hydro-aeroplanes. Some believe that he was influenced by seeing Jean Conneau, a naval officer, in a landplane setting down in Italy during the Paris–Turin–Rome race in 1911.

The first contest was tagged on to the end of a motorboat meeting at Monaco in 1913, but it was a great success with Maurice Prevost winning the trophy (which contrary to popular opinion was not a cup, but a silver figure sweeping down towards the waves) with a Deperdussin Monocoque floatplane. The following year it became an event in its own right and was won by a Sopwith Tabloid. One of the conditions of the contest was that the trophy could be won outright if won by one nation in three consecutive contests.

Schneider himself died in 1928, apparently in poverty.

Schneider Trophy Races (1913–31) Sometimes referred to, completely inaccurately, as the Schneider Cup, the correct title was the Jacques Schneider Air Racing Trophy for Hydro-Aeroplanes, and it was first competed for in April 1913 at Monaco. **Schneider** was motivated by a belief that the hydro-aeroplane held the key to the development of the aeroplane. The contest was announced at a banquet held on 5 December 1912 to celebrate that year's **Gordon Bennett** air race for landplanes. The contest was to be held annually between competing national teams selected by national aero clubs, and under the overall supervision of the **Fédération Aéronautique Internationale (FAI)**. The winning country each year would be responsible for hosting the contest the following year. Three victories by any country within five years would qualify for an outright award of the trophy.

The Trophy cannot be described as an object of beauty. It consists of a base of marble decorated with bronze, upon which a silver nude winged figure is depicted kissing a zephyr recumbent in the crest of a wave, which also contains two other zephyrs and the head of the sea god, Neptune, all

in silver. It is the possession of the Royal Aero Club of the United Kingdom.

The first Schneider Trophy contest was appended to the Monaco Hydro-Aeroplane Meeting which lasted from 3–17 April 1913. Bad weather meant that the meeting was not a great success, and the eliminating events to whittle down the French entry to the required three competitors were unnecessary as the weather damaged all but three of the aircraft beyond repair. There was only one competitor from outside France, the American Charles Weyman, who used a Nieuport, as did one of the French contestants. The course was 10-km long and had to be covered twenty-eight times, and the aircraft had to taxi on the water for the first half-lap of this Grand Prix course to prove that they were true hydro-aeroplanes. Maurice Prevost was first away in his Deperdussin Monocoque, followed by Roland Garros in a Morane-Saulnier monoplane, but Garros drowned his engine in spray and had to abandon the race. Espanet and Weyman followed in their Nieuport monoplanes but Espanet had to retire in the eighth lap due to engine trouble. Prevost was nearly disqualified as he misread the rules and taxied over the finishing line. He then wasted time in procrastination as defeat by the American seemed certain, but Weyman was forced to retire in the twenty-fifth lap with an oil leak and so Prevost took off again. He flew once again around the course and over the finishing line before landing. Even by the standards of the day Prevost's average speed had been low but this was due to the delay in arguing over the rules which cut it to 45 mph from the 61 mph that it might have been. Garros, too, had in fact managed to get back in the air and eventually finished second.

The Aéro-Club de France decided that the second contest would also be at Monaco, with the event being held on 18 April 1914. The event was amended with the taxi session replaced by two touchdowns. This time the French and American contestants were joined by British, German and Swiss. The Germans and Swiss were rejected by the French contingent as being too slow, and the British Sopwith Tabloid biplane was regarded with amusement because of its small size. Weyman was back, still with a Nieuport, while the favourite was Maurice Prevost who had improved his Deperdussin Monocoque by replacing the 160 hp engine with one of 200 hp, but it failed in the qualifying tests. Another American contestant, Charles Thaw, was so embarrassed by the condition of his Curtiss flying boat that he borrowed a Deperdussin Monocoque. The three French contestants went first, followed by Howard Pixton in the Tabloid, whose performance from the beginning was so good that Weyman and Garros decided that participation was pointless. In the end, the Tabloid won with an average speed of 86.78 mph, ending the race by landing in seas that had suddenly become rough as if to prove that this was no outlandish racing machine, but only after remaining in the air to set a new world air speed record for hydro-aeroplanes of 86.7 mph.

Within four months Europe was at war, and the contest was suspended until September 1919, when the host was the Royal Aero Club which chose Bournemouth as the venue. The event was recorded as being one of the worst organised. Not the least of the problems was that Bournemouth lacked suitable facilities and the competitors had to be based at Cowes, on the Isle of Wight, and fly to Bournemouth before starting. The course was 20 nautical miles, running from Bournemouth to Swanage, then to Christchurch and then back to Bournemouth. Aircraft had to alight twice during the first lap. The UK fielded a complete team for the first time, and the Italians made their first entry. The French sent just two competitors. On 10 September the race was postponed from 14.30 to 18.00 due to thick sea mist, but as visibility improved the start was advanced to 16.30 and then delayed again to 16.45 at which point the French, struggling to repair damage to the floats of their aircraft, withdrew. The mist returned, forcing two of the British competitors to abandon the contest, while the third, flying a Supermarine Sea Lion, landed in Swanage Bay for the pilot to check his bearings, but his aircraft sank as soon as it returned to Bournemouth. Sergeant Guido Janello, flying a Savoia S13 flying boat continued and seemed unaffected by the problems, but his final lap seemed too short, so he was sent around again to avoid any risk of disqualification. It was only then that it was discovered that he had been flying around the reserve marker boat in Studland Bay instead

of that at Swanage, so he was disqualified. Despite Italian protests the competition was declared null and void, but as a consolation the Italians were allowed to stage the 1920 event, choosing Venice as the venue.

There was no British team for the 1920 contest at Venice due to a shortage of funds and the absence of a suitable aircraft. The French were also unable to compete. Each aircraft was required to carry 300 kg of ballast as a result of Italian pressure, but this was dropped for 1921. Originally planning to fly three aircraft, two of the Italian aircraft dropped out leaving just one aircraft, a Savoia S12 flying boat flown by Lt Luigi Bologna of the Marine Militaire Italia, to fly ten laps of 37.2 km each on 20 September. Determined to finish the course, Bologna flew at a steady speed and his average worked out at an unspectacular 107.22 mph. This left Italy with a chance to win the trophy outright and, in 1921, no less than sixteen Italian aircraft were put forward at the start of the eliminating tests. The event remained at Venice but was brought forward to 11 August, with a course of sixteen laps of 24.6 km each, and alighting tests during the first lap. The Italian team eventually emerged as two Macchi M7 and a Macchi M19 flying boat. France entered **Sadi Lecointe** in a Nieuport-Delage seaplane. The seaplane's floats collapsed during the alighting test, while the M19 reached 141 mph on the first lap before catching fire and one of the M7s ran out of fuel on the last lap. Once again, just one aircraft finished: Giovanni de Briganti in his M7 with an average speed of 117.9 mph.

The 1922 event remained with Italy but was moved south to Naples and set for 12 August. On this occasion there were Italian, French and British contenders, although the latter was a solitary Supermarine Sea Lion II flying boat and, unlike the other competitors, was without government support. The French CAMS36 flying boats were eliminated during the preliminary tests. The Italians had three aircraft, a Macchi M7, an M17 and a Savoia S51, all flying boats. The S51 was damaged before the contest and, although able to take part, could not show off its full potential. From the start, the Sea Lion showed speed and exceptional manoeuvrability, allowing **Henri Biard** to fly the aircraft close to the pylons marking the course. All four aircraft completed the course, but the Sea Lion won with an average speed of 145.7 mph. Italian hopes of winning the trophy outright were ruined.

Over the post-First World War period, the contest had been ridiculed in some circles for the lack of real competition and the solitary finalists had also undermined the spirit of the original concept. This changed with the 1923 contest, which was held at Cowes. The contest was set for 28 September, with the alighting tests being held the previous day. This was the longest course yet at 37.2 nautical miles, although only five laps would be flown. The Italians could not take part for want of government support, and this left British, French and American entries. The British entry was once again a solitary aircraft, Henri Biard flying a Sea Lion III flying boat, but this was because the Blackburn Pellet failed the navigability tests. Once again, the French saw aircraft eliminated by the pre-contest trials but on this occasion did at least have the CAMS38 flying boat left to take part. The United States had two USN Curtiss CR-3 seaplanes, one of which won with Lt David Rittenhouse flying his CR-3 at an average speed of 177.38 mph. The other aircraft followed close behind with an average of 173.46 mph, leaving the Sea Lion III plodding along at 157.17 mph.

The Europeans failed to send a team to Baltimore for the 1924 event, but the British were last to withdraw and the National Aeronautical Association sportingly offered to cancel the contest rather than simply fly over the course as the Italians had done in 1920. The British Royal Aero Club accepted the offer.

The 1925 contest was also set for Baltimore with seven laps of 50 km each over Chesapeake Bay. A 6-hour mooring-out period was set to eliminate unsuitable aircraft. Scheduled for 24 October, the event was delayed until 27 October by bad weather. Three Curtiss R3C-2 biplane seaplanes were entered, with two flown by US Army officers and one by a USN officer. Italy entered two Macchi M33 flying boats and, for the UK, Henri Biard flew a Supermarine S4 cantilever monoplane seaplane; the other two team members had Gloster III biplane seaplanes. One Macchi was withdrawn because of engine

trouble, the S4 crashed during trials due to wing flutter and one of the Gloster IIIs was damaged while alighting during the navigability trials. A US Army officer, **Lt James 'Jimmy' Doolittle**, won with an average speed of 232.57 mph.

The UK could not send a team in 1926 for want of government support, but this time the event could not be cancelled as the Italians fielded a team. Recognising the mounting costs the FAI decided that after 1927 the contest would become biennial. The event was moved to Hampton Roads, Virginia, and once again the course was 50-km long with seven laps. With the strong support of the Italian dictator, Benito Mussolini, Italy sent three Macchi M39 monoplane seaplanes, while the Americans used three USN officers to fly three Curtiss biplanes, two of which were R3C-3s and one an R3C-4. One of the R3C-3s was damaged during the trials and replaced by a standard Curtiss Hawk. During the contest both teams lost aircraft due to damage, but Major Mario de Bernardi won with an average speed of 246.5 mph.

In 1927, for the first time, the British team had official support and had pilots and mechanics from the RAF's High Speed Flight. Moved to Venice, the course was once again seven laps of 50 km each. Official support for the US team was withdrawn, and a private-venture entry failed to complete the elimination tests. Italy had three Macchi M52 seaplanes, with the British having two Supermarine S5 monoplane seaplanes and a biplane Gloster IVB. Once again, bad weather delayed the start. On 26 September the contest got under way with all three Italian aircraft suffering technical failures, but the two S5s finished the race with Flt Lt S.N. Webster winning, flying an average speed of 281.65 mph.

For 1929 the venue was Calshot, at the mouth of Southampton Water and an RAF flying boat base, but the start and finishing lines were placed at Ryde on the Isle of Wight. This was again a course of seven laps of 50 km each, but the mooring-out tests were augmented by taxiing trials. This was another government-sponsored two-nation event with the US contender not finishing the eliminating tests due to engine problems. The British had intended to enter three aircraft but the failure of the Gloster VI monoplane meant that just two Supermarine S6s formed the team.

The Italians had also suffered problems in finding a suitable type and entered two Macchi M67s and a Macchi M52R.

The contest started on 7 September but both M67s suffered engine failure leaving Flg Off H.R. Waghorn to win with an average speed of 328.63 mph, flying an extra lap by mistake and then running out of fuel.

The 1931 contest was an anti-climax. The Italians could not compete because of persistent troubles with the Macchi-Castoldi MC72. Instead of cancelling the event, the British took advantage and, using the 1929 course, on 13 September Flt Lt J.N. Boothman flew a Supermarine S6B to win the trophy outright for the UK at an average speed of 340.08 mph. Later that day, Flt Lt G.H. Stainforth took the S6B to a world speed record of 379 mph.

Ironically, the British had nearly failed to compete as the government had withdrawn their support. Only the generosity of Lady Houston, widow of a shipping magnate, with a patronage of £100,000 (worth about £6.1 million today) enabled the event to go ahead, while the RAF was allowed once again to provide the personnel.
See Table 21: Schneider Trophy Races 1913–31.

Schwartz, David (1845–97) Austro-Hungarian airship pioneer. Despite his nationality most of his work was in Germany where he built two all-metal airships during the 1890s. His first airship was structurally weak, while the second was based on the shape of an artillery shell, although its cross section was ovoid rather than round and was covered in sheet aluminium. The 12 hp Daimler engine was expected to drive three airscrews. Schwarz died in 1897 but his wife took control of the project, with the craft ready for its first ascent on 3 November of that year before a crowd of spectators among whom was **Count von Zeppelin**.

Not surprisingly, no one was present with any experience of flying an airship, and in the absence of the inventor, who would have been the logical choice, a volunteer was sought from among the spectators. There is no definitive record of the identity of the volunteer, who has been variously named as Jaegels or Platz, and whose occupation has also been given as soldier or engineer, or one of the mechanics who had helped build the airship. He got the airship into the air, moving slowly, but

soon lost control. Completely at a loss over what to do, he released too much hydrogen and the airship dropped like a stone, wrecking itself on the ground. The fortunate pilot was able to jump clear at the last minute.

Scott, Charles W.A. (1903–46) British airshow pilot. A former RAF pilot who had found peacetime flying boring, Scott went to Australia in 1927 to fly for the Queensland & Northern Territory Aerial Service, predecessor of today's airline Qantas. Obscurity did not suit him so he began to make record-breaking flights winning the England to Australia record in 1931 and, before the year was out, breaking the Australia to England record. Even greater fame followed in 1934 when he was one of the two pilots in the de Havilland DH-88 Comet racer that won the MacRobertson Trophy. He then went into the airshow circuit in the UK, later purchasing and operating the flying circus founded by Sir Alan Cobham. He is believed to have rejoined the RAF during the Second World War.

Postwar, he faded back into obscurity until he committed suicide in 1946 while in Germany.

Scott, Maj George Herbert (1888–1930) British airship pioneer. Commissioned into the Royal Navy as an engineer, in 1914 he transferred to the newly formed RNAS and was trained as an airship commander. His first dirigible was the semi-rigid Parseval P-4 and, in 1917, he was given command of the R-9, a rigid airship.

Postwar, as a member of the new RAF, in July 1919 he took the R-34 from Scotland to New York and back, despite having to cope with fierce storms and high winds, and deal with a stowaway. In 1930, as a civilian pilot, he commanded the private enterprise R-100 on a further transatlantic voyage, this time to Canada and back, before being asked to command the government-sponsored R-101 on its journey to India. He was among those killed when it crashed in October 1930.

Scott, Robert Lee (1908–2006) American ace. After enlisting with the US Army, he was eventually sent to West Point and graduated with a commission in the USAAC in 1933. His duties included flying the airmail services that were at one time entrusted to the corps, and afterwards he became a flying instructor. He left the USAAC to join the American Volunteer Group and became a member of the famous Flying Tigers, flying in China before US entry into the Second World War. He accounted for thirteen Japanese aircraft and wrote a wartime book, *God is my Co-pilot*, about his adventures before his unit was absorbed into the USAAF.

Postwar, he remained with what had become the USAF and was in command of a fighter wing in West Germany during the Korean War.

Scott, Sheila (1927–88) British aviatrix. An actress who qualified as a pilot in 1959, initially flying and racing Tiger Moths. It was in a more modern aeroplane, a Piper Commanche, that she made the round-the-world flight which made her famous in 1966. Leaving London Heathrow Airport on 18 May, she returned on 20 June having set a record for the longest solo flight in a single-engined aeroplane of 28,656 miles. She later set records for solo flights from London to Cape Town, and for the same flight in the return direction. In 1971 she made a second round-the-world solo flight, but on this occasion flying over the North Pole. She claimed to have extra-sensory perception (ESP) experiences, and credited one of these with saving her life during this trip: when her aircraft radio failed, she could not receive the message from an American tracking station that would tell her when to turn so as not to miss a refuelling stop – a voice inside her head told her when to turn and she did so, arriving safely to refuel.

Scottish Aviation British manufacturer. An overhaul and refurbishment business that entered aircraft manufacture during the 1950s with the Pioneer and Twin Pioneer STOL transports for the RAF, before moving on to sub-contract work on the Lockheed C-130K Hercules and the then Handley Page Jetstream. It acquired the jigs and production rights for the Beagle Bulldog after the manufacturer's bankruptcy, and then for the Jetstream after Handley Page collapsed. It then became part of **British Aerospace**.

search and rescue (SAR) Originally known as air-sea rescue, the aeroplane soon showed that it

had potential in this field, for even at low altitude the horizon is extended and this, combined with speed, means that a larger area can be searched more thoroughly than by surface vessels. Search is only one part of the role, as the aim has always been to produce aircraft that could provide the rescue function as well, although in many cases the ability to drop inflatable life-rafts has also been a help. Suitable flying boats have been available for SAR since the 1920s.

While many of the flying boats and amphibians used were also engaged in maritime reconnaissance, some aircraft became synonymous with SAR, including the Supermarine Walrus and Sea Otter which served in the Second World War, and the Grumman Albatross. In the UK, SAR in coastal waters was ultimately under the control of RAF Fighter Command, while in the open seas it was part of the duties of Coastal Command. In the United States, this was, and remains, a United States Coast Guard function, although the USAF's Military Airlift Command includes a strong SAR element.

The helicopter, with its ability to hover, was soon engaged in SAR duties, from the Sikorsky S-51 onwards. In many cases, specific SAR helicopter units are operated rather than relying on other operational units to deploy aircraft. The usual practice is for a member of the crew to be winched down to pick up survivors and in some cases, as in the Royal Navy, such personnel are also qualified frogmen with the ability to dive under upturned boats. Other methods tried, albeit with limited success, have been nets such as the Sproule net. One problem is that survivors are often too weak, or suffering from sea sickness or hypothermia, to be able to help themselves.

Modern SAR techniques are helped by such matters as lights fitted to lifejackets or life-rafts, or by homing beacons. By contrast, during the Second World War the need for camouflage meant that often life-rafts, including the Carley floats carried on the sides of warship superstructures, were difficult to spot even at close range.

A more modern concept, pioneered during the Vietnam War, is combat rescue, which involves helicopters, accompanied by aircraft which may include attack helicopters, lifting downed aircrew from enemy-controlled territory. The most ambitious operation of this type occurred shortly after the Islamic Revolution in Iran when US personnel were held hostage. The attempt failed, however, due to equipment malfunctions and poor technical preparation.

Ideally, a SAR force needs three distinct sizes of helicopter starting with a small type such as the MD Explorer or the EC-145, which can lift people off rooftops or from mountain sides with relatively small rotor disc space requirements and limited downwash. At the other extreme a large helicopter is beneficial, such as the Sikorsky Super Sea Stallion, because of its long range and ability to take the entire crew of a merchant vessel in one lift. In between come helicopters such as the Sikorsky Sea King and the Agusta-Westland Merlin, and most SAR operations are equipped with such machines for all duties as a cost-effective compromise.

Seeckt, Hans von (1866–1936)

German military leader. Field Marshal Mackensen's chief of staff during the First World War, postwar he was ordered to reduce the German Army to the limit of 100,000 men as stated in the **Treaty of Versailles**. He kept this obligation but, in order to avoid further disadvantages, i.e. that of Germany not having a military air service, he secretly kept a cadre of pilots. When Hitler came to power **Milch** inherited the core of the future Luftwaffe enabling Germany to rapidly develop an air force.

Seguin, Laurent (1883–1944) and Louis (1869–1918)

French engineers. In 1895 Louis Seguin established a company manufacturing motor car engines, but it was not until 1905 that he was joined by his half-brother Laurent. The company was re-formed as the Société des Moteurs Gnome and continued to serve the motor industry. Just two years later, realising the demand for a reliable but lightweight aeroplane engine, they decided that aviation offered an opportunity and built a **rotary engine** prototype with just five cylinders, followed by a seven-cylinder engine that weighed just 165 lb but produced 50 hp.

Rotary engines, today confused with the Wankel cycle, at the time were engines in which the cylinders revolved around the crankcase, rather than being fixed and driving a rotating crankcase. Known simply as the Gnome, their engine was manufactured under licence in many countries to meet the immense demand during the First World War when most aircraft engines were of rotary configuration.

Postwar, as aircraft engine power increased, the centrifugal force of ever-larger cylinders whirling around the crankcase became a serious limitation and the radial and in-line engines became the power unit of the day.

Selfridge, Lt Thomas E. (1882–1908)

American pioneer. Selfridge was commissioned into the United States Army. In 1907 he met **Alexander Graham Bell** in Washington, and after learning of his interest in aviation, Bell invited him to join the **Aerial Experimental Association (AEA)** and even arranged for President Theodore Roosevelt to have Selfridge seconded as his assistant. At the AEA, Selfridge oversaw the construction of the group's first aircraft, the *Red Wing*, which made the first publicly observed flight in the United States on 12 March 1908, flown by **Casey Baldwin**. Oddly, Selfridge never flew this aircraft, and his own first flight did not come until 19 May, in the second AEA aircraft, the *White Wing*.

Later that year he was recalled from the AEA to serve as a member of the Aeronautical Board, which the Signal Corps had formed to perform trials on a number of flying-machines, including a dirigible from Baldwin-Curtiss and a military aeroplane offered by the **Wright** brothers. His AEA connection, and therefore a **Curtiss** connection, meant that his early dealings with the Wright brothers proved difficult, especially with Orville who found that while Selfridge knew much about aviation he was always seeking more. Nevertheless, Orville had to accede to Selfridge's request for a flight in the Wright machine, and on 17 September 1908 the two men took off, but once in the air one of the propellers on the aircraft shattered, sending it into a dive with Selfridge striking his head on a strut as it crashed. Rescuers found him lying in the wreckage bleeding profusely from the head and he later died.

He was the first man to be killed in an aeroplane crash.

sesquiplane A biplane with the lower wing-span less than that of the upper.

Seversky American manufacturer. Founded by émigré-Russian Alexander de Seversky fleeing the Bolshevik Revolution, the company built a number of monoplane designs between the wars including the three-seat SEV-3MWW floatplane amphibian and the USAAC's P-35 fighter. The company was taken over by **Republic Aviation**.

Seversky, Alexander Prokofieff de (1894–1974) Russo-American designer and manufacturer. The son of the first Russian to privately own and fly an aeroplane, de Seversky was sent to the naval academy. He was commissioned into the Imperial Russian Navy at the age of 20 and went to sea. In 1915 he transferred to the Imperial Naval Air Service, was trained as a pilot and after qualifying was posted to a bomber squadron. While bombing German ships in the Gulf of Riga, his plane was shot down and the bomb it was carrying exploded as it ditched in the sea, blowing off one of de Seversky's legs. After his recovery he became an aircraft inspector, but once he had been fitted with an artificial leg he pressed to be returned to combat and was posted to a fighter squadron in summer 1916. By summer 1917 he was an ace with a tally of thirteen enemy aircraft.

By chance during summer 1917 he was posted to the USA as a member of the Russian Naval Air Mission, and when the Bolshevik Revolution started and his country began armistice negotiations with Germany, he offered his services to his host country. He became an adviser to **Billy Mitchell** for the infamous bombing trials of 1921, and the following year went into business starting a company that produced the first automatic bomb sight, which he sold to the American government for US $50,000 (worth about £250,000 at today's values). In 1931 he founded the aircraft manufacturing business that bore his name, specialising in military aircraft of which the most important was the P-35, predecessor to the P-47 Thunderbolt, produced by the company after the name was changed to **Republic Aviation** in 1939.

He was an adviser to the US government and in 1942 published his book *Victory Through Air Power*, arguing that aviation could win the war.

Shin Meiwa Japanese manufacturer. It produced the PS-1 maritime-reconnaissance flying boat for the JMSDF, which remains in service today.

Short, Horace Leonard (1872–1918), Albert Eustace (1875–1932) and Hugh Oswald (1883–69) British manufacturers. The two younger brothers bought a second-hand balloon in 1897 and taught themselves how to pilot it. They went to France in 1900 and learnt balloon production from Edouard Surcouf at his Paris works, and on their return became balloon manufacturers, winning a contract to supply the British Army in 1904 while also producing balloons for civilian owners, including Henry Moore-Brabazon (*see* **Lord Brabazon of Tara**) and **Charles Rolls**. Their elder brother Horace joined them in 1908 and they diversified into aircraft manufacture, becoming the first British company to do so. Once again, Rolls was an early customer, as was Frank McClean. In 1909 Horace obtained a licence from **Wilbur Wright** to build their designs, and after building six, were able to design aircraft of their own, with Biplane No. 2, built for Moore-Brabazon, their own first successful design.

In 1913 they built a seaplane, the Short Folder biplane, which was not only successful in its own right, but had the novel feature of folding wings so that it could be stored aboard ships. Other hydro-aeroplanes were built by the company during the war years, and postwar it became firmly established as a flying boat builder, most famously with its Empire flying boat for Imperial Airways, of which twenty-six were ordered off the drawing board in an unprecedented display of confidence, and which were used for the Empire Air Mail Scheme, for trials in transatlantic air services and inflight refuelling. The Short Mayo composite aircraft, which was a flying boat launching a four-engined seaplane in mid-air, established a world distance flying non-stop record between Scotland and South Africa. During the Second World War, the Sunderland maritime-reconnaissance flying boat was one of the few early in the war with an adequate range and their Stirling landplane bomber was the first of the RAF's heavy bombers.

Shorts British manufacturer. Formed before the First World War by the **Short** brothers (see above), the company was known as Short Brothers for many years until it moved production from Kent to Belfast during the Second World War. The company initially was a licensee of the **Wright** brothers while its Triple Twin of 1911 was the first twin-engined aircraft to fly and had three propellers, but after these were reduced to two it was renamed the Tandem Twin. The Short S27 was the first to fly from British warships and the Short Type 38 was the first to be both radio-equipped and fitted with a machine gun in pre-First World War experiments by the RFC. During the war, the 184 and 225 float-biplanes were used for naval reconnaissance. Postwar, the Silver Streak was the first to have a stretched skin, all-metal monocoque construction, and the Short version of the Seaplane Experimental Station's F5 flying boat was the first to have a metal hull.

Between the wars the company produced a number of light aircraft, but its main preoccupation was the design and production of large flying boats for both civil and military users. These included the Calcutta for Imperial Airways and the Rangoon for the RAF, the Scipio four-engined flying boat and its landplane development, the Scylla, and the Empire flying boats for the Empire Air Mail service, used by both Imperial Airways and Qantas. Unusual aircraft included the Short Mayo composite aircraft in which a flying boat launched a four-engined seaplane in mid-air and which set a world distance record of more than 6,000 miles flying from Dundee to South Africa.

During the Second World War, the Sunderland flying boat was the first to offer the long range needed by the RAF for long-range maritime-reconnaissance, and the company produced Britain's first heavy bomber, the Stirling. Following the war, a stretched version of the Sunderland, the Shetland, was cancelled although BOAC bought a new commercial flying boat, the Solent. The company also produced a landplane, the Sturgeon, as a target tug for the Fleet Air Arm. There was also the Sealand amphibian which was produced in small numbers.

The company also built Bristol Britannia transports for the RAF, and from this aircraft developed the Belfast, a large heavy lifter, and conducted experiments with a VTOL jet-fighter, the SC-1. A move was made into guided weapons production with the highly successful Blowpipe man-portable, Seacat shipboard and Tigercat surface-to-air guided missiles. Engine pods were also built for aircraft such as the Lockheed TriStar.

The most successful aircraft venture post-Second World War was a series of utility aircraft and lightweight regional airliners, starting with the Short Skyvan, which first flew in 1963 and was a high-wing twin-turboprop monoplane with room for up to eighteen passengers, followed by the larger 330 and 360 with retractable undercarriages. The former was used by the US Army as the Sherpa. Nationalised for many years, the company was bought by **Bombardier** and now builds aerostructures for the new parent company's regional and executive aircraft.

shuttle services Pioneered by Eastern Air Lines in the United States, which introduced services linking New York, Boston and Washington, a shuttle service offers passengers a flight without the need to pre-book or confirm a reservation, and with a guaranteed walk-on seat. This requires back-up aircraft to be available at very short notice if there are too many passengers for the scheduled departure. The service on the eastern seaboard of the United States at one time enjoyed competition and the operators have changed frequently, but it is now branded as Shuttle America. British Airways introduced a similar service between London, Belfast, Glasgow and Edinburgh, later adding Manchester to the shuttle network, but this has now been abandoned. There have also been shuttles between Toronto and Montreal in Canada. The early shuttle operations even had passengers buying tickets on the aircraft, but on some routes, including the UK, this was abandoned in favour of conventional catering.

The problems with shuttle operation are partly operational, as keeping a spare aircraft at both ends of the route is of little benefit if take-off and landing slots are in short supply. They are also economic, as keeping aircraft and crew waiting, possibly not being needed, is costly. This is why the concept has seen limited application, and plans for international shuttles between London and Paris never came to fruition.

Siegert, Wilhelm (1872–1929) German bomber pioneer. After learning to fly in 1910, he joined the

Military Air Service and on the outbreak of the First World War was posted to a bomber unit, although the aircraft could only carry small bombs. On 24 December 1914 he led a force of thirty Aviatiks to bomb the English Channel port of Dover, inflicting little damage. Given the limitations of the aircraft, plans for raids on London were postponed until later in the war. Siegert ended the war as an inspector of fighter pilots.

Sigrist, Frederick (1880–1956) Engineer and manager. Starting as an engineer aboard **Thomas Sopwith**'s yacht in 1909, his responsibilities extended to his employer's aircraft when Sopwith started to buy aeroplanes. When Sopwith started to build aircraft, Sigrist became the workshop manager and started to exhibit a flair for design. He became an expert at construction and reputedly received a commission for every fuselage sold. He became the company's manager during the First World War and remained with the business when it was reformed as **Hawker** after the war. He eventually retired as a millionaire to Bermuda.

Sikorsky American manufacturer. Formed in 1923 as the Sikorsky Aero Engineering Corporation by **Igor Sikorsky**, the company initially specialised in flying boats and amphibians, including the five-seat S-39 of 1931 and the VS-44. The much larger S-41 four-engined flying boat of 1934 and the S-43 twin-engined amphibian were both used by Pan American. The company started its connection with United Aircraft in 1929.

Despite the success of the flying boats, the real claim to fame came with the development and production of the first operational helicopters, following the work of Igor Sikorsky with the single-rotor VS-300 in 1939. The result was the R-4, which undertook trials with the US and British armed forces, and prepared the way for the first production machine, the R-5 or Sikorsky S-51, also known as the Dragonfly. Many of the helicopter designs were built under licence abroad, notably by **Westland** in the UK. Successors to the S-51 have included the S-55 and S-58, the turbine S-61, also known as the Sea King, the S-62, S-64 and the large S-65, also known as the Sea Stallion, including a three-engined development as the Super Sea Stallion.

More recent machines have included the S-71 and S-76, the latter a smaller helicopter that can also be used for business owners.

Sikorsky, Igor Ivanovitch (1889–1972) Russian-American pioneer. Learning from his university-educated mother about **da Vinci**'s designs inspired Sikorsky to take an interest in aviation. He met many of the pioneers on a visit to Paris in 1908. On returning home he built two helicopters, neither of which were successful, before turning to fixed-wing aircraft, but again it was not until his fifth aircraft that he had a machine capable of sustained flight. His sixth aircraft, the S-6, appeared in 1912 and won a substantial money prize at a military competition.

He then moved to the Russo-Baltic Railway Wagon Company, where he designed and built the first four-engined aircraft, the *Bolshoi*, or 'Grand'. The aircraft first flew on 13 May 1913 and was a revelation as in addition to four 100 hp Anzani engines it was the first to have a fully glazed cabin, and the interior fittings included a sofa, armchairs and a table. It even had a cabin for the pilot and co-pilot, more than twenty years before such features became commonplace. An even larger aircraft followed the next year, the *Ilya Mourametz*, or 'Giant', which was a development of the *Bolshoi* and made its first flight on 14 January 1914, while on 11 February it carried no less than sixteen passengers on an 18-minute flight at an altitude of 1,000 ft. The aircraft still had four 100 hp engines, although manufactured by Mercedes, and undertook a number of long-distance flights, including one from St Petersburg to Tsarkoie Selo and back. One commentator was moved to describe the aircraft as a giant 'airbus'. That summer the *Ilya Mourametz* flew from St Petersburg to Kiev and back again, a distance of 1,600 miles, although it made several stops en route. There are claims that on this flight the first meals were served in the air. The aircraft's debut as an airliner was abandoned on the outbreak of the First World War but more than eighty were built during the conflict as bombers for the Imperial Russian Flying Corps.

In November 1917 the Bolshevik Revolution forced Sikorsky to flee to Paris, and in 1918 he went to the USA, arriving with less than

US $100 to his name. In 1922, with the help of other Russian émigrés, he founded the eponymous aircraft manufacturer, which soon established a reputation for a series of flying boats and amphibians that made it one of the leaders in this field during the 1920s and 1930s.

Today, Sikorsky's real fame rests on the invention of the practical single-rotor helicopter with the first being his VS-300, first flown in 1939. While the Second World War raged, work on the development of the helicopter continued with the USCG and the Royal Navy's Fleet Air Arm operating a joint development unit. Postwar, it was a Sikorsky S-55 helicopter that operated the first scheduled helicopter services, although even today such services are still few and far between due to the high cost of helicopter operations.

simulator Modern pilots receive extensive training in simulators which save expensive fuel and costly flying hours, and the most modern of which display considerable realism in both the manoeuvres that can be conducted and in their visual display. Much safer to crash than the real thing. While actual flying cannot be dispensed with altogether, this does reduce costs and is especially good for routine checks of competency.

The concept evolved between the wars with the invention of the **Link** trainer, named after its inventor. The early versions were simple and basic, looking like children's playthings with students learning little more than the movement of the controls and radio communication, often sitting in a room alongside others similarly engaged.

Skalski, Stanislaw (1915–2004) Polish ace. The Polish Air Force in 1939 operated antiquated equipment for the most part, and most of its aircraft were intended to provide reconnaissance for ground forces. Skalski was a fighter pilot with an obsolete PZL P11 fighter, but even so, he accounted for six German aircraft when Poland was invaded in September. He then fled to England where he joined the RAF, flying with No. 501 Squadron during summer 1940, and later with No. 303 (Polish) Squadron. He saw action in the main theatres of war in Europe and in North Africa, and ended the war with a confirmed total of 22½ confirmed kills, the highest of any

Polish pilot. He returned to Poland postwar but was imprisoned for protesting about the Soviet occupation of his country.

Slessor, MRAF Sir John (1897–1979) British air commander and strategist. When the Second World War broke out in Europe in September 1939, Slessor was in charge of planning at the Air Ministry. In April 1941 he was given the operational appointment of commanding No. 5 Group, Bomber Command, but in April 1942 he became Assistant Chief of Air Staff (Policy), and the following February he succeeded **Joubert** as Commander-in-Chief, Coastal Command. From March 1943 he began to receive the long-range aircraft he needed and by May the Atlantic gap had been closed. His aircraft accounted for an average of seven U-boats a month.

Slessor was knighted in 1943. He became commander-in-chief of all RAF units in the Mediterranean and the Middle East in January 1944, as well as being **Gen Eaker**'s deputy in those areas. He was also responsible for the creation of the Balkan Air Force in June 1944. Later, he returned to the Air Ministry and at the end of the war was the air member for personnel.

Slingsby British manufacturer. Originally a glider manufacturer, Slingsby now produces a basic trainer, the T67M260 Firefly, used by a number of air forces as a trainer and screening aircraft.

Smith, Gp Capt Irving Stanley (1917–2000) New Zealand bomber leader. Born at Invercargill, New Zealand, he started work as a coach painter, but when war broke out he received a short service commission in the RNZAF and volunteered to train in the UK. On completing his flying training he was posted to No. 151 Squadron flying Hawker Hurricanes. On 15 August 1940 he flew three sorties, shooting down two Messerschmitt Bf109s and damaging a third. He scored a total of six kills in the Battle of Britain before his squadron was withdrawn and rested, by which time he was one of only four survivors from the original squadron. His squadron was partially equipped with Boulton Paul Defiants to become a night-fighter squadron. In March 1941 he was awarded the DFC, and despite the limitations of the Defiant, on 10 May he shot down a Heinkel He111. He became the squadron commander in February 1942, and in April the squadron was re-equipped with the de Havilland Mosquito, with Smith destroying two enemy aircraft during the night of 24 June. By this time a wing commander, he was awarded a Bar to his DFC in July 1942.

In March 1943, he was posted to Fighter Command HQ, but requested a return to operations. His first move was overruled and it was not until February 1944 that he took command of No. 487 Squadron, a Mosquito bomber squadron. On 18 February he led a raid of eighteen aircraft on Operation Jericho, tasked with breaching the walls of Amiens gaol to release the French resistance members held prisoner there. Despite flying through a blizzard, he succeeded in blowing holes in the walls while aircraft behind him had to blow off the ends of the cell block walls and force the cell doors off their hinges with the blast. There were heavy casualties inside the prison, but 258 prisoners escaped. He later led a raid on a barracks at Potiers, and then destroyed the SS headquarters at Vincey.

He became chief instructor on the Mosquito at High Ercall, Shropshire, and was granted a permanent commission. Postwar, he remained in the RAF serving in Malta and later commanded No. 50 Squadron flying Gloster Meteor jet fighters. Promoted to group captain, he commanded RAF Jever in Germany, later returning to staff duties before being invalided out of the service in 1966 and taking up farming in Norfolk.

Smith, Sir Ross MacPherson (1892–1922)

Australian ace and long-distance pilot. On the outbreak of the First World War he joined the Australian cavalry and saw action in Gallipoli, before transferring to the Australian Flying Corps in 1916. He became an ace, shooting down nine German and Turkish aircraft, and is reputed to have flown Lawrence of Arabia on secret missions, and on another occasion landed behind enemy lines and rescued a downed fellow pilot. He was wounded in aerial combat, and despite having a grazed cheek and skull, and bleeding heavily, he still managed to return safely to base.

Postwar, he achieved fame through his record-breaking flights. Between 12 November and 10 December 1919 he flew with his brother Keith and two others in a Vickers Vimy bomber on the first flight from England to Australia, taking twenty-eight days for the 11,300 miles. He would doubtless have gone on to greater glory but for the fact that he was killed on 13 April 1922 when the Vickers Viking he was testing crashed.

SNECMA

French manufacturer. Now part of the **SAFRAN** group, SNECMA (Société National d'Etude et de Construction de Moteurs d'Aviation) is the main French aero-engine manufacturer and was formed in 1945 from the amalgamation of smaller aero-engine manufacturers, including Gnome et Rhone, which played a major part in rotary engine development, and the aero-engine division of Renault. Later, it acquired Bugatti and Hispano-Suiza.

SNECMA collaborated with **Rolls-Royce** on the engines for the Concorde supersonic airliner and built Rolls-Royce Tyne turboprops under licence for both the C-160 Transall transport and Breguet Atlantique maritime-reconnaissance aircraft, both Franco-German. It also built **Pratt & Whitney** engines under licence for the Sud Aviation Caravelle airliner and **General Electric** (GE) engines for the original Airbus A300B.

Its major project at present is **CFM**, a joint venture with GE which builds the engines for the Boeing 737 family (excepting the -100 and -200) and the A340, and which are an option on the Airbus A320 narrow-body range.

Sommer, Roger (1877–1965)

French pioneer and manufacturer. He became interested in aviation during the early years of the twentieth century, and in 1908 built an aeroplane that failed to fly. He next purchased an aeroplane from **Henri Farman** in 1909 and taught himself to fly. He became an exhibition pilot while also setting a number of records, usually short-lived, and when he took Gertrude Bacon up as a passenger in 1909, she became the first English woman to fly in an aeroplane. That same year he set up his aircraft factory and started to build a series of successful aircraft, as well as establishing a flying school at Douzy.

The Sopwith Triplane, or 'Trike', was a successful early fighter, despite the drag, although this could have provided the essential manoeuvrability.

Sopwith, Sir Thomas Octave Murdoch (1888–1989) British pioneer and manufacturer. Trained as a civil engineer, he came into contact with **Charles Rolls** at university and became interested in ballooning and motoring. He purchased a Howard Wright monoplane in 1910 and attempted to teach himself to fly, on one occasion crashing without injury. When he finally did learn to fly, he became an exhibition pilot and also started racing. In December 1910 he won a race with a long-distance flight from Eastchurch, on the Isle of Sheppey, to Thirlmount in Belgium. In 1911 he toured the United States winning a number of prizes, and in 1912 began aircraft manufacture.

He already employed an engineer, **Frederick Sigrist**, who had looked after his yacht and his aircraft, and who became his factory manager, while **Harry Hawker** became his test pilot. The company built the Sopwith Tabloid that won the **Schneider Trophy Race** in 1914 and became one of the scout aircraft of the First World War, during which a succession of the company's aircraft were used by the RNAS including the Camel, Triplane or 'Trike', and the Snipe. During the postwar slump in demand, the company went into voluntary bankruptcy, was reorganised and emerged as Hawker. Sopwith remained chairman of Hawker until 1963, and lived to be the first aviation centenarian.

Sopwith Camel Appearing in 1916, the Camel biplane was one of the most successful fighters of the war operating over the Western Front and at sea, where in trials it was launched from a lighter

towed by a destroyer. Powerplants varied, including the 110 hp Rhone to engines of 230 hp.

sound barrier The speed of sound is 760 mph at sea level decreasing to 660 mph in the stratosphere, but regardless of the actual height or speed, the speed of sound is always expressed as Mach 1.0.

Breaking the sound barrier was the target for the postwar generation of air speed record setters. The first aircraft through the sound barrier was the Bell XS-1 in October 1947, launched from a Boeing B-29 Superfortress bomber while flying at altitude, which meant that the aircraft was ineligible for the official world air speed record. The first aircraft to take off under its own power and break the sound barrier was the de Havilland DH-108 Swallow, a tailless research aircraft which broke the sound barrier on 6 September 1948. The aircraft itself suffered from many problems and did not lead to a production machine.

Soviet Union, German invasion of, (1941) Germany invaded the Soviet Union on 22 June 1941, starting at 0315 hours, attacking along a line drawn from the Baltic in the north to the Carpathian mountains in the south. The attack was not unexpected, and Stalin had ordered that all units were to be decentralised and camouflaged, but this message was received too late for the various headquarters to pass it on to all units in time. The USSR had some 18,000 aircraft, although only a fifth of these could be regarded as modern, and many of the pilots were still undergoing training. Half of the aircraft were deployed in the West. Against this figure of around 9,000 Soviet aircraft, the Luftwaffe had 1,945 aircraft, with 1,400 immediately ready for combat, including 510 bombers, 290 dive-bombers, 440 fighters, 40 fighter-destroyers (fighter-bombers) and 120 long-range reconnaissance aircraft. This force was in three air fleets: Luftflotte 1 under Gen Keller was assigned to Army Group North; Luftflotte 2 under FM Kesselring was assigned to Army Group Central; and Luftflotte 4 under Gen Lohr was assigned to Army Group South. The total Luftwaffe strength was augmented by that of Germany's allies, giving another 1,000 aircraft. Romania sent 423 aircraft while Finland, still recovering from its war with the Soviet

Union, sent 317, although only 41 of these were bombers. The Regia Aeronautica (Italian Air Force) sent 100 aircraft to operate in the southern zone, operating as the Comando Aviazione (the air command of the Italian Expeditionary Force) but these did not arrive until late July. Luftflotte 4 also had the Hungarian Express Corps with a fighter and a bomber squadron, as well as some reconnaissance units, and the Croatian Air Legion, with a fighter group and a bomber group, another fifty or sixty aircraft.

The Luftwaffe caught most of the Soviet airfields by surprise and a second wave was launched as the main attack, with 637 bombers and 231 fighters attacking thirty-one Soviet airfields. Later in the morning, 400 bombers attacked thirty-five Soviet airfields. Altogether, these sixty-six airfields accounted for 70 per cent of the Red Air Force's strength in the West. One Red Air Force officer, Lt Gen Kopets, lost 600 aircraft without making any impact on the Germans, and committed suicide on 23 June.

In the first few months of the air campaign in support of Operation Barbarossa, the Luftwaffe came across large marching columns of Russian troops and substantial troop concentrations, with the ground on either side of the roads baked hard in the summer heat, also being used as a roadway, so that often the roads were as much as 100 yd wide. Yet, because of a shortage of the right type of bombs, the Luftwaffe was unable to press home all of the advantages granted to it by aerial supremacy. There is little doubt that the inability to disrupt these troop concentrations was a contributory factor at Moscow and Stalingrad.

The failure to take Moscow and Leningrad before the onset of the Russian winter put the invaders in a difficult position: unprepared for the severity of the weather and with supply lines overstretched. During the winter of 1941/2, the temperatures in the theatre stayed between −30 and −50°C for periods of several weeks, relieved only by those occasions when temperatures plunged to −70°C. Problems were at their most serious when aircraft were on the ground, being prepared for operations, with extensive icing of wings and tailplanes. Even canvas covers used to protect smaller aircraft froze and became impossible to handle. An attempt to prevent ice forming using water-repellent oils failed due to the shortage of lubricant supplies. The cold also affected engines when they were started up, needing a lubricant diluted with gasoline added to the engine while starting. It took some 20 minutes of flying time for the gasoline additive to evaporate and for the engine to run at normal oil temperature. To improve matters, sometimes fires were started under aircraft and start-up equipment. Propellers sometimes iced up during flight, and on occasion crews were injured and aircraft damaged by flying chunks of dislodged ice. In the air, aircraft guns would not work, usually because the oil lacked resistance to the cold, while electrically guided weapons suffered from the effects of condensation. Given a depth of snow of 3 ft or more, short-fused bombs, whether high explosive or fragmentation, were much less effective as the snow muffled the effects of the explosion. It was also noted that up to 75 per cent of the detonators on fragmentation bombs failed to work in deep snow, although they remained active and acted as land mines. Frozen hard ground would simply shatter high-explosive bombs without them exploding.

The Germans used one or two-piece sheepskin flying suits, which proved to be cumbersome if the wearer had to walk any distance, such as after an emergency landing. Thermal suits, apparently, were worse, requiring attention in regulating temperatures, while they were so fragile that they could be damaged in an emergency landing, after which, of course, they provided the wearer with little protection against the cold.

Between the start of Operation Barbarossa and mid-May 1942 the Luftwaffe lost almost 3,000 aircraft and another 2,000 were badly damaged. Of the losses, 1,026 were bombers and another 762 were fighters. Meanwhile, the Russians had gathered 3,164 aircraft on the Soviet Western Front, of which more than 2,100 were of modern design. A new commanding officer, Gen A.A. Novikov, took command of Red Air Force units on the front. A further indication of the way the tide was turning came from the battles around Kharkov in mid-May, when the Germans had just 1,500 aircraft, and the Soviets twice as many.

On 28 June 1942 the Germans started their second summer offensive on the Eastern Front, supported by the Luftwaffe's 8th Air Corps under

Gen Fiebig. The commander of German ground forces in the region, Gen von Weichs, moved his troops out from Kursk against Soviet troops at Bryansk under Gen Golikov.

For the most part, by June 1943, the Luftwaffe units on the Eastern Front were confined to tactical operations in support of the increasingly beleaguered ground forces. The intensity of the Allied bombing campaign had forced the Luftwaffe to deploy its best fighter aircraft to protect German cities, so on the Eastern Front the mainstay of the German defences was the Bf109, while the Russians were receiving new equipment, much of it from the United States and the United Kingdom, including 18,000 aircraft during the period from June 1941, onwards.

From the start, the Luftwaffe suffered from the lack of a long-range heavy bomber, with much of the USSR's industrial capacity having been moved east of the Urals and therefore mostly out of range. One of the few Luftwaffe strategic bombing raids on the Eastern Front was by the bomber wings of the 4th Luftflotte, under **FM von Richtofen**. On 3 June 1943 they raided the Molotov Collective Combine in Gorki, one of the few major armaments plants left west of the Urals. This was a major tank factory, reputedly producing 800 T-34 tanks per week, covering about 2.5 sq miles. At 2000 hours, 168 bombers, mainly He111s of the 3rd, 4th, 27th, 55th and 100th Bomber Wings, took off from their base at Briansk, just within reach of the target. Most of the aircraft were carrying 1.7- to 2.4-ton mine bombs, but there were also large quantities of fragmentation, high-explosive and incendiary bombs.

This was intended to be a precision bombing attack using the new Lofte 7D homing device, which was newly operational, although they also navigated using the Moscow transmitter, avoiding the city by flying in a wide arc to keep clear of its anti-aircraft defences. At midnight 149 aircraft reached the target and began dropping 224 tons of bombs from altitudes between 13,000 and 20,000 ft. Five aircraft were shot down. This was the first in a series of raids designed to help prepare the way for the summer offensive. The second raid was on the night of 4/5 June, sending 128 aircraft to the target, where they dropped 179 tons of bombs for the loss of just two aircraft. A third raid followed on the night of 5/6 June, with 154 bombers dropping 242 tons of bombs for the loss of one aircraft, and finally, on the night of 7/8 June, twenty bombers dropped 39 tons of bombs.

The result, according to German intelligence, was that production was suspended for six weeks, but others claimed that little disruption occurred. The following night, 9/10 June, 109 bombers were sent on another long-range operation, to bomb the synthetic rubber plant at Yaroslavl. They dropped 109 tons of bombs.

On 12 July Soviet forces mounted a massive counter-offensive. From this time onwards the Germans were on the defensive. Hitler had other priorities by this time, following the Allied invasion of Sicily two days earlier; he transferred important elements of the Luftwaffe from the Eastern Front to Italy, doubtlessly to the immense pleasure and relief of those involved.

Spaatz, Gen Carl 'Tooey' (1891–1974) US air force leader. Born of German immigrant parents, he was among the early US military airmen and first saw action on the border with Mexico in 1916, before being posted to France when the USA entered the First World War. In 1940 he was sent to London as an observer with the rank of colonel, and his report to Roosevelt convinced the president that the UK could survive the war and that aid was justified. He was promoted to brigadier in 1941 and became chief of staff at the USAAF HQ, and then rose to major-general in January 1942. In July he took command of the Eighth USAAF bomber units in England, under **Gen Eaker**. He became Allied Air Forces commander under Eisenhower in North Africa and was promoted to lieutenant-general in March 1943. When **MRAF Tedder** took command of all Allied air forces in the Mediterranean, Spaatz became his deputy. In December 1943 he commanded the newly formed US Strategic Air Forces in Europe, created from the merged Eighth and Fifteenth USAAF, reporting directly to the combined chiefs of staff. He led the Combined Bomber Offensive (*see* **Allied Bomber Offensive**) and was helped by the arrival of the first long-range fighters in early 1944, which he used not by acting as a close escort for the bombers but by sending them ahead to find the

German fighters in the air and on the ground and destroy them. His insistence on attacking German oil targets meant that the Germans were forced to concentrate fighters over the refineries rather than sending them to France to oppose the Normandy landings; Germany then suffered an acute shortage of oil. Spaatz was promoted to general in March 1945.

After Germany surrendered he was sent to the Pacific to command the US Strategic Air Forces in the Pacific. Postwar, he succeeded **Gen Arnold** as Commander of the USAAF and became the first commander of the USAF when it was formed in 1947. He retired in 1948.

Spanish Civil War (18 July 1936–1 April 1939)

Both sides had the benefit of support from other European nations, with Italy and Germany sending forces to fight alongside the Nationalists, while the Republicans had support from volunteers from a number of other European nations, and the support of the Soviet Union.

The origins of the Spanish Civil War pre-dated the conflict by many years. The country had remained neutral during the First World War, but there were serious internal divisions between what might simply be described as the supporters of the status quo, the Nationalists, and anti-monarchist and anti-clerical factions, compounded by separatist movements and militant trade unionism, who found expression on the Republican side.

Initially, both sides used aircraft that had been in service with the nation's armed forces, but as the war progressed, the Nationalists had German and Italian aircraft, while the Republicans had aircraft from France and the Soviet Union.

Luftwaffe fighter pilots benefited from their experience with the Condor Legion during the Spanish Civil War. They had developed a defensive formation which started with the *Rotte*, a pair of aircraft operating together but widely spaced, at about 200 yd, with the pilots concentrating their search towards each other so that each covered the other's blind spots below and behind. Two *Rotten* created a *Schwarm* of four fighters, with the extremities 600 yd apart. In order to be able to maintain formation when turning, the crossover turn was developed, which meant that the aircraft effectively reversed their positions during the turn. The next stage was the *Staffel*, consisting of three *Schwarme*, or twelve aircraft. In addition to the Condor Legion, there were Italian pilots of the Corpo Truppe Volontarie.

The Spanish government, the Republicans, sought help from France, and although initially this was forthcoming, in due course opinions changed and getting aircraft across the border proved difficult.

Other problems included a shortage of pilots, even though initially the balance of aircrew from the Spanish Air Force was in favour of the government with a ratio of 3:2. Pilots were offered a renewable monthly contract of 50,000 pesetas and life assurance of 500,000 pesetas. The problem in translating this into meaningful values is considerable since the value of the gold peseta, used for international trade, varied wildly due to the civil war. The gold peseta was approximately equivalent, in the exchange rates of the time, to 32 to the pound sterling in 1936, and 38 to the pound in 1939, or in US dollar terms (at the time the exchange rate was 4 US dollars to the pound sterling), the gold peseta varied from 5.18 to the dollar in 1933, to 8 to the dollar in 1937 and 9.55 to the dollar in 1939. The paper peseta, used in everyday transactions, was worth little more than half that of the gold peseta. To compare this against the wage rates in Spain at the time, the average daily wage for a workman was just 5 pesetas.

The conflict is best remembered for the destruction of the city of Guernica by Nationalist bombers on 26 April 1937. The city had symbolic significance to the Basques, but was small with just 5,000 inhabitants and was of no strategic importance. Gen Emilio Mola, commander of nationalist forces in northern Spain, sent bombers from their base at Burgos, using the new Heinkel He111 and Dornier Do17 aircraft, as well as Junkers Ju52/3M bomber-transports. On reaching the city they dropped a mixture of high explosives and incendiaries in wave after wave for the next 2 hours, creating the conditions of a firestorm. As the citizens panicked and attempted to flee into the countryside, they were strafed by Messerschmitt and Fiat fighters. More than three-quarters of the city was destroyed.

The attack confirmed fears in France and Great Britain that the 'bomber would always get through', overlooking the absence of anti-aircraft and fighter defences.

Speer, Albert (1905–1981) German architect and industrial planner. An early admirer of Hitler, Speer joined the Nazi Party in 1932 and then became a member of the SS, organising and stage-managing the 1934 Nuremberg Rally. When the minister for armaments and munitions, and head of the Todt forced labour organisation, was killed in a plane crash in February 1942, Speer was appointed in his place and in 1943 he was given overall control of the German war economy. He proved himself to be an efficient administrator, even an industrial genius, who managed to increase armament production between 1942 and 1944, while his production of synthetic oil enabled the German war machine to continue until early 1945. When Hitler committed suicide he became minister for the economy in Karl Dönitz's government. At the Nuremberg war trials he attempted to dissociate himself from Hitler's regime and maintained that he knew nothing of the final solution, but even so he served a twenty-year sentence for the use of forced labour. On his release he attempted to convince the world in two books that he was an apolitical bureaucrat.

Sperrle, FM Hugo (1885–1953) German air commander. In 1936 he was sent to head the air element of the German Condor Legion that was fighting alongside the Nationalists in the **Spanish Civil War**, returning in 1937 to be promoted first to major-general and then to lieutenant-general. On the outbreak of the Second World War he was given command of Luftflotte 3. His command was not used during the invasion of Poland, but supported Rundstedt's Army Group A in the Battle of France. He was promoted to field marshal in July 1940 in recognition of his service in France. During summer 1940 he argued that pressure should be maintained on the RAF rather than switching to the cities, but he was overruled.

The strength of Luftflotte 3 was drained away to meet the demands of Operation Barbarossa, the invasion of the Soviet Union, and Sperrle became disillusioned, although his command was given the role of providing air defence to occupied France and the Low Countries and making occasional

bomber raids when resources allowed. By June 1944 his resources were so scant that he could do little to support the defending ground forces following the Normandy landings, for which he was blamed and dismissed in August.

Sperry, Dr Elmer Abrose (1860–1930) American inventor of the gyroscope. After studying electricity at Cornell University in the late 1870s, he invented a dynamo and an arc lamp, both of which entered production and, with several other inventions, provided sufficient funds for his other interests, which included an electric car. He started research on gyroscopes in 1896, and in 1910 the USN adopted his accurate marine gyroscopic compass.

He became involved with aviation around 1912 when he collaborated with **Glenn Curtiss** on an automatic stabiliser for aircraft, with an early automatic pilot demonstrated on a Curtiss flying boat in 1913. His son, **Lawrence Sperry**, flew the aircraft 'hands-off' past a large audience in Paris while the mechanic climbed out onto the wing to show that even unbalancing the aircraft did not affect its stability. Sperry became more closely involved with aviation, inventing the directional gyro and gyro horizon, and the drift indicator, which helped **James Doolittle** make the first 'blind' flight in 1929.

Sperry, Lawrence Burst (1892–1923) American aircraft instrument pioneer. After delivering newspapers and repairing bicycles, he became interested in aviation around 1908. His first aircraft was a glider, which was not very successful, and his second was a powered biplane that made a few hops in 1910. His father, **Dr Elmer Sperry**, sent him to **Glenn Curtiss** to learn to fly in 1913, and also made him project engineer on the prototype automatic pilot, which he demonstrated successfully later that year.

He continued working with his father and also made significant inventions of his own, including the first retractable landing gear in 1915, and a flying bomb. After the First World War, he put the Army Engineering Division's Messenger biplane into production and took it on a sales tour of Europe in 1923. He disappeared flying the aircraft over the English Channel that year, and although the wreckage was found, his body remained missing.

spin A condition into which an aircraft falls while autorotating. It can be induced on purpose, especially during training but, particularly during the early days, it was usually accidental. The first pilot to recover from a spin was the Englishman Frederick Langham flying an Avro biplane in 1911, but he could not recall how he managed it. In 1912 Lt Wilfred Parke RN, flying an Avro Cabin biplane, was able to put the aircraft into a spin and demonstrate recovery.

Springs, Capt Elliot White (1896–1959)

American ace. After being educated at military academies and Princeton, where he learnt to fly, he joined the US Army in 1917 and was seconded to the RFC. He completed his training under the guidance of British aces, and shot down his first aircraft while flying an SE5a on 5 June 1918, following this with three further kills before being shot down and wounded. He returned to service with a **Sopwith Camel** unit and shot down another eight German aircraft.

Postwar, he returned to his father's weaving textile mill in South Carolina, but was fired for not attending to his duties. He went to Paris and became an author, writing his first book about a wartime aviator, *War Birds: Diary of an Unknown Aviator*, which was a great success. He wrote further books before returning to take over his father's business when his parent died, and this time built it up into a large corporation.

Spruance, Adm Raymond A. (1886–1969)

American naval commander. He was a rear admiral commanding the cruiser squadron which provided a surface screen for **Halsey**'s carrier force during the first few months of the war in the Pacific. When Halsey fell ill, Spruance was put in command of the carriers and was responsible for the reversal of Japanese fortunes at the **Battle of Midway**. His genius for strategic thinking and his fighting abilities led to him spending fourteen months as chief of staff to **Chester Nimitz**, before being promoted to vice-admiral and given command of the Central Pacific Force. It was designated US Fifth Fleet under his

command, and then Third Fleet when commanded by Halsey. He gathered together a dedicated and talented team of senior USN and USMC officers, as well as having overall command of Task Force 57, the British Pacific Fleet. He planned the capture of Tarawa and then the Marshall Islands which saw him promoted to admiral. He took part in the capture of the Marianas and of Iwo Jima and Okinawa but was criticised for not capitalising on his victory in the Battle of the Philippine Sea. Posterity has defended him as his duty was to protect the landings on Saipan, which he did.

staggerwing A biplane with the lower wing having a leading edge ahead of that on the upper wing. Aircraft include the Airco DH-2 fighter of the First World War and the Beech 17, an up-market light aircraft first launched in 1937 and which remained in production as a military communications aircraft during the Second World War.

Steinhoff, Gen Johannes (1913–94)

German ace. An outstanding pilot, in 1940 he was serving in Jagdgeschwader 26 (JG 26) Squadron at Abbeville in France, before being one of the leaders of the NJG 1 night fighter unit and, later in the war, the JV 44 jet fighter unit. It was while he was flying with JV 44 on 18 April 1944 that his Me262 crashed and he suffered severe burns, especially to his face.

Postwar, he worked in advertising and was among those who rejoined the Luftwaffe when it was re-formed in 1955 becoming Deputy Chief of Staff.

Stinson *See* below

Stinson, Eddie (1894–1932), Katherine (1891–1977) and Marjorie Claire (1896–1975)

American pioneers and barnstormers. Katherine become involved with aviation as a stunt and exhibition pilot to earn enough money to become a pianist, going solo after 3½ hours and becoming the fourth American woman to gain an aviator's certificate. Her mother, who had paid for the flying lessons, bought her a secondhand Wright B biplane in 1912, and she was soon a star attraction at flying displays, earning as much as US $500 per appearance (£100 at the then rate of exchange, equivalent to £5,700 today). She became the first woman to fly airmail in September 1913 when she flew from a fairground outside Helena, Montana, to government offices in the city centre. She visited China and Japan in 1916, where a woman pilot made a great impression.

Marjorie followed her sister, learning to fly in 1914 and then becoming an exhibition flyer. The following year, with their brother, the two sisters and their mother founded a flying school at San Antonio in Texas and when the United States entered the First World War this provided basic training for military pilots.

Their brother, Eddie, learnt to fly in 1915, and after working at the family flying school during the war, followed his sisters into exhibition flying, although he also drove a fast racing car around fairground circuits and earned up to US $1,500 a time. He became an alcoholic and wasted much of the money, but then decided to increase his fees by introducing a novel act; fitting motorcycle brakes to the wheels of his aircraft and offering to land on any racetrack – these were the first practical aircraft brakes. In 1925 he founded the eponymous aircraft manufacturer, initially building airliners but later switching to light aircraft. He was killed flying one of his own aircraft in 1932, when it ran out of fuel, and in 1940 the company was acquired by Vultee.

Stout, William Bushnell 'Jack-Knife' (1880–1956)

American engineer. Graduating in mechanical engineering from two US universities, in 1912 Stout became aviation correspondent for the *Chicago Tribune*, and later founded his own journal, the *Aerial Age*. He earned his nickname as a journalist because of his cutting comments. He later worked briefly as an engineer for Packard and when the USA entered the First World War, became a consultant for the Aircraft Production Board.

A firm believer in metal for airframes, a shortage of money meant that his first design, the Batwing, a cantilever monoplane completed in 1918, was built of wood. After a further development of this aircraft flew, he received an order for a cantilever construction torpedo-bomber from the USN,

which emerged as the twin-engined ST-1, built of aluminium. Encouraged by this, he sent duplicated letters to 100 wealthy businessmen asking for US $1,000 apiece to enable him to start his own business, and being typically frank, he warned them that they might never see their money again. Around twenty of them sent cheques, including Henry Ford and his son Edsel. The Stout Metal Plane Company was established and, in 1923, it produced the Air Sedan, its first aircraft, built with a corrugated aluminium skin. The 2-AT that followed used the same construction and was a single-engined airliner.

His success led Henry Ford to buy the company in August 1925. The 3-AT trimotor transport appeared in late 1925 but this aircraft, often described as ugly, was a poor performer and was destroyed in a hangar fire. Ford and Stout fell out shortly afterwards, and when the Ford Trimotor was developed from the 2-AT it was by a team of Ford designers, although Stout has usually been given the credit for it.

Stout's next venture was an airline, founded in 1926, operating from Detroit to Cleveland, Grand Rapids and Chicago, but which was merged into United Aircraft and Transport in 1929. Meanwhile, he continued building aircraft on a small scale, including the Sky Car and the Amphibian, both light aircraft, as well as designing road vehicles and railway trains. His Scarab motor car was an art-deco design with a rear engine, but only five were built.

strategic air war

A concept that emerged during the First World War in which military aviation becomes a means of war in its own right, over and above the need to provide support to armies and navies. The first application was the use of Zeppelin airships to bomb London and urban centres on the east coast of England, later followed by bombers operated by both sides. The doctrine was followed both by the RAF and the USAAC, later the USAAF, during the interwar period, but not by German or Soviet forces, in which close support of ground forces was seen as the overall priority. When the Luftwaffe started to attack British cities in the **Blitz** it lacked heavy bombers and, while it inflicted considerable damage, it never proved capable of providing a true 'knock-out' blow. The Anglo-American bombing campaign (*see* **Pointblank Directive**) on the other hand did significantly reduce German production, especially when it turned to oil and rubber production, but it still did not win the war on its own, as **'Bomber' Harris** believed it could. The true 'knock-out' blow was the use of the atomic bomber against **Hiroshima** and **Nagasaki** in August 1945, although even this nearly failed as an anti-surrender faction among the Japanese military attempted a push.

Stringfellow, John (1799–1883) British visionary. Although his business was as a lace manufacturer, he had a talent for designing and building small and lightweight steam engines. He was the partner of **Samuel Henson** in the Ariel project. Henson emigrated to America after the project failed, but Stringfellow remained in Britain and designed further model aeroplanes, although still without success. He became a member of the Aeronautical Society in 1868, continuing to predict that heavier-than-air flight would soon be a reality.

Student, Lt Gen Kurt (1890–1978) German air force leader. He was a pilot during the Battle of Tannenberg, the First World War action in which the aeroplane played an important role, and by the end of the war he was commanding Jagdgruppe III. Postwar, with Germany banned from military aviation under the **Treaty of Versailles**, he was the Weimar government's 'aviation adviser'. This allowed him to prepare for the rebuilding of German air power, with the leading designers working outside the country and the interest in aviation being kept alive, while future pilots were having their skills honed through gliding clubs. The Luftwaffe effectively came into being shortly after Hitler came to power in 1933, but was not publicly revealed until 1935. Student was given the task of organising a paratroop division, with these specialised forces being part of the Luftwaffe rather than the army, as is the case in most countries.

He led his forces personally in the Battle for the Netherlands and Belgium in the first ever airborne assault. In May 1941 his troops mounted an airborne assault on the island of Crete, but without adequate naval and army support they suffered such massive casualties that Hitler banned further airborne assaults, although towards the end of the war that resolve seemed to be weakening. The loss of much of the British and Greek forces' equipment during the evacuation from Greece, including radios, put the Allies at a disadvantage, otherwise the German paratroops and glider-landed troops might have failed completely.

With his forces grounded Student led them, and conventional forces, in a number of actions, most notably at the Battle of the Bulge and at **Arnhem**.

Stumpff, Gen Hans-Jurgen (1889–1968) German air commander. He was appointed the Luftwaffe's chief of personnel in 1935 and chief of staff in June 1937, but was replaced by **Gen Hans Jeschonnek** in February 1939. In spring 1940 he was put in command of air operations during the Norwegian campaign. After the fall of Norway, he remained in the country in command of Luftflotte 5, which could only play a small part in the Battle of Britain as its bases were too far away for fighters to escort the bombers. He organised the attacks on the Arctic Convoys from mid-1941 until the end of 1943 and provided air support for German and Finnish troops fighting Soviet forces. In January 1944 he was recalled and given command of Germany's air defences with the home air fleet, Luftflotte Reich, which included Luftflotte 3 commanded by **Sperrle** from September. He was one of three senior officers to sign the surrender document on 8 May 1945. He was also one of the few senior German officers to have an unblemished reputation.

Sud Aviation/Sud Est *See* Aérospatiale

Suez Campaign (1956) While nominally an independent kingdom, Egypt had been virtually a British colony for many years. British forces occupied the country in 1882, mainly through concern for the security of the Suez Canal. The Khedive was bankrupt and sold his share in the Suez Canal Company to the British, to whom it was invaluable as a means of fast communication between the United Kingdom and India and

Australia. The occupation was controversial. It was anathema to nationalists but it had allowed Egypt to leave the Ottoman Empire. In 1946 Britain agreed to pull out of Egypt although troops remained in the Suez Canal Zone until 1954. Before this, in 1952, a coup had overthrown the monarchy and the new regime soon produced a dicatator, the arch-Arab nationalist, Col Gamal Abdel Nasser.

Egyptian nationalisation of the Suez Canal in 1956 outraged British and French opinion – the two countries who owned the international waterway – and alarmed the Israelis, who saw this as a threat to Israeli shipping. The Israelis were also concerned at Egypt's growing military strength.

At first, world opinion was on the side of Britain and France, who agreed to take military action to regain the canal. Had both countries been able to act decisively in July, all might have been well, but time passed and support faded. The problem was that the British armed forces, still overstretched in the twilight of the colonial era, and with a massive new postwar commitment in the part-occupation of what was then West Germany, did not have the manpower or equipment.

The plan which the British and French developed centred on an Israeli pre-emptive offensive against Egypt in Sinai which would be followed by Anglo-French intervention in the Canal Zone. Successive British governments have denied British complicity in the Israeli attack. The French started a re-equipment of Israel's armed forces. British and French forces established a joint command and redeployed naval and air forces to the central and eastern Mediterranean. The United Kingdom had the advantage of a major naval base at Malta, with airfields on both Malta and, even closer to the Canal Zone, Cyprus.

On 29 October Israel launched her attack against Egypt, and two days later British and French shore and carrier-borne aircraft launched an attack, the opening of what had been codenamed Operation Musketeer, bombing Egyptian military targets. The landings did not start until 5 November, by which time world opinion was strongly opposed to the action. The operation was notable not just for the paratroop operations by both countries, but for the use of helicopters to ferry Royal Marine commandos ashore from two British aircraft carriers, HMS *Ocean* and *Theseus*.

The military success was accompanied by a diplomatic debacle with the USA threatening to withdraw support for sterling and the franc unless there was an immediate cease-fire, followed by the withdrawal of British and French forces.

Sukhoi Russian design bureau. The youngest of the former Soviet design bureaux, the first Sukhoi design noted in the West was the Su-7B ground-attacked aircraft, followed by its interceptor development, the Su-9, which appeared in 1956. In more recent years, the bureau has become more usually associated with air superiority fighters than ground-attack aircraft, with such examples as the Su-35 Super Flanker. An unusual aircraft has been the experimental Su-37 Berkut with forward-swept wings, first flown in 1997.

Sukhoi, Pavel Osipovich Soviet designer. A graduate of the Zhukovski Air Academy, at first he was employed by the **Tupolev** design bureau, where he worked on the ANT-5 (later reclassified as the I-4) fighter, which was the mainstay of Soviet air defences in the late 1920s and early 1930s. His ANT-25 long-range monoplane set a record flying non-stop over the North Pole from Moscow to San Francisco in 1937. The great publicity and acclaim that this flight generated caused Stalin to grant Sukhoi the privilege of his own design bureau.

Sukhoi's early record as an independent designer during the Second World War was poor with just one successful aircraft, the Su-2 bomber, and after the war he lost his bureau. Following the death of Stalin in 1952 he was reinstated and set about designing the series of ground-attack fighter-bombers that bore his name. He was awarded the Order of Lenin.

Supermarine British manufacturer. During the First World War, the company produced its first design, the Baby biplane flying boat, and postwar this was followed by a series of flying boats, including the Sea Eagle, Southampton and Walrus, all of which were biplanes. Some of these aircraft were the work of the company's designer, **R.J. Mitchell**, but the company's, and

Mitchell's, real fame lay in the development of cantilever monoplanes for the **Schneider Trophy Races**, including the ill-fated S4 of 1925 through to the successful S5, S6 and S6B that finally won the contest outright for the UK. These were important milestones towards the development of the famous Spitfire fighter for the Second World War. Between the wars, the company was acquired by **Vickers**, famous for airliners and bombers.

Following the war the company built the Royal Navy's first jet fighter, the Attacker, however, a supersonic fighter for the RAF, the Swift, had to be withdrawn due to aerodynamic defects. Then, in 1958, the company produced the Royal Navy's first swept-wing fighter, the Scimitar. With its parent, the company was merged into the **British Aircraft Corporation** in 1960.

Swedenborg, Emanuel (1688–1772) Swedish visionary and mystic. After graduating from the University of Uppsala, he spent five years travelling throughout Europe and meeting many of the leading scientists of the day. He began to develop theories of navigation and flight, as well as religion and government. He published his ideas once in Sweden, but despite acclaim from across Europe, he had to work as a civil servant with the mining board. He put this position to good use, pressing his country to develop iron and copper industries, and arguing in favour of decimal coinage.

He proposed an aeroplane with a fixed mainplane and flapping wings for propulsion in 1714, the first time that the significance of a fixed wing had been recognised, separating the fixed wing for lift from the flapping wings for propulsion. His findings were lost and did not become known to the other pioneers of aviation such as **Cayley**, or later **Chanute** and the **Wrights**.

He achieved fame through his works on religious philosophy which even became established as a separate religious denomination.

T

Tallman, Frank (1919–78) American stunt pilot. His father paid for his flying lessons as a reward for good grades while at high school, and he went solo on his sixteenth birthday. He became a flying instructor with the USN at Pensacola, Florida, during the Second World War. Postwar, he moved to Hollywood to become a stunt pilot in films, acquiring a large and varied collection of aircraft, and becoming a competitor to the established film stunt flyer, **Paul Mantz**. They merged their businesses into Tallmantz Aviation in 1961.

Tallman continued to fly many of the stunts himself for films such as *Catch 22*, and was surveying locations for a new film when the Piper Aztec in which he was flying crashed into mountains in California.

Tank, Prof Kurt Waldemar (1898–1983) German engineer and designer. After gaining experience in building all-metal aircraft with the Rohrbach-Metallflugzeugbau, which he joined in 1924, when that company collapsed in 1930 he joined the troubled Bavarian Aircraft Company (BFW) leaving in 1931 to work for **Focke-Wulf**. At the time, the company was very much a minor part of the German aircraft industry and had lacked direction and professionalism. His first design for his new employer appeared in 1933, the Fw56 Stosser, a parasol monoplane trainer. This was followed by the Fw58 Weihe and then the elegant Fw200 Condor airliner, whose sleek lines were ahead of their time.

During the Second World War, the Condor became a maritime-reconnaissance aircraft operating out over the Atlantic and Bay of Biscay and also off the coast of Norway. Tank became head of the company in 1942, with Heinrich Focke concentrating his energies on helicopter development while Wulf had died earlier in a crash. Tank is best remembered for his Fw190 fighter, which was superior to the Bf109 and of which 20,000 were built.

Postwar, he emigrated first to Argentina and then later to India, where he worked on the indigenous Hindustan HF-25 Marut.

Taranto (11/12 November 1940) An attack on the Italian fleet in its forward base at Taranto had been planned at the height of the Abyssinian crisis in 1935. At that time, the Mediterranean Fleet aircraft carrier was HMS *Glorious*. In 1940 the plan was revived, and originally it was intended that two carriers, *Illustrious*, newly arrived in the Mediterranean, and *Eagle*, should be used, giving a total of thirty Fairey Swordfish biplanes for the operation, and that the date for the attack should be 21 October, the anniversary of Nelson's famous victory at Trafalgar. Fate intervened, however, with first a serious hangar fire aboard *Illustrious* delaying the operation, and then the *Eagle* suffering extensive damage to her aviation fuel system as a result of the mining effect of near-misses by heavy bombs. In the event, a number of aircraft were transferred from *Eagle*'s 813 and 824 squadrons to 815 and 819 squadrons aboard *Illustrious*, giving a total of twenty-four aircraft for the operation. On the day before the operation, one aircraft ditched in the sea because of fuel contamination, and the next day the same thing happened again. In the end it was discovered that one of the carrier's aviation fuel tanks had been contaminated by sea water and all of the aircraft had to have their fuel systems drained. Just twenty-one aircraft were available for the operation.

The operation was rescheduled for the night of 11/12 November 1940. Due to the range involved the Swordfish biplanes carried extra fuel tanks, placed in the observer's cockpit in the torpedo-carrying aircraft and under the fuselage for the bombers and flare-droppers. The observer in the torpedo-carrying aircraft was moved into the rear-most cockpit as telegraphist/air gunners were not carried on the operation. The attack took place in two waves, with twelve aircraft in the first wave and nine in the second. Attacking against a heavily defended target, the first wave concentrated on the ships and the second wave on the shore installation. Three of the Italian Navy's six battleships were sitting on the bottom of the harbour when the raid ended, although two eventually returned to service, while other ships were damaged and fuel tanks ashore set on fire. Just two aircraft were shot down and the crew of one of these, the leaders of the first wave, Lt Cdr Kenneth Williamson and his observer Lt Norman 'Blood' Scarlett, were taken prisoner.

The Italians were forced to move their warships away from Taranto at first, although the next nearest port, Naples, was within reach of Malta-based Wellington bombers.

Tatin, Victor (1843–1913) French pioneer. A watchmaker by trade, he had helped **Etienne Marey** study bird flight. In 1876 he built a flap-wing model that actually flew, but after that he concentrated on fixed-wing aircraft. His 1879 model monoplane used a compressed air motor to turn two propellers and had a three-wheel undercarriage; it flew for around 100 ft while tethered to a pole. Despite these advances he did not persist in his work, abandoning it until around 1900 when he helped **Alberto Santos-Dumont** design his airships and advised **Louis Blériot**, meanwhile working with **Henri de La Vaulx** on his 1907 monoplane. His most notable achievements, however, were with the Clement-Bayard concern for which he designed the dirigible *Ville de Paris* and a monoplane that appeared in 1909. He later worked with **Louis Paulhan** on *L'Aéro-Torpille* of 1911.

Taylor, Charles E. (1867–1956) American machinist and member of the **Wright** brothers' team. In 1901 he was a machinist for an electric company, but lived a short distance from the Wright brothers, who asked him to work for them in return for a 20 per cent pay rise. He not only accepted their offer, but also managed their bicycle business while they were conducting their trials. It was Taylor who actually built the engine designed by the Wrights for their first powered aircraft, the *Flyer I*, as well as its metal parts. Once the Wrights began travelling in 1908, Taylor went

with them and provided engineering support for their exhibition flights both in Europe and then on their return to the USA. He also provided travelling ground support for **Calbraith Rodgers** on his transcontinental flight, repairing his aircraft after each accident.

In the period after the First World War, the original company founded by the Wrights went through mergers and takeovers and Taylor left. He was later found by Henry Ford – looking for someone to restore the original Wright workshop – working as a machinist for North American.

He died in poverty, despite being left an annuity by the Wrights.

Taylor, Clarence Gilbert (1898–1988) American manufacturer. During the early 1920s he started an aircraft factory with his brother, Gordon. Their first product was a light aircraft named the Chummy which they built to order, although only five had been sold by 1929 and Gordon had been killed test-flying one of the aircraft the previous year. These were the depression years so orders were few and far between but it also meant that efforts were made to attract and stimulate employment, with Bradford, Pennsylvania, offering Taylor money in 1929 to relocate his business.

After the move, **William Piper** acquired an interest and asked Taylor to redesign the Chummy to make it lighter with a less expensive engine. The result was the E-2. Despite this, the company went into liquidation in 1931, but was acquired by Piper, who retained Taylor as designer and as a junior partner. In 1931 twenty-four E-2s were sold, and the aircraft began to sell well as the decade progressed, but in 1936 Taylor left after another designer was allowed to modify Taylor's original design.

Taylor next founded Taylorcraft and designed a new two-seat light aircraft which sold in reasonable quantities. A British subsidiary was founded in 1938 which became Auster Aircraft in 1946.

Tedder, MRAF Lord Arthur William (1890–1967) British air strategist. He served with the RFC during the First World War and remained with the RAF after the war ended. His outstanding success was as Air Officer Commanding the Desert Air Force during the Second World War, a command with squadrons from throughout the British Empire and which finally solved the problems of cooperation between air and ground forces. He is credited with being a great tactician and takes some of the credit for the victory at El Alamein. In 1943 he was Allied Air Commander in the Mediterranean and then became second in command to Gen Dwight Eisenhower.

Temple, Felix du (1823–90) French pioneer and designer. Commissioned into the Marine Nationale, du Temple experimented with a series of small clockwork and then steam-powered models that were the first to be capable of making short uncontrolled flights as early as 1857–8. Encouraged by this early success, he then built the first full-sized powered flying-machine, a monoplane with dihedral and reverse sweep to the wings, a tailplane with rudder, and a retractable undercarriage, all based on a single tractor propeller powered by a steam engine. No attempt appears to have been made at flight for some years until in 1874 a young sailor, who had volunteered for the mission, drove the machine down-ramp to make the first take-off by a full-sized heavier-than-air powered flying-machine, a powered hop to which the down-ramp run must have contributed. Nevertheless, the lack of sustained controlled flight did not prevent many from claiming this as the world's first flight.

Thomas, George Holt (1869–1929) British pioneer. After making a balloon ascent in 1906 he became passionate about aviation. He booked **Louis Paulhan** to give exhibition flights at Brooklands, south of London, and in 1911 started to manufacture **Farman** aircraft under licence at Hendon, north-west London, as the Aircraft Manufacturing Company, more usually known as Airco. In 1912 he recruited **Geoffrey de Havilland** and the company produced its own designs including the DH-1, DH-2, and the more successful DH-4 bomber.

During the First World War he found time to register the first British airline, Aircraft Transport & Travel (AT&T), which started the first scheduled flights between London and Paris using converted DH-4 bombers in 1919. If all went well flights took 2 hours, but a flight was recorded as completed even if it took two days and frequent landings to rectify technical faults. The company later went into liquidation as it faced subsidised foreign competition.

After the airline collapsed Thomas took up farming.

Thomson, Sir Adam (1926–1999) British airline founder. Born in Glasgow, he graduated from the Royal Technical College (predecessor of Strathclyde University) and at the age of 17, he volunteered for the Fleet Air Arm and was sent to Canada for flying training. Postwar, he wanted to enter civil aviation, but attempts to found a joy-riding business failed for want of financial support. Initially, he worked as a flying instructor for the Ministry of Civil Aviation, but then became a pilot for Newman Airlines, flying to the Isle of Wight and the Channel Islands. In 1951 he joined BEA and in 1953 became a captain with West African Airways, an airline backed by BOAC. He then moved to Britavia to fly military charter flights.

In 1961 Thomson founded his own airline, Caledonian Airways, with a partner, John de la Haye, an ex-BEA steward. They chartered a Douglas DC-7 from the Belgian airline Sabena, paying by the flying hour, and started transatlantic charters for affinity groups and also undertook **inclusive tour** work. The airline grew, acquired Boeing 707s and began to operate migrant charters to Australia. When the Edwards Report of 1969 recommended not only merging BEA and BOAC to form British Airways, but also the creation of a private enterprise 'second force' airline to provide competition, he raised funds to acquire British United Airways, which had been failing, and established British Caledonian Airways (BCal) in November 1970. The new airline inherited BUA's network of British trunk routes, a basic European network, and scheduled services to Africa and South America. It later started transatlantic services. Thomson was appointed a CBE in 1976 and knighted in 1983. The airline grew to account for half of all movements at London Gatwick, despite the collapse of a major inclusive tour customer and the loss of its routes to South America during the Falklands Campaign. The route to Tripoli was also lost as Libya adopted the status of a renegade state. In 1987 the privatised British Airways took over BCal and Thomson retired rather than join the board of BA.

Thulin, Dr Enoch Leonard (1881–1919)

Swedish manufacturer. Thulin learnt to fly on a visit to France, and returned to Sweden in 1913 to build his first aeroplane. He formed a company, AB Enoch-Thulins Aeroplanfabrik, in 1914 to manufacture **Blériot** designs under licence. During the aircraft famine of the First World War, when the belligerent nations did not have the capacity to export, the company produced other aircraft under licence and Thulin also designed some himself, including the Thulin Type K, a monoplane fighter, of which two were purchased by the army.

In 1919 Thulin was killed in a flying accident but his company survived and was eventually absorbed into Svenska Aeroplan AB (**SAAB**).

Tissandier, Albert (1839–1906) and Gaston (1843–99)

French airship pioneers. Gaston served as a balloon pilot during the Franco-Prussian War of 1870–1. Five years later he endeavoured to break the altitude record set earlier by **James Glaisher**, but just failed to match it. During the ascent his two assistants died and when he returned to the ground, he too was barely alive.

He began working with his brother on an airship in 1881. Their early experiments with models proved promising and led them to build a full-sized airship powered by a 1.5 hp Siemens electric motor, which made an ascent in 1883, but it could only managed 3 mph and was difficult to steer.

Tournachon, Gaspard-Felix 'Nadar' (1820–1910)

French photographer. Usually known to his clients simply as Nadar, he became a professional photographer after trying other work, and became adept at self-publicity. He even hosted the first viewing of Impressionist paintings in his studio, which he had painted a bright red. His involvement with aeronautics came in 1855, when he invented and patented a system of cartography based on aerial photography. The following year he took the first aerial photograph while making an ascent in a balloon and became an enthusiast, building a giant balloon of 212,000 cu ft capacity,

named *Le Géant*. Appropriately enough, it could lift fourteen passengers and had bunks, a toilet, photographic studio and a dark room.

At the time of the Franco-Prussian War of 1870–1, during the Siege of Paris, he prepared microfiche messages that were smuggled out of the city by balloon.

tower jumpers

Usually regarded as a medieval European phenomenon, the first recorded tower jumper was the Chinese Emperor Shin, who in 2200 BC supposedly jumped from a tower and glided safely to the ground using two large reed mats as wings. The first recorded instance of a tower jumper in the West was the Moor, Armen Firman, at Córdoba in Spain in AD 852. Later, in 1029 a Benedictine monk, usually recorded as Oliver (but sometimes as Eilmer) of Malmesbury, jumped from Malmesbury Abbey after fitting himself with wings. Oliver was lucky simply to break both legs after a short glide and is supposed to have lived to see the Norman Conquest in 1066, although due to the lack of medical knowledge in his day he was almost certainly a cripple.

There seems to have been an interval of several hundred years before tower jumping was once again in vogue. In 1496, Senacio, who lived in Nuremberg, was reported as having broken an arm in an unsuccessful attempt. Less fortunate was the Italian mathematician, Danti, who attempted to fly at Perugia in 1503 and was seriously injured. John Damian, the Italian-born Abbot of Tungland, was also injured when he jumped from Stirling Castle in 1507. There could be no starker reminder of the dangers inherent in this activity than the fate of the Italian clockmaker, Bolari, who was killed when he jumped from the Cathedral of Troyes in France.

While a more reasoned approach to the problems of becoming airborne started to emerge after this, the age of the tower jumper had not really passed. This was despite the concept being discredited by the work of Borelli, Hooke and Willoughby. In 1742 the Marquis de Bacqueville jumped from a riverside house in Paris with wings attached to his arms and legs, hoping to fly across the River Seine. He fell into a barge and broke both legs. Then in 1772 Canon Desforges of Etampes built a *voiture volante* – a wickerwork basket with a canopy to provide lift and flappers for propulsion – which he launched from a tower. **Jean-Pierre Blanchard**, the famous aeronaut, designed a canopied and flapper-powered flying-machine which was built in 1781, and proved to be as hopeless as its predecessors, and even the advent of the balloon did not discourage the tower jumpers.

In 1801 the 72-year-old Frenchman, General Resnier de Goué, dived from the ramparts of Angoulême into the River Charente and was fortunate enough to escape injury, but he was not so lucky a little later when he repeated this effort over land and broke a leg. Ten years later Albrecht Berblinger, known as the Tailor of Ulm, flapped off the Adlerbastei and into the Danube. He was using a replica of an ornithopter designed by **Jacob Degen**, the Swiss clockmaker, although he had omitted the hydrogen balloon to which Degen had attached his mechanical device.

training aircraft The early pioneers were often self-taught, for, after all, who could have given the **Wright** brothers flying lessons? At first, instruction was given on the production aircraft of the day, but the need for a dedicated trainer soon emerged, with the British Avro 504 and the American Curtiss JN-4 Jenny becoming the favoured types. Between the wars, basic trainers developed as a distinct type of aircraft for both private fliers, for whom these often became their own aircraft even once qualified, and for military and commercial pilots, with one of the most successful being the de Havilland Tiger Moth. Even so, military aircrew in particular had to complete their training on their operational aircraft and, even though they had flown advanced trainers, the switch from, say, an advanced trainer to a Spitfire or a Mustang was a big step. At the end of the Second World War dual-seat versions of the Spitfire were produced for the Irish Air Corps, and likewise the Hurricane for the Imperial Iranian Air Force.

Postwar, the more exacting demands of the jet saw the de Havilland Vampire emerge as a leading jet trainer, but it was also appreciated that new aircraft types had to include dual-seat conversion trainers so that pilots could be converted safely by instructors. Today, even single-seat combat aircraft such as the F-16, F/A-18 and Harrier have dual-seat conversion trainers.

transition 1. The act of passing through the sound barrier from sub-sonic to supersonic flight. 2. The change from vertical take-off to forward flight, or from forward flight to vertical landing.

Tranum, Dr John, 1900–1935 Danish stunt pilot and parachutist. A worthy European equivalent to the American barnstormers or stunt pilots, by 1931 he had made 1,500 parachute jumps, including some in which he parachuted with a woman in his arms and others in which he set his plane on fire and then jumped. He also wing-walked, including walking from the wing of one aircraft to the wing of another.

Seeking to maintain the excitement and novelty of his act, he began high-altitude jumps, often with a delayed opening. In 1935 he attempted to set a record of 33,000 ft for such a jump, but he failed to jump and the pilot decided to land after which he discovered Tranum on the back seat, dead from a heart attack.

Trenchard, MRAF Viscount Hugh Montague (1873–1956) British air strategist. The 'Father of the Royal Air Force' failed to pass the exams for the Royal Navy's Britannia Naval College or for an engineering course, but was commissioned into an army regiment and spent some twenty years soldiering in the British Empire, in which time he was wounded during the Boer War in South Africa. A friend persuaded him that flying would be fun and could also mean faster promotion, so in 1912 he was taught to fly by **Thomas Sopwith** at Brooklands. The timing was excellent, as the newly formed RFC was looking for experienced officers who could fly, and Trenchard was given the key role of setting up the training programme at the Central Flying School, based at Upavon in Wiltshire. In 1915 he was posted to France where he commanded all RFC units on the Western Front.

Even at this early stage Trenchard, known as 'Boom' to his subordinates because of his deep voice, was a firm believer in strategic air power and particularly in the bomber. He also believed that the RFC should re-absorb the RNAS to provide a single strategic air service and end the rivalry and overlap between the two air arms. This view was also taken by the South Africa statesman and soldier General Jan Smuts, who headed a committee charged by the government to prepare a plan for the future of what was then described as the 'air service'.

When the new RAF, the world's first autonomous air service, came into existence on 1 April 1918 it was not to Trenchard's liking as he believed that to reorganise while fighting a major war was foolish. Nevertheless, he accepted the post as head of the RAF, although he had resigned from the RFC on 19 March, but for the sake of appearances this did not take effect until 13 April. He was soon back. He established an officers' training college at Cranwell, an air staff, and planned a substantial air force that would include the fighter defence of the UK and a substantial bombing force. However, cuts in defence expenditure after the First World War meant that at one stage the new service consisted of just twelve squadrons, most of which were based abroad.

In 1931 he left the RAF, just before the start of the expansion of the 1930s, and became Commissioner of Police of the Metropolis, the head of the Metropolitan Police, establishing its training school at Hendon close to the old aerodrome. He retired finally in 1935.

He died in 1956 and was given full military honours at his burial at Westminster Abbey.

triplane An aircraft that has three wings in the mainplane, and which was favoured by both sides during the First World War, with fighters such as the Sopwith Trike and the Fokker Triplane, as well as a Caproni bomber. Postwar, the greater drag of the triplane and the improved take-off and landing performance allowed by widespread use of flaps, made the concept obsolete.

Trippe, Juan Terry (1899–1981) American airline pioneer. He left Yale University in 1917 to join the USN as a bomber pilot, but returned to the university in 1919. When he graduated in 1922, he went to work in the bank that had been run by his deceased father, but left after a year to return to aviation. He founded his first airline, Long Island Airways, in 1923, but just as quickly abandoned it to form Colonial Airways and bid for government airmail contracts. Although the airline was successful and did win

Civil Airmail Route No. 1, New York to Boston, the rate of progress and what he perceived as a lack of ambition among his partners, led Trippe to leave and acquire two competing airlines, Florida Airways and Pan American Airways, which were competing to carry airmail between Key West in Florida to Havana in Cuba, a flight of just 90 miles. Trippe merged the two airlines, adopting Pan American as the title, and ensured that he won the airmail contract in 1927 by negotiating exclusive landing rights in Cuba.

The following year the route was extended into South America. The company expanded rapidly, and in the strictly regulated sphere of international operations at the time, this often involved contact with foreign governments. There were rumours that Trippe himself was involved in intrigue with Latin American dictators. Even in the USA, international routes were awarded at the discretion of the government, and Pan American soon began winning most of the important international routes, but was denied a domestic route network. At first, the main competitor on routes into Latin America was an airline owned by W.R. Grace & Company, an American shipping line, which had developed a network of services on the Pacific Coast of South America. Trippe arranged a merger of the South American interests of the two companies, forming PANAGRA, or Pan American Grace Airways. The airline acquired other airlines, most notably the New York, Rio and Buenos Aires Line (NYBRA), known as 'near beer', after years of intense rivalry and even hostility between the two companies.

Trippe then pushed Pan American's route network out across the Pacific to China and Hong Kong, and was also involved with Britain's Imperial Airways in establishing transatlantic services. Despite all of this progress, on many routes the airline had a competitor – Trans World Airlines (TWA) on the Atlantic and North-west Orient on the Pacific. It was not until 1979, when the airline was allowed to purchase the ailing National Airlines, that Pan American acquired a domestic route network.

Trubshaw, Ernest Brian (1924–2001) British test pilot. Educated at Winchester, his passion for flying was kindled in 1934 when he saw the

Prince of Wales's aircraft land on the beach at Pembrey, Carmarthenshire. He volunteered to join the RAF in 1942 and received flying training in the United States. He was posted to Bomber Command on his return to the UK and flew Short Stirling and Avro Lancaster heavy bombers, before transferring to Transport Command in 1945. Classified as an 'exceptional' pilot, he was assigned to the King's Flight in 1946, and in 1949–50 he taught at the Empire Flying School and the RAF Flying College.

He left the service to join Vickers-Armstrong as a test pilot, and was involved with the development of the Valiant V-bomber, the Vanguard airliner, the VC-10 long-haul airliner and the One-Eleven short-haul airliner. He was awarded the Derry and Richards Memorial Medal in 1962 for testing the delivery system of a nuclear weapon from a Valiant bomber, and again in 1965 for outstanding test-flying when he saved the VC-10 on a test-flight in which half an elevator broke loose, shaking the aircraft so that he could not read the instruments. On analysing the problem he radioed in, describing it in case he could not get the aircraft back to base – he managed to land safely with just half the elevator.

His fame rests on being the British test pilot for the Anglo-French Concorde supersonic airliner, making the first British test flight in 1969. On one occasion he saved the aircraft when the altimeters failed during a test flight. He took the aircraft on a world tour in 1972, and in 1974 set a still-unbeaten transatlantic speed record for a commercial aircraft when he flew from Fairford, Gloucestershire, to Bangor, Maine, in 2 hours 56 minutes. He finished his career in management with **British Aerospace** and as a board member for the Civil Aviation Authority. He flew as a passenger in Concorde in 1999 to celebrate the thirtieth anniversary of the first flight.

Tsiolkovsky, Konstantin Eduardovitch (1857–1935)

Russian designer and rocket pioneer. Poor hearing meant that he was educated by his father and eventually emerged as a mathematics and science teacher, but with a keen interest in flight. He described the construction of an all-metal airship in 1892, and in 1895 designed an all-metal aeroplane, building and testing the wings in a wind

tunnel that he built himself. He later concentrated on rockets and space flight, and saw the need for a rotating space station in earth's orbit.

His papers were usually rejected by the Imperial Technical Society so his ideas did not reach the wider world until after the Bolshevik Revolution in 1917. After his death, the Soviet authorities tried to maintain that he had invented the turbojet and turboprop, but there is no evidence to support this.

Tuck, Wg Cdr Robert Roland Stanford (1916–87)

British ace. At 19, Tuck left the Merchant Navy and joined the RAF, and by May 1940 was a flight lieutenant, commanding a flight of No. 92 Squadron. He had already studied tactics and argued that tight formations were useless and that fighter patrols should consist of more widely spaced aircraft, something which was later found to be true.

He was an ace before the Battle of Britain in 1940, and in one three-day period had shot down six enemy aircraft. After the Battle of Britain, he commanded the fighter wing based in Duxford, and in December took command of a Biggin Hill-based Spitfire wing. His tally rose to twenty-nine confirmed kills, and would have been higher but for being shot down over Boulogne in January 1942 and made a prisoner of war. His aircraft landed in flames, too low to bale out, and as he attempted a dead stick landing in a field, he realised that the AA gun that had shot him down was straight ahead, so he blasted it with his machine guns and killed the entire gun crew.

Postwar, he retired from the RAF and became a mushroom farmer.

Tupolev

Russian design bureau. **Andrei Tupolev** was given the design bureau by Lenin after he had already begun designing aircraft using the designation ANT. The bureau survived his imprisonment in 1936, when Petlyakov took over and put his superior's TB-7 bomber into production as the Pe-8, the only four-engined bomber built by the USSR during the Second World War.

Postwar, the bureau copied captured Boeing B-29 Superfortress bombers and these entered service in 1946. A succession of turboprop and jet designs followed, including the Tu-16 and Tu-20 bombers, and the Tu-104 and Tu-114 jet airliners, the first to enter service after the ill-starred Comet 1. The bureau went on to produce the Tu-22 'Backfire' supersonic bomber, as well as the widely used Tu-134 and Tu-154 airliners, but were much less successful with the Tu-144 supersonic airliner, designed by Andrei's son, **Alexei**. A turboprop maritime-reconnaissance aircraft, the Tu-95 'Bear' was the only swept-wing turboprop aircraft to enter service. It is the fastest propeller aircraft ever built and, having first entered service in 1956, remains operational today. The Tu-160 'Blackjack' supersonic bomber is the largest operational bomber today and is capable of Mach 2.05.

Tupolev, Alexei Andrevich (1925–2001)
Russian designer. Son of **Andrei Tupolev**, he was born in Moscow and graduated from the Moscow Aviation Institute, where he later became a professor at 39 years old. His most notable achievement was the Tu-144 supersonic airliner, which made its first flight on 31 December 1968, eight weeks before the Anglo-French Concorde. He always denied suggestions that his aircraft, nicknamed Concordski by the media, was a copy of Concorde, but the configuration and droop nose bore a very strong resemblance. Although export interest was claimed, the aircraft lost any credibility when a prototype crashed during a demonstration flight at the 1973 Paris Air Show. The aircraft entered service on Aeroflot's domestic services, but after a second fatal accident in 1978 it was confined to freight flights before being taken out of service in the early 1980s. Apart from the accidents, one problem was that the aircraft used turbofans and had to maintain reheat to cruise at supersonic speeds, keeping fuel consumption high and range short.

Tupolev than started work on hydrogen engines, building the Tu-155, the first commercial airliner to take off powered by liquid hydrogen. Despite claims that the aircraft was 'ecologically pure', it never progressed due to a lack of funding.

Tupolev, Andrei Nikolayevich (1888–1972)
Russian designer. A pupil of Zhukovsky at the Moscow Technical High School, which he attended from 1908, he was arrested in 1911 for alleged anti-Tsarist activity, but he was released and later found work at Moscow's Dux aircraft factory.

He supported the Bolshevik Revolution and, as a reward for his pre-revolutionary activities, Lenin made him chairman of the Special Committee for Heavy Aviation. He persuaded Lenin to allocate funds for a Central Aerodynamics and Hydrodynamics Institute in Moscow, where he started work in 1928. Meanwhile, he had designed his first aeroplane, a single-seat monoplane that first flew in 1922, but this appears to have been a clone of the Junkers K-16, by this time being built at an undercover Junkers factory established in Moscow to circumvent the ban on aircraft manufacture in Germany set by the **Treaty of Versailles**. Among the lessons learnt by Tupolev from the Junkers concern was the use of aluminium in aircraft construction.

He started the long series of aircraft that bore his name with the ANT-2 monoplane, the Soviet Union's first all-metal aircraft. As the first prominent Soviet aircraft designer, most of the other famous designers spawned by the USSR owed their training and initial experience to him. In 1936, despite his important position and earlier favour with Lenin, he was arrested at the outset of the Stalin purges. Stalin blamed Tupolev for the poor performance of Soviet aircraft during the Spanish Civil War, and he was imprisoned, yet continued to design aircraft while in gaol. As the Soviet Union could not assign the initials of a prisoner to aircraft, his TB-7 heavy bomber entered service as the Petlyakov Pe-8, after his assistant, but the Tu-2 twin-engined bomber recognised its designer. Freedom came in 1942, when Stalin needed to inject fresh energy into the Soviet aircraft industry, and at the same time he was awarded the Stalin prize. He produced a series of designs that helped the Soviet armed forces as they fought their way westwards into Germany.

Post-Second World War, Tupolev adjusted to the demands of a much-changed technology, designing the Tu-14 jet bomber and Tu-95 turboprop bomber, and the Tu-104, Tu-114, Tu-124, Tu-134 and Tu-154 airliners.

turbojet See jet

Turbomeca French manufacturer. Formed in 1938, after the Second World War the company concentrated on smaller turboprops and turboshafts, although it was also involved with **Rolls-Royce** on the engines for the Anglo-French Jaguar strike aircraft and for the Mitsubishi T2 advanced jet trainer. After collaborating with **SNECMA**, it became part of the **SAFRAN** group.

turboprop *See* jet

Turner, Roscoe (1895–1970) American air racer. He joined the US Army in 1917 and learnt parachuting while serving in an observation balloon unit. Following the First World War he joined a circus as a lion tamer but stunt flying was his ambition. He went into partnership with Harry Rusner, a stunt flyer who needed financial support to repair his aircraft. They developed a double act with a mock fire in the aeroplane and Turner escaping by parachute, while Rusner, unseen by those on the ground, landed the aircraft some distance away to give the impression that it had crashed. Rusner taught Turner to fly in 1921 and he became a barnstormer, although he did set up the Nevada Air Line and ran that for a period in 1929.

Generally, he was regarded as being lightweight, too much of a showman and not enough of a pilot, but he had ambitions to set a record. In 1929 he set his first speed record, flying with a passenger from Los Angeles to New York in 20 hours and 20 minutes, driving the time down with further attempts. He won the Bendix transcontinental race in 1933, and then the Thompson Trophy races in 1934, 1938 and 1939 – the only pilot to win the contest three times. In 1934 he flew with Clyde Pangborn in the MacRobertson England-to-Australia race and they came third in a Boeing 247. He designed and built his own aircraft, one in association with **Laird**, while he also flew a Wedell-Williams racer. One eccentric feature was that he often flew with a pet lion, Gilmore, as co-pilot.

Twining, Gen Nathan F. (1897–1982) American air commander. Having served as a corporal in the US National Guard during the First World War, American entry into the Second World War found him in the USAAF. In 1943 he was given command of the Thirteenth USAAF based in New Caledonia, and in July he took command of all Allied air units during operations in the Solomons. In January 1944 he took command of the Fifteenth USAAF in Italy, and of the Allied strategic air forces in the Mediterranean. He planned the raids on the oilfields at Ploesti. In August 1945 he returned to the Far East, succeeding **Curtiss LeMay** as commander of the Twentieth USAAF on the Marianas, and it was aircraft under his command that dropped the atomic bombs on **Hiroshima** and **Nagasaki**.

Twiss, Peter (1921–) British test pilot. Commissioned into the Royal Navy's Fleet Air Arm, he learnt to fly in 1940. He flew Fairey Swordfish torpedo-bombers before moving on to the more glamorous Hawker Sea Hurricane and Seafire. He also acted as a ferry pilot. Postwar, he applied to join the Empire Test Pilot School and on graduating joined **Fairey** as a test pilot. He became the last British holder of the world air speed record on 10 March 1956 when he flew the Fairey Delta FD-2 at 1,132 mph. He remained with the company until it was merged into **Westland** in 1960.

Tytler, James (1747–1804) Scottish aeronaut. Tytler had the somewhat unusual professional experience of having been a ship's surgeon as well as editor of the second edition of the *Encyclopaedia Britannica*, but then became interested in ballooning. He sought a public subscription in 1784 to build a balloon, but, not completely aware of the designs used by the **Montgolfier** brothers, he built an envelope that was barrel-shaped rather than spherical. On the first inflation, the envelope caught fire. It was repaired and a second attempt was made at launching it, but high winds prevented a successful ascent and the crowd of spectators rioted and wrecked the balloon. On the third attempt, on 25 August 1784, he managed to make the balloon ascend from Heriot's Garden (possibly now Heriot Row), but without a basket or passengers. The fire simply heated the envelope until the balloon was launched and then it drifted until it deflated and descended.

He made a number of further attempts but failed so often that he became an object of ridicule, giving up when his balloon was completely destroyed in a storm in 1785. He was accused of sedition in 1792 and fled to the USA where he settled and became a newspaper editor.

U

Udet, Gen Ernst (1896–1941) German ace. Conscripted as an infantryman at the outbreak of the First World War, he paid for flying lessons in 1915 so that he could transfer to the Military Aviation Service. His father presented him with a parachute, far from standard issue for military aircrew at the time, which almost certainly saved his life on two occasions. His aircraft always carried the marking 'LO!' on the side, short for Eleanor, his fiancée. He became Germany's second highest scoring ace during the war with sixty-two confirmed kills. He famously had an air-to-air duel with **Georges Guynemer** in which his guns jammed and the Frenchman, realising what had happened, spared his life. By chance, he is claimed to have been the first pilot to destroy a tank when his machine-gun fire so unnerved the driver that he overturned into a ditch.

Udet and Eleanor married, but they divorced soon after the war and he became a stunt pilot touring Germany and performing before large crowds. He later won a number of speed contests and went to Hollywood to become a film stunt pilot. In between, however, he built an aeroplane of his own design, the Flamingo, and put this into production but sold the factory to go to the USA.

When the Nazi regime took over in 1933, he was approached to see if he would join the proposed Luftwaffe, but he initially rejected these advances. He did offer a number of suggestions on the future shape and equipment of the new air force, and out of these was born the Junkers Ju87 Stuka dive-bomber, the ideal aircraft for 'lightning war' (blitzkrieg), with close coordination of fast-moving armour and air power. On the other hand, he dismissed the Messerschmitt Bf109 when he first saw it because it had a glazed cockpit and was a monoplane.

As war approached he relented and joined the Luftwaffe becoming head of technical development, a post that he felt was beyond him and which undoubtedly led to his suicide in 1941.

undercarriage Sometimes referred to as 'landing gear', undercarriage development has often influenced aircraft design. Strictly, the term refers to any form of aircraft landing gear, including skids, skis, floats and wheels, but in general use the term refers to wheeled undercarriages. The difficulty in undercarriage and tyre design keeping pace with the increase in aircraft size during the 1920s and 1930s was a factor in prolonging the development of the **flying boat**.

Early aircraft often took off using skids and a set of rails, but as early as 1906, **Alberto Santos-Dumont**'s 14-bis used a wheeled undercarriage without skids, and a number of pre-First World War designs used a wheeled undercarriage with skids to prevent the aircraft toppling over on landing. Pneumatic tyres appeared at an early stage on the Vuia monoplane of 1906. Many of the early designs used wheels similar to those used on bicycles or prams, but soon solid wheels became standard. **Sikorsky** had difficulty finding a suitable undercarriage for his Grand of 1913, and eventually had to use no less than sixteen wheels. At the same time, and even during the First World War, a tailskid was usual rather than a tail wheel, no doubt helped by the use of unmetalled runways. An American, Matthew Sellers, is reputed to have built an aircraft with a retractable undercarriage, but it is certain that a retractable undercarriage was incorporated into the German Wiencziers monoplane of 1911. The first practical retractable undercarriage was that of the Dayton-Wright high-wing monoplane for the **Gordon Bennett** Trophy Race of 1920.

The complication of the retractable undercarriage and the cost in terms of production and maintenance meant that these did not become widespread until well into the 1930s, as aircraft speeds rose and the drag of a fixed undercarriage and its effect on speed and fuel consumption meant retractable undercarriages became increasingly common. In fact, for many aircraft spatted undercarriages reduced drag sufficiently for a retractable undercarrige to be unnecessary.

The RAF's last biplane fighter, the Gloster Gladiator, had an enclosed cockpit but still had a fixed undercarriage, even though the maximum speed was well above 200 mph, the point at which many believed the drag penalty of a fixed undercarriage outweighed the costs of a retractable undercarriage. The Junkers Ju52/3M transport had a fixed undercarriage but the Allied rival, the Douglas C-47 (DC-3), had a retractable undercarriage – the former was dated even before war broke out in 1939, the latter was modern. Lower speeds and the importance of weight meant that helicopters were later in adopting retractable undercarriages than fixed-wing aircraft, but the Sikorsky S-61 introduced this feature in the 1960s, cleverly putting it into sponsons on both sides of the fuselage so that, combined with a boat-shaped underside to the hull, it provided stability while the helicopter was on the surface of water.

Undercarriage design moved ahead during the Second World War. It became standard on combat aircraft. The Vought F4U Corsair introduced a 'fail-safe' undercarriage that automatically dropped if the aircraft suffered a hydraulic failure, doubtlessly saving many aircraft from having to belly-land or have the pilot bale out. The tricycle undercarriage appeared on the Bell Airacobra, but this aircraft was not a great success, so at first the advantages of greater stability and a much improved forward vision for the pilot once the aircraft was on the ground may not have been fully appreciated. Nevertheless, while some Messerschmitt Me262 aircraft had tail wheels, most jet aircraft were designed with a tricycle undercarriage, with the odd exception such as the Supermarine Attacker, one of the Royal Navy's first jet fighters. Incidental advantages of the tricycle undercarriage include making it much easier to stretch an aircraft design, a feature that mattered little in the early days, but commercial jet aircraft and even military transports are routinely produced offering customers a choice of fuselage lengths.

V

variable-geometry Sometimes referred to as 'variable-sweep', or in popular terminology as 'swing-wing', variable-geometry allows aircraft to have the best possible wing sweep for lower-speed operations, like take-off and landing, and for high-speed flight, with the wings swept back to reduce drag. In fact, high supersonic speeds would ideally have little wing area. The concept is far from new, with the first attempt at variable-geometry being on the Swedish Paulson Type 1 of 1918, which also had **variable-incidence**, although many doubt whether this aircraft could have flown.

A leading proponent of variable-geometry was the British inventor/designer, **Sir Barnes Wallis**, who pressed the case for its use after the Second World War but was for many years ignored in his own country. In the United States, **Grumman** used the technique on the XF10F Jaguar jet fighter, that first flew in 1953, but only two prototypes were built and the aircraft did not go into production because of the complications inherent in the design.

The first operational variable-geometry aircraft was the General Dynamics F-111 strike aircraft, first flown in prototype form in December 1964, and which saw service with both the USAF and the RAAF. A variable-geometry version of the Mirage series, the G8, was test flown by **Dassault**, but the projected Anglo-French Variable-Geometry Aircraft or AFVG, was abandoned. Later the UK, Germany and Italy developed the Panavia Tornado in both interceptor and interdictor versions using variable-geometry, and in the meantime, the USN put the Grumman F-14 Tomcast air superiority fighter into service. A sole attempt at a variable-geometry supersonic transport, the Boeing 2707, was abandoned.

The disadvantage of variable-geometry is the weight of the 'hinges' required for the necessary movement of the wings. On the F-111, these add some 2 tons to the aircraft weight, which also means a lower warload or less fuel. Other problems include additional drag near the wing roots and added maintenance. These problems also mean that it became progressively less attractive and less feasible as aircraft weights and sizes increased.

variable-incidence Variable-incidence is the ability of an aircraft to change the angle of incidence between the wings and the fuselage. As with **variable-geometry**, the first design to incorporate this feature was the Swedish Paulson Type 1 of 1918, but this aircraft appears never to have flown. The first production aircraft with the feature was the **Ling-Temco-Vought** (LTV) F-8 Crusader carrier-borne jet fighter, first flown in 1955. The McDonnell Douglas F-4 Phantom II introduced a variable-incidence tailplane. As with variable-geometry, the concept is best confined to smaller aircraft and is too heavy for large transports.

Védrines, Jules (1881–1919) French pioneer. A fitter at the Gnome engine works, in 1910 Védrines joined **Henri Farman** as chief mechanic at his flying school, and later that year learnt to fly. The following year he embarked on a career as a racing pilot, and in May 1912 was the only pilot to finish the Paris–Madrid air race. Unfortunately, the crowds did not expect anyone to finish and had left by the time he arrived, which he mistook for a snub at his working-class origins and was only partly mollified by an audience with King Alphonso.

Intense rivalry emerged between Védrines and **Jean Conneau**, but between them they became the two best racing pilots in Europe. The story is told that when Conneau beat Védrines in the Great Circuit of England Air Race, completing it in just 22½ hours, with Védrines following an hour behind, Védrines burst into tears. He was the first man to break the 100-mph barrier, winning the 1912 **Gordon Bennett** Race with an average speed of 108 mph. In 1913, he flew from Paris to Cairo carrying a passenger. When the First World War broke out, he volunteered for the Aviation Militaire, mainly flying Moranes, and flew a number of missions to land agents behind the German lines. Postwar, he was killed flying between Paris and Rome.

Verne, Jules (1828–1905) French author and visionary. Originally arriving in Paris destined to become a lawyer, he fell in with the literary circle around Alexander Dumas, who had a theatre for which Verne wrote plays. He soon began to specialise in science fiction. His *Five Weeks in a Balloon* was published in 1863, and in 1864 his *From Earth to the Moon*, followed by *Clipper of the Clouds* in 1886, all pursued aerospace themes and did much to inspire the rising generation with a passion for flight. Possibly the last mentioned work was inspired by Gabriel de la Landelle, whose helicopter design resembled a mixed sail and steam ship, with multiple helicopter rotors mounted on the masts rather than sails.

Versailles, Treaty of (28 June 1919) The Versailles Treaty or Settlement brought the First World War to an end when it was signed in June 1919. Its conditions were far-reaching. As far as aviation was concerned, post-First World War Germany was banned from aircraft manufacture and the armed forces could not include an aviation service. Only a coastal defence navy and an army of 100,000 men was permitted.

The conditions of the treaty were broken by many German designers who worked abroad and even established aircraft factories in places as unlikely as the Soviet Union, while the spread of gliding clubs kept Germans interested in flying. After the rise of Adolph Hitler, secret plans were implemented to create the Luftwaffe and Germany began developing and building aircraft.

Whether or not the conditions of the treaty were too austere or unrealistic, the main problem was that there was no real mechanism for their enforcement. The League of Nations proved powerless whenever put to the test, and the occupying powers did not remain for long – unlike the post-Second World War period, although in this case, occupation was largely prompted by the Cold War.

vertical and short take-off and landing (V/STOL) *See* vertical take-off

vertical envelopment The concept of using helicopters to deploy troops to surround an enemy position, as adopted by the US forces during the Vietnam War and by the British during the confrontation between Malaysia and Indonesia in the 1960s. The system offers speed, especially over difficult terrain such as jungle, but suffers from the limited numbers of personnel that can be deployed and restrictions on the weight of equipment. Noise can also be a problem, giving warning of the intention.

vertical replenishment Usually used by navies, this is the ability to transfer stores between ships using a helicopter carrying an underslung load. It speeds up the transfer between ships under way at sea, and requires great skill on the part of the pilot or pilots, as sudden changes of direction or speed can cause the load to swing like a pendulum and is usually disastrous.

vertical take-off/vertical and short take-off The appeal of vertical take-off arose from the shortage of suitable airfields, which also fuelled the interest in the hydro-aeroplane from the earliest days. The advent of the **helicopter** did much to satisfy the need for vertical take-off and landing (VTOL), but it soon became clear that the performance limitations of the helicopter and its high costs would be a problem, especially with regard to range, and engineers began to explore other ways of providing vertical take-off. The first true VTOL machine was the experimental **Rolls-Royce** TMR, the so-called Flying Bedstead, a test-rig that made tethered flights in 1953 and free flights in 1954 using two Nene turbojets, but it lacked aerodynamic surfaces. Successful test flights were achieved by the Fairey Rotodyne twin-engined turboprop transport which had a wing and a rotor powered by tip-mounted jets for take-off and landing, but this proved noisy, despite interest by the airline BEA, the RAF and the USAF. The main cause for the project being abandoned may have been the acquisition of **Fairey** by the helicopter manufacturer **Westland**.

Among many projects for a VTOL jet fighter, the Hawker P1127 Kestrel has been developed into the Harrier and Sea Harrier, for the RAF, the RN and the USMC, and has been adopted by other navies as well. While the aircraft proved that VTOL was feasible, its fuel and warload were both limited by the maximum take-off thrust through the thrust-vectoring nozzles, although it was soon found that a rolling or short take-off improved performance, especially in conjunction with a ramp at the end of the take-off run, usually found on aircraft carriers adapted for this kind of aircraft and known as the 'ski-jump'.

Over the years it has been found that thrust-vectoring is superior to separate lift jets, partly because little additional weight is involved.

Commercial VTOL transports have also proved elusive with **Canadair**, now part of **Bombardier**, testing tilt wings on the CL214, **Dornier** using lift jets and, more recently, tilt engines have been used by Bell-Boeing working on the XV-22 Osprey, which has entered production and is in service as the V-22 with the USMC. Smaller versions of this design are planned for utility and business markets.

Vertol *See* Boeing and Piasecki

Verville, Alfred Victor (1890–1970) French-American designer. Originally trained as an engineer, he was so impressed by an exhibition flight by one of **Glenn Curtiss**'s pilots in 1914 that he went to work for **Curtiss**. He worked on the design of the 'Jenny' trainer and the America flying boat. He went to work elsewhere but in 1918 was seconded to the US Army Aviation Section's engineering division and sent to France to study European progress in aircraft production. His fluent French enabled him to mix easily with French designers, and he became friendly with **Louis Béchereau** at Spad.

Postwar, back in the USA, Béchereau's ideas influenced Verville's design of the VCP-1, a monocoque biplane similar to the latest Spads. A development of this aircraft competed in the 1920 Pulitzer speed event. He went to Europe the following year with **Billy Mitchell** for further study of European progress, and returned to design the Verville-Sperry R-3, which had a

cantilever wooden wing combined with a welded tube fuselage and retracting undercarriage. This aircraft won the 1924 Pulitzer Speed Trophy.

He remained working for the US government in different departments for the rest of his career.

Vickers British manufacturer. Part of a major industrial group that embraced armament manufacture and shipbuilding, the company entered aircraft production during the First World War with the FB5 Gunbus, a pusher-propeller biplane that gave the air gunner a clear forward field of fire. By the end of the war the company was building the Vimy biplane heavy bomber, and in 1919 this became the first aircraft to make a non-stop crossing of the **Atlantic**. Airliner versions of the Vimy followed, and during the early 1920s the Virginia bomber and its Victoria transport variant were in production. A further biplane design was the single-engined Vildebeest torpedo-bomber. An all-metal monoplane airliner was the Viastra of 1931, which was normally twin-engined but single and three-engined versions were also built.

The company acquired **Supermarine** in the early 1920s, and possibly because of this did not venture into flying boat production itself. The late 1930s saw first the single-engined Wellesley bomber, the first with geodetic construction, and then a further aircraft using this system, the twin-engined Wellington, which was the best bomber in RAF service at the outbreak of the Second World War, and which remained in service on maritime-reconnaissance duties until the end of the war.

Postwar, the aerodynamic surfaces of the Wellington were incorporated into the design of the Viking airliner and its Valetta military counterpart. The main success for the company during this period was the four-engined Viscount, the world's first operational turboprop airliner, of which 444 were built between 1951 and 1963. It was the first British airliner to be sold to a US airline. Far less successful was the replacement, the Vanguard, of which only forty-three were sold because of competition from jet aircraft. The VC10, standing for Vickers Commercial 10, and stretched Super VC10, were popular with passengers but came too late to make a breakthrough into the long-haul jet airliner market. The Valiant was the first of a trio of 'V' bombers intended to deliver the independent British nuclear deterrent, and it was also the first to be retired due to fatigue problems.

In 1960 the company was merged into the **British Aircraft Corporation** while its hovercraft manufacturing interests passed to the British Hovercraft Corporation.

Vietnam, air war (1964–75) Formerly part of French Indo-China, a Geneva conference divided Vietnam into two states, communist North Vietnam and democratic South Vietnam, with unification proposed for 1956, following elections. The elections were never held in North Vietnam.

The Soviet Union rapidly built up the armed forces of North Vietnam, with a Vietnamese People's Air Force established with Soviet assistance. In the South, the Vietnamese Air Force was left with the equipment abandoned by the French, Dassault communications aircraft and Morane-Saulnier trainers, although Grumman Bearcat fighter-bombers, Douglas C-47 transport aircraft and light aircraft were soon added. Soon South Vietnam was being driven into the US sphere of influence because of the threat posed by its northern neighbour.

In 1955 the United States started to provide South Vietnam with equipment and training, including military advisers. As communist incursions continued, the number of American military advisers increased, until by the early 1960s they were more akin to regular troops.

In 1963 a new US President, John F. Kennedy, decided to commit regular US forces to South Vietnam to counter the growing communist threat. This decision came about because the US State Department was committed to the 'domino' theory which decreed that as one state fell to communism, it then posed a threat to its neighbour. Logic dictated that communism had to be checked in South Vietnam, otherwise Laos and Cambodia would be threatened, followed by Thailand and Malaysia.

Kennedy encouraged America's allies to support the fight. The United Kingdom at the time was involved in countering an Indonesian threat to the newly created Federation of Malaysia and Singapore, as well as trouble in the Aden Protectorate, and could not spare any forces. America's staunchest ally was South Korea. Until 1970, Australian and New Zealand forces were also involved.

Probably the most controversial aspects of the Vietnam War was the air war, compounded by the use of defoliant weapons intended to remove foliage from trees and expose the Viet Cong to attack – at least in theory. Another controversial feature was the extensive use of napalm, jellified petroleum, with media pictures of badly burnt children. The opponents of the air war conveniently overlooked the occasional aerial combat between the opposing sides, and the extent to which North Vietnam had been equipped with surface-to-air guided missile systems and extensive anti-aircraft artillery, or 'triple A', by the Soviet Union.

The United States government all too often overlooked the way in which air power could make a difference, with repeated attacks on the main entry point of supplies into North Vietnam – the port of Haiphong – and then easing off for long periods at a time. Given the port's proximity to Chinese territorial waters, a classical naval blockade could not be mounted, leaving air power as the sole instrument for stopping supplies.

Further aerial attacks were mounted in retaliation to North Vietnamese attacks on American naval vessels. One of these followed the Gulf of Tongking incident, on 2 August 1964, when the American destroyer *Maddox* was attacked by three North Vietnamese gunboats while still in international waters. Four torpedoes were fired at the *Maddox*, but all missed, although the destroyer was hit on her superstructure by 14.5 mm gunfire. One of the attacking craft was damaged by fire from the *Maddox* and four fighters from the aircraft carrier *Kitty Hawk* were in the air and attacked the gunboats, sinking one of them. Two nights later, a repeat attack was mounted, this time against the destroyer *Turner Joy*, again without damage. On this occasion, sixteen aircraft from two carriers, *Ticonderoga* and *Constellation*, came to the aid of the destroyer. This led to an attack by sixty-seven aircraft from the two carriers on 5 August, against the North Vietnamese naval bases at Ben Thuy, Hon Gay, Quang Khe and Lach Chao, and an oil storage facility at Vinh. The result of this was the loss of seven North Vietnamese Navy gunboats, while another ten were badly damaged, for the loss of two aircraft, with one pilot dead and another taken prisoner. The impact of the attack can be assessed by the fact that the North Vietnamese Navy had just thirty-six gunboats at the time.

Apart from these operations, there were two main types of air attack in support of the ground war: precision attacks against a specific target, and area bombing, designed to break up concentrations of Viet Cong or North Vietnamese troops. The latter involved large Boeing B-52 bombers, which provided the media with pictures of scores of bombs falling from their bellies. American losses on the precision raids were very heavy, although later in the war these eased off considerably with greater use of 'smart', or guided, weaponry, such as stand-off bombs and air-to-surface missiles. These had the dual advantage of reducing aircraft losses due to missile and triple AAA fire, and increasing accuracy.

Innovations of the war included the use of 'gunships', which in this conflict meant transport aircraft equipped with a large number of machine guns able to fire downwards into the jungle to catch Viet Cong and North Vietnamese troops moving along the trails.

Unfortunately, air power was often expected to win the war for the Americans and the South Vietnamese. As in Korea, good, hard targets against which bombers could excel were relatively few. Porters and mules on jungle trails were difficult targets for air power, and all too seldom was any real attempt made to ambush them, in effect turning the tables on the terrorists. Also lacking was a determined effort to win the 'hearts and minds' of the local population, especially in areas frequented by the terrorists, along the lines of the successful campaign mounted by the British in Malaya during the early 1950s.

Faced with a deteriorating situation on the ground, the North Vietnamese launched a conventional invasion through the demilitarised zone, timed to coincide with the run up to the 1972 American presidential elections. A conventional invasion should have played straight into the American hands, and in many ways it did, with the American and South Vietnamese forces soon checking the invaders, who also failed to have in place the support facilities essential for such an undertaking. However, a week was wasted before air power could be authorised against targets in the north, when the use of smart bombs destroyed the transformer house of the Lang Chi hydroelectric plant, without civilian casualties and without damage to the nearby dam. This cut 47 per cent of North Vietnam's electricity. The use of smart bombs meant that the Thanh Hoa bridge, south of Hanoi, which had been the objective for more than 800 sorties between 1965 and 1968 without being touched once, was destroyed. Within weeks of using smart weapons, no bridge was left intact.

These late successes finally 'bombed Hanoi to the negotiating table', but Hanoi always refused to talk unless the bombing stopped. Every time it stopped, restarting it became more difficult politically. This was a classic example of the difficulties faced by a free society dealing with unscrupulous and manipulative opponents.

US involvement in South Vietnam, which had started officially in August 1964, officially ended in January 1973. After this, the term was 'Vietnamization', with the armed forces of South Vietnam taking more of the burden. Both the United States and the Soviet Union were supposed to reduce support for their respective client states at this stage, but only the United States did so. Neither side was to receive replacements for combat losses, but the Soviet Union continued to supply North Vietnam.

As defeat appeared inevitable for South Vietnam, the United States Seventh Fleet was assembled off Saigon for the evacuation of Americans and those South Vietnamese who had fought alongside them; a total of nine aircraft carriers were gathered for this task on 20 April. Two days later, 7,000 United States Marines were put ashore to protect the evacuation, which included 130,000 South Vietnamese who had emigration clearance in the United States. It took until 29 April to complete the operation.

A routine was established for the evacuation. A South Vietnamese helicopter would arrive aboard one of the warships, discharge its passengers, have its doors ripped off so that it would sink more quickly and then be flown into the sea by its pilot who was picked up afterwards. There was no room for all of the aircraft provided to South

Vietnam to be taken away, although in the end the American warships did manage to remove a substantial number.

Vinci, Leonardo da (1452–1519) Renaissance Italian artist and visionary. Better known today as an artist, da Vinci was obsessed with the possibilities for flight and this grew stronger as he aged. Many of his contemporaries regarded him as more of an engineer, if the term was known at the time, than an artist. Much of his work was based on inaccurate imitations of bird flight, and manpower was considered to be sufficient in most of his designs, with the position of the pilot varying between prone, almost with a 'swimming' action, to upright.

Unfortunately, da Vinci's work, which could have done much to help the early pioneers, was unknown and neglected until it was finally published in the late nineteenth century, by which time it post-dated the work of **Sir George Cayley** and **Horatio Phillips**.

His other achievements included a pyramid-shaped parachute design, an elevator control activated by a head harness, a form of retractable undercarriage, a clockwork helicopter as well as a bow-string-powered ornithopter.

Vodopyanov, Mikhail V. (1900–80) Soviet aviator. Originally one of the early Soviet airline pilots, he later became pilot for several Arctic expeditions and in 1934 he flew one of a number of aircraft used to rescue the crew of the *Chelyuskin*, trapped in thick ice off Siberia. The pilots on this expedition were the first to receive the award, Hero of the Soviet Union. Three years later he flew a group of scientists to within 13 miles of the North Pole, where they set up a base camp.

He flew for the military during the Second World War, and Stalin had him set up a bomber squadron that could attack Berlin. The Tupolev TB-7 bomber, with which they were equipped, did not have the radius of action for the mission, but they flew and bombed Berlin and when they ran out of fuel on the return leg, force-landed in occupied territory. According to Soviet legend, the crews then managed to make their way back to the USSR, although whether or not they

were then sent to the Gulag, which was usual for members of the armed forces who were taken prisoner of war, even if they escaped, has never been mentioned.

Voisin, Charles (1888–1912) and Gabriel (1880–1973) French pioneers. Although he claimed to have sought out **Clement Ader** as early as 1904, it was while studying architecture in Paris that Gabriel Voisin heard a lecture by **Ferdinand Ferber**. Later, in discussion, Ferber suggested that he contact **Ernest Archdeacon**, who immediately recruited Voisin as a pilot. The two men formed the Syndicat d'Aviation in 1905 intending to build aircraft. Two float-gliders were built – one for Archdeacon and one for **Louis Blériot** – and were towed behind motorboats on the River Seine. Blériot proposed that Voisin should join him, and Blériot-Voisin was formed using a workshop purchased from Surcouf, the balloon manufacturer. Between them, they produced another glider and a powered aeroplane, but neither was successful. Voisin also worked independently, building the 14-bis for **Alberto Santos-Dumont**, but after this flew in November 1906, his partnership with Blériot broke up. It was at this stage that Charles joined his brother and they took over the old balloon workshops to establish Voisin Frères.

The new company produced its first aeroplane in 1907, built for Henri Kapferer, but this was unsuccessful. Their second aircraft, built for **Léon Delagrange**, was successfully flown by Gabriel in March at Bagatelle. Other aircraft were built that year, including a second for Delagrange, while one for **Henri Farman** became the first in Europe to fly a circular kilometre. What could have been a developing relationship with Farman was ruined when Voisin sold his aircraft secretly to Henry Moore-Brabazon (*see* **Brabazon of Tara**), and Farman felt compelled to form his own aircraft factory. Charles, always the lesser of the two brothers, helped at this time, but was killed in a car crash in 1912.

During the First World War, Voisin built bombers, although of undistinguished performance, but the business did well. Postwar, he started to produce the world's first prefabricated houses, but soon gave this up fearing retaliation from the building trade. In 1919 he started to build motor cars, and continued to do so until 1937, building high-quality and high-performance machines, although the business lost so much money that Voisin lost it in 1929. He managed to get it back in 1933 and Rolls-Royce even set engineers to study work at the plant in 1934.

When the Second World War broke out a German company, Gnome-Rhone, requisitioned the Voisin works and forced Voisin to remain in charge. He was accused of collaboration on the liberation of France and his factory was nationalised by the government. His name was cleared later, and he went back to designing cars, building a micro-car that was produced in Spain. He was in poverty during the 1950s, but was rescued by a former mistress to whom he had once given a cottage; she, being wealthy by this time, returned the property to him.

Voisin was renowned for a lack of integrity, and made claims that did not stand up to scrutiny. He claimed, falsely, that the **Wright** brothers had not made a true first flight because they had used a launching apparatus, despite photographic evidence to the contrary and their own admission that they did not use a launching apparatus until 1904.

von Braun, Dr Wernher *See* Braun, von

von Kármán, Theodore *See* Kármán, von

von Ohain, Dr Hans Pabst *See* Ohain, von

von Opel, Fritz *See* Opel, von

von Parseval, Maj August *See* Parseval, von

von Richthofen, Rittmeister Manfred *See* Richthofen, von

von Seeckt, Hans *See* Seeckt, von

von Zeppelin, Count Ferdinand Adolf August Heinrich *See* Zeppelin, von

Voss, Lt Werner (1897–1917) German ace. Commissioned into the Hussars at the outbreak of the First World War, he transferred to the Military Aviation Service in 1915, initially flying as an observer but then received flying training and joined **von Richthofen**'s unit, Jasta Boelcke, in 1916. A natural pilot, he shot down forty-eight Allied aircraft in just ten months. On 23 September 1917 he was flying on a lone patrol when 'B' Flight of the RFC's No. 56 Squadron, with seven aircraft, intercepted him. The RFC formation was led by **James McCudden** and five of the other six pilots were already aces. His aircraft was hit several times and he continued to fight back but as he began to tire, a British fighter slipped under his aircraft and fired a long burst from its Lewis-gun into the underside of his aircraft, which crashed in flames behind the British lines.

The RFC buried him with full military honours.

Vuia, Trajan (1872–1950) Romanian pioneer. After studying law in Budapest, he qualified as an engineer and moved to Paris, where he became acquainted with members of the Aéro-Club de France. **Victor Tatin** suggested that he design a monoplane, which he completed in 1906 as the No. 1, using a Serpollet 25 hp carbonic acid gas engine driving a tractor propeller. He managed to make a few powered hops in this aircraft, the longest being 6 metres at Issy-les-Moulineaux on 14 October, although he later claimed that it flew. A second aeroplane, the Vuia II, was powered by an Antoinette engine and made powered hops in 1907, with the longest being 20 metres at Bagatelle on 5 July. While Vuia gave up at this stage, his use of the tractor propeller and monoplane configuration is believed to have influenced **Louis Blériot**.

W

Waco US manufacturer. Dating from the 1920s, it became prominent during the Second World War producing large troop and vehicle-carrying gliders, but it also designed a powered transport that entered production with **Fairchild** as the C-123 provider.

Wallis, Sir Barnes Neville (1887–1979) British designer. Lacking the education to get into university, he started work in a shipyard, working with an engineer called H.B. Pratt. When Pratt left to work on the **Vickers** airship programme in 1913, Wallis went with him. It took just two years for Wallis to be recognised as an airship designer in his own right, with one of his first being the R-80. When the First World War ended, Wallis became the chief designer at Vickers and worked on the successful R-100.

Despite the success of the R-100, the R-101 crash in 1930 brought British interest in airships to an abrupt end. Wallis quickly, and successfully, adapted to designing aeroplanes. He had developed the geodetic structure to give strength and lightness to airframes, and applied this to his first heavier-than-air design, the Vickers Wellesley bomber. It was followed by the Wellington, the heaviest bomber in service with the RAF at the outbreak of the Second World War, and known affectionately to the RAF as the 'Wimpy' (after J. Wellington Wimpy, a cartoon character).

Unlike most aircraft designers, Wallis went beyond the airframe and even considered weapons. He designed a bouncing bomb, strictly speaking a mine, which he thought could destroy the dams in the Ruhr. After initial rejection by the RAF, the plan was adopted and in 1943 was used to attack the Möhne, Eder and Sorpe dams (*see* **Dam Busters**). This was the only time this weapon was used, dropped from specially modified Avro Lancaster heavy bombers, while a smaller version, designed to be dropped by de Havilland Mosquito light bombers for attacks on capital ships, was never used. Next he designed the novel earthquake bombs, designed to spin once dropped and burrow into the ground, then exploding and undermining heavy structures that could not be damaged by having bombs fall on top of them. The first of these was the 12,000 lb Tallboy, itself heavy enough by the standards of the day, but it was followed by the 22,000 lb Grand Slam. With bombs such as these, U-boat pens, which were massively reinforced, no longer offered protection.

Postwar, Wallis turned his fertile mind to the problems of supersonic flight. One of these was that the ideal wing profile for supersonic flight, and that for landing and take-off, were completely different. He proposed the **variable-geometry** aircraft, sometimes known as variable-sweep or 'swing-wing' in layman's parlance, but the idea was rejected in the UK. It was taken up in the USA, which produced the General Dynamics F-111, and later the Grumman F-14 Tomcat. In the UK, an early application (although still lagging behind the Americans) was the Anglo-French Variable-Geometry aircraft (AFVG), but this was cancelled and it was not until the advent of the Anglo-German-Italian Panavia Tornado that the British aircraft industry and the RAF finally became involved with this concept.

Wallis also looked at the potential for hydrogen-powered aircraft but many experts believe that the disadvantages, such as the amount of fuel tank capacity needed and the risk of fire, make this concept difficult.

Warren, Edward (1771–1820) Pioneering American aeronaut. Somewhat reminiscent of **Sir George Cayley**'s first full-sized glider experiment, Edward Warren was just 13 years old when he was asked by Peter Carnes to make an ascent in his balloon as Carnes was too heavy. This was the first balloon to be completed in the United States, and in 1784 Warren made the ascent, which is suspected to have been safely tethered. Carnes himself later attempted a balloon voyage in Philadelphia, but crashed into a wall during the ascent.

Warsaw Convention

Warsaw Convention This was an attempt during the interwar years to regulate air transport, but is best remembered for its scale of compensation for the victims, or relatives of the victims, of an air transport disaster, which became increasingly inadequate during the years after the Second World War.

Watson-Watt, Robert Alexander (1892–1973)

Scottish engineer and radar pioneer. Graduating as an engineer from University College, Dundee, he joined the Meteorological Office in London in 1915, where he was charged with developing a long-range electronic method for detecting thunderstorms. He was unsuccessful, but his experience enabled him to develop radio-beacon navigation aids for aircraft. His superiors must have read too much science fiction as he was next asked to develop an anti-aircraft ray gun, which he refused to do, but suggested that it would be technically possible to develop a long-range detecting beam, in short, radar. He contrived an experiment with a cathode ray tube and a radio receiver with which he tried to detect the short-wave transmission of a BBC radio broadcast off a Handley Page Heyford bomber. To everyone's surprise, the experiment was a success. He next worked on developing a radar beam that could detect aircraft while they were still 55 miles away, and a series of transmitting stations was situated along the south coast of England, including one at Ventnor on the Isle of Wight, in what became known as the 'Chain Home' network, during 1938. During the Battle of Britain and the Blitz, they proved invaluable in the defence, ensuring that RAF fighter controllers could always be certain of where the enemy was concentrating his forces. Previously, faith had been placed in huge sound detectors, but these could be easily confused.

Watson-Watt also inadvertently advanced the cause of women in the armed forces believing that they made better operators for his Chain Home stations as they were less 'ham-fisted' than men.

Weick, Fred Ernest (1899–1993)

Weick, Fred Ernest (1899–1993) American engineer. Graduating from the University of Illinois as an engineer, he initially worked for the US Air Mail Service as a draughtsman, then for an aircraft manufacturer before joining the US Navy's Bureau of Aeronautics. In 1925 he went to work for NACA, and his early work aimed at reducing the drag of air-cooled radial engines while also improving their cooling, and the answer was the engine cowl, which became widely known as the 'NACA cowl'. After teething problems with the early cowls, which were so aerodynamic that they broke loose and flew into the propeller disc, the concept became almost universally accepted, except for a few specialised applications such as crop-dusting aircraft.

Weick argued that tricycle undercarriages gave greater stability and much improved forward vision while aircraft were on the ground. To prove his theories he applied a tricycle undercarriage to the W-1 light aircraft. This so impressed a manufacturer, ERCO, that in 1936 he was commissioned to design and develop a light aircraft. The result was the Ercoupe with a tricycle undercarriage, interconnected rudder and ailerons and a very simple wing structure built entirely of metal. It laid down the specification for the modern light aircraft.

Weick later worked for Piper, designing the Cherokee and also crop-dusting aircraft.

Weiss, Jose (1850–1919)

Weiss, Jose (1850–1919) French glider pioneer. Graduating from Lille, having studied science and engineering, he rejected commerce and with support from his wealthy father became a landscape artist in England. He was successful at this, and began building model gliders as a hobby. Developing theories about stability, he presented papers to the Aeronautical Society. He built more than 200 models during the early twentieth century, but in 1909 built his first full-sized glider with wings curved along the forward edge and swept back. The glider flew well when demonstrated at Arundel in Sussex. Frederick Handley Page was sufficiently impressed to offer him a partnership, but none of the powered aircraft designed by them sold and the partnership was dissolved. The early Handley Page aircraft did, however, incorporate many of the features designed by Weiss.

Wellman, Walter (1858–1934) American pioneer aeronaut. A Chicago journalist attracted by ballooning, in 1907 he decided to make the first aerial voyage over the North Pole. He used the semi-rigid dirigible, *America*, which ascended from Smeerenberg on Spitzbergen; but just 35 miles into the trip, a leather drag strap broke and the project was abandoned. A further attempt in 1909 suffered the same problem. Despite these problems, he then planned to make a transatlantic aerial voyage, setting out from Atlantic City on 15 October 1910 in the *America*. Eighty miles out, an engine failed and the lack of balanced power, with drag on one side and propulsion on the other, meant that the airship could not be controlled. At first Wellman refused to send a distress call, not wanting to suffer further humiliation, but when one was sent, it became the first from an aircraft. Wellman and his crew were rescued on 17 October by a passing steamer, many miles off course, although it turned out they had accidentally set a short-lived airship distance record of 1,008 miles.

Wells, Edmund Curtiss (1910–86) American designer. An enthusiastic model builder since childhood, he spent his summer holidays working for **Boeing** while an undergraduate at Stanford. He joined Boeing on graduating and initially worked on biplane fighters for the USN, but in 1934 he was assigned to the team working on the Boeing 299, which eventually evolved into the B-17 Fortress heavy bomber. He next worked on the B-29 Superfortress and the Stratocruiser airliner, the B-47 and B-52 jet bombers. His final project was the Boeing 747 'jumbo' jet airliner, which remains in production today.

Wenham, Francis Herbert (1824–1908) British aerodynamicist. An engineer, he started to study bird flight while visiting Cairo in 1858 and correctly deduced that cambered surfaces provided the greatest lift and that most lift was generated at the leading edge of an aerofoil. These findings were included in a paper, *Aerial Locomotion*, presented to the Aeronautical Society in 1866, and had a significant influence on future designers. Working with John Browning, he designed and built the world's first wind tunnel in 1871–2,

greatly assisting future aircraft development as before this a whirling arm had to be used.

Westland (*See also* Agusta-Westland) British manufacturer. Westland first became prominent with the Wapiti, a general-purpose biplane for the RAF, designed to replace the DH-9A while using as many of that aircraft's components as possible. The Wapiti was developed into the Wallace that entered RAF service in 1933. More interesting, but commercially never exploited, were the company's experiments during the late 1920s and 1930s with G.T.R. Hill's Pterodactyl series of tailless aircraft, including cabin monoplanes and fighters.

The Westland Lysander (nicknamed the Flying Carrot because of its fuselage shape) army cooperation monoplane for the RAF and RCAF was the most famous of the company's products during the Second World War. The twin-engined Whirlwind fighter was used by just two RAF squadrons when it became clear that agile single-engined fighters were needed. Postwar, the company produced its last fixed-wing combat aircraft (although it later produced the Fairey-designed Gannet ASW and AEW aircraft) in the Wyvern, which was the only operational turboprop fighter.

The main business of the company then became helicopter manufacture, building **Sikorsky** designs, from the S-51 Dragonfly to the S-61 Sea King, under licence for service in Europe and the British Commonwealth. The Bell 47 Sioux was also built under licence. Westland made helicopters of its own design, too, such as the Naval Wasp and Army Scout.

The company was also a partner with **Aérospatiale** of France in the Anglo-French helicopter programme that saw Westland building what were basically the French-designed Gazelle and Puma, as well as the Westland-designed Lynx; the Lynx being available in army and naval versions – although only the latter has been an export success. During the 1960s, the company ventured into rocket research, building the Black Knight rocket for space research.

The government-inspired mergers of 1960 saw it acquire **Fairey** and continue production of the Gannet carrier-borne ASW and AEW aircraft, but the acquisition meant that the Fairey Rotodyne, a novel **VTOL** airliner, was abandoned in favour of the Westland Westminster heavy lift helicopter, which was also subsequently abandoned.

Westland also acquired **Bristol**'s helicopter division, which has built the Sycamore light helicopter and the Belvedere twin-rotor helicopter, and **Saunders-Roe**.

Naval Lynx production continues and work is proceeding on an advanced version. Meanwhile, the main work is the Anglo-Italian Merlin helicopter, developed and produced in collaboration with **Agusta**, part of **Finmeccanica**, which bought the company from GKN in 2005.

whirling arm This was a means of testing aerodynamic surfaces and even models before the invention of the **wind tunnel**. The first use of the whirling arm was by Smeaton in the mid-eighteenth century to test windmill sails, but the first use in aeronautics was by **George Cayley**. It was also used by **Langley** from 1887.

Whitcomb, Richard Travis (1921–) American aerodynamicist. A graduate of the Worcester Polytechnic Institute, Massachusetts, he went to work for **NACA** in 1943, specialising in the problems anticipated with supersonic flight. Almost ten years later he developed the area-ruling concept for transonic drag, under which the total area of any section of an aircraft is used when calculating drag and streamlining, with the concept demanding that transonic fuselages be pinched at the point where the wing is attached. The principles were first applied to the Convair F-102 Delta Dagger. Another ten years on and he developed the **NASA** super-critical wing, a concept that enables aircraft, flying at just below the sound barrier, to use less fuel. He also worked on winglets for the tips of aircraft wings, which turn wasted wing-tip vortices into thrust, again reducing fuel consumption and also, incidentally, lowering landing speeds.

Whitehead, Gustav (1874–1927) German-American pioneer. Born as Weisskopf in Germany, he experimented with parachutes and trapped birds to study their wings, but he worked initially as a machinist and then went to sea, getting

shipwrecked in the Gulf of Mexico at the age of 20. He settled in the USA and anglicised his name. Resuming his interest in aviation, he built a Lilienthal-type wing on a fabric-covered fuselage, as well as constructing a 10 hp acetylene engine which drove two propellers. The resulting flying-machine was tested on 14 August 1901 at Fairfield, Connecticut. Many years later, he was to claim that the machine had flown, and that the following year he flew 7 miles over Long Island Sound.

Despite these claimed successes, he then lost interest in aviation and went into concrete production. While his designs seem to demonstrate an understanding of lift and balance, his understanding of control was only partial, and the engine was unlikely to have sustained flight. All that he probably achieved was a series of powered hops.

Whittle, Air Cdre Sir Frank (1907–96) British jet pioneer. Joining the RAF in 1923, even while still at Cranwell, he started to consider the possibilities of jet propulsion. His graduating thesis as an engineer in 1928 was the *Future Developments in Aircraft Design*, describing how a turbine engine might be built. In 1930, he filed his first patent. He was an engineering test pilot and had little time in which to develop his theories, or the financial resources to do so. Unlike **von Ohain**, who received official encouragement for his work, he had to cope with bureaucratic indifference, at best. In 1932, having obtained financial backing from private investors, he took leave of absence from the RAF. He had hoped to have a prototype ready within a couple of years, but it took him until 1937.

With his investors now incorporated as Power Jets, he persevered and in 1939 had the successful first test of what he designated the WU engine, having overcome problems of combustion, metallurgy and difficulties with the bearings. Officialdom began to take notice and, in May 1941, a Whittle engine powered a Gloster Whittle jet, strangely similar in appearance to the Heinkel He178.

Work continued on the engines until Whittle left Power Jets in 1944 on the nationalisation of the company. He left the RAF in 1948 and emigrated to the United States, becoming an adviser to the oil industry before being appointed as a professor at the US Naval Academy. His invention was shared by the UK with the USA during the final years of the Second World War. He received an award of just £100,000 from the British government for his invention and the patents associated with it.

widebody The concept first emerged with the Boeing 747 or **jumbo jet**, and is applied to any aircraft with two aisles. Building aircraft in this way recognises the limitations of fuselage stretches which, for structural and handling reasons, face natural limits. Widebodied fuselages also enhance the passenger environment, giving an air of spaciousness, and such aircraft often make excellent freighters.

Wilkins, George Hubert MC (1888–1958) Australian pioneer. Graduating from the Adelaide School of Mines, Wilkins decided to become a photographer and stowed on a ship to Africa and then to England where he became a newsreel cameraman. He learnt to fly in 1910 and then became involved in filming stunt flying, often climbing onto the wings of aircraft with his camera. He was sent to film the Balkan Wars, and narrowly missed being shot as a spy. He also became involved in polar exploration.

At the start of the First World War he applied to join the Australian Flying Corps, but was turned down because of his poor eyesight. However, he accompanied the Australian forces to France as a photographer and won an MC for taking command of a platoon on the battlefield after their CO had been killed.

Postwar, he made two unsuccessful attempts to fly over the North Pole, but in 1928 he achieved it, with a flight from Point Barrow in Alaska, to Spitzbergen, north of Norway, in a Lockheed Vega flown by Carl Eielson, although the flight was interrupted by a forced landing because of a blizzard which kept them grounded for five days. The snow was so deep when the storm stopped that they had to push their Lockheed Vega to the landing strip.

In 1931 he tried to sail under the polar ice cap, purchasing a surplus American submarine for just a single dollar and renaming it *Nautilus*, but the

voyage had to be abandoned when they failed to penetrate drifting ice and when the steering gear broke down.

Willard, Charles K. (1883–1977) American engineer. Having experimented with engines at the beginning of the twentieth century, he became a member of the New York Aeronautical Society. In 1909, with fellow members, he purchased a **Curtiss** aeroplane on condition that the manufacturer would teach two members of the group to fly. This was the first aircraft to be bought in the United States and Willard was Curtiss's first pupil. He became a stunt flyer or 'barnstormer', supposedly the first in the USA. He was shot by a squirrel gun on one flight and his aircraft was brought down making him the first aeroplane pilot to be shot down. He made the first exhibition flight in Canada and was first to fly over Los Angeles.

In 1913 he went to work for **Glenn Martin** and headed his design office, moving to Curtiss in 1915 to help design flying boats. He then set up LWF Engineering in 1916 with two partners, Lowe and Fowler, whose initials were incorporated with his in the title, but it also stood for the product, laminated wood fuselages. He shared his time between LWF and acting as chief engineer for Aeromarine.

Williams, Alford Joseph, Jnr (1896–1958) American racing pilot. Graduating from Fordham University, he became a baseball player before joining the USN in 1917 where he was taught to fly. He was posted to the major naval base at Hampton Roads, Virginia, where he became a test pilot and was also involved in the development of aerial warfare, including vertical dive-bombing. He remained with the USN after the First World War but was allowed to take part in sporting events, winning the 1923 Pulitzer Trophy and also setting speed records. In his spare time he studied for a law degree.

He left the USN in 1930 and started exhibition flying for Gulf Oil using bright orange Curtiss Gulfhawks for aerobatic displays. He maintained his service connections as a USMC reserve officer, but was forced to resign in 1940 for publicly advocating an autonomous air force. He continued with flying displays during the Second World War as part of an official recruitment campaign, but after the war gave up flying in order to concentrate on farming.

wind tunnel First built by Francis Wenham in 1871, the wind tunnel replaced the **whirling arm** as a means of testing aerodynamic features, and today its use is not just confined to aircraft.

The wind tunnel is considered essential for the development of aircraft, with scale models usually being subjected to exhaustive testing before the design is finalised. While the principles were understood for many years, it took some time before the results could be accurately scaled up, and the early pioneers sometimes found that wind tunnel results did not bear out in the reality of a full-sized aircraft. As aircraft handling varies according to speed, high-speed and low-speed wind tunnels can be used. One means of assessing airflow employed in the early days was to filter smoke into the wind tunnel so that the flow could be easily seen and photographed. Road and railway vehicles, buildings and structures such as bridges are also subjected to wind tunnel tests.

wings and control surfaces The wing is the primary lifting aerofoil of any aircraft, even though it may be a **rotary wing** on a helicopter, and is usually known as the mainplane. Much of the early work on the design of the wing was conducted by **Sir George Cayley**, **Horatio Phillips** and **Francis Wenham**, while **Sir Barnes Wallis** was an advocate of **variable-geometry**. The control surfaces deployed on the wing include the ailerons, or on some early aircraft, wing-warping, as favoured by the **Wright** brothers, and flaps, which extended the surface area of the wing during take-off and landing. Some aircraft have slots, as invented by **Handley Page**.

The rudder is found on the tail fin or vertical stabiliser and the elevators on the horizontal stabilizers, all of which are part of the tailplane. On **delta-wing** aircraft, the role of the elevators and ailerons is combined. While the Wrights and some of the other early designers used a forward tailplane, some modern aircraft have the elevators forward in what is known as a the 'canard' configuration, first seen on the SAAB

Viggen combat aircraft, but now also found on the Eurofighter 2000 Typhoon, the Dassault Raphael and the SAAB Gripen.

Winter War, Russo-Finnish (1939–40)

Although Finland had been part of Tsarist Russia, Finnish nationalism had been a force to be reckoned with long before the Russia Revolution. The Soviet Union had been persistent in its demands to be allowed to use Finnish bases, and this had prompted the Finns to buy new aircraft to keep their small air force up-to-date. Before the Second World War broke out, the Germans impounded thirty-five Fiat G50 fighters, but eighteen Bristol Blenheim bombers were delivered from the UK. On 30 October 1939, the USSR invaded Finland, with numerically superior forces both on land and in the air. At first the Finnish Air Force, the Ilmavoimat, held its own against some 900 obsolete Russian aircraft, but aircraft were diverted from other areas of the USSR and by 1940 there were 2,000 Soviet aircraft on the Finnish front. Despite deliveries of additional Blenheims, Gloster Gladiator, Hawker Hurricane, Brewster 239 and Curtiss Hawk 75 fighters, and Westland Lysander AOP aircraft, on 26 February the Finns lost the island fortress of Kolvisto. They were also forced to retreat from the port of Petsamo, north of the Arctic Circle. A second assault in the south, across the frozen Gulf of Finland, cutting off the town of Viipuri, led the Finnish government to put out peace feelers on 6 March.

Despite this the country remained independent, but was forced to ally itself with Germany for the rest of the war.

Given the closed nature of Soviet society, and the desire to keep bad news away from anyone in authority, statistics are not reliable. Nikita Krushchev estimated that, against a known sixty-one aircraft that the Finnish aircraft destroyed, Russia lost more than 1,000 aeroplanes. More recent and impartial estimates of Soviet losses suggest some 700 aircraft.

Wise, John (1808–79) American aeronaut.

Despite having a poor education, he was experimenting with balloons in his early twenties, and at the age of 27 made his first ascent at Philadelphia in a balloon he had designed and built. He became an exhibition balloonist making some 440 ascents, often as part of an act in which his hot air balloon would ascend, then he would cut away the base and douse the fire, leaving the balloon to make what was effectively a parachute descent. He invented the rip panel for hydrogen balloons, and discovered that there was a steady easterly air current high above North America. He liked to portray himself as a scientist and frequently adopted the title of 'professor', but he also wrote a book, *A System of Aeronautics*, published in 1850.

He approached Congress in 1843 to request funding for a transatlantic balloon crossing, but the idea was rejected. In 1846. Congress also rejected his idea for a balloon bombing attack on Mexican forces during the siege of Vera Cruz.

He decided to make a transatlantic crossing by raising funds himself, but for practice he started making long-distance balloon voyages. In July 1859 he ascended in St Louis and descended at Hendersonville, New York, a distance of 1,193 miles, creating a record that was not broken until 1900, when the **Comte Henri de La Vaulx** travelled from France to Russia. Despite this, it was realised that the greater strain of a transatlantic crossing would be beyond the capacity of a balloon. Such concerns were well-founded, for in 1879, ascending with a companion in the balloon *Pathfinder*, he disappeared over Lake Michigan.

Wittman, S.J. 'Steve' (1904–95) American racing pilot and inventor. After learning to fly in 1924, he operated a small aircraft charter company until 1927, when he became a test pilot for the Pheasant Aircraft Company. He moved to Oshkosh in 1931 to manage the municipal airport and also built his first aircraft, a racer that he named *Chief Oshkosh*. Over the next eighteen years this aircraft became a race winner with the original aeroplane being constantly modified and updated rather than replaced, although its name was changed to *Buster*, with victories including the 1932 Glenn Curtiss Trophy, the 1933 National Air Race for engines of 350 cu in, or 5.75 litres, and the Goodyear Races in 1947 and 1949.

A member of the Experimental Aircraft Association, he designed simple aircraft – the Tailwind series – for the home-build market. He also became an inventor, with his most significant

advance being the first steel spring landing gear, which he patented. This simplified landing gear made it possible and affordable to improve undercarriages on light aircraft.

During the Second World War he ran a flying school providing basic training for military pilots.

World War, First (August 1914–November 1918) The developments in aviation during the First World War are largely covered under the pioneers, manufacturers and, of course, the aces. The war was not widely expected to be one in which aviation would play a major role, although some did view the German **Zeppelin** airships with foreboding, and before the war there had been experiments in firing machine guns from aircraft, in aerial wireless transmission and in dropping torpedoes from aircraft. The war saw the advent of the **fighter** and the **bomber** as distinct aircraft, the start of **maritime-reconnaissance** and the invention of the **aircraft carrier**. By the end of the war, converted bombers were available as the first transport aircraft.

World War, Second (September 1939–August 1945) As with the developments in aviation during the First World War, those in the Second are largely covered under the pioneers, manufacturers and, of course, the aces. This war was foreseen for many years as the war in which aviation would play a leading role, although a few commanders, mainly naval commanders, hugely underestimated the potential and impact of the aeroplane. Many believed that 'the bomber will always get through', but this was proved to be an exaggeration given improvements in air defences and especially radar, but few could have foreseen just how the aircraft carrier and the submarine would eclipse the battleship, as at **Taranto**, the **Coral Sea**, **Midway** and even **Leyte Gulf**. The **Blitz** against British cities was counteracted by the British bomber offensive and particularly the Combined Bomber Offensive (*see* **Allied Bomber Offensive**), as well as individual operations of significance such as the **Dam Busters**. Few foresaw the extent to which **airborne assault** would change the nature of warfare, especially in the assault on the Low Countries (*see* **Netherlands and Belgium, German invasion of**) and **Crete**.

This was the conflict in which warfare finally moved into the modern age and so much that is taken for granted today appeared as a result, including the **helicopter** and the **jet engine**. Desperate measures were resorted to, including the dropping of nuclear weapons on **Hiroshima** and **Nagasaki** and the **kamikaze** attacks by the Japanese. Stand-off weapons appeared, including glider-bombs.

Wright, Orville (1871–1948) and Wilbur (1867–1912)

American pioneers and manufacturers. Despite having little formal education, the Wright brothers became the first men to fly an aeroplane. They were bicycle manufacturers to begin with but became interested in flying when Wilbur read of **Otto Lilienthal**'s death in 1896. In May 1899 he sought a bibliography of aeronautical books from the Smithsonian Institute in Washington, which also advised him to contact **Octave Chanute**, the then leading American glider pioneer. Chanute's book, *Progress in Flying Machines*, inspired Orville to join Wilbur in the quest for flight. That year they built a biplane kite, on which they tested some of their theories, basing it on a design of Chanute's.

They moved very quickly. The first full-sized glider to be built by the Wrights, their No. 1 of 1900, incorporated the principle of inherent instability and required the skill of the pilot to keep it aloft. Wing-warping was used to provide 'control in roll', and at first they thought that this might also steer the aircraft, while like all of their designs, the elevator was forward of the wings. They chose Kitty Hawk on the North Carolina coast for their tests because the Washington Weather Bureau had advised them they could be sure of high winds,

but their test glides in September were hampered by little wind, although the glider was a success.

They moved to Kill Devil Sands nearby for the rest of their gliding and aeroplane experiments. The No. 2 glider of 1902 had a measure of anhedral to reduce stability. Its first glide was on 27 July, with the glider being launched by one of the brothers and an assistant, while the other brother piloted, lying prone across the mainplane. Glides of up to 390 ft were achieved in winds of up to 20 mph. The evaluation of the 1902 programme was such that they did not start work on their No. 3 glider until midsummer, and in addition to various adjustments, they incorporated a double fixed fin to provide stability while wing-warping, but this was replaced by a movable rudder. In the autumn of 1902 they made no less than 1,000 glides in winds of up to 35 mph and for distances of up 622½ ft with a maximum duration of 20 seconds. It was clear that this could be the basis for a powered aeroplane.

Such progress had not gone unnoticed, and observers were encouraged as they were the witnesses who could dispel the cynicism that abounded.

In the search for a suitable engine, the Wrights realised that it did not exist, so they designed a 12 hp water-cooled engine that weighed just 200 lb. No suitable propeller existed either, so they had to design and build this as well. They also built their own wind tunnel. Named the *Flyer I*, the aeroplane was constructed during the summer of 1903 and taken to the Kill Devil Hills in September. It differed from the No. 3 by having a twin movable rudder, while the engine drove two propellers set to contra-rotate to avoid directional stresses. A single rail was laid for the take-off so the aircraft needed just one man to run alongside to steady it.

On 14 December the weather was suitable for a flight attempt. By the toss of a coin, Wilbur was first. After a perfect take-off run, he pulled back too hard on the stick and the *Flyer I* stalled and crashed into the sand, although not badly damaged. On 17 December it was Orville's turn, and witnesses were hastily assembled and a Coast Guard surfman was asked to press the shutter on a pre-set camera. At 10.35, Orville took off into a 25-mph wind and flew an undulating course for

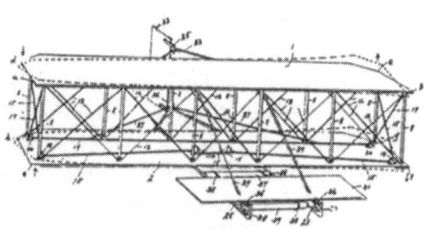

An official patent drawing for the Wright Flyer, with the dotted line showing the effect of wing-warping.

120 ft, taking 12 seconds. The second flight, with Wilbur flying, was for 175 ft, the third for 200 ft and the fourth for 852 ft, and lasted 59 seconds.

Despite their reputation for gliding, the press had not accepted the Wrights' invitation to attend and there was widespread cynicism. Much of this was undoubtedly due to the failure of **Samuel Langley**'s *Aerodrome A*, on which taxpayers' money had been spent. At first, they pressed on with further developments, with the Wright *Flyer II* flying on 26 May 1904, making a catapult take-off on 7 September, flying the first circle on 20 September before flying for more than 5 minutes on 9 November. The following June, the *Flyer III* flew for the first time, but public recognition remained absent and the US War Department refused to even consider buying an aeroplane from them, as did the British War Office, despite a recommendation by **Col John Capper** in 1905.

They stopped flying for three years and when they started again in 1908, they held public exhibition flights in the United States and then in France, near Le Mans. The impact of the French demonstrations cannot be underestimated, with the French realising just how far behind the Americans they had fallen. The Wrights began to sell their aircraft, founded a flying school and licensed other manufacturers, such as the **Short** bothers in the UK, to build them.

They started actions to protect their patents, eventually going to the extreme length of demanding a loyalty on every aeroplane that had ever flown. This encouraged **Glenn Curtiss** to modify the Langley *Aerodrome A* with ailerons in an attempt to discredit the brothers. The brothers were always noted for their integrity, but it does seem that they were anxious at one stage to seek revenge on a world that had ignored their achievements.

Wilbur died from typhoid fever in 1912 and in 1915 Orville sold the manufacturing and patent rights and withdrew from the public eye.

Y

Yakovlev *See* below

Yakovlev, Alexander Sergeyevich (1906–89)
Soviet designer. At just 17, he funded the construction of his first glider by raising a subscription among schoolchildren. He later graduated from the Zhukovsky Air Academy where he studied under **Andrei Tupolev**. He was fortunate in being trusted by Stalin and was awarded his own design bureau, with the first aircraft being the Yak-1 fighter, and his later Yak-9 setting production records for a Soviet fighter of the day.

After the Second World War, although some jet fighters were designed, including the Yak-15 and Yak-17, the Yakovlev Bureau designed transports such as the Yak-40, a small jet airliner and its development, the Yak-42. It also designed VTOL aircraft, including the Yak-38 for the Russian Navy's aircraft carriers.

Yeager, Brig Gen Charles Elwood 'Chuck' (1923–) US ace and test pilot. After leaving high school, he enrolled in the USAAC in 1941 and was selected for flying training. He joined the 356th Fighter Group in England in November 1943, flying North American P-52 Mustangs, and shot down thirteen German aircraft including one of the new Messerschmitt Me262 jets. Shot down over France, he evaded capture with the help of the French Resistance.

Postwar, he became a test pilot and volunteered for the X-1 project. On 14 October 1947 he was the first to break the sound barrier flying an X-1 launched from beneath a Boeing B-29 Superfortress bomber over Rogers Dry Lake in California, at a speed of Mach 1.15. Six years later he flew the X-1A to set a new record of 1,650 mph. These records were in rocket-propelled aircraft released from a bomber in mid-air, and have to be distinguished from those, for example, by **Peter Twiss**, in which the aircraft took off under its own power.

Later, Yeager became an astronaut.

Yost, Paul Edward (1919–2007) American balloon manufacturer. Having learnt to fly aeroplanes in 1939, he distinguished himself in the 1950s by discovering a way to heat a hot air balloon using a propane burner, thus opening the way for the revival and popularisation of the hot air balloon over the last fifty years. He became a balloon manufacturer at Sioux Falls, South Dakota.

In 1976 Yost attempted a transatlantic flight using a helium balloon, ascending from Maine and drifting 2,500 miles – a new world record – before splashing down in the sea. Nevertheless, it was in one of his balloons that **Ben Abruzzo**, **Maxi Anderson** and **Larry Newman** crossed the Atlantic in 1978.

Z

Zahm, Dr Albert Francis (1862–1954) American pioneer. A graduate of no less than three universities, he had started experiments with model gliders while still a student. Later, when a professor at the Catholic University of America, he built a wind tunnel and tested aerodynamic resistance. He watched **Augustus Moore Herring**'s experiments in 1898, and later that year proposed the use of ailerons for control in a paper to the Third International Conference on Aerial Navigation. He wrote a book on the history of aeronautics called *Aerial Navigation*, which also explained the science, and it was published in 1911. In 1912 he suggested creating a national aeronautics laboratory which led to the formation of **NACA** in 1915.

He was one of the early holders of the Guggenheim Chair of Aeronautics at the Library of Congress, where he obtained several important collections on aeronautical history for the institution, including the **Tissandier** collection of aerostatic memorabilia, and was at other times an adviser to **Glenn Curtiss** and director of the USN's aerodynamic laboratory, based at the Washington Navy Yard.

Zeppelin German manufacturer (*see* below), but also in common usage as the name given to any steerable and self-propelled dirigible airship.

Zeppelin, Count Ferdinand Adolf August Heinrich von (1838–1917) German airship pioneer. Commissioned into the Prussian Army, he was sent to the United States during the American Civil War, where he was told about **Thaddeus Lowe**'s work with balloons, and became interested in aeronautics. He served with distinction in the Franco-Prussian War of 1870–1, becoming interested in the development of the airship when he saw the French as being close to solving the problems that had hampered its development. His first airship appeared in 1900 funded by a public subscription and was 420 ft long and built of zinc and aluminium girders with power provided by two 15 hp engines. On 2 July 1900 it made its first ascent but with limited success.

By 1908 a Zeppelin was able to remain in the air for 4½ hours with at least nine passengers, and the following year the Imperial German Navy ordered four Zeppelins. On 19 March 1909, the Zeppelin No. 1 made a trip of 4 hours, covered 150 miles and reached an altitude of 650 ft with twenty-five military personnel on board in addition to the crew. In 1910, domestic air services using these large airships started on a trial basis in Germany, with plans laid for transatlantic flights.

When a Zeppelin exploded, killing twenty-eight men in 1915 during the First World War, the resulting dispute with the Imperial German Navy led to von Zeppelin retiring from the scene. Nevertheless, his company survived and also built heavier-than-air aircraft during the war years.

Appendix I

BC

2200	Chinese Emperor Shin is reputed to have tower jumped
c.852	Legendary King Bladud is supposed to have been killed attempting to fly
c.400	Archytas of Tarentum is reported to have made a steam-jet powered pigeon
	The Chinese invent the kite

AD

c.100	Hero of Alexandria discovers propulsive effects of a jet of steam
852	Armen Firman tower jumps at Córdoba, Spain
1020	Oliver, or Eilmer, of Malmesbury attempts to fly from Malmesbury Abbey
1100	Tower windmills start to appear in Europe
	The Chinese start to use artillery rockets
c.1250	Roger Bacon writes on the prospect of flight
c.1325	Illustration of a string-pull helicopter appears in a Flemish manuscript
c.1326–7	Illustration in the manuscript, *Milemete MS*, of a kite and an aerial bomb
1379	Muratori refers to artillery rockets for the first time in Europe
c.1420	Hoanes Fontana produces an illustration of a bird powered by a 'rocket'
1483–6	In Italy, Leonardo da Vinci designs the first parachute
c.1485	da Vinci designs projectiles with fins
1485–1500	da Vinci designs ornithopters
1495–1500	da Vinci produces the first powered aeroplane design
1496	Senecio is injured in a tower jump
1503	At Perugia, Italy, G.B. Danti is injured while attempting to fly using wings attached to his body
1505	da Vinci writes a treatise on bird flight
1507	John Damian is injured attempting to fly from the walls of Stirling Castle, Scotland, with wings attached to his arms
1536	Bolori killed while tower jumping
1550	Bacon's work is published
1560	Schmidlap mentions kites in a manuscript
1589	Della Porta gives the first description in Europe of a kite
1595	Fausto Veranzio produces an illustration of a parachute
1618	A Dutch engraving shows a conventional kite
c.1628	In Lucca, Italy, Guidotti attempts to fly
1638	The first science fiction by the English bishops Francis Godwin and John Wilkins

1639	Desmarets produces an illustration of a sail-derived parachute
1648	Tito Livio Burrattini makes a model flying dragon
1655	Robert Hooke tests watch-spring-powered model ornithopters
c.1660	Allard attempts to fly at St Germain before Louis XIV
1670	Father Francesco de Lana de Terzi produces his drawing of a lighter-than-air flying ship, and describes aerial bombardment and assault
1673	de Bernoin is killed attempting to fly at Frankfurt-on-Maine
1676	Francis Willughby suggests that man's legs are more comparable with a bird's wings than his arms
1678	Besnier attempts to fly using flappers at Sable-sur-Surthe in France
1680	Giovanni Borelli produces his treatise, *De Moto Animalium*, demonstrating that human muscle power is not sufficient for ornithopter flight
1709	Bartolomeu de Gusmão designs a flying-machine, the Passarola, and is believed to have tested model versions
1716	In Sweden, Emanuel Swedenborg outlines his ideas for an aeroplane
1742	In Paris, France, the Marquis de Bacqueville attempts to fly with wings across the River Seine
1746	Benjamin Robins makes the first use of a whirling arm for aerodynamic tests
1749	Alexander Wilson experiments with a kite to record cloud temperature
1752	Benjamin Franklin studies atmospheric electricity after flying a kite in a thunderstorm
1752–3	John Smeaton uses a whirling arm to test windmill sails
1754	In Russia, Michael V. Lomonosov builds a helicopter model
1764	Melchior Bauer designs a monoplane
1766	Henry Cavendish isolates hydrogen
1768	A.J.P. Paucton proposes the first design for a compound helicopter, with a helicopter screw and a propulsive screw, the 'pterophore'
1772	Canon Desforges builds the *voiture volante* flying-machine
1781	Jean-Pierre Blanchard builds the *vaisseau volante* flying-machine
	Karl Meerwein tests an ornithopter-glider
	Restiff de la Bretonne publishes the book, *La Découverte Australe*
1782	The Montgolfier brothers experiment with paper bags – the first hot air balloon
1783	4 June: at Annonay, France, the first public demonstration of a hot air balloon ascent, unmanned
	19 September: at Versailles, farm animals ascend in a Montgolfière balloon
	October: Joseph Montgolfier suggests that hot air from a balloon can provide propulsion
	21 November: at Paris, Jean-François Pilâtre de Rozier and the Marquis d'Arlandes make the first aerial voyage using a hot air balloon
	1 December: also at Paris, Jacques Charles and Aine Robert make the first voyage in a hydrogen balloon
1784	Launoy and Bienvenu design a model helicopter
	A-J Renaux and Gerard produce designs for ornithopters
	Aries attempts a tower jump with wings at Embrun
	Vallet uses a river boat to run the first test of a full-sized airscrew
	15 September: Vincenzo Lunardi makes the first balloon ascent in Great Britain.
	16 October: Blanchard attempts to propel a balloon with an airscrew
1785	Jean Baptiste Marie Meusnier produces the first design for an airscrew-driven airship

7 January: Blanchard and Dr John Jeffries make the first crossing of the English Channel by air using a balloon

15 June: Pilâtre de Rozier and Pierre Romain are killed in the first serious balloon accident attempting to cross English Channel

1794   The first military use of an aerial observation post, using a hydrogen balloon in the Battle of Maubeuge

1796   Sir George Cayley flies his model helicopter

1797   22 October: André Jacques Garnerin makes the first parachute descent, jumping from a balloon

1799   Cayley produces the first design of a modern aeroplane, with fixed wings, control surfaces in the tailplane and means of propulsion

British troops in India are attacked by rockets by Tipu Sultan's forces

1804   Cayley makes the first tests of aerofoils on a whirling arm

Cayley flies the first modern configuration model glider

1805   William Congreve tests the first modern rocket missiles

1806   The Royal Navy attacks Copenhagen using Congreve rockets

1807   Jacob Degen attempts flight with his flap-valve ornithopter, suspended beneath a balloon

1809–10   Cayley publishes his triple paper on aviation establishing the basis for aerodynamics, with an illustration of his 1796 helicopter

1810   Cayley invents the tension wheel (cycle type)

Cayley flies the first full-sized glider, unmanned

1811   Albrecht Berbinger, known as the 'Tailor of Ulm', attempts flight using a Degen-style ornithopter

1815   Cayley designs the first tandem-wing aeroplane, but does not publish it

1816   Cayley tries to found an aeronautical society

Degen flies a clockwork ornithopter model

1818   Count Adolphe de Lambertye designs an ornithopter with helicopter tenders

1822   George Pocock flies his first man-lifting kite

1827   Pocock successfully uses a kite-drawn carriage, the *char-volante*, on highways

1830   F.D. Artingstall tests a steam-powered model ornithopter

1831   The first publication of a tandem-wing design, by Thomas Walker

1837   24 July: Robert Cocking killed while testing his dihedral parachute based on Cayley's design

1842   W.H. Phillips flies a model helicopter powered by steam jets from rotor tips

1843   Bourne flies model helicopters powered by watch springs

An illustration is published of Dr W. Miller's man-powered ornithopter

March: William Henson publishes his design for an Aerial Steam Carriage, the first to show an airscrew-propelled fixed-wing aeroplane

April: Cayley publishes a convertiplane design, which is also the first biplane design

1847   The first test of a steam-powered model aeroplane using Henson's 1843 design, but it fails to sustain flight

1848   John Stringfellow tests a steam-powered model aeroplane, but it cannot sustain flight

1849   22 August: Austria sends unmanned hot-air balloons carrying bombs against Venice

Cayley test-flies his full-sized glider carrying a young boy

1852   In France, the first aeronautical society is formed, La Société Aéronautique et Météorologique de France

	24 September: Henri Giffard makes an ascent in the first manned steam-powered airship
1853	The first man-carrying flight, although not under control, by Cayley's glider carrying his coachman
	In France, Loup designs airscrew propeller monoplane
	Cayley produces the first design using a stretched-rubber motor for models
1854	Louis Charles Letur is killed in his parachute-glider
1855	In Ireland, Viscount Carlingford designs a monoplane which he later builds and flies as a kite
1856–68	Jean-Marie Le Bris tests his two gliders based on the albatross
1856–96	Louis Mouillard tests his full-sized gliders
1857	Felix du Temple makes the first successful clockwork-powered flight of a model
1858	Over Paris, the first aerial photograph is taken from a tethered balloon
	Pierre Jullien tests a rubber-powered monoplane model
	Francis Wenham tests a multiplane glider
1859	In Ireland, Father E.J. Cordner flies a man-carrying kite
1860	Jean-Joseph Etienne Lenoir invents the gas engine
	John Smythies designs a fixed-wing aeroplane with ornithopter propulsion
1862	Balloons are used for the first time in the American Civil War
1863	Gabriel de la Landelle designs the helicopter
	Ponton d'Amécourt tests a steam-powered model helicopter, later switching to clockwork-propulsion
	J.J. Bourcart builds and tests a full-sized man-powered ornithopter
	The Société Français d'Aviation is founded by Gaspard-Felix Tournachon, known as 'Nadar'
	In France, Jules Verne's *Five Weeks in a Balloon* is published
1864	In France, Nadar founds the first aeronautical journal, *L'Aéronaut*
	Du Vol des Oiseaux by Count Ferdinand d'Esterno is published
1865	Charles de Louvrie produces the first design for a jet-propelled aeroplane
1866	The Aeronautical Society of Great Britain is founded (later the Royal Aeronautical Society) and at the inaugural meeting, Wenham gives a lecture on 'Aerial Locomotion', giving the results of his 1858 tests for the first time
1867	J.W. Butler and E. Edwards devise the first delta-wing design, combining jet propulsion with airscrew jet propulsion with rotor-tip jets
1868	In France, Le Bris concludes his glider experiments
	Boulton designs the first ailerons, but they are impractical
	In the UK, Joseph Meyes Kaufman tests a steam-driven ornithopter with fixed-wings, but is unsuccessful
	Hunter proposes a jet aeroplane with jet lift
	At Guebwiller, France, Bourcart tests a full-sized ornithopter
	June: at the Crystal Palace, South London, the first aeronautical exhibition is held and Stringfellow's triplane is tested, although without success
1870	Harte designs flap-type ailerons, although their purpose is not fully understood
	Gustave Trouve's gun powder-driven model ornithopter flies
	Alphonse Pénaud uses twisted rubber to power models
c.1870	Danjard flies tandem-wing rubber models
1871	Pénaud flies his model planophore
	Wenham and John Browning build and demonstrate the first wind tunnel
	In South Africa, John Household flies a basic glider

1872	Henlein's airship is the first to be driven by an internal combustion (gas) engine
1873	Étienne-Jules Marey's *La Machine Animale* is published
	Charles Renard tests a multi-wing model
1874	D.S. Brown produces multi-wing models and tests them for stability
	Du Temple builds a man-carrying aeroplane that makes a powered hop
	9 July: in London, Vincent de Groof is killed on a semi-ornothopter
1875	Thomas Moy flies his model tandem-wing 'Aerial Steamer'
1876	Pénaud patents the first full-sized amphibian design
	In London, the Aeronautical Society re-issues Cayley's triple paper of 1809–10
	In Germany, Nikolaus Otto invents the four-stroke petrol engine
1877	In France, *L'Aéronaute* publishes Cayley's triple paper
	E. Dieuaide and Enrico Forlanini fly a steam-driven model helicopter
	A Wankel-type engine and helicopter model are designed by Melikoff
1878	The British Army forms the Royal Engineers Balloon Section at Woolwich
1879	Victor Tatin flies a compressed-air-powered monoplane model
	Dandrieux flies 'butterfly' helicopter models
	F.W. Brearey flies his model 'undulator', a wave action aeroplane
	Biot tests a full-sized glider
1881	*L'Empire de l'Air* by Louis Mouillard is published
1882	The Tissandier brothers' airship ascends – the first powered by an electric motor
1883–6	In the USA, Montgomery tests gliders without success
1884	In Russia, Alexander Mozhaiski's steam-powered man-carrying aeroplane takes off, but does not sustain flight
	In the UK, Sir Charles Parsons invents the steam turbine
	Also in the UK, the first double-surfaced cambered wings are patented by Horatio Phillips
	In France, Charles Renard and Arthur-Constantin Krebs ascend in their airship *La France*
	In Germany, Gottlieb Daimler invents a high-speed petrol engine
1886	In France, Jules Verne's *Clipper of the Clouds* is published
1888	Wolfert flies a petrol-engined airship
1889	In Australia, Lawrence Hargrave invents the rotary engine (not to be confused with the Wankel-engine)
	In Germany, Otto Lilienthal's *Der Vogelflug als Grundlage der Fleigekunst* is published
1890	9 October: Clement Ader's steam-powered *Eole* becomes the first full-sized aeroplane to take off under its own power, but it fails to sustain flight
1891	Samuel Langley starts to test steam-powered model monoplanes
1893	Horatio Phillips tests his steam-powered multi-wing model aeroplane
	Parsons builds and tests a steam-powered helicopter
	In Australia, Hargrave invents the box-kite
1894	In the USA, Octave Chanute's *Progress in Flying Machines* is published
	31 July: Maxim tests his steam-powered biplane, which lifts itself off its guide rails
1895	In Germany, Otto Lilienthal flies the first piloted hang-gliders
	James Means commences the publication of *Aeronautical Annuals*
	In Great Britain, Percy Pilcher begins hang-gliding experiments
1896	In the United States, Octave Chanute begins his gliding experiments
	Also in the US, Samuel Langley produces his first successful steam-powered models
	In France, Victor Tatin and Charles Richet fly their successful steam-powered models
	9 August: Lilienthal crashes while gliding, and dies the next day

1897	In France, Clement Ader tests the *Avion III* without success on 12 and 14 October
1898	The Aéro-Club de France is founded
1899	In the USA, Wilbur Wright builds a biplane kite to test wing-warping
	Lawrence Hargrave visits England and lectures
	30 September: Pilcher crashes while gliding and dies on 2 October
1900	The first Zeppelin flight
	The Wright brothers fly their No. 1 glider at Kitty Hawk
1901	The Wright brothers fly their No. 2 glider at Kill Devil Hills, near Kitty Hawk
	In France, Alberto Santos-Dumont circles the Eiffel Tower in his airship
	Samuel Langley flies a petrol-engined monoplane
	Wilhelm Kress's floatplane collapses while taxiing in Austria
	In the UK, the Aero Club, later Royal Aero Club, is formed
1902	The Wrights perfect their technique with their No. 3 glider
	In France, Ferdinand Ferber builds a Wright-type glider
	The Lebaudy brothers complete the first practical airship, *Lebaudy I*
1903	Karl Jatho tests an unsuccessful biplane
	7 October: Langley's *Aerodrome A* crashes on take-off
	8 December: Langley's *Aerodrome A* crashes again on take-off
	14 December: Wilbur Wright crashes *Flyer I* on take-off
	17 December: Orville Wright and then Wilbur make the first sustained powered flights in a heavier-than-air flying-machine
1904	In France, Robert Esnault-Pelterie, Ernest Archdeacon and Ferdinand Ferber work on Wright-type gliders
	In England, Samuel Cody experiments with man-lifting kites for the British Army
	26 May: The Wrights' *Flyer II* takes to the air
	7 September: The Wrights start catapult take-offs
	20 September: Wilbur Wright flies the first circle
	9 November: Wilbur Wright makes the first flight of more than 5 minutes
1905	In France, Voisin-Archdeacon and Voisin-Blériot float-gliders fly
	16 March: in the US, Moloney flies a Montgomery glider launched from under a balloon
	June: the Wrights' *Flyer III* flies
	4 October: Orville Wright makes the first flight of more than 30 minutes
	14 October: in France, Fédération Aéronautique Internationale is formed
	16 October: The Wrights stop flying until 1908
1906	The Wrights' patents are granted
	March: in Transylvania, Vuia's tractor biplane is tested unsuccessfully
	12 September: in Denmark, Jacob Ellehammer makes a tethered hop flight of 140 ft
	12 November: in France, Alberto Santos-Dumont flies for 721 ft
1907	In the UK, Phillips makes tentative flights
	Ellehammer conducts tests with a biplane
	February: the Voisin-Delagrange pusher-biplane is tested without success
	29 September: in France, a Breguet man-carrying helicopter makes a tentative flight
	October: Henri Farman flies
	November: Santos-Dumont's No. 19 monoplane is tested
	10 November: Henri Farman flies for 1 minute in a Voisin
	13 November: Paul Cornu's helicopter makes an untethered flight
1908	13 January: Henri Farman flies the first European circle at Issy-les-Moulineaux
	6 May: the Wright brothers resume flying with the modified *Flyer III*

14 May: Wilbur Wright takes C.W. Furnas on the first passenger flight

30 May: Farman takes Ernest Archdeacon on the first European passenger flight Delagrange remains airborne in a Voisin for 15 minutes

June: in England, A.V. Roe tests his first biplane

28 June: Ellehammer flies in Germany

4 July: Glenn Curtiss wins the Scientific American Trophy for the first public flight in the United States

8 August: in France, Wilbur Wright flies at Hunaudières

4 September: Orville Wright flies in public at Fort Myer, starting his demonstrations to the US Army

9 September: Orville Wright makes the first flight of more than 1 hour

17 September: the first fatal aeroplane accident. Lt Selfridge is killed while flying as Orville Wright's passenger

16 October: the first British flight by S.F. Cody at Farnborough

31 December: Wilbur Wright makes the first flight of more than 2 hours

1909   In Germany, Jose Weiss flies his bird-form gliders

23 February: John McCurdy makes his first flight in Canada in his *Silver Dart*

March: Ambroise Goupy's aircraft *Goupy II* flies

April: the first aerial cinematograph shots from a Wright A over Rome

25 July: Louis Blériot flies the English Channel from Calais to Dover

27 July: Hubert Latham fails in his second cross-Channel attempt

August: in France, the first aviation meeting is held at Reims, sponsored by the champagne industry

27 August: at Reims, Henri Farman makes the first flight of 100 miles, taking 3 hours

2 October: Orville Wright is first to fly at 1,000 ft

23 October: Mme Baroness de la Roche becomes the first qualified woman pilot

1910   Henri Coanda tests the first jet-propelled aircraft, without success

Zeppelin starts airship services within Germany

February: in Germany, Hugo Junkers patents the cantilever wing

10 March: in Argentina, Emil Aubrun makes the first night flight using a Blériot

28 March: in France, Henri Fabre makes the first hydro-aeroplane flights

28 April: Claud Grahame-White makes a night flight in England

2 June: Charles Rolls makes the first double crossing of the English Channel

July: in the USA, Glenn Curtiss conducts the first bombing trials

12 July: Charles Rolls is killed in a flying accident at Bournemouth

17 August: flying a Blériot, John Moisant and his mechanic make the first passenger crossing of the English Channel

27 August: in the USA, using a Curtiss biplane, McCurdy experiments with air-to-ground radio

23 September: Georges Chavez makes the first transalpine flight, but is fatally injured in a landing accident

14 November: flying a Curtiss biplane, Eugene Ely, USN, makes the first take-off from a ship

1911   The Wright brothers win the first round of battle over their patents

John Montgomery is killed while flying one of his own gliders

Experimental airmail flights

January: in the USA, bombing trials take place at San Francisco

Glenn Curtiss tests the first practical floatplane

McCurdy flies for 30 miles over water from Key West to Havana

18 January: Ely makes the first take-off and landing on a ship

12 April: Pierre Prier makes the first non-stop London to Paris flight

August: H.N. Atwood makes the St Louis–Chicago–New York flight

3 August: a Fabre-Voisin seaplane flies

September–November: Calbraith Rodgers flies from Long Island to Long Beach in eighty-two days

22 October: the Italians use the Blériot monoplane on reconnaissance sorties against the Turkish Army during the Balkan Wars

24 October: Orville Wright makes a record gliding flight of 9 minutes

October–November: in France, the Concours Militaire meets at Reims

1912   The Royal Aircraft Factory BS1 flies, paving the way for the First World War fighting scout

Curtiss flies the first flying boat

Avro flies the first cabin biplane

Wilbur Wright dies from typhoid fever

February: Jules Védrines takes the speed record over 100 mph flying a Deperdussin Monocoque

March: the first hydro-aeroplane meeting takes place at Monaco

1 March: in the USA, Capt Albert Berry makes the first parachute drop from an aeroplane

13 May: the Royal Flying Corps is established

In August: S.F. Cody wins the first British military aeroplane competition at Larkhill

12 November: Lt T. Ellyson USN makes the first catapult launch from a warship

1913   First Sopwith Tabloid, Royal Aircraft Factory BE2c, Avro 504 and Dunne No. 8 all fly

The Schneider Trophy Race is inaugurated

13 May: in Russia, the Sikorsky *Bolshoi* flies

Orville Wright wins the appeal against the judgements on his and Wilbur's patents

20 August: in the Ukraine, flying a Nieuport, Petr Nesterov loops the loop for the first time

September: in France, Célestin-Adolphe Pégoud loops the loop flying a Blériot

23 September: Roland Garros makes the first non-stop flight across the Mediterranean

1914   In the United States, P.E. Fansler starts a trial airline service

Sikorsky's *Ilya Mourametz* flies

4 August: the First World War starts

The first air raid by Zeppelins on the Belgian port of Antwerp

The RNAS attacks Friedrichshafen using Avro 504s

1915   The first Zeppelin raid on London

Junkers flies the J.1, the first all-metal cantilever aeroplane

April: flying a Morane, Roland Garros tests firing a machine gun through a propeller fitted with deflector plates

July: Fokker introduces the first practical interrupter gear to fire through a propeller on his E.1 fighting scout

1916   17 May: the Porte Baby flying boat carries a Bristol Scout which is then air-launched – the first time this has been done

12 September: in the USA, the Hewitt-Sperry pilotless radio-guided bomb is tested

1917   The Junkers J.7, the first low-wing cantilever monoplane, is flown

13 June: London is struck by the first mass bombing raid

1918	1 April: in the UK, the RFC and RNAS merge to form the first autonomous air service, the RAF
1919	The first regular, scheduled commercial passenger and airmail services start, linking London with Paris and Amsterdam, flown by Aircraft Transport & Travel
	The International Air Transport Association (IATA) is formed
	May: the US Post Office inaugurates airmail services
	16–17 May: the first transatlantic flight takes place in stages via the Azores to Lisbon, by USN Curtiss NC-4 flying boat captained by Lt Cdr Albert Read
	14–15 June: the first non-stop transatlantic flight by Capt John Alcock and Lt Whitten-Brown in a Vickers Vimy from Newfoundland to Ireland
	2–13 July: the first non-stop transatlantic crossing by an airship, followed by the first return crossing, by the British R.34
	12 November–10 December: Ross and Keith Smith and crew fly a Vickers Vimy to make the first flight between England and Australia
1920	Split flaps are invented by Orville Wright and J.M. Jacobs
	The first practical retractable undercarriage appears, on a Dayton-Wright RB
	March: Frederick Handley Page introduces wing slots
	September–October: the first test flights take place of the Zeppelin-Staaken E4/20 18-seat four-engined all metal airliner
1921	In Paris, a record flying leap of 40 ft is undertaken by a winged pedal cycle, piloted by Pourlain
	22/23 February: in the USA, the first transcontinental airmail flight takes place linking New York and San Francisco
	21 July: a surrendered German battleship, *Ostfriesland*, is sunk by US Army Air Service bombers led by Brig Gen William Mitchell
1922	1 October: in Mesopotamia, for the first time an air force, the RAF, takes command of a military operation
1923	Turnbull demonstrates the first variable-pitch propeller
	9 January: Juan de la Cierva makes a successful flight of the first practical gyroplane, the C.3 Autogiro
	2/3 May: in the USA, flying a Fokker T-2, Kelly and Paul MacCready make the first non-stop transcontinental flight
	27 June: in the USA, the first inflight pipeline refuelling occurs with two de Havilland DH-4s
1924	The first variable-pitch, constant speed propeller is demonstrated by Hele Shaw-Beecham
	The Fowler wing-flap is invented
	The Junkers G.23 three-engined all-metal monoplane airliner flies, heralding the start of the trimotor era
	1 April: in the UK, Imperial Airways is founded
	7 April–28 September: Americans Smith and Nelson pilot the first round-the-world flight
1925	22 April: the first flight of a de Havilland Moth biplane takes place
	16 November–13 March: Alan Cobham makes a pioneering flight from England to Cape Town
	17 December: in the USA, Brig Gen William Mitchell is found guilty of criticising the state of US military aviation and is court-martialled
1926	In the UK, Dr Alan Griffith offers the first ideas on turboprop propulsion with the start of a development programme at RAE Farnborough

	In the USA, Adolph Rohrbach lectures on stressed skin construction
	9 May: the first flight takes place over the North Pole by Lt Cdr Richard Byrd and Floyd Bennett using a Fokker F.VII/3M
1927	20/21 May: flying a Ryan monoplane, Charles Lindbergh makes the first solo crossing of the Atlantic, flying from New York to Paris
	4 July: the first flight takes place of the Lockheed Vega – first of the 'speedplane' airliners
1928	12/13 April: flying a Junkers W331, Koehl captains the first east–west transatlantic flight
	31 May–10 June: flying a Fokker F.VII/3M, Charles Kingsford-Smith captains the first flight across the Pacific from the USA to Australia
	11 June: in Germany, flying an Opel-Stamer, F. Hermann and Stamer make the first rocket-propelled aeroplane fight
1929	*The Streamline Aeroplane*, a paper by Melvill Jones, is published
	23 October: the Dornier DoX, 12-engined flying boat capable of carrying 169 passengers, first appears
1930	Frank Whittle registers his first patents for the jet engine
	5–24 May: Amy Johnson flies a de Havilland Moth solo from England to Australia
1931	In Germany, Alexander Lippisch flies the first successful delta-wing aeroplane
	In Italy, jet propulsion is used for the first time, powering the airship *Omniadir*
	11 June: Imperial Airways introduces the Handley Page HP42 into service, setting new standards of comfort and safety
	13 September: Great Britain wins the Schneider Trophy Race outright as Flt Lt J.N. Boothman flies a Supermarine S6B at 340 mph
1932	Imperial Airways opens a service from London to Cape Town
	The first flights take place of a Junkers Ju52/3M trimotor transport
	In Britain, Sir Alan Cobham starts to experiment with inflight refuelling
	21/22 May: flying a Lockheed Vega, Amelia Earhart makes the first solo transatlantic flight by a woman
	18/19 August: James Mollison makes the first solo east–west transatlantic flight
1933	8 February: in the United States, Boeing flies the first modern airliner, the 247
	3 April: the Marquess of Clydesdale captains the first flight over Mount Everest
	1 July: in the US, the Douglas DC-1 (Douglas Commercial 1) flies
	15–22 July: the American, Wiley Post, makes the first solo flight around the world
1934	Airlines begin to use constant-speed variable-pitch propellers
	July: the Douglas DC-2 enters airline service
	October: the England to Australia MacRobertson air race takes place
1935–6	These two years see the first flights of many fighters that will be used during the Second World War
1935	July: in the USA, the Boeing 299 makes its first flights – the prototype of the B-17 Fortress bomber
	In France, the Breguet helicopter makes a successful test flight
1936	June: the first Douglas DC-3 airliners enter service
	26 June: in Germany, the first practical helicopter, Focke-Achgelis Fa61, makes its first flight
	4 July: the first flight occurs of the Short S23 Empire flying boat
1937	The Fa61 makes the first helicopter flight of more than an hour
	May: the first fully pressurised aeroplane, the Lockheed XC-35, makes its first flight

	6 May: in the United States, the German airship *Hindenburg* crashes in flames, and brings an end to commercial airship services
	August: in Germany, a modern four-engined transport, the Junkers Ju90, makes its first flight
1937–8	The Spanish Civil War escalates with German and Soviet involvement and becomes an opportunity for both sides to test new aircraft and tactics
1937–9	In these three years there are the first experimental airmail flights across both the North and the South Atlantic using flying boats
1938	23 February: in the UK, the Short Mayo composite aircraft is tested with the flying boat Maia launching the four-engined seaplane *Mercury* in mid-air
	31 December: in the USA, a pressurised airliner, the Boeing 307 Stratoliner, makes its first flight
1939	30 June: the Heinkel He176 flies – the first rocket-powered aeroplane
	27 August: the Heinkel He178 flies – the first jet-powered aeroplane
	3 September: the Second World War breaks out in Europe
1940	13 May: in the United States, the first successful flight takes place by a single-rotor helicopter, the Sikorsky VS-300
1941	9 January: in the UK, the Avro Lancaster four-engined heavy bomber makes its first flight
	February: the Short Stirling four-engined heavy bomber enters service
	15 May: the British Gloster E28/39 jet aeroplane makes its first flight
	September: an example of the Whittle jet engine is flown to the USA where it is copied for the first generation of US jet fighters
1942	In the USA, the Douglas DC-4 four-engined airliner makes its first flights
	18 July: in Germany, the Messerschmitt Me262, the first production jet fighter, makes its first flight
	1 October: the Bell XP-59A, the first US jet fighter, makes its first flight using two Whittle engines
1943	In Germany, the first jet-effect-rotor helicopter, designed by Doblhoff, flies
	9 January: in the USA, the Lockheed Constellation airliner makes its first flight
	15 June: in Germany, the jet bomber, Arada Ar234, makes its first flight
	24 July: in the UK, the prototype of the Gloster Meteor jet fighter makes its first flight
1944	In Germany, the first practical rocket-powered interceptor, the Messerschmitt Me163, enters service
	The first V-1 flying bombs, predecessors of the cruise missile, are launched against targets in London and the South of England
1945	The first turboprop aeroplane is flown – a Gloster Meteor fitted with two Rolls-Royce Trents
	6 and 9 August: the first atomic bombs are dropped on Hiroshima and Nagasaki
1945–6	The first regular peacetime transatlantic scheduled air services are introduced
1949	July: in Hatfield, England, the first flight takes place of the de Havilland Comet – the first jet airliner
	September: in England, the first flight of the Bristol Brabazon eight-engined airliner takes place
1951	In the UK, the world's first turboprop airliner in prototype form, the Vickers Viscount 630 makes its first flight
1952	2 May: the world's first jet airliner service is introduced by BOAC between London and Johannesburg using the de Havilland Comet

	16 August: the first flight takes place of the Bristol Britannia medium and long-range turboprop airliner
1954	The Comet is grounded following a series of accidents attributed to structural fatigue
1955	November: in the Netherlands, the Fokker F27 Friendship turboprop regional airliner makes its first flight
1958	Transatlantic jet airliner services are introduced, first by the de Havilland Comet IV and then by the Boeing 707-320
1960	Hawker Siddeley P1127 makes first hovering flight; forerunner of the Harrier and Sea Harrier, first operational V/STOL combat aircraft
1963	The Boeing 727-100 trijet enters airline service
1964	The first flight takes place of the Boeing 747-100 'jumbo jet' – the first wide-bodied airliner
1968	31 December: the Tupolev Tu-144 supersonic airliner makes its first flight
1969	23 February: the Anglo-French Concorde supersonic airliner makes its first flight
1971	24 March: US Congress cancels Boeing SST, supersonic transport
1976	21 January: British Airways starts Concorde supersonic services with flights between London and Bahrain, while Air France operates between Paris and Rio de Janeiro, with a refuelling stop at Dakar
2000	25 July: Air France Concorde crashes on take-off from Paris with the loss of 109 lives. Within six weeks, the certificate of airworthiness is withdrawn
2001	7 November: Concorde returns to operations from London and Paris to New York
2002	3 July: American Steve Fossett completes the first solo round-the-world balloon flight
2004	24 October: Concorde retired from scheduled airline service
2006	Bell-Boeing V-22 Osprey, first operational vertical take-off transport aircraft, cleared for service with the US armed forces

Appendix II

Table 1: *First World War American Fighter Aces*

Capt Edward V. Rickenbacker, CMH	26
2nd Lt Frank Luke, Jnr, CMH	21
Maj G. Raoul Lufbery	17
Lt G A Vaughn, Jnr	13
2nd Lt F.L. Baylies	12
Capt F.E. Kindley	12
Capt E.W. Springs	12
Lt D.E. Putnam	11
Maj R.G. Landis	10
Capt J.M. Swaab	10

Another 78 pilots scored between 5 and 9 victories.

Table 2: *First World War Austro-Hungarian Fighter Aces*

Hauptmann Godwin Brumowski	40
Offizierstellvertreter Julius Arigi	32
Oberleutnant Frank Linke-Crawford	30
Oberleutnant Benno Fiala, Ritter von Fernbrugg	29
Leutnant Josef Kiss	19

Another 25 pilots gained between 5 and 18 victories.

Table 3: *First World War British and Empire Fighter Aces*

Maj Edward 'Micky' Mannock, VC, DSO★★, MC★	73
Lt-Col W.A. Bishop, VC, CB, DSO★, MC, DFC	72
Lt-Col R. Collishaw, CB, DSO★, OBE, DSC, DFC	60
Maj J.T.B. McCudden, VC, DSO★, MC★, MM	57
Capt A.W. Beauchamp-Proctor, VC, DSO, MC★, DFC	54
Maj D.R. MacLaren, DSO, MC★, DFC	54
Lt-Col W.G. Barker, VC, DSO★, MC★★	53
Capt R.A. Little, DSO★, DSC★	47
Capt P.F. Fullard, CBE, DSO, MC★, AFC	46
Capt G.E.H. McElroy, MC★★, DFC★	46
Capt Albert Ball, VC, DSO★★, MC	44
Capt J. Gillmore, DSO, MC★★	44
Maj T.F. Hazell, DSO, MC, DFC★	41
Capt J.I.T. Jones, DSO, MC, DFC★, MM	40

★ denotes Bar to original decoration.
Another 518 pilots scored between 5 and 39 victories.

Table 4: *First World War French Fighter Aces*

Capt René Fonck	75
Capt Georges Guynemer	54
Lt Charles Nungesser	45
Capt Georges Madon	41

Another 154 pilots gained between 5 and 40 victories.

Table 5: *First World War German Fighter Aces*

Rittmeister Manfred, Freiherr von Richthofen	80
Oberleutnant Ernst Udet	62
Oberleutnant Erich Loewenhardt	53
Leutnant Werner Voss	48
Leutnant Fritz Rumey	45
Hauptmann Rudolph Berthold	44
Leutnant Paul Baumer	43
Leutnant Josef Jacobs	41
Hauptmann Bruno Loerzer	41
Hauptmann Oswald Boelcke	40
Leutnant Franz Buchner	40
Oberleutnant Lothar, Freiherr von Richthofen	40

Another 352 pilots gained between 5 and 39 victories.

Table 6: *First World War Italian Fighter Aces*

Maggiore Francesco Baracca	34
Tenente Silvio Scaroni	26
Tenente-Colonello Pier Ruggiero Piccio	24
Tenente Flavio Torello Baracchini	21
Capitano Fulco Ruffo di Calabria	20
Sergente Marziale Cerutti	17
Tenente Ferruccio Ranza	17
Tenente Luigi Olivari	12
Tenente Giovanni Ancillotto	11
Sergente Antonio Reali	11

Another 33 pilots gained between 5 and 10 victories.

Table 7: *First World War Russian Fighter Aces*

Staff Capt A.A. Kazakov	17
Capt P.V. d'Argueeff	15
Lt Cdr A.P. Seversky	13
Lt I.W. Smirnoff	12
Lt M. Safonov	11
Capt B. Sergeivsky	11
Ensign E.M. Thomson	11

Another 12 pilots scored between 5 and 10 victories.

Table 8: *Leading Second World War American Fighter Aces*

Maj Richard I. Bong, CMH, USAAF	40
Maj T.B. McGuire, CMH, USAAF	38
Capt D. McCampbell, USN	34
Col F.S. Gabreski, USAAF	31
Lt Col G. Boyington, USMC	28
Lt Col R.S. Johnson, USAAF	28
Col C.H. MacDonald, USAAF	27
Maj J.J. Foss, USMC	26
Maj G.E. Preddy, USAAF	26
Lt R.M. Hanson, USMC	25

Table 9: *Leading Second World War RAF Fighter Aces*
(includes non–British nationals)

Sqn Ldr M.T. StJ Pattle, DFC★ (SA)	41
Gp Capt J.E. 'Johnnie' Johnson, DSO★★, DFC★	38
Gp Capt A.G. 'Sailor' Malan, DSO★, DFC★ (SA)	35
Sqn Ldr Pierre Closterman, DFC★, (Fr)	33
Wg Cdr B.E. Finucane, DSO, DFC★★ (Ir)	32
Sqn Ldr G.F. 'Screwball' Beurling, DSO, DFC, DFM★ (Ca)	31
Wg Cdr J.R.D. Braham, DSO★★, DFC★★, AFC	29
Wg Cdr R.R. Stanford Tuck, DSO, DFC★★	29
Sqn Ldr Neville F. Duke, DSO, DFC★★, AFC	28
Gp Capt C.R. Caldwell, DSO, DFC★ (Au)	28
Gp Capt F.H.R. Carey, DFC★★, AFC, DFM	28
Sqn Ldr J.H. Lacey, DFM★	28
Wg Cdr C.F. Gray, DSO, DFC★★ (NZ)	27
Fl Lt E.S. Lock, DSO, DFC★	26
Wg Cdr L.C. Wade, DSO, DFC★★ (US)	25

Table 10: *Leading Second World War and Spanish Civil War Luftwaffe Fighter Aces* (includes non–German nationals)

Maj Eric Hartmann★★★	352
Maj Gerhard Barkhorn★★	301
Maj Gunther Rall★★	275
Oberlt Otto Kittel★★	267
Maj Walter Nowotny★★★ (Aus)	258
Maj Wilhelm Batz★★	237
Maj Erich Rudorffer★★	222
Oberstlt Heinz Bar★★	220
Oberst Herman Graf★★★	212
Maj Theodor Weissenberger★	208
Oberstlt Hans Philipp★★	206
Oberlt Walter Schuck★	206
Maj Heinrich Ehrler★	204
Oberlt Anton Hafner★	204
Hauptmann Helmut Lipfert★	203

★★★ Knight's Cross with oak leaves, swords and diamonds
 ★★ Knight's Cross with oak leaves and swords
  ★ Knight's Cross with oak leaves

Another 89 aces scored between 101 and 197 victories.

The leading Soviet fighter pilot of the Second World War was Guards Col Ivan N. Kozhedub, with 62 confirmed victories.

Table 11: *First World War Fighter Performance*

Camel, Sopwith (UK)	Single-seat tractor biplane. 130-hp Clerget 9B rotary engine. Operational: June 1917. Max speed: 115 mph.
DIII, Pfalz (Ger)	Single-seat tractor biplane. 160-hp Mercedes DIII liquid-cooled engine. Operational: September 1917. Max speed: 102 mph.
DH2, Airco (UK)	Single-seat pusher biplane. 100-hp Gnome Monosoupape rotary (a few had Le Rhone engines). Operational: late 1915. Max speed: 93 mph.
DR1, Fokker (Ger)	Single-seat tractor triplane. 110-hp Oberursel URII rotary engine. Operational: August 1917. Max speed: 115 mph.
EIII Eindecker, Fokker (Ger)	Single-seat tractor monoplane. 100-hp Oberursel rotary engine. Operational: late 1915. Max speed: 87 mph.
Nie 11 Bebe, Nieuport (Fr)	Single-seat tractor biplane. 80-hp Le Rhone rotary engine. Operational: November 1915. Max speed: 104 mph.
SVII, Spad (Fr)	Single-seat tractor biplane. 150-hp Hispano-Suiza HS8A liquid-cooled engine. Operational: September 1916. Max speed: 119 mph.
SE5A, Royal Aircraft Factory (UK)	Single-seat tractor biplane. Usually powered by 200-hp Hispano-Suiza 8B liquid-cooled engine. Operational: March 1917. Max speed: 138 mph.
Type N, Morane-Saulnier (Fr)	Single-seat tractor monoplane. 80-hp Le Rhone rotary engine. Operational: 1914. Max speed: 89 mph.

Table 12: *First World War Bomber Performance*

Ca.33, Caproni (It)	Four-crew, triple-engined (two tractor, one pusher), twin-boom, bomber biplane. Three 150-hp Isotta-Fraschini water-cooled engines. Operational: July 1915. Bomb load: 1,000 lb. Max speed,: 75 mph.
DH4, Airco (UK)	Two-seat day bomber biplane. Engines varied, but included 375-hp Rolls-Royce Eagle VIII. Operational: March 1917. Bomb load: 430 lb. Max speed: 143 mph.
GIV, Gotha (Ger)	Four-crew, twin-engined bomber biplane. Two 260-hp Mercedes DIVa water-cooled engines. Operational: April 1917. Bomb load: 660 lb. Max speed: 72 mph.
Voisin (Fr)	Two-seat, pusher-engined bomber biplane. Engines varied, but included 130-hp Canton-Unne radial. Operational: August 1914. Bomb load: 600 lb. Max speed: 74 mph.

Table 13: *First World War Maritime-Reconnaissance Aircraft Performance*

F2A, Felixstowe-Porte (UK)	Five-crew, twin-engined biplane flying boat. Two 375-hp Rolls-Royce Eagle water-cooled engines. Operational: mid-1917. Bomb load: 460 lb. Max speed: 95 mph.

Table 14: *Second World War Fighter Performance*

A6M2 Rei-Sen (Zero), Mitsubishi (Jap)	Single-engined, single-seat monoplane. 950-hp Nakajima NK1C Sakae radial engine. Operational: November 1940. Max speed: 331 mph.
Bf109, Messerschmitt (Ger)	Single-engined, single-seat monoplane. 1,475-hp Daimler-Benz DB605A liquid-cooled engine. Operational: July 1937. Max speed: 387 mph.
Defiant, Boulton Paul (UK)	Single-engined, two-seat monoplane. 1,030-hp Rolls-Royce Merlin III liquid-cooled engine. Operational: August 1939. Max speed: 304 mph.
Fw190A, Focke-Wulf (Ger)	Single-engined, single-seat monoplane. 1,700-hp BMW 801D radial engine. Operational: June 1941. Max speed: 408 mph.
Gladiator, Gloster (UK)	Single-engined, single seat biplane. 840-hp Bristol Mercury VIIIA radial engine. Operational: February 1937. Max speed: 257 mph.
Hellcat, Grumman F6F-3 (US)	Single-engined, single seat monoplane. 2,200-hp Pratt & Whitney R-2800-10W radial engine. Operational: February 1943. Max speed: 376 mph.
Hurricane, Hawker (UK)	Single-engined, single-seat monoplane. 1,050-hp Rolls-Royce Merlin II liquid-cooled engine. Operational: December 1937. Max speed: 316 mph.
Lightning, Lockheed P-38 (US)	Twin-engined, single-seat twin-boom monoplane. Two 1,600-hp Allison V-1710-111 turbocharged liquid-cooled engines. Operational: May 1941. Max speed 414 mph.
Me163B Komet, Messerschmitt (Ger)	Single-engined, single-seat rocket-powered interceptor. 3,748-lb thrust Walter HWK 109-509A bifuel rocket motor. Operational: May 1944. Max speed: 593 mph.
Me262A Schwalbe, Messerschmitt (Ger)	Twin-engined, single-seat jet fighter. Two 1,980 lb thrust Junkers 109-004B turbojets. Operational: May 1944. Max speed: 541 mph.
Meteor, Gloster (UK)	Twin-engined, single-seat jet fighter. Two 3,600 lb thrust Rolls-Royce Derwent turbojets. Operational: July 1944. Max speed: 598 mph.
Mustang, North American P-51 (US)	Single-engined, single seat monoplane. 1,450-hp Rolls-Royce/Packard Merlin V-1650-7 liquid-cooled engine. Operational: November 1943. Max speed: 427 mph.

Re2000, Reggiane (It)	Single-engined, single-seat monoplane. 1,040-hp Piaggio PXI RC 4oD radial engine. Operational: May 1941. Max speed: 329 mph.
Spitfire, Supermarine (UK)	Single-engined, single-seat monoplane. 1,030-hp Rolls-Royce Merlin II liquid-cooled engine. Operational: August 1939. Max speed: 346 mph.
Tempest, Hawker (UK)	Single-engined, single-seat monoplane. 2,400-hp Napier Sabre IIB liquid-cooled engine. Operational: April 1944. Max speed: 435 mph.
Thunderbolt, Republic P-47 (US)	Single-engined, single-seat monoplane. 2,000-hp Pratt & Whitney R-2800-59 Double Wasp radial engine. Operational: November 1942. Max speed: 426 mph

Table 15: *Second World War Bomber Performance*

Ar234B, Arado (Ger)	Single-seat, twin-engined jet bomber. Two Junkers Jumo turbojets. Operational: July 1944. Bomb load: 4,400 lb. Max speed: 470 mph.
Avenger, Grumman TBF (US)	Three-crew, single-engined torpedo-bomber monoplane. 1,700-hp Wright R-2600-8 radial engine. Operational: February 1942. Bomb load: 2,000 lb. Max speed: 278 mph.
He111, Heinkel (Ger)	Three to five-crew, twin-engined medium bomber. Two 1,300-hp Junkers Jumo 211F liquid-cooled engines. Operational: 1937. Bomb load: 4,400 lb. Max speed: 250 mph.
Fortress, Boeing B-17 (US)	Six to ten-crew, four-engined heavy bomber monoplane. Four 1,200-hp Wright R-1820-65 radial engines. Operational: April 1937. Bomb load: 6,000 lb. Max speed: 295 mph.
G4M2 'Betty', Mitsubishi (Jap)	Six/seven-crew, twin-engined medium bomber. Two 1,350-hp Mitsubishi Kasei 21 radial engines. Operational: 1940. Bomb load: 4,840 lb. Max speed: 325 mph.
Ju87 Stuka, Junkers (Ger)	Two-seat, single-engined, crank-wing dive-bomber monoplane. 1,300-hp Junkers Jumo 211 liquid-cooled engine. Operational: 1937. Bomb load: 2,200 lb. Max speed: 255 mph.

Lancaster, Avro (UK)	Seven-crew, four-engined heavy bomber. Four 1,280-hp Rolls-Royce Merlin liquid-cooled engines. Operational: spring 1942. Bomb load: 14,000 lb. Max speed: 275 mph.
Liberator, Consolidated B-24 (US)	Ten-crew, four-engined long-range bomber and maritime-reconnaissance aircraft. Four 1,200-hp Pratt & Whitney R-1830-65 Twin Wasp radial engines. Operational: late 1940 (RAF). Bomb load: 8,000 lb. Max speed: 297 mph.
Mitchell, North American B-25 (US)	Four to six-crew, twin-engined medium bomber. Two 1,700-hp Wright R-2600-13 Cyclone radial engines. Operational: winter 1941/1942. Bomb load: 3,000lb. Max speed: 303 mph.
Mosquito BIV, de Havilland DH98 (UK)	Two-seat, twin-engined light bomber. Two 1,280-hp Rolls-Royce Merlin liquid-cooled engines. Operational: April 1942. Bomb load: 4,000 lb. Max speed: 420 mph.
SM79 Sparviero, Savoia-Marchetti (It)	Five-crew, trimotor bomber monoplane. Three 750-hp Alfa Romeo 126 RC-34 radial engines. Operational: 1939. Bomb load: 2,200 lb. Max speed: 260 mph.
Superfortress, Boeing B-29 (US)	Ten to fourteen-crew, four-engined heavy bomber monoplane. Four 2,200-hp Wright R-3350-23 radial engines. Operational: March 1944. Bomb load: 20,000 lb. Max speed: 360 mph.
Swordfish, Fairey (UK)	Three-seat, single-engined dive-bomber/torpedo-bomber biplane. 750-hp Bristol Pegasus 30 radial engine. Operational: 1935. Bomb load: 1,500 lb. Max speed: 128 mph.
Wellington, Vickers (UK)	Six-crew twin-engined medium bomber. Two 1,050-hp Bristol Pegasus XVIII radial engines. Operational: mid-1939. Bomb load: 5,100 lb. Max speed: 235 mph.

Table 16: *Second World War Maritime-Reconnaissance Aircraft Performance*

Fw200 Condor, Focke-Wulf (Ger)	Eight-crew, four-engined maritime-reconnaissance landplane. Four 940-hp BMW 323 R-2 radial engines. Operational: 1940. Bomb load: 3,300 lb. Max speed: 240 mph.
PBY-5 Catalina, Consolidated (US)	Six to eight-crew, twin-engined maritime-reconnaissance flying-boat or amphibian (PBY-5A). Two 1,200-hp Pratt & Whitney R-1830-92 Twin Wasp radial engines. Operational: 1936. Max speed: 196 mph.
Sunderland, Short S25 (UK)	Nine-crew, four-engined maritime-reconnaissance flying-boat. Four 815-hp Bristol Pegasus XVIII radial engines. Operational: 1938. Bomb load: 3,000 lb. Max speed: 210 mph.

See also Table 15, Wellington and Liberator.

Table 17: *Second World War Transport Aircraft Performance*

Anson, Avro (UK)	Twin-engined light transport. Two 320-hp Armstrong Siddeley Cheetah IX radial engines. Operational: 1936. Six passengers or light freight. Max speed: 170 mph.
Ju52/3M, Junkers (Ger)	Trimotor transport. Three 575-hp or 725-hp BMW radial engines. Operational: 1933. Eighteen passengers or cargo. Max speed: 180mph.
Skymaster, Douglas C-54 (US)	Four-engined transport. Four 1,100-hp Pratt & Whitney R-2000-3 radial engines. Operational: mid-1942. Up to 50 troops or cargo. Max speed: 274 mph.
Skytrain, Douglas C-47 (Dakota) (US)	Twin-engined medium transport. Two 1,000-hp Wright GR-1820 Cyclone radial engines. Operational: 1938. Accommodates up to 28 troops or 8,720 lb cargo. Max speed: 230 mph.
York, Avro (UK)	Four-engined transport. Four 1,280-hp Rolls-Royce Merlin 24 liquid-cooled engines. Operational: 1943. Up to 50 passengers or cargo. Max speed: 290 mph.

Table 18: *Aeronautical Records*

Altitude: Gas Balloons	
Below 16,000 cu metres	38,677.6 ft (11,780 m) on 10 May 1964, by Tracy Barnes in a Barnes 14A, reg. N66B, ascending from Rosemont, MN, and descending at Gilmanton, WI, USA.
Between 16,000 and 22,000 cu metres	53,193.3 ft (16,201 m) on 18 August 1932, by Auguste Piccard in an FRNS, reg OOBFH, ascending from Dubendorf, Switzerland.
Over 22,000 cu metres	113,826.6 ft (34,668 m) on 4 May 1961, by Malcolm D. Ross in the Winzen Research balloon *Lee Lewis Memorial*, ascending from the USS *Antietam* in the Gulf of Mexico.
Speed	
Piston-engined aircraft	531.4 mph (850.24 kmph) on 21 August 1989, by Lyle Shelton in a Grumman F-8F Bearcat, N7771, over a 3 km course at a restricted altitude at Las Vegas, NM, USA.
Turbojet aircraft	2,206 mph (3,529.56 kmph) on 28 July 1976, by Eldon W. Joersz in a Lockheed SR-71 Blackbird, over a 15–25 km course at Beale Air Force Base, CA, USA.
Airliner over commercial air route	1,055.9 mph (1,689.47 kmph) on 8 October 2003, by Mike Bannister in command of unidentified Aérospatiale/BAC Concorde between London and Boston, MA, USA.
Airliner over commercial air route in excess of 6,500 km (4,062.5 miles)	608.2 mph (973.10 kmph) on 29 October 1977, by Capt Walter J. Mullikin in command of Boeing 747SP flying between London and Cape Town.
Distance	
Without landing	25,132.6 miles (40,212.14 km) on 23 December 1986, by Richard G. Rutan, with Jeana Yeager as crew, in the Burt Rutan Voyageur N269VA, powered by Continental piston engines, flying from Edwards Air Force Base, CA, USA, to Edwards Air Force Base, CA, USA.

(Source: Fédération Aéronautique Internationale)

Table 19: *International Civil Aircraft Markings*

A6	United Arab	HB	Switzerland	SE	Sweden		
	Emirates	HC	Ecuador	SP	Poland		
A7	Qatar	HI	Dominican Republic	ST	Sudan		
A9C	Bahrain	HK	Colombia	7O	Yemen		
A40	Oman	HL	South Korea	6Y	Jamaica		
AP	Pakistan	HP	Panama	SU	Egypt		
B	China /Taiwan	HS	Thailand	SX	Greece		
C	Canada	HZ	Saudi Arabia	7T	Algeria		
CC	Chile	I	Italy	SP	Poland		
CN	Morocco	J2	Djibouti	SX	Greece		
C6	Bahamas	JA	Japan	TC	Turkey		
C9	Mozambique	JY	Jordan	TF	Iceland		
CP	Bolivia	LN	Norway	TG	Guatemala		
CS	Portugal	LV	Argentina	TS	Tunisia		
CU	Cuba	LY	Lithuania	3B	Mauritius		
D	Germany	LX	Luxembourg	3X	Guinea		
DQ	Fiji	LZ	Bulgaria	TI	Costa Rica		
D2	Angola	N	United States of	TJ	Cameroon		
D4	Cape Verde		America	TR	Gabon		
EC	Spain	9A	Croatia	TU	Ivory Coast		
EI	Ireland	9H	Malta	UK	Uzbekistan		
EK	Armenia	9K	Kuwait	UN	Kazakhstan		
EP	Iran	9M	Malaysia	UR	Ukraine		
ER	Moldova	9N	Nepal	V2	Antigua		
ES	Estonia	9Q	Zaire	V8	Brunei		
ET	Ethiopia	9V	Singapore	VH	Australia		
EW	Belarus	9Y	Trinidad & Tobago	VR-H	Hong Kong		
EX	Kyrgyzstan	OB	Peru	VT	India		
EY	Tajikistan	OD	Lebanon	XA	Mexico		
EZ	Turkmenistan	OE	Austria	XU	Cambodia		
F	France (incl. French	OH	Finland	XV	Vietnam		
	Polynesia)	OK	Czech Republic	XY/XZ	Myanmar		
5A	Libya	OM	Slovakia	YA	Afghanistan		
5B	Cyprus	OO	Belgium	YI	Iraq		
5H	Tanzania	OY	Denmark	YK	Syria		
5N	Nigeria	P4	Aruba	YL	Latvia		
5R	Madagascar	P	North Korea	YR	Romania		
5X	Uganda	P2	Papua New Guinea	YS	El Salvador		
5Y	Kenya	PH	Netherlands	YU	Serbia		
4K	Azerbaijan	PK	Indonesia	YV	Venezuela		
4L	Georgia	PP	Brazil	Z	Zimbabwe		
4R	Sri Lanka	RA	Russian Federation	ZK	New Zealand		
4X	Israel	RDLP	Laos	ZP	Paraguay		
G	United Kingdom	RP	Philippines	Z3	Macedonia		
HA	Hungary	S2	Belarus	ZS	South Africa		

Table 20: *Comparative Ranks*

Officers and Warrant Officers

Royal Air Force	Royal Navy	Army
Marshal of the Royal Air Force★	Admiral of the Fleet★	Field Marshal★
Air Chief Marshal	Admiral	General
Air Marshal	Vice-Admiral	Lieutenant-General
Air Vice-Marshal	Rear Admiral	Major General
Air Commodore	Commodore	Brigadier
Group Commander	Captain	Colonel
Wing Commander	Commander	Lieutenant-Colonel
Squadron Leader	Lieutenant-Commander	Major
Flight Lieutenant	Lieutenant	Captain
Flying Officer	Sub-Lieutenant	First Lieutenant
Pilot Officer	Acting Sub-Lieutenant	Second Lieutenant
No equivalent	Midshipman	No equivalent
Warrant Officer	Warrant Officer	No equivalent
no equivalent	No equivalent	Sergeant Major (RSM and CSM)

★Rank discontinued in recent years to accord with absence of five-star ranks in other NATO countries.

The United States Navy has a rank of Lieutenant Junior Grade, between Ensign (the equivalent of Sub-Lieutenant) and Lieutenant.
The United States Navy's five-star rank is Fleet Admiral.
(Source: Imperial War Museum)

Ratings (RN) and Non-Commissioned Ranks

Flight Sergeant	Chief Petty Officer	Staff Sergeant
Sergeant	Petty Officer	Sergeant
Senior Aircraftman	Leading Seaman	Corporal
Leading Aircraftman	Able Seaman	no equivalent
Aircraftman	Ordinary Seaman	Private

Table 21: *Schneider Trophy Races 1913–31*

Winning Speeds

Year	Pilot	Aircraft	Winning Speed (mph)
1913	Maurice Prevost (Fr)	Deperdussin Monocoque	45
1914	Howard Pixton (UK)	Sopwith Tabloid	86.78
1919	Result declared null and void		
1920	Luigi Bologna (It)	Savoia S12	107.22
1921	Giovanni de Briganti (It)	Macchi M7	117.9
1922	Henry Biard (UK)	Supermarine Sea Lion II	145.7
1923	David Rittenhouse (US)	Curtiss CR-3	177.38
1924	Cancelled		
1925	James Doolittle (US)	Curtiss R3C-2	232.57
1926	Mario de Bernardi (It)	Macchi M39	246.5
1927	S.N. Webster (UK)	Supermarine S5	281.65
1929	H.R. Waghorn (UK)	Supermarine S6	328.63
1931	J.N Boothman (UK)	Supermarine S6B	340.8

Selected Bibliography

Anderson, William, *Pathfinders*, London, Jarrolds, 1946

Barker, Ralph, *Strike Hard, Strike Sure*, London, Pan Books, 1974

—— *The Royal Flying Corps in France: From Bloody April 1917 to Final Victory*, London, Constable, 1995

Boyle, Andrew, *Trenchard – Man of Vision*, London, Collins, 1962

Buiton, Theo, *Nachtjagd: The Night Fighters Versus Bomber War over the Third Reich, 1939–45*, Ramsbury, The Crowood Press, 1997

Burden, Ronald A., *Falklands: The Air War*, British Aviation Research Group, 1986

Chesnau, Roger, *Aircraft Carriers of the World, 1914 to the Present – An Illustrated Encyclopedia*, London, Arms & Armour Press, 1984

Clark, Ronald, *Battle for Britain: Sixteen Weeks that Changed the Course of History*, London, Harrap & Co., 1965

Clostermann, Pierre, *The Big Show*, London, Chatto & Windus, 1951

Collier, Basil, *History of Air Power*, London, Weidenfeld & Nicolson, 1974

Copeman, Geoff, *Bomber Squadrons at War*, Stroud, Sutton Publishing, 1997

Craven, Wesley Frank and Cate, James Lea, *The Army Air Forces in World War II*, University of Chicago Press, 7 vols, 1948–1958

Falconer, Jonathan, *RAF Bomber Airfields of World War II*, Stroud, Sutton Publishing, 1995

—— *The Bomber Command Handbook 1939–1945*, Stroud, Sutton Publishing, 1998

—— *The Dam Busters: Breaking the Great Dams of Western Germany 16–17 May 1943*, Stroud, Sutton Publishing, 2003

Freeman, Roger, *The US Strategic Bomber*, London, MacDonald & Jane's, 1975

Fredette, Major Raymond, *The Sky on Fire: The First Battle of Britain 1917–18*, New York, Rinehart & Winston, 1966

Gibbs-Smith, Sir Charles, *Aviation: An Historical Survey from its Origins to the End of World War II*, London, HMSO, 1970

—— *Sir George Cayley's Aeronautics 1796–1855*, London, HMSO, 1962

Gibson, Guy, *Enemy Coast Ahead*, London, Pan Books, 1979

Grey, C.G., *Bombers*, London, Faber & Faber, 1941

Haddow, G.W. and Grosz, Peter M., *The German Giants: The Story of the R-Planes 1914–1919*, London, Putnam, 1962

Hanson, Norman, *Carrier Pilot*, Cambridge, Patrick Stephens, 1979

Harris, Sir Arthur, *Bomber Offensive*, London, Collins, 1947

Hastings, Max, *Bomber Command*, London, Michael Joseph, 1979

Hobbs, Cdr David, *Aircraft Carriers of the Royal & Commonwealth Navies: The Complete Illustrated Encyclopedia from World War I to the Present*, London, Greenhill Books, 1996

Inoguchi, Capt Rikkei and Nakajima, Cdr Tadashi, *The Divine Wind: Japan's Kamikaze Force in World War II*, Naval Institute Press, 1958

Johnson, Brian, *Fly Navy: History of Maritime Aviation*, Newton Abbot and London, David & Charles, 1981

Kay, C.E., *The Restless Sky*, London, Harrap & Co., 1964

Larrazabal, Jesus Salas, *Air War Over Spain*, Hersham, Ian Allan, 1969

Lewis, Bruce, *Aircrew: The Story of the Men who Flew the Bombers*, London, Leo Cooper, 1991

Longmate, Norman, *The Bombers: The RAF Offensive Against Germany 1939–45*, London, Hutchinson, 1983

Lucas, Laddie, *Five Up*, London, Sidgwick & Jackson, 1978

Marshall, Chester, *B-29 Superfortress*, New York, Motorbooks International, 1993

McKee, Alexander, *Dresden 1945: The Devil's Tinderbox*, Souvenir, 1982

Messenger, Charles, *Bomber Harris and the Strategic Bombing Offensive 1939–1945*, London, St Martin's Press, 1984

Morrison, Wilbur H., *Fortress Without A Roof*, London, W.H. Allen, 1982

Morse, Stan, *Gulf Air War Debrief*, London, Aerospace Publishing, 1991

Nichols, Cdr John B., USN (Ret) and Tillman, Barrett, *On Yankee Station: The Naval Air War over Vietnam*, Naval Institute Press, 1987

Piekalkiewicz, Janus, *The Air War: 1939–45*, London, Blandford, 1985

Prange, Gordon with Donald M. Goldstein and Katherine V. Dillon, *God's Samurai: Lead Pilot at Pearl Harbor*, New York, Brassey's, 1990

Price, Alfred, *Battle Over The Reich*, Hersham, Ian Allan, 1973

—— *Blitz on Britain 1939–1945*, London, Purnell, 1977

Renaut, Michael, *Terror by Night*, London, Kimber, 1982

Saundby, Robert, *Air Bombardment: The Story of its Development*, London, Chatto and Windus, 1961

Saward, Dudley, *Bomber Harris: The Story of the Marshal of the Royal Air Force*, London, Doubleday, 1985

Smithies, Edward, *War in the Air*, London, Viking, 1990

Southworth, Herbert Rutledge, *Guernica! Guernica! Study of Journalism, Diplomacy, Propaganda and History*, University of California Press, 1977

Sweetman, John, *Operation Chastise: The Dams Raid: Epic or Myth*, London, Jane's, 1982

Turner, John Frayne, *VCs of the Air*, London, Harrap & Co., 1960

Unknown author, *War Birds: Diary of an Unknown Aviator*, London, Hamish Hamilton, 1927

Webster, Sir Charles and Frankland, Noble, *The Strategic Air Offensive Against Germany 1939–1945*, London, Imperial War Museum, 1994

Winfield, Dr Roland, *The Sky Shall Not Have Them*, London, Kimber, 1976

Winton, John, *Air Power at Sea 1939–45*, London, Sidgwick & Jackson, 1976

—— *Carrier 'Glorious': The Life and Death of an Aircraft Carrier*, London, Leo Cooper Ltd, 1986

Woods, Gerard A., *Wings at Sea: A Fleet Air Arm Observer's War 1940–45*, London, Conway Maritime, 1985

Wragg, David, *Airlift: A History of Military Air Transport*, Shrewsbury, Airlife, 1986

—— *Swordfish: The Attack on the Italian Fleet at Taranto*, London, Wiedenfeld & Nicolson, 2003

—— *The Fleet Air Arm Handbook 1939–1945*, Stroud, Sutton Publishing, 2001 and 2003

—— *Carrier Combat*, Stroud, Sutton Publishing, 1997

—— *Wings Over The Sea: A History of Naval Aviation*, Newton Abbot and London, David & Charles, 1979